Market Analysis for Real Estate

Concepts and Applications in Valuation and Highest and Best Use

Appraisal Institute®

*Professionals Providing
Real Estate Solutions*

Market Analysis for Real Estate

Concepts and Applications in Valuation and Highest and Best Use

by Stephen F. Fanning, MAI

Appraisal Institute • 550 West Van Buren • Chicago, IL 60607 • www.appraisalinstitute.org

Reviewers: M. Lance Coyle, MAI
Randal D. Dawson, MAI
Michael S. MaRous, MAI, SRA
Vice President, Educational Programs
and Publications: Larisa Phillips
Director, Publications: Stephanie Shea-Joyce
Editor: Mark Boone
Manager, Book Design/Production: Michael Landis
Production Specialist: James Sobiesczyk

For Educational Purposes Only

The materials presented in this publication represent the opinions and views of the author. Although these materials may have been reviewed by members of the Appraisal Institute, the views and opinions expressed herein are not endorsed or approved by the Appraisal Institute as policy unless adopted by the Board of Directors pursuant to the Bylaws of the Appraisal Institute. While substantial care has been taken to provide accurate and current data and information, the Appraisal Institute does not warrant the accuracy or timeliness of the data and information contained herein. Further, any principles and conclusions presented in this publication are subject to court decisions and to local, state and federal laws and regulations and any revisions of such laws and regulations.

This publication is sold for educational and informational purposes only with the understanding that the Appraisal Institute is not engaged in rendering legal, accounting or other professional advice or services. Nothing in these materials is to be construed as the offering of such advice or services. If expert advice or services are required, readers are responsible for obtaining such advice or services from appropriate professionals.

Nondiscrimination Policy

The Appraisal Institute advocates equal opportunity and nondiscrimination in the appraisal profession and conducts its activities in accordance with applicable federal, state, and local laws.

Library of Congress Cataloging-in-Publication Data

Fanning, Stephen F.
     Market analysis for real estate : concepts and applications in valuation and
   highest and best use / by Stephen F. Fanning.
       p. cm.
     ISBN 0-922154-86-4
       1. Real property–Valuation. 2. Real estate business I. Title
   HD1387.F328 2005
   333.33'2–cd22

                                                                    200505484

Contents

Foreword vii

About the Author viii

Preface ix

| Part I | Concepts and Techniques of Market Analysis |

Introduction to Part I 1

Chapter 1   Market Research in Real Estate Appraisal 3

Chapter 2   Levels of Market Analysis 17

Chapter 3   Productivity Analysis 31

Chapter 4   Productivity Analysis–Introduction to Location 47

Chapter 5   Urban Structure 69

Chapter 6   The Economic Base 101

Chapter 7   Market Delineation 113

Chapter 8   Estimating Real Estate Demand 127

Chapter 9   Estimating Competitive Supply 141

Chapter 10   Data Sources 149

Chapter 11   Evaluating Market Dynamics,
Market Conditions, and Marketability 169

Part II   Market Analysis Applications

Introduction to Part II 185

Chapter 12   Existing Retail Shopping Center 187

Chapter 13   Existing Office Building 269

Chapter 14   Existing Industrial Building 307

Chapter 15   Existing Apartment Complex 343

Part III   Highest and Best Use Applications

Introduction to Part III 375

Chapter 16   Highest and Best Use Decisions 377

Chapter 17   Mixed-Use Vacant Land 403

Chapter 18   Proposed Retail Shopping Center 449

Chapter 19   Vacant Retail Shopping Center 465

Epilog   Application of Market Analysis Concepts in the
Approaches to Value 501

Appendix A. Market Analysis Guidelines 507

Appendix B. North American Industry Classification System 515

Bibliography 521

Index 529

Foreword

In the 11 years since the publication of the Appraisal Institute's *Market Analysis for Valuation Appraisals,* real estate market analysis has grown to occupy an increasingly important niche in the discipline of real estate appraisal. This heightened interest in the field has prompted the development of *Market Analysis for Real Estate: Concepts and Applications in Valuation and Highest and Best Use.* This new text fills the need for a book that describes market analysis as an integrated process that applies market and marketability techniques to actual situations that appraisers encounter in valuation practice and when performing more complex stand-alone market studies.

Market Analysis for Real Estate: Concepts and Applications in Valuation and Highest and Best Use is an essential text that introduces a six-step process that entails analyzing a property's productivity, defining the market, analyzing supply and demand, comparing supply and demand, and developing a subject capture estimate. The concepts and techniques of market analysis presented in the first part of the book are applied to the second part, which features an existing retail shopping center, office building, industrial building, and an apartment complex. Finally, the third part of the book demonstrates how market analysis conclusions are applied to make highest and best use decisions for mixed-use vacant land, a proposed retail shopping center, and a vacant retail shopping center.

Market Analysis for Real Estate: Concepts and Applications in Valuation and Highest and Best Use is a much-needed resource for every appraiser involved in market analysis for real estate valuation.

Bruce A. Kellogg, MAI
2005 President

About the Author

Steve Fanning, MAI, AICP, CRE, is the owner of Fanning & Associates, which specializes in market analysis, highest and best use studies, and valuation. He has considerable experience in urban planning and community development, having directed several planning agencies in northern Texas. He holds a bachelor's degree and a master's degree and has been an adjunct professor in real estate at the University of North Texas. Fanning is a co-author of an earlier book on market analysis and valuation, *Market Analysis for Valuation Appraisals*, published by the Appraisal Institute, has contributed to *The Appraisal Journal*, and has been active in the development and teaching of Appraisal Institute courses.

Preface

The primary objective of this book is to introduce principles and examples of simplified market and marketability analysis techniques that can be used in the typical appraisal or in more complex stand-alone market studies. While market analysis is fundamental to real estate valuation, the tools and techniques of market analysis are often discussed in a highly technical and recondite manner. Practitioners have long needed a text that presents market analysis as an integrated, "hands-on" process. It is the author's hope that this book will fill the current void in practical literature dealing with real estate market analysis.

Market analysis is a multistep study process analogous to the problem-solving approaches employed in other areas of economic and scientific investigation. In real estate market analysis, the productive attributes of a parcel of real estate are examined in light of the demand for the particular category of real estate and the supply of competitive properties within the defined real estate market.

This book focuses on the role of market analysis in real estate valuation. By identifying the components of value in a real estate parcel, market analysis provides critical support for the value estimate in two ways. First, the findings of real estate market analysis provide data required in the highest and best use determination. Second, the market forecast developed in market analysis is essential to application of the three approaches to value. This book introduces a six-step process for market analysis. The six steps include analysis of property productivity, market definition, demand analysis, supply analysis, comparison of supply and demand, and development of a subject capture estimate.

This book is divided into three parts and an epilog. The chapters in the first part provide an overview of the concepts of real estate market analysis. The six-step process is conceptually developed in this first part of the book. In the second and third parts of the book, case studies illustrating the market analysis process are presented. Many of the tables that appear in the case study applications are included as Excel files on the CD at the back of the book. The four chapters in Part II demonstrate how the conclusions reached in the market analyses of four existing, income-producing properties are used to support market value estimates. In Part III the conclusions of the market analyses of three more case study properties are applied to make highest and best use decisions. The concluding chapter addresses the application of market analysis concepts in the three approaches to value.

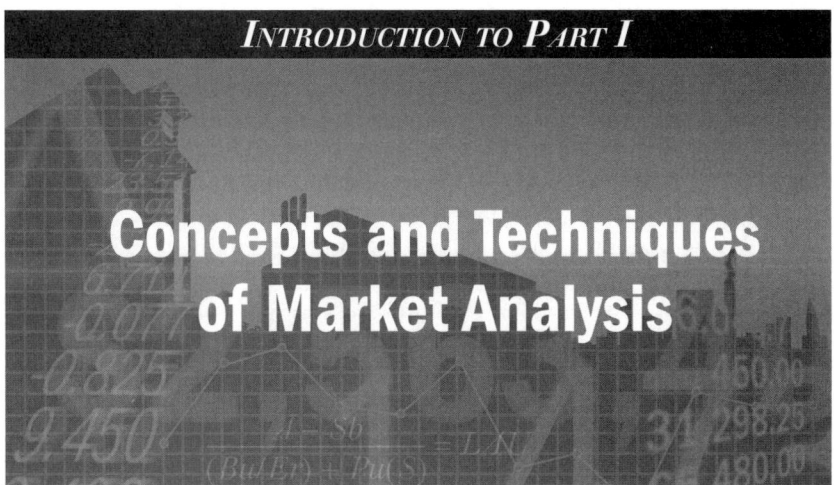

INTRODUCTION TO PART I

Concepts and Techniques of Market Analysis

Part I introduces concepts and techniques that will be encountered in the case studies presented in Parts II and III of the text. Throughout the book, special attention has been paid to practical concerns. Chapter 1 examines the role of market analysis in an appraisal and identifies the three general problem types or scenarios that market analysis investigates. In this first chapter, the six-step market analysis process is introduced. The extent of the market study and the level of detail appropriate to a given appraisal assignment are addressed in Chapter 2. A significant distinction is made between techniques based on inferred or trend analysis and those that involve fundamental analysis or forecasting. Chapter 2 also describes four levels of market analysis and provides a checklist to evaluate the level required, given the nature of the appraisal assignment.

Chapters 3, 4, and 5 discuss the productive attributes of real estate, which include physical, legal/regulatory, locational, and amenity characteristics. Understanding a property's productive attributes helps the appraiser identify the property's market, specifically the demand for the property type and the supply of competitive properties. Chapter 4 develops the concept of situs and Chapter 5 discusses the historical models of urban growth advanced by the social ecologists and rent theorists.

Chapter 6 introduces economic base analysis and offers useful techniques for estimating the population and employment of a community. The chapter demonstrates the various ways in which employment multipliers are estimated and applied. Chapter 7 focuses on the definition and segmentation of real estate markets, while Chapter 8 explores the techniques used to forecast market demand for retail space, office space, and housing. In Chapter 9 the inventory of competitive properties is examined, and techniques for calculating the projected competitive supply are explained.

Chapter 10 discusses types and sources of data, provides models that can be used to refine and test data, and analyzes problem situations that the appraiser may encounter in compiling data. The final chapter in Part I, Chapter 11, considers the effect of market cycles and changing market conditions on property marketability and value.

Market analysis is an eclectic field of study that draws on a number of other disciplines. These related fields include economics, statistical analysis, demographics, city planning, and location theory. Each field employs its own technical terms and usage, which may seem rather esoteric to a novice. The terminology employed in this book necessarily reflects the hybrid nature of market analysis. To assist the reader, terms such as *secular trend, frictional vacancy, centroid, gravity model, friction of distance,* and *location quotient* are defined where they first appear in the text. The topical bibliography at the back of the book will prove useful to readers who want to consult key surveys and anthologies on market analysis, technical literature from ancillary disciplines, and monographs on the market analysis of specific property types.

CHAPTER 1

Market Research in Real Estate Appraisal

Chapter Objectives

- To explain how market analysis relates to the economic theory of supply and demand
- To identify the role of market analysis in the appraisal process
- To compare the scientific method to the appraisal process, and thereby clarify the role of market analysis in appraisal
- To characterize three general scenarios for market analysis– i.e., a site in search of a use or market, a use or market in search of a site, and the consideration of real property as an alternative investment instrument
- To show how market research forms the basis for the six-step market analysis process introduced in this book

Introduction

Market analysis can be a separate study from appraisal but an appraisal cannot be completed without market analysis. This book will examine market analysis concepts and provide specific examples of how simplified market analysis techniques can be directly integrated into the appraisal process.[1]

Economic Theory and Market Analysis

It is essential that appraisers and users of appraisals understand the relationship between market analysis and appraisal. Market research is fundamental to economic decision making. Economics is concerned with choices made in a competitive environment under the constraint of limited resources. In a real estate context, market analysis examines the productive attributes of a property vis-a-vis the relationship of supply and demand, delineating the market in which the property competes. In recent years institutional investors have been requiring that more market analysis be included in the appraisals they commission.

Utility and Scarcity—Value Components of Supply

In land value theory *utility* refers to the function or use of a parcel of land. To derive the market value of a property, the appraiser considers the alternative uses of a property. The market analysis component of the appraisal investigates the support for a single use or a range of uses for a particular site. Determining whether or not there is market support for a probable use, i.e., if the use is financially feasible, is a function of market analysis.

In economic theory, *scarcity* increases the value of a commodity, asset, or resource in limited supply. Real estate may be seen as a commodity, an asset, or a resource depending on the property type and the problem situation.

As analysis of market absorption reveals, a large quantity of properties available in a market characterized by relatively stable demand generally tends to reduce the probable selling price of a typical property. Alternatively, a limited quantity of competitive properties can cause real estate prices to rise.

Desire and Effective Purchasing Power—Value Components of Demand

In value theory, *effective demand* refers to the ability of people who desire a good or commodity to act upon their desire. Consumers' ability to spend is contingent on their purchasing power or disposable income. Demand analysis identifies market segments. The demand

---

1. Although the process is commonly referred to as *market analysis*, all appraisals must include a *marketability analysis* as well. Marketability analysis includes market analysis as well as capture estimation. More information on marketability analysis is presented in Chapter 11.

for specific property uses must be understood to consider alternative uses, to select appropriate comparables, to forecast future rents and occupancies that indicate the financial return for various property types, and/or to identify when a property should be developed for a particular use and when its value should increase.

The balance of supply and demand at any given time is the key to estimating value. In a growth market characterized by increasing demand, the supply of all types of real estate may be relatively limited or inelastic and this scarcity will lead to higher prices in the short run. Supply may change over the long term, however, bringing about a decline in prices. Demand generally has a more immediate impact on value or probable selling price than supply. In an overbuilt market where supply exceeds demand, the quantity of existing and proposed supply will have a more immediate impact on value.

The Role of Market Analysis in the Appraisal Process

Market analysis in appraisal has two basic functions. First, market analysis provides the data input to identify the highest and best use of a property in terms of 1) property use 2) market support (economic demand) and timing (absorption rates), and 3) market participants (probable users and buyers). The second major function is to provide data input and identify the key factors of value that are to be measured by applying the three approaches to value.

Supply and demand considerations direct the collection of data required to develop a picture of the economic environment that affects the property. Such an economic overview includes a description of the general economy and analysis of economic patterns, trends, and cycles. Economic research also provides data and support for the three approaches to value. Market analysis facilitates the selection of comparables, the calculation of adjustments, and the forecasting of income streams and makes it possible to identify the effective demand for and competitive supply of a particular property type in a specific location at a specific time.

A fundamental component of an appraisal is documented evidence that there is an appropriate level of market support for the existing use of the site or for alternative uses. Through supply and demand analysis, the appraiser identifies and tests the level of market support, which is critical in the analysis of highest and best use.

Highest and best use, in turn, links the physical, legal, design, and locational attributes of a property to market demand and financial feasibility. Unlike many other products and commodities, real estate may have alternative uses; demand for a property with certain attributes may be expressed by different groups of users at different prices.

As one approach to market analysis, the analyst identifies how desirable the attributes of the property are to alternative market segments. This approach is especially appropriate in real estate appraisal because a site's address is often the only information an appraiser has to begin his or her investigation. To define the market for the real estate, the attributes of the property are identified and analyzed in a process called *productivity analysis*. Productivity analysis examines a property's attributes to determine the marketability of the property in terms of the specific services it provides and the specific needs it satisfies. (An in-depth discussion of productivity analysis is found in Chapter 3.)

In productivity analysis the appraiser considers the attributes of the site and the improvement, concentrating on how the property's physical, legal, design, and locational attributes are combined to meet the needs of competitive users. Productivity analysis facilitates the determination of highest and best use by identifying a range of possible uses and linking the real estate product to specific market segment.

Productivity analysis is particularly important in the valuation of a complex product like real estate. Real property is an extremely heterogeneous product that is differentiated qualitatively and many real estate markets are characterized by a lack of data. By concentrating on the site's attributes, productivity analysis can enhance the appraiser's understanding of the limited data available and help reduce the complexity of the valuation assignment. In the analysis of alternative uses for a given site, the analyst considers the combination of physical, legal, and locational property characteristics as a package. By considering these attributes collectively, the analyst can assess the marketability of the property and its resulting value.

Because market analysis links the property's attributes to market preferences, it is indispensable to the highest and best use determination and to value measurement. Supply analysis not only identifies competitive properties, but also compares specific competitive attributes. The desirability of a property's attributes forms the basis for identifying the market segment that constitutes the demand for the property. By linking competitive supply to effective demand, productivity analysis helps the appraiser identify the marketability of a given parcel.

Although real estate is physically fixed, the attributes of a property can support a variety of uses. Therefore, real estate is said to be economically flexible. To address the complex physical and economic characteristics of a property, extensive data must be compiled. These data are used not only to fix the parameters of the market, but also to identify possible alternative real estate products. Because a broad range of issues influence real estate markets, a systematic approach to research is required.

The Scientific Method and the Appraisal Process

The appraisal process and the scientific method are two organized methods for solving problems. The scientific method can be applied to investigate economic problems and to document value estimates empirically.

The five-step process described below highlights the similarities of the scientific method and the appraisal process.

Step 1

The scientific method begins with identification of the problem. Sometimes identifying the problem correctly can be 90% of the solution. The appraisal process also begins with the identification of a problem, but the range of problem situations is generally more limited. The problem to be solved in an appraisal is indicated by the use of the appraisal–i.e., the reason the client needs the property appraised. Problem identification directs the collection of information, documentation, and analysis. Appraisals may be undertaken for various purposes, including

- Transactions–the acquisition or disposition of property
- The extension of credit–the estimation of collateral value
- Indemnification–compensation for property loss
- Taxation
- The development or redevelopment of real estate
- Alternative use considerations
- Real estate portfolio analysis and management

This book focuses on the estimation of market value. As illustrated in Exhibit 1.1, the valuation process begins with identification of the property, the property rights to be valued, the use of the appraisal, and the date of the value estimate.

Depending on the problem, a different starting point for the research process or a shift in emphasis may be required. Exhibits 1.2, 1.3, and 1.4 illustrate scenarios that may call for alternative starting points and emphasis in the market research process. These scenarios will be discussed later in the chapter. As mentioned previously, this book will examine the market analysis component of an appraisal to estimate the market value of a specific site.

Step 2

The second step in the scientific method is the formulation of a hypothesis. A hypothesis is a tentative assumption about the relationship between one situation and another. In an appraisal the hypothesis is stated in the purpose of the assignment, which is to estimate a defined value, generally market value. The defined value can vary with the appraisal problem. For example, the purpose of an appraisal required in an indemnification conflict may be the estimation of insurable value. This is an example of a traditional site- or property-specific appraisal. The hypotheses offered in alternative problem situations (e.g., finding the best location for a store, choosing among investments) as depicted in Exhibits 1.3 and 1.4 need to be more flexible.

Generally, the hypothesis set forth in a real estate market analysis concerns supply and demand relationships with respect to a given product. Such a hypothesis is founded upon the productivity analysis of the property and the identified supply and demand relationships that characterize the market.

Exhibit 1.1   Valuation Process

Definition of the Problem

Identification of real estate   Identification of property rights to be valued

Date of value estimate   Identification of use and users of appraisal

Definition of value   Description of scope of work

Other limiting conditions

Extraordinary and hypothetical assumptions

Market/Marketability Analysis

Property productivity analysis

· Physical attributes analysis

· Legal/political attributes analysis

· Locational attributes analysis

Market (supply and demand) analysis

· Inventory and analysis of competitive properties

· Demand studies

· Marginal demand studies

Subject capture analysis

Highest and Best Use Analysis

Conclusions:

· Land as though vacant   · Use

· Property as improved   · Time (probable use date or occupancy forecast)

                                                        - Market participants

                                                        - User of space

                                                        - Most probable buyer

---

Collection and Screening of Specific Comparable Data

Data required for analytic technique to measure value

Land Value Estimate

Application of the Three Approaches

Cost   Sales comparison   Income capitalization

Reconciliation of Value Indications and Final Value Estimate

Report of Defined Value

Step 3

The problem situation and the hypothesis set forth establish the data requirements for the research process. The availability and accessibility of data are major problems in conducting real estate research. Although the data available may not meet the needs of the research assignment, the best information available will have to be used. The data available often determine which valuation techniques are used in appraisal and market analysis. For example, the units of comparison selected in the sales comparison approach and the capitalization technique employed in the income approach may depend on the market data that can be collected. In market analysis, an employment forecast may be used to estimate demand when population forecasts are not available or do not appear to be realistic. The nature of the problem, the formulation of the hypothesis, and the availability of data help the analyst decide what research methodology should be employed.

Step 4

The fourth step in the scientific method is the application of an appropriate methodology. Once the problem is identified and a hypothesis is proposed, specific relationships can be tested. These relationships can be investigated by inductive and deductive means, using analogy, descriptive analysis, statistical analysis, observation, laboratory testing, and cause and effect analysis.

Most valuation techniques and methods of market analysis fall under the categories of analogy, descriptive analysis, and cause and effect analysis.

Step 5

The final step in the scientific method is the reconciliation of the findings to arrive at a solution to the problem. The analyst's objective is to fit the solution to the problem. This is the concluding step in the market research and appraisal processes as well.

The Market Research Process

Most market analyses for real estate can be described as one of three general scenarios: a site in search of a use or market, a use or market in search of a site, or real property as an alternative investment instrument.

In the first scenario—a site in search of a use or market—the analyst must determine whether there is appropriate support for a use and, if so, delineate the market that supports that use. This is the typical appraisal assignment and the focus of this book.

In this case the analytic process begins by identifying the productive attributes of the site to identify the property's productive capacity, the real estate services it can supply, and the market of potential users. Often any number of uses may be suitable for a given parcel of real estate. A land parcel may be an appropriate site for residential, retail, office, industrial, or institutional use. The physical, legal, and locational attributes of the site determine its productive capacity and use.

After completing the productivity analysis, the appraiser begins the second step in the process—identifying the competitive supply and effective demand for the site. Supply and demand analysis is the essence of market research; real estate market research defines the market in a spatial or geographic context.

The patterns of market activity identified in the supply and demand analysis suggest the appropriate decision model. In analyzing a site in search of a use or market, the productive capacity of the property is related to market activity. This analysis sets the stage for the application of appropriate valuation techniques.

Exhibit 1.2   Market Research Scenario 1

Market Research Scenario 1

A Site in Search of a Use or Market

Alternative Use Scoping

Productivity Analysis
A.   Physical attributes
B.   Legal attributes
C.   Location attributes
     Market Appeal and Use Implications

Market Activities
A.   Supply analysis
     1.   Competition measures
     2.   Qualitative measures
B.   Demand analysis
     1.   Consumer profile
     2.   Quantitative measures
C.   Market interaction
     1.   Capture rates
     2.   Absorption rates

Appraisal Analysis
A.   Value theory
B.   Valuation techniques
     1.   Cost approach
     2.   Sales comparison approach
     3.   Income approach
C.   Reconciliation and the appraisal process

Use or Value

The second scenario concerns a use or market in search of a site. This scenario, which is shown in Exhibit 1.3, begins with the investigation of the broader market to identify the types of services or facilities the market is seeking. If the inquiry is focused on use, the analysis begins by addressing demand, e.g., basic and general demographics. If finding an appropriate site is the objective of the analysis, a particular use is identified, market preferences are studied, and the competitive supply is investigated.

As Exhibit 1.3 shows, this type of assignment begins with supply and demand analysis and then proceeds to productivity analysis which addresses the physical, legal, and locational attributes of the site. The market analysis and productivity analysis are then incorporated into the appraisal process.

In comparing the two scenarios described, appraisers will recognize that the first scenario, a site in search of a use or market, is the basis of most appraisal assignments. Appraisers are asked to value a specific site. Although the appraisal process includes the analysis of general data on the city or region, the process focuses on the site. Analyzing the *situs* or totality of a property's locational attributes is difficult if the assignment is not site- or use-specific. The second scenario, a market or use in search of a site, is often the task of a specialist in market analysis. Such an assignment is an extension of the traditional appraisal process, with a different emphasis and different applications of traditional analytical tools.

The third scenario involves the consideration of real estate as an alternative investment instrument. Again, this scenario has a different emphasis. To investigate market support for a real estate investment, the analyst may study an individual parcel of real estate or multiple parcels within a portfolio. Portfolio analysis is growing in importance due to the increased influence of institutional investors in both national and local real estate markets.

Exhibit 1.4 illustrates the analysis of real estate as an alternative investment. The focus of the analysis is to identify whether the levels of return and risk associated with the real estate are appropriate given the requirements of the investors. The decision-making models used by the investors are identified to establish the parameters of the problem. Measures of return and risk are linked to standards of market performance and opportunity cost.

Analyzing real estate as an investment includes the investigation of alternative investments as well as the decision-making models used by investors. Subsequent market analysis addresses competitive supply and effective demand. Because the location of a real estate investment significantly affects its profitability, the final stage of the analysis considers spatial concerns, exploring whether the macro-location of the property will allow it to achieve the desired returns.

The three scenarios described represent general problem situations in the market research process which address the particular needs of different decision makers. This book is concerned with the first scenario, which most closely replicates the variety of problem situations

Exhibit 1.3   Market Research Scenario 2

A Use or Market in Search of a Site

Identification of Market Need

Market Activities

A. Supply analysis
    1. Competition measures
    2. Qualitative measures
B. Demand analysis
    1. Consumer profile
    2. Quantitative measures
C. Market interaction
    1. Capture rates
    2. Absorption rates

Market Appeal and Use Implication
Productivity Analysis

A. Location attributes
B. Physical attributes
C. Legal attributes

Appraisal Analysis

A. Value theory
B. Valuation techniques
    1. Cost approach
    2. Sales comparison approach
    3. Income approach
C. Reconciliation and the appraisal process

Site and Value

appraisers face. The appraisal process is flexible enough to accommodate all three scenarios discussed here. The specific issues to be addressed are treated in different sections of the appraisal report, e.g., site and improvement analyses, neighborhood analysis, city/regional analysis, and highest and best use analysis.

After the enactment of the Financial Institutions Reform, Recovery, and Enforcement Act (FIRREA) in 1989, many appraisers began providing separate market analysis sections in their reports. It is logical to link market analysis to highest and best use analysis, which explicitly addresses the components of value–i.e., utility, scarcity, desire, and effective purchasing power. Market analysis supports the conclusion of highest and best use by assessing the productivity of the property and documenting the level of market support and financial feasibility.

Exhibit 1.4   Market Research Scenario 3

Real Estate as an Investment Alternative

Risk and Return Objectives

Investment/Appraisal Analysis
A.   Decision models and valuation techniques
    1.   Return measures
    2.   Risk measures
    3.   Discounted cash flow analysis
B.   Identification of rates in alternative markets

Market Activities
Market risk and return analysis
A.   Supply analysis
    1.   Competition measures
    2.   Qualitative measures
B.   Demand analysis
    1.   Investor profile
    2.   Quantitative measures
C.   Market interaction
    1.   Capture rates
    2.   Absorption rates

Market Appeal and Use Implication
Productivity Analysis
A.   Location attributes
B.   Physical attributes
C.   Legal attributes

Site and Value

The Six-Step Market Analysis Process for Appraisal

The typical appraisal assignment is performed to derive an opinion of the market value of a specific property and follows the "site in search of use" model shown in Exhibit 1.2. The applications presented in this book reflect this model and employ the six-step process shown in Exhibit 1.5. The process addresses the following questions:

- What attributes does the subject property offer the market?
- Who are the most likely users of these attributes?
- Is the property use needed? (demand analysis)
- What is the competition? (supply analysis)
- What is the condition of the market? (comparing supply and demand)
- How much of this market can the subject capture?

The conclusions of the study are used in the appraisal to address the financial implications for the subject in terms of highest and best use and value.

The six step process is used in studying alternative uses of property. In this context, the process functions as a screening mechanism and alternative use(s) forecast model. The amount and timing of the demand for a particular use is then used in the financial analysis of highest and best use alternatives.

The process is also used in appraisal situations where alternative use is not a major concern, but the value of the current use is. The focus of the six-step process then becomes the identification of market and marketability prospects for the current use. The market/marketability forecast for the subject property is used in the valuation part of the appraisal, which typically involves application of the cost, sales comparison and income approaches to value.

The following outline of the components of the six step process (Exhibit 1.5) is referenced throughout this book.

Summary

The treatment of market analysis in an appraisal is determined by the nature of the assignment and the specific problem confronting the decision maker. Once the purpose and function of the appraisal are identified, the appraiser will select a level of analysis appropriate to the problem. An appraisal should include a market analysis component that not only fulfills regulatory requirements, but also complements the application of the appraisal process.

It is impossible to estimate the market value of a property without considering the supply of and demand for the property within a specific time frame. Market analysis links value theory and valuation techniques and documents the supply and demand relationship on which the value estimate is based. Moreover, market analysis identifies which use among alternative uses the market supports, and thus helps determine the highest and best use of a property.

The steps in the scientific method are analogous to the steps in the appraisal process. Three general scenarios for real estate market analysis can be identified: a site in search of a use or market, a use or market in search of a site, and real property as an alternative investment instrument. The appraisal process is flexible enough to accommodate all three scenarios.

In each market analysis scenario, a general overview of the economic base and a survey of growth patterns in the community are linked to the property's attributes. The economic overview is tied to specific data on the attributes of the subject and comparable properties. The dynamics of metropolitan growth are also related to the subject and comparable properties. These linkages, which are identified in market analysis, are examined to determine the highest and best use of a property. The relationship between the economic base, market activity, and property productivity provides the foundation for the three approaches to value.

Exhibit 1.5   Market/Marketability Analysis

SIX-STEP PROCESS

Step 1. DEFINE THE PRODUCT (Property Productivity Analysis)
A. Physical attributes
B. Legal and regulatory attributes
   1. Private
   2. Public
C. Location attributes
   1. Identification of economic attributes - the association between land uses and their linkages
   2. Identification of the movement of demand in relation to the direction of urban growth

Step 2. MARKET DELINEATION
A. Market area delineation concepts
   1. Time-distance concepts and standards
   2. Area over which equally desirable substitute properties tend to compete with the subject
B. Market delineation techniques
   1. Gravity models
   2. Customer spotting

Step 3. DEMAND ANALYSIS
A. Demand segmentation
   1. Identification of characteristics of most probable user (consumer profile)
B. Tastes and preferences: behavioral, motivational, and psychological factors
C. Inferred demand analysis
   Analysis of historical growth and absorption data
D. Fundamental demand forecast
   Submarket-specific demand forecast
   Major demand drivers
   1. Population creates households.
   2. Income creates retail buying power.
   3. Employment creates office/industrial users.

Step 4. SUPPLY ANALYSIS (Survey and Forecast of Competition)
A. Existing stock of competitive properties
B. Properties under construction
C. Potential competition
   1. Proposed construction
   2. Probable additional construction
D. Attributes and characteristics of competitive properties.
   1. Economic and financial
   2. Locational
   3. Site
   4. Structure

Step 5. ANALYZE THE INTERACTION OF SUPPLY AND DEMAND
A. Competitive environment
B. Residual demand concepts

Step 6. FORECAST SUBJECT CAPTURE (Market Penetration Concepts)
A. Inferred methods
   Comparison of subject to general market Indicators
   · Comparable property data
   · Secondary data surveys and forecasts
   · Subject historical performance
   · Local economic analysis
   · Other
B. Fundamental capture methods
   Estimate subject capture potential of fundamental demand forecast by methods such as:
   · Share of market
   · Adjust by quantifiable rating techniques
   · Subject historical capture rate
   · Other
C. Reconcile subject capture indications derived by analysis of inferred and fundamental methods

USE OF STUDY PROCESS (SIX-STEP) CONCLUSIONS
· Economic demand data for financial testing of highest and best use alternatives
· Economic demand data for the valuation models

CHAPTER 2

Levels of Market Analysis

Chapter Objectives

- To explain the concept of *levels* of market analysis
- To identify the criteria for determining the appropriate level of market analysis for a given assignment
- To describe each of the four component tasks in market analysis
  - productivity (property location) analysis
  - demand analysis (inferred demand or fundamental demand)
  - competitive supply analysis
  - highest and best use conclusion and marketability analysis
- To identify key items to check in evaluating the adequacy of the market analysis in an appraisal

Appraisers need to identify the amount of market research and documentation required in appraisal analyses and appraisal reports. The various levels of analysis that may be appropriate range from the application of relatively general techniques to increasingly complex ones. Two broad categories of analysis may be distinguished: *inferred analysis* and *fundamental analysis.*

Inferred Analysis Versus Fundamental Analysis

Inferred analysis, which is sometimes called *trend analysis,* is similar to the technical analysis practiced by stock market analysts. This type of analysis is an attempt to estimate future changes in value by investigating past market behavior. In a technical analysis, the analyst identifies trends and patterns and infers expected market behavior. In a similar manner, real estate analysts frequently use statistics to draw inferences about a general class of phenomena, studying data from the recent past to predict future occurrences.[1]

It may be inferred, for example, that the future performance of the subject property will follow the past performance of other properties in its class. If the office occupancy rate in City X has increased from 80% two years ago to 90% today, it might be inferred from the macro data for a broad real estate sector that the subject will follow this trend, achieving 95% occupancy next year and full occupancy the following year. The stabilized occupancy inferred from this analysis might be used in the 10-year discounted cash flow (DCF) analysis required in many appraisals of income-producing property.

Fundamental analysis goes beyond trend analysis, forecasting demand based on segmentation of broad demographic and economic data to reflect the subject property's specific submarket. For example, if the subject is a neighborhood retail shopping center, demand is forecast only for neighborhood retail centers in the specific market area of the subject. To estimate the future capture rate of a retail property, a demand forecast of the submarket is completed and the subject is compared only with the specific properties that compete with the subject in that sub-market. Fundamental analysis of real estate markets is based on the principle that real estate value is tied to the services the real estate provides. As applied to the stock market, fundamental analysis may be defined as "an investment analysis technique that emphasizes investigation of the underlying business activity of the firm whose securities are being considered."[2] Fundamental analysis of a stock or parcel of real estate is based on the theory that the worth of an asset is "anchored in something called 'intrinsic value,' which can be determined by careful (fundamental) analysis of present conditions and future prospects."[3]

---

1. Gaylon E. Greer and Michael D. Farrell, *Investment Analysis for Real Estate Decisions,* 2d ed. (New York: The Dryden Press, 1988), 520 and 81.
2. Ibid., 4, 81, and 506.
3. Burton G. Malkiel, *Random Walk Down Wall Street* (New York: W.W. Norton & Sons, Inc., 1990), 28.

A comparison can be drawn between inferred analysis and fundamental analysis using an example from the stock market. An investor who is considering the purchase of IBM stock may infer how IBM stock will perform by examining the daily report of Standard & Poor's 500. If the stock average is trending up, the investor might infer that IBM stock will also rise. Making use of fundamental analysis, the investor can take the study a step further and analyze underlying market demand for IBM products. Such an analysis might segment specific demand for IBM products to determine IBM's market share within the computer industry. The investor might also look into the management and tooling of IBM industrial plants to determine whether they are efficiently run and equipped to produce the products desired by today's computer market. Finally, rival computer manufacturers might be studied to assess the competitive potential of IBM. With an informed market outlook, the investor could reach a decision as to whether or not the purchase of IBM stock at today's price seems like a profitable investment.

In a real estate context, the performance of a property may either be inferred based on macroeconomic trends or forecast through fundamental analysis of the specific property market. The anticipated level of occupancy for an office building provides an example. If the market has been steadily improving and the subject has a good location and a modern design, it can be inferred that the building will maintain a high level of occupancy for the typical 10-year holding period considered in many appraisals. If, on the other hand, the forecast for white-collar employment is lower than current white-collar employment and new competition is likely to emerge over the next few years, then an inferred analysis of occupancy trends might be misleading. An analysis of occupancy trends might produce entirely different expectations than a fundamental analysis of the office building market.

So, inferred analysis may be described as a projection of historical trends focusing on macro data. Inferred analysis is not subject-specific. Fundamental analysis, on the other hand, is based on micro data for a specific real estate submarket and includes a forecast of that submarket's future demand and future competition. Fundamental analysis is specifically focused on the subject real estate.

The two broad categories of inferred and fundamental analysis may be further broken down into sublevels. It is possible to identify many different sublevels, or strata, of analyses because there is considerable variation in assignments. This text will examine four general strata that can be identified as Levels A, B, C, and D. Level A represents the least in-depth analysis and Level D the most elaborate analysis. Data reflecting Level A and B market analysis are generally interspersed throughout an appraisal report, in the sections on area or regional analysis, highest and best use, and the specific approaches to value. Level A and B market analyses reflect inferred analysis. The two more in-depth levels, Levels C and D, are most often presented in a discrete section of the appraisal report devoted solely to market analysis. Levels

C and D represent applications of fundamental analysis. A comparison of the major characteristics of inferred and fundamental analyses appears in Exhibit 2.1.

Exhibit 2.1	Levels of Market Study in Appraisal			
	Inferred Demand Studies		**Fundamental (Derived) Demand Studies**	
Level of Study	**A**	**B**	**C**	**D**
Inferred subject attributes			Quantified subject attributes	
Inferred locational determinants of use & marketability by macro analysis			Quantified and graphic analysis of location determinants of use & marketability by macro and micro analysis	
Inferred demand from general economic base analysis conducted by others			Inferred demand derived by original economic base analysis	
Inferred demand by selected comparables			Forecast demand by subject-specific market segment & demographic data	
Inferred supply by selected comparables			Quantified supply by inventorying existing & forecasting planned competition	
Inferred equilibrium/highest and best use and capture conclusions			Quantified equilibrium · Highest and best use—graphic—map · Timing—quantified capture forecast	
Emphasis is on:			**Emphasis is on:**	
· Instinctive knowledge			· Quantifiable data	
· Historical data			· Forecast	
· Judgment			· Judgment	

Note: An appraisal without a fundamental demand study—i.e., Level C or D market analysis —is designed to estimate value only in a certain and stable market.

Descriptions of Levels

Although market analysis cannot be standardized, clients expect, and reliable value estimates require, some level of market analysis in an appraisal. Naturally, the level of study will vary with the client's needs, market conditions, and the property type. The general categories or levels of market study are described below.

Level A

Level A market analysis is general and descriptive, not subject-specific. This level of analysis relies on historical data rather than future projections. General data and selected comparables are presumed to reflect the market. The conclusions based on such a study might apply to most similar properties in the city. For example, a Level A location analysis provides only a general description of the area or neighborhood. The analysis usually relies on generic data that are updated annually. If general growth trends for the city and region are positive, future demand is assumed to exist. The treatment of the data does not usually relate area-wide demand to the subject property, but leaves the reader to *infer* the level of demand that exists for the subject.

Typically, Level A analyses only indirectly address the supply side of the market by reference to vacancy rates for selected rent or sale comparables. These vacancy rates serve as indicators of oversupply or undersupply. Vacancy projections are based on the assumption that these rates will remain stable.

Exhibit 2.2 is an example of Level A analysis. The chart provides data on the residential building permits issued by a city over the past eight years. An appraiser could use these data to infer demand for all types of real estate. In the example, the trend seems to be a steady decline. Based on a "feel for the market," the appraiser might make judgments about the duration of this downward cycle and its impact on the subject property.

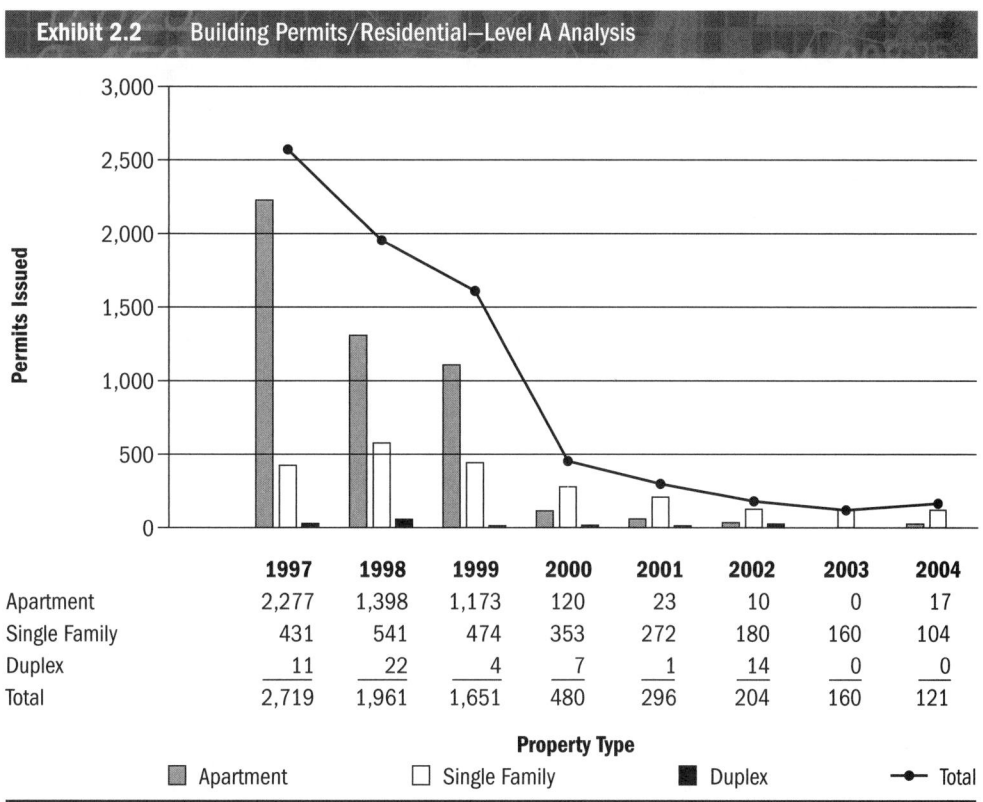

Exhibit 2.2   Building Permits/Residential—Level A Analysis

	1997	1998	1999	2000	2001	2002	2003	2004
Apartment	2,277	1,398	1,173	120	23	10	0	17
Single Family	431	541	474	353	272	180	160	104
Duplex	11	22	4	7	1	14	0	0
Total	2,719	1,961	1,651	480	296	204	160	121

Property Type

■ Apartment   □ Single Family   ■ Duplex   —●— Total

Level B

Level B analyses employ area-wide market data on a general property class. The projected-use conclusions are more subject-specific, and the timing projections depend on interpretation of market-wide data on the property type. For example, a Level B analysis typically employs data from regularly published, area-wide market surveys prepared by proprietary firms or public agencies. These surveys are usually conducted for each class of property–i.e., retail, apartment, office building. The data are updated at regular intervals, either quarterly or semi-annually. However, even periodic updates may lag behind changes in a dynamic market in which data become obsolete all too soon. These public and proprietary surveys typically cover broad areas in an urban setting and the geographic boundaries of the survey rarely conform to the submarket for the subject property.

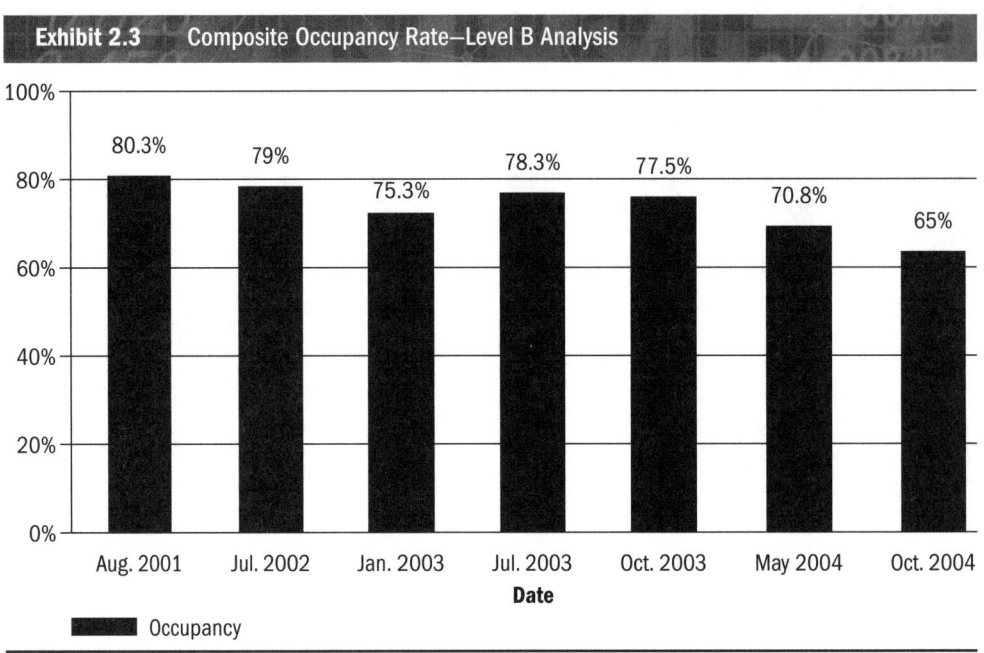

Exhibit 2.3   Composite Occupancy Rate—Level B Analysis

In Level B studies, secondary data are used extensively and must be scrutinized to determine how well they fit the problem. The analyst usually infers that the subject's submarket will perform in a manner similar to the historical performance of the broad class of property to which it belongs. The use of broad-based market survey data increases the reliability of the analysis, but reliance on such data has its limitations. Level B analyses may cover many projects that are not competitive with the subject. Moreover, the historical pattern of the broader market may not reflect the future prospects of the property. The appraiser must carefully evaluate the data used to determine how well they fit the actual assignment.

A graphic analysis of Level B data is presented in Exhibit 2.3. The data show a decline in office occupancy over the past four years. The appraiser might infer that this indicates either a downward trend for the future or the bottoming out of a market that will be improving shortly.

Level C

Level C analysis goes further. Whereas Level A and B analyses use historical absorption rates as indicators of future absorption, a major shift occurs in Level C analyses, which incorporate future-oriented forecasting techniques. Future demand and absorption are forecast by first projecting the growth of population, income, and employment. A Level C study provides detailed submarket data on which to base absorption and *NOI* projections as well as a competitive ranking of the subject property. A Level C study for an appraisal of vacant land, for example, will include a proposed land use plan that specifies the probable property use or most appropriate mixture of uses and the timing of development.

Level C analyses make extensive use of primary data, which are compiled by conducting field work and direct surveys. A Level C inventory includes all properties that currently exist in the defined market as well as all planned properties. (A more complete discussion of primary and secondary data is provided in Chapter 10.)

Exhibit 2.4 depicts a Level C study of *marginal demand*, i.e., any additional demand that exists (based on an inventory of current supply) or that is forecast to develop (based on an inventory of anticipated supply). The Level C study forecasts specific submarket demand for housing units similar to the subject property. In the example, an oversupply is forecast for Years 4, 5, and 6. These supply and demand data could be presented in an appraisal to support future rent and occupancy projections for the subject under the proposed use, the probable timing of the uses of vacant land, and other similar judgments made by the appraiser.

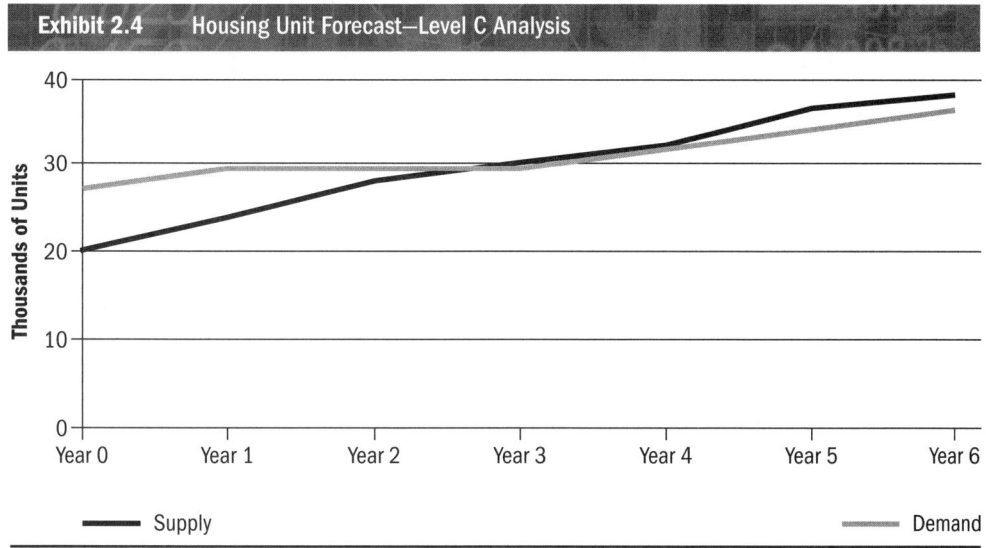

Exhibit 2.4   Housing Unit Forecast—Level C Analysis

Level D

A Level D analysis provides the most detailed type of market study available. While the number of applications for Level D analyses is unlimited, only a few will be mentioned here.

A Level D study might include an analysis of urban planning and land use policy, public and private fiscal capabilities, probability weighting of use projections, and risk ratings. Original economic base analysis is typical of Level D studies. Forecast demand based on employment projections is segmented in great detail. The demand forecast for a shopping center may be broken down into the demand for each retail product line and the total square feet area of each type of competitive store. For example, jewelry stores, sporting goods stores, and shoe stores are analyzed separately for demand and competition.

Level D analyses may also call for attitudinal surveys and direct interviews with market participants active in the market segment identified for the subject property. These techniques are applied in a structured manner that conforms to accepted standards of statistical analysis. For example, a market survey aimed at prospective apartment tenants might quantify the level of demand for fireplaces or other specific amenities that tenants would require as an inducement to relocate to the subject property. Probability weighting and risk analysis are used in deriving marketability conclusions.

Exhibit 2.5 indicates the level or levels of analysis appropriate to typical studies found in appraisal reports.[4]

Criteria for Determining Appropriate Level of Market Analysis

Appraisers use specific criteria to determine the level of market analysis appropriate to a particular appraisal assignment. The appraiser might use the following guidelines to decide which level of analysis to apply:

- The regulatory requirements incumbent upon appraisers, e.g., the Uniform Standards of Professional Appraisal Practice, specific legislation, memoranda or circulars of government agencies
- The needs of the client or user of the appraisal
- The market conditions prevailing at the time of the appraisal
- The complexity of the property being appraised

Regulatory Requirements

The need for market analysis is emphasized throughout the Uniform Standards of Professional Appraisal Practice (USPAP-2004 Edition).[5] For example, Standards Rule 1-3(a) specifies the need for market analysis in all appraisals to support the use determination and estimate of value.

---

4. Stephen F. Fanning and Jody Winslow, "Guidelines for Defining the Scope of Market Analysis in Appraisal Assignments," *The Appraisal Journal* (October 1988).

5. *Uniform Standards of Professional Appraisal Practice*, 2005 edition, published by The Appraisal Foundation.

Exhibit 2.5   Levels of Market Analysis

Work Item	A	B	C	D
Location				
General description—city and neighborhood	X	X	X	X
Specific analysis of site linkages		X	X	X
Specific analysis of urban growth determinants		X	X	X
Detailed competitive location rating			X	X
Detailed probable future land use analysis				X
Demand Analysis				
General evidence of sales/leasing activity	X	X	X	X
General city growth trends	X	X	X	X
Analysis of overall market absorption from secondary data		X	X	X
Demand forecast by specific projections of population, employment, and income			X	X
Demand forecast for subject market segment			X	X
Direct attitudinal survey of target market				X
Competitive Supply Analysis				
Vacancy rates for selected comparables		X	X	X
Vacancy rate from secondary data—broad market surveys			X	X
Field research on all competitive properties			X	X
Research on proposed properties—field inspection, building permit analysis, identification of potential sites			X	X
Detailed competitive amenities rating			X	X
Direct interviews with developers				X
Highest and Best Use Conclusion and Marketability or Timing				
Vacant Land				
Probable use and timing but no specific timetable for development	X			
Generalized land use plan				
Probable use supported by present value analysis		X		
Timing supported by secondary data		X	X	X
Specific land use plan				
Probable use supported by present value analysis		X	X	X
Land plan drawn to site			X	X
Timing based on marginal demand and competitive rating analysis			X	X
Cost estimate for subject development				X
Value impact analysis of alternative marketing/development strategies				X
Improved Properties				
General *ad hoc* judgments	X			
NOI projection supported by performance of selected comparables	X	X	X	X
Use, timing, *NOI* projection supported by analysis of secondary data		X	X	X
Capture rate/*NOI* projection supported by marginal demand of market segment and competitive ratings			X	X
Risk analysis of *NOI* forecast				X
Value impact analysis of alternative marketing/development strategies				X

Appraisers are advised to "identify and analyze the effect on use and value of existing land use regulations, reasonably probable modifications of such land use regulations, economic supply and demand, the physical adaptability of the real estate and market area trends."

Other standards have long addressed the need for market analysis in all appraisals. The final guidelines to implement the Financial Institutions Reform, Recovery and Enforcement Act (FIRREA), set forth in 1990, require that the defined market value be "designed to provide an accurate and reliable measure of the economic potential of property involved in federally related transactions."[6]

Although these standards confirm the need for market analysis in an appraisal, they do not specify the level or extent of market analysis to be developed.

Because current requirements are not specific as to the level of study, the appraiser must be aware of new interpretations of existing standards as well as new standards promulgated in the future. While a Level A analysis might be acceptable in some cases, a Level B or possibly a Level C analysis would be the minimum requirement for the majority of commercial appraisals.

Client Needs

An appraisal serves the needs of the client, who is typically engaged in decision making for lending or underwriting purposes. The basis for property profitability and value is marketability. The level of market analysis performed should match the level of information a client requires to reach a decision. The appraisal may be viewed as a service to help reduce (but not eliminate) risk for the client and the public. The greater the potential risk, the more intensive the level of analysis required. The tolerance the client and regulatory agency have for risk will determine the level of study needed. The appraisal can lend confidence to the client's decision by providing the conclusion of highest and best use, projections of *NOI*, the estimated timing of the project, and documentation for the demand forecast.

Prevailing Market Conditions

In a market characterized by stability or equilibrium, a less intensive analysis may meet the needs of the client. A stable or balanced market usually exhibits three features: a steady number of sales in the recent past, the absence of overbuilding or a supply shortage, and available public studies documenting market equilibrium. If these conditions exist, a Level A or Level B analysis may be acceptable.

An unbalanced market is characterized by few recent sales, much construction activity or an expected surge in such activity, and public studies that report or forecast market disequilibrium. A Level C analysis would most likely be the minimal level of analysis required to satisfy the exigencies of this kind of market.

---

6. *Federal Register,* August 22, 1990, Section C, 1608.2.

Complexity of the Property

The level of market analysis varies with the type and size of the property. Property type refers to the use to which an existing improved property is put, the use proposed for a property that is to be developed, or the absence of any use designation, as is the case of raw land. Size is generally related to property type. For a small, income-producing residential property, a Level A analysis might be adequate. For most income-producing properties, however, a Level B analysis would likely be the minimum. For moderate-sized commercial properties, a Level C analysis would seem to be the minimum, especially if sufficient demand to support the property is in doubt. Complex properties such as mixed-use developments generally require a Level D analysis.

Existing improvements usually have some income history and the use determination is likely to be straightforward. Net operating income is not always certain, however, and it is here that market analysis becomes most significant. When raw land is appraised, questions arise about alternative uses and their timing. A Level B study is generally the appropriate minimum for a parcel of raw land in a fairly stable market with limited alternative use potential. As the size of the vacant tract and the number of alternative uses increase, the level of analysis required will increase. Whenever market conditions are unstable, Level C analysis is considered the minimum regardless of the size of the land parcel. Proposed improvements normally carry a degree of uncertainty and necessitate more in-depth study. Level C analysis would appear to be the appropriate minimum for a proposed project unless it is very small.

Risk is typically related to property size. Small properties usually have shorter marketing periods and more potential buyers. They require smaller financial outlays and carry lower risk. Large properties require longer marketing periods and, thus, entail higher risks. Property value must be considered in light of a reasonable marketing time. The bigger the property, the longer the projection period. A more detailed analysis will be required to enhance the reliability of the appraisal. If the market projection for a big project is faulty, the dollar amount of the error will be high. The appraiser must recognize the direct correspondence between project risk and the required level of market analysis.

Exhibit 2.6 outlines guidelines for determining the level of market analysis appropriate to a given appraisal assignment. Exhibit 2.7 presents a checklist which might be used in an appraisal review to identify inadequate market analyses.

Summary

The four levels of market analysis are distinguished by their relative degree of complexity and manner of presentation. Level A analyses are the most general; Level D studies are the most in-depth. To determine which level is appropriate to the assignment, an appraiser considers

Criterion	Inferred	Fundamental
Market Conditions		
Stable Market		
Steady number of sales		
Absence of overbuilding or undersupply		
Market balance reported in public studies		
Stable prices	X	
Unstable Market		
Sharp increase or decrease in number of sales		
Evidence of overbuilding or undersupply		
Market imbalance reported in public studies		
Unstable prices		X

Note. If the subject is in a stable market, the lowest level of the given range should be selected; if the market is unstable, the highest level should be selected.

Criterion	Inferred	Fundamental
Property Complexity by Type and Size		
Vacant Land		
Simple situation involving single use; clear timing for that use	X	
Complex situation involving multiple use potential; questionable timing for those uses		X
Proposed Project		
Less than 50 lots/25,000 sq. ft.	X	
More than 50 lots/25,000 sq. ft.		X
Improved Property		
Relatively simple assignment		
Less than 5 tenants		
Less than 25,000 sq. ft.	X	
Complex properties		
More than 5 tenants		
Larger than 25,000 sq. ft. or more than $2 million value		X
Highly complex properties		
Hotels, resorts, mixed-use developments, or retail-office space over 25,000 sq. ft.		X
Properties whose future *NOI* is very uncertain		X

Note. If the subject is a small property in a big market, a lower level may be selected; if the subject is a big property in a small market, a higher level should be selected.

four criteria: regulatory requirements, the needs of the client, prevailing market conditions, and the complexity of the subject property.

Each of the four levels may be described in terms of major steps in the market analysis, i.e., property location analysis, demand analysis, competitive supply analysis, and highest and best use/marketability conclusion.

Level A analyses are general and descriptive, not subject-specific. Anticipated market conditions are inferred from historical data rather than forecast. Level B analyses expand upon Level A analyses by ex-

Key parts of the appraisal to check

Identification of the Assignment, Assumptions and Disclosures

❏ Is the market that is forecast consistent with the market for the subject property—i.e., are there any inconsistencies such as the presentation of "filler data" on retail buying power or office vacancy rates in a report on a residential apartment complex?

❏ Are there any special assumptions that make the market forecast untenable—i.e., an assumption that the population will grow by 10%, but no evidence presented to support it?

❏ Are the assumptions underlying the market capture rate estimated for the subject the same as those in the definition of market value?

· Is there any special lender financing?

· Is either party operating under duress?

· Does the marginal demand estimate support the timing?

❏ Is the level of analysis appropriate for the property type and current market conditions?

❏ Who commissioned the appraisal? Appraisals commissioned by third parties are less likely to be biased.

❏ Does the analyst have a vested interest in the property? Appraisers are required to disclose any personal interest in the certification statement.

Market Analysis Component and Specific Approaches to Value

❏ Typical weaknesses of the market analysis (demand and competitive supply analyses)

· Failure to show ranges

· Lack of analysis of different population forecasts

· Overstatement of population forecast

· Overuse of macro data

· Inadequate knowledge or information about the timing of public infrastructure development

· Overly positive analysis of the subject or subject location

· No support for subject capture estimate, i.e., the capture rate given involves a "leap of faith" from the general data

· Only a general area description for the location analysis, without any focus on the subject or competitive properties

❏ Typical weakness of the cost approach

· Estimates of economic obsolescence not consistent with market analysis

❏ Typical weaknesses of the sales comparison approach

· Use of comparables that do not have the same locational and timing characteristics as competitive properties inventoried in the market analysis or lack of adjustments for such differences

· Use of comparable sales that are sales to users while the subject H&B use was investment tract for use in the say 3 to 5 years.

❏ Typical weaknesses of the income capitalization approach

· Forecast of increasing subject rent/sale price or of subject capture is not consistent with market analysis

· Forecast of subject rent/sale price or of subject capture is not based on comparison with specific competition

· Application of a discount rate that is not consistent with the findings of the market analysis; i.e., a low discount rate suggests lower risk, but the forecast and subject capture may be highly optimistic which suggests high risk. This is not consistent.

amining site linkages and determinants of urban growth. Judgments about the use of the subject and the timing for that use are based on data from broad-based market surveys.

Level C analyses, which are based on data generated by the appraiser, include the development of a quantifiable location rating, a demand forecast, a survey of existing and planned competition, and an amenities rating. These facets of the analysis support conclusions about use and timing. Level D analyses examine the policy and budget of a municipality to determine the likelihood of new infrastructure development. Original economic base analysis and direct surveys characterize Level D demand and competitive supply analyses. Detailed development cost estimates, alternative marketing strategies, value impact studies, and risk analyses are associated with Level D analysis.

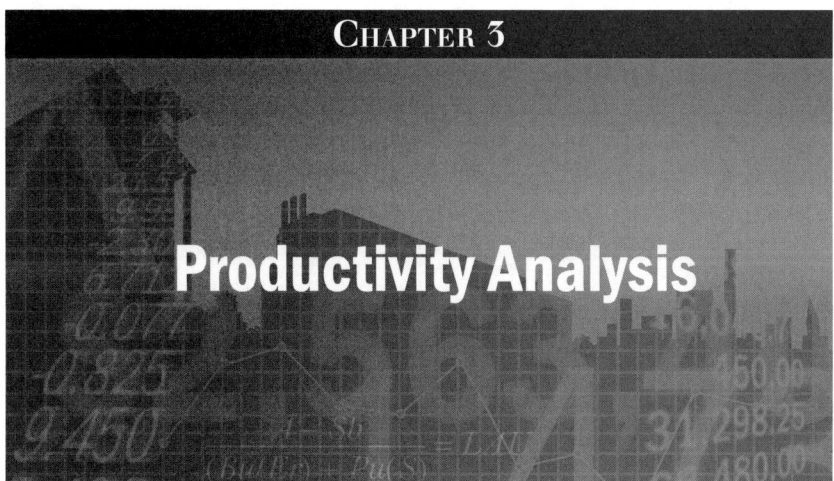

CHAPTER 3

Productivity Analysis

Chapter Objectives

- To introduce the concept of productivity analysis and relate property attributes to market activity and market identification
- To examine the physical features of real property, the first set of attributes studied in productivity analysis
- To discuss the dual nature of real estate–i.e., land vs. capital, commodity vs. resource
- To examine property improvements in terms of their quality, attractiveness, and functional utility and to link these attributes to market activity and property value
- To further define the realty product and its market by relating the legal dimension of real estate to property productivity
- To explore the quantitative and qualitative aspects of real property rights in defining a real estate product and its market
- To discuss the four powers of government, which affect the use and acquisition of private property and alter the market structure, and to examine how a community's regulatory environment is linked to market delineation

Productivity Analysis

Productivity analysis may be defined as analysis of the capacity of a property to house economic activities, supply services, and provide amenities to meet human needs. In other words, productivity analysis examines the ability of a property to serve a market segment.

A property's productive capacity depends on the manner in which the factors of production are combined in the property and the way potential consumers react to the mix of property attributes. The need for productivity analysis arises from several factors, which include the heterogeneous nature of individual properties, the potential for any site to be put to more than one use, and the appraisal practice of analyzing data on comparable properties to arrive at a value estimate for the subject property.

Productivity analysis focuses on the characteristics of a property to establish its competitive position in the market. The major sections of real estate productivity analysis focus on 1)site and building improvements 2) legal attributes and 3) location attributes and urban growth structure. These concepts will be discussed in the next three chapters.

From an historical perspective, productivity analysis is the concept that links Lancaster's New Consumer Theory to real estate.[1] Lancaster's theory is based on the premise that the attributes of a product are priced in the market. Productivity analysis relates the value of a product to the marketability of its attributes. The concept is founded on the economic theory of distribution, which allocates the returns to a product among the factors of production. By identifying a property's attributes and their pricing in the market, an appraiser can compare unique, but similar, real estate products over time.

Property attributes delineate the highest and best use of similar properties. This is true when the similar properties are direct competitors based on their use, and also in limited cases where properties compete even though other attributes make them more suitable for different uses and direct them to different markets. For example, consider an apartment building located on a freeway. A new off ramp is constructed and, over time, the adjacent properties are developed with retail uses. The subject apartment property in still in good shape and producing positive cash flow. The value of the improved property is more than its value would be if it were demolished and put to a retail use, so the apartment building stays even though the highest and best use of the site is for retail use.

The potential for attributes to direct land and property use, and thus delineate the market, is relevant in most market situations. In active markets, the analysis of a property's physical, legal, and locational characteristics helps define the specific product and the services it offers, thus facilitating a more precise identification of the most likely users of the property and a more direct comparison of the subject to

---

1. John C. Lancaster, "New Consumer Theory," *Journal of Political Economy* (April 1966), 132–157.

the most similar properties. In depressed markets, productivity analysis focuses on the potential use of an existing property based on its attributes, allowing the property to be compared with properties that were originally developed for different uses.

Productivity analysis allows the analyst to compare and contrast similar and dissimilar attributes of competing assets, especially durable goods and real property. The analysis of attributes helps appraisers identify appropriate competitive properties, but competitive supply is more than just comparable properties. For example, in studying the supply of competitive housing, the analyst must consider whether or not single-family residences or condominiums are viable alternatives to apartments. In the student housing market, dormitories represent another possible alternative. Assuming that apartment space has a 95% occupancy rate in a medium-sized market, what are the implications if the university, with an enrollment of 40,000 students, decides to build a dormitory to house 5,000 students?

The two functions of productivity analysis are:

1. To identify the extent of the market and the possibility of further market segmentation.
2. To identify the attributes desired in the market. The second task enables the analyst to compare and contrast competitive properties to establish their differences and the market's pricing of those differences. For durable goods and real property, productivity analysis reflects the operation of the principle of substitution.

Productivity analysis does not merely describe the site and improvements, the property rights, and the physical location. *Productivity analysis examines how the market perceives the physical, legal, and locational dimensions of a property.* It addresses the capacity of a property or properties to accommodate specific activities and satisfy market needs.

In real estate, the value of a property is determined by its economic function and the psychological satisfactions it offers. The attributes of a property account for its marketability and form the basis of its value. The value of a property is influenced not only by tangible attributes such as the soil, size, frontage, and construction quality, but also by amenity factors such as a scenic view, a babbling brook, or other natural features. Beyond physical characteristics, value is also affected by the psychology of the people that constitute the market for the property. Therefore, behavior and psychological factors are a central concern of market research.

Productivity analysis is a recursive process with many interrelated parts. The major purposes of site and improvement analysis are:

- To identify those attributes that motivate people to pay for the right to occupy and use a property.
- To identify the components of a real estate product that galvanize market activity as measured in demand, transaction prices, and competition.

- To provide a basis for comparing and contrasting properties and identifying their unique or distinct attributes.
- To relate the attributes that support the specific property use to the valuation techniques employed.

Physical Attributes

Real estate is an immobile asset that can have many uses. The appraiser addresses the flexibility of real estate use in the highest and best use section of the appraisal report. The analysis begins with an investigation of the physical constraints on the possible use of the property because physical attributes can influence use, development plans, location relationships, and value.

In analyzing productivity, the appraiser investigates the physical attributes of the subject property, identifies any limitations on use, and considers the possibility that physical alterations will occur over the proposed holding period. Physical changes can either create a comparative advantage for the property or reduce its market potential. A site's productive potential is analyzed to identify sites with the same or similar attributes, which represent potential competition.

Physical attributes can be divided into natural and man-made features. Natural features, which include geological features, place major constraints on the use potential of a site. Site terrain is a primary concern because to develop a site, the terrain may have to be graded or otherwise modified. Terrain may include natural amenities such as scenic views, creeks, and brooks, which can be important to both residential and commercial uses. Other natural physical attributes that can influence property use and market potential include soil composition and capacity, ground cover, and the site's orientation to sun, wind, infrastructure, and transportation.

Natural physical attributes often impact land use and market potential. For example, in high-tech industries, campus-like sites are preferred for new facilities. Many industrial parks try to provide pleasant environments that foster worker productivity and creativity for new product development. The terrain and the elevation may determine the mix and layout of uses and recreational amenities. Industrial parks try to replicate the facilities provided by large research universities, which are often centered around natural amenities.

Soil composition can be important to any development. Topsoils and subsoils that are especially prone to expansion and contraction may be unsuitable for building. Similarly, shifting soils and subsoils are not fit for construction. The city planners of Austin, Texas, for example, had to consider the limestone under sites to the west of the city and the impervious clay under land to the east. They drew up a city plan that allowed for growth, but preserved sensitive environmental areas. The result was a physically restrained, politically acceptable growth corridor running north and south through the city.

However, knowledge of soil conditions and legal inducements do not always redirect market preferences. Despite the preferential treatment given to development within the identified growth corridor, building in the Austin market has tended to be more active in the southwest and northwest. The preferred direction of growth has been towards the hill and lake country to the west. Despite the high cost of development, the demand for hill country parcels, which offer views and natural amenities, has placed market premiums on available land.

A site's orientation to sun and wind also influence value because site orientation impacts use, desirability, and occupancy. The downtown area of one Georgia community provides a good illustration. The community's major downtown retail center ran along a north-south axis and the stores on the east side of the street were exposed to the afternoon sun. The buildings on the west side were shaded, so most of the pedestrian traffic passed along the stores on that side of the street. The stores on the east side had more sun-faded inventory and incurred higher utility costs. In fact, operating expenses were generally much greater for stores on the east side. Vacancy in the downtown area at that time was 50%, and almost all of the vacant stores were on the east side of the street. Property values, returns, and rents were all based on these unique physical and locational circumstances. The marketability and worth of a building in this community was directly dependent on its location on the east or west side of the street.

The importance of the physical dimensions, location, and legal attributes of a property is addressed in the highest and best use section of an appraisal. The role of these attributes is often reflected in statements such as

- "The parcel is too small for a large high-rise office facility."
- "The property's shape, which limits visibility and access, is inappropriate for a retail enterprise."
- "The topography is too steep for commercial use, but desirable for residential development."

Recognition of the physical constraints on a given site and an understanding of the legal attributes of the site are basic to a determination of site value. In site valuation, the analyst identifies the capacity of a site to capture a certain market share or to even monopolize demand in the given market. Many sites are endowed with unique characteristics. Critics of the appraisal process must recognize that appraisers have to deal with individual situations ad hoc.

Real estate is chiefly identified by structures–i.e., the capital improvements to a land resource–so real estate has a dual nature that comprises both land and capital assets. In an urban context, capital is the dominant concern because economic feasibility is a major criterion of the highest and best use of a land parcel.

Capital additions to land can be divided into two general groupings: site improvements and building structure(s).

Site Improvements

Site improvements are classified as on-site improvements and off-site improvements. On-site improvements, which are the most familiar capital additions to land, directly alter the site. Examples of on-site improvements are grading and leveling, terraced slopes, retaining walls, and drainage systems. Other on-site improvements include site and yard improvements such as landscaping, shrubbery, and surfaced areas (e.g., driveways, walks, and parking areas). An amazing array of underground improvements are also necessary, including utility connections for sewers, water laterals, gaslines, and electrical wires. Expenditures for site improvements must be accounted for in the cost analysis of a specific property and tested for feasibility in light of market economics.

Off-site improvements also contribute to the value of an urban site. Off-site improvements, which are often held in common by the community, are considered in the analysis of the physical and locational attributes of the site. Examples of off-site improvements are the street and road system, the public sewage system and water systems, the disposal plant, the pumping station, sidewalks, and other infrastructure. Any of these improvements may afford competitive advantages to a given parcel and can explain differences in the value of competitive or substitute properties.

Off-site improvements are installed by developers, government departments, or quasi-public agencies such as utility companies and can be paid for by various means. The capital outlay for off-site developments can be covered by incorporating the costs incurred by the developer into the lot prices or by levying a general property tax on the community. Other means of payment include specific user fees such as utility charges and special assessments to recover public expenditures for off-site improvements that only benefit specific sites. Commercial lot development also requires additional capital expenditures to build streets, curbs, gutters, and sidewalks. These expenditures must be recaptured in some manner and the means of capital recovery may be reflected in price differentials.

Both on- and off-site improvements influence the cost of development and, hence, the supply of properties comparable to any given subject site or property group. Property attributes influence the nature of a product and thus define its competitiveness in the market.

The Building Structure

In productivity analysis the analyst investigates the physical attributes of a building improvement in terms of:

- The quality of the facilities
- The attractiveness of the structure
- The functional efficiency of the property

A principal concern of the analyst is understanding market preferences. In other words, why are some projects more desirable than others? The quality of the facilities and their perceived attractiveness are dependent on demand, taste, and preferences.

Quality is often linked to the cost of construction, but it is identified in a market context by structural standards and by alternative developments in the market. The standards define the marketability attributes of a property or property type. Marketability attributes help the appraiser identify the real estate product, its use and market competition, and its potential capture and absorption rates.

Attractiveness is subjective and is not easily separated from the quality of a product. Quality appeals to different market segments, but attractiveness must be considered from the perspective of the market segment that defines the market standard. To do this the market analyst must identify the probable user group.

Functional utility describes the capacity of the property to satisfy contemporary tastes and preferences. The relationship between the property's design and current market standards as reflected in comparable properties is the test of functional efficiency.

Site Analysis and the Immediate Area

The layout of a site and the location of various activities on the property must be related to the shape of the parcel. At this stage in the analysis, the physical and locational attributes of the site cannot be considered separately. The dimensions of the site determine the placement of structures, the layout of yard improvements and parking facilities, and the general maintenance requirements. The shape of the site affects its adaptability to alternative uses and thus its market appeal over time. Some important spatial considerations are listed below.

- The number of sides a site has determines its degree of exposure or seclusion. For a retail use, exposure is desirable. Assuming that access is convenient and the flow of traffic is manageable, a multi-sided site is highly desirable for a retail use. For a residential site, however, privacy, not exposure, is usually desired.
- The functional layout of the facilities on a site is often the key to the site's marketability. The placement of structures and parking areas cannot be separated from the ease of ingress to and egress from the site.
- The degree of "friction" or inconvenience in accessing a site indicates how well the site is linked to its environment. In considering access, the appraiser should determine whether the traffic flow inward or outward is more significant and whether this flow involves goods, services, or people. If the site is primarily visited by consumers, its location should provide convenient access with a minimum of aggravation. The mode of transport for goods will vary with the weight and bulk of the material being conveyed. Service delivery requires reasonable access to the site.

- The flow of traffic within the site should also be considered. On-site "friction" can be reduced by the placement and design of facilities. Good design can ensure that a property has market appeal and is both functional and aesthetic.

Legal Attributes

To understand property productivity, the legal dimensions of the realty must be investigated because legal concerns as well as physical attributes set real estate apart from other types of assets. Legal vehicles are used to transfer and control the physical attributes of property. The right to use realty may be transferred on a temporary basis by means of a leasehold estate, or on a permanent basis by the passing of title to the fee simple estate. Different legal estates exist within a temporal framework.

Legal Concept of Real Estate

The legal status of real estate significantly affects its economic potential. The spatial dimensions of a parcel of real estate are generally defined in a legal description. The fourth dimension, time, is also fundamental to the creation of real estate value. The use and control of space occur within a temporal framework.

Legal concepts of real estate specify the interests of owners, users, and investors in a property. The legal transfer of property rights results in the assignation of surface rights, air rights, mineral rights, and subsurface tunnel rights. It forms the basis for investment strategies, which may be simple or complex. One complex theory, the "Hawaiian technique," put forth by real estate developer William Zeckendorf, demonstrates that the sum of various leasehold interests can exceed the value of the fee simple estate.

The temporal dimension of real estate allows for the creation of alternative property products. The establishment of legal estates makes it possible to create financial interests such as mortgages and investment contracts. A special type of fee simple estate created by law is the *fee simple condominium*; another is the *timeshare interest.* A condominium owner holds rights to a three-dimensional space, usually an apartment unit, within a larger real estate entity. In a timeshare arrangement, an additional legal provision is introduced. The appraiser must estimate the value of the right to use the unit for a stipulated period of time.

Property Rights

Legal arrangements can create new and alternative products which contribute to market segmentation. Market segments may also result from the different ways in which the rights to property are assigned. Space may be transferred in perpetuity, i.e., for an indefinite period, by means of a fee simple estate or for a stated period through a leasehold. The various rights transferred by these legal arrangements are subject to certain constraints. The rights and limitations pertaining to the ownership, transfer, and use of a property can be separated into two general categories–private and public.

The ability to identify the legal constraints on and advantages of property are one of the factors determining use potential. The use of property establishes the supply and demand characterizing a market and depends on an understanding of the specific rights ascribed to the legal estate in property.

Private leases can impact the use and market potential for a property. Consider a neighborhood shopping center that is well designed and in a good location. The owner signed a long-term lease allowing a wrestling exhibition and training studio in the center right next to the anchor space for the grocery store. The wrestling tenants are perceived to be detrimental to the grocery shoppers and the grocery store plans to move unless this adjacent tenant is removed. If the wrestling center can be moved, the center will continue to function as a neighborhood center; if not, the anchor grocery store will move and the center will be transformed into a secondary commercial community center.

A public legal requirement can also impact the use of a property. Consider a strip center build adjacent to a retail mall. The parking was designed according to city standards for retail use which require one space per 200 square feet of retail space. However, some years ago the market changed for retail at this location and the area became a major restaurant location. Unfortunately, the center cannot rent space to restaurants because the restaurant regulations require one parking space for each 150 square feet of space. Thus, the center's productivity attributes are all pointed toward restaurant use, but legal constraints prohibit this use because of the parking regulations.

The productivity analysis must identify the legal impacts on use and assess what these impacts mean for current market use and whether there is a probability of change.

Public Policy and Market Delineation

The attitudes and policies of a community can delineate a market. In major metropolitan areas, jurisdictions can change within a short distance. The Atlanta metropolitan area, for example, extends over several counties including Fulton and DeKalb counties. In the not-too-distant past, DeKalb County prohibited the sale of liquor while Fulton County did not. Land use along the major thoroughfares in east Fulton County was influenced by the demand for alcohol in DeKalb County. Accessibility to this demand was especially important and the jurisdictional boundaries of the counties helped to delineate two separate markets.

Different jurisdictions also exhibit distinct attitudes toward regulatory enforcement, which also must be considered in market delineation. The enforcement policy of a community can bring a windfall to individual property owners or wipe them out economically.

The state of Texas provides two examples of very different jurisdictions within 170 miles of each other. At one extreme is the city of Houston, which implemented its first full zoning code in 1993. The 1993 zoning restrictions were phased in with temporary controls beginning in 1991. Before 1991 control over land use was a judicial matter handled by the courts through the interpretation of restrictive covenants. The lack of zoning reflected the city's traditional laissez-faire attitude toward property rights. The city's requirements concerning development filled less than two pages of its municipal ordinance book.

At the other extreme is Austin, which is located in an especially attractive setting and has a much better environment than many other communities in Texas. Much of the citizenry and the city leadership favor regulating land use to prevent the uncontrolled degradation of the surrounding countryside. Existing legal controls include zoning, watershed ordinances, hill country ordinances, roadway ordinances, extensive extra-territorial controls, and exactions and dedications. Whereas land use in Houston long remained a private contractual matter subject to the judicial process, Austin has regulated land use with legislative and executive action. An encyclopedic knowledge of development regulations and ancillary literature is required before a developer can build in Austin. Local experts are sought after as consultants to help outside developers get through the legal and regulatory hurdles of the development process.

Despite the differences in regulation and land markets, Austin and Houston both experience economic cycles, though the phases have occurred at different times. The level of regulation in a community affects the cost of producing a real estate product. Compared to Houston, Austin has markedly higher development costs. These costs impact the quantity of supply available over time. Community policy also influences the demand for different real estate products. As a general observation, recreational property now accounts for a larger share of Austin's real estate market.

The purpose of comparing these two cities is to illustrate the importance of regulatory requirements in delineating the market for a property. Failure to identify this factor will result in a flawed understanding of the market for the realty product.

Evaluating Preferences and Market Structure

Attitudes toward the regulation of real estate are not static features of isolated communities. Attitudes change and policies evolve. To identify the changes in a community's orientation, one must investigate recent legislation and litigation concerning land use. A community's inclination to control private real property use changes over time, often in a cyclical pattern. A period characterized by strong emphasis on the rights of government may be followed by a period of weak enforcement of public restrictions. A community may change its attitudes toward property rights or reconsider its position and go in an opposite direction. Many decisions involving the enforcement of rights have been ad hoc in nature.

The cyclical pattern of land use regulation can be traced to the changing attitudes and policies of our national government. Thomas Jefferson and the Founding Fathers believed that it was beneficial for the country to vest individuals with the right to property. This was the prevailing attitude for decades. The government promoted property ownership with land grants and land rushes. A vision of manifest destiny spurred the settlement of the American West. This attitude predominated as long as the country was basically rural. With urbanization, however, the potential for conflict over property rights increased. As people began to live in closer proximity to one another, conflicts over land rights arose.

The government has the power of eminent domain, taxation, police power, and escheat. It uses these powers to deal with potential conflicts between the pubic interest and the rights of property owners. Over time, the courts have revised their position on the extent to which the state may enforce its regulatory powers. Appraisers must understand current attitudes toward the exercise of private property rights and public controls to evaluate the risk, returns, and expectations associated with property ownership and investment. Often the state's current enforcement of its regulatory powers can only be understood in light of past perceptions. These perceptions may explain in part the changes observed in price and yield data over time. The impact of changes in zoning and permitted density may also be related to historical change in the attitudes of a community or the residents of a jurisdiction. Legal or societal values can give rise to different economic values for parcels in the same tract.

Site, Building, and Legal Attributes Interact

The interaction of legal and physical attributes to create real estate is illustrated by the development of the "building envelope" for a specific property, i.e., the area of the property reserved for setbacks, parking, or open space. Consider a 150-ft.-by-100-ft. (15,000 square feet) lot situated on the corner of two major streets. One interior property line abuts a residential neighborhood while the other abuts a commercially zoned lot. The zoning classification suggests that a one-story retail structure could be developed. Several other uses are possible, but the retail facility would generate the greatest potential return to the site.

The zoning of the site requires a 5-ft. setback on the side abutting the residential land. A 10-ft. building line is required at the rear of the property. No building can be constructed within 10 feet of the rear property line, but this area can be used for parking. The 5-ft. area abutting the residential property cannot be used for parking because, by law, no improvements can be made on the setback that abuts a different property use. (See the plot plan in Exhibit 3.1.) Based on the zoning restrictions, the usable square footage is calculated as follows:

$$\begin{array}{lr} \text{Basic land } 150 \times 100 = & 15{,}000 \text{ sq. ft.} \\ \text{Less setbacks } 150 \times 5 = & \underline{750 \text{ sq. ft.}} \\ \text{Land available for use} & 14{,}250 \text{ sq. ft.} \end{array}$$

The development regulations and local zoning require that 300 square feet of parking be allotted for each 300 square feet of net building area planned. The estimated building efficiency ratio (i.e., the ratio of rentable area to gross building area) based on market trends and the ratios found in comparable structures is 90%. Thus 300 square feet of net building area translates into 333.33 square feet of gross building area.

300 sq. ft./.90 = 333.33 sq. ft. of gross building

The allocation of land use for the one-story retail facility is set forth below. If 333.33 square feet of gross building area, the "building footprint," requires 300 square feet of ground parking (including parking stalls and access area), the basic land area equation is

Building footprint	333.33
Surface parking	300.00
Total land required per unit	633.33

Exhibit 3.1   Plot Plan for Proposed Retail Site

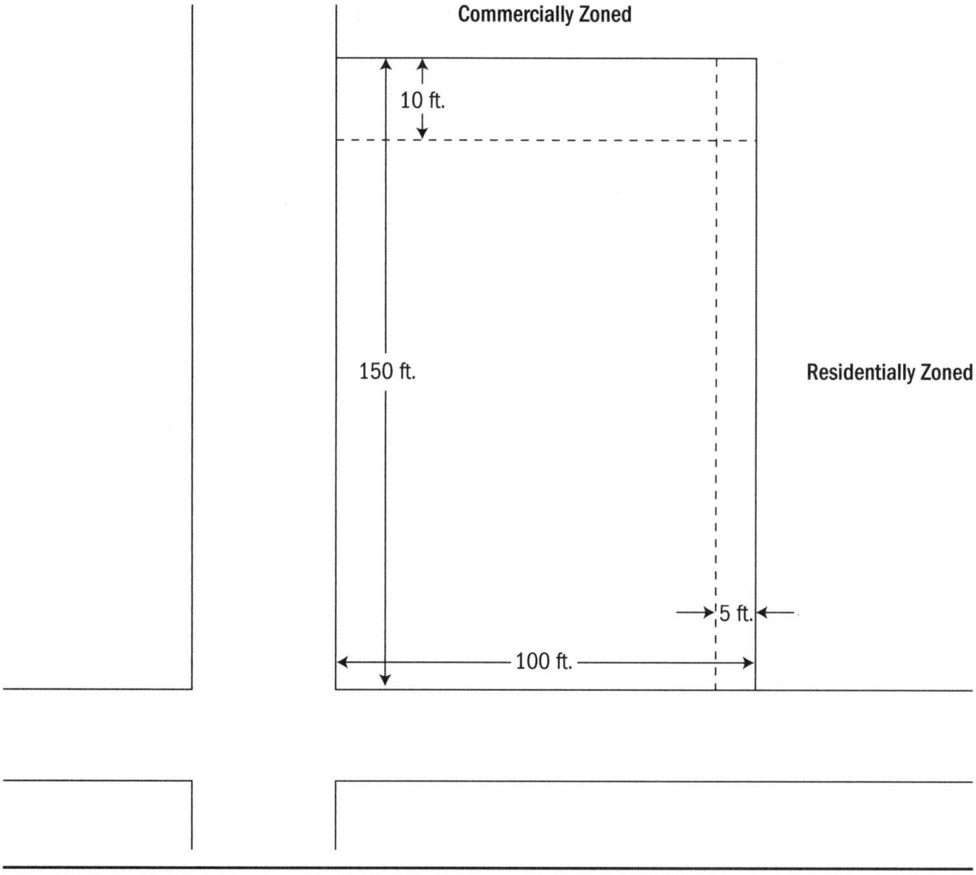

Then land allocation units can be calculated.

$$\frac{14{,}250 \text{ sq. ft. of land available}}{633.33 \text{ sq. ft. required per unit}} = 22.50 \text{ land units}$$

The total land use allocation is calculated as follows:

Building area per floor	333.33 sq. ft. × 22.50 =	7,500 sq. ft. gross
Parking area	300 sq. ft. × 22.50 =	6,750 sq. ft.
Total land available for use		14,250 sq. ft.

This example demonstrates how the physical and legal components of real estate interact to establish the space that will be developed. A general formula for calculating the building envelope is provided below.

$$\frac{A - Sb}{(Bu/Er) + Pu\,(S) + O} = LAU$$

Where: A is lot area

Sb is setback area

Bu is building area

Er is efficiency ratio

Pu is size of parking unit

S is number of stories

O is open space (if any)

LAU is land allocation unit

The data from the example can be substituted into the formula, as follows:

$$\frac{15{,}000 - 750}{(300/.9) + 300\,(1) + 0} = 22.50$$

The land allocation unit (22.50) is then applied to the building and parking areas to check that the allocation for the adjusted lot size is correct.

The example illustrates that physical and legal constraints are important to product definition and estimates of projected income and value. In the example, the calculated building area is 7,500 sq. ft. At a development cost of $45 per square foot, the total building cost would come to $337,500. The land was purchased for $100,000, thus the total investment would be $437,500.

Net floor area can be used as the basis for estimating rental income. The net floor area of the proposed structure is 6,750 square feet. At an annual net rental of $8 per square foot (including an appropriate vacancy and collection loss), the property's probable net operating income would be $54,000. Applying a market-derived capitalization rate of 10%, the potential *NOI* can be capitalized into a value estimate of $540,000. This is $102,500 more than the cost of construction, which indicates that the market will support the retail facility and the project is economically feasible.

Real Estate as a Space-Time Product

Characterizing a real estate product by its spatial and temporal dimensions may be alien to many real estate professionals. Viewing real estate as space used over time to house economic activities or satisfy human needs focuses attention on the behavioral foundation of value. This perception invalidates the common perception that value is inherent in physical objects.

Physical and legal attributes combine to create real estate, which is essentially space used to house alternative uses over time. Physical and legal attributes and constraints also determine the suitability of a piece of real estate for a particular use. The appropriate use of a site depends on the urban structure and the linkage of the site to the market.

Although real estate is physically fixed, it is economically flexible. Despite the fact that a parcel of real estate is immobile, its location is an economic variable that can change over time. Essentially, any piece of real estate is space used to house an economic activity over a period of time. As the surrounding neighborhood changes, the support system for the existing use may change. Change affects the use of the property, the market for the property, and hence the transfer price obtainable for the property. The market for a given parcel of real estate cannot be analyzed without first analyzing the use. When the value defined is market value, highest and best use becomes the standard for estimating the property's value. Highest and best use analysis considers the substitutability of heterogeneous sites.

The combination of locational, physical, and legal dimensions forms the essence of the real estate product, i.e., the use of space over a defined period of time. Thus, real estate is a space-time product representing the combination of locational, physical, and legal attributes. An understanding of real estate's temporal dimension allows alternative products to be identified and further markets to be segmented. These location concepts will be covered in greater depth in Chapters 4 and 5.

Summary

In a real estate context, productivity analysis is the study of a property's capacity to house economic activities, supply services, and provide amenities to meet human needs. Productivity analysis relates the value of a product to the marketability of its attributes. The physical, legal, and locational attributes of real property are linked to market preferences.

The physical attributes of a property may make it appropriate for a specific use. Physical attributes may also act as constraints that limit the use of a property. Physical attributes include natural features and man-made site improvements and buildings.

The ownership, transfer, and use of property are subject to private entitlements and public controls. The rights to most properties fall under the categories of fee simple and leasehold estates. The type of deed further differentiates leasehold properties. Eminent domain, police power, taxation, and escheat constitute the four powers that government exercises over real property. The legal characteristics and physical dimensions of real estate are specified in a property's legal description.

The regulatory environment of a community is closely linked to market delineation within that community. Societal attitudes and judicial interpretation play a significant role in defining a realty product and delineating its market. Attitudes are continually evolving. Past, present, and future perceptions of the relationship between individual property rights and public regulation must be considered in the market research and valuation processes. The benefits that derive from real estate depend on how these rights are exercised. The character of a real property interest, the public constraints on its use, the timing of its development, and the risks associated with contractual agreements must be considered to derive a value estimate that accurately reflects market expectations.

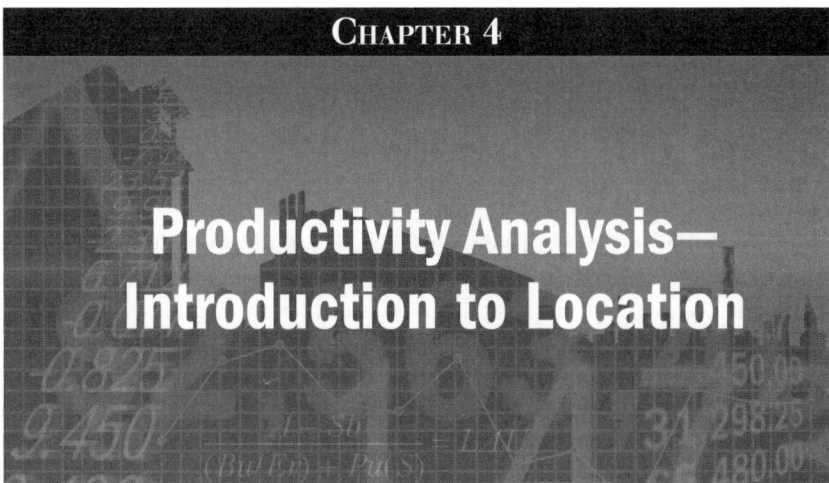

CHAPTER 4

Productivity Analysis—Introduction to Location

Chapter Objectives

- To describe how the location of the site relates to its immediate surroundings
- To discuss the concept of situs
- To explain the relationship between the location of a site and its broader, urban surroundings
- To discuss the various land use environments that affect a location: the physical environment, the social and cultural environment, the psychological environment, and the institutional and political environment

Overview of Location

The most important factor affecting the productive potential of real estate (and, in turn, value) is probably location. As the third aspect of property examined in productivity analysis, location is fundamental to an understanding of real estate and its value. The location of the subject property connects the property with market demand and sets it apart from its competition. Chapter 3 demonstrated that the physical and legal attributes of a property are important to its marketability. Any in-depth discussion of location must be presented in relation to the physical and legal aspects of property. Zoning, for example, has both legal and spatial, or locational, dimensions that influence property value and impact highest and best use. Urban structure cannot be described without reference to the physical terrain, infrastructure, and skyline of the city.

Real estate location attributes determine the type and location of land uses most expected in an area. In the next step of the market/marketability study, the economic demand analysis will identify how much growth might be expected over time.

Location determinants of growth consist of static and dynamic features. Static features include linkages and land use associations. Linkages refer to the movement of people, goods, services, or communication to and from the property site. Common linkages include roads and utilities. Land use associations refer to the current type of development in the area and how land uses relate or support each other. Current land uses in an area set a pattern for the future.

Because locations change over time, the dynamic aspects of location also need to be addressed. Dynamic location features are the land use growth patterns and the direction and rate of growth.

Location analysis addresses these major questions regarding the use potential and competitive position of a property.

- What is the current and expected growth pattern in the area and how does the subject fit in relation to this growth pattern?
- What is the subject's current and future competition?
- How does the subject location compare to competitive areas?

In this chapter the attributes of location are investigated to describe the relationship between the site and its surroundings. In land economics *situs* is the concept that identifies the relationship of the urban environment to a specific use on a specific parcel of land over time.[1]

The second level of location analyzed is the overall urban structure and the interrelationships within a community's land use pattern. The study of location at this level is discussed in Chapter 5. As described in that chapter, urban structure is concerned with the community's economic base; its present, past, and future land use patterns; and the magnitude and direction of expected growth.

The interrelationship of the three levels of location is analogous to the biological interrelationship of a cell, organ, and organism (see Exhibit 4.1). As the exhibit illustrates, a site can be thought of as a cell. In a living organism, each individual cell has a specialized function in relation to the immediately surrounding cells and the overall organism. Despite the cell's unique features, it also has many attributes in common with other cells.

This relationship between the part and the whole applies to a site as well. Each parcel of land has characteristics that are similar, if not identical, to the attributes of other sites. The specific combination of property characteristics, however, makes the site unique and limits the range of possible functions that can be conducted on the site.

To carry the analogy further, a cell with specialized functions is dependent on surrounding cells and relates to the organ of which it is

---

1. Richard B. Andrews, *Urban Land Economics and Public Policy* (New York: Free Press, 1971). Andrews thoroughly developed the concept of economic location within the framework of situs theory.

Exhibit 4.1   Site as a Cell

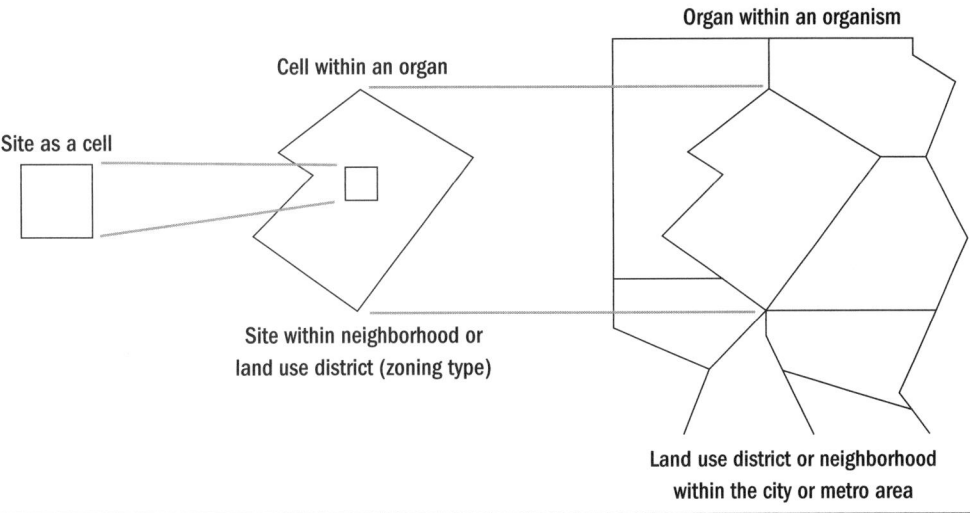

a part. Similarly, a site is linked to the neighborhood, the land use district, or the trade area and to the overall urban environment. The concept of situs analyzes the linkages of a site to the urban environment and can be used to explore the site's economic situation.

As the final step in the analogy, the cell, or site, is linked to the overall organism, which may be the city, community, metropolitan area, or metropolitan statistical area (MSA). An understanding of the development and economic base of the overall community provides insight into the spatial dimension and market dynamics of the market. Urban economic analysis is the basis for the supply and demand relationship that defines real estate value.

The link between an urban location and real estate value was first recognized by Alfred Marshall. In his *Principles of Economics*, published in 1890, Marshall established the foundation for the valuation approaches adopted by the appraisal profession in the 1930s and identified location as the essence of urban real estate. The term Marshall used was *urban situation value.*[2]

The biological analogy presented here suggests a process for analyzing location by directly linking productivity analysis with the supply and demand relationship identified in the market. The supply of and demand for real estate must be considered within a spatial context. To project supply and demand, the analyst must consider locational attributes to identify existing and proposed competition and to assess the magnitude of demand and the direction of development.

Market/marketability analysis may be seen as employing three filters or channeling agents. These filters are a location filter, which the

---

2. Alfred Marshall, *Principles of Economics,* 18th ed. (London: Macmillan and Company, 1920).

analyst uses to process location and other productivity attributes, a supply filter, and a demand filter. By applying these filters, the analyst can remove irrelevant data from the market analysis and focus on the essential factors influencing the use and value of the site.

Location: Site and Situs

The study of location in productivity analysis corresponds to the typical appraisal problem, i.e., a site in search of a use or market. Generally, location analysis for an appraisal begins with a specific site. The appraiser inspects the site, investigating both the locational characteristics of the neighborhood and the locational attributes of the site. This is the stage of productivity analysis in which locational, physical, and legal attributes are interrelated and often cross-categorized.

Location analysis is concerned with the placement of spatial attributes and how these attributes relate to specific functions. It is difficult to analyze location without reference to a specific use. Just as the analysis of use requires an investigation of location, the analysis of location must be undertaken within the context of a specific use. Only the use type must be specified; the use need not exist at the time of the analysis. For example, in highest and best use analysis, various use scenarios are considered as though the site were vacant. One might begin by analyzing the property from the perspective of a potential office building use and then find that the site is inappropriate because the area lacks adequate support facilities. In this hypothetical case, a retail use might be considered next and subsequently be eliminated for the same reason. A residential use, however, might ultimately pass the location test. Thus, the analytical process can be seen as a funnel or sieve in which various uses are sifted until one appropriate use is able to pass through all of the filters. An analyst could consider an office use, retail use, residential use, and mixed use for a given property even though the site is currently improved with a warehouse.

As these examples illustrate, even a generic location is considered in light of its suitability for a specific land use. Highest and best use is thereby tied to market analysis and valuation.

The Concept of Situs

Situs theory rests on the belief that land uses are interdependent and economic activities are interrelated. It focuses on the movement between centers of activity, or loci, and the accessibility of these loci. Situs may be defined as the relationship between the total urban environment and a specific land use on an individual land parcel at a specific time.[3] This definition encompasses several elements fundamental to appraisal and market analysis. One key idea is that the land use of a given parcel and the locus of the parcel are separate.

---

3.   Andrews, *Urban Land Economics and Public Policy*.

Any given site may have a range of possible uses that are suited to the site legally, physically, and locationally. Although the site is physically fixed, it is economically flexible in terms of use. *Economic location*, the concept that a site functions as a locus of economic activity in association with other loci within a dynamic urban structure, is a central concern in market delineation and valuation.

In everyday practice, it may be difficult to separate the concepts of economic location and physical location. Physical location refers to the position of one site relative to that of another. The term *physical location* is often used interchangeably with *proximity* and *accessibility*. In this chapter, the concept of location is extended to include the economic concerns of appraisal and real estate market analysis. The general concepts of location, proximity, and accessibility will be examined from various technical perspectives to better understand the real estate product and the market in a spatial context.

The definition of *situs* refers to the relationship of uses as a function of time as well as space. As forces outside the land parcel alter the relationships of uses, the activities conducted on the site and the economic nature of the site itself begin to change. From an appraisal standpoint, the location analysis of a site cannot be separated from the life cycle of the neighborhood. The concept of situs is the building block that undergirds all these economic issues and links highest and best use and market analysis to the valuation process.

Situs Process

Situs is not just a theory relating the individual site to its immediate neighborhood or overall urban environment; it is also a practical analytical process. The situs links the data and the concerns raised by the data into an overall study of location, land use, and market analysis. The situs process includes gathering, classifying, and analyzing information and comprises four steps.

1. Identification of the activities in the area
2. Study of the nature of the associations between these activities
3. Analysis of the accessibility of the site to the surrounding area
4. Evaluation of the impact of the total area on the site use

To identify the activities in an area and analyze the associations between them, the appraiser must demarcate the spatial boundaries of the subject neighborhood. Understanding the spatial nature of real estate allows the analyst to define the physical limits of the real estate market. Boundaries identified with natural features can often be drawn for real estate markets, but such boundaries may not be appropriate for defining markets for consumer goods or commodities. The market boundaries for other products are often determined by the productive capacity of the manufacturer or the limitations of the distributor that warehouses and sells the product. For real estate, however, the locational or spatial dimension of the site is a key determinant of the product. While this fact complicates productivity analysis, it can facilitate delineation of the market.

Market Boundaries

The productivity of real estate is strongly influenced by its economic and physical location. Analyzing economic location goes beyond identification of the physical position of one property in relation to another.[4] The analysis of economic location begins with identification of the economic activities in the neighborhood or trade area, which is delineated by physical, political, and socioeconomic boundaries or by the time-distance relationships represented by travel times to and from common destinations.

The geographic extent of the market for a property is determined by the real estate itself and by features such as the amount of space involved, the price level or price range of the property, and the current or intended use of the space. Therefore, the geographic extent of the market for office buildings in major commercial cities is generally broader than the market for single-family residences in rural communities.

Boundaries can be established using various criteria. The boundaries for neighborhoods and trade areas can be based on geographical features such as lakes, hills, and mountains. Markets can also be delineated by topographical features that prevent development or impede transportation between sections of a community. Man-made features such as expressways, divided highways, one-way streets, walls, building bulk lines (zoning mandates), bridges, infrastructure, and designed environments (e.g., landscaped lakes, parks) can create market boundaries, as can political or legal jurisdictions. Different incorporated communities within a metropolitan area may impose different legal restrictions on land use. A slight difference in location, e.g., a location within the limits of an incorporated community versus one outside the jurisdiction of the community, can alter the maintenance costs and lot prices prevailing in the market. Location can also determine the services available to a real estate product. The combination of cost and available services can help delineate the competition and market for a particular facility.

The time/distance variable is a major economic determinant of a market trade area. The cost of transporting people or goods from a facility to other specific locales must be considered in relation to the cost to access competitive sites. The economic and psychological dimensions of a market area are often defined by the effort required to travel between one location and another. The distance workers are willing to commute often sets the boundaries of a neighborhood. This issue is further discussed in Chapter 5 in the analysis of accessibility and the rent theorists' school of urban structure.

Neighborhoods are also defined by the homogeneity or compatibility of the land uses. The next step in location analysis, therefore, is to identify the major characteristics of a neighborhood.

---

4. Terry V. Grissom, "A Feasibility Process: The Benefits of Land Economics and Risk Management," *The Appraisal Journal* (July 1984).

Identification of Activities

Identifying the activities in an area may require a simple survey of existing land uses or a major economic base analysis. The key activities that characterize a neighborhood are those that attract people to the specific location. These activities, which function like economic magnets, may be represented by major employers, recreational facilities, institutions, services, or physical features such as rivers and roads. A shopping center, for example, usually generates further activity in an area.

Primary activities often define the character of a neighborhood and form the basis of the neighborhood's economy. For example, the central business district of most communities is typified by high-rise office buildings. The activities of the office building tenants determine the overall character of the area. The office buildings along Madison Avenue and along Wall Street in Manhattan are used by different tenant-occupants. The needs of these tenants and the character of surrounding land uses are different. The tenants on Madison Avenue are mostly marketing and advertising agencies, while Wall Street tenants provide financial services. Although both areas are dominated by business enterprises, the associated activities nearby vary.

The identification of primary activities in a city is the foundation for economic base analysis. These activities must also be identified for specifically defined trade areas and neighborhoods.

A thorough understanding of a neighborhood is only gained through the identification of its key activities, which begins with a functional study of the general land uses in the area. After driving through the area, the analyst can prepare a schematic drawing of immediate land uses, which will facilitate decision making. A simple land use survey such as this can be developed into a more sophisticated study. Rapid changes rarely affect an entire area within a short period of time. If changes are occurring in the neighborhood, the analysis should focus on identifying these changes.

The identification of primary activities and the related land uses that develop around them leads to our second concern–the association of land uses.

Identification of Associations

The various activities in a neighborhood are associated. Activities may be complementary, subservient, or competitive. Some activities even repel one another. Categories of land use associations are identified in Exhibit 4.2. The nature of the relationship among any set of land uses is determined by their economic function.

Competitive automobile dealers, for example, generally locate next to one another. Car dealers find it mutually advantageous to be close to their competitors and they often locate on cheaper, out-of-the-way land. In most cases, a car is not bought on impulse. It is a durable good purchased after one or more comparative shopping trips and locating dealerships together is more convenient for car buyers.

The first general category presented in Exhibit 4.2 is a dominant use/subordinate use relationship in which the subordinate enterprises serve the operation of the dominant activity. For example, assume a major printing and publishing company locates in a community and hires 1,000 employees in various occupations. In due time, the analyst can expect ink supply companies to locate in the area to serve the large publishing company. This subservient activity may employ 100 more people. This same relationship can be seen in the proximity of machine shops to manufacturing plants, the location of food jobbers in areas with inexpensive access to fast-food restaurants and supermarkets, and the proximity of law offices to courthouses, public records offices, and law libraries.

In the dominant use/subordinate use relationship, the subordinate land use activity is directly involved in the dominant activity—e.g., a distributor supplies materials needed for manufacturing, a lawyer litigates cases at the courthouse.

The second type of land use association is a dominant use/ancillary use relationship in which the ancillary activity serves the clients or employees of the dominant use. Examples are cigar, gift, or florist shops located on the first floor of an office building. The ancillary character of the land use is emphasized when the shop has an internal orientation, with little or no external access or exposure from the outside of the building. If the shop fronts on the lobby, atrium, or foyer of the office building, it probably serves an ancillary function within the overall structure.

Exhibit 4.2	General Categories of Land Use Associations

I. Dominant Use/Subordinate Use
II. Dominant Use/Ancillary Use
III. Codominant Uses (or Dominant Use)/Satellite Uses

Other examples of ancillary uses are restaurants, bookshops, and computer stores located near a university. Bookshops and computer stores overlap in the categories of goods sold. Books and computer software can be seen as direct inputs into the education of students, who represent the "product" of the university. Many items purchased at these ancillary facilities do not directly contribute to educational programs, but rather to the personal development of the students.

The third general category of land use associations consists of codominant and dominant uses that relate to satellite uses. This category is exemplified by the facilities at a shopping center or mall. The codominant uses are the large department stores, which draw consumers to the center and serve the same demand as the satellite uses. The customers who buy at the large department stores also patronize the adjacent shops where similar products are sold.

In this type of relationship, the satellites capitalize on the power of the dominant anchors to draw customers to the area. Often the satellite use in a dominant use/satellite use relationship takes on characteristics of an ancillary use, but the key to the satellite function is dependence on the drawing power of the dominant/codominant use.

Codominant or dominant use and satellite use relationships are not limited to shopping centers. They can be identified in a range of neighborhoods or trade areas. For example, the basic economic activities, or codominant uses, in Austin's central business district are government offices and financial institutions. The various state, federal, and local government offices often serve the same clientele as the financial service businesses (banks and savings and loans). The law firms, lobbyists, and professional groups located near government offices can be considered satellite functions. Ancillary services in the CBD such as retail shops, restaurants, hotels, and recreational facilities are direct recipients of the business drawn to the dominant activities.

By understanding the quality and extent of land use associations, the analyst gains insight into the stability, durability, and development potential of a given property or neighborhood. Studying the associations among the land uses in an area over time will help the analyst forecast the direction of growth and future land use patterns.

Analysis of Accessibility

Accessibility addresses the degree of convenience or inconvenience involved in moving people, goods, and services between different loci of activity. The degree of friction, or inconvenience, is measured in terms of time, cost, and aggravation. Accessibility translates into negative transportation cost. The greater the site's accessibility to major activities and complementary land uses, the lower the cost to get to the property and the higher the potential site return in income and market value. The importance of accessibility to a specific use is reflected by what one user (or buyer) will pay for one site over another site.

The interrelationship of activities, associations, and accessibility affects the allocation of land uses. An understanding of these relationships helps identify the highest and best use or probable use of a site.

The analyst should be concerned with accessibility on two levels. At the macro level, the flow of people between one area and another is considered. At the micro level, the analyst examines the subject site, ingress to and egress from the property, and the immediate area. Various concepts have been developed by urban land economists, geographers, and landscape architects to facilitate this analysis.

Macro-level Accessibility

Macro-level accessibility reflects the trade-off between the transportation cost to the site and the specific features and amenities the site offers. Macro-level accessibility is reflected in site rents or sale prices and can be linked directly to the drawing power of dominant or codominant land uses.

In gravity models of retail attraction, drawing power operates in inverse proportion, like the relationship between distance and mass in Newton's law of gravity. Newton's law states that the force of gravity between particles is proportional to the product of their masses and the inverse square of the distance between them. Thus, in a real estate context, the greater the number of competitors (dominant and codominant uses) in an area, the greater the total volume of potential consumers seeking access to the area.

Drawing power is contingent on specific land uses. As mentioned earlier, automobile dealerships cluster near their competitors. This clustering is called the *economics of agglomeration.* An economic advantage is created for automobile dealers when many dealers offering slightly different products locate near one another. Since the purchase of an automobile requires premeditated travel and comparative shopping trips, a number of dealers located together creates a collectively dominant land use association and generates a gravitational pull. The accessibility of several alternative facilities in one location more than offsets any friction or inconvenience the customer experiences reaching the location.

Thus, even on the macro level, the analysis of accessibility must be use-specific to identify the relationships and linkages between activities. The focus of analysis at the macro level is the competition between uses within the overall urban structure. This competition is based on the ability of a land user to pay a competitive price for a desirable location. If a land use is outbid by other land uses for a given site and a less desirable site is obtained, then an additional transportation cost may be incurred because of the lack of accessibility. The economic trade-off between site rents and macro-level accessibility explains the economic structure of cities, which is addressed in Chapter 5.

To investigate the importance of accessibility to a specific area, the analyst must describe or explain the character, direction, distance, and frequency of trips to and from a particular land use. On a macro level this can be done by focusing on the relationship between a neighborhood or trade area sector and the overall city. This relationship is important for two reasons:

1. The neighborhood is a focal point for inward and outward trips relating to specific land uses or aggregations of land uses.
2. The neighborhood monopolizes certain "packets" of movement and accounts for the majority of high-frequency, short trips.

Thus, while travel within a neighborhood defines the micro level of accessibility (down to site ingress and egress), travel between neighborhoods forms the basis of macro-level accessibility.

A neighborhood's drawing power and macro accessibility can be determined by studying the size and traffic volume of connecting arterial streets, the nature of linkages outside the area, the number and types of establishments within the neighborhood, and the competition in other neighborhoods. Analysis of macro-level accessibility entails the identification of key roadways and public transportation lines, the study of traffic counts, and the measurement of travel times and distances to other centers of activity associated with the neighborhood.

The accessibility of a neighborhood will often determine the desirability of the neighborhood and its status within the overall community. Ease of access and desirability are indicators of the area's potential for growth and the future direction of that growth.

Movement patterns between neighborhoods are used to identify areas of potential development. Urban geographers use the term *zones of conflux* to describe land segments where activities with considerable drawing power are located. In these areas arterial streets and other infrastructure have been developed to direct or pull vehicular traffic into the area. Most cities have zones of conflux where such characteristic economic activity and infrastructure combine. When these factors are present and identifiable in specific locales, the analyst can determine likely growth patterns and location rankings. The process is to identify the major economic activities within the area, the association between these activities and related activities, and the relationship of the activity center to major or heavily traveled roadways. The zones of conflux will be found where the volume of activity exerts a strong pull and major roadways intersect or converge.

Micro-level Accessibility

After the drawing power and accessibility of the area are considered, the next objective of location analysis is to analyze micro-level accessibility. Micro-level accessibility is concerned with linkage relationships, i.e., the movement between, or proximity of, associated activities. The linkage relationships classified in Exhibit 4.2 are characterized by continuing or recurring interaction, which necessitates movement between the sites. Proximity may be a secondary component in the transportation of persons and goods.

Linkage relationships have various orientations. Movements can have an inward or outward orientation—i.e., to or from a land use or establishment. It is possible to categorize movements more specifically as assembling movements, dispersive movements, and random movements.

An *assembling movement* is characterized by convergence on a focal point. This type of movement is illustrated by a commuter's journey to work in the central business district or the convergence of shoppers on a shopping center. In contrast, a *dispersive movement* spreads out from a focal point. On a micro level, dispersion is represented by outward movement from a given site, subdivision, or neighborhood. On a macro level, dispersion is reflected in commuters leaving the subdivisions and bedroom communities in the metropolitan area to journey to work. Often, assembling movements and dispersive movements are flip sides of one another. Commuters' journey to work can be an assembling movement from the perspective of employers in the labor market, but a dispersive movement from the perspective of residential neighborhoods.

A *trapping point* is a configuration of uses that is especially conducive to assembling movements. Trapping points are micro-level zones of conflux. A well-known site supported by good infrastructure and design features exerts a strong gravitational pull, bringing people, goods, and activities to the area. Cincinnati's Fountain Square, Manhattan's Times Square, San Francisco's Fisherman's Wharf, and Boston's Faneuil Hall and Quincy Market are all trapping points.

In a *random movement* pattern, goods or persons are dispersed at various locations along the route. A random movement can occur at either end of the route–i.e., at its terminus or where it converges with another route.

Whatever the pattern, it is difficult to analyze a movement without linking it to a specific use or activity. An understanding of existing activities and movement patterns helps identify the support network that surrounds a given site or will sustain a proposed use and market for that site. These factors must be considered to analyze a property's viability in terms of a highest and best use. The nature and orientation of the movement patterns must be identified along with the frequency and volume of trips. To measure specific activities on sites, trip patterns can be identified by survey or observation. For example, the number of trips made to a supermarket each week by its clientele and the typical dollar amount spent per trip indicate the nature and frequency of one movement pattern. Traffic volume counts may be used as a secondary data source.

The quantifiable measures of access are dollar costs, the time and distance traveled, the frequency of the trips, and the degree of irritation experienced. The importance of each of these factors varies with the mode of transportation involved.

The dollar costs of movement may be fixed or variable. For public transportation, these costs are measured in taxes and/or user fees. The former are fixed; the latter vary with the level of service provided. For private transportation, fixed costs include registration fees for an automobile license and title, the cost of insurance, and a personal property tax. Variable costs include expenses incurred for gas and oil, maintenance, driving fines, and parking fees. Collectively, all the expenses incurred to access a site over and above the costs of accessing a more convenient location represent the opportunity cost of occupying that site. In effect, a higher cost of accessibility offsets the lower site rent.

Accessibility on both a macro and micro level is a key attribute that strongly influences a property's use, marketability, and value. The land economist William Alonso propounded a theory of rent that segmented site value into two components–accessibility and location. In situs theory, however, accessibility is treated as a dimension of location. For purposes of analysis and decision making, the two attributes should be addressed as separate, but related, factors.

Impact of the Overall Environment on Site Use

The final element in the analysis of situs is the relationship between the total urban environment and the specific neighborhood. Like neighborhood analysis, the analysis of the urban environment considers social, physical, economic, and institutional features. These features are set, but the environment is also described in terms of access, specifically the surroundings through which goods and people must travel to reach a site. Certain amenities and noneconomic attributes are also classified as environmental components of situs. Thus, *environment* is a loosely defined term for the area surrounding a property. Although external to the site, the environment reflects certain spatial aspects of the site's physical and legal productivity attributes.

Environmental attributes are generally characterized as immobile externalities. Nevertheless, environmental attributes combine with accessibility to define the gravitational draw of an area.

In general, environmental factors are often identified as area amenities. Investigation indicates that the environment encompasses many other spatial considerations–e.g., land use; physical, social, cultural, psychological, and economic factors; and institutional or political concerns.

The key to analyzing the environment is understanding that all the above-mentioned topics affect realty markets. Often the economic environment is said to be the focus of real estate decision makers. In a broad sense, the economic environment encompasses all the other dimensions. In fact, all these environmental attributes are so closely interwoven that any "true" breakdown for discussion purposes would be artificial. Most of the breakdowns available are the result of independent investigation into different real estate issues by various disciplines.

Physical Environment

The physical environment is characterized by both natural and artificial features. Natural features include the topography (grade and elevation), vegetation and ground cover, the atmosphere (climate), the condition of the surface and subsurface soils, any bodies of water, and any natural phenomena in proximity to the neighborhood.

Most land uses adapt well to flat or gently rolling, well-drained land. Extreme grades are often an impediment to land use. Topography influences the potential for development and may often direct the nature of the land use pattern. For example, the development of El Paso, Texas, reflects the economic significance of the city's proximity to the Rio Grande and the Franklin Mountains. The extreme variation in terrain, from lush river valley to rugged mountains and desert, have strongly influenced the economic delineation of El Paso's neighborhoods.

The following features are considered in the analysis of the physical environment:

- Atmosphere and micro climate
- Surface infrastructure (street system and sidewalks)

- Topography
- Wind direction
- Soil composition and capacity to support structures
- Installation of subsurface utilities (water, sewer, gas, etc.)
- Vegetation (an aesthetic amenity that can enhance the area's competitiveness)

Of course, the natural physical environment must be linked to the artificial, or built, environment. The natural terrain directs the development, design, and cost of improvements in an area. Sometimes an artificial environment may be directly substituted for the natural environment. Where natural vegetation is lacking, for example, extensive landscaping may be required to make the subject area competitive.

The built environment is a major factor affecting the physical character of many neighborhoods. The environment can be described and analyzed based on the age and size of the structures in the area, the density of development and occupancy, and the degree of maintenance. The dominance of a specific architectural design and quality may reflect the age of neighborhood buildings. Analysis of the built environment can provide further insight into the impact of development on the area and indicate whether the development complies or conflicts with local building controls.

The physical environment influences and interacts with the land use pattern in an area and forms the basis for its future development potential. Both the existing pattern and future potential often depend on the tastes and preferences of the resident population. These tastes and preferences are linked to the social and cultural environment within the subject area.

Social and Cultural Environment

The social and cultural environment of an area is represented by the residents, clients, or employees that live in or frequent the area on an on-going basis. The interaction of these groups of individuals may be observed in the ancillary land use associations characteristic of the neighborhood. For example, a neighborhood bar situated across from a manufacturing plant can give a neighborhood a social dimension that would be absent in a new industrial park. A bar often extends the duration of activity in an area beyond the workday into the evening hours.

Studying the social and cultural environment provides information on the land use potential of an area that could not be gleaned from data on the quantity of land uses only. Investigation of the social dimension can indicate:

- The efficiency of the land use associations. An efficient land use pattern is one characterized by a high degree of compatibility and consistency.
- The lifestyle of the occupants or the clientele that frequents the neighborhood.

- The cultural environment, which is strongly influenced by the occupational and economic status of area households

Collectively, the lifestyles of the residents direct the quantity, quality, and efficiency of the potential land use associations in an area.
The social and cultural environment is constantly changing. If shifts
in behavior are readily apparent and easy to detect, the pattern of
change is usually linear and can be forecast.[5]

Analysis of the social environment goes beyond investigation of the
demographic variables typically studied in market analysis. The
lifestyles and levels of communication among residents, neighborhood
associations, and other political groups must also be addressed. Other
concerns focus on the emphasis placed on tradition and custom and
the fit between customers or clients and the products, services, and
existing or proposed activities in the area. The degree of economic or
political power in a neighborhood also depends on the social group or
groups that are active there.

The social and cultural environment is reflected in the lifestyles
and behavioral patterns observed in the neighborhood. These behavioral patterns are more thoroughly investigated in the context of the
psychological environment.

Psychological Environment

The psychological environment focuses on how neighborhood behav-
iors are perceived. While the social environment reflects the group's
value system based on common heritage, experience, and culture, the
psychological environment describes how individuals or households
respond to the group value system and what prompts individuals or
households to choose, safeguard, and promote a neighborhood. Often
psychological tendencies evolve into formal traditions.[6]

A sense of prestige is one element of a psychological environment.
To understand this attribute, *prestige* must be distinguished from *status*. Prestige is an abstract quality that describes the high regard which
both direct users and third parties have for a specific area, district, or
neighborhood. Status is a more general condition that can prevail over
a range of urban areas. High status areas are usually characterized by
wealthy occupants or clients (e.g., Rodeo Drive in Los Angeles). Prestigious and high status areas may overlap, but prestigious areas are
not necessarily always wealthy neighborhoods; similarly, high status
neighborhoods may not have prestige.

The prestige associated with certain neighborhoods often rubs off
on nearby properties. Many residential and retail facilities situate themselves as close as possible to traditionally prestigious districts. Because
the rub-off effect skews the land use pattern, understanding prestige is
useful in inferring or predicting the direction of growth.

---

5. Richard B. Andrews, *Situs Theory*, Part III, *Situs: Its Relation to Environment*. Monograph published by the Center for Urban
    Land Economics Research, Graduate School of Business (Madison: University of Wisconsin, 1982), 33.

6. Ibid., 48.

The psychological environment is often considered only in connection with residential locations, but prestige and status are relevant to the location of office and retail facilities as well. Certain types of businesses identify with specific office districts and the psychological environment of business activity is often defined by a street address. A location on New York's Wall Street, for example, commands premium rent because it is advantageous for financial operations. Similarly, advertising is linked to Madison Avenue. The locale must relate to the activity for which the neighborhood has drawing and holding power since the public's perception of the area affects business potential.

The prestige associated with retail or commercial areas is more fragile than the prestige attached to residential neighborhoods. In commercial areas additional factors are at work–competition from alternative sites, shifts in consumer and client preferences, the introduction of new retailing methods, changing perceptions of the area, and the relocation of anchor stores.

Other psychological factors that affect how an area is perceived include sentiment, heritage, and territoriality. Sentiment is reflected in the desire to preserve the old downtown areas of small rural communities despite competition from new shopping centers. Displacement can occur as a result of the functional and external obsolescence of the old downtown, but sentimental resistance by local residents may be sufficient to reverse the neighborhood's decline. Only a vibrant economy can ensure the area's survival, however.

A sense of heritage, which is often based on sentiment, may also prolong the stages of a neighborhood's life cycle. When several generations have lived in the same home or operated businesses in the same facilities, they have a vested interest in maintaining the area. In many American communities the sense of heritage has been eroded by increased mobility. Modern families often relocate to other parts of the country during economic downturns.

Territoriality is the psychological perception that specific individuals or activities belong in a particular area. If this perception is strong, it may lead to political action that contributes to the homogeneity of land uses, income groups, and demography in a specific area. The boundaries of a neighborhood are often established along distinct lines and become entrenched over time by tradition, custom, and sentiment.[7]

The psychological environment represents a mental map of the area, the "aura" associated with a neighborhood which forms the basis for its holding power and promise. Expectation is the key to potential growth. Psychological expectations underlie the subjective decision making that directs market expectations. Market expectations, in turn, set constraints on a neighborhood's economic environment.

---

7. Ibid., 54.

Economic Environment—The Economics of Land Use

The economic environment of an area is reflected in the sale prices of properties, rental rates, land use patterns, and the mix of market participants in the neighborhood. Sale prices and rental rates, which are often stated in ranges, are tied to specific land uses and distinct property attributes. Market participants in an area are generally grouped into consumer, speculator, and investor categories. A descriptive analysis identifying each type of land use in the area and the market players involved is often sufficient to establish the economic status of the area as well as its potential for, and direction of, growth.

Price becomes a symbol for the expectations of an area—its capacity to absorb and support alternative land uses. But price is also an independent factor in real estate decision making. The analysis of prices in relation to land uses and the economic environment can become ensnared in a causal dilemma: Does use determine price or does price determine use?

Price and use are interwoven. The principles of competition and substitution affect land use patterns in a neighborhood as well as the uses of specific sites. On a micro level, a site's capacity to support a use indicates the return to the site or the price paid for the site. The use of a site is determined on a locational basis by its economic environment, other activities in the vicinity, and the associations between these activities.

On a macro level, the competition among uses is reflected in the prices paid for sites. These prices determine the sites' use potential. The economic topography of an area, which is the result of the competition for uses, may be depicted with land price gradients and bid-rent curves. These conceptual tools are used to analyze the competition among uses within the overall urban structure; they are addressed in the discussion of urban structure in Chapter 5.

A neighborhood functions like an organ within the overall organism of the city. Thus, the economic environment of a neighborhood is also shaped by citywide competition. The relationship between micro-level and macro-level accessibility depends on both the linkages between activities outside the subject neighborhood and activities within it. Economic events in the metropolitan area can have a profound effect on price ranges in specific neighborhoods.

The sale prices and rents in an area cannot be separated from the objectives of the market participants. Economics is concerned with choice and economic decision making is a process in which choices are made among limited options. The options in real estate are most often constrained by location because there is only so much space available in a given area at a given time. If the needs of area users exceed the inventory available, i.e., if demand exceeds supply, then prices and/or rents will rise. If the available space greatly exceeds the amount of space required, i.e., if supply exceeds demand, then prices and rents should decline. Markets react or change direction over time and the analyst must determine how long it will take buyers and sellers in the area to adjust.

The market participants that create demand in an area should be identified as consumers (direct users), speculators, or investors. Classifying potential buyers in this way helps focus on their objectives with regard to area properties. Further investigation may indicate the area's potential for change, the likely pace of growth, and the range of prices likely to be paid for neighborhood sites. Generally, an analyst expects direct users to offer less for properties than speculators. However, financial analysis of a speculative purchase may indicate that favorable financing and tax deductions have influenced the price paid and effectively lowered the speculator's actual cost below what the agreed-upon price would suggest.

Investor objectives also influence the expectations for properties in a given location. This may be reflected by differentials in economic units—e.g., sale prices, adjustments for market conditions, capitalization and discount rates, and the rates of return characteristic of properties in the area. Another indication that change can be precipitated by investor activity is seen in the alternative forecasts of potential income developed for a given site. Speculation and investment generate growth and set the pattern of land use in an area. A fair level of investment activity and numerous property transactions generally indicate change in the economic environment of a neighborhood.

The availability of commercial credit in an area is an essential attribute of the economic environment. Commercial credit is a good indicator of financial support for the existing or proposed land uses in a neighborhood. The volume of capital available to businesses in a community reflects perceptions of the strength and durability of its economy. The terms of the loans offer further insight into the potential risk associated with specific economic environments.

Mortgage delinquency and foreclosures in a neighborhood are signs of an economic environment in transition. Such financial data must be segmented to pinpoint the areas of occurrence and the types of properties involved. In addition to the location and type of property, the analyst must consider the levels of debt incurred by the properties and the quality of their management. If a consistent pattern of mortgage delinquencies for specific property types in a given location is observed, this information can be used to project neighborhood trends.

Rental delinquencies and the availability of property insurance should also be investigated. Both are leading indicators of the economic environment of a property. Here too the analyst must check the pattern of delinquencies against the location, type, and management of the properties.

The availability of insurance depends on the ranking of the area, which determines the periodic insurance payment. The cost of insurance affects income projections for properties. The analyst must identify the levels and types of insurance available in an area; the relationship between insurance coverage, vacancy rates, property uses; and institutional perceptions of risk in the area.

Property maintenance is a function of both the economic environment and the physical environment. Maintenance also has a psychological dimension. The level of stewardship in an area is often higher if properties are owned by user-occupants rather than absentee landlords.

Maintenance requires the periodic investment of additional capital and labor. If expectations of future returns do not justify such an investment, expenditures are not made. Returns may come in monetary form (rent and capital gains) or in personal satisfaction (e.g., the pride of ownership, a better standard of living, or a legacy bequeathed to future generations). In any case, the willingness to invest in existing structures indicates a positive perception of the economic environment. Rental or mortgage delinquencies, a high level of income loss, and lack of maintenance in an area all suggest diminished expectations. They also indicate economic or external obsolescence, which must be investigated as part of the valuation process.

Technology is the last major factor to be considered in relation to an area's economic environment. The economic potential of an area is often linked to its ability to adapt to changing market demand standards based on perceived needs. When business activities change so do their space requirements; the changes they make will alter building structures in the neighborhood. For example, the advent of the Internet has created new standards for office space and popularized the office hotel. Under this plan, employees can share the same space because each employee works in the office only occasionally. Most often, employees work from their homes over the Internet. The valuation process addresses changes in response to the economic environment under the category of functional obsolescence.

The economic environment of a neighborhood overlaps all the other environmental dimensions–physical, social, psychological, institutional, and land use. The economic environment provides decision makers with important data that translate into units of comparison. With these units, decision making can be based on quantifiable rates of return, sale prices, and comparative costs.

Institutional and Political Environment

Like the economic environment, the institutional and political environment of a neighborhood has social, cultural, and psychological dimensions. The institutional environment comprises public laws and rules of behavior as well as city planning and services. Although many of the concerns of the institutional and political environment are also considered facets of the social, economic, and psychological environments, the institutional environment may be distinguished by the level or degree of political organization.

The level of political organization is reflected in the size of the city's bureaucracy, the strength of district representation in elections, the area's contacts at city hall, neighborhood associations, and the power of city planners. Various organizations influence the availability of community services in a specific neighborhood, which must compete with other neighborhoods for limited services and benefits.

The public services a neighborhood receives depend on the institutional or political clout it wields. A neighborhood may be defined by the scale and cost of these services, which generally vary within a community. The availability of services is linked to their cost, which is represented by the taxes, special assessments, and user fees levied in the area. In fact, the nature of the public services desired can often be related to specific locations and specific uses within these locations. For example, police protection may be most important to residents, while street maintenance may be of prime concern to commercial users in the neighborhood.

Housing and building codes control the form and structure of cities. The implementation and enforcement of these codes and the link between code compliance and the provision of public services reinforce the city planning process. The perceptions and philosophies of the strategic planners in a community help determine the environment in which land use decisions are made.

It is important to recognize that strategic planning is not limited to the public sector. Private developers and financial institutions help formulate land use policies and are integral to the decision-making process. Many municipal utility districts were formed before individual property owners had an opportunity to provide input and consider whether their properties should be included or excluded. The neighborhood environment must be analyzed with political awareness.

The institutional and political environment of a neighborhood can only be understood within the context of the overall urban plan. Each site is linked to the neighborhood as the neighborhood is linked to the total urban structure.

Summary

Location is a complex subject which has many dimensions. Although an understanding of location is essential to any analysis of property productivity, the locational attributes of property are often approached in a subjective manner. The linkages between a specific site and the overall city can be investigated in the contexts of situs and urban structure.

The concept of situs addresses the individual site within its environment. Situs theory separates the site into two components: the land use function and the land parcel. These two distinct property dimensions are then related to the overall urban environment within a specified time frame.

Based on this theoretical link between the site and the urban environment, the situs concept can be adapted and applied step by step. First, the subject area is delineated and the activities within the area are identified. Next, the association and accessibility of activities are examined. Finally, the activities are studied in terms of various components of the environment—the land use; social, cultural, psychological, and economic factors; and institutional and political dimensions. Although the environment is generally thought of as set, it is actually a dynamic force that shapes the potential of the site and the neighborhood.

Location analysis must also address the overall urban environment. The urban structure and land use patterns are tied to the economic base. Understanding the overall urban environment is the key to forecasting the potential of specific land parcels and neighborhoods. For purposes of real estate decision making, it is useful to consider the impact of individual land use decisions and property transactions in aggregate. Over time, urban land use patterns are directed by market trends, cultural preferences, institutional constraints, and technology. These key issues are identified in the environmental component of situs.

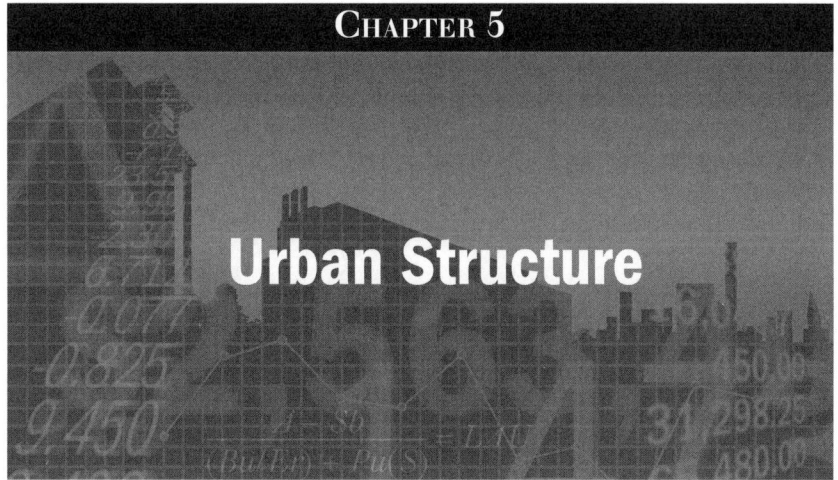

CHAPTER 5

Urban Structure

Chapter Objectives

- To explain how social, physical, economic, and institutional support systems in urban areas ultimately determine land use and define highest and best use
- To examine the various theories or models of urban growth and how they relate to real estate appraisal
- To explore models of rent theory and how they help an appraiser understand land use patterns, land use succession, and property values
- To describe the relationship of real estate productivity to real estate market structure

Despite its fixed location, real estate is economically flexible. Although a parcel of real estate is physically tied to a particular place, location is an economic variable subject to change with the passage of time. Essentially, real estate is space used to house economic activities over discrete segments of time. As the surrounding neighborhood changes, the support system for the existing use may change. Change affects the use and future revenue potential of the property, the market for the property, and the transfer price obtainable for the property at any given site. Therefore, the market for any given parcel of real estate cannot be analyzed without first considering its use and revenue potential—now and in the future. A major part of this determination is the current and future urban structure because the urban structure is a major determinate of a site's use and, hence, its revenue.

To understand real estate markets, spatially defined land use patterns and associations must be examined. Situs theory addresses the relationship between a land use and the specific location. (*Situs* is defined in Chapter 4.) The linkage between the land use on a given site and the broader urban structure further defines the product and its value. The geographical, or spatial, dimension is the key to urban structure.

The term *urban structure* refers to the social, physical, and economic aggregation of land uses in a community, which serves as the support system for the land use on any given site. This support system directs the quantity, quality, and duration of returns to the site.

Urban structure connotes an orderly arrangement of discrete economic functions within an overall system. As economic interrelationships become more complex, functions tend to become more specialized and rational patterns of land use evolve. Urban activities such as retailing, manufacturing, and recreation tend to concentrate in specific areas.[1] This is how major land use clusters have formed in most cities in the past and this pattern continues today.

As the urban network develops, site function becomes more specialized. Each individual parcel of land may be considered a "packet of functions,"[2] the locus of specific economic activities. A site can accommodate a variety of activities depending on surrounding land uses. Highest and best use analysis requires the identification of economic associations, the nature of which can vary. Associated activities can be complementary, competitive, or conflicting.

The urban structure reflects each community's cumulative land use needs over a number of years. For example, in some urban areas the skeleton of the street and utility systems may be a relic of the past,[3] while in other areas the street and utility plan may be current. Older buildings may intermingle with modern facilities. To understand the current pattern of land uses and land prices, an analyst must identify

---

1. Richard U. Ratcliff, *Urban Land Economics* (New York: McGraw-Hill, 1948), 368.

2. Robert M. Haig, "Toward an Understanding of the Metropolis," *The Quarterly Journal of Economics* (February 1926): 414–20.

3. Ratcliff, 370–72.

the factors influencing the urban structure, its origins, and the changes it has undergone over time.

Forces Influencing Urban Structure

Although similar forces may be at work in most cities, differences in topography and size can cause variations in urban structure. The original siting of a city is usually attributable to some primary activities such as commerce, manufacturing, or political and social functions. Many cities developed at shipment points or where transportation routes converged—e.g., where water routes met overland trails or railroads.

Economic activity draws people into an urban area, but topography often puts constraints on development. The direction of and potential for growth are forecast based on an understanding of both the urban economy and topography. Generally, the geographical features that most strongly influence the direction of urban growth are bodies of water and variations in terrain. Cities originate at the most convenient point of contact with the outer world and grow along the paths of least resistance toward poles of greatest attraction.

Many land economists perceive that the prices paid for land are based on the ease of accessibility between the land and prominent areas of activity. Therefore, the price per square foot of site area is inversely related to the transportation cost or cost to access that site. A convenient location is highly desirable, so high prices are paid for sites that provide the greatest number of people with the easiest access. Sites in the central business district (CBD) and other areas of great activity can command premium prices. The premium paid for convenience is related to the supply of land available in the city. Land in the center of the city is limited, so its price is driven up. Intensity of demand decreases along the urban periphery because the number of competing sites increases as a square function of the distance ($S_n \propto 1/D^2$) from the central point. Often land prices along the periphery of a city simply represent the cost of platting, opening streets, and/or discounting the returns expected from the projected development.

Proximity to the CBD or the core of economic activity has been the strongest factor influencing land prices. One general pattern of growth is along transportation corridors (radii or axes); nearby sites become desirable because of their accessibility. Various models of urban growth will be discussed in this chapter. Two key ideas to remember are 1) the urban structure influences individual land use decisions and land values, and 2) the basic economic functions of a city influence the urban structure.

As demand pushes up the price of land in a desirable location, topography generally becomes less important. Nevertheless, certain amenities associated with the terrain may make particular locations especially attractive. For example, high-income residential users are able to outbid lower-income groups for land along high ground and near scenic riverfront locations. Thus, terrain also needs to be considered in delineating the competitive supply.

Quality-of-life issues also impact urban growth. The need to live close to work and the desire for family privacy continue to shape urban growth and create land use conflict. These factors shaped such trends as the growth of the suburbs in the 1950s. The suburbs offered big single-family houses on large lots for privacy and interstate highways allowed residents to commute to work easily. In turn, dependence on the automobile has led to massive public expense for infrastructure and a deteriorating quality of life plagued with pollution and traffic congestion.

Other factors that impact the urban structure over time are:

- Government regulations and planning objectives
- Population changes
- Financing terms
- City size and age
- Tax rates
- Effective buying power (income levels)
- Supply of available land
- Transportation
- Expanded urban services
- Technology
- Employment centers
- Major groups of economic activities
- School systems
- Social issues
  - Crime
  - Desire for association
  - Cultural/entertainment activities

These factors affect different cities in different ways. Their impact on particular neighborhoods or submarkets within a city may also vary. All of the factors listed can be grouped under the principal categories of physical characteristics, economic base, market forces, the institutional framework, technology, and cultural norms.

Exhibit 5.1 illustrates how the forces that influence urban development and land markets affect the overall urban structure. The economic base, market forces, the institutional framework, technology, and cultural norms must all be considered in relation to physical topography. The physical attributes of property provide the foundation on which the other forces operate; the pattern of land prices is thereby linked to the physical terrain. As the forces interact within the physical terrain, they influence the development of a city and shape aggregate patterns of land prices. These forces are discussed below.

The economic base of a community or neighborhood strongly influences the land use activities and land use patterns in the area. Before space set aside for a specific use can be absorbed, there must be demand for the activities, goods, or services associated with that use.

Exhibit 5.1   Forces on Urban Structure

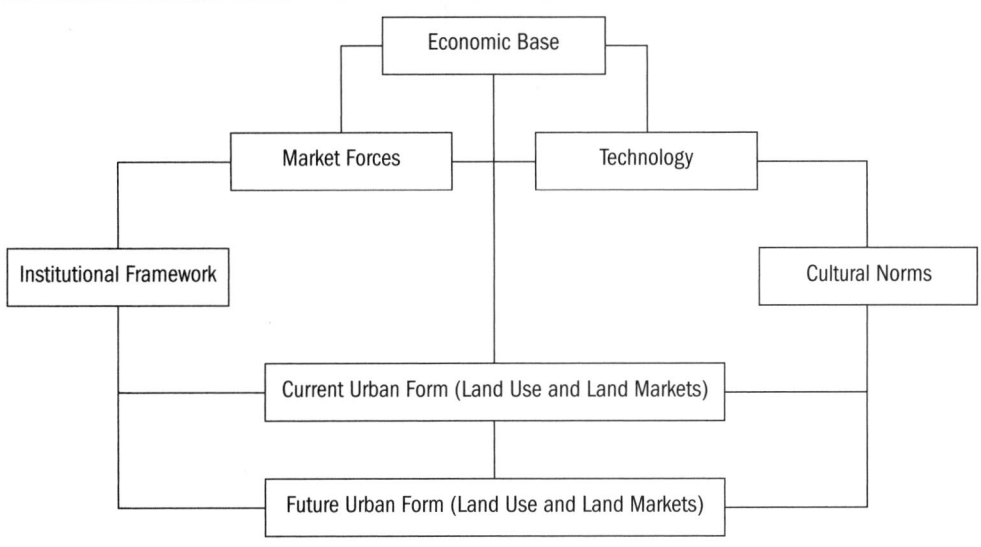

The number of people employed in a given activity serves as evidence of the demand for that use. The activity is conducted because the output, be it a product or a service, is demanded by consumers.

Market forces determine the supply of and demand for a property. Appropriate market support is needed if the property is to capture its market share and achieve the anticipated absorption rate for the specific use within a given time frame. Market forces also affect other economic variables such as land prices, returns (rents/incomes), and development costs.

The institutional framework consists of a mix of elements, including the procedures that govern property transactions; zoning, planning, and legislative controls; and regulations that impact land use decisions. Lending policies, insurance requirements, and public safety codes also fall within the institutional framework.

Technology refers to changing modes of manufacturing, communication, and transportation. The ongoing development of products and processes alters the way work is performed. New modes of communication enable, and sometimes even force, people to interact. Changes in technology impact land values because they affect accessibility and the aesthetic or functional desirability of existing real estate.

Cultural norms reflect individual lifestyle desires and the community's attitude toward protecting these desires. A community's desire to protect the environment can alter the possible uses for a parcel of land. The desire for privacy in housing affects land use patterns, crime, schools, and development, all of which are factors in the trade-off between convenience, quality of life, and economic needs.

Social Ecology Models

Various models can be used to describe the nature of urban land use and growth patterns. No single model adequately explains the full urban structure of most cities. Often a city's structure can best be represented by a combination of several models. Nevertheless, structural models provide useful insights into urban land use and growth patterns. In turn, these models help the analyst forecast the changes in urban structure that might be expected in the future.

Four classic urban growth models are often grouped together and described as *social ecology models.* Many analysts consider the models of the social ecology school as a unified body of work on urban structure. Developed between the 1920s and 1940s, the models have undergone little change over the last 60 years.

The social ecologist sees a city as a system of interrelated land uses. The social ecology models include three discrete patterns—the concentric zone model, the sector (wedge) model, and the axial (radial corridor) model—as well as one hybrid, the multiple nuclei model. The models' names describe their formulation and point of origin. The models are used to predict where growth is likely to occur.

Understanding the direction and type of urban growth is a key element of market analysis. The social ecology models describe the physical and spatial dimensions of urban structure and may be used to segment markets because it is within this spatial context that the ever-changing relationship of supply and demand is forecast.

Represented graphically, three of the models are circular while one has an irregular center surrounded by disconnected points. The models originated with theorists in different disciplines and they tend to emphasize different structural dynamics. The concentric zone model was developed by Ernest W. Burgess, a sociologist; the sector model by Homer Hoyt, a land economist; the axial model by Richard M. Hurd, a mortgage banker; and the multiple nuclei model by Chauncy D. Harris and Edward L. Ullman, two geographers. Elements from each of the models appear in different combinations in most cities.

Concentric Zone Model

After studying several urban areas, Ernest W. Burgess concluded in 1923 that a city expands radially from its center to form a series of concentric zones.[4] Exhibit 5.2 illustrates the concentric zone model.

Zone 1 is the central business district, or CBD, where diverse economic activities take place. The CBD contains office buildings for financial and professional services, retail stores, theaters, museums, and warehouses. This area is the urban core, the heart of the major retail and service activities of the city.

Growth from the city core encroaches upon Zone 2, which surrounds the CBD and tends to exhibit an unstable land use pattern. Zone 2 is a

---

4. E. W. Burgess, "The Growth of the City," *The City* (Chicago: University of Chicago Press, 1925).

Exhibit 5.2   Concentric Zone Pattern of Land Use

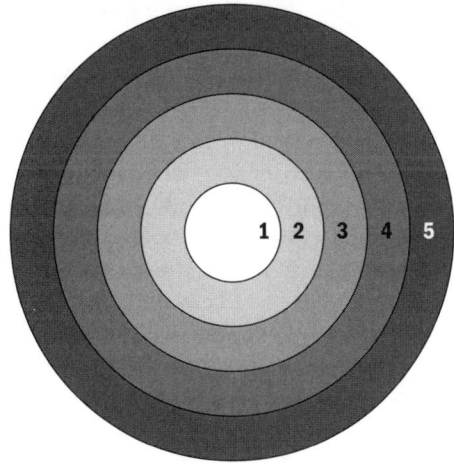

Concentric Circle Theory

1. Central business district (CBD)
2. Zone of transition
3. Zone for worker homes
4. Zone for middle- and high-income units
5. Commuter zone

Source: T.V. Smith and L.D. White, eds., *Chicago: An Experiment in Social Science Research* (Chicago: University of Chicago Press, 1929), 114–123.

transitional zone with light manufacturing and substandard dwellings on its periphery; this may be an area of considerable poverty and crime.

Zone 3 is a relatively stable area because Zone 2 has absorbed most of the growth from the city core. Successful businessmen may have originally settled in Zone 3. When manufacturing was displaced from the city core and relocated to Zone 2, Zone 3 remained essentially untouched. As industry expanded, however, Zone 3 became populated mainly by blue-collar workers who preferred to live near their work. The middle-class population moved out to Zone 4, where lots and houses were larger than in Zone 3. Zone 4 is an area of middle-class homes. Better transportation systems allowed more prosperous households to move into Zone 5, an area surrounded by farms and recreational areas. Zone 5 is an area of nonurban land uses. Because many of the people who live in this area work in the city core, Zone 5 may be identified as the commuter zone.

Beyond the major built-up urban area lies the urban-rural fringe, a transitional zone between urban and rural uses. Although difficult to define, such an area outside a growing urban area often becomes a speculative land market. Analysis and valuation of properties in the urban-rural fringe can be difficult because a range of potential highest and best uses can be projected for any given lot.

Burgess put forth his theory as a very general model. As such it has been criticized for offering only limited insight into the analysis of cities. Critics contended that Chicago, the reference point for the model, had a more defined CBD than other American cities, even in the 1920s. The growth of Chicago's core was constrained by natural features (Lake Michigan) and limited public transit (i.e., elevated trains and highways). In fact, to this day the central business district of Chicago is a commercial anachronism, very different from most cities where CBD growth has sprawled in various directions.

Other critics faulted Burgess's model for neglecting to consider both topography and the impact of the automobile on land use. Burgess focused on residential land use rather than commercial and industrial uses, which has also been seen as a weakness of his model. Nevertheless, since residential use is the major land use in cities, the concentric zone model still offers useful insights into the patterns of urban growth and market delineation.

Burgess's zones impose an order on land use patterns, which facilitates the comparison of cities and submarkets within cities. Focusing on residential markets, Burgess identified social status and income as key factors in land use development patterns. As a sociologist, Burgess studied the link between land use and social class or status.

The value of the zonal theory derives from its insight into the structural relationships between zones. The concentric zone model illustrates the tendency of each zone to expand outward until it spills over into the next zone. The outward movement from each zone is initiated by conditions in the previous zone. The dynamics of urban growth create an overflow effect. As its density increases, the central city can no longer be contained within its former boundaries. Vacant land is quickly absorbed and any available space is priced at a premium. Population spills over into the suburbs and outlying areas. The overflow effect can produce exponential growth. Before internal growth reaches the city boundaries, the suburban ring is characterized by relatively light development and low density, generally scattered over satellite communities. As development expands beyond the central city, the suburban population increases at a faster pace and eventually suburban population growth is greater than the growth in the central city.

The concentric zone theory offers both a general model of land use zones and the dynamic of the overflow effect to explain urban growth. Although it fails to consider the impact of topography, radial growth, and multiple clusters, the concentric zone model does provide a general framework within which these issues may be considered. The most important insight to be gleaned from Burgess's theory is that each inner zone tends to exert pressure on the next outer zone, thereby affecting the land use(s) and residential character of that zone. Thus, each ring builds on the previous ring.

Overflow Characteristics in Urban Structure

Early twentieth century research[5] identified three distinct tendencies or patterns of growth for commercial and apartment districts. These tendencies are still seen in the twenty-first century. In one pattern, districts "slide" along an axis, outward from the core, in one or more directions. This sliding pattern may extend away from the original nucleus or from a point along the axis. The pattern may be distinct or it may be integrated into a second pattern.

The second pattern is "coalescence," the merging of two nuclei that have the same land use but originate in different locations. Sliding and coalescence help explain the dynamics of changing "highest and best use" patterns in transitional areas. The sliding pattern may be observed in commercial development along an arterial. Coalescence is illustrated by the growth corridors which bring cities or suburban communities toward one another, e.g., the development along I-35 between Austin and San Antonio, Texas. The growth of commercial activity along major arterials that carry a heavy flow of intercity traffic illustrates the integration of sliding and coalescence patterns.

The third category of movement is "jumping," which describes a situation in which commercial or apartment units in one area jump to disconnected points outside the zone. These outlying points may become new nuclei. "Jumping" also describes the movement of an entire original nucleus to an outlying location.

Sector or Wedge Model

The sector, or wedge, model of urban growth was proposed in 1934 by Homer Hoyt, MAI, to describe more accurately how an urban area takes form.[6] The sector model was based on a study of 64 cities initially developed for the U.S. Federal Housing Administration (FHA). The study evolved into a theory of urban growth which recognizes the importance of transportation to a city's activities. In this regard, the sector theory is an improvement over the concentric zone theory. Industrial land use is also better addressed in the sector model.

The sector theory expands the concept of the overflow effect by considering the movement patterns of high-income residents and the effect of filtering. *Filtering* refers to the relationship between social and economic mobility and the quality of the housing stock. Generally, people are upwardly mobile, moving up to higher-priced housing in neighborhoods that confer status or prestige. As the high-quality housing stock ages, however, it declines in prestige and desirability. Older housing is purchased by members of a lower, upwardly mobile income stratum. Filtering suggests that urban growth is driven by high-income residential markets.

---

5. Charles C. Colby, "Centrifugal and Centripetal Forces in Urban Geography," *Annals of the Association of American Geographers* (March 1933): 1–20.

6. Homer Hoyt, "Recent Distortions of the Classical Models of Urban Structure," *Land Economics* (May 1964): 199–211.

In the sector model, the overflow effect is observed as the tendency of sectors to expand along transportation routes. Retail businesses predominate along main thoroughfares that provide the most convenient access. The sector model also addresses the impact of topography–e.g., the elevation of terrain, the location of bodies of water–on the direction of growth and patterns of development.

Like the concentric zone model, the sector model has a single center. It traces a city's origins to an economic activity or siting factor such as the location of a transshipment point. (A transshipment point is an area where a change in the mode of transportation occurs: a change from ship to wagon or rail, as in early New York and Chicago; from cattle trail to railroad, as in Fort Worth; or from riverboat to ship, as in New Orleans.) Homer Hoyt found that within the core area different land uses often competed for location. He then hypothesized that once a land use had established itself in a sector of the core, that use would expand outward as the city grew. Distinctive land use wedges were seen as growing out from the center core along major arterials.

Hoyt's theories of growth centered on high-income housing. Once a high-income residential district was established, the most expensive sites for new homes would lie along the outer edge of this sector. If a sector of an urban area initially develops as a high-, medium-, or low-income residential district, it will tend to retain that character and growth of the city will cause the sector to expand outward. Exhibit 5.3 illustrates the sector theory.

Exhibit 5.3   Sector Pattern of Land Use

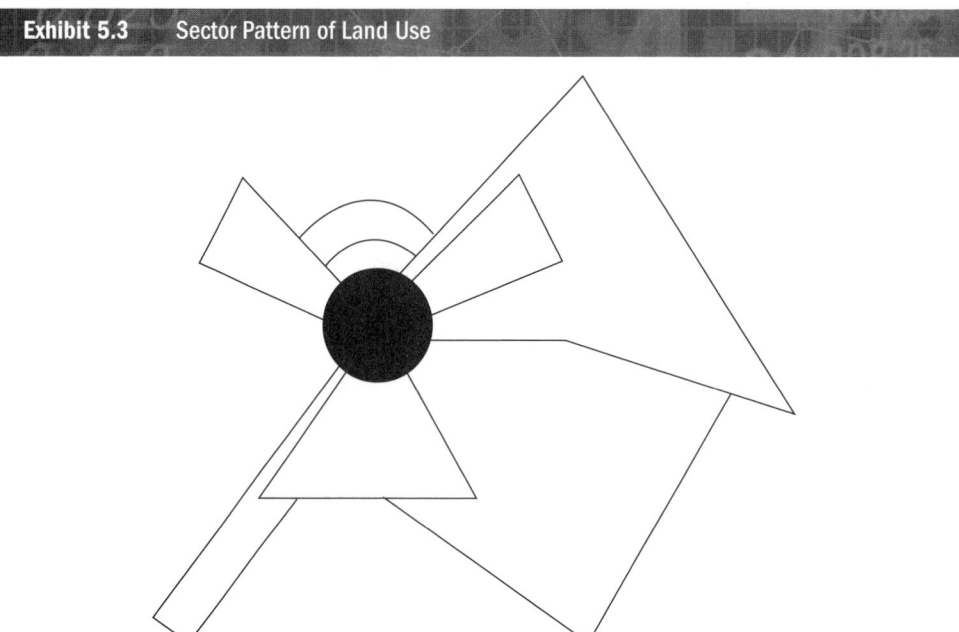

Source: Homer Hoyt, "The Structure and Growth of Residential Neighborhoods in American Cities," Federal Housing Administration (Washington: U.S. Government Printing Office, 1939).

According to the concept of filtering, groups of people tend to segregate themselves on the basis of income and social position. People form groups based on their work and residence. The tendency of different income groups to segregate is largely a function of economics. The wealthy can afford to live where they choose and make choices that may not always reflect rational economic motives. The low- and moderate-income residents of a city, however, are constrained by economics and concerned with accessibility and purchasing power (i.e., their ability to pay the rent). The sector theory holds that although the choices of high-income city residents may not always reflect economics, this group is the most influential in determining the direction of urban growth.

Several residential sectors usually develop within an urban area. As the population of a sector increases, pressure builds up and pushes the sector outward. Each residential group seeks to maximize the number of amenities and amount of space that it can afford. Residential groups generally socialize with those at a similar educational, cultural, or social level, but the overriding factor in differentiating residential groups is income.

Hoyt observed that low-income districts tend to be located farthest from high-income districts, and that low-income housing is usually found on the least desirable land, alongside railroads, commercial districts, or industrial areas. Eventually, as the perimeter of the urban area expands, the urban core may be occupied by the poor or abandoned altogether. The zone of high-income housing, on the other hand, becomes concentrated in one sector of the city rather than in a concentric ring as proposed by Burgess. High-income residential districts tend to be found upwind and upstream from concentrations of industry.

The sector model makes the following assumptions about high-income residential locations.

1. High-income residential growth proceeds from a given point of origin along established lines of travel or toward existing commercial or office-building nuclei. This phenomenon, referred to as scatteration, is seen in the tendency of residential development to fill in vacant areas around a mall located at a major intersection in the urban-rural fringe. The mall developers considered the micro-location appropriate because they anticipated that residential growth would follow. Situs theory shows that land uses are interdependent—i.e., the presence of a mall will attract residential development.

   The concepts of scatteration and situs answer one of the criticisms of the sector model, namely that it does not deal with interstitial areas—the land lying between the transportation routes along which the high-rent commercial enterprises are situated.

2. Expensive homes are built on desirable high ground, which is free of flooding and offers panoramic views. As this sector grows, it spreads along scenic waterfronts (lakes, bays, rivers, or oceans) which do not have industrial uses.

3. Higher-income residents seek out sections of the city that are open to the country rather than dead-end areas where expansion is blocked by barriers.

4. Higher-priced residential neighborhoods grow toward the homes of prominent members of the community.

5. The development of office buildings, banks, and stores pulls the higher-priced residential neighborhoods along in the same general direction (scatteration).

6. High-priced residential areas develop along the most convenient lines of transportation.

7. High-income neighborhoods continue to grow in the same direction over long periods of time.

8. Deluxe, high-rent apartment areas tend to be established near the business center in old residential areas.

9. Real estate promoters can sometimes bend the direction of high-priced residential growth by means of advertising and marketing campaigns. Their efforts may counteract the tendency of residential development to direct overall urban growth toward desirable topography and along major arterials.

These nine observations can be used to help forecast the direction of growth and land use patterns in a given city or neighborhood.

Hoyt noted that the age and condition of structures in residential areas are important determinants of the typical prices and rents in the area. In fact, the housing policy that guided the FHA, which was founded in 1934, was based on the concept of filtering. The sector model influenced the urban land use pattern of many communities during the late 1940s and early 1950s.

Multiple Nuclei Model

In 1945 Chancy Harris and Edward Ullman proposed the multiple nuclei model as a modification of the concentric zone and sector models.[7] The multiple nuclei theory holds that a city does not necessarily expand from a single central core, but rather that urban areas develop from several nuclei created by governmental or economic activities. The multiple nuclei theory emphasizes the influence of the automobile on urban growth patterns, not the overflow effect. In this model, cities take on a cellular structure, with distinctive land uses grouped around nuclei or growth points.

The grouping of land uses is tied to the needs of specialized economic activities. On a micro level, the nature of these land group associations is explored by *situs* concepts identifying the four factors that influence the spatial distribution of activities within a city:

1. Certain activities require specific site characteristics, which may be natural or man-made. For example, a site may be desirable because it hap-

---

7. C.D. Harris and E.L. Ullman, "The Nature of Cities," *Annals of the American Academy of Political and Social Science*, 1945.

pens to have appropriate natural grading in relation to its frontage along an arterial. Man-made curb cuts can enhance a site's accessibility.

2. Cohesion often helps generate profits. The economic concept of agglomeration demonstrates that profits can be made by grouping land uses. The uses so grouped may be mutually supportive, complementary, ancillary, or competitive. Significant benefits can be gained from closely observing major competitors, especially their turnover of durable goods and services.

3. The relationship between land uses can be either beneficial or detrimental. As Hoyt observed, high-income residential districts are rarely located next to heavy industry.

4. Not all economic land uses can meet the rents or prices paid for desirable sites within specific neighborhoods or within the overall community. The nature of an activity generally determines its ability to pay for a location. The principle of substitution explains the tendency of similar land uses to group. Low-cost housing and bulk storage facilities are examples of lower-end groupings that result from price competition.

The principle of land use association and the economics of agglomeration determine the highest and best use of the sites within a district and the land use groupings of a city. The multiple nuclei model also identifies land use groupings linked to activities outside the city's core.

Exhibit 5.4 illustrates the multiple nuclei model. The number of nuclei tends to increase as the urban area grows. The multiple nuclei model recognizes that the internal geography of cities owes much to the relationship between the unique characteristics of sites and general social and economic factors. The history of a city is especially important to an understanding of its existing and future land use patterns. The origin of a city and its economic base define the urban geography. As land use groupings become distinct, these nuclei articulate the existing urban structure and establish a basis for the pattern of its future development. The timing of a city's growth spurts, which are often cyclical, also influence the pattern of urban geography.

Harris and Ullman based the multiple nuclei model on four assumptions:

1. Certain activities require specialized facilities—i.e., financial institutions need easy access to law offices.

2. Certain land uses are priced out of locations in specific areas. Low-income families who cannot afford desirable housing are seldom found in proximity to high-priced housing.

3. Dissimilar activities are often detrimental to one another. The odors from a petrochemical complex would be incompatible with high-class restaurants or retail stores which require a cleaner environment.

4. Similar activities often group together because they benefit from proximity. Automobile dealers tend to cluster together to facilitate comparison shopping.

Exhibit 5.4 Multiple Nuclei Pattern of Land Use

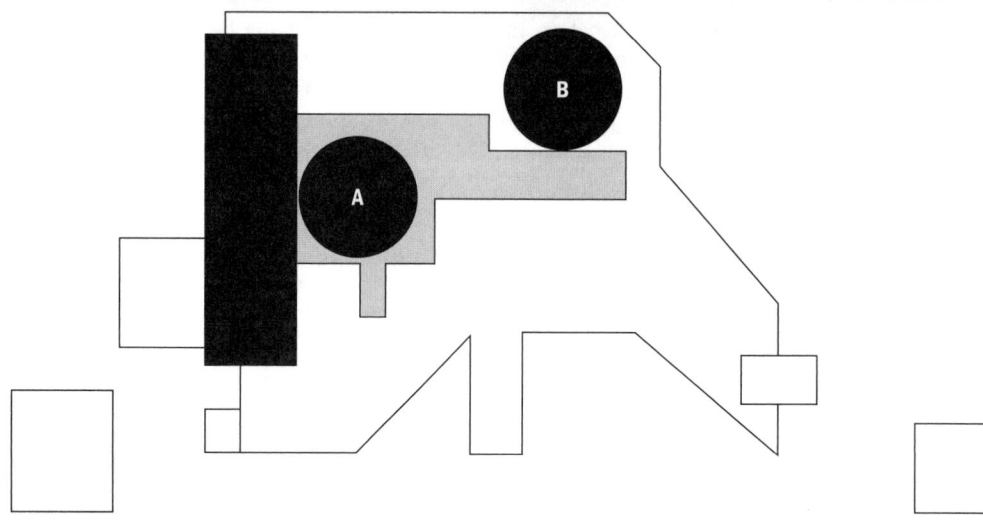

Source: Chauncy D. Harris and Edward L. Ullman, "The Nature of Cities," *Annals of the American Academy of Political and Social Science* (November 1945), 7–17.

The multiple nuclei model is broad enough to address unique urban situations and to incorporate the concept of situs. The model is premised on the competition of land uses for locations and attributes current changes in the urban structure to the effect of the automobile. The automobile and the overflow effect tend to promote decentralization. The greater mobility provided by automobiles helps explain land use activities in interstitial areas, and thus strengthens the multiple nuclei model against one of the principal criticisms of the sector model. The effect of the automobile is especially evident in the "newer" cities of the West and South, but can also be seen in suburban areas of older northern and Midwestern cities. The multiple nuclei model recognizes accessibility as a key factor in urban development. Accessibility is also emphasized by the rent theorists in their analyses of urban structure. The importance of transportation to land use patterns is central to the fourth social ecology model, the axial model.

Axial (Radial Corridor) Model

The axial, or radial corridor, model is often regarded as a subset of the concentric zone or sector models, even though it was advanced in 1903 and thus precedes the two other models.[8] The sector model owes much to the radial corridor model. Many attribute the radial corridor model to Richard Hurd and his classic text, *The Principles of City Land Values*. This model locates urban development along major transporta-

---

8.   Richard Hurd, *The Principles of City Land Values* (New York: The New York Times Press/Arlo Press, reprinted 1974).

tion routes such as highways, railroads, and waterways. Exhibit 5.5 illustrates the radial corridor model.

Hurd devised the axial model to facilitate decision making for investment and mortgage underwriting. Approaching the study of cities historically, Hurd identified city origins and urban development patterns. His practical approach resulted in the following observations about urban land use patterns.

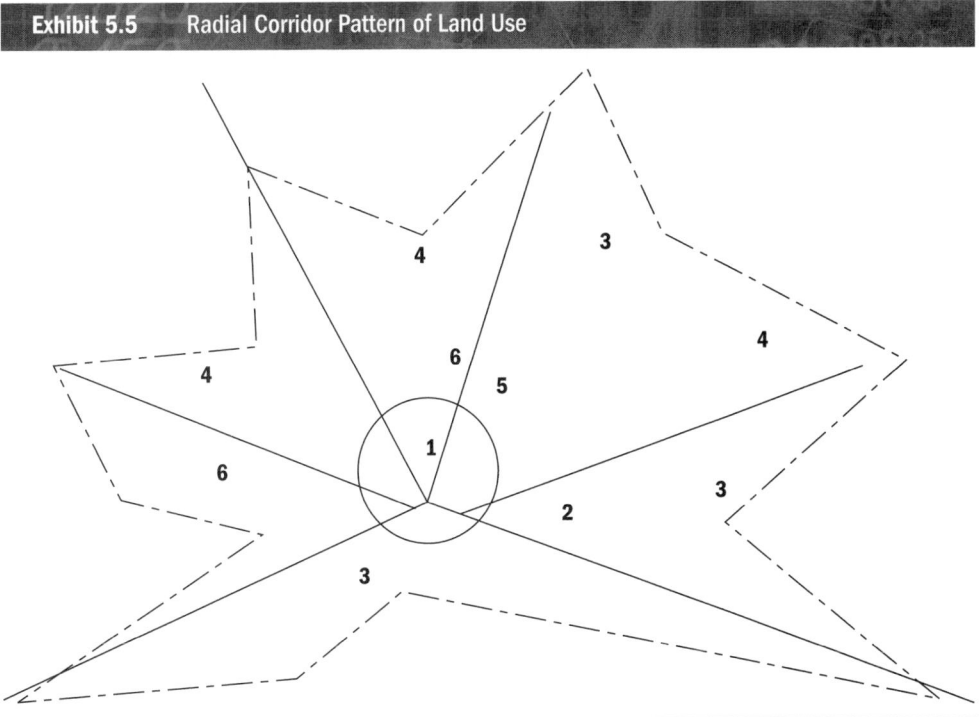

Exhibit 5.5   Radial Corridor Pattern of Land Use

- Cities tend to be organic in their composition and growth. Hurd believed that cities grow in conformity with biological laws, in particular with the law of evolution. Increasing differentiation is accompanied by increasing integration.
- The organic view of urban growth applies to the origins of cities. According to Hurd, cities originate at points where contact with the outside world is most convenient. In other words, accessibility accounts for both the economic base and location of a transshipment point.
- The same factor–accessibility for economic activities–underlies the origins of all modern cities. Given their common origins, cities may grow from a central core via the overflow effect or in an axial pattern.

The axial theory lacks an explanation of interstitial development because Hurd advanced the theory before the advent of the automobile.

Like other social ecology models, the axial model characterizes urban development as centered upon a point of origin. Growth moves axially in various directions away from this point. The axial pattern is created by pressure at the center and the process of aggregation at the edges. The city grows outward in an organic, or cellular, manner from center points at which key activities are located. These points can be at the city center or at various subcenters.

In Exhibit 5.5, the central business and industrial districts are shown as Area 1. Retail and service-oriented businesses are located along transportation routes from the central core. Area 3 usually is an apartment district inhabited by lower-income families who live there because of the low rent and availability of public transportation. The middle-class population is found in Area 4, far from the busy commercial and industrial areas yet close to transportation corridors and public facilities such as hospitals and schools. Secluded higher-income residential areas are located in the open space beyond Area 4.

Urban growth causes each area to encroach on the adjacent area. As a result, industrial parks and commercial facilities may develop in Areas 3, 4 and 5.

The Social Ecology Models Summarized

The social ecology models examine the relationship between socioeconomic factors and land use patterns. While these models are basically descriptive, they do consider the dynamics of growth and offer causal explanations for land use patterns. Understanding organic or cellular growth as originating from one center or from multiple centers is useful in the delineation of trade areas. Theories of central place (i.e., city centers where activities are concentrated command the highest rents) and efficient location (i.e., the loci of greatest activity command the highest rents) cannot be separated from the social ecology models. Moreover, demographic distribution cannot be considered apart from economic location.

Model Name	Major Determinate of Urban Form	Urban Type
Concentric Circle (Burgess)	Social	Central Core
Sector or Wedge (Hoyt)	High-Income Housing	Central Core
Multiple Nuclei (Harris & Ullman)	Automobile	Multiple Economic Activity Nodes
Axial/Radial Corridor (Hurd)	Transportation Routes	Central Core

The rationale for the social ecology models is economic activity, thus the analytical models formulated by the rent theorists are necessarily linked to the descriptive models of the social ecology school. The social ecology models also provide intuitive insights useful in decision making.

Rent Theorists' Models

Bid-Rent Curves

The rent theorists represent another school of thought on urban structure. For the rent theorists, the city structure reflects a trade-off between rents and transportation costs. Rent is basically the payment for location, over and above compensation for use and occupancy of the land parcel. Thus, the economic return to a parcel of land involves two factors: the overall accessibility of the site and the competitive price that has to be paid to occupy a given place in the urban terrain. In the calculation of rent, payment for the use and occupancy of the site is extracted to arrive at a measure of the price of location. The rent theorists view the entire city from the perspective of the economics of location; they identify the amount of income spent on location as an economic good in its own right. The basic model developed by William Alonso, a land economist, illustrates this concept of the city.

According to the basic model, the choice of location reflects an allocation of income dollars between rent and transportation costs at varying distances from the CBD. The vertical axis in Exhibit 5.6 represents the income to be spent on location. The selection of a site reflects a trade-off between the rent paid for the location and the transportation costs. The model suggests that the further one moves from the center of the city or focal point of the neighborhood, the lower the rent per unit of area (per square foot) and the greater the transportation costs.

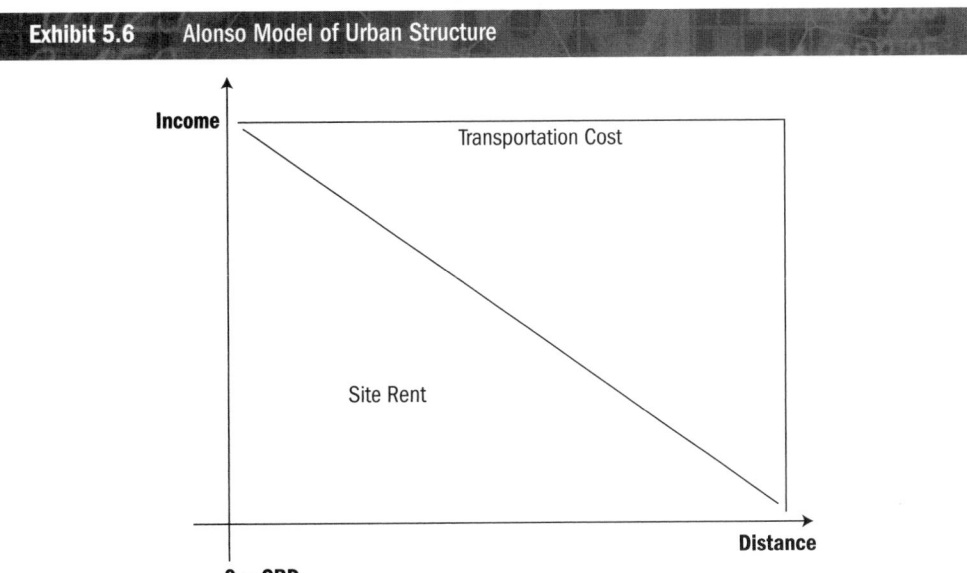

Exhibit 5.6 Alonso Model of Urban Structure

Alonso's analytical model of urban structure demonstrates that economics underlies the choice of location. Basically, Alonso's model is limited to a demand perspective, i.e., the trade-off between the advantages of location and the costs of transportation to and from the urban center. Transportation costs may actually be viewed as negative accessibility. In the formation of a city, sites are chosen on the basis of trade-offs between location and accessibility. Thus, the economics of choice upon which the Alonso model is based elucidates real estate decision making. Study of the trade-off between location and accessibility within the overall city provides one approach to analyzing the competition among alternative land uses within a given area or neighborhood.

Trade-offs between location and accessibility are graphically illustrated by the slopes or gradients of the bid-rent curves plotted for different land uses. (Bid-rent curves plot the rents offered at different locations in a city.) For example, the trade-off between location and accessibility may produce a curve such as Bid-Rent Curve 1 in Exhibit 5.7, which depicts citywide office demand. Office demand in the area tends to be highest in the CBD. Five miles from the CBD of the city, the income spent on site rents for office use is zero dollars. A preference for office location in the CBD is indicated by the relatively high site rent paid at point 0. This bid-rent curve illustrates the importance of a central location for office uses.

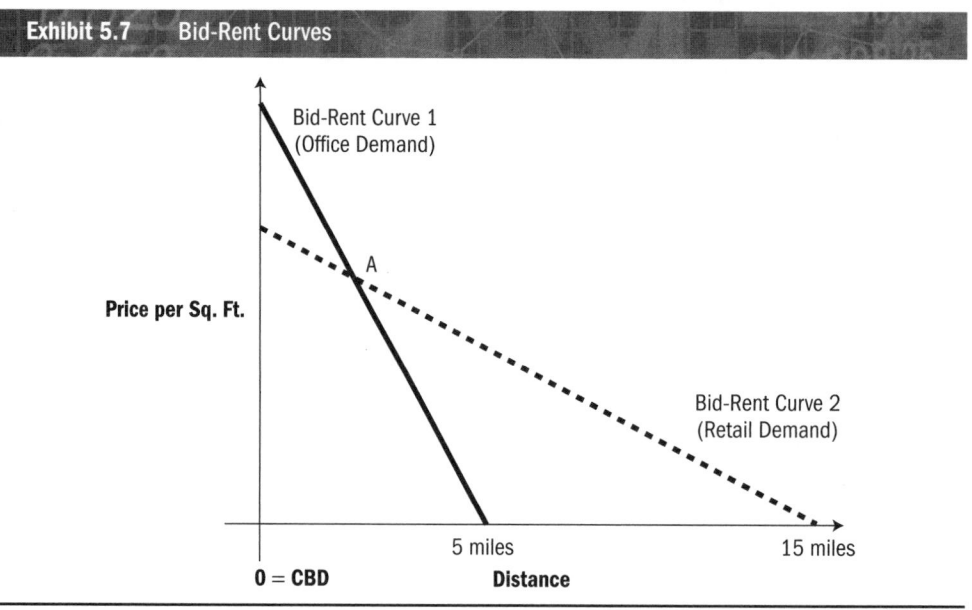

Exhibit 5.7   Bid-Rent Curves

Bid-Rent Curve 1
(Office Demand)

A

Price per Sq. Ft.

Bid-Rent Curve 2
(Retail Demand)

5 miles   15 miles

0 = CBD   **Distance**

Bid-Rent Curve 2 in Exhibit 5.7 depicts the trade-off of location and accessibility for retail facilities in the city. This second curve illustrates that retail space users do not attach the same importance to a central-city location as do office space users. Retail space users assign a higher premium to locations five miles away from the CBD; at a distance of 15 miles, however, the retail price for location is zero dollars. The competition between land uses is reflected at point A, where the dominant use shifts from office to retail activities in the overall land use pattern of the city.

A study in the early 1990s of land sales in Austin, Texas, provides an empirical test of a rent theorists' model, investigated the sales price per square foot of land under different uses. Exhibit 5.8 shows that the commercial market tends to predominate up to a distance of six miles on the south side of Austin. It is essential to note that a residential market does exist within this area, but in most situations commercial activities are able to outbid residential uses. It is important to keep in mind that any given site might prove an exception to the general pattern because of the specific attributes of the parcel.

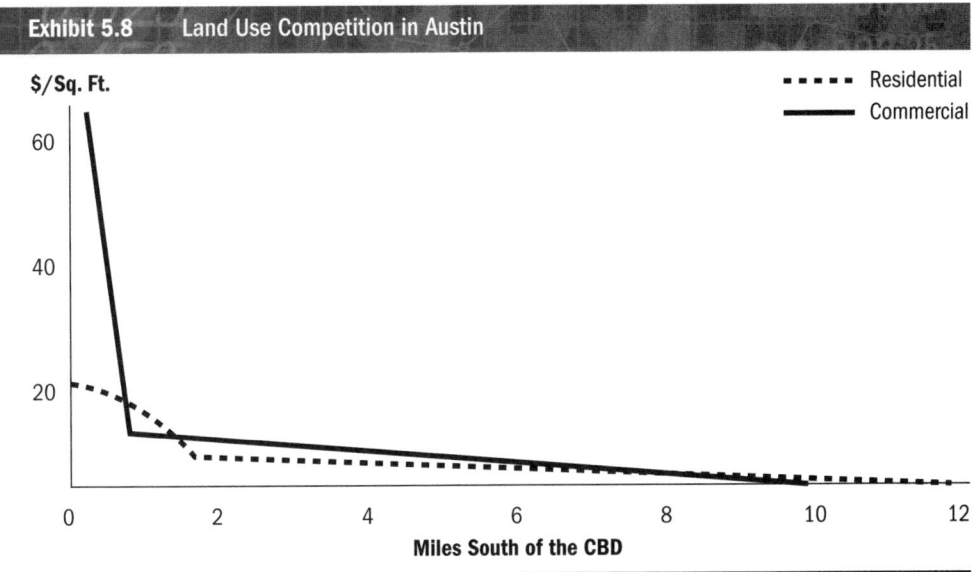

Exhibit 5.8   Land Use Competition in Austin

Empirical comparison of the commercial and residential land markets in Austin reveals that the trade-off between site location and accessibility is not the direct linear relationship illustrated in the Alonso model. The trade-off depicted by the Alonso model is based on a demand perspective, i.e., the allocation of income between two distinct goods. The curvilinear character of actual bid-rent curves reflects both supply and demand. Supply is represented in the limited availability of sites near the CBD and demand in the allocation of income between two goods. The impact of available supply on bid-rent curves is addressed by Richard F. Muth in his economic model of the city. Muth plotted the physical limits of supply in a mononuclear city as asymptotic curves, which show a rapid decline from the high site rents in the central city to the lower rents paid along the fringe of the city. This pattern is attributable in part to the potentially geometric increase in land available as the distance from the city core increases, assuming that there are no topographical barriers or transportation obstacles limiting the city's expansion.

Applicability and Theoretical Foundation

Although the rent theorists' models are based on valid assumptions, they lack the flexibility and descriptive insight of the social ecology models. The rent theorists do provide an analytical framework that is absent from the ecology models, however. The rent theorists' models represent aggregate or macro-level applications of gravity and central place theories, which are key to the delineation of retail trade areas. Moreover, the rent theorists provide alternative insights into the decision-making process applied to location. Whereas the social ecologists consider the overall urban environment, the rent theorists identify the economics of location as the key to urban land use patterns.

Theories of urban structure demonstrate the impact of geography on real estate markets. These theories allow us to segment markets and to identify substitutable tracts and land use support systems.

Both the social ecology and rent theorists' models can be used to identify land use clusters and the direction of urban growth. Exhibit 5.9 shows a bid-rent analysis typical of many cities. In this case, the city is Austin, Texas, in the early 1990s. At that time, the highest sale prices per unit were found in the CBD. Prices decline in all directions from point A (the intersection of 6th Street and Congress Avenue), which indicates the center of the CBD. However, current and growing multiple nuclei development is evident with the various land price peaks noted at point B (near I-35 and Highway 290) and to the northwest and southwest at points C and D, respectively. The northwest corridor along Highway 183, indicated by point D, is noted as the dominate center outside the CBD. As this exhibit demonstrates, the direction of growth for the land market can be better understood by using several theories in combination.

Link Between Multiple Nuclei and Rent Theory Models

The conceptual link between multiple nuclei models and rent theory is depicted in Exhibit 5.10. The figure shows the economic boundaries of specific retail nuclei. Using rent theory, the economic boundary between two competitive facilities is established where the combined costs of rent and travel for one site intersect with the combined costs for rent and travel for the other site. The two sites are identified as locations A and B. The sites are depicted in both the multiple nuclei schematic at the top of the figure and the rent theory graph below.

The rent for the location of activity A is amount E. The rent for the location of activity B is amount C. The transportation costs are represented by the lines radiating from rents E and C to points A and B. The combined costs are the sum of the location rents and the delivery costs. Delivery costs include both the cost of delivering a good to a customer and the cost of acquiring a good by a customer. For example, the cost of a can of peas is not just the retail cost of the can, but also the cost in time and travel to purchase the peas. Point X, where the costs intersect on the graph, is the point of indifference, i.e., at this point it costs a consumer

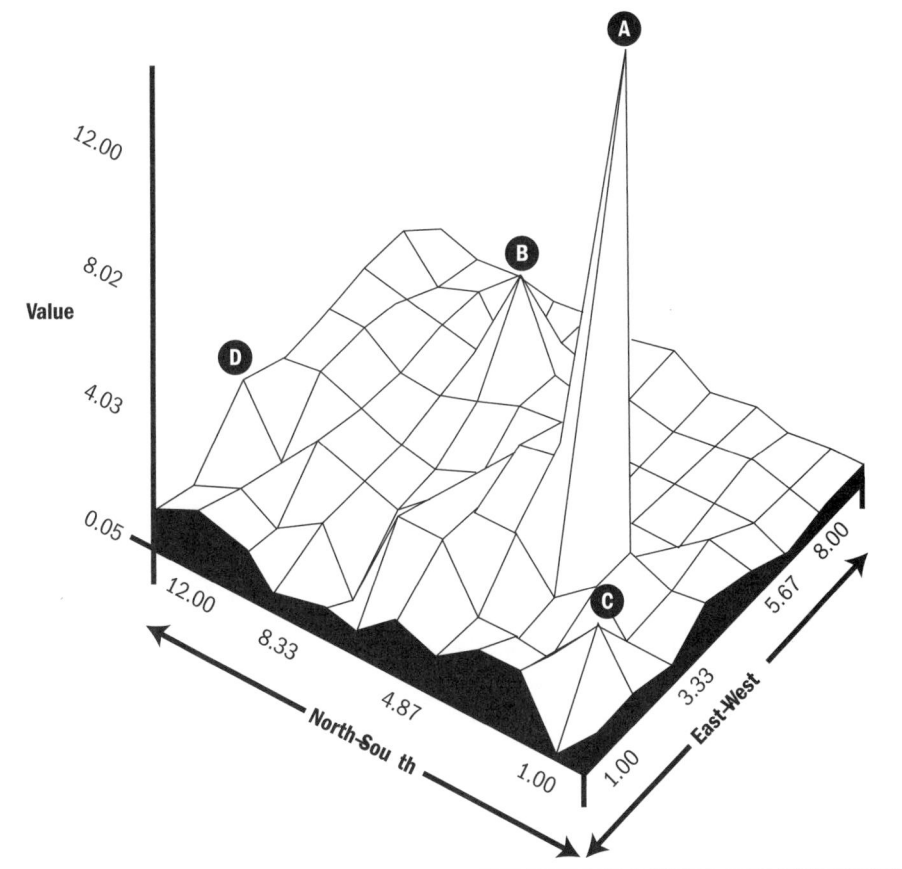

Exhibit 5.9 Bid-Rent Analysis of Austin, Texas

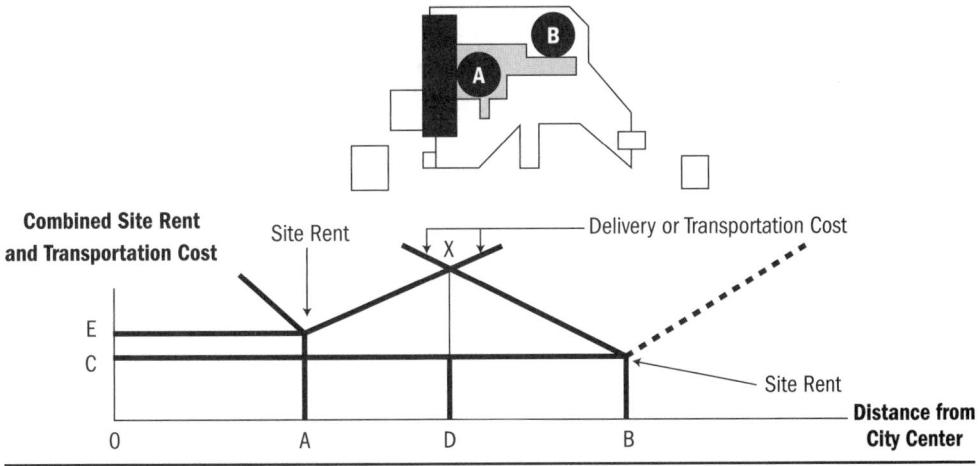

Exhibit 5.10 Linkage of Multiple Nuclei Models and Rent Theory

located at point D the same amount to acquire goods from point A or B. To the left of point D, it is less costly to make purchases at point A. To the right of point D, it is less costly to acquire goods at point B.

Exhibit 5.10 illustrates the application of urban structure theory to market delineation. It shows how rent theory can be used to explain and document the impact of socioeconomic and physical factors in the ecology models. The ecology models may also be used to adjust a model that has been developed using rent theory.

Recent Trends in Urban Growth Concepts and Models

During the last few decades, new urban growth trends have emerged. Some of these trends are so pronounced that they are considered by some to be new urban growth structures. In reality, however, it seems that most, if not all, of these trends are simply extensions of classic urban growth models or new growth regulation methods, not new urban growth forms. Regardless, emerging trends do impact urban growth structure and provide insight into how classic growth concepts still provide the foundation for forecasting future urban growth. The following discussion highlights some recent urban growth trends.

Suburban Urban Core Cities (Edge Cities[9])

In the 1950s, the suburbs were born, spurred on by government assistance in home buying, the building of interstate highways, and a surge in automobile production. During the 1950s and 1960s, the suburbs were largely residential islands, dependent on the central city for all the residents' economic and social needs. The 1970s and 1980s saw changes, transforming purely residential suburbs into suburban cities, small urban centers with their own economic and social bases.

In his book *Edge City*, Joel Garreau provides an in-depth study of this evolution of suburban growth. He states "Americans are creating the biggest change in a hundred years in how we build cities. Every single American city that is growing, is growing in the fashion of Los Angeles, with multiple urban cores." He further states that the retail mall has become the new village square and that, as of the early 1990s, two-thirds of all office space can be found in these edge city nodes.[10] And all this has occurred since about 1970. Garreau identified some 200 nodes in the United States, including

- Tyson Corners just outside of Washington, D.C. This 2,128-acre node had the largest concentration of retail space in the area in 2000 and more than 89,000 jobs.
- The Perimeter Center at the northern tip of Atlanta's Beltway. This area is larger than downtown Atlanta.

---

9. Joel Garreau, *Edge City—Life on the New Frontier* (New York: Doubleday Books, 1991). The term "edge city" was first used in this book.

10. Ibid., 5.

- Irvine, in Orange County south of Los Angeles.
- Las Colinas, between Dallas and Fort Worth, Texas. The urban core of this planned community had as much employment as downtown Fort Worth in 2000.

Joel Garreau's definition of an edge city is an area with[11]

- At least five million square feet of leasable office space
- At least 600,000 square feet of retail space
- A population that increases at 9 a.m. on workdays, indicating a job center, not a residential suburban area
- A local reputation as a destination for mixed-use jobs, shopping, and entertainment
- A history indicating that the area was residential or rural, not urban, 30 years ago

The advent of edge cities is another example of the interface of jobs, linkages, and housing. The multinucleated metropolitan areas, or edge cities, with jobs, shopping, and entertainment now scattered in the metropolitan outer rings, are created by different urban growth generators than were active in the past. The cities of the past were located to facilitate linkages to material sources for production and linkages for distribution of goods and services. The linkages formed the basis and the workers followed, creating the residential growth areas of the cities. Now it seems that edge cities are the result of jobs following the residents. This phenomenon is restricted for the most part to metropolitan areas and is the outgrowth of the suburban bedroom communities created in the 1960s.

Historically, the suburban growth cycle started with people moving to large cities to find work, and jobs were usually located in the downtown area. To live close to work they resided in dense, noisy urban residential areas. With the advent of the interstate highway system in the 1950s, however, people could travel long distances to work in a short time. This led many households to heed the call to the suburbs, which offered houses on large lots, less noise, less crime, and more privacy. Movement to the suburbs continued throughout the 1960s and 1970s and, in many places, continues today.

In some areas, however, the ever-increasing numbers of households in the metropolitan area's outer rings created commuter overload on transportation routes into the downtown area. Transportation arteries became clogged with traffic and many large urban areas were on the verge of gridlock. Many employers found it difficult to get workers to drive into the city and an alternative was found in the creation of the edge city. These edge cities reversed a prior urban growth concept and, in this case, the jobs were following the residents.

---

11. Ibid., 425.

The birth of suburban core cities can be attributed to these factors:[12]

- The economy shifted from manufacturing to service.
- The boss wanted to live closer to his job.
- Transportation linkages changed, particularly multi-modal train shipments which made trucks the dominant supplier mode.
- Most people wanted privacy, whether this means getting to work by car or a home on a big lot with a high fence.
- Technology advances provided ways to communicate information so that retailers do not need to be near their customers.
- Land was cheaper in the suburbs.

Suburban residents still wanted the advantages of urban amenities such as cultural activities and entertainment, so they settled around the suburban core centers.

Edge Cities and Classic Urban Structure Models

The edge city trend follows the principles of the multi-nuclei model discussed previously. One difference is that the multi-nuclei model is not predicated on a central city, whereas nearly all edge cities are located in urban metropolitan areas with a recognized central city acting as the hub for the edge city spokes. Thus, the edge cities of today may be found in the exurbs in the past; in turn, today's exurbs are the suburbs of the future. The growth cycle in metropolitan areas appears to be that suburban residents commute to areas of job concentration, which causes congestion and other urban problems. These residents then move even further out to secure more privacy and escape urban problems. The movement outward is always to an area that offers a reasonable commute time, but a less dense environment. And the cycle begins again.

Exurbia—Suburbs of the Suburbs

Another level of metropolitan growth rings, called "exurbia, has now emerged. Exurbia is generally defined as the emerging residential areas beyond the built-up (urbanized) suburbs and edge cities. These outer residential rings may extend up to 100 miles beyond the central city's downtown area.[13] Within this outer layer is a mixture of both residential, suburban-type developments and areas with rural character. These areas have emerged primarily as an outgrowth of multi-nucleated metropolitan areas. Because jobs are now farther out, one can live farther out (in the never-ending quest for residential privacy) and still be within a short drive of jobs in the new edge cities.

According to some researchers, the movement of population to these second tiers of suburbia is not solely related to total job proximity.[14]

---

12. Points made by Christopher Leinberger of Charles Lesser & Co. at a conference in Pacific Grove, California, in 1989, as reported by the *Chicago Tribune*.

13. Ibid., 252.

14. Jack Lessinger, *Regions of Opportunity.* (New York: Times Books, 1986).

Quality-of-life issues are sometimes equally important. Noise, pollution, crime, and congestion (both traffic and housing density) are associated with urbanized suburban and edge city locations as well as locations in the central city.

Growth in these outer rings has also been made possible by the improvement of infrastructure such as rural utilities and by the continued improvement of interstate and major highways.

The Rebirth of the Central City (Back from the Edge)

Edge cities and exurbia not withstanding, major metropolitan area central cities do not seem to be dead. Urban analysts like Roberta Gratz in the book *Cities Back from the Edge*[15] have asserted that many Americans are ready to give up their suburban dreams for dense, compact cities modeled on places like Prague or Toronto. Gratz notes that changes such as technology that allow a more mobile work force have not made the central city unnecessary as some predicted.[16] She argues that people still need the attachment of urban living. A new generation of urban dwellers started invading downtown areas in the 1990s and created condo building booms in cities like Chicago and Miami in the early 2000s. Demand[17] came first from young professionals, but older, affluent residents followed, hoping to experience "a more pluralistic way of life." Over time, however, this culture-based growth may not be self-sustaining, says Joel Kotkin in his book, *The City*.[18] Lifestyle and linkages seem to be the driving force. (Note that these trends reflect the classic concepts—lifestyle-concentric circles, linkages, and multi-nuclei and radial corridors models.)

It appears that some current urban forms are the combination of the multi-nuclei and radial corridor models, with edge cities and metro central cities providing differing nodes that emphasize different types of job centers and different lifestyles for the workers. The financial district is often downtown and the telecom corridor is located in the edge city. Urban centers offer high-density in contrast to lower-density living in the edge cities and exurbia.

New Urbanism

The opening of developments like Celebration in Orlando, Florida, in the early 1990s started a new wave to get back to the cities of our roots. In the first part of the twentieth century, neighborhoods were walkable, with corner grocery stores and social interaction. This movement is called new urbanism, which is defined by the Appraisal Institute as:

> A twentieth century urban planning movement emphasizing walkable, sustainable, mixed-use communities of greater density than traditional suburban subdivisions.[19]

---

15. Roberta B. Gratz, *Cities Back from the Edge: New Life for Downtown* (Washington, D.C.: Preservation Press, 1998).

16. Ibid., 334.

17. Demand eventually evolved into an investor speculation binge.

18. Joel Kotkin, *The City : A Global History* (New York: Modern Library Chronicles, 2005), 153.

19. *The Dictionary of Real Estate Appraisal*, 4th ed. (Chicago: Appraisal Institute, 2002).

New urbanism is as much a movement as it is an urban growth form. It is an attempt to hold back and reverse the suburban growth sprawl that started in the 1950s.

New urbanism, which started in the early 1990s (at least by that name), has now evolved into a very active movement. One of the leaders is The Congress for the New Urbanism (CNU). The following list established by the CNU indicates their criteria in judging whether or not a project is truly a "new urbanism" project.

- The project should not be gated. It should have sidewalks, and a grid layout, not a tree-like street system. The purpose of the grid is to make the project as a whole connect well with surrounding neighborhoods, developments, or towns while also protecting regional open space.
- The project should not be a single-use project made up of all housing, retail space, or offices. The various land uses should be seamlessly integrated—from different housing types to workplaces to stores.
- The project should have a neighborhood center within an easy and safe walk from all dwellings in the neighborhood. Buildings should be designed to make the streets feel safe and inviting. Front doors, porches, and windows should face the street to create openness and avoid a streetscape of garage doors.
- The project, and particularly the neighborhood center, should include formal civic spaces and squares.
- Lastly, the project should pass what they call "the popsicle test." A child in the neighborhood should be able to bike to a store to buy a popsicle without having to battle highway-size streets or freeway-speed traffic.

According to Mark Hinshaw, "We are now well beyond the experimental stage that produced high-profile, prototypical communities such as Seaside and Celebration. New urbanism has become mainstream, finding its way into plans, policy, and codes of many local governments."[20]

In summary, a new urbanism project, neighborhood, or city has more mixed use, more density, and fewer automobiles. The ingredients for new urbanism are not really new. New urbanism strives to have mixed land uses integrated into a neighborhood that is accessible (walkable) and functional (integral). Residents of these new towns could sit on their porches and talk to the neighbors who walk by. The new urbanism would encourage people of different socioeconomic strata to interact, like in cities of old where the rich banker's house was just down the street from the poor janitor's apartment. That banker and janitor might meet on the street or at the local café before work.

The new urbanism is characterized by developments such as retail space on the first floor of an apartment building, a town center of store

---

20. "The Case for True Urbanism" *Planning* (June 2005): 25.

fronts with apartments or offices above, and buildings close to the street with parking in the back. All this mirrors cities at the turn of the century. The new urbanism is really not new since many of the same principles were established in the subdivision work of Olmsted and Stein and Wright in the first quarter of the century. The old "neighborhood unit" concept called for walkable shopping districts for each neighborhood.[21]

Sustainable Growth

Some cities describe their new comprehensive land plans as being based on "sustainable growth concepts."[22] *Sustainable growth* is defined by the World Commission on Environment and Development as, "Development that meets the needs of the present without compromising the ability of future generations to meet their needs."

Sustainable growth is considered by many to be a subset of new urbanism. The focus of sustainable growth is the environment, but it is not a "no growth" movement. It is an environmentally sound growth movement to promote

- Reduced sprawl developments
- Fewer automobiles and less pollution
- More pedestrian development and thus more density
- More node development and thus more density and intensity–i.e., develop up, not out

The sustainable growth concept is not just an environmental movement, it is a movement to reduce pollution and infrastructure costs and to encourage jobs, particularly more jobs closer to residential areas.

Smart Growth

Another growth term and concept is called "smart growth." No one seems to have a good definition of what this means, but everyone is for it. As Anthony Downs noted,[23] who could be against smart growth? If you were against it, you would be for "dumb growth."

Smart growth is similar to sustainable growth in that its proponents generally reject the undesirable impacts of "suburban sprawl." Smart growth differs somewhat from sustainable growth insofar as the advocates of the concept fall into the "no or slow" growth camps, while sustainable growth proponents want growth, but only if it's environmentally sound.

The smart growth movements generally favor

- Limiting the outward expansion of infrastructure to reduce sprawl.
- Limiting new infrastructure costs on existing residences. If costs are incurred, let the new people pay for it.

---

21. Theodore C. Koebel, Ph.D., *Analyzing Neighborhood Retail and Service Change in Six Cities.* Published by the Center for Housing Research, Virginia Polytechnic Institute and State University, 1996.

22. City of Fort Worth, Texas, 2005, Comprehensive Plan.

23. Anthony Downs, "What Does Smart Growth Really Mean?" *Planning* (April 2001).

- Reducing dependency on automobiles by requiring higher-density, limited, mixed-use developments.
- Preserving large amounts of open space.
- Redeveloping inner-core urban areas and developing in-fill sites.
- Creating pedestrian-friendly developments.

Smart growth is not considered by most to be a pure urban growth form, but it does impact the direction and structure of growth through the regulatory aspects of the movement.

Conclusions on Urban Growth Concepts

Recent growth concepts appear to be responses to urban growth trends, not new forms of urban structure. The old basic determinants of urban structure—i.e., jobs (economy), social activities, natural land features, and transportation linkages (linkages of goods, people, information, utilities, etc.) have traditionally explained why and where cities grow. It appears that the fundamentals have not changed.

Future Urban Structure

Will the city of the future be a ghost town run by robots while we sit home with our electronic entertainment centers and Star Trek replicators that provide for all our needs and desires? Our cities may change, but probably not to this extreme. The current technology already gives people the opportunity to live rather secluded lives, but this has not changed our urban structure.

With the Internet we can work at home, transfer information, and accomplish our daily work better than we could years ago in a typical office setting. We can also shop online and order just about anything we need to entertain or sustain ourselves. Even with these innovations, however, major office complexes go up and new large retail centers are being built. It appears that we still need social contact to make a business deal or serve a customer. We need the social and recreational aspect of shopping and to meet in groups at the local hangout or golf club. Cities and the needs of people for the city's amenities have not changed that much, but they are changing somewhat.

In the book *The City,* Joel Kotkin notes some potential future changes and challenges for our cities.[24]

- The dominant megatropolis may in some cases be in crisis. Some large central cities seem to have reached their marginal productivity, and migration to smaller cities may be seen in the future. The mega cities, burdened with congestion, pollution, and crime, may be losing their economic advantage.
- Technological advances allow us to transmit information across the world instantly. A customer who calls a major company in New

---

24. Kotkin, 153.

York about service may be talking to an employee at his home in Montana and never know the difference. This technology linkage may be undermining the historical advantage of urban centers.

- The resurgence of cities may not be sustainable. At the close of the twentieth century, many large cities were in the cycle of significant intercity population and economic growth. However, the source of urban population growth–young professionals–have been moving back to the suburbs when the children came along. Other cities have changed their focus and become cultural and entertainment cities like Orlando, Florida. These cities are being defined not by their export of goods and services, but by their galleries, unique shops, lively street life, and tourist trade. Over time, this form of culturally based growth may not be self-sustaining.

- The gentrification of a city may lead to its decline. Many cities have seen more redevelopment of older neighborhoods, warehouses, and old apartments into new high-income condos. The demographic trend has been to squeeze out not only the poor, but also the middle class. This poses a question for cities concerning their long-term sustainability and quality of life without a middle-class base.

- In the years following 2001, many people and businesses are rethinking the advisability of locating close to high-profile buildings that could be potential terrorist targets.

These trends may alter the shape of the future city, but whether we migrate to the dense urban core or choose the less-dense urban periphery, economic linkages coupled with social needs and community identity will continue to shape our urban structure for years to come.

Land Use Succession and Urban Growth Forms

The theory of land use succession describes how time affects location decisions and the land market. Land use succession underlies the neighborhood life cycle, which identifies specific economic changes that impact the highest and best use of properties in the neighborhood. While locational analysis links land use to surrounding activities in an ecological chain, land use succession identifies the breaks that occur in this chain over time. Observing changes in the economic activities and physical condition of properties in the area may help the analyst forecast possible changes in the subject property.

The neighborhood surrounding a university provides a good example of land use succession. Initially, older single-family homes may be converted to boarding houses that rent to students. This conversion of space does not change the use or basic structure of properties, only the residential density. As the demand for residential space near the university increases, however, the boarding houses are razed and new apartment buildings are constructed. The use remains the same, but now the structures change. Over time, the apartment buildings deteriorate and incur obsolescence. They cannot readily compete with the newer facilities built to accommodate students in the expanding neighborhood. In the next phase of the neighborhood's life cycle, the existing structures are converted into condominiums. The residential use continues with only superficial changes in the structure of the buildings, but the economic and legal framework has changed significantly. The succession of land use generally begins with a simple break in the chain. At first the activities and associations vary only slightly. Once the system is altered, however, the potential for change increases exponentially.

Land use succession may follow different scenarios. Residential facilities may be converted into office space, changing the use while the structure stays intact. Over time market preferences might support the construction of new office facilities in the previously residential neighborhood.

Various factors can be studied to help document expected trends. Such indicators allow citywide forecast data to be broken down into useful information relating to the subject neighborhood and site. In his classic text on urban land economics, R.B. Andrews identified 10 indicators of possible changes in land use (see Exhibit 5.11).[25]

Exhibit 5.11 Potential Indicators of Land Use Change: Good and Bad

1. Investment return	6. Use controls
2. Market competition	7. Situs quality
3. Vacancies	8. Property turnover
4. Physical	9. Family cycle
5. Structure density	10. Structure value

Along with indicators of land use succession, analysts study two general economic factors that account for land use changes: the functional weaknesses evidenced in existing properties and external pressures that force a change in the existing land use pattern.

Conclusions

The economic location of real estate is considered on three levels: the specific site and its internal layout, the situs or linkage between the specific site or land use and the immediate neighborhood, and the total urban structure in which the site and neighborhood function as components of an aggregate market. These three levels can be seen as a continuum from the micro level of site analysis to the macro level of total urban structure. The locational or spatial dimension of real estate is basic to understanding this distinct product and its characteristic market. Within the market analysis process, the analyst proceeds

---

25. Richard B. Andrews, *Urban Land Economics and Public Policy*, Chapter 2 (New York: Free Press, 1971).

from investigation of the city and region to the study of market structure and decision-making criteria.

Identifying the pattern and extent of change enhances productivity analysis which, in turn, strengthens market analysis. By linking land use succession to the spatial concerns of situs and urban structure, the analyst ties the key components in an urban real estate product to supply and demand issues. These concerns are at the heart of market analysis, property valuation, and investment analysis.

Summary

Urban structure refers to the aggregation of land uses that act as a support system for the land use on any given site. The development of an urban structure is influenced by physical characteristics, the economic base, market forces, the institutional framework, technology, and cultural norms. Urban structure models fall into two broad categories: social ecology models and rent theorists' models. The social ecology models include the concentric zone, sector (or wedge), multiple nuclei, and axial (or radial corridor) models. Each model uses a different set of dynamics to explain urban development. The rent theorists' models focus on the trade-off between rent and transportation costs, or location and accessibility. The rent theorists' and social ecology models can be applied in combination to an analysis of urban growth patterns.

Real estate is essentially space used to house economic activities over discrete segments of time. Analysts study land use succession to understand the effect of time on real estate markets and to identify changes in the predominant land use patterns in neighborhoods. The productivity of real estate must be analyzed in light of its unique characteristics. Real property is a space-time product that is physically fixed but economically flexible. Its value depends on the support system or aggregation of land uses represented by the urban structure. Because of the spatial or locational dimension of real estate markets, they are not efficient markets. An understanding of this spatial or locational dimension is essential to the analysis of real estate productivity.

The urban setting is like an economic terrarium, the arena in which the real estate game is played. By studying macro data relating to the key features that influence the neighborhood and the subject parcel, the analyst clarifies the relationship between the urban setting and a specific site. Understanding a site's location in relation to the urban structure is the basis for real estate forecasting.

CHAPTER 6

The Economic Base

Chapter Objectives

- To compare and contrast economic base analysis with traditional analysis of the area, region, and city
- To demonstrate the fundamentals of economic base analysis and how it is performed
- To explain the strengths and weaknesses of the various techniques employed in economic base analysis

Introduction

Economic base analysis is used to understand the extent and nature of the local economy and to generate primary data for real estate market research. An area's economic base consists of the industries and economic activities that generate employment and income in the area. Typically, population growth and decline in an area may be considered functions of employment opportunities. As employment opportunities increase, people move to the area; when opportunities decline, they move away. A collapse of the economic base created the ghost towns of the Old West. When the gold ran out, the miners, saloon keepers, and the general store left.

When employment opportunities are growing, the economy of the area is healthy. A city can assume some measure of control over its economic destiny by attracting industries with long-term growth prospects and diversifying its economic base.

A real estate appraiser examines an area's economic base to understand the economic strengths and weaknesses of the community. In economic terms, this is called studying the city's *comparative advantage*. A comparative analysis is undertaken to identify the resources and productive capabilities of a city and determine what it can produce relative to other geographic areas. The appraiser then relates this information to local real estate and translates economic base data into a demand projection for the subject property. Knowledge of the economic base is used to project the demand for housing; office, retail, recreational, and industrial space; and other types of real estate.

The appraiser focuses on the generation of income that will be spent on real property. Ideally the analysis would trace all income flows for a city, but such an analysis would be expensive. Studying economic base indicators is more cost-effective.

Economic base analysis focuses on employment, which becomes a proxy for income. As people move into the area to find employment, they generate demand for housing, retail stores, office space, recreational facilities, and public services such as schools, fire stations, post offices, hospitals, and roadways. The infusion of people produces a multiplier effect and has a broad impact on employment and income.

The types of employment available in an area indicate how much income prospective employees will earn. Income levels, in turn, influence market segmentation, economic stability, and the demand for real estate. For example, average monthly wages of $3,000 indicate one level of housing and retail demand, while incomes of $10,000 per month would identify a different market segment to be served by real estate developers and retailers. Similarly, job opportunities in the warehousing and distribution industries create a different type of local real estate demand than jobs in service industries such as banking, finance, and real estate consulting.

The economic base defines the linkages between the local economy and the broader state, national, and international economies. As these economies wax or wane, the demand for the goods and services exported by the local economy increases or decreases, depending on how closely the local economy is tied to these larger economies. Thus, fluctuations in the state, national, and even international economies will affect the income generated in the local economy and the local demand for real estate.

How does an appraiser develop an economic base analysis, make a population or employment forecast, and use this information to estimate demand for the subject property? The process has five basic steps. The appraiser

1. Identifies the basic components of the economy that generate sales to areas outside the local community (These components are the basic sources of employment.)

2. Determines the prospects for growth (or decline) in basic employment

3. Estimates an employment multiplier

4. Develops a population or employment forecast

5. Develops a real estate demand forecast

This chapter will address the first four steps in the process, which are associated with economic base concepts. Demand estimation will be addressed in subsequent chapters.

Basic and Nonbasic Sources of Employment

To understand economic base concepts, it is helpful to begin with some background information on the circular flow of the economy. For purposes of simplification, the local economy can be divided into two major components: households and businesses. Households account for the productive resources of land, labor, capital, and entrepreneurship, which are sold to the business community in return for money (incomes). The business sector employs these resources to produce goods and services, which may be categorized as either *basic* or *nonbasic*. Basic goods and services are exported to areas outside the local community—i.e., to other cities and communities in the state or to national or international markets. From the sale of basic goods, money flows into the local economy. Nonbasic goods and services are both sold and consumed by the local population.

Because export industries cause money to flow into the local economy, they are called *basic*. They are the base, the foundation, on which the local economy is built. Nonbasic industries develop to provide goods and services for those employed in the basic economy.

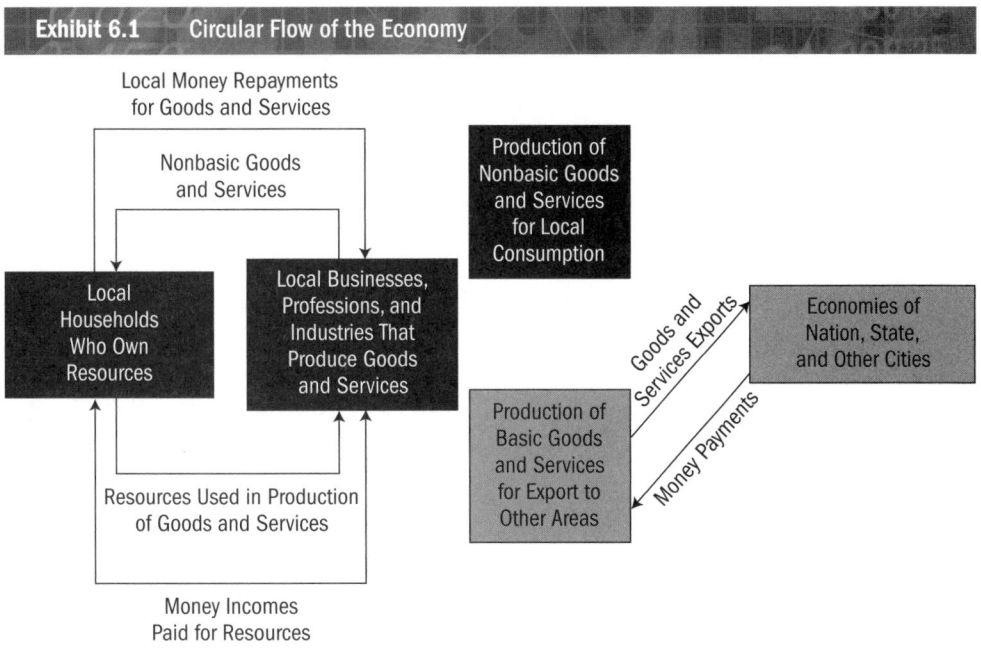

Exhibit 6.1   Circular Flow of the Economy

Although basic employment industries are frequently called "export industries" on the assumption that the goods and services they produce are exported to other areas in return for money that flows into the local economy, this description is not quite accurate. The tourism industry, for example, does not produce a product for export. Rather, it caters to people who visit an area. Tourists bring money from outside the area and spend it locally. The same type of economy exists in small college towns. Students from outside the area bring money with them and spend it locally. Degreed students are the exported "product;" they leave the area and the skills they acquire from their education are consumed elsewhere. The key to distinguishing basic employment is identifying activities that cause money or income to flow into the community. Some examples of basic employment follow.

- Mining and extractive industries (oil in Houston)
- Manufacturing (cars in Detroit and steel in Pittsburgh)
- Tourism (in Hawaii, Las Vegas, Orlando and New Orleans)
- Federal government (military bases in Norfolk and San Diego and government bureaucracy in Washington D.C.)
- State and local government (state-funded universities, state-supported hospitals, and state and local government offices)
- Retail and financial services that attract consumers to a particular city (a major retail center in a rural area)

Nonbasic employment includes all industries that are not basic employment and is frequently referred to as the "service sector." Again, this is an oversimplification because some segments of the service sector may be considered basic activities. Nevertheless, the service sector is usually associated with nonbasic employment. Nonbasic employment may include:

- Local professionals such as attorneys, physicians, real estate brokers, and appraisers
- Employees of service-oriented businesses such as gas stations, hardware suppliers, grocery stores, clothing stores, and other retailers
- Local construction workers
- Local government workers employed in sanitation departments, municipal offices, public schools, and city hospitals

Together, basic and nonbasic employment constitute the work force in a community. This is stated in the equation:

$$B + NB = T$$

where B = workers in basic employment
NB = workers in nonbasic employment
T = total employment

A simple *employment multiplier* reflects the relationship expressed below:

$$K = T/B$$

where K = the employment multiplier

       T/B = the relationship between total employment and basic employment

For example, if $T = 140{,}000$ and $B = 51{,}700$, $K = 2.71$.

The multiplier indicates that any increase in basic employment has a multiple impact on the local economy. As new jobs in basic industry are created, additional jobs in nonbasic industry are generated to support and supply the new individuals employed in basic industry.

Another way of looking at the relationship between basic and nonbasic employment is to consider the number of nonbasic jobs that are generated by the creation of each new basic job. This relationship is represented by the following equation:

$$NB/B = m$$

where m = the simple multiplier effect of basic employment on nonbasic employment

Using the data set forth earlier

$$88{,}300/51{,}700 = 1.71$$

Thus, for each new basic job created, 1.71 nonbasic jobs will be created indirectly.

Estimating Employment Multipliers from Basic Employment

To estimate the employment multiplier, basic employment must first be estimated by one of several methods. All the methods described here require the application of judgment. The only alternative to these methods is a detailed economic base study, which can be very expensive.

Method 1: Existing data

The appraiser may have access to planning agency data that are already disaggregated into basic and nonbasic employment data. Regional planning agencies such as regional councils of governments often conduct studies in which data are broken down into basic and nonbasic employment categories. These data are available at a modest cost.

Method 2: Whole industry

A second approach is to study industry-specific employment data. Certain industries can be identified as wholly export industries in the basic employment category. For example, employment in manufacturing, wholesaling, and the federal government is generally considered basic. By designating certain categories of industry as basic, a simple employment multiplier can be calculated. The inherently flawed assumption that a number of employment categories are wholly basic industries is offset by the countervailing assumption that the remaining industries are wholly nonbasic. To some extent these assumptions offset one another and nullify any significant error.

Method 3: Major employer

Another way to estimate basic employment is by compiling a list of the major employers in the area. Ordinarily a firm that is a major employer may be assumed to be a basic industry. Usually the chamber of commerce maintains a list of major employers that can be used as a starting point. An appraiser can generally compile a comprehensive list of the major employers in a city or region by conducting some research, contacting state commerce and labor departments, and checking the telephone book. Other possible data sources include *Forbes* and *Fortune* magazines and Dun & Bradstreet.

Method 4: Refined lists of major employers

Major employers may sell many of their goods and services to local consumers and therefore not represent wholly basic employment. To determine if this is the case, the appraiser may choose to refine the list of major employers by conducting telephone interviews. Through interviews appraisers can often get information about

- The percentage of sales to buyers outside the defined market area
- The firm's current total employment
- The number of employees who are directly involved with production intended for sale outside the market area

Although gathering detailed information is time-consuming and expensive, this process produces more accurate results than the preceding methods. The primary shortcoming of this method is that the survey is limited to major employers. A comprehensive survey of all employers would be more desirable, but from a cost-benefit perspective, this approach may be appropriate.

Method 5: Location quotient

A final method that may be used to identify basic industries is a location quotient (LQ). A location quotient is a ratio of the percentage of local employment in a given industry to the percentage of national employment in the same industry. It is derived with the following equation.

$$\frac{LE_i / LE_t}{NE_i / NE_t} = LQ_i$$

where LE_i = local employment in industry i
LE_t = total local employment in all industries
NE_i = national employment in industry i
NE_t = total national employment
LQ_i = location quotient for industry i

A numerical example appears below. Assume that

$$LE \text{ in manufacturing} = 42{,}700$$
$$LE_t = 140{,}000$$
$$NE \text{ in manufacturing} = 20{,}017{,}000$$
$$NE_t = 147{,}000{,}000$$

The location quotient for manufacturing is calculated as follows:

$$\frac{42,700/140,000}{20,017,000/147,000,000} \quad \frac{0.305}{.13617} = 2.24$$

A location quotient in excess of 1.00 suggests that the local industry is producing goods for export. In the example, the LQ for manufacturing employment in the community was 2.24. Of this total, 1.24 points (2.24 – 1.00) may be interpreted to represent employment devoted to producing goods that are exported to consumers outside the local economy; the remainder represents employment that produces goods for local consumption. Conversely, an LQ below 1.00 suggests that the local economy probably imports goods that are produced outside the area, and that nonbasic employment accounts for more local jobs than basic employment. Lastly, an LQ of exactly 1.00 suggests the community produces an amount equal to what is locally consumed.

The location quotient technique has some implicit assumptions that should be recognized: 1) that consumption patterns are constant and do not vary from one geographic location to another; 2) that labor productivity is also constant in all parts of the country; and 3) that each industry produces a single, homogeneous good. The result of these model assumptions is that the LQ may understate the amount of basic employment.

Exhibit 6.2 provides a sample of how some simple methods may be applied to estimate basic employment in an area.

Exhibit 6.2	**Basic Employment Breakdown and Derivation of Multipliers**					
Industry Category	Total Employment	Whole Industry Export Jobs	Major Employer Export Jobs	Refined Major Employer Export Jobs	Location Quotient	Location Quotient Export Jobs
Agriculture	4,500		3,400	1,200	1.82	3,690
Construction	5,400		00	00	0.79	
Manufacturing	32,700	32,700	20,200	18,300	1.71	23,217
Transportation	14,100		4,200	3,800	0.26	
Wholesale	12,100	12,100	8,800	7,300	1.63	7,623
Retail	19,300		5,100	4,300	0.59	
Finance	7,700		7,500	4,800	0.94	
Service	14,900		3,100	1,500	0.92	
Fed. government	6,900	6,900	6,900	6,900	1.88	6,072
Local government	10,300		00	00	0.52	
Miscellaneous	12,100		00	00	1.06	726
Total employment	140,000	51,700	59,200	48,100		41,328
Employment multiplier		2.71	2.36	2.91		3.39
Total population	250,000					
Population multiplier		4.84	4.22	5.20		6.05

Using four different methods–the whole industry, major employers, refined list of major employers, and location quotient–various employment and population multipliers can be developed. Which multiplier is correct? Which one does the appraiser use? All four employment (and all four population) multipliers are conceptually correct, so the selection must be left to the appraiser's judgment. As in other parts of the appraisal, the appraiser's judgment in choosing a multiplier will depend on a variety of factors such as the availability and reliability of the data, the level of study required, and the needs of the client.

From a conceptual standpoint, the multiplier derived from the refined list of major employers may be the most accurate. The whole industry multiplier or the major industry multiplier will be the least expensive for the client. The whole industry multiplier may be adequate for a quick, rough estimate. Some favor the location quotient multiplier, but when so doing the weakness must be recognized in the final determination.

Applying the Employment Multiplier

Once basic employment has been estimated, any expected change in basic employment can be translated into a corresponding change in total employment and population.[1] Employment and population serve as surrogates for the potential demand in the community. In the following example, the employment multiplier (K) and the expected change in basic employment (cB) are used to derive the change in total employment.

Assuming

$$K = 2.71$$
$$cB = 4,800$$

The expected change in total employment (cT) can be calculated with the following equation:

$$K = cT/cB$$
$$K \times cB = cT$$
$$2.71 \times 4,800 = cT$$
$$13,008 = cT$$

Thus, the 4,800 jobs in basic employment anticipated for the local economy will likely generate a total of 13,008 new jobs. Of these, 8,208 (13,008 – 4,800) will be in nonbasic employment. Obviously, basic and

---

1. At this point, a critical assumption comes into play—namely, that the average employment multiplier will reflect the pattern of change in employment, which economists call the *marginal change in employment*. This assumption, which may or not be valid, is expressed in the equation,

    $$T/B = cT/cB$$
    where T = total employment
            B = basic employment
           cT = expected change in total employment
           cB = expected change in basic employment

    This assumption *can* result in biased projections, but it is usually made for the sake of expediency and economy.

nonbasic employment jobs will not come on line simultaneously. The creation of nonbasic jobs will lag behind the creation of basic employment jobs as the local economy will take some time to respond to the basic employment stimulus.

Assuming that the percentage of the population in the work force is 56%, the multiple of people per worker, or population multiplier (k), can also be calculated.

$$1.00/0.56 = k$$
$$1.79 = k$$

The expected increase in total population resulting from the change in basic employment can be estimated by applying the population multiplier to the expected change in total employment ($k \times cT$).

$$1.79 \times 13,008 = 23,284$$

The total population at the beginning of the period was 250,000. The expected change in population will bring it to 273,284 (250,000 + 23,284).

Using another simple relationship, total anticipated population may be estimated with a different equation.

$$k = P/B$$

where k = population multiplier
       P = total population in the community
       B = basic employment

Thus, when $P = 250,000$ and $B = 51,700$, k is calculated to be 4.84.

$$4.84 = 250,000/51,700$$

If the employment multiplier (K) is calculated with the equation

$$K = T/B$$
where $T = 140,000$
       $B = 51,700$
       $K = 2.71$

The expected change in total employment can be estimated by applying the employment multiplier (K) to the expected change in basic employment (cB). In the previous example, the expected change in basic employment (cB) was 4,800. Thus,

$$K \times cB = cT$$
$$2.71 \times 4,800 = 13,008$$

The expected change in total population can be estimated by applying the population multiplier to the expected change in basic employment.

$$k \times cB = cP$$
$$4.84 \times 4,800 = 23,232$$

After the multiplier effect works its way through the economy, total expected population will be:

$$250{,}000 + 23{,}232 = 273{,}232$$

The slight difference in the answers derived from these two methods (23,232 here and the 23,284 previously) is due to rounding.

Refinements to the Economic Base Concept

It has been demonstrated that basic and nonbasic employment and employment multipliers can be used to project changes in employment and population. The appraiser can refine such estimates by considering more than one period in the economic base analysis. By analyzing local trends and evaluating their likely duration, appraisers can develop more reliable population and employment projections. Exhibit 6.3 shows such a projection for a city that had a population of 250,000 in 1997.

Exhibit 6.3 Projecting Population and Employment Using Economic Base and Trend Analyses

	1980	1990	1997	1980 Empl.	Pop.	1990 Empl.	Pop.	1997 Empl.	Pop.	1980–1990	1990–1997	1997–2003 %	Est.	2003–2009 %	Est.
Agriculture	8,100	6,000	4,500	8.4	3.9	5.2	2.5	3.2	1.7	-25.9	-25.0	-25.0	3,400	-25.0	2,600
Construction	4,200	5,200	5,400	4.4	2.0	4.5	2.2	3.9	2.2	23.8	3.8	4.0	5,600	4.0	5,800
Manufacturing	19,500	28,600	32,700	20.3	9.3	24.9	12.2	23.4	13.1	46.7	14.3	9.0	35,600	7.0	38,100
Transportation	10,300	12,700	14,100	10.7	4.9	11.0	5.4	10.1	5.6	23.3	11.0	10.0	15,500	10.0	17,000
Wholesale	9,600	10,100	12,100	10.0	4.5	8.8	4.3	8.6	4.7	5.2	19.8	12.0	13,600	8.0	14,700
Retail	10,600	15,400	19,300	11.0	8.8	13.4	6.5	13.8	7.7	45.3	25.3	20.0	23,200	15.0	26,700
Finance	3,500	4,200	7,700	3.6	1.7	3.6	1.8	5.5	3.1	20.0	66.6	30.0	10,000	10.0	11,000
Services	8,900	9,300	14,900	9.4	4.2	8.1	4.0	10.6	6.2	4.5	60.2	30.0	19,400	20.0	23,200
Fed./state gov't.	6,000	6,500	6,900	6.3	2.9	5.7	2.8	4.9	2.7	8.3	6.1	6.0	7,300	5.0	7,700
Local gov't.	4,900	6,500	10,300	5.1	2.3	4.8	2.3	7.4	4.1	12.2	87.3	15.0	11,800	5.0	12,400
Miscellaneous	10,400	5,500	12,100	10.0	4.9	10.0	4.9	8.6	4.8	10.6	5.2	5.1	12,100	5.0	12,700
Total employed	96,000	115,000	140,000	100.0		100.0		100.0							
Projected employment													157,500		171,900
Actual population	210,000	235,000	250,000												
Employment participation rate				45.8		48.7		56.0					.59		.62
Projected population													266,949		277,258

In comparing historical data, the old SIC code organization may have to be used, like in the exhibit above. More recent trend studies can make use of the NAICS organization because some historical data are being compiled using the NAICS classifications.

By examining data covering several periods, an appraiser can plot trends in employment growth or decline. In Exhibit 6.3 absolute employment figures (i.e., the actual number of people employed) are presented along with figures for the individual employment categories as percentages of total employment and population. Absolute changes in employment (i.e., the actual changes in the number of people employed) are also given. Extrapolating from these trends, an appraiser can project three, five, and 10 years into the future. Ordinarily, appraisers use information about the local economy to interpret trends and make projections.

For example, if a new major airport is planned, the appraiser may undertake primary research to obtain estimates of the number of people to be employed at the airport. Such estimates can be used to make adjustments to the general projection pattern. Similarly, if an employment category has experienced unusual growth in the recent past, the appraiser may deduce that this rate will be difficult to sustain and reduce the rate over the projection period. These types of adjustments call for appraisal judgment.

Employment (labor force) participation rates, which break down employment data by marital status, sex, age, and number of dependents, can be used to convert employment estimates into population projections. The analyst can use the completed projections along with other data to estimate demand for the subject property.

Employment Data and North American Industrial Classification System (NAICS)

Most sources of employment data now use the new NAICS classification, which replaced the Standard Industrial classification System (SIC). One of the major sources of employment data is *County Business Patterns* from the U.S. Bureau of the Census. This is an annual series that provides subnational economic data by industry and is useful for studying the economic activity of small areas over time. However, because of the change to NAICS in 1998, comparing historical employment became more difficult. Data for 1997 and earlier years are based on the Standard Industrial Classification System. This series has been published annually since 1964. The U.S. Bureau of the Census does provide tables on the relationship between the NAICS and SIC systems.

Summary

Economic base analysis is an essential tool used by appraisers to examine employment as an indicator of demand for real estate. To perform an economic base analysis, the appraiser

1. Identifies the components of the economy that generate sales to areas outside the local community to determine basic employment
2. Investigates the prospects for growth in basic employment
3. Estimates the ratio of basic to nonbasic employment to derive an employment multiplier
4. Develops a population/employment forecast

Basic employment may be estimated using existing data for basic and nonbasic categories of employment, industry-specific employment data, surveys of major employers, or a location quotient. An employment multiplier, which represents the ratio of total employment to basic employment, may be used with current and projected data to estimate future employment and population.

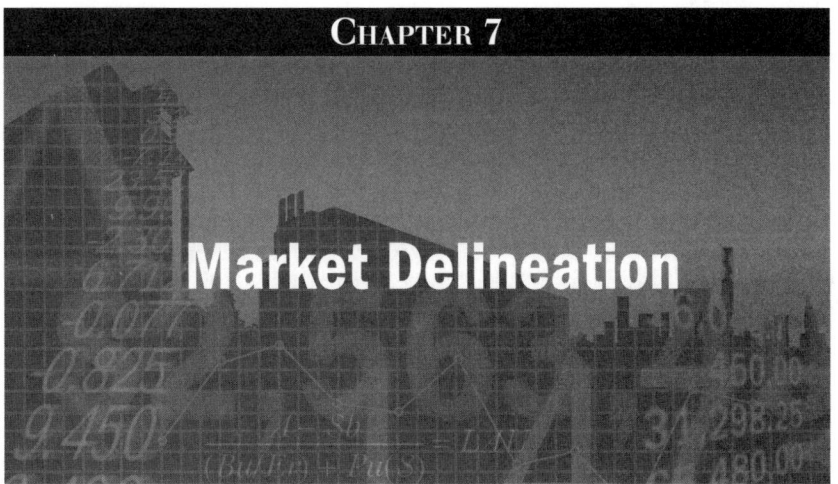

CHAPTER 7

Market Delineation

Chapter Objectives

- To explain why a market must be defined
- To present techniques for identifying, segmenting, and delineating a market

Introduction

The purpose of market delineation is to determine where demand comes from and which properties compete for this demand.

The potential users of property and where they come from must be determined before the quantity of demand for the property can be measured. Identification of potential users is one part of overall market delineation; the other part is the competition for that demand. The two together–demand sources and competition constitute total market delineation, which determines the economic basis for the property use.

Part of market delineation is to define the market area. The Urban Land Institute defines a market as "The geographic region from which a majority of demand and the majority of competition is drawn."[1] In analyzing residential and retail properties, we often find that properties actually have two market areas–the area where the customers come from and the area where the competition is located. On the other hand, office and industrial properties may not have a market area per se since the demand drivers for these properties usually come from di-

---

1. Adrienne Schmitz and Deborah L. Brett, *Real Estate Market Analysis: A Case Study Approach* (Washington, D.C.: Urban Land Institute, 2001).

verse locations. Thus, delineating the market areas for these uses usually starts with identifying the competitive cluster of buildings that compete for some of this diverse market of users.

Market analysis in real estate valuation is unique because it requires the appraiser to analyze the buyer/seller market as well as the user market. The market area for the buyer/seller market is usually different from the market area for the user market. The market area for the buyer/seller market could be international, say, for a hotel, while the user market area for the hotel could be the county. Thus, market delineation for valuation has two main parts 1) analysis of the user market (demanders and competition) and 2) analysis of the buyer/seller market.

The discussion in this chapter, and in the other chapters of this book, focuses on delineation of the user market. The buyer/seller market is covered briefly in Parts II and III of the book in the chapters on highest and best use and the market analysis applications.

In the typical assignment, the appraiser may not formally define the market for the subject property. After examining the subject, the appraiser generally proceeds to the selection of comparables, choosing properties that reflect the subject's prospective sale price or potential net operating income (productivity). The appraiser may also estimate the depreciated cost of constructing the subject improvements using data from comparable properties.

In the process of selecting comparable properties and analyzing the data obtained from these comparables, the appraiser does, in effect, define and segment the subject's market. This is typically not stated in the report and sometimes not fully recognized by the appraiser. In many cases this approach is adequate–i.e., for a Level A market analysis. A Level C analysis, however, requires a more formal and specific identification of the subject market segment. This chapter presents concepts for this more sophisticated market analysis process.

Reason for Defining the Market Area

The users of property must be identified in order to measure the depth of the demand for the property type. Defining the market area provides a key link between the property productivity analysis and the economic demand forecast for the property.

The economic demand conclusions reached are then applied in the approaches to value to support the revenue forecast in the income approach, to inform the economic obsolescence analysis in the cost approach, and to set parameters for the selection and analysis of comparables in the sales comparison (buy/sell) approach. The comparable sales selection provides another level of market area analysis by determining the type of property and the geographic area in which the property competes for buyers.

General Procedures for Defining the Markets

The delineation of both the user market and the buy/sell market in an appraisal is integrated into the six-step market analysis process and analysis of highest and best use (see Exhibit 7.1). The user market is identified before the buy/sell market is determined because the user market sets the basis of highest and best use, which in turn sets the parameters of the substitute property comparables identified in the buy/sell market.

Exhibit 7.1   Market/Marketability Analysis

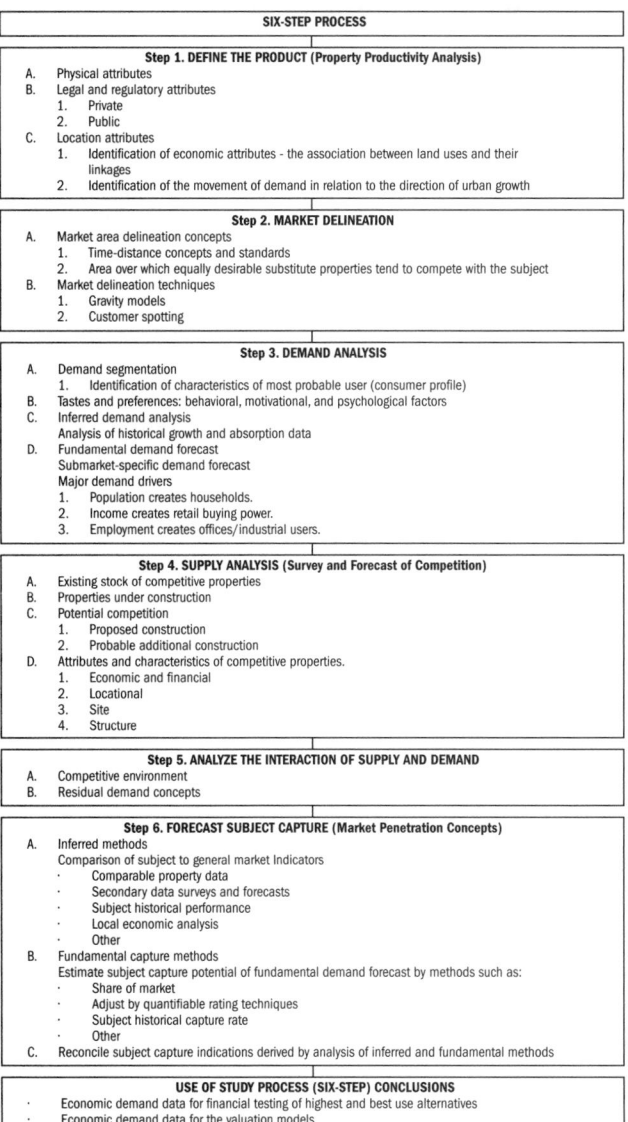

SIX-STEP PROCESS

Step 1. DEFINE THE PRODUCT (Property Productivity Analysis)
A. Physical attributes
B. Legal and regulatory attributes
    1. Private
    2. Public
C. Location attributes
    1. Identification of economic attributes - the association between land uses and their linkages
    2. Identification of the movement of demand in relation to the direction of urban growth

Step 2. MARKET DELINEATION
A. Market area delineation concepts
    1. Time-distance concepts and standards
    2. Area over which equally desirable substitute properties tend to compete with the subject
B. Market delineation techniques
    1. Gravity models
    2. Customer spotting

Step 3. DEMAND ANALYSIS
A. Demand segmentation
    1. Identification of characteristics of most probable user (consumer profile)
B. Tastes and preferences: behavioral, motivational, and psychological factors
C. Inferred demand analysis
    Analysis of historical growth and absorption data
D. Fundamental demand forecast
    Submarket-specific demand forecast
    Major demand drivers
    1. Population creates households.
    2. Income creates retail buying power.
    3. Employment creates offices/industrial users.

Step 4. SUPPLY ANALYSIS (Survey and Forecast of Competition)
A. Existing stock of competitive properties
B. Properties under construction
C. Potential competition
    1. Proposed construction
    2. Probable additional construction
D. Attributes and characteristics of competitive properties.
    1. Economic and financial
    2. Locational
    3. Site
    4. Structure

Step 5. ANALYZE THE INTERACTION OF SUPPLY AND DEMAND
A. Competitive environment
B. Residual demand concepts

Step 6. FORECAST SUBJECT CAPTURE (Market Penetration Concepts)
A. Inferred methods
    Comparison of subject to general market Indicators
    · Comparable property data
    · Secondary data surveys and forecasts
    · Subject historical performance
    · Local economic analysis
    · Other
B. Fundamental capture methods
    Estimate subject capture potential of fundamental demand forecast by methods such as:
    · Share of market
    · Adjust by quantifiable rating techniques
    · Subject historical capture rate
    · Other
C. Reconcile subject capture indications derived by analysis of inferred and fundamental methods

USE OF STUDY PROCESS (SIX-STEP) CONCLUSIONS
· Economic demand data for financial testing of highest and best use alternatives
· Economic demand data for the valuation models

The property productivity analysis (Step 1) defines the real estate product available to the user market. This user market is then identified in market delineation (Step 2) and the demand generated by these consumers is measured (Step 3). The extent of the competition (Step 4) is determined and measured. The competitiveness of this market is considered next (Step 5) and then the ability of the subject to capture part of the user market is considered (Step 6). All of these data now feed into the highest and best use analysis and valuation of the property. Revenue expectations for property use(s) lead into the highest and best use financial analysis of alternatives to determine which use is the highest and best use. The most profitable use among the probable alternatives becomes the highest and best use and the value of that use is measured by various methods. At this point, the buy /sell market can be analyzed to identify buyer/seller types that would be attracted to this type of property and the geographic area within which properties would compete for buyers.

Market Segmentation by Property Type

The market segment is defined in terms of the property type, i.e., residential, office, retail, manufacturing, warehouse, or recreational. Each of these broad categories are then subdivided to define the market segment served by that property type. For example, a recreation property like a golf course is a property type but, depending on the design and location of the course, it can serve many different market segments. The specific golf course market segments—and there are at least twelve[2]—may consist of families from a nearby neighborhood or it may consist of high-income golfers scattered across the United States.

Exhibit 7.2 lists subcategories for three major property types. Similar breakdowns can be developed for manufacturing, warehouse, and recreational properties and for other property types.

Market Segmentation (User Market Analysis)

Real estate is a multifaceted product. Each parcel of real estate is a composite of various physical, locational, legal, and design attributes, which together account for the productivity of the property and determine its market segment. The most direct way to define a subject property's market segment is by means of a thorough productivity analysis. The characteristics that account for property productivity will attract certain types of users. Thus, one common way to segment a market is to examine demographic data on consumers most likely to be drawn to this real estate product. This demographic analysis will shed light on the most probable users of the property.

User Demographic Analysis For Market Segmentation

Demographic data provide a wealth of information about the prospective customer base in a geographic area. Information can be obtained

---

2. Stephen Fanning, "Segmentation of Golf Course Markets," *The Appraisal Journal* (January 2003).

Residential	Office	Retail	Specialized Area
Single-family	Single-tenant	Shopping Centers and Retail	Automobile
Detached	Multitenant	Clusters (Nucleations)	Print district
Attached	Low-rise	Convenience	Entertainment
Townhouse	Mid-rise	Neighborhood	Medical district
Plex	High-rise	Community	Furniture district
Duplex	Class A, B, C	Regional	
Triplex	Prestige/image	CBD	
Quadraplex	CBD/suburban	Strip Commercial (Ribbons)	
Patio house	Node/freestanding	Shopping street	
Multifamily		Urban/suburban	
Garden apts.		Arterial highway	
Mid-rise			
High-rise			
Other			
Mobile home			
Manufactured home			

on the size and growth rate of the population, the overall labor force and its growth rate, the employment breakdown by industry, and the number of households and rate of household formation. A profile of the population can be compiled by age, sex, income distribution, social status, activity patterns, marital status, and tastes and preferences. With this information the real estate analyst can target the specific user segment most likely to desire this particular real estate product. The consumer profile provides the base for the next step in the market study, which quantifies how much real estate product demand can be realized from this consumer base of most likely users.

The user demographic analysis, or consumer profile, is traditionally part of demand analysis. Like a number of market analysis steps (i.e., location analysis) this step is related to demand and competition to some extent. Segmenting the market of potential users is an important part of the market analysis process.

To see the impact of the market segmentation analysis, consider an upscale boutique in a retail shopping center. The type of individuals who would shop at this store would include affluent residents living some distance from the shopping center as well as other individuals who regularly come to the area such as tourists and office building workers from other parts of the metropolitan area. A nearby area of predominantly low- and middle-income households would not likely shop at this store. Thus, the boutique's primary market area may be some distance from the store, not the area immediately around the shopping center.

Techniques for Defining the Subject User's Market[3]

Two types of techniques may be used to define a property's market area: general techniques that can be adapted to a variety of real estate problems and specific techniques designed to define the market areas for particular types of property. The appraiser must use judgment to determine which techniques are applicable to the problem.

The market delineation of potential property users is more than drawing a line on a map. Market area delineation has two major purposes. First, it identifies the customers for the subject property type. Second, and equally important, it identifies where these customers come from. The results of the market delineation then feeds into the next step which is measuring the depth of the demand from this market segment

General Techniques

There are three general techniques for defining market areas: 1) delineation of the market area in relation to customer location; 2) identification of the market area by the location of substitute properties; and 3) specification of the market area based on analogs or analogous situations.

Market Definition by Location of Consumers

If the subject property is a subdivision or an apartment complex, the census tracts represent the area from which the subdivision or complex will draw prospective homebuyers or renters, who are part of the population of the census tracts. If the subject is a neighborhood shopping center, the census tracts represent the area from which its retail customers will be drawn. Population and employment projections for census tracts that delineate the market area will constitute the population and employment base for that market area. The appraiser must then determine the segment of the market that the property will capture.

Exhibit 7.3	The Use of Census Tracts to Define a Market

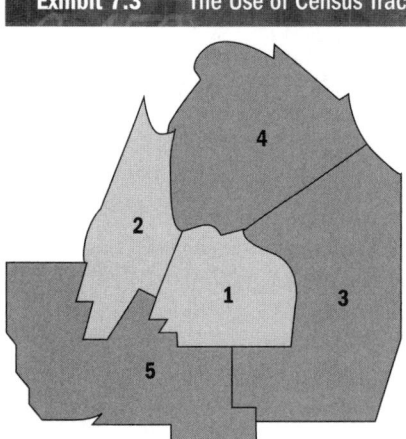

Market Area	Census Tracts
Primary	1, 2
Secondary	3, 4, 5

3.   See Chapter 12, pages 216–226, for a more detailed discussion of a case study example.

Market Definition by Substitute Properties

The principle of substitution is applied in defining market areas for subject properties. A residential buyer will purchase the least expensive unit from among equally desirable, substitute units. The substitute units may be assumed to constitute the market in which the subject property will compete. The appraiser delineates the market area by identifying substitute properties and their geographic distribution in relation to complementary population areas and employment centers. If the subject property is a subdivision, the appraiser identifies competing subdivisions in the area. The geographic distribution of these subdivisions defines the market area. Then the appraiser identifies the census tracts that correspond to the defined market area. By matching the census tracts with the distribution of substitute properties, an estimate of the population/employment in the market area can be derived. Exhibit 7.4 demonstrates how this method is applied.

Exhibit 7.4   Defining a Market Area Based on Substitute Properties

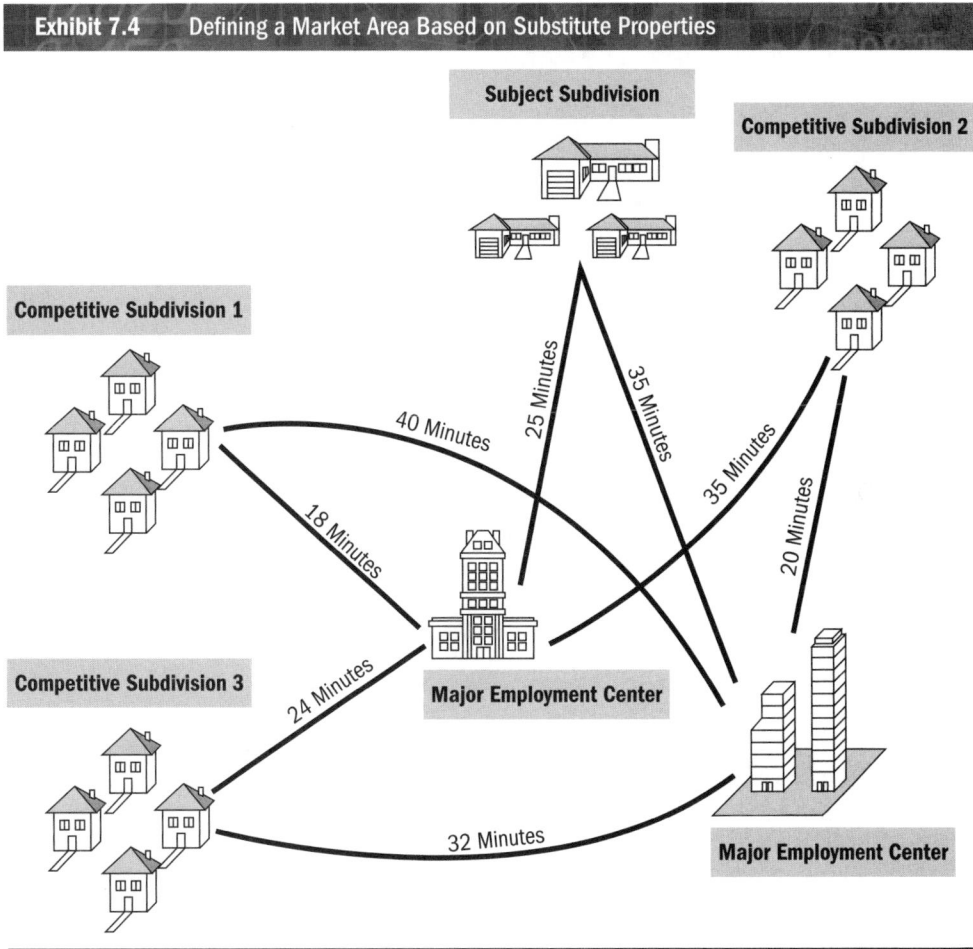

Market Definition by Analogs

The third general method of market definition that can be readily adapted to various appraisal problems is use of an analog, i.e., a comparable setting or situation. The use of an analog is similar to the use of comparable properties in the sales comparison approach. First, the appraiser finds a property in a setting analogous to that of the subject property. Assuming that the market area for the analog is known, the market area for the subject can be projected by extension. This technique is most frequently used to estimate the size of the market for retail centers. For example, consider a corner parcel of vacant land that has the potential to become a major retail node in the area. The appraiser researches similar retail nodes and identifies these with an analogous market area, which in this situation is a complementary residential neighborhood. Once the size of the analogous market area has been established, the analyst can estimate the subject's market area.

Specific Techniques

Specific techniques are useful in determining the market areas for two particular property types—retail space and offices.

Defining a Retail Trade Area

Reilly's Law.[4] One traditional technique for estimating a retail market area is Reilly's law of retail gravitation, which is used to delineate the boundaries between trade areas. This model is called a "gravity model" because it is based on Newton's law of gravity, which states that the attraction between two particles is in direct proportion to the product of their masses and in inverse proportion to the square of the distance between them. Simply stated, Reilly's Law states that the trade area boundary between two competing retail centers is a function of their sizes and the distance between them. This relationship is expressed in the following equation.

$$\text{Breaking point time from B to A} = \frac{\text{Driving time from A to B}}{1 + \sqrt{\dfrac{\text{Center A Size}}{\text{Center B Size}}}}, \text{ where } A > B$$

Exhibit 7.5 shows data on a subject shopping center and three competing centers. The drawing power of each center relative to the subject is calculated using the equation. Once the breaking point between the subject and each competing center has been calculated, the subject's market area can be delineated (see Exhibit 7.6).

Exhibit 7.5 Reilly's Law

Center	Drive Time from Subject	Center Size in Sq.Ft.
1	42 minutes	350,000
2	34 minutes	180,000
3	28 minutes	210,000
Subject	0 minutes	560,000

---

4. William J. Reilly, *Methods for the Study of Retail Relationships,* monograph no. 4, University of Texas Bulletin No. 2944 (Austin: University of Texas Press, 1929; reprinted 1959).

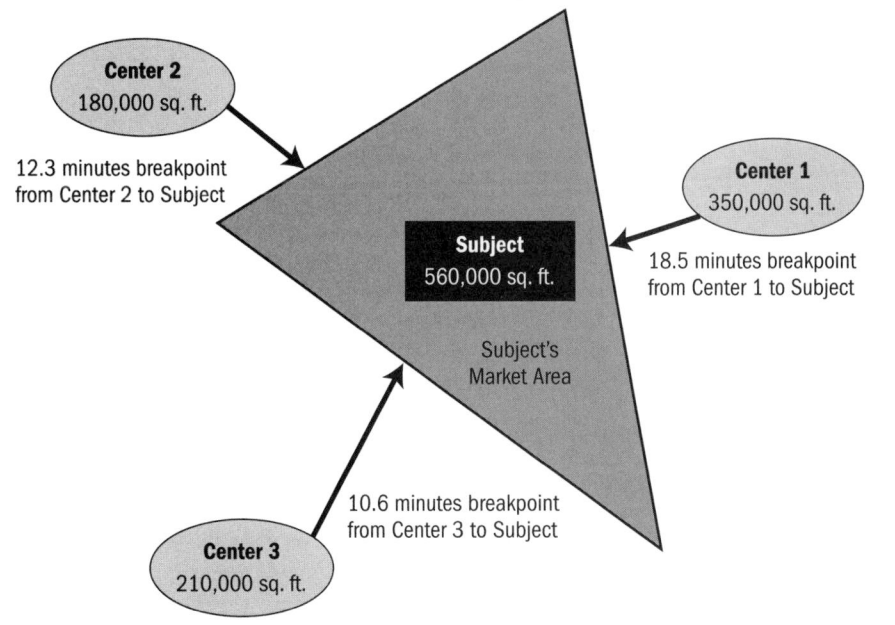

Center 2
180,000 sq. ft.

12.3 minutes breakpoint
from Center 2 to Subject

Center 1
350,000 sq. ft.

Subject
560,000 sq. ft.

18.5 minutes breakpoint
from Center 1 to Subject

Subject's
Market Area

10.6 minutes breakpoint
from Center 3 to Subject

Center 3
210,000 sq. ft.

Applebaum customer spotting technique. The Applebaum customer spotting technique[5] is another method for measuring the size of a trade area. The technique is so named because customer data are "spotted" or located on a map. This method was developed more than 40 years ago and is still widely used. However, the technique has been expanded to a much greater extent than Mr. Applebaum envisioned. Today, with customer loyalty cards and computers, the accuracy and detail of the customer spotting technique is very sophisticated and extensive Level D type analysis is possible.

Since most appraisers do not have access to the store loyalty card data, however, approximation methods must be employed. The analyst may gather the data by interviewing customers. Alternatively, data may be obtained by taking a sample of the license plate numbers of the automobiles in the store's parking lot at different hours on different days. From the license plate numbers, the analyst can find the addresses of the vehicle owners and spot the customers' residences on a map. Once all the data are spotted, it is possible to identify the boundaries for the trade area. The area from which 70% to 80% of the store's customers are drawn is considered the primary trade area. Exhibit 7.7 demonstrates the Applebaum technique.

---

5. William Applebaum, "Method for Determining Store Trade Areas, Market Penetration, and Sales," *Journal of Marketing Research* (May 1966): 126–141.

Exhibit 7.7   Application of the Applebaum Spotting Technique

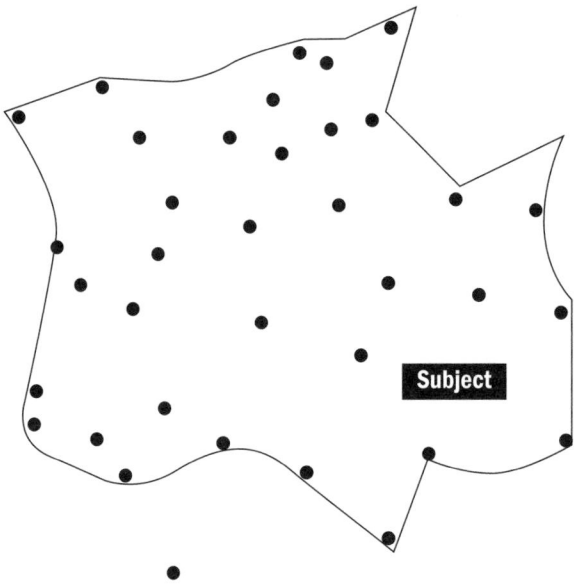

Subject

*   Each dot represents three customers' addresses. Most of the customers live to the north and northwest of the store.

Nelson technique.[6] Another classic concept still in use today was developed by Richard L. Nelson, who offered another technique for estimating the size of a retail trade area. Nelson's technique is similar to Applebaum's, but Nelson relied on a set of *a priori* assumptions to develop his model. Nelson intended his model to be a means to an end, i.e., the basis for additional, in-depth research into store location. The appraiser, however, may use the model simply to estimate the size of a trade area. Nelson assumes that shoppers are drawn to a retail center for the following reasons

- The availability of merchandise (The greater the variety of stores, the broader the selection.)
- The competitive pricing of the center
- Physical amenities such as eating establishments, decor, and interstore circulation.
- The degree of convenience, including factors such as accessibility, adequacy of parking, and favorable traffic conditions.
- The dominance of the trading center in the area
- The lack of intervening facilities (Shoppers will not go past one retail center with equivalent shopping facilities to get to another center.)
- The proximity of the center (Shoppers will go to the closest center with adequate facilities.)

6.   Richard L. Nelson, *The Selection of Retail Locations* (New York: F.W. Dodge Corporation, 1958), Chapter 17.

- Force of habit (Shoppers tend to follow customary travel and circulation patterns.)

With these working assumptions, the analyst investigates the retail site, the population and income in the area, nearby competitive stores, traffic patterns, ingress to and egress from the site, and physical barriers that may impede accessibility.

The analyst should also be alert to other factors that can influence shoppers' habits. A variety of subjective features must be considered in defining a retail trade area. Such features may include the image of the shopping center, the type of customer to which it appeals, the income and socioeconomic status of potential shoppers, and possible social or psychological barriers. The "subjective distance" of the center is also a factor. *Subjective distance* refers to the perceived convenience of access to a retail facility in terms of time and distance. By studying all these features, the analyst can plot the likely boundaries of the trade area. Ongoing analysis will delineate the trade area more precisely.

Defining an Office Market Area

Office projects do not have narrow, geographically defined trade or market areas like shopping centers or residential developments. The appraiser has to begin with an analysis of the entire metropolitan area. Although the analysis must cover a citywide market, that market can be segmented by focusing on the particular features of the site, the realty product and the sub-area location. Significant categories for defining office building markets include:

- General location—city core vs. suburban
- Single-tenant vs. multitenant occupancy
- Class or quality of office building—Class A, Class B, and Class C buildings
- Specific location—i.e., the office node and the class of office building within the node

City Core vs. Suburban Location. The central business district (CBD) is still a major office market area in most metropolitan areas of the United States. The CBD is easily identifiable. It has the highest single concentration of economic activity, is the principal focus of automobile and pedestrian traffic, and accommodates a large daytime population. Most CBDs are on an extended vertical, but limited horizontal, scale and are characterized by highly intensive land use. Because of these conditions, the highest land values in the city are usually found in the CBD.

Many central business districts were transformed between 1960 and 2000 and their character changed from a diversified economic center replete with commercial, retail, and office space to simply a concentration of office buildings. Retail activity abandoned the CBD for the outlying suburbs, while an unprecedented office building boom took place in both the CBD and suburbs. In the last several years, many major cities have reversed this trend somewhat. Workers frustrated with long commuting times and a desire for urban living have brought many CBD back to life with new housing and new retail space.

The suburban office market lies outside the central city in both incorporated and unincorporated areas with high concentrations of population. As noted in the Chapter 5, the suburbs have captured much of the office market for several reasons: cheap land, lower taxes, lower construction costs in office parks, and, perhaps most importantly, lower commuting costs for employees who work in suburban offices. Many suburbs are now becoming self-sustaining cities.

Single-Tenant vs. Multitenant Occupancy. A single-tenant office building is occupied by only one tenant, whereas a multitenant structure has multiple tenants. Usually a single-tenant office building serves as the headquarters of a company or the regional headquarters of a large corporation. Multitenant office buildings obviously represent a different market segment.

Class or Quality of Office Space. Office buildings are rated as Class A, B, or C according to their construction quality, condition, and appeal. Class A office space is most frequently located in the CBD. Construction materials, workmanship, and design are of the highest quality. Class A buildings are relatively new structures. The best Class A buildings command the highest rents and occupy the most desirable locations in the city. Occupancy of Class A office space enhances the prestige or image of a corporation.

Class B buildings are also of high-quality construction and occupy good locations. Built within the past 10 to 15 years, their high level of maintenance ensures that physical depreciation has been kept to a minimum. Class B office buildings may incur some functional obsolescence. While rents for Class B space are below rents for Class A space, tenant standards remain high.

Class C office buildings are older (up to 25 years old), but they are still able to maintain steady occupancy. Class C buildings will suffer both physical depreciation and functional obsolescence. Their rents are lower than rents for Class B space.

Office Node and Class of Office Building within the Node. Office parks are, in effect, office nodes or clusters of office buildings. The largest single node in a metropolitan area has traditionally been the CBD itself. Suburban office development is also centered on nodes with office parks situated at convenient locations adjacent to or near airports and regional shopping malls and along freeways with easy access. Thus, the market area may be defined with respect to a specific node and to other competitive nodes.

Within an office node, the appraiser must identify the class of the buildings. Typically, a node will consist entirely of Class A, Class B, or Class C structures. Occasionally, there may be a mix of space classifications.

Summary

To define the market for a property, the appraiser carefully analyzes its physical, locational, legal, and design attributes..

Demand is a reflection of the attributes of a product. By examining a product's attributes, we can identify the market segment to which the product will appeal. The attributes supplied by the product have a pronounced influence on the market segment that generates demand for the product.

Defining a market could just as easily be called *analyzing a market segment* because the analysis focuses on property features that will appeal to specific, segmented demand groups. Thus, *market segment analysis* implies *property user analysis,* which implies *demand analysis.* Once the property features are identified, the various end users that make up the market segment can be identified.

A market is defined based on analysis of several factors:

- Geographic area. Locational attributes define a market area.
- Property type (e.g., residential, retail, office, manufacturing, warehouse, recreational) and physical attributes. With regard to land, physical attributes include the load-bearing capacity of the soil, the topography, the site size, and the grade. For improved properties, the size of the structure(s), the construction materials, and the quality of workmanship are significant.
- Legal/regulatory attributes. Public regulations include zoning, building, and subdivision codes. The property rights or legal attributes of current tenants also determine to a large degree the market segment for the property.
- Design/amenity attributes. Spectacular architectural design, a panoramic view, or special amenities can make a property more or less appealing than competitive properties.
- Other property attributes such as single-tenant or multitenant occupancy and the customer base. Those who will likely use the property can be segmented demographically according to age, sex, employment, income level, social status, and activity patterns.

CHAPTER 8

Estimating Real Estate Demand

Chapter Objectives

- To contrast general area analysis as currently practiced with demand forecasting for a segmented market
- To explain the importance of examining demand
- To provide definitions of *real estate demand* and *market segmentation* and to explain the role that property productivity analysis plays in defining the market segment
- To present a variety of techniques for examining demand in a market under investigation

Introduction

The price of a commodity, service, or product is created by the interaction of supply and demand. Market analysis investigates supply and demand as economic forces that establish the conditions of the market in which real estate competes. These conditions, in turn, establish the price of the real estate product. An opinion of value reflects the anticipated benefits to be derived from the real estate product, so the appraiser must act as an economic forecaster. Demand estimation and economic forecasting differ considerably from general area analysis. To conduct a demand analysis, the appraiser needs working definitions of *demand* and *market segment* as well as a set of cost-effective techniques for estimating demand. After constructing a model to analyze demand, the appraiser inputs primary or secondary data, tests the estimates produced by the model, and develops the demand forecast.

Reasons for Examining Demand

The general area analysis undertaken in many appraisals has serious shortcomings. The appraiser may fail to focus on the relationship between area trends and the value of the subject property. In many appraisals the area analysis section begins with information on international and national economic developments such as job outsourcing overseas or downsizing in the real estate industry.

When information about local activity is presented, it often comes from prepared statements provided by the local chamber of commerce or a regional planning agency. Little, if any, analysis focuses on how area or citywide trends will affect the value of the subject property. Typically appraisers describe area trends by citing volumes of data on area growth over the past 25 years. They reason that past development indicates that growth will likely continue in the future. While such a presumption may be justified, it is problematic.

Often area analysis is based on the premise that general population and employment growth in the region will automatically result in growth in the submarket for the subject property. This premise is not logical because the effect does not necessarily follow the cause. The metropolitan area may be experiencing excellent growth, but the subject's market area may not benefit. Conversely, the general area may be experiencing negative or limited growth, while the subject's submarket may grow rapidly.

The neighborhood analysis section of an appraisal is often the last opportunity for the appraiser to examine demand. Unfortunately, like the area and city analysis sections, the neighborhood analysis often does not relate to the demand for the subject property. In many cases the reader must make inferences from the discussion and the data to understand how the property's value may be affected by area, city, and neighborhood trends. In effect, the reader must draw his or her own conclusions about the economic demand for the subject property when, in fact, this is what the appraiser is supposed to be doing for the client.

Examining demand for a real estate asset means that the appraiser must begin with the specific property and focus on how various economic and demographic trends in the area will affect its value. Thus in the area, city, and neighborhood analyses (or whatever the appraiser calls the market/marketability section of the report), the starting point should be the real estate. The pivotal question is: How do area, city, and neighborhood trends affect the anticipated benefits from, and value of, the subject property? These trends reflect the dynamics of the forces of supply and demand embodied in the physical, locational, legal, and market appeal attributes of the property. They have a decisive impact on the value of the subject property, which is fixed at a point in time and in space.

The area, city, and neighborhood analyses should not relate the impact of various trends to the subject's value. By beginning the analysis with the property, the appraiser can simultaneously identify the property's productive attributes and the market segment to be studied.

Using this approach, the appraiser also establishes a tentative highest and best use for the property early on. If the market analysis determines that there is appropriate market support for this use, the tentative highest and best use becomes the highest and best use conclusion. Thus, to forecast the demand for the subject, the appraiser focuses the analysis on the specific property and seeks to answer the following questions:

- How strong is the current demand for the subject property?
- How will that demand change over the projection period?
- How will that demand be affected by the various physical, locational, legal/regulatory, and design/amenity attributes of the property?

Defining Demand

Real estate demand can be defined generally as the quantity of a particular type of real estate product or service that will be purchased or leased, in a given market. Because real estate demand is derived from the demand for the product or service that the real estate provides, the analysis is tailored to the property type. To estimate the demand for

- Retail property, an estimate is made of the demand for retail services by customers
- Office space, an estimate is made of the demand for services provided by businesses housed in offices (These businesses' demand for employees who will use the office space must also be estimated.)
- Housing, an estimate is made of population, employment, and households in the area
- Industrial space, the demand for the industrial products produced in the area is estimated along with industry's corresponding demand for employees
- Recreational space, the ability of the recreational use to attract local residents and vacationers is estimated

Although this list could be expanded, it demonstrates that the demand for real estate must be estimated from the number of businesses, employees, and residents that use, or are housed in, the real estate facilities in the area. An individual parcel of real estate is fixed in location and has certain attributes that generate demand. In most appraisal assignments, the real estate product already exists. The improvement is standing and occupies a specific number of square feet. Its building materials, quality of construction, and design are fixed. The services that the property provides its users are evident. The appraiser, therefore, is estimating the demand for an existing real estate product that usually cannot be extensively modified.

Demand and Market Segmentation

Property productivity analysis and market segment analysis both identify the physical, locational, legal, and design/amenity attributes of the subject property. These qualities of the subject account for its utility and productivity. The analyst asks these questions:

- What demand is there for the attributes of the property? Who can use these attributes?
- How will the productivity attributes of this particular property attract users to the real estate?
- How many people can afford to pay for the attributes of this particular property?
- How much are people willing to pay for these attributes?

By identifying the subject's attributes, the appraiser has also defined the market segment to which the property will appeal. Thus, real estate *market segmentation* means dividing market demand into meaningful user[1] groups based on the property's attributes–i.e., identifying different user groups attracted to the physical, locational, legal/political, and design/amenity attributes of the real estate.

A spreadsheet can be constructed to analyze the productive attributes of a property. Often productivity analysis is conducted with a mental spreadsheet, but sometimes it may be helpful to construct a formal spreadsheet like the one shown in Exhibit 8.1.

Exhibit 8.1	Spreadsheet Analysis of Productive Attributes of Subject and Competition			
		Competitive Properties		
Item	**Subject**	**1**	**2**	**3**
Physical attributes				
Size in sq. ft.	560,000	350,000	180,000	210,000
Construction–Quality	Excellent	Similar	Good	Good
Age	2 years	5 years	8 years	15 years
Condition	Average	Similar	Similar	Inferior
Conclusion		Similar	Inferior	Inferior
Locational attributes				
Access/linkage	Good	Superior	Similar	Inferior
Market area density	Fair	Superior	Similar	Inferior
Market area income	Excellent	Similar	Inferior	Similar
Direction of urban growth	Fair	Superior	Similar	Inferior
Conclusion		Superior	Similar	Inferior
Legal attributes				
Zoning	Beer/wine sales (allowed)	Similar (Allowed)	Similar (Allowed)	Inferior (Not Allowed)
Conclusion		Similar	Similar	Inferior
Design/Amenity attributes				
Design	Good	Similar	Similar	Similar
Amenities	Excellent mix of shops	Inferior	Inferior	Inferior
Conclusion		Inferior	Inferior	Inferior

1. Users are people such as shoppers and office workers–i.e. people who use the property–as opposed to people who buy property as an investment based on what a user will pay the investors over time to use the property.

Once the spreadsheet is constructed, the analyst can begin to identify the different buyer or user groups to which the property attributes appeal. Exhibit 8.2 lists some of the variables used for market segmentation.

Exhibit 8.2   Variables Used in Market Segmentation

Socioeconomic Variables	Geographic Variables (Location and Size of Area)	Buyer/User Behavior Variables
Age	Nation	End user
Sex	State	Speculator
Family size	Region	Investor
Household size	County	Image-sensitive, prestige seeker
Income	City size	Price-conscious economizer
Occupation	Sector of the city	Convenience or quality seeker
Education	Neighborhood	
Stage in family/life cycle		
Social		

Different productivity characteristics will attract different types of users. Further market segmentation can be based on other property attributes such as:

- Single-tenant or multitenant occupancy, i.e., single-family or multifamily residential, single-tenant or multitenant office buildings/retail properties
- Customer base, i.e., the probable users of the property based on a demographic breakdown (age, sex, employment, income range, social status, and activity patterns)
- Quality of the construction

Techniques for Examining Demand

A demand estimate may be based on secondary or primary data on population and employment. Frequently, a combination of the two types of data is used. Generally secondary data serve as the basis for certain judgments about underlying demand projections, while primary data are needed to refine the analysis. Before demand can be examined further, two relevant terms must be defined: estimate and forecast.

An *estimate* refers to the current population, employment, and demand. Estimates are used to update data from the last census. A *forecast* refers to the future population, employment, and demand. A forecast attempts to measure changes that may occur, given certain functions inherent in the methods and data employed to make the projection. Typically several projections are made, each based on a different set of criteria. Often minimum, maximum, and midpoint projections are made and each is plausible to a degree. Forecasting requires the application of judgment. A forecast is *the* projection, or set of projections, deemed most likely to occur. It is based on the set of data conclusions that the analyst considers most probable.

Sources of Demand

As previously noted, the demand for a particular property type bears a specific relationship to population and employment. Identifying and understanding the relationship between demand drivers and the particular type of real estate is the first requirement in demand estimation. Some examples of major demand drivers are:

- Increase in population
- Increase in employment
- Redevelopment growth-i.e., old, outdated facilities need to be replaced
- Relocation growth-i.e., people/commercial establishments simply move away from older areas to relocate to another part of the city perceived to be more desirable
- Speculative demand

This last type of demand is generated by speculative investors who buy lots, condominiums, or other properties in down markets and expect to resell them for a profit to other investors or to users. At some point the opportunity to sell the properties in the investor market dries up and then the only recourse is to sell them in the user market. Thus, the economics of the speculative/investment market is ultimately dependent on the long-term economics of user demand. In other words, the long- term value is based on long-term use and the long-term property absorption will, over time, revert back to the long-term user demand. This means that short-term demand in the speculative real estate market cannot be accurately forecast with fundamental analysis, but the long-term economics can be reliably predicted no matter what the short-term speculative market indicates.

Types of Demand Methods

The number of methods that can be used to develop demand estimates is limited only by the availability of data and the resourcefulness of the analyst. The techniques described in the following sections may be used to derive demand estimates for commonly appraised properties. The analyst should focus on demonstrating the existing relationships between population, employment, and income. Using primary data to refine the demand estimate will add greater precision to the results.

Retail Space Demand Estimates

Demand estimates for retail properties focus on the demand for retail services. Two simple relationships can provide insight into the demand for a retail property.

1. The ratio of retail space in the market area or city to the population of the market area or city. This relationship is expressed by the following equation:

$$R_m/P_m = r_m \qquad R_c/P_c = r_c$$

2. The ratio of retail space in the market area or city to the number of households in the market area or city, which is expressed as

$$R_m/H_m = r_m \qquad R_c/Hc = r_c$$

The symbols used in these equations are explained below.

R_m and R_c = number of square feet of retail space in the market area and the city, respectively
P_m and P_c = population of the market area and the city, respectively
H_m and H_c = number of households in the market area and the city, respectively

Two other useful ratios are sales per capita in the market area or city

S_m/P_m = sales per capita in the market area
S_c/P_c = sales per capita in the city and/or sales per household in the market area or the city.
S_m/H_m = sales per household in the market area
S_c/H_c = sales per household in the city

where S_m and S_c = volume of sales (in dollars) in the market area and in the city, respectively
P_m and P_c = population of the market area and the city, respectively
H_m and H_c = number of households in the market area and the city, respectively

If the ratio for the market area exceeds the ratio for the overall city, there may be strong demand for retail services in the market area; conversely, if the ratio for the city exceeds the ratio for the market area, the demand for retail in the market area may be saturated. The following example shows how the ratio is used for this type of analysis. In this case, the market area may be oversaturated because its ratio is higher than the ratio for the city.

Market Area Ratio

Occupied retail space in the market area = 425,000 sq.ft.
Market area population = 10,000 people

Thus, the market area ratio is 42.5 sq. ft. of occupied retail space per person (425,000/10,000).

City Ratio

Occupied retail space in the city = 1,000,000 sq. ft.
City population = 40,000 people

Thus, the city ratio is 25 sq. ft. of occupied retail space per person (1,000,000/40,000).

The market situation should be very carefully examined. If the market area has an average income level that is substantially higher than income levels for the overall city, the market may be able to support extra retail facilities. The actual occupancy in each area should be compared because one area may have extensive vacant space. Or one market area may have a superior retail center that is drawing in customers from the other side of the city. These factors can cause ratios to vary from area to area.

The next step is to determine the market share that the retail outlet is likely to capture. To project the demand for retail space in a market area, the ratio technique shown in Exhibit 8.3 may be successfully employed.

Exhibit 8.3	Projection of Supportable Retail Space in Square Feet		
Year	**Space Requirement Per Capita in Sq. Ft.**	**Population in Subject's 1.5- Mile Primary Trade Area**	**Total Supportable Retail Space in Sq. Ft.**
Current	11.0	9,774	107,514
Year 1	11.0	10,817	118,987
Year 2	11.0	20,798	228,778
Year 3	11.0	23,211	255,321

The retail sales data in Exhibit 8.3 were found in *Reported Gross and Taxable Sales*, provided by the State Comptroller of Public Accounts. The categories included miscellaneous general merchandise; auto and home supply stores; men's, girls', and boys' clothing; women's clothing; sporting goods; grocery store; drug store; and miscellaneous retail. These sales totaled $797,500,000. County population is estimated by the Council of Government to be 290,000. Therefore, the county per capita demand for neighborhood shopping is $2,750 per person ($797,500,000/290,000).

The required sales per square foot for neighborhood shopping center retail space in this sample market area is $250. (Sources such as the Urban Land Institute's *Dollars and Cents of Shopping Centers* should be referenced for actual data.)

The demand per capita divided by the retail sales per square foot in neighborhood shopping center retail space ($2,750/$250) indicates 11.0 square feet of retail space per capita. Given this information and the population estimates shown in the exhibit, the total supportable retail space can be calculated.

Basis of Retail Demand. The formula that follows shows the basis of retail demand as it may be approximated by various methods such as the ratio methods described previously. Retail demand is a function of household buying power and how much of household income is spent on retail goods. The amount of money spent on retail goods is converted into an estimate of retail space by applying a conversion factor that reflects how much sales volume is needed for the typical store to want to do business in this market. The formula follows.

$$\frac{(cH \times AHi \times CR)}{SR \text{ per sq. ft.}} = \text{New retail space demand per year in sq. ft.}$$

where

cH = change in number of households in market area per year

AHi = Average (or median) household income per year

CRi = Capture rate of household income by retail facilities

$$SR = \text{Sales required per square foot to attract a retail facility to this market area}$$

The application of this techniques is demonstrated using a five- year projection period and the following data:

Given: $cH = 6{,}918$ household change over next five years

$AHi = \$65{,}000$ average household income

$CRi = 38\%$ of income spent on retail

$SR = \$250$

The demand for retail space can be calculated as follows:

$(6{,}918 \times \$65{,}000 \times .38\ )/\$250 = 683{,}498$ sq. ft. of new retail space needed over the next five years, or 136,700 sq.ft. per year on average

Office Space Demand Estimates

The demand for office space is generated by the services provided by businesses housed in offices and, more directly, the demand of these businesses for employees who use the office space. In the short run, the ratio between the general population and the number of people employed in offices remains relatively constant. Office space demand can be analyzed by means of the following relationships:

$$OS_m/P_m = (OS/P)m \qquad OS_c/P_c = (OS/P)c$$
$$OS_m/OE_m = (OS/E)m \quad \text{and} \quad OS_c/OE_c = (OS/E)c$$

where OS_m and OS_c = square feet of office space in the market area and the city, respectively

P_m and P_c = population of the market area and the city, respectively

OE_m and OE_c = office employees in the market area and the city, respectively

$(OS/E)m$ and $(OS/E)c$ = office space per employee in the market area and the city, respectively

The demand for office space may be stated in the generalized equation

$cOE \times SF,OS/E \times CRm$ = square footage of office space demand in the submarket

where $\qquad cOE$ = change in the number of office employees over a given period

$SF,OS/E$ = the number of square feet of office space per employee

CRm = capture rate for the submarket

The key to applying this method is understanding the sources of office employment. The analyst must investigate the various employment categories in the market because certain types of employment require more office space than others. Most of the work force in service-sector employment categories (finance, insurance, real estate, and government) uses office space.

For example, assume the data indicate an increase of 8,700 in area employment over the five-year period. From data on individual employment categories, the analyst discovers that 69% of these employees are likely to be housed in offices and that, on average, each office employee uses 235 square feet of space. The analyst then estimates that the expected capture rate in the submarket is 9.5% of the total office market. Thus,

$8{,}700 \times 0.69 \times 235 \times 0.095 = 134{,}017$ square feet of office space demand in the submarket during the five-year period, or an average of 26,803 sq. ft. per year

Equipped with this demand estimate, the appraiser can better understand the competitive position of the subject property. If the subject has 4,000 square feet of vacant space yet to be absorbed, the analyst can use the following equation to make an informed estimate of the required absorption period for the property.

4,000 sq. ft./26,803 sq. ft. annual demand = 14.9% capture if the property is to lease up in one year

After thorough analysis, the appraiser may determine that the property is not advantageously located or is not competitive in other ways. It may be concluded that the property will require two or more years to be fully leased. In other words, the appraiser may decide that because the property is not highly competitive, it probably cannot capture 14.9% of the market in one year. It may have the capacity to capture 7% or 8% of the market given the competitive environment.

Housing Demand Estimates

Estimates of housing demand are based on population, employment, and income data and the number of households in the market area. The following generalized equation can be used to obtain an estimate of the demand for new housing units:

$$(cH + nR) - (V_a - V_n) - (UC_a - UC_n) = \text{demand for new housing units}$$

where cH = change in the number of households in the community or market area over a given period

nR = net removals of units (demolitions) from the housing inventory

V_a = actual vacancies

V_n = frictional vacancy (normal vacancy in a balanced market)

UC_a = actual housing units under construction

UC_n = the normal (average) number of units under construction

The following example demonstrates how the equation is used. Assume that 16,949 is the population forecast and 2.45 is the number of persons per household in the market area.

$$cH = 16,949/2.45 = 6,918 \text{ new households}$$

The following additional data are given

nR = 324 removals (demolitions)

Va = 8,000 units actually vacant

Vn = 6,500 units frictional vacancy (i.e., 5% of total units)

UCa = 800 units actually under construction

UCn = 1,200 units normally under construction

The demand for new housing units is estimated by inputting the data into the equation.

$$(16,949/2.45 + 324) - (8,000 - 6,500) - (800 - 1,200) = 6,142 \text{ new housing units in demand over the next five years}$$

This estimate can be allocated to single-family and multifamily units based on the percentage breakdown for the community. If, for example,

72% of the households in the community are single-family detached dwellings and there are 2.59 persons per single-family household, the above equation can be adjusted as follows:

$$(0.72 \times 16,949)/2.59 + (0.72 \times 324)$$
$$- 0.72(8,000 - 6,500) - 0.72(800 - 1,200) = 4,153 \text{ single-family units}$$

Thus, over the five-year period, demand for 4,153 single-family dwelling units will come on line, averaging 831 units per year. With the additional information that 12% of the households have incomes of $50,000 or more, the analyst can further refine the estimate. According to the general rule of thumb, a household can meet payments on a mortgage equal to twice its annual household income. Thus, a household that can make a 20% down payment will be able to purchase a house in the $125,000 range. Of the 831 units demanded each year, approximately 100 units will be in the $125,000 range.

Two calculations are performed

$$(\$50,000 \times 2)/0.80 = \$125,000 \text{ house price}$$
$$\text{and}$$
$$831 \times 0.12 = 99.7 \text{ or } 100 \text{ units demanded}$$

Relationship of Demand to Urban Growth Patterns

Two basic concepts characterize the relationship between demand and urban growth.

1. The rate of growth in the economic base determines the increase in demand for real estate and the rate at which land is absorbed for use.
2. The direction of growth determines where demand for real estate and land use will accelerate and where land will be absorbed. As a corollary, when growth moves in a direction away from the real estate, demand and absorption rates will fall off.

In deriving a market value opinion, an appraiser makes a prediction or forecast about the future net benefits accruing from a property and the anticipated supply and demand situation. Because appraisers are predictors or forecasters, they must understand the dynamics of urban land use. If the appraiser is developing a 10-year cash flow analysis for an income-producing property, for example, an understanding of how urban land use patterns may change will enhance the accuracy of the income forecast. If the value of a tract of vacant land is being sought, an understanding of urban growth patterns will help determine when the parcel will likely be absorbed.

While employment and population are the forces that generate demand, it would be impossible to exclude locational considerations from demand analysis. In the world of real estate, demand shifts over time and space. Real estate products and services, however, are created at a specific point in space and the real estate remains bound to that location. The real estate supply is immovable, but demand consists of people and people are mobile. As people move into an area, they spread out in predictable directions and real estate development takes place. This is how urban land use patterns evolve over time: new neighborhoods grow as old ones decline. Chapter 5 of this text discusses urban land use patterns and the dynamics of real estate demand.

Demand estimates must also take into account macro demand concepts, which relate to the metropolitan area beyond the immediate neighborhood. Over time, real estate market demand moves in generally predictable directions within an urban area. As demand moves in one direction, the urban structure changes and property values are affected. The direction in which demand is moving will influence the subject's value. If demand is moving toward the subject property and population density is increasing in the vicinity, the subject's value will rise. As demand moves away from the subject, its value will decline.

To gain a better understanding of these dynamics, the appraiser should be familiar with urban growth patterns, which reflect the channeling of demand forces. The social ecology models discussed in Chapter 5—the concentric zone theory, the sector (wedge) theory, the multiple nuclei theory, and the radial (axial) corridor theory—are especially relevant in determining the direction of urban growth.

Predicting the Direction of Urban Growth

Because an opinion of property value rests on the anticipated benefits to be derived from the property, the appraiser needs to predict the direction of urban growth and determine where population density and demand will increase. The critical features an appraiser should examine are proposed developments in the urban infrastructure, specifically transportation and utility linkages. The development of linkages integrates individual sites into the metropolitan matrix.

The social ecology theories of urban growth provide insight into the direction of urban growth. Briefly stated, the concentric zone theory suggests that an urban area usually expands outward from a principal node or nucleus. The sector theory indicates that upper-, middle-, and low-income residential development tends to occur in select sectors of the urban area. The radial-corridor theory supports the sector theory and expands on it by suggesting that development will occur along major transportation arteries. Concentric zone and sector theories postulate that new urban development occurs at the urban periphery, while the radial-corridor theory indicates that development tends to follow transportation corridors. The multiple nuclei theory explains why certain land uses attract or repel other land uses.

No one theory provides all of the answers, but considered together the models should help the appraiser interpret growth or decline in the demand for real estate. Given a specific set of circumstances, the appraiser should be able to observe the dynamics of one or more of these urban growth patterns at work.

Demand and Urban Growth Rate

The rate of growth in the economic base determines the demand for real estate and the rate at which land is absorbed for use. The economic base concept attributes a city's growth to the goods and services that it exports. The more goods and services that are sold outside a community's immediate environs, the more money is brought into the community. To produce more goods and services, the work force must expand and more people must move into the area. This growing population creates greater demand for real estate because more people need places to live, work, and play.

Summary

The general area or city analysis found in many appraisals is often far too general to be of much assistance in real estate market analysis. Serious practitioners need to be more specific, more critical, and more precise in their analyses, focusing on the subject property and the factors that contribute to its value. The study of value-creating factors makes the appraiser an applied economist, studying and interpreting the forces of supply and demand.

To study the value-creating components of a property, the appraiser must analyze how the forces of supply and demand come to bear on the property in its fixed location. Through productivity analysis the appraiser focuses on the components of the property that make it productive and in this way identifies its prospective uses. Tentative property uses indicate the property's prospective users and the market segments that constitute demand for the property. Once these market segments have been identified, the appraiser can estimate the demand for the specific property.

This chapter has presented some general concepts and techniques employed in estimating demand. These tools reflect the fundamental relationships between the demand for real estate and employment and population in the market area and the overall city. The use of simple equations for estimating demand in retail, office, and housing markets has been demonstrated. Because real estate demand has a spatial dimension, urban growth patterns have been reviewed and related to real estate demand.

Finally, the chapter emphasizes an important relationship–i.e., the rate of growth in the economic base determines the increase in the demand for real estate. By coupling economic base analysis with an understanding of land use patterns, the appraiser will be able to identify the rate and direction of urban growth and, ultimately, the rate at which land is absorbed for use. Once the rate and direction of urban growth have been determined, the appraiser can make use of various models to estimate demand.

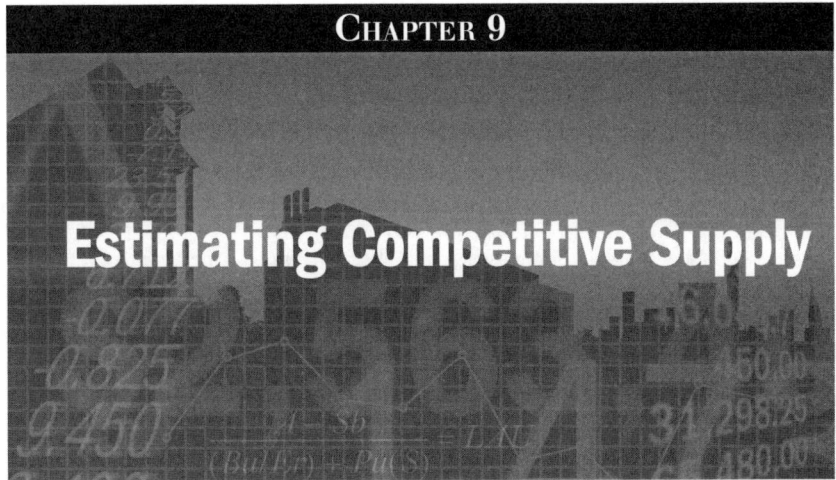

CHAPTER 9

Estimating Competitive Supply

Chapter Objectives

- To contrast general area or regional analysis as currently conducted with competitive supply projections
- To explain the importance of examining competitive supply
- To provide a definition of projected competitive supply for the defined market segment
- To present a variety of techniques for projecting competitive supply in the market under investigation

Introduction

Competitive supply is the other side of the demand-supply equation. Appraisal theory and practice have long called for examination of economic trends, including indicators such as population, employment, purchasing power, and interest rates. Unfortunately, many appraisers have interpreted this to mean that they should load the general area analysis or regional analysis section of the appraisal report with volumes of regional or city data.

The discussion of area trends in a report most often consists of boilerplate—i.e., standard data pertaining to the entire region or city. This information is often taken from the appraiser's files, which are updated perhaps once or twice a year. Such material is rarely examined in connection with the market value of the subject property. Interpretation of the trends described and their impact on the subject is left to the reader. The following quotation shows that the Appraisal Institute has long mandated that appraisers focus market analysis on the specific submarket and competition of the subject. The fifth edition of *The Appraisal of Real Estate*, which was published more than 35 years ago, reminds appraisers of what should be considered.

> The appraiser's knowledge should include some recent history of these [trends], their present status, and a logical idea of what to expect of them in the foreseeable future. However, the appraiser should reflect in his value estimate *only those trends which presently affect [the] market value [of the subject].*[1]
>
> Another problem with regional analysis, as it is typically performed, is that it often considers only demand-side factors, ignoring supply-side factors. For example, a report may include demand-side data such as the names of the major employers in the area, exhibits on population/employment trends, or graphs plotting the growth in demand deposits at local banks. These data demonstrate that demand is growing, but shed no light on the market supply. The unspoken assumption is that because there is growth in demand, demand must exist for the subject property in its submarket. This argument does not necessarily hold true. Competitive supply must be examined.

Defining Competitive Supply

The real estate supply being examined consists of the competitive properties in the market area. The quantity of competitive supply is, in turn, a function of the prices being paid for properties and the costs of building new units. There are two components of supply to be considered: the existing supply—i.e., the stock or inventory of the specific type of real estate being studied—and the new supply that will enter the market during the projection period.

Competitive Supply for the Defined Market Segment

Property productivity analysis defines the physical, locational, legal, and market appeal attributes that the subject property can provide. These attributes are shared by competitive properties. When these attributes are examined, the productive capabilities of the property and the likely users of the property will come into focus. Thus, productivity analysis helps define the attributes that competitive properties must have and the market segment in which the subject property competes.

One way to identify competitive property attributes is to use a spreadsheet that lists the productive attributes of property. Exhibits 12.5 and 12.13 in Chapter 12 are examples of spreadsheets. The spreadsheet may also list financial attributes, which include the price or rent levels of the properties, any special financing (e.g., below-market financing or rent concessions), and any special assessments for public utilities. A property's productivity characteristics will attract certain types of users.

Further market segmentation can be conducted based on other property attributes such as:

- Single-tenant or multitenant occupancy, e.g., single-family or multifamily residential, single-tenant or multitenant office buildings/retail properties

---

1. *The Appraisal of Real Estate,* 5th ed. (Chicago: Appraisal Institute, 1967), 80.

- Customer base, i.e., the probable users of the property based on a demographic breakdown of their ages, sex, employment, income range, social status, and activity patterns
- Construction quality and property condition
- Financial attributes

Competitive Supply and the Level of Market Analysis[2]

Level A market analysis is the traditional level of market analysis employed by many appraisers. Level A analysis draws on readily available regional and city data. A description of the general area is provided as a backdrop for the analysis of data on comparable properties, which are taken as representative of conditions in the market. The analysis focuses on the generators of real estate demand in the area. The appraiser's analysis of the data does not usually relate areawide demand to the subject, but leaves it to the reader of the appraisal to infer the level of demand that exists for the subject. Typically, Level A analyses refer to the supply side of the market only indirectly, by citing vacancy rates for selected rent or sales comparables. The vacancy rates of these comparable properties serve as indicators of any oversupply or undersupply in the market. These rates are taken as representative of the market. Projected vacancies are based on the assumption that these rates will remain stable.

Level B market analysis incorporates and builds on the Level A analysis. Level A is descriptive and historical, using past data on selected comparables to represent the market. Level B is more analytical. The appraiser studies broad-based surveys of the market to estimate supply and uses quantifiable data to make judgments about property use and the timing of development. In Level B supply analyses, regularly published market studies are examined to provide an idea of the number of similar-use properties in a designated geographic area. Thus, Level B analysis can be further contrasted with Level A analysis, in which conclusions about the entire market are based on the vacancy rates of selected comparables. Level C analyses are much more sophisticated and require more extensive data.

Estimating Supply with Secondary Data

Secondary data consist of published information collected for purposes unrelated to the specific research at hand. Using such data saves time and expense. However, this advantage must be weighed against the potential inaccuracies that can arise from data that are not tailored to fit the market area defined in the problem.

Sources of Secondary Supply Data

A variety of secondary data is available in most major cities and can be used to estimate the supply of a given property type. An office brokerage

---

2. Four levels of market analysis were described in Chapter 2. The three levels discussed below (Levels A, B, and C) represent the kinds of analyses typically undertaken for valuation appraisals.

or leasing company may conduct semiannual surveys of office buildings to determine the amount of space on the market, changes in the quantity of available space, and vacancy rates. Similarly, a retail brokerage firm may conduct surveys of retail space. In some metropolitan areas, commercial market research firms collect statistics on various types of real estate and sell these data to appraisers, brokers, leasing agents, developers, and others. City and regional planning agencies also collect and process data that may be of use to real estate appraisers.

Level B analyses make extensive use of secondary data but, in using such data, the appraiser must carefully consider the purpose for which the data were collected and what the data do and do not indicate about the market. The boundaries of any designated submarket must also be identified. The analyst must then consider the data in terms of the appraisal problem to be solved.

The analyst should determine whether or not the collector or disseminator of the data has skewed the information or interpreted it to serve some special interest. For example, consider three office market reports, published by three different brokerage firms in a major Southwestern metropolis. As is typical, these reports contain divergent data on vacancy rates, absorption rates, and the amount of office space that is coming on line. When the nature of these data is carefully investigated, the appraiser discovers that the studies cover different, but overlapping, components of the office market. The first company tracks only Class A buildings that contain 100,000 or more square feet of space. The second company reports on office space in the CBD in both Class A buildings with 20,000 or more square feet of space and Class B buildings. This second company openly acknowledges that its survey covers only 50% to 60% of the market. The third company tracks all Class A buildings from which it can readily obtain data, but the survey does not indicate what percentage of the market this group represents. This third report subtly identifies the buildings the company has leased and notes that they have occupancy rates higher than the market average. The appraiser must take note of these qualitative differences in data and select the data that best address the problem.

Estimating Supply with Primary Data

Level C analyses make extensive use of primary data and employ secondary data much more sparingly. To estimate the supply of real estate in the market area, Level C analyses depend on field work and direct surveys.

The supply of real estate includes all properties that currently exist in the given market because any available property may be bought, sold, or leased at any moment. In addition to existing units, supply includes new properties that may be developed or built within a given time frame. (A corollary to the quantity of units being developed is the number of units that may be demolished and permanently removed from the market.) Thus, the first component of supply is the stock or inventory of existing units in the market; the second component comprises the properties coming into the market over the projection period. Both components must be investigated. A third component, competitive sites suitable for development, is also considered.

Existing Stock or Supply of Competitive Properties

To estimate the stock of competitive properties, the analyst delineates the market area and does field work to survey the competitive projects in the area defined. The analyst identifies units that may be considered competitive with the subject and personally inspects each property to collect the required data. Basic information may include

- Name and address of the project
- Name and phone number of the contact person
- Project size
- Occupancy level
- Parking facilities
- Amenities
- Rent levels

Of course, much more information may be gathered. The definition of the problem will suggest the quantity of information needed to solve it.

While conducting the field work, the analyst organizes the data on a worksheet. After systematic collection and analysis, the data will indicate which properties are competitive with the subject.

Building permit data can also be used to estimate the existing supply of a given property type. These data, which can be obtained from city governments, may be used to track the number of new buildings being constructed in the market area. Such data should be used with caution, however, because not all permits are acted upon–i.e., some buildings for which permits are issued are never built. The best way to ascertain whether or not a building has been constructed is to personally inspect the area. Another method involves taking a sample of the permits issued over a given period, checking to see how many were acted upon, and developing an adjustment factor. For example, if 86% of the permits tracked have been put to use, an adjustment factor of 86% may be applied to the total number of building permits issued in the market area. As market conditions change, the adjustment factor will have to be updated to ensure its reasonableness.

Competitive Supply Under Construction or Planned

The second component of supply is the number of new properties currently under construction or in planning. Projects currently under construction are identified by inspecting the market area and contacting knowledgeable people. To survey planned projects, the analyst may conduct telephone interviews with developers, city planning officials, plat map compilers, and others who may be aware of planned construction projects.

Competitive Sites in the Market Area

The final step in the supply estimate is a comprehensive survey of sites in the market area that may be developed into competitive properties in the near future.

Design/Amenities Rating

In addition to quantitative analysis of the inventory of competitive properties, in-depth supply studies involve qualitative analysis to assess the relative competitiveness of the subject. This information is needed to estimate the subject's market capture rate. The analysis is conducted by assigning design/amenities ratings, which rank the subject and competitive properties according to features such as design, quality of construction, condition/maintenance, profile/visibility, access, proximity to support facilities, and the quality of the management and tenants. Features that strongly influence a tenant's decision to lease space in a property may be accorded greater weight in this ranking.

Relationship of Supply to Value

The price of property is determined by the interaction of supply and demand. Demand is a function of the size of the population and the income levels in a market area. Supply is developed to meet the population's demand for places to live, work, and play. Without supply, there can be no market; similarly, a market cannot exist without demand. It takes both supply and demand to create a market, a price, and a value.

Summary

The area or regional analyses conducted by appraisers often do not specifically address market conditions. Perhaps the most obvious shortcoming of area analyses is their failure to focus on the subject property. Data may be incorporated into an appraisal report without any attempt to relate market conditions to the value of the subject property. The readers of the report must draw their own conclusions as to what the data mean with regard to the property's value.

Another problem arises when area analysis concentrates on the demand for the real estate, but ignores the supply of competitive properties. Demand-side data on population, employment, and income are included in most area analyses. These data may indicate that demand is growing or declining, but they say nothing about supply.

The competitive supply of real estate is determined by the price of similar properties and the cost to build new units. As the price paid for a particular type of property increases, the number of properties of that type placed on the market also increases, all else being equal. As the price paid declines, the quantity of properties declines as well.

Competitive supply may be estimated by a variety of techniques. Secondary data generated by market research groups often provide excellent information, but a more in-depth analysis may require primary data, which can only be obtained by conducting personal surveys and field work.

CHAPTER 10

Data Sources

Chapter Objectives

- To review definitions of *primary* and *secondary data*
- To define other essential terms employed in data analysis, i.e., *model, data, information*
- To provide the rationale for using different data sources
- To offer strategies for finding different data sources

Introduction

This chapter discusses the uses, and evaluation of data for the supply and demand analyses within an appraisal. Appraisers make use of both primary and secondary data in the models they use to generate information essential to decision making.

A *model* is an artificial representation of, or abstraction from, reality that describes a particular aspect of the world. Models are generally used for decision-making purposes. For example, a road map can be considered a model. A road map of the United States can show a driver how to get from New York City to San Francisco. It represents a high level of abstraction. As you travel through the various states, you may find you need a state map. And if you are to be in a particular city for a while, you might want a local city map. Each map reflects a different level of abstraction. None depict the actual world as we see it when we drive down the road. Reality is far too complex for a map to reflect its totality.

Appraisers use models to understand the market. In market analysis an appraiser might forecast the demand for retail space using per capita expenditures in the area divided by the average sales per square foot of space, which would result in the overall market demand for retail space in square feet. Or the demand for office space may be forecast by multiplying the typical square foot area per employee times the number of employees in the employment groups that have a large percentage of workers who occupy office space. In measuring value, the appraiser might use models such as the sales comparison approach, in which similar properties that have been sold are compared to the subject, or the income capitalization approach, in which discounted cash flow analysis is used to forecast future incomes and discount them to present value.

Models do not replicate the complexity of the real world. In fact, if there are too many variables to incorporate into the model, the model becomes unmanageable. For example, in the sales comparison approach, the appraiser collects data on comparable sales which are adjusted for differences using a matched pairs model. Even when data on very comparable matched pairs are available, the adjustments are only approximations and the effect of the distinguishing feature cannot be totally isolated. Other differences can affect the final outcome. However, for a matched pairs model to be effective, only significant, critical variables need to be identified in the model. This point is important. Just as the road map forces the user to focus on the critical route, blocking out the scenery and detours, an appraisal model forces the appraiser to focus on *critical variables* while downplaying the role of other variables.

Data are observations and evidence that relate to some aspect of the appraisal problem. *Information* is produced through interpretation of data for purposes of decision making. The data the appraiser collects are incorporated into and filtered through various appraisal models, which generate information that can be used in solving the appraisal problem. *Primary data* are collected directly by the appraiser and used in the appraisal models that will be tested. *Secondary data,* which are generated for reasons other than the appraisal problem at hand, often must be adapted for use in the selected models. Appraisers must become adept at generating primary data such as comparable sales, rents, incomes, expenses, capitalization rates, and property specifications. Much of the market analysis within an appraisal, however, will make use of secondary data that have been collected for purposes other than the appraiser's specific research problem.

Secondary Data

The following discussion will first focus on secondary data that are published and readily available.

The use of secondary data saves time and expense. The secondary data most commonly used for real estate analysis consist of statistics published by the Bureau of the Census (U.S. Department of Commerce) and the Bureau of Labor Statistics (U.S. Department of Labor) on population, incomes, birth rates, death rates, employment, retail sales, interest rates, housing starts, and building permits.

The appraiser tries to find data that meet the needs of the job at hand, given the time and budget constraints of the assignment.

The data for a market study included in an appraisal is more focused than the data used for most other market studies. The appraiser is focused on a specific property in a specific location serving a specific submarket. This is the biggest data problem in appraisal because much of the data available is developed for large geographic areas such as cities, counties or states.

The appraiser looking for secondary data to be used in a sub-market supply and demand study needs both existing and forecast data focusing on small areas. The required data might include the following:

Demand Side Data
- Employment (by industry sector)
- Population (households, income, age, etc.)
- Daytime visitors to the area-current and forecast
  - Tourist
  - Daytime employment in area
  - Visitors to the local hospital district
  - Other data

Supply Side Data
- Inventory of total competitive space
- Inventory of occupied space
- Historical occupancy and supply
- Planned new space

If only county or citywide data are available, the appraiser must segment the data by some means. For example, one of the most useful employment data sources is the County Business Pattern Survey from the U.S. Census Bureau. For the appraiser to use these data in an office demand study, the county data must be segmented to the subject submarket to forecast employment demand in the area. One method might be to segment countywide employment based on the amount of office space in the subject submarket compared to the county. The following example demonstrates use of this method.

Office Demand Segmentation Example

· Current countywide employment (Data Source: County Business Patterns from U.S. census)	150,000 jobs
· Current office space in county (Data Source: XYZ Brokerage Company)	18,750,000 sq. ft
· Countywide office space/job (18,750,000/150,000)	125 sq. ft./job
· Current office space in subject quadrant of county (Data Source: XYZ Brokerage Company and/or appraiser's survey)	3,750,000 sq. ft.

· Subject quadrant capture rate (3,750,000/18,750,000)	20%
· Forecasted countywide employment in 5 yrs.	175,000
(Data Source: Council of Governments and private vendor)	
· Times ratio of sq. ft. of office space per job	× 125
Countywide office space demand in 5 yrs.	21,875,000 sq. ft.
Times subject quadrant capture ratio	× 20%
Subject submarket office space demand in 5 yrs.	4,375,000 sq. ft.

Data Sources

There are hundreds, perhaps thousands, of data sources available. All of the data referenced here can be found on the Internet under the name of the provider. Major government home pages for the U.S. Bureau of the Census, Bureau of Labor Statistics, and the Bureau of Economic Analysis are good places to start. These sites have links to related sites. Corresponding agencies on the state level will have more local data. State agencies with data useful for market analysis include the state comptroller (for sales tax data), economic development department, and state employment commission. Other agencies such as the state natural resources and utility departments have population and employment forecast. Many university real estate centers also have comprehensive lists of real estate data sources on their Web sites. At the local level, typical data sources include the regional council of governments, regional transportation planning agency, and local economic development and planning departments.

These sources change often, with new data becoming available and new ways to report data. The sources described below will give the reader some idea of the wide variety of data available. The list describes only the most common public sources and a sample of the commercial sources; it is not intended to be comprehensive. The analyst will recognize that many private sources of data are not cited. A search on the Web will reveal many sources of proprietary data that can be obtained for a fee. The analyst must try to find data that meet the needs of the job at hand, given the time and budget constraints of the assignment. The following sections list major data sources.

Population and Demographic Characteristics
1. The U.S. Census of Population and Housing

Kind of data: Demographics, housing, population, incomes.

Geography covered: U.S., states, census tracts, zip codes and block data.

Frequency: Every 10 years for comprehensive census data. After 2000 the census bureau started the American Community Survey (ACS). This program is a comprehensive effort by the bureau to replace the long form, which was administered to one in seven people during the decennial census, with data from an annual large-sample survey. This survey provides current annualized data for all areas with 65,000 or more persons, annual data based on three-year averages for areas with between 20,000 and 65,000 persons, and annual data based on five-year averages for areas as small as individual census tracts. Data at the tract level will not be available until 2010 and then annually thereafter. Other statistics like county- and MSA-level data are already available for many areas.

Source: U.S. Bureau of the Census (www.census.gov)

Buying Power, Consumer Spending

1. Bureau of Labor Statistics–Consumer Expenditure Survey

Kind of data:	Consumer spending.
Coverage:	Regional, MSA for major cities.
Frequency:	Biennially.
Source:	U.S. Department of Labor, Bureau of Labor Statistics (www.bls.gov/cex)
Content:	The survey indicates how much households (BLS uses the term "consumer unit") spent for major items such as housing, transportation, retail spending, health, savings, education, and insurance. Subgroup detail data for each group are available.
Methodology:	
Diary Survey	Consumer units complete a record of expenses for two consecutive one-week periods.
Interview Survey	An interviewer visits each of the consumer units in the sample every three months over a 12-month period. The expenditures are based on consumer recall for the period.
	The results of these two surveys are reconciled into the final report.

2. Annual Retail Trade Survey

Kind of data:	Retail establishment sales, number of establishments, annual payroll.
Coverage:	U.S., state, county, MSA, city, and zip code.
Frequency:	Every five years, years ending in 02 and 07.
Source:	U.S. Bureau of the Census (www.census.gov/econ).
Content:	Retail sales by seven-digit NAICS code, number of establishments, and payroll. The report, released each spring, contains estimates of

annual sales, per capita sales, gross margins, monthly and year-end inventories, and sales/inventory ratios by kind of business.

Methodology: A mandatory survey of all major business establishments and sample survey of small businesses.

Employment
1. County Business Patterns

Kind of data: Employment.

Coverage: States and counties.

Frequency: Annual.

Source: U.S. Census Bureau (www.census.gov/epcd/cbp)

Content: The series provides employment data by county, both current and historical. The series excludes data on self-employed individuals, employees of private households, railroad employees, agricultural production employees, and most government employees.

2. Bureau of Labor Statistics

Kind of data: Employment data (usually the most current).

Coverage: U.S., states, counties, and some MSAs. The data are only for workers covered by federal unemployment insurance, so they exclude many categories such as the government and armed services.

Source: www.bls.gov/cew

3. State Agency–Employment and Wages by Industry and County

Kind of data: Employment, income, earnings.

Coverage: States and counties.

Frequency: Quarterly, semiannually–varies from state to state.

Source: State Department of Labor or Employment Commission. Offices of these departments exist in each state. Statistics are compiled by at least one of these agencies, and sometimes by both.

Content: Varies from state to state, but generally the data will cover monthly employment and earnings by industry group.

Methodology: Typically data are compiled from quarterly contribution and wage reports submitted by employers subject to the State Unemployment Compensation Act.

Private Demographic Vendors

Many private vendors compile and make projections on demographic characteristics. Using these companies is convenient since they have already found the data and have compiled them into various tables and charts for the appraiser. They prepare an assortment of studies that can be tailored to the user's needs, including demographics, housing, income, age groups, sex, five-year forecasts, and other breakdowns of data. The studies can be provided for a market area defined by the user. In addition, such firms provide market segmentation studies that further identify consumer characteristics on the basis of psychographic profiles and other criteria.

The data methodology varies from company to company, so the analyst should discuss the methodology used with a demographer on staff. Essentially, these companies update data from the previous census and make forecasts. They determine the population distribution for small market areas by means of a smoothing technique using centroids. (A centroid, which represents the center of mass, is graphed as the point at which population is concentrated. A centroid is plotted by coordinates, which are the averages of the coordinates for a given set of points.)

Typically the analyst will want to discuss the updating, forecasting, and smoothing techniques applied to disaggregate data for small areas with a demographer in the firm to decide which data set best suits his or her needs. There are often significant variances between the results provided by different companies for the same defined market area.

One example of a good, semi-private demographic vendor is STDBonline.com . This site has nearly all the demand-side data needed for most Level C market studies. The Site to Do Business Online(STDB®) was developed by the CCIM Institute. The Appraisal Institute has arranged for its members to enroll as CCIM Institute Organizational Affiliate Members and access the site for a discounted fee.

STDB® is an integrated market analysis system that combines demographic information, mapping technology, and reporting tools for use in appraisal and consulting assignments. The site includes market analysis templates for single-family, multifamily, retail, office, and industrial properties as well as access to flood maps, aerial photography, and more. It puts critical and reliable information from a variety of sources in one location.

The information on the Site to Do Business includes aerial and floodplain maps, comprehensive U.S. Census demographics with current and five-year forecasts of population, household and income data, current employment by industry, detail lists of business establishments in the area, consumer spending estimates by category, household financial and wealth estimates, shopping center lists, major employer lists, mosaic tables and charts, traffic counts, crime indexes, and other information. The list of available data seems to grow daily. The data comes in many pre-analyzed forms like mosaics, ranks, and narrative summaries.

The best news for property-specific valuation studies like appraisals is that STDB® is a geographic-based system that provides users with numerous methods of displaying and analyzing information for small geographic areas, including MSAs, counties, zip codes, rings, and self-defined polygon areas.

As of 2005, STDB® does not have employment projections. Thus, these data would have to be added to compile a complete data set for a demand forecast for a major property type.

Forecasted employment data sources can be obtained from state economic development or labor departments, from local and regional planning agencies involved in transportation planning, and from commercial data vendors. Local regional planning organizations and local planning departments are usually the only public sources of small-area employment data. The state economic development agencies usually have county- or MSA-level data only. A couple of commercial data sources that provide employment forecasts for counties and MSAs are Woods & Poole Economics out of Washington, D.C. (*www.woodsandpoole.com*) and Economy.com, Inc. out of West Chester, Pa (*www.economy.com*). Woods & Poole provides data at the county level, while Economy.com will provide MSA-level data. For most Level C office or industrial studies, the forecast of employment starts at the county level and then is segmented to the subject submarket by the analyst. Any source that will give county-level data is usually acceptable.

University Real Estate Centers
Nearly all states have at least one university with a designated real estate center. These centers usually provide research and services to the general public. Many of these centers have developed comprehensive lists of data sources. Many include a short description of the data source and its web address.

Appraisal Institute Lum Library
The Appraisal Institute's Y.T. and Louise Lee Lum Library maintains a list of data sources and information databases that are available to Appraisal Institute members and associates.

Secondary Data of Construction and Space Inventory
The U.S. census provides data on existing housing and housing permits. Various agencies and private vendors provide building activity data at the city or metro level. However, these data are not typically very useful to the appraiser of a specific property. The metro data can be used by investors deciding which cities to invest in and which to avoid, but the appraiser must consider the specific property and the specific submarket in which the property competes. Thus, appraisers need small-area data much more than metro-area data.

Submarket inventories of existing space by product type are limited. However, some major brokerage firms do maintain such databases and some private vendors maintain localized detailed inventory data and will provide them for a fee. Typically, national data are limited so the appraiser will usually have to find data from different sources in different cities (or generate the data through primary research. The Site to Do Business (STDB®) has major shopping center data from the National Research Bureau, but no other inventory data.

Some private national data sources with inventories for major markets are:

- Society of Industrial and Office Realtors (*www.sior.com*)
- REIS (*www.reis.com*)–for office, industrial, multifamily, and retail
- Torto Wheaton Research (*www.torwheatonresearch.com*)–mostly industrial and office
- CoStar–office , industrial and retail
- Xceligent Corp. (*www.xceligent.com*)–selected markets office, industrial, and retail.

Sources for specialty real estate data are:

- Smith Travel Research(*www.str-online.com*)–for hotels
- Pellucid Corporation (*www.pellucidcorp.com*)–for golf facilities and consumer survey data

These data sources are continually changing, requiring researchers to update their sources regularly.

Many appraisers have problems with national sources because of cost and geography. Also, the data are often limited to only large buildings and/or only multitenant buildings. Thus, in most cases the data are only a starting point for the competitive space inventory. Most information on competitive space has to be secured from local or regional sources. There are good local sources, but usually only in major metropolitan areas. Some of the best local sources are local planning and economic development agencies.

Evaluating Secondary Data[1]

Appraisal standards state that an appraiser who uses secondary data has a responsibility to investigate the sources and reliability of the data. Analytical data, even a population forecast from a public agency such as a university, cannot be assumed accurate for an appraisal. Appraisal standards require the appraiser to take responsibility for any analytical data used in an appraisal, including the population or employment forecast. One of the first duties of an appraiser, therefore, is to evaluate the secondary data to be used. A review of the secondary data will sometimes uncover problems but, in most cases, these are the only data available and they will have to be used. Nevertheless, analysis of the data's reliability is important. As Joseph Rabianski points out, "The analyst will not be able to remove or overcome some

---

1. A more detailed discussion of analyzing data can be found in Joseph S. Rabianski, Ph.D., "Primary and Secondary Data: Concepts, Concerns, Errors and Issues," *The Appraisal Journal* (January 2003): 43.

of the errors, but knowledge of their existence will help in drawing informed conclusions and establishing some level of confidence in the judgments that result."[2]

Several rules should be followed in evaluating secondary data. First, the appraiser must determine who compiled the data and for what purposes. For example, the Texas Department of Water Resources makes 30-year forecasts of county populations. These forecasts are designed so that any error will be in overestimation because the department does not want Texans to run out of water. If an appraiser were to base population and absorption forecasts on these data, the results would be especially optimistic.

Second, the appraiser should examine the methods used to collect the data. Collection techniques and their reliability can vary immensely. For example, substantial differences may exist in the data compiled by two agencies that collect building permit data and forecast housing starts. One agency may make a mechanical, rule-of-thumb adjustment to update data, while the other sends its staff out to neighborhoods to count the actual number of units being constructed. Similarly, population forecasts may differ significantly. A data supplier may base a population forecast on the number of building permits issued, adjust this figure for buildings that were not built, and check this number against data on water connections. The local chamber of commerce, on the other hand, may employ a straight-line projection technique based on the growth rate over the last two years. Both techniques are legitimate and can produce accurate results, given the assumptions and purposes of the analysis.

Third, the appraiser should examine the market area covered by the data and compare it with the market area defined in the analysis. When the market areas do not correspond, a bias is introduced into the analysis. The appraiser may need to adjust or modify the data so that the two market areas correspond more closely and the bias can be reduced. Just as adjustments are made to comparable sales data, the appraiser will frequently need to make adjustments to the secondary data used.

Fourth, the appraiser should conduct his or her own analysis to check the reasonableness of the data. When analyzing a population forecast, for example, the appraiser first secures more than one source. Then the appraiser contacts the agency or private firm that provided the forecast and asks about its data sources and methodology. Next, the appraiser decides if the sources and methodology seem reasonable. (If a private vendor will not talk about its data sources or methodology, do not buy the data.) Finally, the appraiser compares the forecast to what is known about the history of the area. For example, the forecast may call for 5,000 more people in the next five years, but the area only grew by 2,500 people in the past five years. Is there physical space to add 5,000 people? Is it reasonable to expect the area to grow

---

2. Ibid., 49.

twice as fast in the next five years? If the appraiser has doubts, he or she must use judgment. One good way to handle such a forecast is to create a range using the highest and lowest forecasts available as the top and bottom of the range. Then the appraiser can use judgment to find the best number for the midpoint.

Using Secondary Data for Estimating Demand

Demand forecasts are developed from projections of population, employment, and income. The kind of secondary data used by appraisers generally includes small-area projections, such as census tracts, up to countywide data. Sometimes subcensus tract data may be available. One source of small-area employment data is the transportation planning agency (usually the council of governments for a region). These agencies are required by the Federal Transportation Act to have a small-area employment forecast as part of their transportation planning before they can receive federal highway funding. These forecasts are sometimes called *traffic survey zones*. A single census tract may be divided into three, eight, or even 20 or more traffic survey zones. Obviously, such small-area data can be tailored to fit a defined market area more easily than data on a larger area.

Projections are often made by city and regional planning offices as well as other public or private agencies. After examining the methodology used to develop the projections that are available and rejecting those based on methodologies unsuitable to the needs of the assignment, the appraiser may wish to take a simple average of the acceptable projections for the point estimate and use the high and low for the forecast range. Averaging may be appropriate because the strengths and weaknesses of each projection may cancel each other out to some extent. In other words, any discrepancies between the projections should be offset by averaging them.

Once a preliminary estimate has been derived, the appraiser may wish to compare the projection with data from an analogous city. This is done by comparing the city's forecasted population increase with the population history of another city that has grown by a similar amount over the same period. If the history of the other city or area matches the subject, then the forecasted population for the subject market area could be considered reasonable.

If, however, the data appears to fall outside the range indicated by the appraiser's judgment or the historical data from the comparable city analysis, the appraiser may conclude that the estimate is too high or too low. Then, with a clear rationale, the appraiser may make adjustments upwards or downwards just as estimates derived from different valuation approaches are reconciled into a final value estimate. From small-area population and employment estimates, the appraiser develops a demand estimate. The appraiser may then decide which level of demand analysis is appropriate.

Level A Market Demand Analysis & Use of Secondary Data

Level A market analysis is the traditional descriptive type of study undertaken by many appraisers. Based on readily available macro secondary data on the region and city, a general area description is provided as the backdrop for the analysis of data on comparable properties. These secondary data provide something like a chamber of commerce city overview describing general market conditions. The level of current demand may be estimated based on evidence of sales and leasing activity involving similar properties over the past year. The existence of future demand is frequently assumed if growth trends in the region and city have been positive.

Level B Market Demand Analysis

Level B market analysis incorporates and builds on a Level A. Such an analysis includes more submarket-specific secondary data. Level A analysis is descriptive and historical, drawing upon selected comparables and macro secondary data to represent the market. Level B analyses are more analytical, relying on more specific secondary data surveys of the market to estimate demand. One example of secondary data used in this level of study would be a brokerage company's list of property vacancies by submarket. In Level B studies, secondary data are used extensively and must be scrutinized to determine how well they fit the problem at hand.

In a Level B demand analysis, the analyst examines secondary data from regularly published, area-wide market surveys. Using public and proprietary surveys saves time and money. These data are readily available in most cities because data services or state agencies in most urban areas routinely survey real estate submarkets, gathering data on office, retail, and apartment space. Data of this nature are more specific than the general data typically included in a Level A analysis and these data are updated at regular intervals–i.e., quarterly or semiannually.

There are some disadvantages to using this type of survey data. The surveys cover broad areas in an urban setting and the geographic boundaries designated for the survey rarely conform to the geographic submarket for the subject property. Therefore, survey data must be used with caution lest the appraiser draw an inappropriate conclusion. Although proprietary and public survey data are updated more frequently than census data, the data may soon become obsolete. Semiannual or quarterly updates may lag behind change in a dynamic market. Demand is usually projected by estimating net lease-up (i.e., the difference between new leases and leases that are not renewed) or time on the market (the period it takes for new properties to sell). Thus, the current market leasing or sales pattern is projected as the level of marginal demand that might be expected over the next few years.

A further caveat is needed. Although the use of broad-based market survey data increases the reliability of the analysis, it also has its limitations. Data of this type may cover many projects that are not competitive with the subject. The appraiser must carefully evaluate the data being used to determine how well they fit the specific appraisal assignment.

Level C Market Demand Analysis

In a Level C study, the analyst adds to the detailed analysis of historical secondary data from Level A and B studies by including a forecast of demand drivers and by refining the supply-side data with primary research methods. Secondary data are still central to a Level C study, but they are more submarket-specific and used for forecasting. For example, the retail sales data maintained by state comptrollers for sales tax purposes are used in a retail demand model as a measure of per capita spending. Thus, the secondary data are not used in the appraisal for the purpose for which they were originally collected. Similarly, supply-side secondary data such as building inventory data from leasing agents can be used as a starting point, but in a Level C study the analyst goes beyond the original ground surveys to supplement and verify the data. The following example illustrates the use of secondary data in a retail demand study in an appraisal.

Sample Level C Analysis Using Secondary Data

The assignment is to appraise a tract of land. After analyzing the productivity attributes of the property, the appraiser concludes that the property is best suited for development of a neighborhood supermarket, pending a supply and demand analysis. Two sets of population data are used in the supply and demand analysis: one was published by a local planning agency and covers a subcensus tract area called a traffic survey zone (TSZ); the other was published by a private demographics firm. The former contains population projections for the entire city. The latter includes forecasts for the specific market area (the northeast quadrant of the city), along with updates of income and age breakdowns and other standard demographic data. The different population forecasts are analyzed and reconciled into a final population forecast.(See the retail case study in Chapter 12 for the specific steps in the analysis.)

After these forecasts and data have been reconciled, the next step for the analyst is to estimate the net demand in the trade area for supermarket space. Exhibit 10.1 illustrates this process. Note that the data used in each step are secondary data.

This study was based entirely on secondary data and the appraiser's judgment. The conclusion of the study is that the market area is currently only slightly oversupplied. With a new store, however, the area will be oversupplied with grocery stores unless additional demand is generated from outside sources.

Primary Data

Primary data are generated by the researcher for the specific study at hand. Primary data may be obtained in three ways: through respondents, analogs, and experiments.

Exhibit 10.1 Grocery Store Residual Demand Study by Per Capita Expenditure

Line		Current	+5 Yrs	+10 Yrs	Data Source/Comment
1	Population within 1.5 miles of the subject—primary market trade area	6,144	7,841	9,840	Current population based on U.S. census data. Forecasted population based on appraiser's reconciliation of forecasts from various secondary sources
2	Grocery store sales per capita	$1,559	$1,559	$1,559	Grocery store sales per capita based on city data from the state comptroller, who collects data as part of sales tax function
3	Total neighborhood grocery store sales potential	$9,578,496	$12,224,119	$15,340,560	Line 1 × Line 2
4	Median grocery store sales per sq. ft.	$335	$335	$335	Urban Land Institute, *Dollars and Cents of Shopping Centers* *
5	Supportable grocery store sales from resident population in primary market area	28,593	36,490	45,793	Demand = Line 3 divided by Line 4
6	Square feet of grocery store space in primary trade area	30,000	30,000	70,000	The proposed subject store is the only store in the primary market area.
7	Planned new space in market area	0	40,000	0	New 40,000 sq. ft grocery store forecast to be built in five years. From city planning department development activity report
8	Residual demand	-1,407	-33,510	-24,207	Demand minus supply

* Sample data only. Consult most recent edition of this publication for current data.

Respondents

An appraiser may either *communicate* with respondents or *observe* respondents. Communication with respondents simply means asking questions of people who may have the answers. Interviews may be informal or formal. Appraisers most often conduct informal interviews, calling real estate market participants for information on sale prices, rents, and occupancy rates. Appraisers also interview property managers, tenants, owners, investors, and developers in the field on topics such as investor motives, costs, vacancies, rents, and finishing expenses. Sometimes formal questionnaires are developed and sent to select individuals who constitute a statistical sample. The special research skills required to develop and administer questionnaires are not addressed here. Nevertheless, questionnaires are an important tool used by marketing researchers, but usually only for in-depth, Level D analyses.

Appraisers often obtain primary data through observation. An appraiser may count the number of competing properties in the area or drive around a neighborhood to determine its character. Similarly, the researcher may count the number of customers going into a store or the number of vehicles passing an intersection. Often an appraiser will pace off or measure the number of front feet occupied by a storefront or the square feet in a warehouse. All these techniques depend on observation.

Analogs

Frequently, studying an analogous or comparable situation can shed light on an appraisal problem. For example, an appraiser may use case histories of comparable areas to estimate the amount of land that is likely to be absorbed over a specified period given the projected population. The appraiser may also examine the amount of land that was put to various uses as the population of the comparable area increased. Thus, an appraiser who is estimating the demand and absorption rate for a large, single-family subdivision may examine a similar community which is currently the size that the subject community is expected to be by the end of a designated period. By examining the amount of land allocated to single-family residences in the comparable community, the appraiser may be able to estimate the amount of land that will be needed for single-family housing units in the subject community. The appraiser can then estimate the capture rate for the subject subdivision to determine how many units may be absorbed over a specified period.

Experimentation

Sometimes appraisers may derive data through experimentation with a model. Such a model can be developed based on information obtained from an analog, as discussed above. By changing the assumptions and corresponding variables entered into the model, the appraiser can simulate alternative scenarios. A simple example is illustrated in Exhibit 10.2.

| Exhibit 10.2 | Experimental Model Based on Land Uses in Analog City XYZ | | | | |

| Analog City XYZ | 1990 | | 2000 | |
Land Uses	Acres	% of Total	Acres	% of Total
Total acres	16,000	100.0	20,000	100.0
Single-family	4,252	26.6	5,680	28.4
Multifamily	960	6.0	1,140	5.7
Retail	1,152	7.2	1,580	7.9

| Subject City ABC | 2000 | | Projected 2010 | |
Land Uses	Acres	% of Total	Acres	% of Total
Total acres	13,500	100.0	17,000	100.0
Single-family	3,267	24.2	4,590	27.0
Multifamily	851	6.3	1,020	6.0
Retail	932	6.9		
Retail Scenarios				
#1			1,173	6.9
#2			1,224	7.2
#3			1,275	7.5

The assumption underlying this example is that the subject parcel of land will eventually be developed for a retail use. The appraiser's objective is to estimate how many additional acres of land under retail use can be absorbed during the coming years. Equipped with such information, the appraiser can determine the likelihood of the subject being developed as a retail use. By examining city planning data about land uses in analog City XYZ, the analyst is able to estimate the land use breakdown in the subject City ABC. Stated differently, the appraiser finds that City XYZ is very similar to City ABC and realizes that the patterns of land absorption in City ABC will resemble those observed in the analog city.

If development proceeds according to the adage, "retail follows rooftops," the appraiser should be able to estimate the number of residential acres that will be absorbed over a period of time by applying a rate comparable to the growth rate for the analog city. Assuming that the cities' land use patterns will be similar, the appraiser can then forecast the amount of retail land to be absorbed in the subject city. Based on the changes in land use in City XYZ, the appraiser estimates the percentage changes for City ABC and then estimates the number of acres for each type of land use. By changing the critical ratio between land uses, the appraiser can literally use the model to run experiments, each with different outcomes.

Using the figures shown for the three retail scenarios in Exhibit 10.2, City ABC may be expected to bring between 241 (1,173 – 932) and 343 (1,275 – 932) additional acres under retail use. With these data the appraiser can estimate the likely absorption for the subject property, whose highest and best use is for future retail development.

Issues with Primary Data

If obtained in a reliable manner, primary data will provide the most accurate estimates of likely outcomes of the real estate market. The more reliable the data, the less risk accompanies the forecast. However, all analytic techniques have pitfalls. As is true for secondary data, the primary data are only as good as the structure of the research.

Sources of Primary Data

Primary data may be generated in any number of ways. The methods that can be applied are limited only by the imagination and initiative of the analyst and the constraints of time and expense. The traditional methods for generating primary data have already been discussed. These include telephone and field interviews with people directly or indirectly involved with the subject or the comparables as well as the use of analogs and experimentation.

Using some common sense and using secondary data for primary research, however, the appraiser can come up with new and innovative ways to obtain more and better information. The following list presents examples of data-gathering approaches that have been used successfully at one time or another. First, a problem is set forth and then a possible solution is suggested. Only one possible solution is given for each problem, but there could easily be more than one solution.

- **Problem:** To establish a vacancy rate for an apartment submarket within the city.

  One solution: The appraiser checks with the local post office or postmaster in the city. Post offices do weekly updates on all addresses to which mail is delivered. New construction addresses are added and address changes are noted. The data available may be used to establish the vacancy rate for the multifamily submarket under study.

- **Problem:** To estimate vacancy rates for two apartment complexes. These rates are critical to the appraisal.

  One solution: If the units are individually metered, the appraiser could obtain a utility company's readouts covering the past 12 months for the two complexes under investigation. The number of electrical hookups should be an excellent indicator of the number of vacancies in the past year.

- **Problem:** To estimate the demand for elderly housing in a small suburban community. The estimate is needed for the appraisal of a proposed housing project for the elderly.

  One solution: The local property tax office can provide information about the number of houses in the area whose residents pay reduced taxes because they are over age 65. The number of these units is an indication of the number of households that may be seeking elderly housing units in the coming years.

- **Problem:** To estimate the number of properties that compete with an old office warehouse building in an older part of the city. The appraiser also needs to estimate the square foot area of these competitive properties.

  One solution: The fire department catalogs the different buildings in the city and notes their condition for fire-fighting purposes. Therefore, the fire department may be able to provide the appraiser with a comprehensive list of older warehouse properties.

- **Problem:** To estimate the appropriate timing for the development of a vacant land parcel. To complete the appraisal assignment, the appraiser needs data on where city growth will likely occur over the next 10 to 20 years. In what direction will the city be growing, and when will specific parcels be ready for development?

One solution: Utility companies, telephone companies, and school districts all make long-term projections about the direction and rate of urban growth. These companies have a vital interest in mapping the future growth of an area and are usually quite willing to share their forecast data.

- **Problem:** To estimate the market area of an existing retail shopping center.

One solution: On several randomly selected weekdays and weekends, the appraiser copies down the license plate numbers of cars parked in the competitors' parking lots. Many municipal offices can provide a breakdown of these license plate numbers by geographic area and perhaps even provide the addresses of the vehicle owners.

The Use of Modeling to Refine Data

Another method for generating data is to use a model to refine secondary data into data that satisfy the analyst's specifications. However, an additional element of uncertainty is introduced in applying this method because the secondary data from which the refined data are extracted were not specifically compiled for the model, and faulty assumptions may have been built into the model itself. The analyst must be extremely careful in using this technique.

The following equation, which is a model used for estimating apartment marginal(residual) demand, provides an example of a Level C market forecasting method.

$$(D_{NG} + D_{MU} + V_N) - (CS_V + Sp_{PN}) = D_M$$

Where: D_{NG} = demand from new growth

D_{MU} = move-up demand

V_N = normal vacancy

CS_V = competitive vacant space

Sp_{PN} = planned new supply

D_M = marginal demand, or the net difference between projected growth in demand and supply

The equation provides information about the relationship between demand and supply. One way to test the data inputs in the demand forecast is to apply the same data inputs to historical population data. This is sometimes called *calibration*. The input data from secondary data sources are applied to historical points in time so the known quantities of demand and supply can be compared. For example, assume the subject of the appraisal is an existing apartment building and a market study of future supply and demand is needed to assess its rent and vacancy prospects. The area added 700 apartment units over the last five years and the population increased by 5,000 people. If 5,000 people are forecast to be added to this market over the next five years, and the results of the forecast model do not match what actually occurred in the past, then the data or model may need to be re-examined and refined. The analyst will have to question whether the factors influencing household formation have changed. Is the interest rate so low that the housing mix is changing to single- family units? Is the city restricting new multifamily development? These and similar questions will have to be addressed to lend confidence to the reliability of the model. This technique is sometimes called "calibrating the model."

In another situation, one or more of the input datum may vary in magnitude. For example, one source may say that the population will increase by 10,000 people, while another calls for a 5,000 increase. In this situation, the appraiser can experiment with different scenarios based on assumptions about the variable data input. A range of possible outcomes, with a high end and low end, will be the result.

These and other techniques can be used to generate missing data that are needed to complete the market analysis.

Summary

The analyst generates primary data through interviews with respondents, the use of analogs, or the creation of models with which the analyst runs experiments. Published secondary data are readily available but they are compiled for purposes other than the specific research problem. The analyst should investigate why the secondary data were compiled, the methodology used to gather the data, and how well the area described by the data corresponds to the market area of the subject property.

Level A demand analyses rely entirely on general secondary data for the city or region. The difference between Levels B and C demand analyses depends on the extent to which the appraiser uses primary and secondary data. In Level B analysis, demand is estimated based on secondary data. The area for which the secondary data were compiled does not usually correspond to the specific market area of the subject property. Level C analyses generate primary data for the defined market area which are required to forecast subject-specific demand. Level C techniques that rate or weight the physical, legal, locational, and amenity features of the subject and its competitors can provide the appraiser with greater insight into the competitive position of the subject property. With these insights, the appraiser can form better judgments about absorption rates, prices, rents, and leasing activity.

CHAPTER 11

Evaluating Market Dynamics, Market Conditions, and Marketability

Chapter Objectives

- To explore the dynamics of real estate market cycles and explain why the cyclical patterns in the real estate market are forecast
- To investigate the relationship between the national business cycle and the local real estate cycle
- To describe the underlying causes of long-term and short-term real estate cycles and their interaction
- To explain why it takes the market some time to adjust itself to shifts in supply and demand within real estate market cycles
- To define market conditions and explore why they are evaluated
- To establish a systematic framework for examining market conditions which should enable the analyst to identify the appropriate stage in the real estate market cycle
  - To determine the extent of excess supply or demand in the specific market
  - To evaluate market conditions and determine the direction and intensity of market forces
  - To evaluate how market forces will influence the indicators of value–sales, costs, and income
- To describe marketability analysis as the full six-step process, which culminates in an estimate of occupancy or market capture
- To demonstrate two methods for deriving a capture rate

Introduction

Real estate analysts need to understand the dynamics of market cycles and how these cycles affect real estate demand and value estimates. In this chapter the business cycle and the real estate cycle are described and the fundamental causes of the cycles are investigated. Also examined are the interaction of the national business cycle and local real estate cycles and the mechanisms by which the market adjusts to shifts in supply and demand. With an understanding of these processes, the analyst will be able to determine the impact of market cycles and market conditions on property values.

Reasons for Forecasting Cyclical Patterns in the Market

Real estate markets operate through the dynamic interaction of supply and demand, which can be perceived as cycles of activity. Real estate values are likely to change during different phases of a cycle so analysts must understand and address the effects of these cycles. When supply and demand are out of balance, an excess of supply or demand creates market conditions that cause property values to change. Cyclical activity and market conditions must be examined in all appraisals; if they are not, the value estimate might be misstated. Specifically, market dynamics and market conditions exert major influences on the rate of absorption, the timing of lease-up and sales, and the establishment of sale prices. A forecast of the dynamics of the cycle affecting the subject property is absolutely essential to arrive at a reasonable value opinion.

Business Cycles

The economy tends to move through predictable, recurring stages of business activity. Collectively, these stages constitute the business cycle. There are four stages in the business cycle:

1. Expansion: a period of economic upswing characterized by growing employment, production, and income and basically stable or moderately rising prices.
2. Slowdown, peak and downturn: a period characterized by movement toward full employment and manufacturing capacity, positive but declining rates of economic growth, and a rising rate of inflation. Once the peak of the cycle is attained, the economy begins a moderate downturn, which accelerates and sets the stage for an economic contraction.[1]
3. Contraction: a period of economic downturn characterized by declining employment, production, and income accompanied by price stabilization and then price deflation.

---

1. Economic contraction reflects a composite index of leading and lagging economic indicators, which track phenomena such as the number of bankruptcies, foreclosures, and unemployed workers.

4. Slowed contraction, trough, and upturn: a period characterized by a bottoming out of the economic downturn, stabilized rates of unemployment and unutilized manufacturing capacity, and a slowdown in deflation. Once the trough, or low point, of the cycle is reached, the economy begins a moderate upturn, which accelerates and sets the stage for the next economic expansion.

Shifts in supply and demand over time explain the dynamics of national business cycles. As a simple example, assume that the federal government decides to reduce taxes. The population has more money to spend and the demand for goods and services, relative to the supply, begins to increase. The market responds to the excess of demand over supply, and an expansionary stage in the business cycle occurs. If the government decides to increase taxes, on the other hand, the opposite chain of events will be set in motion.

Relationship Between National and Local Business Cycles

Reverberations from the national business cycle are transmitted to the local economy through the linkages that tie the local economic base to the national economy. Basic industries and employment in the community produce goods and services that are exported to the national market. Thus, as the national economy moves through the phases of a cycle, local employment and local demand are affected.

During an economic expansion, for example, the demand for basic goods and services produced in the community grows. Increased demand results in expansion of basic employment, production, and income in the community. The expansion of employment in basic industries has a multiplier effect, bringing about an expansion in nonbasic employment as well. People seeking employment will move into the community. Conversely, when the national economy contracts, the demand for basic goods and services produced in the community declines. The reduction in demand results in a contraction of the local economy. Employment declines, and ultimately there may be an outward migration as people seek employment in other communities.

The strength of the relationship between the local economic base and the national economy is pivotal. If the local economy is closely tied to the national economy, it will be especially responsive to phases in the national cycle. If, on the other hand, nonbasic employment constitutes the economic base of the community, the local economy will not be seriously affected by changes in the national economy. For example, employment in a small town with a major university depends mainly on the number of students that attend the university. The local economy is largely independent of the national business cycle.

Real Estate Cycles

Like the business cycle, the real estate cycle consists of four stages:

1. Expansion: a period characterized by rising occupancy and absorption rates, increasing prices, and ultimately greater construction and development activity.

2. Slowdown, peak, and downturn: a period characterized by positive, but declining, absorption rates and a slackening of construction and development activity. Prices, which are already high, are rising and occupancy rates remain high. Once the peak of the cycle is attained, absorption rates and construction and development activity begin to decline.

3. Contraction: a period characterized by declining occupancy and absorption rates, decreasing prices, and, ultimately, a falloff in construction and development activity.

4. Slowed contraction, trough, and upturn: a period characterized by a bottoming out of the construction downturn and stabilization of both absorption and occupancy rates. Once the trough, or low point, is reached, the real estate industry begins a moderate upturn, which sets the stage for the next expansion.

The analyst should look for indicators of long- and short-term real estate cycles and attempt to identify the current stage of the cycle.

Long-Term Real Estate Cycles

Long-term, or secular, real estate cycles are primarily a function of nationwide changes in population and income. If the birthrate and real income are rising nationally, demand for real estate will grow. The relationship is simple and direct: a growing population with higher income needs places to live, work and play. If the birthrate and real income are declining nationally, the demand for real estate will fall off.

One example of a long-term real estate cycle is the wave of demand that was unleashed by the post-World War II baby boomers, the generation of individuals born between 1946 and 1966.

A lack of real estate development during the 1930-1945 period had created great pent-up demand. As soldiers returned to civilian life after the war, the rate of household formation picked up. American industry, which had remained productive throughout the war, was converted to peacetime production. Birthrates and incomes both began to rise and real estate demand took off.

As the postwar years wore on, the baby boomers matured. They became a part of the workforce and began to seek housing. Again there was a tremendous surge in the demand for real estate. By the mid 1980s, most of the baby boomers had been absorbed into the workforce, and many had their own homes. The demographic blip began to recede and the unprecedented boom in real estate of the postwar period finally ended.

The relationship between the economic base of a community and a long-term real estate cycle at the local level becomes clear if local growth in population and income is examined vis-à-vis activity in the local real estate market. If the local economy is able to generate new jobs, people seeking employment will move to the area. The types of employment determine the levels of income in the community while the rate of job creation influences the size of the in-migration. Other factors such as climate may also have an impact on the rate of population growth–e.g., the warm Sunbelt states attract many people.

Once real estate has been financed and developed, it becomes a long-term investment. A real estate analyst assesses the long-term health of the local economy by examining the components of the economic base on which long-term growth depends. The analyst will seek answers to questions such as these: Which industries are likely to grow? Which are likely to stagnate? How will these industries influence the long-term, local demand for real estate?

Short-Term Real Estate Cycles

The primary determinants of the short-term demand for real estate are the availability of credit (or capital) and the level of interest rates. In comparison to other types of business and corporate transactions,[2] purchases of real estate generally require a considerable amount of debt financing. Interest represents the price paid for credit. Interest charges, therefore, become a primary concern for real estate investors. The development and acquisition of real estate are extremely sensitive to changes in interest rates. As interest rates rise, the demand for real estate plummets; as rates decline, demand increases. In the first part of this decade, capital abundance created what Sam Zell called "wealth of liquidity."[3] He noted the conversion of oil and natural resources wealth into hard currency, tax cuts, and low interest rates have created a "monetization bubble," which could reshape many previous assumptions about real estate cycles.

Real estate activity, as measured by the number of housing starts, takes the lead in upturns and downturns of the national business cycle because interest rates are responsive to the phases of the business cycle. When the economy is in a trough, interest rates generally bottom out as a result of monetary and fiscal policies aimed at reviving the economy. Real estate is very sensitive to interest rates. Low interest rates, therefore, stimulate real estate activity, which helps lead the economy out of recession. A real estate expansion generally precedes an upturn in general business activity.

Similarly, once an expansionary phase of the business cycle is well underway, interest rates begin to rise, first slowly and then more rapidly. As the business cycle approaches its peak, interest rates rise sharply.

---

2. Leveraged buyouts are a notable exception.

3. Sam Zell, Chairman of Equity Investments. Quoted from an address to the annual meeting of the Counselors of Real Estate (CRE), in Chicago in Spring 2005.

The real estate industry, being especially sensitive to rising interest rates, responds before the general economy. Even before business activity peaks, real estate may begin its downturn, leading the economy into the recession. The sequence is illustrated in Exhibit 11.1. This abstract relationship is valid in theory, but somewhat variable in practice.

Interaction of Long-Term and Short-Term Cycles

The long-term real estate cycle is a function of growth in population and income; the short-term cycle depends on the availability of mortgage credit and the level of interest rates. The short-term cycle, which has a narrower amplitude and a shorter duration, tends to oscillate over the long-term cycle.

Cycles and Time Lags

As short-term shifts in demand and supply produce successive phases of a cycle, time lags will occur as the market attempts to adjust. Real estate markets do not transmit information instantaneously. When there is excess demand, prices and rents begin to rise before the need for new construction is perceived. Once new construction is initiated, another lag will occur because it takes time to complete the building process.

An excess in supply results in an alternative scenario. While prices and rents continue to rise, excess space is being built or coming onto the market. Even after the excess in supply becomes apparent, projects

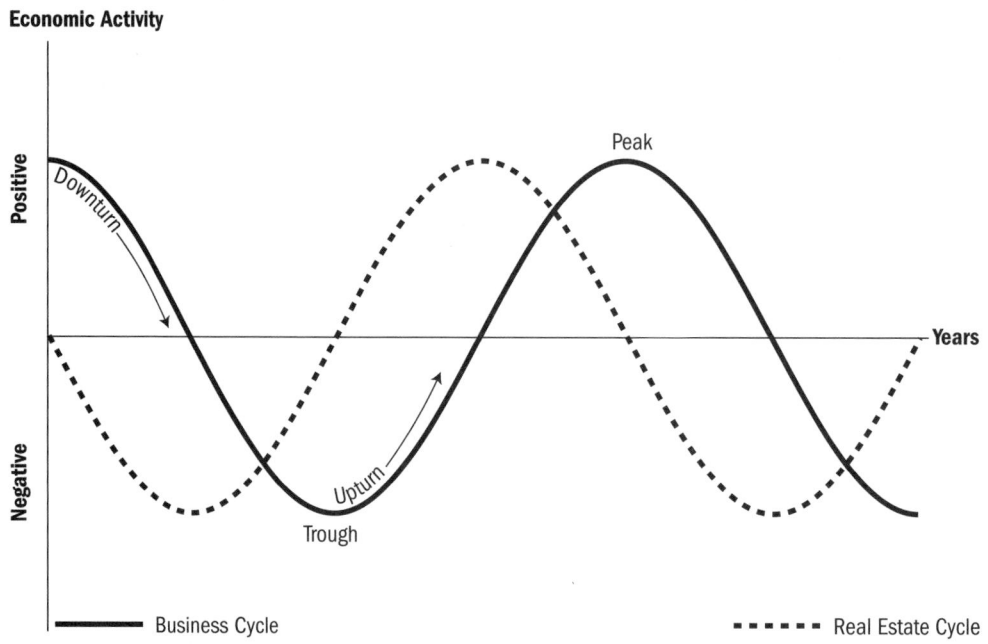

Exhibit 11.1   Relationship Between the Business Cycle and the Short-Term Real Estate Cycle

currently under construction have to be completed, adding still more stock to the existing surplus. Thus the real estate market tends to lag in responding to shifts in supply.

Recognizing the "Bubble" Market

Sale prices go up and down over time. If they fluctuate at a steady rate, then the market is considered normal. However, prices (and rents) very seldom change at the same rate every year. In oversupplied markets, they may go down and then level off for many years. Even when demand exceeds supply, it typically takes two to three years for most market rents to respond to the change and increase. If the market is in a very active job growth cycle or redevelopment is increasing in a city, the rents or sale prices will typically spike—and then level off.

When markets experience very dramatic price spikes for a long period, they are sometimes called "bubbles" in the market. These conditions are not based on real estate fundamentals but on unique situations or motivations in the buy/sell market such as tax avoidance through 1031 exchanges or, more commonly, simple greed. Some buyers think they can resell property to another investor and make big profits. Consider the condo craze in Miami, Chicago, and other major cities in 2004-2005. These markets saw condo construction and sale prices increasing at extremely high rates in spite of the fact that job growth was increasing only slightly if at all. Most buyers were investors who intended to resell the condos for a profit. Bubble markets are based on high investor expectations and are hard to predict. One thing is certain: Over time, the bubble markets will eventually cycle back to fundamental economics. The price paid for real estate over the long term depends on how much the owner can realize in user rents.

Market analysts should be aware of bubble markets because they seem to contradict the fundamental demand data generated in a market study. These phenomena are signs of a bubble markets.

- Rents are not rising at the same rate as prices.
- Buyer is likely an investor looking for a quick re-sell.
- Market indicators, particularly jobs, are not increasing at the same rate as the product being added to the market.
- Hyper-appreciation markets are moving in waves across the country based on quick profit expectations, not changing market fundamentals. For example, some buyers base their judgments primarily on the observation that investors made a lot of money in a particular market last year and they think they should be able to do the same in the local market.
- Multiple buyers are active in the market. For example, in the condo market of 2004, the same entity would buy multiple units.
- Extreme spikes in building permits.
- Sale prices at or above replacement cost.

- High real estate appreciation rates. This is the final, and probably the most conclusive, test. When the newspaper reports how much some real estate appreciated last year and readers say, "That doesn't make sense," the market is probably experiencing a bubble. If the numbers look crazy, they probably are.

Market Conditions (Residual Demand Analysis)

The term *market conditions* refers to the imbalance between supply and demand in the market. When the demand for a particular property type exceeds the available supply, real estate buyers will bid prices and rents upwards. When the supply of property exceeds the demand, downward pressure will be exerted on prices and rents. In either case, appraisers must consider market conditions in analyzing comparable sales, rents, occupancy, and construction costs.

Identifying, evaluating, and forecasting market conditions are essential for the following reasons:

- Market conditions determine the period over which the appraisal may be valid. If market conditions are stable, the appraisal may be valid for an extended period of time. If conditions are changing rapidly, the appraisal will be reliable for a shorter period. When estimating property value, an appraiser should specify the period for which the estimated value is expected to be valid or the period within which the property is expected to sell.
- The rate of absorption for new properties is a function of market conditions. If demand exceeds supply, absorption should be rapid. When excess supply exists, absorption will be slow. The appraiser must also estimate the holding, marketing, and lease-up costs incurred over the anticipated absorption period. In oversupplied markets, appraisers can adjust the property value estimates indicated by the cost approach to compensate for the reduction in value attributable to shifts in supply and demand.[4]
- The extent of excess demand or excess supply determines the direction and rate of change in prices, rents, occupancy and costs. An understanding of the demand and supply relationship helps the appraiser forecast cash flows and probable sale prices more accurately.
- Finally, market conditions must be identified to arrive at adjustments in the sales comparison approach. The sale data on which the appraiser relies all reflect previous transactions. If market conditions have changed, the appraiser must adjust the comparable sale prices to bring them into line with what the properties would sell for today.

---

4. This is referred to as an adjustment for *external obsolescence*. The term *externality* is used by economists to refer to a cost or benefit that accrues to someone other than the person who created it when no contractual agreement exists to allow one party to compensate the other. An externality may also be caused by factors outside the market—e.g., the air pollution generated by automobiles.

Market conditions may be evaluated in three steps:

1. Identify the appropriate market segment by both property type and geographic area.
2. Identify the current stage of the real estate cycle and an appropriate time frame for the cycle. Typically, the appraiser seeks to estimate a current sale price, so the short-term real estate cycle will usually be considered.
3. Identify the supply and demand conditions prevailing in the market–e.g., excess demand, excess supply, market balance.

Equipped with an understanding of market conditions, the appraiser is ready to apply the information in reconciling value indications and estimating a final value. Three critical items must be considered.

1. The time frame for the demand-supply forecast
   - What is the relevant time frame for the demand-supply forecast and the value estimate?
   - In what stage of the cycle is the current market?
   - How will the cycle change within the time frame?
2. Current and forecasted demand-supply conditions
   - Does an excess in demand or supply exist today ? If so, how great is the excess?
   - Is excess demand or supply expected in the future? If so, how much and when?
   - What are the short- and long-term consequences of excess demand?
   - What are the effects on prices, rents, absorption, and vacancies?
   - What are the short- and long-term consequences of excess supply?
   - What are the effects on prices, rents, absorption, and vacancies?
3. How do market conditions relate to the value of the subject property?
   - How does the local real estate cycle relate to the value of the subject property?

Marketability Analysis

A subject property is affected by the overall market demand and dynamics, but any specific property can perform better or worse than the overall market. Marketability analysis explains why this happens.

A marketability analysis is a demand and competition study for a specific property. In contrast, a market analysis encompasses the demand for and supply of all competitive properties. Robert Dunham, MAI, explains it like this: "Market study is a use in search of a site, while marketability study is a site in search of a use."[5]

A marketability study must encompass a market study because the market study establishes the market demand and sets the competitive tone for a specific property's prospects for capturing the demand.

---

5. Robert Dunham is an Appraisal Institute course developer and instructor.

A marketability study is defined as:

The process that investigates how a particular piece of property will be absorbed, sold, or leased under current or anticipated market conditions; includes a market study or analysis of the general class of property being studied.[6]

The marketability study culminates with an estimate of occupancy and the projected rents for the subject, which are usually calculated by multiplying demand by the capture rate.

Capture rate is defined as:

The estimated percentage of the total potential market for a specific type of property. .....Short-term capture is referred to as *absorption;* long-term capture is referred to as *share of the market.*[7]

Other terms that have basically the same meaning include *market penetration* and *market share:* these terms refer to a particular property's amount of sales or occupancy based on the market demand.

The capture rate of the subject property is derived by comparing its competitive attributes to the attributes of all the competitive properties in the area competing for the same market demand.

Related terms that are sometimes confused with *marketability study* are *market residual demand* and *market gap analysis.* Residual demand is the measure of unmet (or over-met) demand in the market area; it is not property-specific. Gap analysis is usually used to describe the market residual demand for a very specific segment of a market, say jewelry stores, but is not specific to a particular property.

Marketability Analysis and Valuation

Property productivity analysis of site, legal, and location attributes provides the link between the subject property and the market. The marketability study connects the subject property to the market by measuring the difference between the subject property's productivity attributes and the competition's. This analysis forms the basis of the subject property's forecast of future revenues. Valuation is most concerned with the present value of future benefits so this becomes the heart of the valuation study.

All appraisers complete a marketability study whether they formally document it or not. A revenue forecast in the income capitalization approach is a marketability conclusion. The estimate of economic obsolescence in the cost approach is another marketability conclusion. The selection of comparable properties and their comparison in the sales comparison approach also requires marketability conclusions.

Marketability Analysis and the Six-Step Process

The marketability analysis encompasses the market analysis. The marketability analysis includes Steps 1 through Step 6, in which the analyst compares the subject to the competition and completes the

---

6. *The Dictionary of Real Estate Appraisers,* 4th ed. (Chicago: Appraisal Institute, 2002).

7. Ibid.

final quantification. Steps 2 through 5 of the six-step process is the market analysis.

The whole six-step process can be considered the marketability study because it is focused on the subject from the beginning. The process starts with the subject, defining the property type and scope of the market analysis. All the market analysis supply and demand estimates are based on the subject type property and the market it specifically serves. The more precise the market segmentation, the more reliable is the final step in the process—the forecast of subject capture.

Subject Capture Rate

The concept of the capture rate is illustrated with the following example. Assume the subject is one of 10 properties in the market competing for apartment renters. The market has an estimated demand of 1,000 renters. If the *subject is equal to all other competitive apartment projects* in terms of property productivity attributes and all the apartment projects charge the same amount of rent, then the market penetration for the subject and the competitive properties should be equal. In this case, the subject capture rate would be calculated as a pro rata share as follows:

Total competitive properties including the subject =	10
Subject is equal thus its capture rate would be:	10% (1 divided by 10)
Total market demand is:	1,000 renters
Then subject current occupancy should be:	100 renters
1,000 renters × 10% capture =	100 renters

If the subject is not equal to all the other competitive properties, however, the pro rata capture rate needs to be adjusted.

A good place to start is the current actual capture rate. Using the last example, if the subject's actual occupancy was 70 renters, then the subject's actual current capture rate would be 7% (70 divided by 1000). The next step is to analyze the current actual capture rate and what the potential capture rate could or should be in the future. This adjustment is based on detailed comparisons with competitive properties. In a full Level C analysis, these comparisons involve a quantifiable rating of the subject compared to the competition to determine the subject's competitive advantage (or disadvantage). In such an analysis, the focus is on the factors that have the greatest impact on revenue, since this has the biggest impact on value. The marketability study includes the overall market analysis because revenue depends not only on how competitive the property is, but how much demand there is in the market for the property type. All of the application chapters in Parts II and III of this book have detailed examples of competitive rating techniques.

Long-Term and Short-Term Capture Rates

Capture rates can vary over the life of the property. Often short-term capture rates for a new property are higher than long-term rates. New properties may have higher capture rates for several reasons.

- New properties are vacant and they have more space to offer the user market. (This factor is most evident in a growing market.)
- Customers go to a new retail center just to see what it is like–i.e., the "novelty effect."
- New properties usually have the best current location in the area.
- New buildings have less functional obsolescence.

Two Alternative Capture Methods

There are two different capture methods–capture from total demand and capture from new demand in the market. These methods have significantly different implications. A property's current capture rate is calculated as the current occupied space in the subject property divided by the occupied space in the market. If this current capture rate is forecast to be the same in the future, the capture method implies that the subject will not "steal tenants" from competitive properties. However, if the conclusion is that the subject capture rate will increase in the future, then the implication is that the subject will steal tenants. This second, "steal tenants" conclusion becomes significant because it determines which demand line is used in the capture calculation. If the analyst decides that the subject will capture some demand from existing tenants, then the capture rate needs to be applied to total demand. On the other hand, if the analyst decides the subject will only capture demand from the new tenants entering the market, then the capture rate is applied to new demand only. The methods provide significantly different results.

Consider the following example. Assume the subject property is a 100,000-sq.-ft. retail center, currently 68% occupied. Given the competition, the subject is capturing about 25% of the market demand. However, the analyst's future capture analysis concluded that it should capture 30% of market demand in the future. Different future subject occupancy forecasts will be derived depending on the capture method used.

Capture Method 1—Capture From Total Demand

The major assumption of this capture method is that the subject can "steal" existing tenants from other competitive properties. Thus, the capture rate is applied to total demand (Line 1) to derive the percentage of subject occupancy (see Exhibit 11.2). Using this capture method, the subject property will be 99% occupied in 10 years.

Capture Method 2—Capture from New Demand Only

This method assumes that the subject center and all competing centers will maintain their current tenant base (i.e., current occupancy amount) and additional tenants (occupancy) will come only from new demand in the market. Exhibit 11.3 shows the subject future occupancy forecast derived using this capture method. Now the subject only reaches 86% occupancy in 10 years. When the first method was applied, subject occupancy of 99% was forecast.

Exhibit 11.2 Property Marketability by Total Market Capture

Line	Year	Current	In 5 Yrs.	In 10 Yrs.
1	Total forecast demand for occupied space in sq. ft.	270,000	300,000	330,000
2	Less existing sq. ft. of competitive space	330,000	330,000	330,000
3	Less forecasted new competition	0	0	0
4	Market residual demand in sq. ft. (Line 1 minus Lines 2 & 3)	-60,000	-30,000	0
5	Market occupancy rate	82%	91%	100%
6	Subject capture rate applied to total demand	25.185%	30%	30%
7	Subject forecasted sq. ft. occupied (Line 1 times Line 6)	68,000	90,000	99,000
8	Subject percentage occupied	68%	90%	99%

Exhibit 11.3 Property Marketability by New Demand Capture Method

Line	Year	Current	In 5 Yrs.	In 10 Yrs.
1	Total forecast demand for occupied space in market in sq. ft.	270,000	300,000	330,000
2	Less existing sq. ft. of competitive space	330,000	330,000	330,000
3	Less forecasted new competition	0	0	0
4	Market residual demand in sq. ft. (Line 1 minus Lines 2 & 3)	-60,000	-30,000	0
5	Market occupancy rate	82%	91%	100%
6	New demand in sq. ft.	NA	30,000	30,000
7	Subject capture rate applied to new demand	NA	30%	30%
8	Subject forecasted sq. ft. occupied (Line 6 times Line 7 plus previous year occupancy)	68,000	77,000	86,000
9	Subject percentage occupied	68%	77%	86%

Often the second method–capture of new demand only–is applied to new construction. The subject starts with 0% occupancy and only captures from new demand. In this situation, the second method would be considered a very conservative marketability method.

Different situation will require different methods. The important point is to recognize the different implications of each method.

Levels of Marketability Analysis
The examples shown and the focus of this book is a Level C analysis, which is a fundamental demand forecast. More detail would be found in a Level D analysis. There could be variations of the amount of detail in a Level C marketability analysis.

Marketability Analysis without a Competitive Property Inventory (Partial Level C Analysis)
In a partial Level C marketability analysis, the demand side is forecast but the supply side is limited due to a lack of data. Even with limited competitive data, marketability analysis can be completed to meet a "reasonableness test." Assume the following data are available:

- The total market demand is 170,000 square feet.
- The subject current occupancy is 68,000 square feet. Using these data, the current capture rate can be calculated.

Subject current market capture rate = 40% (68,000 sq. ft./170,000 sq. ft.)

- The competition is estimated in general by driving around the neighborhood and counting the number of centers. Their square feet areas are not known, but general judgments can be made about center sizes, quality, and tenant types.

Precise marketability analysis conclusions cannot be derived from these data alone. However, general reasonableness can be determined. If the subject is one of three centers in this neighborhood competing for retail demand, and it captures 40% of the market, it is capturing more than its pro rata share, which would be 33% of the market assuming all the centers are of equal size and tenant types. Since the subject's actual capture rate is 40%, something about the subject is superior to the competition. The appraiser determines if this is a reasonable conclusion to use in a forecast. For example, if the subject is larger than either of the other two competitive centers, but its tenants are similar, the 40% capture rate is reasonable. Based on these type of observations in the market, the analyst can make general judgments about whether the current capture rate will change or stay the same in the future.

Marketability Analysis with a Competitive Property Inventory (Full Level C Analysis)

A full Level C marketability analysis would include a complete inventory of competitive space with the total square feet area of each center. It would not include the detail of a Level D study, which would have an inventory of the competition by each tenant type as well. The general study procedure for a full Level C marketability study is:

- Calculate the subject's current capture.
- Calculate the subject's pro rata capture share.
- Complete a detailed, quantifiable competitive property rating comparison. (See application chapters for examples.)
- Survey market participants (e.g., leasing agents).
- Reconcile the studies into a forecasted capture rate- usually with a range.

Marketability Analysis with a Detailed Competitive Property Inventory (Level D Analysis)

A Level D marketability analysis includes Level C analysis plus Level D techniques. Such an analysis can include many different studies, but most Level D analyses center around retail "customer penetration studies."[8] These types of studies require customer exit survey data and/or

---

8. Examples of customer penetration studies can be found in *Market Research for Shopping Centers* (New York: International Council of Shopping Centers, 2005), 29.

loyalty card data as well as analysis of the customers' locations and purchasing amounts by location in the trade area. These data are compared to the calculated potential retail sales in the trade area and actual sales reported in sources such as the sales tax data. This type of study can give a very accurate measurement of a store's current capture overall, by location, and by age, ethnicity, and income groups.

Summary

Real estate market activity is cyclical and subject to the effects of both national business cycles and real estate cycles. As the market adjusts to changing conditions over the successive stages of a cycle, supply and demand shift. Business cycles are characterized by four stages: 1) expansion; 2) slowdown, peak, and downturn; 3) contraction; and 4) slowed contraction, trough, and upturn. The effects of a national business cycle are transmitted to the local economy through the linkages that tie the national economy to the basic industry and employment base of the community.

The real estate cycle passes through four comparable stages. The two types of real estate cycles are long-term, or secular, cycles which reflect long-term trends in population and income, and short-term cycles, which are generated by the availability of credit and the level of interest rates. Real estate activity generally responds to an increase or decline in interest rates before the overall economy. Thus real estate activity may be considered a leading indicator of economic trends. Generally the real estate market does not readily adjust to short-term shifts in supply and demand and construction activity lags.

An understanding of market conditions is essential to 1) determine the period for which an appraisal may be valid, 2) estimate the rate of absorption, 3) forecast the direction and rate of change in prices, rents, and costs, and 4) estimate the adjustment for market conditions in the sales comparison approach.

A marketability analysis is conducted to forecast how a particular property will perform under current and anticipated market conditions. Such a study encompasses market analysis plus an additional sixth step–the forecast of market capture.

A capture rate can be derived by applying one of two methods. The capture rate can be calculated from total demand or from new demand only. Some marketability analysis may be performed in a Level C analysis but a full marketability analysis with a detailed competitive property inventory would usually be part of a Level D analysis.

Market Analysis Applications

In Part II of this book, the six-step market analysis process for valuation appraisals is demonstrated using three sample applications. Every appraisal typically includes an inferred market analysis or trend analysis, and many appraisal problems also require fundamental analysis. The examples provided here primarily illustrate fundamental analysis. Although only brief coverage is given to inferred analysis, it is an integral part of any complete study.

The difference between fundamental and inferred analysis is discussed at length in Chapter 2 of Part I. In preparing a fundamental, forecast-oriented market analysis, the analyst segments demand and competition in the subject submarket and ranks the marketability attributes of the subject against those of its competition. Fundamental, forecast-oriented studies emphasize micro-market analysis, while inferred studies rely on historical data and focus on macro-market analysis. All appraisal assignments differ. For some appraisals, inferred market analysis is adequate, but many assignments require both methods of analysis.

The three applications in the following chapters pertain to existing properties and present case studies of market analyses appraising a community shopping center, an office building, and a multitenanted apartment complex. Each chapter begins with a discussion of concepts unique to the specific property type, followed by a step-by-step analysis of the market for the subject property. Lastly, the findings of the market analysis are put to use in the appraisal. Many of the tables that appear in these applications can be found on the CD at the back of the book.

The market or marketability analysis section of an appraisal is discussed here,[1] but a complete appraisal is not presented. Most apprais-

---

1. The term *market analysis* or *marketability analysis* is used in this book to describe the process of forecasting the revenues and expenses of a property to estimate its market value. Other terms for this forecasting process are *feasibility* or *economic feasibility study, market* or *market demand study,* and *financial projection study.* These studies generally produce similar results.

als include an economic overview of the broad market for the subject market and a description of the subject property, which precede the market and marketability analysis section of the report.

The basic six-step process presented in the case study applications for performing a market analysis entails the following steps:

1. Property productivity analysis. The analyst examines the productivity attributes of the subject property. These are the features that shape the productive capabilities and potential uses of the property, i.e., its physical, legal, locational, and amenity attributes. Identifying the potential uses of the property enables the analyst to target potential users or the specific market segment to which the property is most likely to appeal.

2. Specification of the market of most probable property users. The analyst pinpoints the precise market segment to establish the behavioral components of market demand.

3. Demand analysis and forecast. The analyst estimates existing and anticipated market demand by examining population and employment data based on economic base analysis.[2]

4. Competitive supply analysis and forecast. An inventory of existing and anticipated supply is developed to establish marginal demand.

5. Supply and demand relationship. Supply and demand are compared to determine whether marginal demand exists or to forecast when the market is expected to move out of equilibrium.

6. The capture estimate for the subject. The analyst ranks the productive attributes of the subject property against those of competitive properties considering market conditions, demand, and the competitive supply. This ranking is used to forecast the market share the subject is likely to capture.

The data studied and the conclusions reached in the analysis are used in the appraisal to test alternative highest and best use conclusions and in applying the three valuation approaches. The appraiser may also draw on components of the market analysis to develop a final value conclusion in the reconciliation.

---

2. Time and budgetary constraints typically prevent the analyst from investigating all the demand-side variables in a market study. It is imperative that the analyst select the variables most relevant to the assignment.

CHAPTER 12

Existing Retail Shopping Center

Chapter Objectives

- To define the retail shopping center and describe its trends
- To describe the principal types of retail shopping centers
- To discuss the concept "trade area"
- To introduce the market analysis process for a shopping center using a case study approach
- To explain how to use conclusions derived from the market analysis to test highest and best uses

Introduction

This chapter presents a step-by-step procedure and techniques for performing a market analysis as part of a valuation appraisal of an existing retail shopping center. First, trends in retail shopping centers, then concepts and terms unique to retail properties will be discussed. Next, an overview of the analytical process will be provided. Finally, the process will be applied to the appraisal of a specific retail subject, discussing each step in detail. The application presented is a Level C fundamental market analysis. The procedure described is only one of the many variations that could be applied. The analytical techniques used depend on the characteristics of the subject property, the market conditions on the date of the appraisal, the availability of data, the needs of the client, and the judgment and experience of the appraiser.

Trends in Retail Shopping Centers

A shopping center is a tract of land, under individual or joint real estate ownership or control, improved with a coordinated group of retail buildings that contain a variety of stores and offer free parking.[1] In recent years individual supercenters have emerged with full-line grocery, department store, auto, nursery, and convenience items (all under one roof) and function as a shopping center. Thus, in this book the term *shopping center* refers to the traditional multitenant shopping center and other one-store concepts that function similarly to or compete with a traditional shopping center. The key is that shopping centers are planned and managed as a unit, and their location, size, and retail mix are determined by the trade area they serve.

Until the mid-twentieth century, retail activity in the United States was concentrated in the downtown areas of cities and towns. After World War II the production and use of the automobile increased significantly and along with government programs like the interstate highway system and new government housing programs contributed to the change in urban development patterns toward the suburbs. Consequently, retail activity has been dispersed throughout metropolitan regions and into specialized areas and outlying centers.

The nature of retail activity continues to change. During the 1960s and 1970s, the retail trend was toward enclosed malls. The 1980s brought a dispersion of neighborhood and community centers throughout the metropolitan areas. The 1990s introduced the power center, a concept that included a number of major stores and very little small in-line space. The 1990s were also the advent of the entertainment center, a mix of retail, restaurants, and entertainment. Entertainment ranged from restaurants, to movie houses, to massive game rooms, the idea being that kids would lure their parents to the center so that the retailers could entice them to part with their money. The outlet mall, a large concentration of major retail stores selling their seconds merchandise also came during this time. Typically, these stores were located on the outskirts of major metropolitan areas that serve a large trade area.

A trend that emerged about 2000 was the stand-alone community department store, which located full-line department stores in neighborhoods. These stores usually carried economically priced merchandise.

Another significant trend of the 2000s was the lifestyle center, whose aim is to attract higher-income shoppers through convenience and tenant mix. The likely tenant types at lifestyle centers are more upscale/specialty stores such as home furnishings, women's fashion, bookstores and restaurants, and some major department store anchors.

The lifestyle center is designed as an open-air mall where shoppers can drive up to the stores. These centers typically vary in size from 300,000 to 500,000 square feet. The upscale architectural design is intended to create a nostalgic experience, the goal being to create a downtown shopping experience reminiscent of the 1940s and 1950s. This

---

1. *The Dictionary of Real Estate Appraisal,* 4th ed. (Chicago: Appraisal Institute, 2002).

open-air center has proven to be successful in the cold climates of the North as well as the hot humid climates of the South. This type of center has also proven to be economical, as typical sales for the first half of 2005 were about $298 per square foot compared to about $245 for traditional regional malls. Higher dollars per visit, along with lower operating costs have made lifestyle centers very attractive.

Another trend in recent years represents competition for community shopping–the discount store supercenters. These stores of about 180,000 square feet offer similar merchandise to large community shopping centers.

It was once thought that Internet sales would outstrip the demand for bricks-and-mortar stores. However, at least at this time, they have not fulfilled this prediction. Internet retail sales in the United States are indicated in Exhibit 12.1, based on a February 2003 report issued by the U.S. Bureau of the Census derived from data from 11,000 surveys disseminated by the *Monthly Retail Trade Survey*. The sales exclude travel tickets, securities, and event ticket sales.

Exhibit 12.1   Internet Retail Sales in the U.S.

Year	Internet Sales (in Billions)	Percentage Change	Share of Total U.S. Retail Sales
1999	$15.0	-	.5%
2000	$28.9	92.3%	.9%
2001	$35.9	24.2%	1.0%
2002	$45.5	26.5%	1.3%

Source: U.S. Census

At each step in the appraisal process, the appraiser must remember that retail centers have changed in the past and will continue to do so. Their dynamics may depend on changes in linkages to demand and product distribution, in demographics, or in retail marketing techniques. Consequently, the changing nature of retail centers forces analysts to reconsider their criteria for each assignment.

The challenge is to assess how the shopping center being valued compares with competitive properties, both existing and anticipated. Although current competition may be investigated directly, future competition requires more study because of the ever-changing nature of shopping centers.

General Concepts

The first concept to understand about retail market analysis is to realize that a shopping center cannot create new demand. It can only harvest customers from four methods:

- Attracting them from other competing businesses in the trade area because of better linkages (ease of access) to them
- Providing products that other centers do not provide

- Filling a vacuum created by obsolete buildings or the competition's marketing weaknesses
- Realizing sales growth from new sources of demand entering the trade area

The second major concept is for appraisers to realize that, traditionally, retail has followed, rather than led, community growth. A shopping center is like a magnet—the more customers it can attract, the better it will be. Thus, it needs households and linkages to those households (or other demand sources).

The next concept to understand is that the ability of a shopping center to capture a share of market demand depends on the size of its trade area and how it compares to its competition in terms of the merchandise it offers and its linkages to customers. Thus, the market analyst must also consider the existing competition as well as planned and potential competition.

The retail cluster is another important concept. Clustering may result when stores that sell similar goods (e.g., auto dealerships, furniture, and appliance stores along arterial streets) locate near each other to offer customers a wider selection. Although they sell similar goods, consumers can differentiate their products, and the storeowners believe that the benefits of increased consumer traffic outweigh the negative effects of proximity to competitors. This concept is also called the principle of cumulative attraction,[2] which recognizes that a location in a retail cluster with similar but not identical retailers attracts more customer traffic than a single retailer would. The benefits of increased customer traffic outweigh the negative effects of the store's proximity to possible competitors.

Shopping centers represent another type of retail cluster. A shopping center usually contains stores that do not directly compete with one another, although some stores may sell products that are close substitutes.

Finally, the drawing power of dominant centers is subject to the principle of interception, or the principle of intervening opportunities, which recognizes that most shoppers will not bypass a dominant center to get to a subordinate center.

These and other concepts show how shopping centers differ from other types of real estate. Moreover, the principles and concepts underlying the operation of shopping centers are not static. Additional specialty stores and a broader product mix in community centers, for example, may counteract the effects of the principle of interception.

The appraiser's dilemma is apparent. In appraising a shopping center, he or she must consider whether or not the subject real estate is still competitive today and is likely to be in the future. If the subject is on the verge of becoming outdated, comparable sales that are two or three years old may be of little use. The subject's historic income may be misleading because future income may be declining. Major renovation or alternative uses may have to be considered. Thus, under-

---

2. Richard L. Nelson, *The Selection of Retail Locations* (New York: F.W. Dodge, 1958).

standing the retail business and the real estate product (the shopping center) that houses it is the key to estimating the subject's value.

Types of Shopping Centers

Shopping centers are usually classified according to two criteria: their size in square feet of gross leasable area (GLA) and their tenantry. In this discussion, tenantry is synonymous with products sold or services rendered. A subcategory of tenantry is the anchor or principal tenant and the tenant mix. Secondary criteria are drive time and customer base.

The principal determiners of the type of shopping center are the tenants, the products sold, and whether they are convenience goods, shopper goods, or specialty goods. Determining the type of center is critical to the market study. The type of center establishes the customer category and the distance to which the customer will travel to it. The customer type and location determine, in large part, the trade area. The trade area sets the limits of the demand calculations. Consequently, the leading edge of the market study is the type of shopping center, as it delineates the trade area.

There are generally two major classifications of shopping centers: convenience goods centers and shopper goods centers. Shopper goods centers are general merchandise stores that sell apparel and accessories, furniture, and home furnishings. They include discount stores and other specialty stores. The industry code for these types of stores is GAFO,[3] which represents sales at stores that sell merchandise normally sold in department stores. The acronym stands for General Merchandise, Apparel, Furnishings and Other. Convenience stores include supermarkets and other food stores, drugstores, home improvement stores, and hardware stores. The supercenter (discount stores) marketing concept includes both shopper goods and convenience goods stores.

Centers that specialize in selling primarily shopper goods find that their customers come from greater distances than those for retail facilities that primarily sell convenience goods.

Traditional shopping centers include convenience centers; neighborhood, community, regional, and superregional shopping centers; and specialty or theme centers. Variations and new types of centers are continually evolving. Some examples are off-price outlets and discount centers, festival shopping centers, lifestyle centers, supercenters, hypermarts, supermalls, power centers and thoroughfare- or highway-related commercial developments. (See Exhibit 12.2, Principal Types of Shopping Centers.)

Trade Area(s) Concept Defined

The trade area is defined as the geographic area from which a retail facility consistently draws most of its customers (also called market

---

3. GAFO stores include General Merchandise Stores (NAICS 452); Clothing and Accessories (NAICS 448); Furniture and Home Furnishings (NAICS 442); Electronics and Appliance Stores (NAICS 443); Sporting Goods, Hobby, Book and Music Stores (NAICS 451); Office Supplies, Stationery and Gift Stores (NAICS 453).

Exhibit 12.2   Principal Types of Shopping Centers

Type	Tenantry	Size	Trade Area
Convenience center	Stores that sell convenience goods, e.g., groceries, pharmaceutical; not anchored by a supermarket	Less than 30,000 sq. ft.	Less than 5-minute driving time
Neighborhood shopping center	Stores that sell convenience goods and stores that provide personal services, e.g., dry cleaning, shoe repair; a supermarket is often the principal tenant	30,000 to 150,000 sq. ft. of gross leasable area; 4 to 10 acres	Less than 5-minute driving time; 1 to 1½-mile range; 5,000 to 40,000 potential customers
Community shopping center	Stores that sell convenience goods, personal services, and shopper goods, e. g., apparel, appliances; a junior department store or off-price/ discount store is often the principal tenant; other tenants include variety or super drugstores and home improvement centers	100,000 to 300,000 sq. ft. of gross leasable area; 10 to 30 acres (includes mini-malls)	5- to 20-minute driving time; 3- to 6-mile range; 40,000 to 150,000 potential customers
Regional shopping center	Stores that sell general merchandise, shopper goods, and convenience goods; one or more department stores are the principal tenants	300,000 to 1,000,000 sq. ft. of gross leasable area; 30 acres; contains one or more department stores of at least 100,000 sq. ft.	20- to 40-minute driving time; 5- to 10-mile range; 150,000 to 400,000 potential customers
Superregional shopping center	Stores that sell general merchandise, apparel, furniture, home furnishings, and services as well as recreational facilities	Over 800,000 sq. ft. of gross leasable area; contains at least three major department stores of at least 100,000 sq. ft. each	In excess of 30-minute driving time; typically 10- to 35-mile range; over 500,000 potential customers
Specialty, or theme center	Boutiques and stores that sell design items, craft wares, and gourmet foods; a high-profile specialty shop is often the principal tenant; festival malls and fashion centers are types of theme centers	Same range as a neighborhood or community shopping center	Similar to that of a regional shopping center
Lifestyle centers	Stores that sell upscale home furnishings, women's fashion, department stores and restaurants	300,000 to 500,000	Similar to regional shopping center
Power center	A minimum of three, but usually five or more, anchor tenants that are dominant in their categories	Typically open-air centers of more than 250,000 square feet; almost all space designed for large tenants	A minimum of 15 miles—typically a 20-minute range and a population of 400,000 to 500,000
Off-price outlet and discount center	Name brand outlet stores and/or wholesale grocery and hardware stores	60,000 to 400,000 sq. ft.	Similar to superregional center
Strip commercial (a continuous row or strip along a main thoroughfare)	Convenience stores, fast-food restaurants, car dealerships, and service stations	Varies according to trade area	Neighborhood or community
Highway commercial	Motels, restaurants, truck stops, service stations; may stand as a single establishment within a cluster of other highway-related service facilities	Varies	Passing motorists in need of highway-related services

area).[4] The definition's focus is on the origination of most of the subject's customers and sales. However, for the market residual demand study, the competition must also be considered. In some instances, retail properties have two market areas: 1) the origination point of most of the customers and 2) the location of most of the competition. Thus, the trade/market study area, in practice, is usually combined, forming the overall market study area as defined by ULI: the geographic region from which the majority of demand and the majority of competition are located.[5]

The extent of this area is the result of many factors, among them accessibility, the extent of physical barriers, the location of competing facilities, and drive time. The usual focus of the market study is the primary trade area, which is a subset of the trade area, defined as "the geographic area around a retail facility from which approximately 60% to 70% of the facility's customers are drawn."[6] Some sources say 70% to 85%. Regardless, this is the area where most of the customer/sales originate for the subject center.

The next layer of the trade area is called the secondary trade area where about 15% to 20% of the sales are generated. The last layer is the tertiary trade area, where an additional 5% to 10% of sales are generated. For a typical center this accounts for about 95% of sales; the sales from other various sources usually are not well defined. The customer base for each layer of the trade area(s) can reside in these areas or can be derived from nonresident groups in the area such as daytime employees, tourists, and other groups who live outside the area but who regularly frequent the subject trade area.

Different types of shopping centers have distinctly different tenant compositions and trade areas (see Exhibit 12.3). The general guidelines for delineating the trade areas shown in Exhibit 12.3 must be modified to fit the characteristics of the specific shopping center, pri-

Exhibit 12.3	Trade Area Breakdown by Total Sales and Driving Time		
	Primary	**Secondary**	**Tertiary**
	The geographic area immediately adjacent to the facility from which approximately 60% to 80% of its customers are derived	The geographic area adjacent to the primary trade area from which an additional 20% to 40% sales/customers customer's are derived	The farthest outlying segment of the trade area from which the remaining percentage of the facility's sales/customers are derived
Neighborhood shopping centers	Under 5 minutes	5 to 15 minutes	
Community shopping centers	5 to 20 minutes	20 to 35 minutes	
Regional shopping centers	20 to 40 minutes	40 to 60 minutes	
Superregional shopping centers	More than 40 minutes		

4. Adrienne Schmitz and Deborah L. Brett, *Real Estate Market Analysis: A Case Study Approach.* (Washington D.C.: ULI- Urban Land Institute, 2001).

5. Ibid.

6. Ibid.

marily as they relate to the type of products sold and the factors in the area that will dictate linkages to its customers. Detailed discussion on procedures for defining the trade area is presented in the following section on Step 2, Market Delineation.

Some important industry terms pertaining to shopping centers are defined below:

Building Terms	
Gross leasable area (*GLA*)	The total floor area rented to tenants, including basements and mezzanines. Gross leasable area is measured from the outside wall surface to the center of interior partitions.
Gross building area (*GBA*)	Gross leasable area plus all common areas.
Gross sales area (*GSA*)	Gross leasable area minus storage and work areas.
Sales per square foot	The annual store sales divided by the floor area that generates the sales. The number is used in the market analysis calculation to convert economic data to real estate. It is important to identify the type of floor area measurement used in the economic data. The Urban Land Institute's *Dollars and Cents of Shopping Centers* uses sales per gross leaseable area to the tenant (GLA).
Common area	The total area within a property that is not intended for sale or rent but is available for common use by all owners, tenants, or their customers, e.g., mallways, parking, and restrooms; not included in gross leasable area.
Parking area	The area of a facility designated for parking employees' and customers' cars, including parking surface, aisles, stalls, and islands.
Parking ratio	The ratio of parking area to GFA or GLA. This figure is used only as a rough estimation of the parking area needed.
Parking index	The number of car parking spaces per 1,000 square feet of GLA.

The Market Analysis Process for a Retail Shopping Center

Exhibit 12.4 is an overview of a fundamental, Level C market analysis of a shopping center. The six-step process includes analysis of the subject property, analysis of the subject's trade area, an estimate of existing and potential demand, an inventory of competitive supply, analysis of market equilibrium, and the estimated subject capture. The market analysis provides essential data used in the three approaches to value. Each of the six steps is divided further into sub-steps. For example, the nine sub-steps of Step 3.2, identified as Steps 3.2(1) through 3.2(9), describe the segmentation process used to estimate demand in the retail center's primary and secondary trade areas. The case study application follows the sequence of steps shown in Exhibit 12.4.

Introduction to Case Study

The case study that follows is an application of the six-step process to a valuation appraisal of a specific retail property. General procedures for each step are introduced and applied to the case study. The purpose of the case study is to lend support to the highest and best use

Exhibit 12.4   The Market Analysis Process for a Shopping Center

Step 1: Analyze the subject property (property productivity).

    1.1 Analyze the site and building for competitive strengths and weaknesses.

    1.2 Analyze the location of the subject property.

        1.2(1)   Investigate land use(s) and the linkages of the subject property.

        1.2(2)   Determine the position of the subject property within the patterns of urban growth.

        1.2(3)   Identify the location of the competitive supply.

        1.2(4)   Rate the subject location in comparison with competing areas.

Step 2: Analyze the market of users.

    2.1 Define the trade area.

    2.2 Profile customer characteristics.

Step 3: Forecast demand.

    3.1 Analyze trends (inferred analysis).

    3.2 Analyze demand by buying power segmentation method (fundamental analysis method 1).

        3.2(1)   Forecast number and size of households in the primary trade area.

        3.2(2)   Estimate average (median) household income and total income for primary trade area.

        3.2(3)   Estimate the percentage of household income that is spent on retail items.

        3.2(4)   Estimate the percentage of retail purchases typically made at a shopping center of the subject's type.

        3.2(5)   Estimate the percentage of sales retention in the primary trade area from the total potential sales for the primary trade area.

        3.2(6)   Estimate the supportable square footage of retail space by dividing total demand by required sales volume per square foot.

        3.2(7)   Repeat Steps 3.2(1) through 3.2(5) for the secondary trade area and/or other demand sources.

        3.2(8)   Determine total demand in the primary and secondary trade areas.

        3.2(9)   Estimate the square footage of nonretail users of neighborhood shopping centers.

        3.2(10) Adjust the estimate of supportable retail space to reflect the frictional (normal) vacancy rate for the market.

    3.3 Analyze demand by ratio method (fundamental analysis method 2).

    3.4 Analyze demand by sales per capita method (fundamental analysis method 3).

    3.5 Reconcile findings and forecast final demand.

Step 4: Measure competitive supply.

    4.1 Inventory existing competition, competitive properties under construction, proposed competitive properties, and likely additional competitive space.

Step 5: Analyze market equilibrium or disequilibrium.

    5.1 Estimate residual or marginal demand.

Step 6: Forecast subject capture.

    6.1 Analyze capture by inferred methods, including

        ·   Historical capture of subject

        ·   Capture of comparable properties

        ·   Secondary data surveys and forecasts

        ·   Impact of residual or marginal demand on subject

        ·   Local economic analysis

    6.2 Forecast capture by fundamental methods.

    6.3 Reconcile subject capture indications derived by inferred and fundamental analyses.

The forecast capture rate for the subject is then employed as a basis for the highest and best use conclusion. In particular, a forecast of timing is needed to test feasibility. Forecast capture is also essential data in the three valuation approaches, such as the revenue forecast for the income approach.

Note the numbering system employed in this six-step process. Sub-steps are indicated with sequential numbers in parentheses. Thus, Step 1.2 is followed by Steps 1.2(1), 1.2(2), 1.2(3), and so on.

conclusion and to furnish information for the valuation approaches applied to the market value estimate.

The question of use is not a major element of this study because the subject retail center is relatively new and currently occupied. The value of the land as though vacant is far less than the value of the property as improved. Alternative uses that would require remodeling are not feasible. Thus, the highest and best use as if vacant would be a minimal Level A study since it is not critical to the overall property value conclusion. Thus, for brevity the Level A highest and best use "as if vacant" is not shown.

The part of the appraisal in this case study that has the most impact on value is the ability of the subject to re-lease back to previous levels and then to maintain its tenant base. Since this question is paramount to the value, this part of the appraisal will receive the most study, which in this case is a Level C market study.

The market study also lends support to the sales comparison approach by answering the following question: Are the comparables' prospects for future benefits similar to those of the subject? If not, the market study will indicate the need for an adjustment. Information from the market study can also be used in the cost approach to help estimate external obsolescence.

Case Study Description

The subject of the case study is a shopping center located in a small town on the fringe of a major metropolitan area. It is an older town that has historically had its own economic base. In recent years it has been influenced by the job opportunities from the nearby metro area. The metro area extended to the town and during the last decade began to impact the town more in terms of housing and business growth coming from the influence of the metro area. Thus, the town is expected to continue at its recent growth rate.

The property is a multitenant six-year-old retail center with 110,000 square feet of gross leasable area. It is currently leased at 80% of total occupancy, has a typical design for this city, and is in good condition. The mix of tenants at the subject center includes an anchor supermarket, a drug store, video store, three fast food restaurants, an auto parts store, a dry cleaning establishment, a variety store, junior department store—selling primarily ladies' and children's apparel—a small hardware/home garden store, a hobby shop, and office space for a veterinarian, real estate agency, and insurance sales.

The subject had a good leasing history during its first four years, and occupancy reached 95%. Last year, however, two specialty stores (an electronics store and a shoe store) moved out, and the space has not been re-leased. Although the center's rental rates may be considered competitive, they are among the highest in town. The rents have not been lowered since the center opened and have generally increased with the rate of inflation.

A new mall has been announced in the southern part of town and a new discount supercenter is planned ½ mile west of the subject at the site of a new loop being built around the town. The new bypass is scheduled to open and will direct traffic away from the subject. These factors contribute to the uncertainty surrounding the subject's future.

The property is located in a city of 55,000 people in the outer edge of a major metropolitan area. Over the past decade the community has experienced steady growth, averaging 5% per year. The economic base of the community includes a good mix of manufacturing industries (electronics, office equipment, appliances) and suppliers (food and paper). Given its solid economic base, the town is expected to continue to grow at a rate similar to that experienced over the past decade.

The property is in a good area of town on the corner of a major and secondary thoroughfare. One thoroughfare feeds into the central business district, which is approximately four miles to the east. Except for commercially zoned areas along the thoroughfares on which the shopping center stands, the surrounding area is zoned for residential use and is improved primarily with single-family dwellings. The housing density is fairly uniform.

Immediately north of the subject is moderate-to-low-income housing that is approximately 30 years old. South of the subject is a 20- to 30-year-old subdivision of moderate-to-high-income housing. These residential subdivisions are in good condition due to a high level of maintenance.

The subject is located in one of four major retail areas that serve the community. A new mall four miles south of the subject is under development and a 180,000-sq.ft. supercenter is planned to be built on the new bypass one-half mile west of the subject. The new supercenter is expected to open in three to five years—i.e., when the new bypass is completed. There are also scattered, stand-alone retail stores in town, but all are considered secondary and small in nature. Planned for the southern part of town, adjacent to a major north/south highway and new loop is a new mall. In years to come, satellite stores in this area will probably include some competitive convenience shopping.

Step 1: Analyze the Subject Property (Property Productivity)

Step 1.1: Analyze Site and Building for Competitive Strengths and Weaknesses

The first step is to inspect the subject. The immediate focus is twofold: 1) analysis of tenant types and 2) analysis of the facility's ability to serve different retail types. The initial focus on the tenants determines in large part the type of center, i.e., how far customers tend to come to it. This will help to determine the retail submarket that the subject shopping center serves.

The property productivity step then enables the analyst to estimate the subject's present and future competitiveness for that submarket. In this case study, the purpose is neighborhood center use.

For this analysis, the subject property is compared to the most typical neighborhood centers in the town using current industry standards. The analysis includes performing an inventory of the subject's attributes and making a preliminary assessment of its functional problems and competitive advantages. The importance of comparing the subject to current industry standards (or the ideal improvement) underscores the dynamic nature of retail real estate. Properties can become outdated quickly, which significantly affects future demand and, in turn, value.

Current Industry Standards

The industry standards described here are not applicable to every retail use. The items cited represent typical concerns that might appear on an appraisal checklist. Such a list should be updated continually to reflect trends in the industry. Trade associations, trade magazines, the Urban Land Institute Shopping Center Development Handbook series, interviews with leasing agents, and a study of newer retail centers might reveal additional information on industry standards. If new types of centers cannot be found in the subject area, a national search for data may be needed.

The following is an overview of the attributes to be considered in the first part of the productivity analysis, which focuses on the subject improvements. The analyst's objective is to determine to what extent the subject's improvements meet current retailing needs.

Site Efficiency Analysis

This can be analyzed by comparing the ratio of the following site factors to the building size:

- Landscaping and walkways
- Parking area
- Buffers and setbacks

The landscaped and walkway area is generally about 10% of the gross leasable area. Thus, a 110,000-sq.-ft., one-story center would have about 11,000 square feet of landscaping and walkways.

Approximately 5 to 6 1/2 parking spaces per 1,000 square feet of GLA is a good rule of thumb. This guideline assumes that half of the cars parked are compact models. Thus, for a property with 110,000 square feet of GLA, approximately 750 parking spaces would be needed $(110,000 \div 1,000 \times 6.5)$.

With efficient use of space, 325 square feet per car is needed for the parking and maneuvering of compact cars. For larger cars and less efficiently designed space, 400 square feet is required. Thus, the area needed for 650 parking spaces would range between 243,750 square feet (750×325) and 300,000 square feet (750×400).

A 15-ft. perimeter around a site is usually set aside for buffers and setbacks.

Building Area
As a rule of thumb, the ratio of gross building area to land area should be about 10,000 to 15,000 square feet of GBA for each 43,560 square feet (one acre) of land for retail, not including parking garages.

Parking
The availability of parking space is critical. Parking area is related to the GFA or GLA of the center and the tenancy. A neighborhood center with convenience stores has a high rate of turnover for each parking stall and thus may require less overall parking area than a larger center with specialty shops and stores selling shopper goods.

Parking areas should be conveniently located in relation to the shopping center's stores. The preferred distance between the parking area and stores falls between 300 and 350 feet, with 400 feet as the maximum distance.

For marketing purposes, some stores provide more parking than required by zoning ordinances or actual use. For example, some supercenters (big box stores) want to project the image of easy ingress and egress, so they strive for several vacant spaces visible from the road. Some municipalities trying to counter a "sea of asphalt" restrict the number of spaces by establishing zoning requirements for the maximum number of parking spaces.

Frontage and Visibility
Shopping centers should have sufficient frontage to ensure ease of access. Visibility is dependent on location. Both frontage and visibility can be critical to the success of a retail center. A center with poor visibility may never be able to compete, regardless of the marketing strategies implemented.

Topography
The site's topography should be level or slightly sloping. Steep grades make it hard for vehicles to maneuver and may create runoff problems. Difficult maneuvering can drive customers to competitive centers that are more easily accessible. Runoff problems increase maintenance costs and can create an unseemly appearance that deters customers.

Utilities
Utilities should be adequate and convenient. The costs of linking up utilities may render a project infeasible. In some municipalities the requirements for utility service vary with the center's tenants; i.e., restaurants may require more utility service. The setup of utilities at the subject property could restrict future tenant flexibility.

Landscaping

The use of landscaping to upgrade a center's exterior appearance and define traffic lanes has recently begun to change the image of shopping centers—especially more expensive ones. Good landscaping can help draw customers, improve a center's image, generate higher rents, and improve traffic flow and parking access. Poorly planned landscaping, on the other hand, may obstruct the center's visibility, impede circulation, and result in higher maintenance costs.

Design and Building Layout

The design and layout of the building or buildings in a shopping center must project a modern, functional appearance if it is to compete effectively. Its design and layout should reflect current marketing trends. A flexible layout is important because marketing concepts change continually.

Amenity Features

Amenities are features that enhance a property's attractiveness or increase the satisfaction derived from its use. Although they do not constitute an essential part of the property, they can give a shopping center a competitive advantage in attracting customers. They range from indoor amusement parks complete with roller coasters as found in the Mall of America in Minnesota to the small, attractively landscaped eating areas in neighborhood centers that emphasize street-level walking and eating areas.

Store Size

According to the NRB Shopping Center Census for 1999-2004 the average size of shopping centers has increased from 120,460 sq. ft. to 124,451 sq. ft.

However, the variety of the retail tenant mix (or merchandise mix) is more important in drawing customers than the size of a particular store. The size and design of stores change over time. As retail-marketing techniques evolve, the appraiser must assess an existing center's overall capability of competing with more modern facilities.

Store Width

There is no standard width for a particular store tenant.[7] Landlords often try to restrict the widths of mall stores to provide mall frontage to as many tenants as possible.

Store Depth

Store depth typically ranges from 40 to 120 feet, depending on building requirements and feasibility. The ability to provide stores of varying depths is an asset to any center. Small stores may be carved out of deeper space, leaving rear areas for larger neighboring stores. Greater store depth is needed if shopper traffic moves along two frontages, if deliveries are made at the back of the store, or if the center has no

---

7. Data on median store sizes (in gross leasable area) by tenant classification are provided in *Dollars and Cents of Shopping Centers,* published triennially by the Urban Land Institute.

basements and ground-level storage facilities have to be provided. Less depth is required if storage and service facilities are in a basement area or if pedestrian traffic passes on only one side of the store.

Signage
Shops should be clearly identified by signage that conforms to the center's design and image. Poor sign control can be counterproductive; inappropriate signage may block views, emphasize the wrong anchor, and give the center a cheap or second-rate appearance.

Truck Service Facilities
Delivery areas for the loading and unloading of trucks should be screened from the view of customers.

Tenant Mix and Marketing Attributes
A center's ability to attract customers is a function of the type, mix, location, action, and reputation of the tenants. Anchor tenants, major stores within a shopping center that attract or generate the vast majority of customers for the facility, have long been the key tenants in a center, but this may be changing.

The presence or absence of secondary stores, of which there are two types, is also important. One type includes stores that complement and broaden the selections of the anchor store. The second type consists of convenience stores that serve customers who shop at the anchor and complementary stores. These convenience stores may include fast food restaurants, pharmacies, and card shops. Whether a secondary store is to be considered complementary or not depends on the mix of stores in the vicinity and its location within the center.

The location of tenants should ensure proximity of compatible stores and take advantage of access linkages. Richard Nelson refers to this design factor in the context of "pedestrian interruptions." For example, it is desirable to have a women's apparel store adjacent to a men's apparel store; but if the stores are separated by a driveway to the parking area, the benefit is canceled out.

The principle of compatibility is closely related to the principle of cumulative attraction. Similar tenants grouped together can be beneficial for all. For example the electronic stores and video stores may be grouped together.

The store's activity can also impact a shopping center's ability to attract customers and affect its ability to charge rents. A fine restaurant that caters to high-end adult dining adjacent to a teenage nightclub is not considered a compatible tenant location due to each tenant's activity.

The image of a shopping center depends on consumer perceptions of its tenants. The factors influencing these perceptions include the age of the center, the price and quality of the goods sold, the security provided, and the promotional activities of the retailers. A new center can generally expect to attract customers for a period because of its newness. A center in a high crime district cannot expect to compete with a store in a safer area. A center that is actively promoted by its developer may attract a larger share of the potential market than its size would warrant.

Legal Constraints and Opportunities

Legal constraints and opportunities vary. Long-term leases may be detrimental. For example, a center may have tenants located in the wrong place but be unable to move them because of their leases. Zoning restrictions may also create leasing problems. For example, a center designed for small retail shops may be prevented from leasing to restaurants for which there is market demand, because the parking was originally planned for retail shops. According to the municipal zoning regulations, there are not sufficient spaces for restaurant parking.

Introduction to Case Study Property Rating

The purpose of rating the subject property is to document, organize, and assess the subject's strong and weak points systemically. A rating is different from a description of the subject. This step is analytic, not descriptive. The subject's attributes and location are not easy to analyze quantitatively, so the appraiser begins by recognizing how the data from this analysis, combined with data produced in subsequent analyses, will eventually be used.

This analysis provides input for identifying competitive centers because the subject's attributes (along with location) determine, in large part, what are considered competing centers. It also helps the appraiser determine the subject's specific advantages or disadvantages. Using this information, the appraiser can establish a relative scale for rating the subject, and in combination with future analyses, it helps narrow the study and refine the data until it is possible to arrive at specific estimates of functional and economic obsolescence in the cost approach, adjustments in the sales comparison approach, and rents and occupancy rates in the income capitalization approach.

In this case study, the subject is rated according to the typical center being built in the nearby metro area, which is considered the current industry standard. Most of the current retail centers in the subject city are more than 10 years old. Some appraisers choose to compare the subject property to the most dominant competition in the area. Either technique can be used, but the dynamic nature of retail shopping centers is one reason to base the comparison on current industry standards. In retailing, the primary competition can be expected to differ from potential future centers as much as other current centers. Fundamental market analysis techniques are future oriented. For this reason, the case study property is rated according to current standards, not in relation to the current older competition in the city.

The rating scale applied is both narrative and quantitative. In practice, an appraiser might select either form or apply several other rating methods.

The rating process that begins at this early stage in the market analysis is further refined in the subsequent stages of location analysis and competitive supply analysis. The successive ratings rank the subject with the competition and contribute data to support the share-of-the market forecast required in the appraisal. This rating grid, like the others employed throughout the market analysis, represents a screening process in which the characteristics of the subject and the competition are analyzed successively and ranked until the appraiser is ready to formulate conclusions to be used in the three valuation approaches. This is the first step in a rating process in which data are scaled, refined, and evaluated. These successive ratings build upon one another and help form the final value opinion. As the late James Graaskamp wrote, "In fact, each step in the appraisal process is a screening and ranking of alternatives."[8]

Subject Property Rating and Highest and Best Use Analysis

In an appraisal assignment highest and best use must be considered. The property rating can help document whether or not the subject suffers from severe obsolescence. If so, alternative use would have to be considered in more detail. In the subject case this is not found, and since the property has some long-term leases based on physical and legal attributes, the consideration of alternative use is not likely.

The land as if vacant consideration can also be reviewed by a preliminary test to determine if more detailed analysis is warranted, called threshold testing. The building is compared in value to a very low-priced retail center. The land is tested at a high-priced land sale. If the land value compared to a high-priced sale does not come close to a building sale at the low end of the range, then it is very unlikely that the subject would be demolished for alternative use even if there were no legal constraints such as tenant leases in force. Exhibit 12.5 shows this analysis:

Exhibit 12.5	Highest and Best Use Land As If Vacant Test of Reasonableness		
Land As If Vacant Alternative		**As Improved Alternative**	
Land size	10.5 acres, or 457,380 sq. ft.	Building size	110,000 sq. ft.
Times high land price per sq. ft.	× $6.50	Times low price per sq. ft./ building	× $40
Less demo cost	− $50,000		
Land value test	$2,922,970	As improved value test	$4,400,000

In this case the highest and best land use as if vacant in the appraisal would probably be a Level A analysis. This is justified on the basis that the highest and best use for alternative use is not the most critical element of value. Thus, the case study presented here reserves the bulk of the analysis to the most critical element of value–the ability of the subject to sustain a strong tenant base in the retail center.

---

8. *The Appraisal of 25 N. Pickney Street: A Demonstration Case for Contemporary Appraisal Methods,* (Madison, Wis.: Landmark Research, Inc., 1977).

Case Study Application of Step 1.1: Property Analysis

The appraiser inventories the subject's attributes and rates the relative impact of each. First, the analyst determines which items to rate. The list will vary with the type of center.

Next, the appraiser compares the subject's attributes item by item to current industry standards. To help in this assessment, the analyst can develop a comparison grid for the subject and newer centers that serve a similar market (see Exhibit 12.6). A comparison grid listing the major attributes of the centers can be used to determine whether the subject is similar or dissimilar in each attribute. This comparison can suggest the attributes that the subject center may be lacking and identify whether the subject is typical, inferior, or superior. If, for example, the new trend is toward bigger anchor stores and the subject's anchor is smaller, the subject would be rated inferior.

The next step is for the analyst to weight the factors. Factors are weighted in two ways. First, the number and type of factors to be rated in each category are themselves a form of weighting. The more factors in a category, the greater the weight given to that category. In Exhibit 12.6, for instance, the category titled "Tenant Mix and Marketing Features" contains six factors to rate. For the other categories, between two and five factors are listed. Thus, more weight has been given to "Tenant Mix and Marketing Features" than the others.

Factors are weighted another way by assigning a numerical score to attributes judged inferior or superior. This ranking technique measures the item's impact on the subject's productivity, i.e., retailing ability. After initial scores are assigned to all of the factors, they are refined further. In the initial comparison, the analyst considers whether the subject is equal, inferior, or superior. The adverse or beneficial impact of inferior and superior characteristics is then judged to be slight, moderate, or high. All factors judged equal must have the same impact score. If a factor is superior to another, it must have a higher impact score; if it is inferior to another, it must have a lower score.

In this case, the subject's street visibility and the size of its anchor were both judged inferior to current industry standards. However, the size of the anchor store could have a much more detrimental impact on the center's success than the lack of high street visibility. Thus, the size of the subject's anchor is given a more detrimental rating, but street visibility is given only a slightly detrimental rating.

The magnitude of the difference among the assigned scores should be noted. Many scoring systems can be used. In this system, a single point represents the difference between an average and an inferior or superior rating. A one-point differential allows for smoothing in situations where the distinctions among attributes are very fine.

The scores assigned to the subject are compared to the score given the industry standard. Using the categories in Exhibit 12.6, the industry standard score is 110, calculated by multiplying the 22 factors rated by an average score of 5 for each factor. The final step in the ranking is to calculate each item's score by multiplying the number of factors in each score category by the scoring number given that category.

Note the column on the left designated "Veto Factor." This column highlights a feature or features that are so detrimental, and so significant, that they put the subject at a distinct competitive disadvantage. In short, this column specifically identifies an item that would necessitate an alternative use or a major corrective program.

Exhibit 12.6 is an interpretation of the rating analysis.

Sub-rate (rate factors by inserting "X")	Veto Factor	Inferior			Typical	Superior		
		High	Moderate	Slight	Neutral	Slight	Moderate	High
Site								
Size				X				
Land-to-building ratio					X			
Parking								
Number				X				
Location					X			
Convenience					X			
Interior circulation					X			
Topography								
Circulation impact				X				
Drainage					X			
Exterior access (curb cuts)					X			
Landscaping						X		
Building Improvements								
Exterior appearance					X			
Construction quality					X			
Signage appearance					X			
Design flexibility					X			
Street visibility			X					
Tenant Mix and Marketing Features								
Anchor's size		X						
Anchor's drawing power				X				
Tenant compatibility mix					X			
Image of center					X			
Shopper access shops to shops					X			
Center's amenities features					X			
Legal								
Zoning/easements/legal attributes					X			
Rating Conclusions								
Sub-rate number of items		1	1	4	15	1	0	0
Times category score		0	2	4	5	6	8	10
Category score		0	2	16	75	6	0	0
Total subject score	99							
Percentage above or (below) average	-10%							

Exhibit 12.6   Neighborhood Retail Shopping Center—Property Rating

The subject property, a six-year-old, 110,000-sq.-ft. neighborhood-type shopping center, was rated for all factors. When compared to a modern retail center, it was considered average or standard in all respects except for the following characteristics.

- Size of site and parking. The site is 10.5 acres, which makes it too small to accommodate the buildings and required parking. Thus, the parking meets city zoning standards but is below typical industry standards.
- Topography (grade). Traffic from the street must climb a steep grade to reach the center, thus restricting ease of access.
- Visibility. Due to the steep grade, subject visibility is poor.
- Anchor size. The anchor, a nationally recognized grocery store, is small compared to newer grocery store anchors built in the nearby major metro area. Nor does it provide the variety of goods found in the newer anchor grocery stores built in the last two to three years in major urban areas. This rating reflects industry standards, not the current competition. In this case, the subject anchor is typical of its own local competition. However, the analyst compares it to newer stores in other areas since the subject is in a growing town, and it is only a matter of time before larger stores that offer a broader mix of products are built. When the new loop is built in five years, a major supercenter discount/grocery store is planned to be built there. Thus, the analyst starts assessing the current and future competitiveness of the subject.

The supply analysis performed in Step 4 will consider existing and planned competition in greater detail. This initial rating is one of the building blocks that the analyst will use to form a judgment about the planned competition in the supply analysis.

- Landscaping. The subject site was carved out of a hill covered with many large trees. This is one of the most attractively landscaped sites in town.

These factors are rated on a relative scale to assess the subject's advantage or disadvantage in the market. The factors considered standard each received an average score of 5. Of the four nonstandard factors, three are negative and one is positive. The ratings were weighted to reflect the relative importance of each factor to the future marketability of the subject.

The market trend toward bigger anchors with a broader product mix is by far the most important factor, but how do topography and visibility rate? Is topography (ease of access) more or less important than visibility? Comparison of rents, discussions with retailers, and similar research can provide a clue. In this case, topography and visibility were rated as having less of an impact than the anchor store, which by receiving a score of "0," was rated the most negative impact.

Interpreting Property Analysis Data

How does an appraiser interpret the results of this analysis? At this preliminary stage, no final judgments are made. It is the first in a series of screenings that continue throughout the appraisal and help the appraiser arrive at a final value conclusion. The analysis does indicate that the subject center is slightly inferior compared to current industry standards. (This fact may or may not account for its occupancy rate of only 80%.) The ratings also provide a relative scale for the subject's competitive position. The subject rating was 90% of the industry standard. If the subject had been rated typical for all factors, it would have received a score of 110; however, it received a score of 99, which is 90% of 110(99/110). Expressed negatively, the subject is rated slightly inferior (10%) to the typical modern center.

Market Segment Indicated by Property Analysis

The property productivity analysis also helps define the market that the subject serves. The property was rated against other neighborhood shopping centers based on their tenants. The final rating indicated that the center was slightly inferior, but it also means that the center is still more than adequate to accommodate neighborhood-type tenants. If the potential anchor problem is not considered, then based on current competition, the subject is considered one of the better neighborhood centers in the city. In the next step, location analysis, the analyst examines the impact of location on the subject's competitiveness as a neighborhood retail center.

Step 1.2: Analyze the Location of the Subject Property

A shopping center's success is dependent on a location that is proximate to an adequate customer base and the ability to draw those customers. When more customers spend money at the stores in a facility, the value of the shopping center's real estate tends to increase. A center's ability to attract customers depends in part on the distance of the shopping center from its customers. In retailing, this distance is measured in time. A final consideration is the proximity of competing centers that might interfere with the subject's draw. All of these issues relate to location.

For shopping centers, the urban setting is the economic turf on which the competition for customers occurs. Because value is the present worth of future benefits, the appraiser must understand the current and future urban setting. This section describes a means of assessing the effect of location on the subject's productivity. Location analysis focuses on:

- Static factors, such as roads, utilities, and rivers. The emphasis is on how competitive the subject location is for the current use.
- Dynamic factors i.e., direction of growth issues. The emphasis is on how competitive the location will be in the future for the current use.

The following questions help structure the analysis to make these determinations.

- Where does the subject fit in the overall growth pattern? To answer this question, the analyst studies the current and future land use pattern and the direction of growth.
- Where does the subject's market come from? The center's linkages to demand are identified.
- Where is the subject's competition located? The analyst studies the market's linkages to demand compared to the competition's linkages to these customers.
- How does the subject's location compare to demand sources and to the location of the competition now, and how is it projected to compare in the next five to 10 years?

These questions can be addressed with quantifiable data and graphic analysis.

Quantifiable Techniques
The following are examples of quantifiable data used for location analysis.

- Demographic data compared by small geographic areas such as census tracts. For example, current household incomes are compared to determine if the subject's income pattern is positive for retail development. This can be accomplished using data in a table or by GIS (Geographic Information Systems) mapping and tables.
- Comparison of population groups by different areas of town. Many demographic services consolidate data by population groups. These groups have common composite characteristics such as age range, number of children, extent of education, and so on.

Graphic Location Analysis Techniques
A number of geographic location analysis techniques also can help the analyst make locational determinations. One technique involves using maps of the current and forecast land-use patterns and transportation routes that the analyst can use to predict land-use patterns that will emerge over the next 10 years. For appraisals, the short-term future land-use pattern is the most critical. Known changes in transportation, land use, and institutional activity are the main factors that affect the current land use pattern over the short term.

Growth areas are isolated by placing dots on a map to represent new developments within the past five to 10 years. These dots can identify new retail and residential areas. The clustering of the dots indicates the boundaries, direction, and intensity of growth.

A map can also be drawn to identify the location of the highest density of household demand and the driving time from demand sources to area shopping centers. Another technique features the use of a map to identify the location of existing and potential neighborhood shopping centers in the city. Rings are then drawn around these centers (for neighborhood centers it is usually a 1.5-mile radius). The ring study can be interpreted to identify areas of considerable competition, little competition, and underserved areas. For example, an area with many overlapping rings would be considered a very competitive area of town, whereas one with housing development but no overlapping neighborhood center ring touches would be considered an underserved area.

The focus of these techniques is on existing and future linkages between the subject center and areas that generate demand, i.e., residential subdivisions, office clusters, centers of major economic activity, and other retail developments. The subject's current and future linkages are compared to the competition's to determine the relative drawing power of each center. Traffic counts and the traffic volume that passes a site are also important. The appraiser investigates current land use trends in the neighborhood, which may lead to changes in the customer base of retail centers. A question for the appraiser to answer is whether the direction of growth is away from the subject. The age and condition of nearby buildings and the relative degree of conformity that characterize the neighborhood also indicate change. The maps created in this step provide a base for further analysis of locational factors.

Step 1.2(1): Investigate Land Uses and the Linkages of the Subject Property

Richard B. Andrews' theory of situs[9] relationships can be adapted to prepare a checklist for this investigation. The concept affirms that certain types of land uses require the support of complementary land uses nearby (i.e., within the neighborhood), while other land use associations can be located more distantly from one another. (For a discussion of this concept, see Chapter 4.)

The subject property has the same size and tenant mix as a neighborhood retail center. Because of its location on a major east-west thoroughfare and its proximity to office buildings, however, it may have the drawing power of a community center. What key land use associations should be identified, and how is the subject affected by them? Do the essential linkages between the subject and complementary land uses exist? A list of requisite support facilities and demand generators based on situs relationships can be developed. A possible list for the subject center is shown in Exhibit 12.7.

In conclusion, the subject is rated higher than the city average in most respects and therefore should be a highly competitive center.

Step 1.2(2): Determine the Position Within Urban Growth Patterns

The analyst next examines the rate and direction of urban growth by noting where retail clusters are forming, where new and existing centers of economic activity (i.e., peak value intersections, critical mass centers, and development nodes) are developing, and where housing is being built.

---

9. Richard B. Andrews, *Urban Land Economics and Public Policy* (New York: The Free Press, 1971).

Exhibit 12.7 Rating of Current Land Use Linkages of the Subject

Desirable Nearby Land Uses	Poor	Fair	Average	Good	Excellent
Number of residential units to support a retail center (measured in travel time and travel distance)					X
Traffic volume by the subject site					X
Complementary retail uses in the immediate area			X		
Service support, i.e., post office, branch bank, transit stop					X
Complementary neighborhood support, i.e., churches, schools, community recreation centers				X	
Quality of adjacent land uses			X		
Desirable Area-wide Land Uses					
Proximity to traffic generators such as employment centers and major residential areas					X

Urban growth is influenced by the natural and manmade features of an area, its economic base, and local political situation. For example, a political entity can influence the direction of growth by approving a larger share of infrastructure development for certain areas of the city.

Anticipated development of residential subdivisions and business centers and projected linkages (e.g., new freeways and major thoroughfares) indicate changes in land use patterns. These changes will affect the market area and the linkages on which a retail center depends. For example, the current rent structure and occupancy level of a community retail center may be jeopardized if new roads redirect traffic to another area. The direction of growth determines both future population patterns and the timetable for population increases in market areas. Growth also affects income potential. In growth areas, retail sales increase; when growth slows, retail sales generally level off. Thus, locations closer to expanding centers or at peak value intersections experience higher rates of occupancy and, consequently, higher land values, than locations in declining nodes or at less intensely developed intersections. The study of growth patterns also helps the analyst assess the validity of the population projections used in the demand analysis in Step 3.

Location Analysis Techniques

The map shown in Exhibit 12.8 is the result of one type of graphic analysis applied to the subject market area. Growth was plotted by mapping recent preliminary plats as well as actual development that occurred in the last five years. The map also identifies the location of the competition. Together these data describe the general pattern of growth expected in the next five to 10 years.

A source of real estate market data is the GIS, which spatially delineates legal, physical, and economic factors on a map base. The GIS system makes possible the depiction of productivity, location, and market factors in an appraisal report.

Exhibit 12.8 Map Showing Direction of Growth and Location of Competition

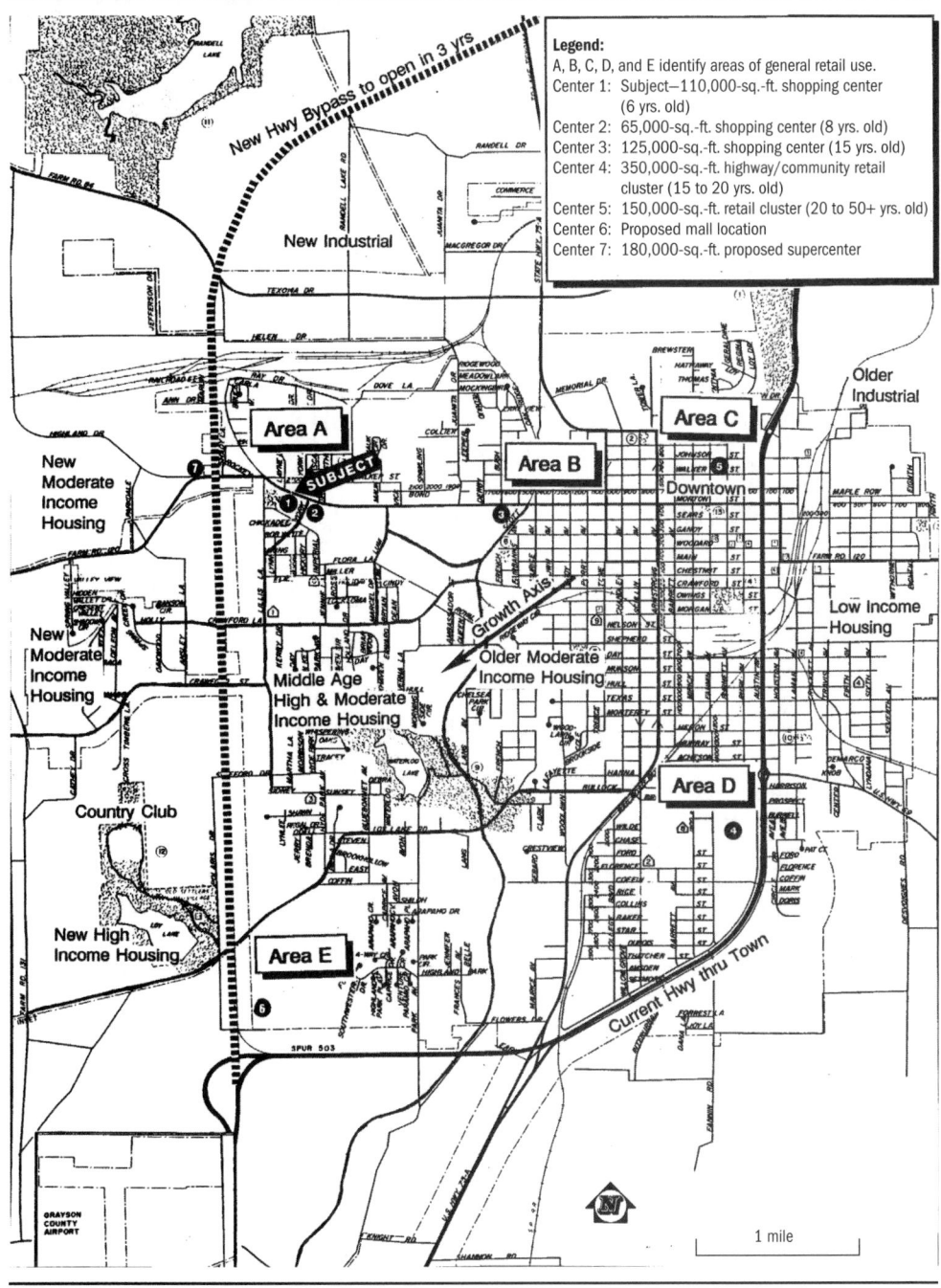

Legend:
A, B, C, D, and E identify areas of general retail use.
Center 1: Subject—110,000-sq.-ft. shopping center (6 yrs. old)
Center 2: 65,000-sq.-ft. shopping center (8 yrs. old)
Center 3: 125,000-sq.-ft. shopping center (15 yrs. old)
Center 4: 350,000-sq.-ft. highway/community retail cluster (15 to 20 yrs. old)
Center 5: 150,000-sq.-ft. retail cluster (20 to 50+ yrs. old)
Center 6: Proposed mall location
Center 7: 180,000-sq.-ft. proposed supercenter

Rate of Growth Analysis Technique

The appraiser can compare aerial photographs of the area taken over a period of time to determine the amount of acreage that has been developed. Census tracts or other population data should be analyzed for long-term trends. Appraisers are cautioned to look beyond short-term cycles, which may not be typical. The appraiser may also consider using an analogue to which the subject area can be compared. The analog can be an adjacent area or an area in a nearby city that has already reached the population anticipated for the subject's city in the next five to 10 years. If the location and economic base of the subject city are similar to the analog, a comparable rate of growth can be anticipated.

Step 1.2(3): Identify the Location of Competitive Areas

In this step of the market analysis, competitive areas may be approached either in a general or a detailed manner. The location of the competitive area would be both within and outside the subject primary trade area. The location analysis is an area-wide or, in this case study, citywide assessment of the areas that have the greatest retail potential. The primary question to answer is whether the subject is in a good location today and whether it will be in five or 10 years.

Besides the location of current competitive centers, the appraiser may note current vacant corners that are anticipated to have retail in the next 10 years. Center 7 is currently a vacant site. The appraiser notes the center's approximate size, typical tenants, amenity features, and major anchors. As a general rule, the survey of competitive centers should identify all potential competitive areas, both primary and secondary. The subject case study property is located in a small town, and even convenience shoppers could utilize nearly any, so a citywide survey is considered reasonable. In a larger metropolitan area, however, the appraisal of a neighborhood shopping center would probably not require a comprehensive survey of the whole city but would consider the areas within the subject's broad market area or quadrant of the metro area.

Case Study Application of Step 1.2(3): Identify Location of Competitive Areas

The locations of all similar retail centers in the city are plotted on a map and survey sheets with basic data (i.e., size, tenants, amenities, and anchors) are attached. The locations of the various retail nodes in the city are indicated on the map in Exhibit 12.8 as area A, B, and C.

Step 1.2(4): Rate the Subject's Location in Comparison with the Competitive Areas

The location analysis ends with a location rating. The success of a retail center depends on its location and individual property characteristics such as tenant mix and amenities. Changes in the location can rapidly reduce a shopping center's appeal. A well-designed center that has very little competition in the immediate area may be harmed by changes in city growth patterns that drain clientele from the center's trade area. In a fundamental market analysis, the analyst may need to quantitatively rate the locational attributes of the subject and competitive properties in the subject's primary and secondary trade areas.

In a later stage in the market analysis, the competitive location rating is used in the demand calculations as part of leakage analysis–the estimate of the share of the market in the primary trade area that the primary trade area is likely to retain.

The analysis in Step 1.2(4) also provides input for Step 2, the definition of the subject's primary and secondary trade areas. The location rating also helps the analyst assess the likelihood that new competition will develop in other parts of the city and whether or not this new competition will draw customers away from the subject. This is especially important in cities where residential growth into new neighborhoods occurs due to relocation from older neighborhoods. This situation often makes the current neighborhood center obsolete, as the major retailers follow the money to the new residential areas. Using a rating technique is one approach to location analysis. Ten factors that affect the subject and competitive facilities are considered in the location rating.

The area rated is a cluster or retail node and not a single center in the area. For example Area "A" in the following rating includes the subject, the center located across the street, and the potential supercenter to be located ½ mile from the subject to the west. Thus, area "A" includes the centers on the previous map identified as 1, 2 and 7. The 10 factors described below are used in the case study rating chart shown in Exhibit 12.9.

1. The number of households in the trade area. Each competitive center's trade area is defined, the number of housing units in each trade area is estimated, and each center is rated based on whether the number of units in its trade area is approximately equal to, greater than, or less than the number of units in the trade area of other competitive nodes.

2. Proximity to new retail development. The locations of all retail stores less than five years old are identified on a map. Areas (nodes) with the greatest retail concentrations receive the highest ratings.

3. Location in the path of growth–i.e., new or projected residential development. The direction of urban growth is identified. (See the urban growth theories discussed in Chapter 5.) Finalized plats in the area are reviewed, and preliminary plats are examined to project growth five to 10 years in the future. Each area is rated based on the relative amount of plat activity.

4. Proximity to major roads. Nodes are rated for advantages such as a location on a major thoroughfare or intersection and disadvantages such as a location on a collector road or one-way street.

5. Traffic counts by each center. Sites with the heaviest traffic volume are rated the highest. Forecast traffic counts are used to derive a 5- to 10-year rating.

6. Proximity to the market. People tend to travel along the same routes to existing shopping areas. All things being equal, the retail nodes along the route closest to the broadest customer base (the intercept location) tend to capture more of the market. The appraiser determines the location of the greatest concentration of customers and identifies the traffic routes over which these customers travel, establishing the primary axis for customer shopping trips. The subject location is compared with the locations of the competitive centers to determine which facilities should attract the most customers.

7. Size and drawing power of the anchors. Current trends show that location and anchor type are critical to a center's retailing ability. The number and mix of anchor stores may be as important as their size. In this case, the diversity of the merchandise available was considered a principal factor in rating a center's drawing power. The product mix may be provided by one anchor or by several stores at a particular location node.

8. Tenant mix and compatibility in the retail node. The appraiser considers the tenant mix of non-anchor stores and the compatibility of all merchandising operations, including those of the anchors.

9. Effective age and reputation of the centers in the retail node. Both the appearance (level of maintenance) and the image (prestige and safety) of the shopping area are considered.

10. Special amenity features. Amenity features may be associated with the center or the trade area. A center may have a community attraction such as a performance area. A trade area may be located next to a scenic lake or near recreational activities that draw people.

Factor	Rating Criteria	Area A*	Area B	Area C	Area D	Area E†	Rank by Importance
	Exhibit 12.9 Competitive Location Analysis Chart						
1	Proximity to households in city	1	1	1	1	2	6
2	Proximity to new retail	3	1	2	1	4	5
3	Location in path of new residential growth	3	2	1	1	4	5
4	Proximity to major roads—access and visibility (existing or approved)	3	2	2	1	4	4
5	Traffic count through node	3	2	2	1	4	6
6	Proximity to market (interceptor sites)	2	1	1	1	3	3
7	Size and drawing appeal of anchors	3	2	1	1	4	7
8	Tenant mix and compatibility	3	2	1	1	3	3
9	Effective age of centers	3	2	2	1	3	2
10	Special amenity features	1	1	1	1	2	1
Total	(individual score times weighting)	109	69	59	42	146	Total all scores 425
	Percentage of Total Scores	26%	16%	14%	10%	34%	

* Area A includes the proposed supercenter.

† Area E includes the proposed mall.

The rating also assumes the bypass is complete. In the ranking, a score of 3 is better than 2; 2 is better than 1. If two centers are similar with respect to a specific item, they may have the same rating.

Rating Procedure

The appraiser rates each area as equal, superior, or inferior to competing retailing areas, a procedure that involves six steps:

1. First, two clusters are rated, e.g., Area A is compared to Area B and judged equal to, better than, or worse than the other trade area. At this stage, the degree of difference between the two areas is not specified.

2. The procedure is repeated with another cluster–e.g., Area C is rated relative to Area A. Again, the degree of difference is not specified.

3. Next, the ratings of the second and third clusters are reconsidered. For example, Area B and Area C both were compared to Area A, but not to each other. The degree of difference between two centers, which may have received superior or inferior ratings compared to Area A, are now measured quantitatively–e.g., 3 indicates the area is better than 2, 2 is rated better than 1, and the same score goes to areas that are equal.

4. The ratings are completed by analyzing the specific relationships between all possible pairs of competitive areas. Five competitive areas are studied in the following example (see Exhibit 12.9), so 10 possible sets are compared.

5. The factors are weighted after all the combinations have been compared. The ranking number for each factor is then multiplied by the weight assigned to the factor. The weighted scores for each area are totaled and converted into a percentage using the sum of all weighted scores as a base. Each area score is divided by the base number to obtain a percentage.

6. The individual score for each area is calculated by multiplying each area score by its weight. The total score for each area is shown at the bottom of Exhibit 12.9.

Suggestion for Rating Technique

The amount of data and analysis required for each factor rated will vary with the complexity of the assignment and the importance of the factor. As a general rule, the ratings developed in a Level C analysis can be based on a moderate amount of data on the factors rated rather than an exhaustive analysis of each factor. For example, in rating the number of households, the analyst will usually need to know which trade area has the most households, not exactly how many households each area has. Typically, a minor difference in the number of households will not produce a major miscalculation in the trade area's overall buying power. Usually the only data needed to analyze and rate this factor is an aerial photograph or a detailed street map of the area that shows the findings of a customer-spotting survey. As a general guide, an appraiser refines the trade area circle by modifying its boundaries to take into account major streets and physical features.

Trade areas are then compared visually. If the comparison is too close to call without counting each rooftop, the areas are rated similar.

The rating technique described here is intended to target major differences, not to gauge the differences with mathematical precision. A Level D analysis usually requires greater exactitude, but most Level C assignments do not. As with other sections of the appraisal, the extent of data collection and analysis required is determined by the client and the appraiser in light of the costs and benefits that greater precision will bring to the analysis.

Application of Step 1.2(4)

The subject area was rated against four competitive areas in Exhibit 12.9. The ratings scores at the bottom of the table suggest that the subject is the second best retail node in the city. The rating also suggests that for typical retail (nonregional), the subject's future share of citywide retailing will be approximately 26%.

Step 2: Delineate the Market

The purpose of delineating the market area is to set the limits of the market demand calculations and to determine which properties are competitive for this demand. The terms *trade area* and *market area* are sometimes used interchangeably. The terms are not as important as the study area scope. In this discussion the former refers to the area used to calculate the market demand for which the subject will compete; the latter refers to the area used to calculate the market residual demand. Thus, for this case study, market area is the area where nearly all the customers are located and the area where most of the competition is located.

Market delineation begins with the subject trade area estimate. The trade area analysis identifies the most likely customers for the subject in terms of their location and demographic characteristics. Market delineation is more than simply drawing a line on a map. It also identifies the segment of the population in this market area that constitutes potential customers for the center.

The trade area delineation determines the next step, demand analysis, a measurement of the customers' desire and ability to buy retail goods. The defined trade area also establishes the geographic area over which the primary competitive set is located, identified in Step 4–the supply analysis. The combination of these two–supply and demand–establishes the market poles to compare in Step 5–residual demand analysis, whose purpose is to assess the competitiveness of the trade area in which the subject center competes. Consequently, the size of the trade area is dictated, for the most part, by the location of most of the customers/sales to the subject center and secondarily by the location of most of the subject's competition.

Step 2.1: Define the Study Area

The area of the subject's likely customers is drawn on a map to identify districts for which demographic data will be analyzed and forecast data will be generated. In the past, trade area boundaries were more distinct because each shopping center served its own area. Today, many shopping centers (including neighborhood shopping centers) are located in close proximity to each other and all serve the same or multiple overlapping trade areas. With the variety and volume of shopping centers, the many multipurpose centers, the overlapping trade areas, and the consumers' loyalty for specific store brands, the study becomes more complex than simply measuring the typical distance around the subject.

The three basic methods of analyzing the trade areas of retail centers are: trade area circles, customer spotting, and gravitational models. All three should be applied, if possible, so that the results of the different methods can be reconciled. Thus, the basic analytical techniques only become the start, which in the final determination requires the reconciliation of location factors, competition, and marketing factors.

Procedures and Issues for Defining the Trade Area

The trade area boundary is largely set by the location of the subject's customers and sources of sales. All the demand drivers should be considered, whether they are nearby permanent residents, or nonresidents in the area such as second-home residents, workers in nearby office buildings, tourists, or business travelers.

Next is the determination of alternatives where customers can shop for the same product or services. The users set the initial line that is adjusted for many factors, such as access, but it is also adjusted for the competition. The trade area that covers the largest part ($\pm$ 70% to 85%)of the customers and most of the competition is ideal.

General Procedure for Defining the Trade (Study) Area

Listed below are general procedures for defining the primary trade or study area. They are expanded in the application part of this chapter.

1. Identify the center type determined in Step 1: Property Productivity analysis.
2. Draw a trade area circle for the type of center studied. Start the trade area delineations with a rule-of-thumb distance from the subject. For example, in suburban areas, this would usually be about 1.5 miles for a neighborhood retail center.
3. Adjust the trade area circle boundaries for drive time and access abnormalities caused by natural and manmade barriers such as freeways, rivers, and access. The required drive time will vary by type of center. For example, the drive time for neighborhood retail is usually about 10 minutes. Drive time is more critical than distance.
4. Adjust boundaries to the location of $\pm$70% to 85% of the subject center's customers/sales, known as a customer-spotting technique. For a Level C study, this typically constitutes talking with subject

center's managers to determine the approximate location of most customers. Note sales volume by location is more important than number of customers by location.

5. Adjust the boundary for competition by gravitational models concepts. The major competition on the peripheral of the subject trade area boundary often can set the limit of the study boundary based on Reilly's Law of Retail Gravitation. To paraphrase Reilly's Law, a center's ability to draw customers is proportional to the size of the center and the distance of the center from its competitors.[10] Most of these customers would go to the nearest center. However, frequently, the study boundary line will be adjusted to include these competitive centers due to overlapping customers and the need to judge the competitiveness of the market. As a rule of thumb, if a competitive center's trade area overlaps with the subject center by more than half, the center is typically included in subject trade area and study boundaries. If an adjacent area center has its own trade area and overlaps only slightly with the subject trade area, then the subject trade area boundary would be located about halfway between. The following describes the trade area procedural steps.

Identification of the Subject Center Type by Trade Area

Shopping centers may be differentiated by size and tenancy as illustrated in Exhibit 12.2. Each type has a trade area of a typical size that can be depicted as a range or circle. A shopping center that has a supermarket as an anchor tenant and in-line tenants who sell predominantly convenience goods would be classified as a neighborhood shopping center, which typically has a trade area of 1 to 1½ miles. For example, the subject case study has the size and tenant mix of a neighborhood shopping center and has some tenants with shopper goods. Thus, it functions in part as a community center. The sizes of the primary trade areas for three basic types of retail are shown below:

Type of Shopping Center	Distance	Travel Time
Neighborhood shopping center	1 to 1.5 miles	5–10 minutes
Community shopping center	3 to 5 miles	10–20 minutes
Regional shopping center	10 to 15 miles	20–30 minutes

Note: Drive times are the major determining factor.

The type of center could also be identified in terms of the retail node or cluster of which it is a part. Retail establishments are often found in clusters within small geographic areas.

A property is studied to determine its tenant types and building type and whether it is part of a cluster. This is accomplished mainly through the property and location analysis described previously. Once this is determined, as in the case of the subject, the analyst can proceed to the next step, drawing primary and secondary trade area circles to start the mapping process.

---

10. William J. Reilly, *Methods for the Study of Retail Relationships*, monograph no. 4, University of Texas Bulletin No. 2944 (Austin: University of Texas Press, 1929; reprinted 1959).

Trade Area Circles

The delineation of trade area circles begins with preliminary zonal boundaries, which the analyst adjusts and refines. It should be recognized that regular trade area circles drawn with the retail facility at the center are based on erroneous assumptions.[11]

These assumptions include:

- Easy accessibility to the retail facility from all points on the plane
- A uniform distribution of consumers
- Consumers that share the same characteristics, e.g., income and preferences
- Transportation costs that are directly proportional to distance

Because none of these presuppositions reflect real-world practices, an ideal geometrical shape such as a circle cannot describe a trade area. Thus, the shape and size of the trade area circle must be adjusted.

Adjusting Trade Area Circles

Trade area circles are refined to take into account the following:

- The specific characteristics of the area in terms of land uses, terrain, and transport systems
- The distribution of population and purchasing power
- The fit of the available data (e.g., county, census tract, and block data)
- The interrelationships among the area's geography, demography, and economy (e.g., population density and its effect on purchasing power)

The specific characteristics of an area that the appraiser considers include the system of transportation (mode, capacity, accessibility, and quality); the transportation network (area served and current or committed development); any physical barriers to the flow of traffic (natural features and man-made barriers); and psychological barriers (undesirable land uses).

The next potential problem encountered in drawing the trade area boundary is that the initial line drawn is not likely to conform to the geographic areas for which data are available. Secondary data from the U.S. Bureau of Census are generally obtainable for counties, census tracts or zip code areas, and blocks. Commercial vendor data are available for these areas as well as individually drawn trade area boundaries. The general method of the commercial vendor is that if a trade area boundary touches a block data point, then all the block data are included. Thus, the typical vendor computer generated data for an individualized line does not technically follow the drawn line exactly. Rarely do trade areas and census tracts coincide. The appraiser must understand the relationships that affect the subject property and make judgments concerning the use of aggregate census tract data.

---

11. Neil Carn, Joseph Rabianski, Ronald Racster, and Maury Seldin, *Real Estate Market Analysis: Techniques and Applications* (New York: Prentice-Hall, 1988).

Customer Spotting

Adjusting boundary for the location of customer/sales volume is called customer spotting. Customer spotting is tracking data on specific customers to determine where the majority live. Many retailers issue customer discount cards for this very purpose. These data not only pinpoint where customers live, but also what they tend to buy and, most importantly, how much they spend.

Sometimes the data are available in general from the store manager such as number of customers by zip codes. The appraiser can then spot the customer concentration on a map to see where most of the customers reside.

Most appraisers cannot obtain these data, so alternative methods must be used. Typically for a Level C study, it entails surveying managers to obtain opinions of areas where customers originate. A more detailed, Level D, method is a structured customer survey. Another Level D method, less cumbersome than a structured customer survey, and some consider more accurate, is a structured survey of license plates in the subject parking lot. The license plates are checked with the state for addresses to determine the origin of customers. Not all states provide this data. Site observation surveys such as these require special care on the part of observers to avoid any suspicion of unlawful activity.

Gravitational Models

The trade area circles should be adjusted for competitive centers. This is based on the principle that a shopper will not drive by one center that sells a similar product (tenant types) to shop at another center. Gravitational models attempt to address this weakness. The gravity model traditionally employed in market analysis is Reilly's Law. Distance, however, is of greater consequence than size. (An application of Reilly's Law can be found in Chapter 7.)

By calculating the trade area boundary between all major competing retail stores or clusters, the appraiser can draw a gravitational boundary for the subject trade area. The case study application of Step 2.1 shows how the boundary is determined.

As noted earlier, not all retail follows Reilly's Law, and therefore should be adapted accordingly. For example, customer brand loyalty is one factor that does not follow Reilly's Law.

Another factor in most markets is that retail is so clustered that significant competition can be next door or just down the street. The rule of thumb suggested earlier is that if a competitive facility trade area shares half or more of the subject trade area customers, the competitive facility is usually included in the subject primary trade area study. However, the inclusion or exclusion of areas must not distort the subject demand calculations by making the area so small that the income is not enough to support any store which is not realistic nor so large that it suggest enormous demand, even though from such a large area the customers on the fringe would probably never go that distance to shop at the subject. Thus, the impact on the demand sources is the key determinate of whether or not to include competition in the trade area demand calculations.

Regardless of the subject trade/study area boundary, there is nearly always a store just outside the line competing for some of the subject trade area's customers.

Relationship of the Competition to the Trade Area Residual Demand Studies
The market analysis compares demand with supply to determine if a market is over- or undersupplied, called the residual demand study. The study quantifies demand for a property type in a trade area, which is used as the basis of the forecast for the subject property's future rents and occupancy.

The ideal residual demand study locates all the competition within the trade area boundary, making the residual demand calculation simple: demand minus supply equals residual demand. However, it is rare for the subject trade area to contain all competition for customers in the trade area. Typically, a competitive store (with its own trade area that overlaps the subject trade area) lies just outside the subject trade area boundary. Both stores share common customers.

These fringe, or peripheral, competitive facilities typically will draw some of the consumers who live on the edge of the subject trade area. These consumers will cross over to the competitive facility because it is closer. Conversely, the subject primary trade area may have a competitive store that lies just inside the edge of the subject trade area boundary, which captures from some of its competitors' customers. Thus, this crossover customer base must be addressed in the analysis.

For example, most of the subject neighborhood shopping center customers may live within 1.5 miles of the center. This would be called the primary trade area for the subject. Within the subject primary trade area there may be only one competitive center. However, on the fringe of the subject primary trade area (in the secondary trade area of a 1.5- to 2.5-mile ring of the subject primary trade area) there could be other neighborhood centers that serve their own trade area of which a part overlaps the subject primary trade area. These fringe stores are also trying to attract the subject's customers. Thus, the residual demand study must account for this competition as well as the competition within the primary trade area.

The market delineation step defines the trade area (consumers) and market area (competition) that are to be studied. This example suggests that the area to be studied should be the 2.5-mile radius, since it attracts most of the subject's customers and all of the subject's direct competition. However, the residual demand study element can overstate supply, since the stores located within the 2.5-mile radius also have their own 1.5-mile trade area, of which a part also lies outside the 2.5-mile ring of the store's trade area. If the study area is expanded further to accommodate the trade areas of all of the peripheral competitive stores, then the problem is repeated since the new boundary will probably find another layer of competitive stores just outside the new 2.5-mile ring. Thus, in a metro area there is virtually no end to the competition since the process of including all the competition in the trade area expands with each new ring.

Factoring in the Peripheral Competition

The competition that lies just outside the subject trade area can be handled in a number of ways. One way is to repeat the demand and supply estimates for each trade area ring–primary, secondary, and tertiary. As the rings go out they have less impact on the subject. [See Step 3.2(6)]. Another way is to consider the peripheral competition in the leakage analysis step [Step 3.2(5)]. This method is used in the case study that follows.

Still another way is to adjust the competition's square footage(Step 4.1) on a pro rata basis using the amount of overlap to the subject trade area. Regardless of the method used to account for the peripheral competition, the following principles must be maintained in defining the trade area/study area.

- The reliability of the demand calculations is most important and thus the study area should reflect where nearly all of the subject customers originate.
- As much of the subject competition should be included in the study area if it does not distort the first principle.
- In the residual demand study part, the supply data must be consistent with the demand calculations data in terms of type of retail and geographic area, no matter which method is used.

Alternative Approach for Market Study and Trade Area Delineation

An alternative method is to omit the residual demand (market condition) study. This method is not included in this book because the residual demand study is used in many places in the appraisal. However, if the subject future market penetration occupancy and/or sales is the only question, then the subject trade area demand would be divided between the competition no matter whether the competition was located in or out of the subject trade area.

This is simply a variant of the procedure presented in this book, as the competition located outside the trade area is accounted for in the demand estimates by the leakage factor. Note that the leakage factor method shown in this book is not as prescriptive as this alternative method. This alternative method would focus demand calculation completely on the subject trade area in terms of the customers' origination, and the marketability analysis (rating competition) would require rating and analyzing all the subject's competition, whether they are located in the trade area or not.

Case Study Application of Step 2.1: Trade Area Delineation

The subject property is located at the intersection of two major thoroughfares, functions as part of a retail cluster, and sells some shopper goods. As a result, it has the size and tenant mix of predominately a neighborhood shopping center, but it also has the locational characteristics of a community shopping center.

The appraiser's first task is to forecast the typical tenants expected in the subject center over the next three to 10 years. The key word is *typical* tenants, one of the subtle differences between a market study in appraisal and a study conducted in other fields. A market analysis for an appraisal is based on what is probable, i.e., average or typical retail management, whereas specialized market studies consider specific managers, individual retailing objectives, and specific retail types.

The type of tenants that currently occupy the subject center will likely continue their leases because:

- The subject has had a fairly successful track record with these tenants.
- The manager of the grocery store confirmed that 70% to 80% of the customers live within about 2 miles. This seems reasonable, given that the subject's tenants stock convenience goods that are typically bought by local customers.
- The location rating indicates that the new mall area will probably serve the future shopping needs of the community. It is unlikely that the subject or the adjacent center will attract more retail tenants oriented toward shopper goods.

Therefore, the primary trade area for the subject is preliminarily identified as the immediate residential area within a one- to two-mile radius. This approximation will be refined using a gravitational model, the land use patterns, and natural and man-made barriers.

Adjustment for Competition by Gravitational Models

The gravitational model is used to adjust the preliminary trade area boundary established by the trade area circle and customer-spotting analyses. In the case of the subject property, distance and travel time were similar for all parts of the city. The gravitational model was used to compare the drawing power of the stores in four areas by size. Because the central business district has very little retail space, it was not analyzed in detail. The gravitational model is based on the following formula:

$$\text{TAB} = t/(1 + \sqrt{Sb/Sa}) \text{ where } b > a$$

And where TAB is the trade area boundary, measured as either the travel time or distance from Store A to Store B

t is the travel time (or total distance) between Store A and Store B

Sb is the size (area) of Store B

Sa is the size (area) of Store A

The subject property is located in Area A. The following specific data on distance and square footage were input into the formula.

Distance between Area A and Area B = 1.7 miles
Distance between Area A and Area E = 5 miles
Distance between Area A and Area D = 4 miles

Size of stores in Area A = 175,000 sq. ft.
Size of stores in Area B = 125,000 sq. ft.
Size of stores in Area D = 350,000 sq. ft.
Size of stores (planned) in Area E = 400,000 sq. ft.

The formula indicates that the trade area boundary of Area A is located at the following distances:

Area A compared to Area B = 0.92 mile from A
Area A compared to Area E = 1.66 miles from A
Area A compared to Area D = 2.0 miles from A

Adjusting for the Competition Based on Competitive Surveys

The competition can also show the adjustment needed by comparing the distances between the same brand-name stores; i.e., if a major grocer in town has three stores, and each is about 1.5 miles from the other stores, it indicates that 1.5 miles is the primary trade area for the grocery stores. Exhibit 12.10 shows a graphic example of this analysis using ring study analysis. The many overlapping rings to the east of the subject suggest that the subject trade area boundary would be less than a mile, similar to the previous calculations of Reilly's Law. However, currently to the west there is very little coverage, so the subject primary trade area should be extended farther to the west.

Exhibit 12.10 Grocery Store Ring Study

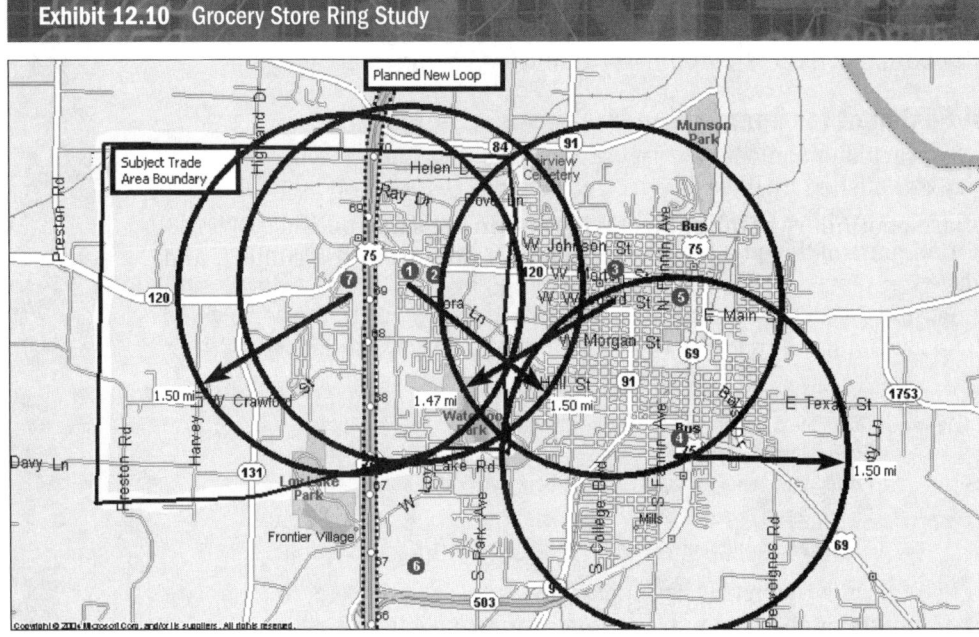

Conclusions of Subject Case Study Primary Trade Area
The results of the alternative analytical techniques are as follows:

- The radius of the trade area circle extended 1 to 1.5 miles.
- Customer spotting indicates that 70% to 80% of the subject's customers come from within two miles. (This refers to the number of customers, not the dollars spent per customer.) The breakdown of purchases by area can be ascertained only by using Level D survey techniques. Customers outside the primary trade area may drive to the grocery store and make big dollar expenditures, while nearby customers may make frequent trips but spend fewer dollars per trip. Thus, customer spotting cannot be considered in isolation from other factors.
- The radius of the gravitational models extends approximately one to two miles.
- A major grocery store in town has two stores located about 1.5 miles apart. The other two major grocery store brands, including the subject only have one store.

None of the techniques identifies a trade area that corresponds to specific census tract boundaries and none of the results is definitive. After reconciling the findings, the boundary for the subject center primary trade area has been adjusted in a number of ways.

- The boundary has been adjusted to reflect major natural and man-made barriers including parks, lakes, and major thoroughfares.
- The current market area was extended to the west to include the most urbanized area of existing housing because the subject has better linkages to these customers than the competition does. The final primary market area has a conservatively drawn southern border because a planned mall (Center 6) will open in three years, and Center 4 is now serving this area. It appears that Center 4 will be impacted by competition from Center 6 to a far greater extent than the subject.
- If the proposed supercenter Center 7, is developed, the western trade area boundary of the subject will remain the same because the new competition will be located only a half mile from the subject, and the manager felt that, based on their other stores, they would continue to serve this area to the west based on proximity and subject brand loyalty. However, the subject's capture will be reduced due to increased competition in the market area (subject capture will be considered in Step 6).

The final primary trade area boundary represents the area where nearly all of the customers/sales originates and most of the competition is located. It is indicated by the area drawn on the map in Exhibit 12.11.

In retail analysis, the greatest capture and competition are usually found in the primary trade area. Thus, the boundary of the primary trade area defines the area from which data are drawn to forecast buy-

Exhibit 12.11 Trade Area Boundary

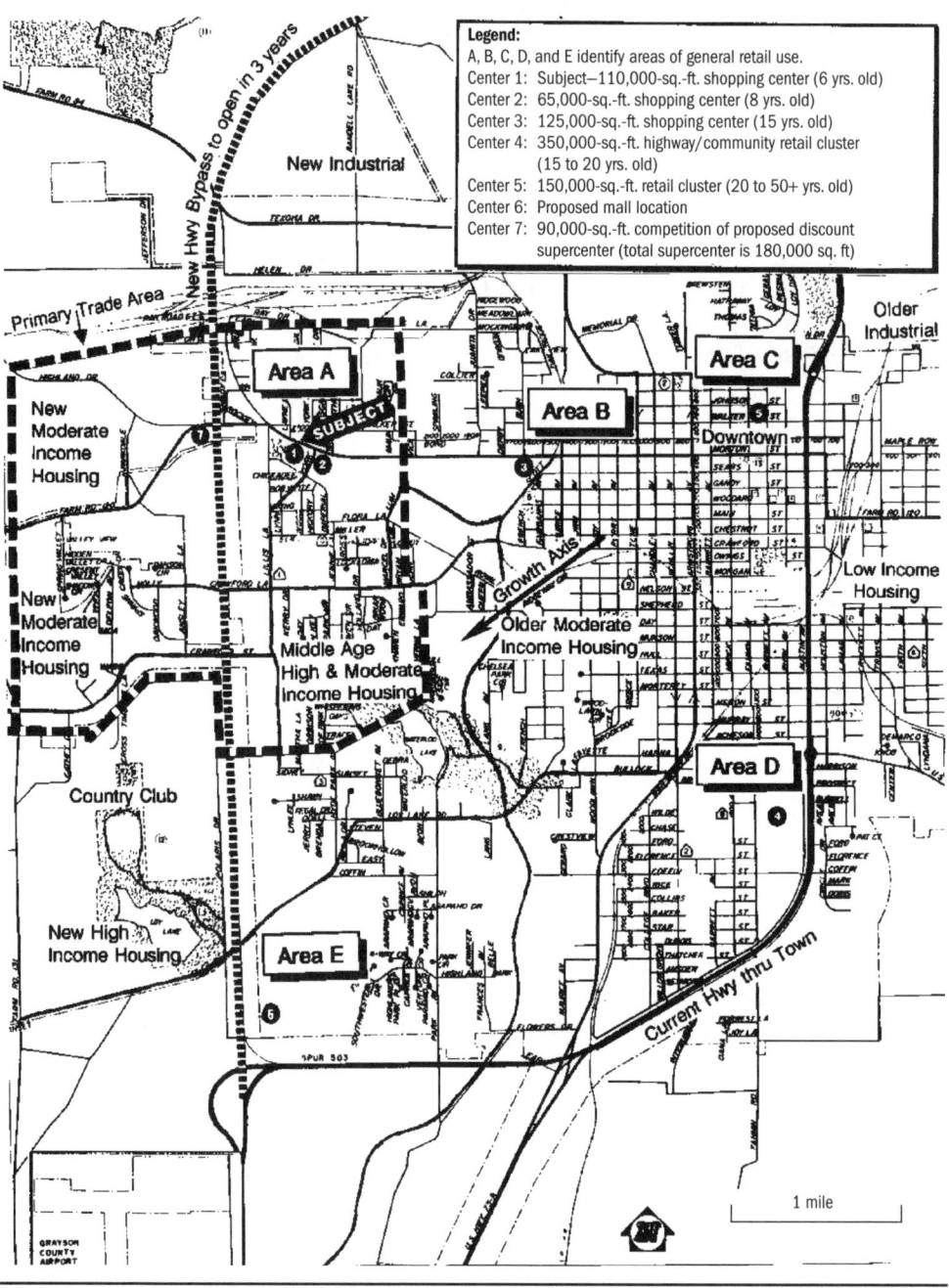

Legend:
A, B, C, D, and E identify areas of general retail use.
Center 1: Subject—110,000-sq.-ft. shopping center (6 yrs. old)
Center 2: 65,000-sq.-ft. shopping center (8 yrs. old)
Center 3: 125,000-sq.-ft. shopping center (15 yrs. old)
Center 4: 350,000-sq.-ft. highway/community retail cluster
(15 to 20 yrs. old)
Center 5: 150,000-sq.-ft. retail cluster (20 to 50+ yrs. old)
Center 6: Proposed mall location
Center 7: 90,000-sq.-ft. competition of proposed discount
supercenter (total supercenter is 180,000 sq. ft)

ing power and other demographic characteristics. It also indicates the place from which the appraiser gathers precise data on supply (competition). This is not to suggest that the appraiser can guess at the number of households and the extent of competition in the secondary area. However, less precision is needed in the secondary trade area because any error in the data will have less impact on the study.

Step 2.2: Consumer Profile

After the customers' locations have been identified, their demographic characteristics are compiled. These data reveal the type of customers that the subject store can expect to attract. The data will also be used to complete an inferred demand analysis and as the basis for making a population and income forecast for the future in the following demand step.

Step 3: Forecast Demand

Demand is analyzed using methods employed in inferred (trend) and fundamental analyses. A Level C analysis uses both types of methods and reconciles the conclusions into a final demand forecast. Demand can be inferred from trends based on the economic base and city growth, from citywide retail center occupancy trends, competitive centers' occupancy trends, and consumer profile trends.

Step 3.1: Analyze Trends (Inferred Analysis)

The economic base of the subject community was described at the beginning of this chapter. The community had a good employment mix and good prospects for continued growth. On average, the population has increased 5% per year for the last decade. Local industries continue to grow, and there is no indication that the trend will change in the next 10 years. Therefore, population growth of 5% per year is a reasonable expectation for the city; this growth indicates that demand for retail goods should also grow in the years to come.

Retail occupancy citywide has been steadily increasing over the past 10 years–from approximately 80% in the early part of the decade to about 90% today. Because the city is expected to continue to grow, it can be surmised that citywide occupancy will continue to increase and that the subject will realize a share of this increase.

The center across the street from the subject is operating at 95% occupancy. Similar centers around the city also have good occupancy rates, which suggests that demand is strong in the city for centers like the subject.

The dominant consumers in the area had average and median household incomes higher than the city, their age and number of persons per household indicated a significant number of households with children, and their education level was higher than the city average. All these factors are very positive for a neighborhood center anchored by a grocery store.

Fundamental Demand Analysis

A Level C market analysis requires fundamental studies in addition to inferred analyses. Three different fundamental forecast models are generally used:

- Forecast by buying power analysis
- Forecast by per capita expenditure method
- Forecast by occupied space ratio to population

Given the complexity and dynamics of today's retail industry, a reconciliation of multiple methods is recommended as a more reliable way to forecast sales. Thus, ideally, analysts would use all three as a check on the other method. However, the availability of data and time and budget constraints may require the analysts to choose one of the models that seems most reliable.

Step 3.2: Demand Forecast by Buying Power Analysis (Fundamental Analysis Method 1)

The fundamental demand for retail space is a function of the:

- Number of households
- Average (or median) household income
- Percentage of household income spent on retail purchases
- Percentage of retail purchases typically made at neighborhood shopping center (i.e., subject-type shopping center)
- Percentage of purchases made at the shopping center allocated to the primary and secondary trade areas
- Volume of sales per square foot of retail area required for the facility to remain profitable or supportable
- Demand from nonretail service tenants typically found at neighborhood shopping centers
- Normal vacancy rate of a balanced market

These variables are determined in Steps 3.2(1) through 3.2(9).

Step 3.2(1): Forecast Number and Size of Households in Primary Trade Area

The appraiser starts by compiling population forecasts for the market area. Typical data sources include government agencies, public utility companies, and commercial data vendors. Projections vary widely, so the appraiser should not simply accept the first one found. Multiple projections should be analyzed to determine the most reliable forecast. This judgment is critical because the population forecast is one of the most sensitive variables in an appraisal. A procedure for analyzing forecasts is described in the seven steps outlined below.

1. The first step is to compare forecasts with local area trends to determine the reasonableness of the forecasts. To evaluate forecasts in

terms of economic base factors, the appraiser must ask how the change in employment breaks down by sectors and whether trends in household growth and buying power are consistent with employment trends and trends in the regional economy.

In evaluating forecasts in terms of locational factors, the appraiser questions whether the development of the city infrastructure is consistent with the forecast and whether the land use pattern is consistent with the area's demographics. For example, a forecast of a significant percentage increase in high-income population cannot be applied to an area of the city dominated by moderate-income housing.

2. The appraiser then talks to the forecaster to identify the data sources employed and determine if they are reliable and appropriate. The methodology used to develop the forecast should be scrutinized based on the following questions:

- Is the technique state-of-the-art?
- Are the assumptions reasonable?
- Is the method appropriate? For example, the use of linear regression to analyze rapid growth or decline could overstate the rate of change. It may not be reasonable to apply a previously compounded rate to estimate future change because the base has changed. The appraiser should ascertain that the population figures forecast for sub-areas add up to the population forecast for the overall area.

3. The next step is to analyze the forecaster's motivation. Most water districts make high forecasts of the number and size of households to ensure that the community does not go without water. A health department may make low forecasts to curtail the costs of public hospital services and efficiently ration health care to the indigent. Chambers of commerce sometimes make high forecasts to promote their cities.

4. The fourth step is to compare the forecasted population to the known change for the last 10-year growth as estimated by the last U.S. Census. This comparison can be a simple inferred method that answers the question of whether the forecast is reasonable, given the last 10 year's growth. Say, for example, that the population is forecasted to increase by 5,000 in the study primary trade area boundary for the next 10 years. The actual last 10-year increase according to the U.S. Census was only 2,500 (half the population increase forecasted for the next 10 years). The analyst would then ask whether it is reasonable to expect the next 10 years' forecast growth to be twice the number of the last 10 years. If not, the appraiser should adjust the forecast in the reconciliation. This analysis technique is a benchmark of a forecast to known comparable data.

5. The fifth step is to make a simple, original forecast to get a feel for the numbers. This can help the appraiser judge the sensitivity of the variables.

6. Next, the appraiser compares the absolute growth of an analogous city with the absolute growth forecast for the subject city. Ideally, the analogue should be located nearby and have a similar economic base that has reached the population level forecast for the subject city. The time frame of the forecast can then be compared to the actual growth of the analogous city over a similar time span. This analytical method can be used to test the reasonableness of the absolute growth forecast.

7. Finally, the appraiser reconciles the data, considering their reliability and applicability, and chooses a final forecast range for the market study. (This step is similar to the reconciliation procedure in the sales comparison approach.) It should be noted that appraisal forecasts typically cover a longer time frame than those for specialized market studies. A specialized study usually has a short-term focus. For example, the analyst may question whether the retail center can lease up within the next three years and whether current demand exists for a clothing store. The questions an appraiser asks relate to a longer term and are more concerned with probability, i.e., what is the present value of future benefits, given the most probable tenants, the most probable competition, and the most probable customer base over the economic life of the project? The emphasis is different because a typical appraisal is performed for lending purposes, and lenders make a long-term commitment. For this reason, most lenders now require a 10-year discounted cash flow (DCF) analysis for appraisals. A specialized market study, on the other hand, may be undertaken to assess the prospects of selling men's clothing at a particular location for the next five years. A more advanced, Level D analysis is more specific and usually requires a shorter time frame than a Level C analysis.

Case Study Application of Step 3.2(1): Population Forecast
The appraiser estimates from census data the number of households in the subject's primary trade area at 3,072 (i.e., total primary trade area population of 7,373 divided by 2.4, the average household size). Data from a commercial source were compared with both local forecasts, and the appraiser's own simple forecast, in this case based on trend analysis and comparison with an analogous city. The appraiser concluded that the subject primary trade area should continue to grow by 130 to 210 new households per year, on average for the next decade. Thus, in five years the number of households is projected to be between 3,700 and 4,100 (rounded), and a point estimate of 3,920 is chosen. (This figure is shown under Step 3.2(1) in the summary of demand analysis in Exhibit 12.16.) To simplify the presentation, only one forecast is shown in this table. In practice, the development of high-, low-, and mid-range forecasts is recommended.

Step 3.2(2): Estimate Household Income and Total Income for Primary Trade Area
Total potential retail sales volume is a function of population, income level, and the propensity to spend income, which, in turn, depends on

the level of income and the characteristics of the population (age, family size, tastes, and preferences). Data on household income can be obtained from the following sources:

- The U.S. Census of Population, which provides data on the mean or median income per capita and per family gathered in each decennial census and updated annually by sample survey
- Current Population Reports, which publishes data on per capita income every two years
- The U.S. Commerce Department's Survey of Current Business, provides data on per capita income for counties and metropolitan areas
- The "Annual Survey of Consumer Buying Power" in *Sales and Marketing Management* magazine, which presents data on household income for counties, metropolitan areas, and major cities.
- Commercial data vendors

Most appraisers use commercial data sources for small area current income estimates. Since these data sources are some form of extrapolation from U.S. Census data, they should be checked for reasonableness. One such method is to associate income levels with area housing prices. Current income may be inferred from the sale prices of houses in the trade area. If the average sale price is $200,000, and it is assumed that 28% of gross income is spent on housing, the typical area household income can be estimated by performing the following calculations:

$200,000 house, minus 10% down payment = $180,000 mortgage @ 6% for 30 years requires $1,079.19 monthly payment Plus 20% for ad valorem taxes and insurance indicates a total yearly expenditure on housing of approximately $15,500.

$15,500 ÷ .28 = $55,400, the approximate total annual household income required to support housing in the $200,000 price range

Income Weighted by Location in the Primary Trade Area

If the trade area is part of a number of census tracts, the most accurate procedure is to calculate the income for specific subsections using block data. This is particularly important for convenience-type centers because the majority of their customers will come from the immediately adjacent area. The commercial vendor's ring studies (or polygons) usually sort by block data, but the computer program is an approximation method. The analysts can also manually estimate population in the subject primary trade area as shown in the Exhibit 12.12. To perform this analysis, the block data can be used to show income by location. (Note: some vendors will provide automated data by specific rings—i.e., 0 to ½ mile or ½ mile to 1 mile, which should provide similar results.)

In a Level D analysis the trade area would also be weighted toward the households that are closer to the subject shopping center as opposed to those that lie on the outer fringe of the trade area.

Aggregate income data can be compiled by weighting the income in the primary trade area by the percentage of the population in the census tract that is in the subject primary trade area. This procedure is illustrated in Exhibit 12.12.

This method will provide a check on some of the automated ring and polygon data and can also be used in Step 6, the capture estimate, to determine the probability of capturing the trade area dollars at the subject center. For example, the following illustration shows that the subject lies in census tract 101, with 45% of households in the primary trade area with the lowest household income. The analyst can use this data for possible refinement, such as using the median instead of mean data, or adjust the capture for the subject in Step 6. The subject capture adjustment, if any, will depend on the capture method used, and the degree and location of the competition in the trade area.

Exhibit 12.12 Income by Location in Primary Trade Area

Census Tract #	Number of HH in Census Tract		Estimated Percentage of Census Tract HH in Subject Primary Trade Area	Number of HH in Primary Trade Area	Avg. HH Income	% of HH in Primary Trade Area
101*	3,448	×	40%	1,379	$45,600	45%
102	3,193	×	35%	1,117	$54,480	36%
103	2,600	×	20%	520	$64,800	17%
105	1,105	×	5%	55	$115,200	2%
Totals/Wt. Avg.‡	10,346		100%	3,071	$53,330†	100%

*   Subject located in census tract #101.

†   Weighted average of household income in primary trade area.

‡   Numbers rounded.

Mean Versus Median Income

Both the mean and the median are measures of central tendency. In most communities, the mean income will be greater than the median income. This is true because most communities have a few people with large incomes and a great number of people with low and moderate incomes. In other words, the distribution of incomes is skewed toward the few higher incomes. If income were distributed evenly, then the average income (mean) and midpoint income (median) would be the same. This is rarely the case. Thus, some analysis of the difference between the mean and median income is advisable to determine which measure of central tendency gives the more reliable picture of purchasing power for the subject type market study.

The compilation of census data generally shows that family income is higher than household income. A household of only one individual may comprise a household, but a family must have two or more members. Income distribution can affect retail-spending patterns. Generally, higher income households spend less on retail than lower income groups. Use of average household or per capita incomes will give the total income in an area, but use in retail calculation may give an inflated number if a few very high-income households in the area skew the data.

When median income is significantly lower than mean (average income), then some analysts suggest that the median should be used for neighborhood convenience type shopping studies and the mean for shopper type market studies such as regional shopping center studies, which typically stock mostly shopper goods. The reasoning is that lower income consumers spend a bigger percentage of their income on neighborhood convenience goods than do higher income people. This determination is related to the data source for the next step in the calculation–the percentage of income spent on retail. When using percentage from one data source for another use, the base number used for the percentage calculation must be examined. As will be seen in the following discussion on this subject, most data sources are national or regional survey data such as the Bureau of Labor Statistics Consumer Spending Survey. This type of data is taken from large population areas and typically shows no significant difference between mean and median data, whereas for some small population areas data might have a wide variance.

The question relates to whether or not high-income households spend the same percentage of their income on total retail as low-income households. It is a known fact that low-income households spend a greater percentage of their income on food, for example, than do high-income households. The Bureau of Labor Statistics found in 2002 that low-income households spent 20% of their income on food while high-income households spent 12%. Overall, the 2002 Consumer Expenditure Survey found that households earning median incomes ($20,000 to $29,999) spent about 52% of their income, before taxes, on retail goods, while households earning more than $70,000 spent about 26% on the same goods.[12] The average of all households surveyed was 38%. Thus, in some cases the median income may be better measured if the data are significantly skewed one way or the other.

Inflated Dollars Versus Constant Dollars

Forecasts of income are generally based on rates extrapolated from data for larger areas and adapted to reflect the profile of households in the trade area. In an inflationary environment, real income does not necessarily increase. If the appraiser uses income projections based on inflationary dollars, then he or she should also employ data on the required volume of sales per square foot that reflect inflationary expectations. Alternatively, an appraiser may use a constant dollar approach, which considers real growth only, not inflation.

---

12. Bureau of Labor Statistics, *2002 Consumer Survey.* Average annual expenditures. Items considered retail-type goods included all types of food, alcoholic beverages, housekeeping supplies, household furnishings, apparel and services, vehicle purchases, gasoline, 20% of other vehicle expenses, 80% of entertainment, personal care products, and tobacco.

When considering forecasting incomes above inflation, analysts will typically require some Level D type analysis because, in general, historically real growth in income has not been significant, at least not on a national basis.

Consider the data from the Department of Labor from 1982 to 2005 of average weekly earnings for private non-agricultural workers. The average income in 1982 was $267.26, and in 2005 it was $536.17. At first glance it appears that average weekly earnings increased by more than 100% during these 23 years. However, if the income is compared on a constant dollar (taking inflation out) based on the consumer price index for urban wage earners and clerical workers (called the CPI-W), the total change over the 23-year period is 3.6%, or .16% per year, on average.

Granted, there are many local exceptions to this general national data. Some areas such as the Silicon Valley experienced an increase in income attributed to the new jobs from the high-tech industries. Areas that experience gentrification are another example of incomes in a local area exceeding the rate of inflation. However, both of these examples were caused by a significant change in the local economic base or land use pattern. If this were not forecast for the subject area, then real growth higher than the rate of inflation would be less likely.

Case Study Application of Step 3.2(2): Estimate Household Income

The appraiser estimates local mean household income to be $53,300. The primary trade area median income is $46,900, which suggests that the household incomes are skewed, but not significantly so. Exhibit 12.12 shows the income distribution in the primary trade area.

Step 3.2(3): Estimate the Percentage of Household Income Spent on Retail Items

To estimate the percentage of household income spent on retail purchases, nonretail expenditures are deducted from gross income to arrive at retail buying power. An example of representative breakdown of gross household income is shown in the following exhibit from the Bureau of Labor Statistics consumer survey data. The consumer survey is based on journals of a household's actual expenditures.

Other data sources (not shown) are state sales tax data and U.S. Economic Census of Retail Trade conducted every five years by the U.S. Census. These retail sales data can alternatively be compared on a percentage basis to the total household income for the same geographic area. The resulting calculation is an estimate of the percentage spent on all retail or specific segments. Some analysts make this a one-step calculation and combine Steps 3.2(3) and 3.2(4)[13] However, when using these data for the estimate of household retail spending percentage, the analyst should recognize the potential weaknesses. First, the alternative data method is based on total reported sales in an area, which means that it could include sales from households who

---

13. *Market Research for Shopping Centers,* International Council of Shopping Centers, 2005, page 30–31.

live outside the geographic area. For example, if using retail spending data from the Minneapolis, Minnesota, MSA, the reported sales data would include sales from such shopping centers as Mall of America. This mall generates sales from households that come from all over North America; thus, data on a per-household-basis from this geographic area would probably overstate the GAFO[14] retail spending percentage for the typical household that lives in Minneapolis. This is why the segmentation method presented in this book makes this estimate a two-part process of using BLS data for overall retail spending [Step 3.2(3)] and then using sales tax data for the percentage spent on specific retail items that are the subject of this study [Step 3.2(4)].

Exhibit 12.13 Household Income and Buying Power

Dallas/ Ft. Worth Consumer Expenditure Survey 2002

Item Description	Income	% of Gross Income	% of Disposable
Gross Income Before Taxes	$62,185		
Taxes	$11,904	19%	
Net Disposable Income	$50,281		
Average Annual Expenditures of Disposable Income			
Food and alcoholic beverages	$7,767	12%	15%
Housekeeping supplies	$583	1%	1%
Household furnishings and equipment	$1,765	3%	4%
Apparel and services	$2,528	4%	5%
Vehicle purchases	$5,160	8%	10%
Gasoline and motor oil	$1,506	2%	3%
Other vehicle expenses (50%)	$1,516	2%	3%
Personal care products and services	$648	1%	1%
Tobacco products	$256	0.4%	1%
Entertainment (80%)	$1,760	3%	4%
Total Retail Type Expenditures	$23,489	38%	47%
Housing	$13,406	22%	27%
Public transportation	$352	1%	1%
Health care	$2,432	4%	5%
Entertainment	$2,201	4%	4%
Reading and education	$518	1%	1%
Cash contributions	$1,446	2%	3%
Personal insurance and pensions	$6,126	10%	12%

Source: Bureau of Labor Statistics Consumer Expenditure Survey 2001-2002 for Dallas/Ft. Worth.

Note: Percentage numbers rounded to whole numbers.

14. GAFO stands for general merchandise, apparel, furniture and other miscellaneous goods (i.e., electronic). These are typical segments of sales for mall major stores.

Application of Step 3.2(3)

The appraiser estimates that approximately 40% of the average household income in the subject trade area is spent on retail purchases. This estimate is based on the analysis of primary market area incomes in the previous step, which suggested that more lower-income households than higher-income households are located in the subject primary trade area. Lower-income households typically spend a greater percentage of their income on basic retail goods. In the subject center, there are more stores selling necessary retail goods than stores selling luxury items. The breakdown of retail expenditures in Exhibit 12.13 was based on metropolitan data. Such data can be used only as guidelines for the subject trade area.

This step estimates the percentage of gross income spent on retail. The following steps in the model require the estimated percentage of expenditures for subject type center (neighborhood shopping). Thus, the model uses a percentage of a percentage in calculating neighborhood-shopping expenditures. This means that the base number of the different calculations must contain the same assumptions. Total retail expenditures in both bases for the percentage calculations must be exactly the same for the model to be most reliable. For example, note that the data in Exhibit 12.13 included car sales; thus, for the step allocated percentage of retail sales for neighborhood shopping, the base list of retail sales where the percentage is calculated must also include car sales.

Step 3.2(4): Define the Market Study Type—Estimate the Percentage of Retail Purchases Typically Made at Neighborhood Shopping Centers (i.e., the Subject's Type Center)

This step defines the type of market study being developed. For example, if a market study of only grocery stores were needed, the percentage of total retail spending on grocery purchases would be the percentage used at this step. Since data to estimate demand for neighborhood shopping in general (i.e., the subject and the subject's competition) is desired, then retail purchases in this market that would be realized at the typical neighborhood shopping center are needed since this was determined to be the subject type center and submarket that it serves.

The percentage of retail purchases typically made at a certain type of shopping center varies with its tenants. A Level D fundamental demand study can segment the demand on a tenant-by-tenant basis according to the specific type of retail item sold by each tenant.

Then the demand for each retail category (identified by SIC code or NAICS[15]) can be studied and compared to the competition posed by

---

15. SIC stands for Standard Industrial Classification, which was published by Executive Office of the President Office of Management and Budget in 1987. In 1997 this was changed to the NAICS, which stands for the North American Industry Classification System. The NAICS is also updated periodically. In 2000 the Census Bureaus started using the NAICS system for their retail trade survey. However, state sales tax data have been in transition on a state-by-state basis. Some states' data used the new classification and some have not. For example, in Texas in 2004, employment data was utilizing the new classification, but the state retail sales data still used the old SIC categories. Thus, until all data changes over to the new system, the appraiser will have to deal with a dual system.

corresponding retailers to assess current residual demand (gap analysis) on a category-specific basis. Studies like this are usually performed to solicit new tenants based on the identified gap in the market.

This type of study is conducted in a more detailed, Level D analysis. It is not described in this book because a Level D study is not used by appraisers but is principally used by retailers making management decisions to introduce new products to the market or expand current capture by stepping up marketing efforts.

In some Level C analyses key tenants may require analysis on the basis that if they have problems, the whole center may have problems. For example, for a neighborhood center, the analysts might want to segment only the grocery store, drug store, and hardware store. The procedure would entail calculating the demand for these key tenants and comparing the trade area demand to the competition. This would yield a residual demand study for only the key tenants of grocery, drug, and hardware store. If the market for these tenants were oversupplied, it would be a risky market in which to operate unless the subject's center has a dominant tenant in this category. This type of study is based on the premise that, as these tenants go, so goes the subject shopping center.

In most assignments, however, such as the subject neighborhood center, the appraiser is primarily interested in a mid-range (5- to 15-year) economic forecast for the center as a whole for whatever tenants might be expected during this time. This range is compatible with the economic modeling typically used in the income approach. Given the longer time frame of the forecast, a center's value will be most influenced by the general tenant types in the center; it is unlikely to be affected to a large degree by any one tenant.

In a Level C analysis conducted for an appraisal, the segmentation of purchases usually begins with the major tenant types most likely to occupy the subject over the next 10 years. The analyst examines the subject to identify major tenant types that sell convenience goods and shopper goods. If the facility principally sells convenience goods such as groceries and pharmaceuticals and personal services such as dry cleaning and shoe repair, the percentage of retail purchases captured will differ from that of a facility that sells shopper goods such as appliances and apparel. The appraiser can also look at other neighborhood centers in the area to determine the norm for those centers. National survey data are also available in such publications as the Urban Land Institute's *Dollars and Cents of Shopping Centers*. The data are updated every two years and contain information on the typical tenants found in neighborhood, community, and mall shopping centers. These data provide a good list to start with when comparing the subject's and competition's actual and potential tenants that are to be identified for the market study.

Next, the appraiser identifies unique tenant types (current and prospective over the next 10 years) on a category-by-category basis. After each category is noted, the anticipated percentages of expenditures made at these shops are totaled. These data are input in calculating demand.

Using this technique the analyst develops information about the percentage of expenditures from general tenant types that is anticipated at the subject over the next few years (usually a 10-year DCF period). The analyst does not forecast specific tenants or specific tenant-by-tenant space demand, as might be done in a more detailed, Level D study.

There are many variations of this procedure. For example, one Level D type of refinement uses general segmentation as a base but takes the analysis a step further and segments demand between large space tenants and small space tenants. This is more commonly found in market studies for large malls. Mall market studies typically focus on the residual demand for the GAFO tenant groups.

Data on Retail Expenditures

Data on expenditures for convenience and shopper goods are needed to complete this step in the analysis. Sources of this type of data include:

- U.S. Census Bureau-Economic Census of Retail Trade. Census conducted every five years for years ending in "2" and "7." The data give the number of establishments, annual sales, annual payroll and number of employees by type of business for the U.S., states, counties, MSAs and limited data by zip code.
- U.S. Department of Labor, Bureau of Labor Statistics, Consumer Expenditure Survey.
- Local sales tax data, which are compiled in most states by SIC or NACIS; state data geography varies from city level to zip code level in some states.
- Commercial data vendors provide current year and projected expenditures for individual categories for most household spending. The methodology typically is to use the BLS Consumer Expenditure Survey, which is determined for each small area based on the household income in the area.

The percentage of income spent on convenience goods and shopper goods depends on local income levels and general economic conditions and can change over time. Percentages that characterize consumer expenditures at a national or regional level may have to be adjusted to reflect local patterns. A typical expenditure pattern is illustrated in Exhibit 12.14.

Explanation of Exhibit 12.14

The percentages shown may vary over time because the spending habits of the population change. For example, more is now being spent on home computers than was spent in previous years. Percentages may also vary from area to area.

The categories shown in the exhibit are grouped by the 1987 SIC and the NAICS. The state data source is usually sales tax data. Because of the major recordkeeping change required of the states and businesses some states have been slow to change. Also, some of the commercial data ven-

Exhibit 12.14 Percentage of Retail Sales—Example Metro Area

Industry Group	SIC	2002 NAICS*	Expenditures as % of Total Retail Sales	Applicable to Neighborhood/ Community Market Study
Lumber and building materials	521	4441	5.10%	
Hardware and paint and wallpaper stores	523-525	44413	1.20%	1.20%
Retail nurseries and garden stores	526		0.75%	0.75%
Totals 52—Building Material	**52**	**444**	**7.05%**	**1.95%**
Department stores	531	4521	10.40%	
Variety stores	533	4529	0.54%	0.54%
Misc. general merchandise	539	4529	2.10%	2.10%
Totals 53—General Merchandise Stores	**53**	**452**	**13.04%**	**2.64%**
Grocery stores	5411-12	4451	10.56%	10.56%
Other	542-549	44511	4.35%	4.35%
Totals 54—Food Stores	**54**	**445**	**14.91%**	**14.91%**
Motor vehicle dealers	551-552	44111-12	14.50%	
Auto and home supply stores	553	44131	4.50%	4.50%
Gasoline service stations	554		2.20%	
Other	555-559	4412	1.01%	
Totals 55—Automotive	**55**	**441**	**22.21%**	**4.50%**
Men's and boys' clothing	561	44811	0.24%	0.24%
Women's clothing	562-563	44812	1.75%	1.75%
Family—general	564-569	44814	2.02%	
Totals 56—Apparel and Accessories	**56**	**448**	**4.01%**	**1.99%**
Furniture stores	5712	44211	1.49%	
Specialty home furnishing stores	5713-572	44221	1.47%	
Radio, TV, and electronic stores	5731	443112	2.72%	2.72%
Computer and software stores	5734	44312	2.50%	
Record and prerecorded tape stores	5735	45122	0.30%	0.30%
Musical instrument stores	5736	45114	0.20%	
Totals 57—Home Furnishings	**57**	**451**	**8.68%**	**3.02%**
Restaurants	5812	7221	9.75%	9.75%
Drinking places	5813		0.75%	0.75%
Totals 58—Eating and Drinking Places	**58**	**722**	**10.50%**	**10.50%**
Drug stores	591	4461	3.18%	3.18%
Liquor stores	592	44531	1.20%	1.20%
Used merchandise stores	593	45331	0.40%	
Sporting good and bicycle shops	5941	45111	1.40%	1.40%
Book stores and stationery stores	5942-5943	451211	0.85%	
Jewelry stores	5944	44831	0.76%	
Hobby, toy, and game shops	5945	45112	0.50%	0.50%
Camera, novelty, luggage, and sewing stores	5946-5949	44313	0.97%	
Florists	5992	45311	0.24%	0.24%
Tobacco and newsstand	5993-5994	451/453991	0.08%	
Optical goods stores	5995	44613	0.14%	
Misc. retail stores, NEC	5999		9.88%	9.88%
Totals 59—Miscellaneous Retail	**59**	**445-453**	**19.60%**	**16.40%**
Total Retail Sales All Categories			**100%**	**56%**

* Note the NAICS codes do not directly match all SIC codes. The NAICS includes more categories than SIC. Appendix B gives a more complete comparison and more comprehensive list of NAICS codes. Also reference the latest version of NAICS on the U.S. Census Bureau Web site.

dors still convert the new NAICS retail data to SIC categories to show historical trends. The data presented here are based on the SIC classification. The appendix of this report provides an overview of the NAICS changes. A detailed explanation of each category is provided for each classification manual available from the U.S. Bureau of Census Web Site.

Case Study Application of Step 3.2(4): Estimate Percentage of Retail Spending at Subject-Type Center

The appraiser estimates that about 56% of household retail purchases are made at shopping centers similar to the subject center. The appraiser studies the subject's tenant mix and nearby centers, the trade area, and area trends to determine the subject's most probable future tenants and to estimate the percentage of retail expenditures typically made at this type center. The total percentage is estimated by adding the respective percentages of select items listed in Exhibit 12.14. An estimate obtained in this way cannot be considered conclusive since shopping center tenancy varies over time, and this is a forecast of the most probable. Moreover, there is no standard shopping center. However, this does specifically define the type of market study being completed by the categories selected. The previous exhibit shows an example of the process of defining the type of market study.

The following categories from Exhibit 12.14 were excluded from the analysis: other building materials, department stores, automotive sales/ service stations, furniture and appliances, and some miscellaneous retail. The remaining categories indicate approximately a 56% capture rate.

If the assignment warranted a Level D study, the appraiser would investigate all retail categories, estimate the demand for each, and compare each category with its respective competition.[16] This level of study would help identify retail gaps (undersupplied retail categories), which could be used to target the most probable future tenants for the subject.

Step 3.2(5): Estimate the Percentage of Sales Retention in the Primary Trade Area from Total Potential Sales for the Primary Trade Area

This analysis considers the leakage of customers out of the primary trade area to peripheral competition located outside the subject primary trade area. It takes into account location and linkage factors and other factors such as type of retail vendors. This is based on the fact that where people shop depends on a number of factors, and location linkages is only one of them. For example, some customers will prefer a certain food store brand and will drive some distance just to shop there. Others will go to a center or large discount store located outside their primary trade area because they can combine several shopping needs at a large center with many product lines. That is why, for example, some grocery store chains locate in regional power centers. Leakage analysis starts with locational and linkage considerations but includes the marketing and brand appeal of competing centers in adjacent market areas.

---

16. An example of this study can be found in Michael D. Beyard, W. Paul O'Mara, et al. *Shopping Center Development Handbook,* 3rd ed. (Washington, D.C.: Urban Land Institute, 1999).

Thus, the percentage of retail leakage outside the primary trade area includes purchases made to competition that lies just outside the primary trade area, which may be closer to the consumer than the other stores in the trade area. It also includes purchases consumers make while on trips, purchases of specific items or alternative brands not available in the primary trade area, purchases made near workplaces, and purchases made at competing centers that provide special amenities or offer a variety not found in the primary trade area.

The estimated retention of potential retail sales in the primary trade area is a difficult number to support in any study. At best, only a range can be estimated. Nevertheless, the techniques described below may be considered.

Many state and local governments compile sales tax data using similar categories and often break this information down by zip code for small geographic areas. The tax data can indicate the actual dollars spent, which can be compared to the estimate of potential retail purchases. The data compiled in sales per capita show the categories and the magnitude of sales leakage out of an area. The difference is one measure of the leakage out of the trade area. For example, consider the following restaurant sales data:

Restaurant Sales Per Capita

State	Metro	County	City
$1,195	$1,413	$1,035	$742

The data show that the city's sales are 62% of the state's, 52% of the metro area's, and 71% of the county's. Thus, there is leakage out of the city of at least 29% based on the county as the standard (100% county standard minus 71% city sales = 29%). A variation of the above procedure is to utilize the Bureau of Labor Statistics Consumer survey, which give typical household retail spending by various broad categories. These data can be used to estimate an area's potential retail sales and then convert the survey estimate data to sales per capita to compare to the preceding actual sales from the sales tax data.

Another method for estimating the retention of sales is to compare the trade area circles, such as in the previous trade area delineation analysis step. This method begins with identifying all the subject's competing centers, whether inside or outside the subject primary trade area. Next, the "rule of thumb" trade area circles are drawn for each of the competitive centers to determine whether trade area circles of nearby competitors overlap the final boundaries chosen for the subject. If they do, the percentage of households involved must be determined. The number of shared households indicated by overlapping circles, can be used as the starting point to estimate the percentage leakage.

A third technique uses the location rating of citywide retail areas developed in Step 1.2(4). This rating combines locational and marketing factors such as the quality of the adjacent area's competitive stores. The subject did not rate as the best retail location in town, but it came in at a close second. On the other hand, if the subject had rated considerably lower than nearby competitors, the retail sales retention could be lower.

The final retention estimate represents a probable range. As in many other steps of the market analysis, estimates derived from alternative techniques should be compared, and the final capture forecast should be based on the reliability and comparability of the data analyzed.

The techniques described can be applied in the analysis of an existing retail center or a specific proposed retail development. A more detailed analysis would include marketing features compared to the competition. The leakage might be attributed to poor design, insufficient marketing, or the tenant mix of the center. When these deficiencies are corrected, the center's retention might increase. This type of problem usually requires a Level D analysis. The effect of marketing usually is not considered within the scope of a typical valuation appraisal.

A general estimation procedure can be used in some cases. If the buying power and competition in the primary and secondary areas are similar, then the leakage out of the primary trade area should approximate the leakage into the primary trade area.

Case Study Application of Step 3.2(5): Percentage of Sales Retention

The appraiser estimates that the subject center will retain 75% of the total potential sales in its primary trade area for the next few years and rise to 85% when the new supercenter is built in about 5 years. The basis for raising the percentage is the potential drawing power of the new supercenter, which should help retain current potential customers who leave the subject primary trade area to shop. Even though the competitors around the new mall could draw some of the demand from the subject primary trade area, the proposed new supercenter is expected to keep the retention of nearby customers high.

Step 3.2(6): Convert Retail Buying Power to Real Estate Square Foot by Dividing Total Demand by Required Sales Volume Per Square Foot

The retail buying power is converted to real estate measurements so that the data can be used to forecast occupancy and rents in the market. The conversion factor is called "required sales per square foot," which is the most probable level of sales required per square foot of space at a specific rent for a store to turn a profit.

Required sales per square foot can be obtained from industry data on median sales per square foot of GLA. Such data are often quoted along with data on the median rent per square foot of GLA. Required sales volume per square foot of retail space is closely related to rent per square foot of retail space. If rents increase, greater sales volume is required to support the store. If rents decline, less sales volume is necessary for the store to remain in business.

Sources of Sales Per Square Foot Data

Publications such as *The Dollars and Cents of Shopping Centers* provide such data for different tenant classifications. Exhibit 12.15 shows typical store sales per square foot and rents for the types of tenants most frequently found in neighborhood shopping centers. This exhibit is dated and is included for example only. It is one of many exhibits in this book that the appraiser should reference. Thus, purchase of the most recent ULI survey and a complete review of the survey data is required to apply this data source.

Other data sources include the International Council of Shopping Centers, shopping center directories published by Chicago-based National Research Bureau (NRB), and many periodicals such as the summer issue of *Stores* magazine, which shows sales for all major chain retailers, as well as *Chain Store Age*. Some university real estate centers and various trade association Web sites also have these data. The

Exhibit 12.15 Tenants Most Frequently Found in Neighborhood Shopping Centers

Tenant Classification	Avg. Number of Stores	Median GLA (Sq. Ft.)	% of Total GLA	Median Sales Volume Per Sq. Ft. of GLA per Year	Median Total Rent Per Sq. Ft. of GLA*
Food					
Supermarket	0.5	33,080	58%	$335.71	$6.75
Food Service					
Restaurant without liquor	0.2	2,400	4%	$175.28	$11.03
Restaurant with liquor	0.4	3,360	6%	$271.60	$15.50
Sandwich shop	0.2	1,350	2%	$207.24	$15.00
Pizza	0.3	1,500	3%	$237.91	$13.74
Chinese fast food	0.2	1,491	3%	$130.68	$12.24
Clothing and Accessories					
Women's specialty	0.1	1,483	3%	$448.81	$27.00
Gifts/Specialty					
Cards and gifts	0.1	2,533	4%	$228.55	$12.65
Jewelry					
Jewelry	0.1	1,209	2%	$432.54	$15.66
Drugs					
Drugstore/pharmacy	0.3	9,000	16%	$380.80	$9.90
Subtotal/Averages of Retail		57,406	100%	$284.91	$13.95
Wt. Avg. of Retail Sales (Wt. by GLA)				$321.65	**$9.43**
Personal Services					
Women's hair salon	0.3	1200		$151.91	$11.90
Dry cleaner	0.4	1,500		$166.72	$15.36
Unisex hair	0.2	1,276		$218.20	$14.17
Videotape rentals	0.2	3,705		$86.66	$12.60
Mailing/packaging	0.1	1,258		$235.93	$15.53
Nail salon	0.2	930		$82.50	$14.03
Financial					
Banks	0.2	4,096			$14.68
Finance company	0.2	1,555			$12.00
Insurance	0.2	1,067			$10.96
Offices (other than financial)	0.5	1,660		$197.17	$12.16
Totals other space		18,247	24%		
Totals/Averages All Categories		75,653		**$234.60**	

*Supportable sales volume per square foot is related to the rents for retail space. If rents go down, less sales volume would be required to support the store and vice versa.

© 2002 The Urban Land Institute, *Dollars and Cents of Shopping Centers*. Used with permission. Data presented are dated for example only. Appraiser should reference the most recent publication for actual use.

following is an example analysis of ULI data. The appraiser could also construct a composite data analysis from various sources to conduct similar analyses.

Forecasts of the sales required per square foot of retail space can be made in current (inflated) or constant (real) dollars. If the analyst uses inflated dollars, the estimates of income and expenses must also be expressed in inflated dollars. The need for more GLA comes from a forecast of real growth in sales, not from inflation.

Case Study Application of Step 3.2(6)—Estimate of Required Sales Per Square Foot

The required sales volume per square foot of tenant space for the subject center can be estimated by weighting the anticipated rent from each of the tenants by the respective size of the tenant space. After adjusting for rent differences between the local market and the data, the estimate of the average sales volume required was approximately $300 per square foot of GLA. The final judgment on required sales involves using data from Exhibit 12.15 and other data from *The Dollars and Cents of Shopping Centers* and thus cannot be taken directly from Exhibit 12.15.

The appraiser then divides the total retail sales potential by the dollar sales required to support one square foot of retail space to derive the supportable square footage of retail space. (See Step 3.2(8) in Exhibit 12.16.)

Step 3.2(7): Repeat Steps 3.2(1) Through 3.2(6) for the Secondary Trade Area and Nonresident Sources

This step is shown in Exhibit 12.16 as one number on line 12. However, it requires the same steps described for the primary trade area, except that it is now applied to the secondary trade area. Also, the nonresident demand sources are included as tourists and daytime employment in the area such as office workers. In Exhibit 12.16 the first 11 steps involve demand from nearby local residences.

In the subject's case, there were no nonresident demand sources in the primary or secondary trade areas but only demand from residents from the secondary trade area. Currently, there is very little secondary demand. However, it is estimated that when the new supercenter opens, the additional capture of residents who live outside the primary trade area, i.e., inside the secondary trade area, is highly likely.

The procedure for secondary trade area demand estimate is to repeat the same previous steps completed for the primary trade area, except that now they are applied to the secondary area. The extent of this demand can be estimated as inflow to the subject trade area the same way as the primary trade area retention estimate step 3.2(5). In the case study it was insignificant. Thus, it could have been considered offset by the outflow from the primary trade area and might have been a good breakeven approximation.

The level of analysis needed for the secondary area and or nonresidents depends on how much it is considered a significant part of the subject trade area demand. In the case study it was not significant to measure but in some locales such as Orlando, Florida the buying power from nonresidents exceeds the residents' retail buying power.

If the nonresident demand is significant, then several procedures for estimating it could be considered. First, this involves estimating the type and number of nonresidents in the primary (and secondary, if significant) trade area. This can be accomplished by using estimates by commercial vendors such as Site To Do Business (stdbonline.com), which provides a current estimate of daytime employment.

A forecast for this increase can be made by the appraiser's ascertaining the city employment growth rate. Other sources such as the number of tourists might be found by analyzing hotel occupancy data in the primary or secondary trade area. Tourist estimates are also made by many local and state economic development departments. Second-home residents are not counted as part of the U.S. census population for an area, but they do count the number of second-home housing units; thus, an estimate of second-home residents per unit would give a good approximation.

After the number of nonresidents is estimated, an estimate of retail buying per person must be made. Secondary data on this item is limited, but usually local economic development departments and state tourist agencies have estimates. Their data can be checked by calculating the current buying power of residents and comparing it to the actual retail sales in the area by sales tax data from the state.

With these two numbers—nonresident population and spending per resident—the calculation for supportable retail space from nonresident sources is the same as resident calculations presented in this case study.

Step 3.2(8): Determine Total Demand in the Primary and Secondary Trade Areas
In this step, the appraiser adds the retail sales potential of the primary and secondary trade areas or sources. (See Exhibit 12.16.)

Step 3.2(9): Estimate Square Footage of Nonretail Users of Neighborhood Shopping Centers
The space in neighborhood centers includes tenants who provide personal services, financial services, or office uses such as dental offices. The demand for this space is not allocated in the previous retail buying power. The exhibit from the Urban Land Institute's shopping center survey shows the type of tenants most frequently found. A calculation of the ULI data-mean square footage of these uses compared to the overall square footage suggests that about 24% of the space is being used for nonretail tenants.

Case Study Application of Step 3.2(9): Estimate of Nonretail Uses
A survey of the shopping centers in the subject city found that about 15% of the neighborhood center's space is used for the nonretail uses, and this will be applied in the demand model.

Step 3.2(10): Adjust the Estimate of Supportable Retail Space for Frictional Vacancy (Balanced Market Vacancy Rate)

This step recognizes that in a balanced market some vacant space for move-ins, move-outs, and short-term growth is necessary to maintain rents at competitive levels. Economists sometimes refer to normal vacancy as *frictional vacancy*, sometimes called the normal or balanced market vacancy. The concept "frictional vacancy" is demand-side data; "current vacancy" is supply-side data.

The rate applied to the subject shopping center is 5%, the industry rule-of-thumb.

Step 3.3: Analyze Demand by Ratio Method (Fundamental Analysis Method 2)

In the ratio method the analyst applies the current amount of occupied retail square footage per capita to the future population forecast. This method is applicable when the amount of currently occupied space is known.

The following ratio analysis makes use of the supply (competition) survey in Exhibit 12.22. The survey shows that currently occupied competitive (neighborhood/community type retail) space in the city totals 722,500 square feet (competitive space plus space in the subject). The population of the same geographic area as surveyed was 55,000 people. Thus, there is approximately 13 square feet of competitive retail space per person in the city (722,500 / 55,000).

The typical suburban city in a metropolitan area has about 22 to 36 sq. ft. per capita of all types of retail. The subject citywide neighborhood (convenience retail) is about one-half the typical city total retail. The subject is also located on the outskirts of a major metro area; thus, it loses significant retail to the adjacent central city (see the following per capita sales data). Therefore, the subject 13 sq. ft. per capita is reasonable.

In the subject's primary trade area (Area A), there are currently 7,373 people and 149,750 square feet of occupied neighborhood/community retail space. This indicates a ratio of approximately 20 square feet of retail space per person.

The basis for using the ratio method is that the underlying factors in the market will maintain a constant ratio to population for the future. Exhibit 12.17 shows the results of the ratio demand method.

Step 3.4: Forecast Demand by Per Capita Sales Method (Fundamental Analysis Method 3)

This method uses actual retail sales data and population data to find retail sales per person in a geographic area, according to the following procedure:

- Find the actual retail sales data by type of retail business. Sources include sales tax data, U.S. Census retail sales survey, and commercial vendors.

Ref. Work Step	Line No.	Year	Current	in 5 Yrs.	in 10 Yrs.	Comment
3.2(1)	1	Total number of households in primary trade area	3,072	3,920	4,920	Reconciled forecast of vendor's forecast and appraiser's forecast
3.2(2)	2	Average household income	$53,300	$53,300	$53,300	Based on vendor data estimate and compared to CPI increase in area from last census. Constant dollar model
	3	Total household income in primary trade area	$163,737,600	$208,936,000	$262,236,000	Line 1 × Line 2
3.2(3)	4	% Income spent on retail	40%	40%	40%	Bureau of Labor Statistics
	5	Total retail sales potential	$65,495,040	$83,574,400	$104,894,400	Line 3 × Line 4
3.2(4)	6	% of retail sales by subject type shopping center	56%	56%	56%	Spending pattern % for neighborhood-type retail
	7	Total subject-type shopping center sales	$36,677,222	$46,801,664	$58,740,864	Line 5 × Line 6
3.2(5)	8	% of potential retention of sales in primary trade area	75%	85%	85%	With new supercenter in area should retain more customers in Yrs. 5–10
	9	Retail sales potential in primary trade area from resident household	$27,507,917	$39,781,414	$49,929,734	Line 7 × Line 8
3.2(6)	10	Sales required per sq. ft.	$300	$300	$300	Source: *Dollars & Cents of Shopping Centers*
	11	Supportable sq. ft. of retail space from households in primary trade area	91,693	132,605	166,432	Line 9 divided by Line 10
3.2(7)	12	Plus demand of neighborhood type retail space from secondary trade area and/or sources	27,508	39,781	49,930	Demand from residents in secondary area plus nonresidents in primary or secondary trade area
3.2(8)	13	Total occupied retail demand from primary and secondary trade area	119,201	172,386	216,362	Line 11 + Line 12
3.2(9)	14	Percentage of service/office use/medical use	15%	15%	15%	Estimate based on analysts' org. survey and *Dollars and Cents of Shopping Centers*
	15	Plus demand for nonretail use	21,035	30,421	38,182	(Line 13/.85) minus Line 13
	16	Total demand for occupied sq. ft. of retail and service/office space from primary and secondary trade area	140,236	202,807	254,544	Includes all types of retail and non-retail typically found in a neighborhood shopping center
3.2(10)	17	Plus frictional vacancy @ 5%	7,381	10,674	13,397	(Line 16/.95) minus Line 16
	18	Total forecast demand (sq. ft.) in primary trade area	147,617	213,481	267,941	Market demand for neighborhood shopping center space

Exhibit 12.17 Retail Market Analysis—Ratio Method

Item					Comments/Source
1	Existing occupied sq. ft. retail (and office in retail) in primary trade area	149,750			Survey data
2	Current population in primary trade area for same time	7,373			Census, commercial data, and Council of Governments
3	Ratio of occupied retail sq. ft. per capita (population and/or employees)	20.31			Calculation
	Forecast New Demand	**Current**	**+5 Yrs.**	**+10 Yrs.**	
4	Forecast population in primary market area	7,373	9,409	11,808	Census, commercial data, and Council of Governments
5	Ratio of occupied sq. ft. per capita	20.31	20.31	20.31	Calculation from Line 3
6	Demand for occupied shopping center space	149,750	191,102	239,827	Calculation
9	Plus frictional vacancy @ 5%	7,882	10,058	12,622	Calculation
10	Total forecasted demand (sq. ft.) in primary trade area	157,632	201,160	252,450	Includes all types of retail and nonretail users typically found in neighborhood shopping centers

- Analyze the data to find the sales most typical for a neighborhood shopping center (or whatever type of retail market study is being performed).
- Estimate the population for the same geographic area covered by the sales data. The population figure must also be based on the same year as the sales data being used.
- Calculate the sales per capita for the different retail categories.
- Repeat the process for various geographic areas.
- Use the geography that best represents the retail of the subject locale as the sales potential proxy.
- Apply the sales potential proxy of sales per capita to the subject current and forecasted population.

Analysis of the Per Capita Retail Sales Data

The sales data can be used for many purposes from inferring demand to establishing the fundamental demand shown in Exhibit 12.19.

The concentration of sales in one area compared to another shows sales leakage out of one area. Leakage to another area means that area has superior retail establishments or product choices.

The data in Exhibit 12.18 show that the metro area has a number of malls and major department stores, as its per capita department store sales of $1,739 per person are higher than state department store sales, which is $1,546 per person. It also shows that the subject city's department store sales of $754 per person are half the state's, which means that the subject city lacks many large stores. This is probably why a mall and supercenter are planned for the subject city since the data suggest it is underserved, given its size and population growth.

The subject area is slightly below average in local convenience retail. For example, the grocery store sales in the subject city at $1,247 per person are below the county's, which is $1,559 per person and is below the metro. Thus, one can infer that the subject county must have other large and more popular grocery stores that are probably located in areas closer to the metro area and lure sales from the subject city.

Choosing the "Best Fit" Sales Per Capita Data Proxy for the Type of Market Study

The data are analyzed to ascertain which geographic data best represent the subject market's situation. For example, the subject county data may represent the subject's best potential in the near future even though sales per person are below current sales. On the other hand, the subject city could not expect to achieve the sales of shopper goods stores such as those in the metro area since the metro area draws from such a large area outside its own local population.

Exhibit 12.18 shows the sales per capita data and the proxy data estimated that best represents the subject market's potential for neighborhood shopping goods stores.

The data source in Exhibit 12.18 is state sales tax data and results from a study performed by a market analyst. The state did not have data categorized by NAICS code, so the SIC code was used. The U.S. Census Web site provides tables to convert SIC data to NAICS if needed. The data shown in Exhibit 12.18 are actual data for the locale but they are shown for example only. Because data can vary from locale to locale, an analyst should get current data specific to the study's locale.

Forecasting Demand by Sales Per Capita

The next step in the per capita demand estimate is to apply the total real sales per capita estimate to the forecasted population for the trade area(s). Exhibit 12.19 shows this calculation.

Step 3.5: Reconcile Findings and Forecast Final Demand

Each forecast method has its strengths and weaknesses, so it is recommended that throughout the study, alternative methods be used and the results reconciled into a final conclusion. In the market analysis component of a valuation study, inferred (trend) analysis and fundamental analysis by various methods is recommended.

In the reconciliation of data into a final demand forecast, the analyst should consider the strengths and weaknesses of each method. The strength of inferred methods such as recent trend analysis is that the data are verifiable. The appraiser knows the previous occupancy rate of the subject, the previous occupancy rate of the competition, and any specific increases that have been realized. The method's weakness is that the data are historical and supply oriented. This is a seri-

Exhibit 12.18 Retail Sales Per Capita

Industry Group	SIC #	State	Adjacent Metro Area	County	Subject City	Selected for Neigh. Retail
Lumber and building materials	521	$582	$755	$741	$571	$0
Paint, glass, and wallpaper stores	523	$49	$42	$34	$26	$34
Hardware stores	525	$117	$88	$42	$42	$42
Retail nurseries and garden stores	526	$75	$65	$54	$56	$56
Totals—Building Material		$823	$949	$871	$695	$132
Department stores	531	$1,546	$1,739	$1,184	$754	$0
Variety stores	533	$45	$65	$61	$52	$61
Misc. general merchandise	539	$320	$225	$192	$153	$192
Total—General Merchandise Stores		$1,911	$2,029	$1,437	$959	$253
Grocery stores	5411	$1,454	$1,512	$1,559	$1,247	$1,559
Other	542-549	$512	$503	$390	$499	$499
Totals—Food Stores		$1,966	$2,015	$1,949	$1,746	$2,058
Motor vehicle dealers (new and used)	551-552	$1,829	$2,476	$2,496	$1,811	$0
Auto and home supply stores	553	$453	$592	$308	$215	$308
Gasoline service stations	554	$550	$328	$200	$237	$0
Others	555	$156	$204	$231	$266	$0
Totals—Automotive		$2,988	$3,600	$3,235	$2,529	$308
Men's and boys' clothing	561	$37	$45	$48	$28	$48
Women's clothing	562	$82	$86	$96	$63	$96
Family—general	563-569	$420	$622	$682	$413	$0
Totals—Apparel and Accessories		$539	$753	$826	$504	$144
Furniture stores	5712	$310	$358	$333	$198	$0
Specialty home furnishing stores	5713-572	$291	$387	$290	$198	$0
Radio, TV, and electronic stores	5731	$356	$465	$355	$209	$355
Computer and software stores	5734	$428	$607	$316	$104	$0
Record and pre-recorded tape stores	5735	$28	$30	$20	$18	$20
Musical instrument stores	5736	$35	$40	$39	$30	$0
Totals—Home Furnishings		$1,448	$1,887	$1,353	$757	$375
Restaurants	5812-5817	$1,195	$1,413	$1,035	$742	$742
Drinking places	5813-5814	$78	$76	$48	$48	$48
Totals—Eating and Drinking Places		$1,273	$1,489	$1,083	$790	$790
Drug stores	591	$425	$490	$277	$314	$314
Liquor stores	592	$94	$126	$42	$96	$96
Used merchandise stores	593	$105	$96	$43	$47	$0
Sporting good and bicycle shops	5941	$96	$147	$110	$115	$115
Book and stationery stores	5942-5943	$181	$266	$183	$138	$0
Jewelry stores	5944	$97	$139	$101	$80	$0
Hobby, toy, and game shops	5945	$69	$72	$96	$72	$72
Camera, novelty, luggage, and sewing stores	5942-5949	$139	$163	$133	$47	$0
Florists	5992	$34	$34	$17	$31	$31
Tobacco stores and newsstands	5993	$14	$20	$12	$16	$0
Optical goods stores	5995	$29	$25	$19	$76	$0
Misc. retail stores, NEC	5999	$1,568	$1,419	$918	$598	$598
Totals—Miscellaneous Retail		$2,851	$2,997	$1,951	$1,630	$1,226
Total Retail Sales All Categories		$13,799	$15,719	$12,705	$9,610	$5,286

Exhibit 12.19   Neighborhood Retail Demand by Per Capita Expenditure

Line	Year	Current	In 5 Yrs.	In 10 Yrs.	Source/Comment
1	Population in primary trade area	7,373	9,409	11,808	Current population based on U.S. census data Forecasted population based on reconciliation of various forecasts and rounded
2	Neighborhood-type retail sales per capita	$5,286	$5,286	$5,286	See previous selection table for items considered neighborhood shopping oriented
3	Total neighborhood retail sales potential	$38,973,678	$49,735,974	$62,417,088	From residents in primary market area
4	% of retail sales retention in primary trade area	75%	85%	85%	With new supercenter in area should retain more customers in Yrs. 5–10
5	Neighborhood retail sales expected	$29,230,259	$42,275,578	$53,054,525	From residents in primary market area
6	Required sales per sq. ft.	$300	$300	$300	*Dollars and Cents of Shopping Centers*
7	Supportable retail sq. ft. from resident population in primary trade area	97,434	140,919	176,848	Divide Line 5 by Line 6
8	Plus demand for neighborhood retail from secondary trade area or other sources	29,230	42,276	53,055	Estimate based on location rating and analysis of sales tax expenditures per zip code
9	Total occupied retail sq. ft. demand from primary and secondary trade areas	126,664	183,194	229,903	Total occupied retail space in sq. ft.
10	Percentage of nonretail service/office use	15%	15%	15%	Estimate based on analyst's org. survey and *Dollars and Cents of Shopping Centers*
11	Plus demand for nonretail service office sq. ft.	22,353	32,328	40,571	Line 9/(1 – Line 10) – Line 9
12	Total demand for occupied retail and service/local office sq. ft. in primary trade area	149,017	215,523	270,474	Demand for total occupied space—retail + service, + local office
13	Plus frictional vacancy @ 5%	7,843	11,343	14,235	
14	Total demand for retail/service/local office sq. ft. in primary trade area	156,860	226,866	284,710	Market demand for neighborhood shopping center space

ous shortcoming because the concept of market value derives from future benefits. Another weakness is that the data are typically macro data and generally not specific to the subject's submarket.

The strengths of a fundamental analysis are twofold. The analysis is future oriented, and it is possible to segment forecast demand to reflect the specific submarket of the subject. The weakness of fundamental analysis stems from the need to make judgments about the future demographics of the subject's submarket at each sub-step in the analysis process. Thus, there is potential for error at several points. A parallel can be drawn to sales comparison analysis, in which the best value indicator is usually the sale that requires the smallest gross adjustment (unless an especially high level of confidence can be placed in the adjustments applied to other sales). Similarly, in market data analysis, fewer judgments may reduce the margin of error. On the other hand, methods that allow for variances expected in the future such as the buying power segmentation fundamental analysis method provide the ability to adjust to the ever-changing demographic landscape.

The ratio method combines certain advantages of both fundamental analysis and inferred trend analysis. In the ratio method current occupied space (a known fact) is compared with current population (a known fact), and then applied to a future-oriented population forecast. It is a simple method and requires few adjustments. The first weakness of the ratio method is that it does not segment, in detail, all of the factors that make up retail demand. The dynamics of today's market can change tomorrow. Fundamental analysis using the buying power segmentation method, which segments demand data, provides a means to forecast change. By contrast, the ratio method is static, basically assuming that future economic relationships (ratios) will follow current economic relationships.

The sales per capita fundamental demand method is similar to the ratio method but relies on actual sales data being realized in the market. The major weakness of this method lies in the selection of a "proxy" sales per capita. It is up to the analyst to assess whether the proxy sales per capita is the best indicator of future relationships in the subject's submarket.

Having summarized the strengths and weaknesses of the methods applied, the analyst can now consider the demand indicated by each (see Exhibits 12.20 and 12.21).

Exhibit 12.20 Inferred Demand Methods

Analysis Types	Indicated Demand
City growth trends	Positive for increase neighborhood retail
Citywide retail occupancy	Positive—increasing last 10 years
Competitive centers	Positive—average 90% occupancy
Consumer profile	Positive—moderate income families

Exhibit 12.21 Fundamental Methods

	Supportable Occupied Sq. Ft.			
Analysis Types	Current	5 Yrs.	10 Yrs.	Average Increase/Yr.
Buying power segmentation	140,236	202,807	254,544	11,431
Ratio method	149,750	191,102	239,827	9,008
Per capita sales method	149,017	215,523	270,474	12,146
Average of three methods	146,334	203,144	254,948	10,861
Plus 5% frictional vacancy	7,702	10,692	13,418	
Total forecast demand (sq. ft.) from primary trade area	154,036	213,836	268,367	

Conclusions of Demand Forecast

The inferred methods do not provide a specific number, but from the data it can be inferred that demand for the subject will increase. The reliability of the fundamental analysis can be checked by comparing the calculated average current demand of the three methods, which was 146,334 square feet, shown in Exhibit 12.21, to the current actual occupancy of 149,750 square feet. The close correlation (2.3%) of these figures lends credence to the multiple estimates required by the fundamental demand models.

Step 4: Measure Competitive Supply

A preliminary investigation of the competition was made for the location analysis and trade area definition in the first and second steps of the market analysis. In Step 4, competitive supply is analyzed in greater detail. There are three reasons for undertaking an in-depth supply study.

First, the analysis of competitive supply differentiates the competition in comparison to the subject more precisely. The rating that results generates more detailed information, which enables the appraiser to forecast the subject's prospects for earning income (rent) and capturing a specific share of the market.

Second, the inventory and forecast of competitive supply is used in the equilibrium analysis to determine marginal demand. Marginal demand represents the "window of opportunity" for increased probability of new development, rent increases, and occupancy increases, i.e., the point when all available and projected retail space has been absorbed and new net demand becomes apparent. Identifying this point is very useful; the information is employed in many parts of the appraisal. It may signal when rent increases and new competition can be anticipated. In the sales comparison approach, it supports the adjustment for a change in market conditions (time adjustment). In the cost approach, it provides a means of identifying and measuring external obsolescence.

Third, supply data on the overall retail activity in the city can be used in inferred demand analysis. For example, if retail centers have an overall occupancy of 90% and no new centers are planned, it might be inferred that the subject will increase its current occupancy. On the other hand, if a major center is planned (such as the new supercenter in the case study), the appraiser might infer that occupancy at the subject will decrease in the near future.

Step 4.1: Inventory Existing and Proposed Competitive Space

As part of the analysis of location, land use, and linkages, which constitute the first step of the market analysis, the location of the competitive shopping centers in the primary and secondary trade areas of the subject were identified. By this stage, the analyst is ready to examine the attributes of the specific competition in greater detail.

The survey includes all of the subject's direct competition, whether located inside or outside the subject's primary trade area, but is limited to the competition, i.e., competitive facilities that sell similar readily substitutable items. For example, the stores in a neighborhood multitenanted shopping center compete directly with stores in other neighborhood multitenanted centers and with large, freestanding discount outlets in the area, all serving the same customers as the subject. However, caution should be exercised in making judgments about competitive space in large stores such as super discount stores that have many shopper goods sections typically found in regional shopping center. Therefore, when appraising a neighborhood or community shopping center, a portion of the space in a large regional discount store should be counted as competitive space, but not all the space.

On the other hand, a center located down the street from a subject neighborhood center may be a multitenant power center, while the subject is a neighborhood center anchored by a grocery store. Even though the power center is in close proximity, none of the shopper-type goods in the center compete with the subject's wares. Further, it is unlikely that the center would be redeveloped into competitive neighborhood space in the future because of store sizes; thus, it is not counted as competitive space in this market.

The survey of the competition must be directed toward the geographic area of either the subject study area or peripheral area competition. The competitive facilities used for the residual demand study must correspond to the area used in the demand forecast, otherwise, the estimate of marginal demand will be distorted. Nevertheless, data from the peripheral competition outside the primary trade area is needed for locational analysis and analyses of the primary trade area and leakage. In metropolitan areas, these data are usually available from secondary sources. The detailed data survey conducted for the study is usually concerned only with the primary trade area of the subject. A citywide survey of a small town such as the one in which the case study is located can be accomplished within a reasonable amount of time. However, because competition in the primary trade area will affect the subject the most, the survey usually concentrates on the competition in the immediate area, even in a small town.

Small, stand-alone retail stores that are not adjacent to a shopping center are considered satellite stores. Any small store that functions as a neighborhood shopping center should be included in the survey. In this case study application, the central business district (Area C) and the highway strip commercial (Area D), which are groups of stand-alone stores, have been included because they function as neighborhood/community shopping center nodes. At this point the appraiser may also select the competing centers to be used in the detailed market rent analysis developed in the income approach.

Planned and Potential Competition

Planned and potential competition that may enter the market over the next five to 10 years must also be considered. This competition may be extremely difficult to identify. The analysts might begin by investigating vacant competitive sites in the area and by asking such questions as: Who are the owners? and Are they developers? Not all potential sites can be developed. For example, a parcel of land may be tied up in an estate. The analysis should also look into possible zoning problems. What is the likelihood of a competitive site being rezoned if current zoning does not allow for retail development?

The analyst should consult with municipal departments that issue building permits and are involved in city planning. They can sometimes provide information on who may be considering pursuing development in the area.

A survey of preliminary plats may reveal long-term development patterns. Preliminary plats are more reliable than zoning plans because platting usually indicates a nonspeculative venture with money paid in advance. Not all preliminary plats will be developed, but final plats often show a strong correlation with preliminary plats. Historical data may also indicate the number of preliminary plats that become final and the number that are actually developed.

An analyst can clip announcements of building starts and proposed developments from local newspapers and keep them on file to furnish data for subsequent assignments. Many papers now have historical stories on the Internet that can be searched by topic.

The last recommended step is to complete a test residual demand study with no new development shown. If the residual demand is increasing significantly in the market to exceed current supply, it is likely that new development will occur in this market in the future.

Case Study Application of Step 4.1: Estimate Competitive Supply

The inventory of existing, competitive retail space in the city that serves the target market totals 800,000 square feet. This total includes the four existing community-shopping areas and the 110,000 square feet in the subject property. Only 175,000 square feet of the total are within the subject's primary market area. A survey of citywide retail space revealed a 90% occupancy rate.

Area B has a retail center that serves in part some of the subject trade area customers. However, the overlap of shared customers is less than 50% and thus is not considered a major part of subject primary trade area. Nevertheless, it is included in the competitive analysis.

A major discount retailer has concluded a land purchase only one-half mile from the subject and has announced plans to construct a 180,000-sq.-ft. supercenter discount store one-half mile west of the subject on the new proposed highway bypass in three to five years. (This property was identified as Center 7 on the maps presented earlier.) It is estimated that only about 50% of the store will compete for neighborhood convenience goods. The remainder of the store is considered shopper goods and thus not directly competitive with the subject type neighborhood market study.

A regional mall has been announced in the southern part of the city adjacent to the current major highway through the city and the proposed new bypass. It was estimated that up to 300,000 square feet of grocery stores, junior department stores, and discount stores would develop adjacent to the mall and will be competitive with the subject neighborhood convenience/community shopping.

Exhibit 12.22 summarizes the results of the citywide survey of retail activity. Detailed survey sheets are not shown here, as this material is typically presented in the income approach section of the appraisal report, where actual rents and expenses are analyzed for the DCF forecast.

Step 5: Analyze Market Equilibrium or Disequilibrium

The purpose of the market analysis section of an appraisal is to analyze the condition of the subject market and the subject's ability to capture a share of that market. The various steps in the analysis contribute information that will be used to answer these questions. One additional analysis is required—the residual demand analysis or marginal demand analysis, which identifies the phase of the supply-and-demand cycle that the overall market is currently experiencing. This determination is useful to the final step in which the analyst assembles various blocks of market data and makes a judgment concerning the subject's market share and future rent prospects.

Step 5.1: Estimate Residual (Marginal) Demand

Residual or marginal demand is estimated by comparing the inventory of existing and anticipated competitive supply against the estimate of current and potential demand. The prospective date when positive marginal demand will register in the market corresponds to the point when all available and projected retail space will have been absorbed, thus opening a window of opportunity for new development as well as rent and occupancy increases.

Exhibit 12.22 Summary of Survey of Competitive Retail Space (Neighborhood and Community Type Retail)

Existing	Size (in Sq. Ft.)	Occupied Sq. Ft.	Vacancy Rate	Typical Rental Rate	Typical Tenants
Area A					
Center 1 (Subject)	110,000	88,000	20%	$12 to $16	· Grocery · Restaurants · Variety/junior department
Center 2	65,000	61,750	5%	$10 to $15	· Convenience
Subtotal Primary Trade Area	**175,000**	**149,750**	**86%**		
Area B					
Center 3	125,000	118,750	5%	$12 to $15	· Hardware · Variety/junior department · Grocery
Area C					
(Central business district)					
ID 5	150,000	120,000	20%	$10 to $12	· Jr. department stores · Restaurants · Jewelry stores · Specialty
Area D					
Highway strip					
Center 4	350,000	334,000	5%	$9 to $11	· Grocery · Discount store · Restaurants · Specialty
Total	**800,000**	**722,500**	**10%**		
Proposed					
Area A					
New supercenter. Estimated 50% of 180,000 sq. ft. to be competitive space Center 7	90,000				Discount store that includes grocery, drug, convenience items, family clothes, automotive repair, and shopper goods
Area E					
Estimated competitive space in proposed mall and anticipated satellite, in 5 to 10 years Center 6	300,000				Adjacent to mall—expect: · Convenience goods · Specialty stores · Jr. department stores · Restaurants · Office/home supplies · Grocery stores · Discount stores
Total	390,000				

Note: The survey includes only major retail centers or clusters and the neighborhood centers cited above. Small convenience centers, small stand-alone retail space, and noncompetitive specialty retail space such as auto dealers are not included.

Case Study Application of Step 5.1: Primary Trade Area Residual Demand Analysis
The analyst compares the estimate of supportable retail space with the existing and projected supply to gauge marginal demand. Exhibit 12.23 shows the demand-supply situation.

Exhibit 12.23	Residual Demand Analysis			

	Supportable Occupied Sq. Ft.			
Analysis Types	**Current**	**5 Yrs.**	**10 Yrs.**	**Average Increase/Yr.**
Buying power segmentation	140,236	202,807	254,544	11,431
Ratio method	149,750	191,102	239,827	9,008
Per capita sales method	149,017	215,523	270,474	12,146
Average of three methods	146,334	203,144	254,948	10,861
Plus 5% frictional vacancy	7,702	10,692	13,418	
Total forecast demand (sq. ft.) from primary trade area	154,036	213,836	268,367	
Less existing sq. ft. of competitive space	175,000	175,000	265,000	
Less forecasted new competition	0	90,000	0	
Net (excess) shortage of supportable sq. ft. of retail space	-20,964	-51,164	3,367	

Note: This only shows the mid-range forecast. The high- and low-range forecasts are not shown for brevity. The results of the high- and low-range population forecasts indicated that demand would vary about 10% higher or lower than the above point estimate.

The calculations shown in Exhibit 12.23, based on the averages of the three demand methods, conclude that residual demand in the primary trade area creates an oversupply during the next one to five years, but should then register a slight positive residual demand for the next five to 10 years. However, the conclusions are based on averages of the three demand methods, with the per capita method showing substantially more demand than the other two methods. Using only the ratio method, the trade area would be oversupplied for the next 10 years.

This residual demand forecast will be used in the next analysis step–subject capture–by indicating how competitive the market is. The residual demand study is also used in the valuation models to support the market conditions adjustment, the projected rent increase in the DCF analysis, and the estimate of economic obsolescence.

Step 6: Forecast Subject Capture

Retail capture (sometimes called market penetration) is extremely challenging due to the dynamic nature of retailing. Consumer tastes and preferences can change rapidly and the effect on retail property can be immediate, whereas changes in office and housing markets tend to be felt more gradually. The capture rate is not only difficult to estimate, but it is one of the three most sensitive variables in the analysis. (The other two highly sensitive variables are the population forecast and the estimate of sales retention in the trade area.) As with other sensitive variables, using a variety of techniques is recommended. Reconciling the results of alternative techniques into a probable range derives the final capture rate estimate.

Level A and B analyses rely on an estimate of inferred demand. In Level C and D capture analyses; inferred methods are augmented by fundamental forecast data and specific quantifiable rating data.

Step 6.1: Analyze Capture by Inferred Methods

The inferred demand data presented here are based on the following facts:

- In its first three years of operation, the subject achieved 95% occupancy, but in the last year occupancy had fallen to 80%. The subject is in one of the best retail locations in the city. This part of the city is growing. Thus, it is reasonable to estimate that the subject should be able to lease back up to the 90% range in the near future.
- Comparable properties show occupancy rates of 90% to 95%, with the center across the street operating at 95% occupancy.
- Secondary data indicate that citywide occupancies have been 90%. This is a positive sign for the subject's realizing 90%+ occupancy again.
- Economic base and general growth trends suggest that the general economic outlook for the city is good. Population is forecast to increase at a healthy rate of 4% to 6%. The subject is located in the general direction of growth. This is positive for leasing back up.
- A new supercenter is planned about ½ mile west of the subject. The center is planned in 3 to 5 years when the new loop is finished. This suggests that this part of town is good for local and community retail. The unknown is the competitive impact on the subject and whether it will bring new customers into the area. It can be a positive factor for the subject, enabling it to capture some of the new customers, or a negative one, as the supercenter might lure away some of the subject's current customers.

In summary, all of the inferred demand data are positive for the subject's leasing back up to the 90% range. The only question seems to be the impact of the new competition expected in the next few years.

Step 6.2: Forecast Capture by Fundamental Methods the Market Outlook (Residual [Marginal] Demand Study)

In Step 5 the analyst forecast an oversupply of competitive retail space for the next four to six years. The 10-year forecast indicated a slight positive residual demand. This suggests that the subject should be increasing occupancy for the next five years until the new competition comes on line, which will contribute to a very competitive market. The following analysis of the subject's specific capture or market share refines the general indications of the marginal demand study for the market.

Quantitative Ratings

Two quantitative ratings have been derived up to this point in the market analysis. First, in terms of current industry standards, the subject was rated slightly inferior. Second, when the subject and its locational attributes were rated against the citywide competition, its location was rated the best currently, but only second best in five years.

Each analytic technique produced its own conclusions. In each, the subject was ranked using different comparative data and varying levels of detail. The initial analysis identified attributes of the subject that were above or below average. The second analysis examined the relative strength of the subject's location. This test is important because real estate is extremely location sensitive. If the subject's location is poor, leakage can be expected to increase, and the subject's future capture may be weak. The next analysis will assess the subject's relative strength compared to its primary competition. Each quantitative analysis conducted builds on the previous analysis. These consecutive ratings form a foundation for the final capture analysis.

Capture Estimate by the Size-of-the-Center (Pro Rata Share) Technique

The next step in the capture analysis is called the *pro rata share* or *size-of-the-center technique*. This method is based on the following numeric calculation:

> If Center "X" has, for example, 100,000 square feet and its
> existing competition has 400,000 square feet, then
> Center "X" should draw a 20% share of the market (100,000 ÷ 500,000).

Of course, the base estimate of subject capture must be adjusted for several factors. For example, if the subject property were a proposed project or a new center with low occupancy, its estimated share of the market would have to be adjusted for the time it would need to become established in the market; i.e., if the center were equally competitive, it might achieve a 10% share in the first year, and a 20% share in the second.

Two other possible factors to adjust for are the correspondence between the trade area of the subject and its competitors and any unique features that diminish the comparability of the subject and its competitors. If a competitor serves an area larger than the subject's trade area, the estimate of the competitor's capture must be adjusted to be consistent. Moreover, the base for the data employed in the demand calculations must match the base for the data on the competition. This pertains to both the geographic area and the type of the retail product.

Matching the data on which the percentage spent at the subject center is based with the square footage of space inventoried for the competition provides a specific example. In the subject case study it will be competing with a new supercenter discount store. Not all of the space in the discount store competes with the subject space. The discount store probably will provide auto services and will stock appliances as well as many other shopping goods. These categories were excluded from the calculations used to identify the subject trade area. Thus, it is reasonable to exclude the square footage in these centers devoted to noncompetitive retail sales from the inventory of the competition. Unique characteristics of the center such as design and amenities may also necessitate adjustments.

The Two Alternative Scenarios of Capture Rate[17]

The capture rate can be applied to two estimates in the demand analysis: 1) total supportable (occupied) square feet or 2) the net excess or shortage of retail space. These applications involve two different competitive pictures of the market and the subject.

If the capture rate is applied to the total supportable (occupied) square feet, then the analyst is determining that the subject is competitive enough to "steal" tenants from other stores. This assumes, for example, that current tenants in the competing center can move at any time, given lease requirements. This assumption may not be totally realistic in the short run, but given the typical valuation analyst's time frame of a 7- to 10-year DCF, the longer-term valuation may make the total capture assumption reasonable. This method recognizes the dynamic nature of retail by providing consideration of the retail tendency of lateral movement from location to location.

The second option is to apply the capture rate to fill up the subject vacant space by capturing *only* the residual demand (net excess or shortage of space). Because the residual analysis determines the supportable space left after all supportable space allocated to existing retail facilities has been deducted, the following assumptions are used in its application:

- The subject center will continue to maintain its current tenants.
- The subject center will not capture tenants from other existing centers; i.e., the subject will not capture move-up demand.
- All increased occupancy in the subject will come from new demand (residual demand).

Case Study Application of the Pro Rata Share Technique

The subject center contains 110,000 square feet of space, and the existing competitors within the primary trade area contain 65,000 square feet. Therefore, the subject represents 63% (110,000 ÷ 175,000) of the effective retail space in the primary trade area.

In the subject's case, the need for some adjustment is apparent. Based on its size, the subject should be capturing 63% of the market. The subject's actual capture was a fair (proportional) share of the market, but its current actual capture is less than a pro rata share. Consider the following calculations.

The previous estimated current demand for occupied space was 146,334 sq. ft. of potential occupied demand in this market based on

---

17. See Chapter 11, page 180, for more detailed examples of the two different capture rate implications.

the average of three methods. If the subject captured its pro rata share based on size, then it should have the following occupancy:

Current potential demand	146,334 sq. ft.
Subject capture rate	× 63%
Indicated subject capture	92,190

However, the current subject actual occupancy is 88,000 sq. ft., or 60% of the calculated "potential demand." This makes the subject operate at about 5% less than estimated by pro rata share of market demand.

Current Actual Capture Rate

Current actual demand as measured by current occupied space in market area is 149,750 sq. ft. At 88,000 square feet, the subject makes its current actual capture rate at 59% (88,000/149,750). This shows the subject is operating less than its pro rata share in the market.

Pro Rata Share of Future Space and "Potential Demand"

Now the analyst must consider future demand when the proposed new competitive center is scheduled to be built. If it is concluded that 90,000 square feet of retail space in the new center will be competitive with the subject, then the subject's pro rata share will drop to 42%. (110,000/265,000) However, this is not expected to occur for three to five years.

Thus, the subject's capture potential in Year 5 by the pro rata share method is:

Potential demand	203,144 sq. ft.
Subject capture rate	× 42%
Indicated subject capture	85,320 sq. ft. in Year 5

This suggests that if the subject can maintain an equally competitive position in the market when the new competition comes on line in Year 5, its occupancy would drop slightly. In Year 10, as demand increases, it should gain occupancy–if competitive positions of all centers are equal. Since the competitive positions of all centers are not equal, then a competitive rating technique is used to refine the pro-rata share method.

Analysis by Competitive Rating Techniques

The competitive rating techniques can be used to adjust the preceding share-of-the-market technique.

In competitive supply analysis, the analyst investigates the property's characteristics in detail by comparing it only to retail centers in the primary trade area that are directly competitive. The peripheral competition is not compared here because the demand estimate segmented out (leakage step) the part of the demand expected to be captured by these peripheral competitive centers. The subject's market penetration is measured in terms of location factors (already considered on a macro scale but now considered on a micro scale) as well as specific building and marketing features such as:

- Size
- Quality of merchandise sold
- Image
- Tenant mix
- Reputation and merchandising characteristics of the anchor

For a share-of-the-market analysis, a rating is assigned to each center in the geographic area where demand data are forecast. The rating at this point assumes that rents and building expenses are the same for each of the buildings rated.

Case Study Application of Capture by Rating Method

A detailed rating of the subject's primary competition is presented in Exhibit 12.24. The rating is based on both qualitative and quantitative analyses. The quantitative technique applied employs a ranking system like the one used in the location rating. That is, each factor is ranked against each competitor based on the rating equal to, the same, or worse than. Thus, the lowest score "1," is the worst or lowest ranked for a particular factor, and the highest score is the highest ranked for that factor.

Exhibit 12.24 Competitive Retail in Primary Market Area-Marketability Rating

ID #		1		2		7	
Rating Criteria		Subject		Across Street		Planned Supercenter	
Size of Center		110,000		65,000		90,000	Rank
Location Factors	Rating	Description	Rating	Description	Rating	Description	of Factor
Current household density in 1 mile	2	moderate	2	similar	1	inferior	13
Median household income in 1 mile	1	$46,900	1	$46,900	2	$59,525	11
5 yrs. household density in 1 mile	1	moderate	1	similar	1	similar	12
Proximity to roads	1	average	1	similar	2	adj.to freeway	10
Traffic volume by site	1	average	1	similar	2	freeway and major	8
Ease of access to site	1	average	1	similar	1	similar	9
Proximity to other demand sources	1	good	1	similar	1	similar	6
Center Factors							
Size of center	3	110,000	1	65,000	2	90,000	5
Exterior appearance bldg. and site	3	very good	2	good	1	fair	2
Visibility from street	1	good	1	good	1	good	7
Adequacy of parking	2	good	1	fair	2	good	4
Image of center	2	good	1	average	1	good	3
Bldg. design flexibility	3	good multitenants	2	good	1	big box design	1
Anchor drawing power	2	good	1	across st.	3	very good	14
Tenant/product variety	2	grocery anchor	1	no major anchor	3	significant mix	15
Total Score	176		127		207		510
% of Scores	35%		25%		41%		
Pro Rata by Bldg. Size	42%		25%		34%		
Total Competitive Space	265,000						

Note: Higher number in ranking is better; i.e., 2 is better than 1.

Center 2, which is located across the street from the subject, is the only current competitive center in the subject's primary trade area. In three to five years it is expected to have new competition in this area identified as Center 7, the proposed new discount supercenter store to be built on the nearby loop. Exhibit 12.24 shows the ranking scores for these three centers.

Capture Potential by Competitive Rating

The previous rating adjusts the pro rata share to a capture rate based on competitive attributes. The subject capture rate as adjusted is now applied to the potential demand forecast as illustrated in Exhibit 12.25.

The above capture forecast applied the subject capture rate to the average of the three forecast demand models. This is the preferred method if the appraiser gives equal weight to all three models.

Exhibit 12.25 Subject Occupancy by Capture Rating			
	Supportable Occupied Sq. Ft.		
Demand Methods	**Current**	**5 Yrs.**	**10 Yrs.**
Buying power segmentation	140,236	202,828	254,544
Ratio method	149,750	191,112	239,834
Per capita sales method	149,017	215,523	270,474
Average of three methods	146,334	203,144	254,948
Subject capture rate	60%	35%	35%
Indicated Subject Occupancy (Sq. Ft.)	88,000 (r)	71,100	89,231

For brevity, only the mid-range forecast (point estimate) is shown. In practice, the high and low range should also be presented which, in this case, varied ±10%.

Market/Marketability Study Recap

Exhibit 12.26 shows a recap of the complete fundamental demand, residual analysis, and subject capture. The recap is applied to the buying power segmentation model. The conclusions shown in Exhibit 12.25 and Exhibit 12.26 are interim analysis steps, as they become one of the analysis techniques that are brought forward to the final reconciliation and capture conclusions shown in Exhibit 12.28.

Step 6.3: Reconcile Subject Capture Indications

Now the ratings and other results of the analyses must be reconciled. This process is similar to the appraiser's reconciliation of the value indications derived from the three approaches to value, or the adjustment of comparable sale prices in the sales comparison approach. The appraiser forms a judgment based on the most reliable data. In a Level C or D fundamental analysis, additional techniques are employed beyond the general inferred methods used in Level A and B analyses. These fundamental methods provide the best means of arriving at a final judgment for reconciliation.

Exhibit 12.26 Recap of Market/Marketability Analysis

Ref. Work	Line No.	Year	Current	In 5 Yrs.	In 10 Yrs.	Data Source/Comment
3.2(1)	1	Total number of households in primary trade area	3,072	3,920	4,920	Reconciled mid-range forecast of vendor, Council of Government and appraiser's forecast
3.2(2)	2	Average household income	$53,300	$53,300	$53,300	Based on vendor data estimate and compared to CPI increase in area from last census to current; constant dollar model
	3	Total household income in primary trade area	$163,737,600	$208,936,000	$262,263,000	Line 1 × Line 2
3.2(3)	4	Percentage of income spent on retail	40%	40%	40%	Bureau of Labor Statistics
	5	Total retail sales potential	$65,495,040	$83,574,400	$104,894,400	Line 3 × Line 4
3.2(4)	6	Percentage of retail sales by subject-type shopping center	56%	56%	56%	Spending pattern percentage for neighborhood-type retail
	7	Total subject-type shopping center sales	$36,677,222	$46,801,664	$58,740,864	Line 5 × Line 6
3.2(5)	8	Percentage of potential retention of sales in primary trade area	75%	85%	85%	With new supercenter in area should retain more customers in Yrs. 5–10
	9	Retail sales potential in primary trade area from resident household	$27,507,917	$39,781,414	$49,929,734	Line 7 × Line 8
3.2(6)	10	Sales required per sq. ft.	$300	$300	$300	Source: *Dollars and Cents of Shopping Centers*
	11	Supportable sq. ft. of retail space from households in primary trade area	91,693	132,605	166,432	Line 9 ÷ Line 10
3.2(7)	12	Plus demand of neighborhood type retail space from secondary trade area and/or sources	27,508	39,781	49,930	Demand from residents in secondary area plus nonresidents in primary or secondary trade area
3.2(8)	13	Total occupied retail demand from primary and secondary trade area	119,201	172,386	216,362	Line 11 + Line 12
3.2(9)	14	Percentage of service/office use/ medical use	15%	15%	15%	Estimate based on analyst's original survey and *Dollars and Cents of Shopping Centers*
	15	Plus demand for nonretail use	21,035	30,421	38,182	(Line 13/.85) minus Line 13
	16	Total demand for occupied sq. ft. of retail and service/office space from primary and secondary trade area	140,236	202,807	254,544	Includes all types of retail and nonretail users typically found in neighborhood shopping centers
3.2(10)	17	Plus frictional vacancy @ 5%	7,381	10,674	13,397	(Line 16/.95) minus Line 6
	18	Total forecast demand (sq. ft.) in primary trade area	147,617	213,481	267,941	Market demand for neighborhood shopping space
4.1	19	Less existing sq. ft. of competitive space	175,000	175,000	265,000	Survey of space like Line 6 in primary trade area
	20	Less forecasted new competition	0	90,000	0	New 180,000-sq.-ft. supercenter in Year 5 but only partly competitive for neighborhood retail
5.1	21	Net (excess) shortage of supportable sq. ft. of retail space	-27,383	-51,519	2,941	Market residual demand for neighborhood shopping
	22	Subject capture rate	63%	35%	35%	Capture of market demand (Line 16)
	23	Subject forecasted square feet occupied	88,349	70,983	89,090	Line 16 × Line 22
6.2	24	Subject percentage occupied	80%	65%	81%	Subject capture estimate @ mid-range forecast

Fundamental analysis methods such as the residual analysis and specific capture rate analysis can be used to check the results of inferred methods. In an oversupplied or undersupplied market, more weight may be given to fundamental methods; in a relatively stable market more consideration may be given to inferred methods.

Case Study Application of Step 6.3
This chapter has presented several inferred and fundamental analysis techniques which, taken together, constitute an incremental approach to capture analysis. Exhibit 12.27 summarizes the techniques applied and the conclusions reached. The following is a procedural checklist for performing the capture rate reconciliation.

- Complete a pro rata share analysis and make adjustments using a quantifiable property rating technique.
- Review the property rating with the implications of the location and property rating in the preceding step.
- Check the consistency (or reasons for inconsistency) between the results of these methods. Do the location and property rating seem consistent with the detail competitive rating in Step 6?
- Use residual analysis as a check on indications from share-of-the-market analysis and the competitive rating. Residual analysis can be used as support in determining the ease of entering the market, and the prospects for future rent (decrease or increase), and future occupancy. This type of analysis is combined with capture rate techniques to gauge the competitive nature of the market. For example, an over-supplied market may suggest that more weight be given to competitive rating analysis, while an undersupplied market may indicate that market capture estimate by size may need to be given more weight.
- Compare quantified forecast data methods with inferred demand data analysis. Sometimes a survey of the brokers in the area can be more reliable than the quantifiable forecast.
- As in any reconciliation in an appraisal, the analyst must bring to bear on the final capture forecast range all pertinent specific and general data and his or her informed understanding of national, regional, and local economic trends.

Consideration of Competition Outside the Primary Trade Area
This case study did not consider comparing the subject's capture rate potential directly to competition that lies just outside the subject primary trade area. The method used here was to consider the peripheral competition as part of the leakage out and the "inflow" from the secondary trade area as part of the demand calculations. Thus, for the data model used here the peripheral competition has already been considered. As noted earlier, this is only one of several ways to handle the impact of peripheral competition that also competes for some of the customers in the subject trade area. Other methods would involve not considering the leakage factor and then including the competition

Exhibit 12.27 Summary of Capture Incremental Analysis

	Analytical Technique	Conclusion
1	Property rating	Subject is slightly inferior to industry standard. The quantitative estimate is 10% inferior.
2	Location and competition rating	Subject is currently considered the best location in the city. In five years it should rate as the second best retail area citywide.
3	Primary competition rating	As one of two centers at this location, the subject is rated superior; in five years, with the third center, it is rated second best.
4	Supply survey analysis	
	Citywide	90% occupancy.
	Primary competition	95% occupancy.
5	Residual analysis	The market is characterized as moderately competitive for the next five years and highly competitive after the new mall and adjacent new supercenter are completed.
6	Current pro rata share capture rate	63% capture of Area A demand.
7	Future pro rata share capture rate	42% capture of Area A demand when new supercenter is built.
8	Capture rate by attributes rating	59% currently and 35% after new supercenter is built.

on the peripheral as part of the capture rating shown in this section. Still another method is to repeat the study for the primary and secondary trade areas and include the competition in each area separately.

Conclusion of Capture Forecast

The subject is capturing about what would be expected in the current market. Rent levels could be affecting subject capture. Downward rent adjustments could tend to increase occupancy. However, this part of the appraisal does not consider rents in detail. The capture analysis up to this point assumes that all centers operate at what would be market rents for their buildings. In other words, rent is neutral for this aspect of the occupancy forecast. The income capitalization section of an appraisal report will usually include a detailed rent and expense analysis, which should support the appraiser's final judgment as to the subject's rents and, in turn, occupancy. These conclusions may, therefore, be considered only tentative, pending the completion of additional steps in the appraisal. Exhibit 12.28 summarizes and concludes the capture estimate.

The analysts gave weight to the inferred conclusions—particularly the growing market and good location—and equal weight to the fundamental demand and capture conclusions for the final reconciled subject occupancy forecast.

Use of Conclusions

These conclusions are pivotal to an appraisal. They can be used to test alternative highest and best uses and provide forecasts required for

Exhibit 12.28   Subject Capture Study Re-cap and Conclusions

Trend (Inferred) Methods	0 to 3 Yrs.		4 to 6 Yrs.		7 to 10 Yrs.	
	Occupancy	Rents	Occupancy	Rents	Occupancy	Rents
Subject history: 80% to 95%	87%	rising	90%	rising	95%	rising
Comparable across street: 95%	95%	rising	95%	rising	95%	rising
Citywide occupancy: 90%	90%	stable to rising	90%	stable to rising	95%	rising
Economic base good: 4% to 6% population growth	rising	rising	rising	rising	rising	rising
New supercenter in subject area	NA	NA	falling	falling	falling	falling
Fundamental Methods						
Market conditions indicated by residual or marginal demand	stable	stable	falling	falling	rising	rising
Fundamental forecast conclusions	80%	stable	65%	falling	81%	rising
Final reconciled point estimate conclusion*	**85%** average	**stable**	**75%**	**falling**	**85%**	**rising slightly**

Rents compared in real terms as to rising and falling.

* Final conclusions consider inferred and fundamental analyses.

the valuation models. In this case, alternative uses were unlikely, given the high occupancy of the subject and the absence of any indicated demand for an alternative use.

This market study will furnish the forecast needed to perform a DCF analysis in the income approach. The conclusions of the residual or marginal demand study will be used in the sales comparison approach to adjust sales for market conditions as of the date of the appraisal. The quantitative ratings of the subject property's attributes are also useful in the sales comparison approach. In the cost approach the analyst makes use of data from the residual or marginal demand study to estimate economic obsolescence. Lastly and most important, market analysis provides a basis for reconciliation, helping the appraiser judge the applicability and reliability of each valuation approach in light of the appraisal problem and the market conditions prevailing on the date of the appraisal.

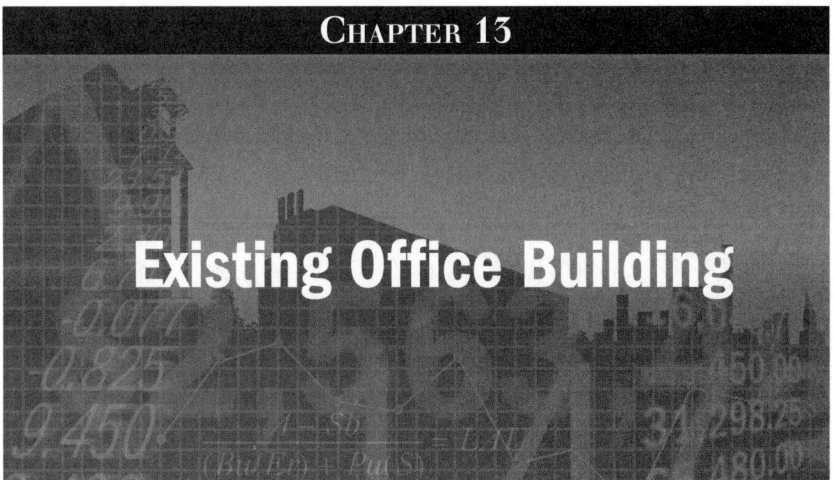

CHAPTER 13

Existing Office Building

Chapter Objectives

- To describe the office building market and its classes of buildings
- To discuss user and tenant categories
- To describe the market analysis process for an office building
- To introduce the market analysis process for an existing office building using a case study approach
- To develop a market/marketability study conclusion for an existing office building

Introduction

This chapter presents a step-by-step procedure for analyzing the market for an office building as part of a valuation assignment. The steps are:

- Analyze property productivity.
- Delineate the market of property users.
- Forecast demand.
- Measure competitive supply.
- Analyze market equilibrium/ disequilibrium.
- Forecast subject capture.

First, basic concepts and terminology are introduced, followed by a description of the analytical process. Finally, a case study application of the market analysis of an office building is presented as it might appear in an appraisal.

The Office Building Market

In the past two decades, extensive office building development has occurred throughout the United States. The demand for new office space has been fueled by the expansion of the white-collar workforce—especially service sector jobs associated with business, finance, and the professions. This demand led to rapid office building in the early 1980s, and a surplus of office space in many American cities ensued by the late 1980s. By the late 1990s, the economy entered an upswing, and most of the surplus space became occupied. The Internet and high-tech companies were booming, a situation that created significant job increases in most markets, followed by a new wave of office building. The 2000 economic slowdown and the dot.com bust resulted in an oversupply of office buildings as had occurred in the 1980s. By the mid-2000s, positive economic signs have spurred new office construction once again.

The advent of the so-called flex space, which also occurred during the last decade, ushered in a change in tenant types such as high-tech companies, which blurred the distinction between office building and industrial space. Office buildings have maintained specific nodes, but the former prestige of the metro central business district (CBD) has been eroded as many large companies opted to relocate to the outlying areas to occupy office space in office concentrations that function as self-contained CBDs.

In the face of these changes, some office categories have become specialized and target-specific submarkets, such as office buildings for medical and medical support activities. All of these factors require the appraiser to focus more closely on the submarket instead of the metro market because the submarkets can vary significantly from the macro market areas in terms of location and building market segment.

Concepts and Terminology

Market analysis for an office building requires the segmentation of demand and supply. The terms and concepts used in this segmentation are described below.

User or Tenant Categories

The market for office space can be subdivided according to the users, or tenants, who occupy office buildings. The institutional/professional category includes banks, insurance companies, and investment firms, which generally occupy prime downtown office space. Accounting and law firms may also require offices in the highly visible buildings of a CBD, which may comprise the traditional downtown areas of older cities.

In many metro areas, however, suburban nodes have developed to such a degree that they function as CBDs. The general commercial category of office space is comprised of smaller buildings occupied by firms that have a strong sales orientation and require convenient automobile access and adequate parking facilities for both workers and clientele. Medical and dental offices are usually located in professional buildings, often near hospitals or residential areas that account for their patient base. Government offices are centrally located in or near city halls, civic centers, courthouses, and county seats. They may be owned or leased by the municipality or the county. Industrial space includes pure industrial office space, which is actually part of a manufacturing plant; quasi-industrial office buildings that are located in industrial parks but house high-tech firms; and research-and-development space for industries unrelated to manufacturing.

Classes of Office Buildings

Office buildings are typically segmented by Class A, B, or C space based on their quality. Quality typically means the buildings that command

---

Key Terms

Key office building terms are defined by BOMA (Building Owners & Management Association) below:

Gross Building Area
Total area of all floors measured from the exterior of the walls plus the superstructure and substructure floor areas (also known as construction area).

Gross Measured Area
Total area of all floors of a building enclosed by the dominant portion of an exterior wall excluding all construction outside the building's vertical line.

Floor Rentable Area
GMA less major vertical penetrations on that same floor. All area within permanent outer walls to the office side of permanent partitions; no deductions for columns necessary to the building but vertical penetrations (stairs, elevator shafts, flues, air shafts, vertical ducts) are excluded; toilets, HVAC rooms, electric and telephone closets and other areas that serve the floor are included.

Building Rentable Area
The sum of all the floor rentable areas.

Floor Usable Area
The sum of usable areas of office areas, store areas, and common areas of a floor. Office areas shall mean the measured area where a tenant normally houses personnel and furniture. Store area shall mean the area suitable for retail occupancy. Floor common area shall mean the areas of a floor such as washrooms, janitorial closets, electrical rooms, telephone rooms, mechanical rooms, elevator lobbies, and public corridors, which are available primarily for the use of several tenants of the floor.

Building Usable Area
The sum of all the floor usable areas plus all building common areas. Building common area shall mean the areas of a building that provide services to building tenants, but which are not included in the office area or the store area of any specific tenant. Building common areas may include, but shall not be limited to, main and auxiliary lobbies, atrium spaces at the level of the finished floor, concierge areas or security desks, conference rooms, lounges, vending areas, food service facilities, health or fitness centers, daycare centers, locker or shower facilities, mail rooms, fire control rooms, fully enclosed courtyards outside the exterior walls, and building core and service areas such as fully enclosed mechanical or equipment rooms.

Efficiency Ratio
The rentable area (the space used and occupied by tenants) divided by the gross building area (total building area measured from the exterior of the walls, including below-grade space but excluding unenclosed areas).

Rentable area measurement can vary significantly from market to market since the above terms are not used in all markets. The data on the supply side is often gathered from secondary sources. Their measurement criteria should be determined to ensure consistency with the demand forecast square feet. The demand calculation method measures the demand for the square feet of space occupied by employees. The supply side data should be adjusted to the same measurement as the demand side data.

---

the highest rent. These higher-rent buildings typically have better locations, construction, condition, management, tenants, and amenities. Class A space is usually competitive with the rents for space in new buildings. In many markets they are considered the top 1/3 of the market in terms of rents commanded.

Class B buildings have good location, management, and construction. Tenant standards are high, but rents are lower than rents for space in newly constructed buildings. Class B buildings may suffer some physical deterioration or functional obsolescence.

Class C buildings are generally older (15 to 25 years), have reasonably high occupancy levels, and are still part of the active supply of office space. Moreover, older buildings may need to be brought into compliance with current building codes and often suffer considerable physical deterioration and functional obsolescence.

In addition to these three classes of office buildings, there are other specialized segments such as rehabilitated buildings and trophy buildings.

Rehabilitated Buildings

These buildings have good locations and can be restored to a satisfactory condition without changing the floor plan, form, or style of the structure. Sometimes these buildings are Class C buildings that with a little rehab, can be Class A buildings. If a market study is requested for a Class A building, then the building should be analyzed as potential new competition.

Trophy Buildings

These buildings are nearly considered collectors' items. They are typically buildings of the highest quality, suitable for the most selective investors. Generally, they are one of a kind, have notable architectural design, and outstanding locations. Constructed with the best quality materials, expert workmanship, expensive trim and interior fittings, and first-rate maintenance, they are attractive to tenants seeking prestige.

The actual segmentation of Class A, B, and C space is market-specific. For example, the Class A buildings in Dallas, Texas, may exceed Class A standards in El Paso, Texas. Therefore, it is imperative that the appraiser classify demand and supply in the subject market consistently.

Segmentation by Location of Office Buildings

Office buildings for multitenant professional space tend to locate in specific nodes such as the CBD, suburban business park, or the new town center in a major city. On the other hand, professional and medical offices used for dentistry or insurance, for example, tend to locate close to the neighborhoods they serve. In this way, they function similarly to community retail. Other nodes may form based on the tenant types that form clusters based on business advantages. These include the high-tech corridors found in such cities as Austin, and Dallas, Texas and San Jose, California.

Segmenting the Office Study

The classification of office space provides a framework in which appraisers can analyze the supply of competitive office buildings within the overall metropolitan area as well as the specific district or node in which the subject property is located. An appraiser should identify the percentage of office space of each class within both the metropolitan area and the subject node.

Generally, buildings compete with other buildings in the same class. However, the segmentation of the competitive supply for the subject should include an analysis of the class that lies above and below it. For example, an oversupply of space in Class A buildings would be more critical to new office construction than excess space in Class B or C buildings. Furthermore, excess space in Class A buildings could affect Class B buildings either by lowering their net operating income prospect, (i.e., rents lowered in response to excess Class A space), or increasing the fix-up cost needed to compete with Class A space.

When a firm moves, it generally rents or buys 10% to 20% more space than it currently occupies, a phenomenon known as move-up demand. Move-up demand can impact the competitive supply and the market segmentation. In prosperous times, some tenants may move up from Class B to Class A space or from Class C to Class B space.

The Market Analysis Process for an Office Building

Generally speaking, the office market demand forecast considers changes in total employment segmented to office-based employment and then converted to real estate by the average square foot per employee.[1]

An overview of the complete six-step market analysis process applied to this office building is presented in Exhibit 13.1. Each of the six steps is further divided into substeps. The results of the process are applied to the appraisal in testing highest and best use alternatives and then in applying the three approaches to value. The case study example follows the sequence described.

The market analysis process is not static. It varies with the availability of data, the techniques that the appraiser chooses, and the changing conditions of the market. For example, different techniques might be used to analyze markets of different sizes. Demand is typically estimated on a county or citywide basis, but capture estimates vary according to the size of the city and the growth pattern for office complexes. In large metropolitan areas, demand is usually segmented to reflect the specific node and building class. For smaller cities, the appraiser may make a citywide forecast of demand along with an analysis of competitive buildings.

---

1. Market analyses for office and industrial properties have many similarities, as many of the properties serve both market segments. Thus, the chapter on industrial market study should be referenced with this chapter to learn other analysis techniques that could be adapted for office market studies and vice versa.

Exhibit 13.1 Market Analysis Process for an Existing Office Building

Step 1: Analyze productivity attributes of the subject property.

    1.1 Identify the type of office building by tenancy and class.

    1.2 Analyze the site and building. Rate the subject in relation to the typical competition and/or the industry standard.

    1.3 Analyze the location.

        1.3(1) Analyze the macro location. Identify the clusters or nodes of office buildings within the metropolitan matrix and the pattern of urban growth. Rate the cluster or node in which the subject is located relative to other competitive clusters or nodes within the metropolitan area in terms of land use linkages and the direction and rate of urban growth.

        1.3(2) Analyze the micro location of the subject, i.e., the characteristics of the subject's location within its node.

Step 2: Delineate the market of property users.

    2.1 Identify the market of property users by studying the tenants in the building and the clientele they draw. Most office markets do not have a contiguous market area; the market area is generally diffused over a broad metropolitan area. The tenancy and clientele will vary with the character of the cluster or node.

Step 3: Forecast demand.

    3.1 Conduct trend analysis using inferred methods.

    3.2 Conduct fundamental analysis using the segmentation method.

        3.2(1) Forecast the workforce.

        3.2(2) Estimate percentage occupying office space.

        3.2(3) Estimate the size of the workforce occupying space in the subject's class of office building. Multiply the figure derived in Step 3.2(1) by the specific percentage for that class of building.

        3.2(4) Estimate the requisite space per office worker.

        3.2(5) Calculate the demand for the specific class of office space by multiplying the number derived in Step 3.2(3) by the figure derived in Step 3.2(4).

        3.2(6) Adjust demand for the "normal" vacancy rate.

    3.3 Conduct fundamental analysis by the ratio method.

    3.4 Reconcile the results of the various methods applied and forecast demand.

Step 4: Measure competitive supply.

    4.1 Inventory current competitive supply. This will include office building space within the subject's building class as well as competitive buildings that are under construction and proposed. The competitive supply inventory may also be affected by demolitions, renovations, and the adaptation of space under other uses to office use.

Step 5: Analyze market equilibrium/disequilibrium.

    5.1 Compare supply and demand to determine marginal demand.

Step 6: Forecast subject capture.

    6.1 Derive a preliminary (inferred) estimate of subject capture. Analyze the competitiveness of the subject vis-à-vis the competition in view of the marginal demand forecast. Examine historical occupancy rates for the subject and competition against historical marginal demand.

    6.2 Derive a capture rate for the subject by fundamental rating analysis.

    6.3 Reconcile the subject capture indications. Reconcile the competitive rating with the inferred capture rate or the subject derived in Step 6.1 and 6.2.

Note the numbering system employed in the six-step process. Sub-steps are indicated with sequential numbers in parentheses. Thus, Step 1.2 is followed by Steps 1.2(1), 1.2(2), 1.2(3), and so on.

To obtain an estimate of subject capture, aggregate demand is segmented according to three different ratings:

- A preliminary rating of the site and building relative to the typical competition and industry standards (Step 1.2)
- A rating of the office building nodes in the city (Step 1.3(1)) and
- A rating of the subject compared to competitive buildings in the same node (Step 6.2)

Case Study Description

The following application is a Level C market analysis for the market value appraisal of an existing office building. The subject is a five-year-old, 100,000-sq.-ft., 80% leased, multitenanted Class A office building. It is in the central business district of a mid-sized town of 180,000 people that also has two suburban office building nodes. The town has experienced steady growth over the past decade, and it is expected to continue. The building houses institutional/professional, general commercial, and quasi-industrial tenants.

An alternative use for the subject is not considered because the building is relatively new, has lease commitments, and the land as if vacant does not have a value remotely close to the property as improved. This means that the highest and best use considerations of alternative use in an appraisal would be minimal, and therefore, for brevity, are not presented here. Thus, the critical value question pertains to the future income prospects of the subject as currently operated. Specifically, it involves whether or not the vacant space can be leased and when, whether the current tenant base can be maintained and the amount by which the rents will increase (if at all) for the foreseeable future, and if the current improvements will need any substantial upgrade to compete in this market.

Consequently, the main purpose of the following study is to support

- The future rent and occupancy forecast needed in the income approach as well as future extra reserves for functional obsolescence, if any, for building improvements
- The adjustments made to comparable sale properties from different markets in the sales comparison approach
- The estimate of economic obsolescence (if relevant) in the cost approach.

Accordingly, the appraiser must forecast the demand for Class A space and estimate the share of this demand that the subject will likely capture over the next 10 years.

The central business district in which the subject is located is one of three office nodes in the city. It contains banking institutions, investment and accounting firms, law offices, advertising and public relations agencies, and municipal offices leased by the city. Class A office buildings account for 15% of the buildings in the CBD, Class B space makes up 40%, and the remaining 45% is Class C space. A combination of retail buildings, a courthouse, two hospitals, a sports complex, a public library, and a newspaper office lend diversity to the CBD. The CBD has about 24% of the total Class A space in the city. Although the CBD it is not characterized by dynamic growth, it may be considered a stable area with good potential for long-term redevelopment.

A node of office buildings associated with a regional shopping center is located southwest of the CBD. The office buildings contain professional offices with typical tenants that include corporate headquarters, financial planners, accounting firms, advertising agencies, and architectural firms. This area contains the largest concentration of Class A space in the city.

A node to the northeast is noted for concentration of high-tech, and research and development firms. About half of the buildings are single-tenanted office buildings, and the rest are multitenant buildings. About one-third of these are Class A buildings, and the others are Class B buildings usually associated with research and development activities.

The following presents an application of the six-step process to the case study. The concepts that apply to each step are discussed first, followed by the case study application of that step.

Step 1: Analyze Property Productivity

Step 1.1: Identify the Type of Office Building by Tenancy and Class
The subject is a Class A office building with institutional/professional, general commercial, and quasi-industrial tenants.

Step 1.2: Analyze the Site and Building
A rating is developed by comparing the subject office building to the typical competition and the industry standard. The purpose of this rating is to assess the subject building's major strengths and weaknesses. In this step the appraiser focuses on the subject building; ratings are also derived in location analysis and capture analysis in Step 6. Besides providing a general orientation to the subject property, the property rating helps identify the characteristics to look for in determining the properties that constitute the competitive supply. Subsequent ratings will enable the appraiser to estimate subject capture and to segment demand by location and building class.

The subject should be analyzed according to its comparability with the current competition and the competition in the near future.[2] An office building's overall productivity depends on the successful integration of diverse components into an efficient product. These components include physical items such as building design and construction materials as well as nonphysical items such as management and the reputation of building tenants. The following discussion highlights the factors to be considered in a typical office building analysis.

---

2. Current industry standards can be obtained from brokers, developers, and reference sources. The following is a reference source for a more detailed discussion than can be found in this book—Urban Land Institute's *Office Building Handbook*, 2nd ed., 1998.

Building Design and Construction Materials. The structural and design features of office buildings are constantly changing in response to new technology and human preferences. In building design, flexibility and efficiency are critical. Flexibility refers to the adaptability of the space to changing tenant requirements. The efficiency of a building's layout is measured by the ratio of rentable area to gross building area. The higher the ratio, the greater the efficiency.

Signage. Signs are an integral part of the design of an office project. Poor signage reflects on the quality of the buildings. Functional exterior and interior signage is essential to direct pedestrian and vehicular traffic to and within the office complex.

Exterior Lighting. Exterior lighting refers to the pedestrian walkways and parking areas that promote public safety and enhances the image of the office complex.

Street Layout. Access to the office building or office park is important and helps a building maintain a competitive advantage.

Utilities. The availability and capacity of the utility lines providing service to a project are important factors. The capacity of existing utilities to provide adequate electricity, gas, cable, and telephone service should be investigated. Utility lines installed underground are generally preferable to poles running along easements or within street rights-of-way.

The importance of electrical and telecommunication infrastructure should not be overlooked. The once-advertised "smart building" as a unique amenity has now become somewhat of a necessity. Providing adequate support for the ever-growing demands of the computer age have become more a market norm than it was in the past.

Parking. In urban areas the need for parking is tempered by the availability of mass transportation and the limited area of an urban site. In suburban areas, on-site, surface parking is essential to the success of an office park. There is no standard indicator of the number of parking spaces required, but a general rule of thumb would allow four spaces for each 1,000 square feet of rentable area, or approximately one space for every two employees. A ratio of 3.5 spaces per 1,000 square feet would be the absolute minimum, unless public transportation is available to the site. In addition to the amount of parking, the cost of parking is a major issue.

Lotting and Building Lines. In urban areas an office building typically covers 100% of the site at grade, although prestige buildings usually have some of the ground plane devoted to plazas, landscaping elements, or arcades. In suburban projects approximately 25% to 30% of the site is generally covered by the building. A typical two-story garden office will have about 10,000 to 15,000 square feet of building area on one acre of land, without structured parking.

Landscaping and Grading. Landscaping gives identity to a project, gives an image of quality, and can impart a sense of unity to a complex made up of uncoordinated buildings.

Office Space Layout. Efficient and flexible office space is critical to future changes in the market and, in turn, occupancy and income for the subject. For maximum efficiency, the interior layout of the building must address five factors:

- The availability and placement of space
- The users for whom the space is designed
- The activity taking place in the space
- The need to accommodate future change, and
- Energy efficiency

The availability of space is determined by fixed building elements–i.e., floor areas, ceiling heights, and the location of the building core and supporting columns. Layouts can be described as closed-office, open-office, and combination open- and closed-office. The closed-office layout is the traditional office building design, characterized by closed offices located around a central building core. The open-office layout, in which partitions are used to create modular units, originated as a means to facilitate office design changes.

Tenant Finish. Tenant finish refers to the modifications or remodeling that a tenant requires before occupying leased space. Normally, the cost of some changes is covered by the developer or landlord. A building's design should be analyzed in terms of its ability to accommodate alteration. A building that is easily adapted to changing tenant needs has a competitive advantage over one that is not.

Floor Sizes. Optimum floor sizes in mid- and high-rise speculative office buildings can range from 16,000 to 30,000 square feet per floor. Since such buildings may be occupied by a single anchor tenant or multiple tenants, a floor area design that is flexible enough to accommodate both full-floor users and small space users has a competitive advantage.

Stairways, Corridors, and Elevators. In a low-rise garden office building, the stairway or escalator often creates a visitor's first impression. Stairways should be well lighted and clean. Each floor should be marked on stairwell doors and a floor directory should be provided. Corridors must be maintained. The elevator service in mid- and high-rise buildings must meet the needs of the users. The elevators should be dependable and waiting time should not be excessive. The preferred elevator ratio is one elevator per 30,000 sq. ft.

Heating, Ventilation, and Air Conditioning (HVAC). Generally HVAC equipment is accommodated in the space between the ceiling of one floor and the floor of the next. HVAC systems control the level of heating and cooling in the building's interior and perimeter space. Most systems divide a building into zones. The recommended standard is one thermostat zone for each 1,200 square feet of area.

Amenities. The support facilities provided in an office building or within walking distance give the building a competitive advantage. These facilities may include convenience retail stores, professional and business services, cafeterias and restaurants, transient lodging, conference halls, and physical fitness centers. Providing support facilities within a project contributes to tenant satisfaction. Other types of special amenities include cultural or aesthetic attractions such as prominently displayed art, special exhibits, and garden atriums.

Security. Tenant security may be considered a special amenity. Security includes both low-profile measures such as entry card systems and high-profile measures such as closed-circuit television and alarm systems. Security concerns are governed by the number of entrances and exits to the building, the absence or presence of fencing, the accessibility of the parking area, and the presence or absence of security personnel.

Nonphysical Items. Although the layout and physical condition of an office building are important considerations, nonphysical items such as building management and the quality and mix of tenants are equally significant.

Building Management. Professional on-site management is generally preferable to off-site management. Most Class A buildings are managed on site and, thus, have a competitive advantage over those that are not.

Hours of Operation. Some buildings turn off the A/C at night and weekends to save costs. Others, for competitive advantage, will keep A/C and heating on 24-7. This can be a competitive advantage in some markets.

Tenant Quality. A location near a building occupied by a major tenant such as a Fortune 500 company is a competitive advantage. This is attributable to the sense of prestige and stability that the market associates with long-term, major tenants and to the economic advantage of being able to serve such companies. Class A buildings are characterized by their long-term tenants.

Case Study Application of Step 1.2: Property Rating

The subject property contains 100,000 square feet of rentable area, has a high efficiency ratio, and is in excellent condition. Based on information gathered from a preliminary analysis of office buildings in the subject's class, the appraiser was able to rate the subject according to the property characteristics described above. Exhibit 13.2 lists the rating factors for the subject. In a Level C study, a quantitative method is generally applied to structure the analysis and help the reader follow the reasoning. In this case the subject was considered average in

Exhibit 13.2   Office Building—Property Rating

Sub-rate (rate factors by inserting "X")	Inferior			Typical	Superior		
	High	Moderate	Slight	Neutral	Slight	Moderate	High
Site							
Parking (adequacy and cost)				X			
Access				X			
Visibility				X			
Proximity to support facilities				X			
Building Improvements							
Construction quality				X			
Design and exterior appearance				X			
Size (leasable area)				X			
Security features				X			
Efficiency ratio				X			
Condition and effective age				X			
Obsolescence				X			
Quality of tenant finish				X			
Property Management and Tenancy							
Management				X			
Quality of tenants				X			
Hours of operation				X			
Rating Conclusions							
Sub-rate number of items	0	0	0	15	0	0	0
Times category score	0	2	4	5	6	8	10
Category score	0	0	0	75	0	0	0
Total subject score	75						
Percentage above or (below) all average	0%						

all categories, and a rating of 5 was assigned for each factor. (For a more complete discussion of this rating method, refer to the retail shopping center application in Chapter 12.)

Step 1.3: Analyze the Location

Because the demand for office space is diffused over a broad citywide or metropolitan area, the analysis must first consider the subject's macro location.

Step 1.3(1): Analyze the Macro Location

Macro location analysis encompasses the overall metropolitan matrix, reflecting urban growth patterns, the clusters or nodes of office buildings, and the quality of the vital linkages that connect these buildings to the community and support facilities. The analyst's objective is to identify the subject node and to determine how it currently compares to competitive office nodes and to predict how it will compare in the future.

Urban growth patterns are examined to discern the direction and rate of development. The appraiser investigates where office, retail, and residential growth has occurred in the last five to 10 years; where large public expenditures on infrastructure development have been made; and where future growth is most likely to occur.

In location analysis for office buildings, the metropolitan market is divided into clusters or nodes of office buildings. In most metropolitan areas, office buildings tend to cluster around established centers of economic activity or principal transportation arteries. Nodes can change over time. Many CBDs declined in the 1970s and 1980s but have experienced a rebirth in office space in many markets. This is occurring in part as an outgrowth of new residential construction in downtown areas. It is a mutually correlated phenomenon in most cases since the urban core office users were having difficulty keeping employees until the wave of downtown condominium building provided nearby potential employees. Moreover, the downtown condo market that occurred in the 1990s in many major cities resulted largely from market demand for housing close to jobs to shorten workers' commuting time. Thus, current and future nodes should be considered.

Within a metropolitan area, many of these office nodes continue to form as they were described by McMahon[3] some years ago. Some of the tenant types have changed over time, such as the high-tech nodes of the 1990s, but the same node-forming principles still apply.

An uptown node is such an area. Uptowns result from an intra-urban shift. Often this type of node is located along an arterial that provides access to the suburbs. Its shape is likely to be linear, reflecting the importance of the artery along which it has developed.

Another type of node accommodates a specialized activity. For instance, offices that serve attorneys and title companies often cluster around major government buildings such as courts and public records repositories. Medical offices tend to be located near hospital complexes, assuring doctors easy access to patients. University areas attract research and development firms that seek proximity to technical expertise and laboratory facilities. Companies that depend on air service may rent space in office buildings near airports.

Office parks house tenants oriented toward research and development activity or local manufacturing. Major corporations that lack local connections may choose to locate in office parks to take advantage of their attractive park-like surroundings or may be lured by an enticing rental offer negotiated with the developer.

Shopping centers are nodes of activity that support office building development. They may be especially attractive to tenants who have modest requirements for space. Generally, the users of such offices serve the needs of the residential households within the trade area of the shopping center.

Case Study Application of Step 1.3(1): Macro-Location Analysis

The three office nodes in the city are rated according to their competitiveness. The node in which the subject property is located may be ranked

---

3. John McMahon, *Property Development: Effective Decision Making in Uncertain Times* (New York: McGraw-Hill, 1976).

against competitive nodes for its quality of linkages, ease of access, reputation, visibility, and the availability of support facilities. The appraiser focuses on the time workers and management spend commuting to the buildings in the node. The appraiser also focuses on traffic conditions, proximity to mass transit systems, airports, and to clients or associated facilities such as courthouses and hospitals, nuisances in the area, scenic or natural advantages that the node may possess, and the size of the node, which strongly affects its drawing power.

Based on information about the three competitive office building nodes, the appraiser assigned the macro locational ratings shown in Exhibit 13.3. These ratings will support the allocation of citywide demand among the CBD and the competitive office nodes.

The comparative ratings suggest that the CBD remains a competitive office location, but is not as highly rated as the suburban nodes. Its strength lies in its appeal to prestigious tenants. This may change over time, as outlying nodes attain locational advantages. Thus, the location rating is future oriented because value is the present worth of future benefits.

After completing the macro locational analysis of the node where the subject property is located, the appraiser investigates the micro location of the subject building.

Step 1.3(2): Analyze the Micro Location

Micro location refers to the following attributes: the subject's relative location within the node, traffic conditions around the subject

ID #	Rating Criteria	Downtown (Subject Node)	Southwest Node	Northeast Node	Importance Factor
1	Current travel time to employee housing	1	2	2	6
2	Expected travel time to employee housing in 5 years	1	2	3	5
3	Current travel time to executive housing	1	3	2	10
4	Expected travel time to executive housing in 5 years	1	3	2	3
5	Current travel time to airport	1	2	3	4
6	Expected travel time to airport in 5 years	1	2	2	2
7	Support facilities in area (e.g., hotels)	2	3	1	9
8	Proximity to country clubs, upscale shopping and restaurants	1	3	2	1
9	Quality of node's tenants	2	1	2	13
10	Reputation (prestige) of area	1	1	2	11
11	Area of most new buildings (last 5 years)	1	2	2	8
12	Area of most public expenditures in next 5 years	1	2	2	7
13	Amount of Class A occupied office space in the area	1	2	2	12
	Total Score	113	181	182	476
	Percentage of Total Scores	24%	38%	38%	

Exhibit 13.3 Office Location Ranking Analysis

Note: Based on ranking method where 1 = worst.

site (e.g., one-way streets and curb and median cuts), pedestrian access to and from the support facilities for the subject building, adjacent land uses, the availability and convenience of parking, nuisances, natural amenities (e.g., a scenic view from the subject), the subject's future location within the projected pattern of growth for the node, and any special building amenities the subject may possess. This information will be used to rate the subject relative to the competitive supply in Step 6.2.

Case Study Application of Step 1.3(2): Micro-Location Analysis
The subject is easily accessible within the CBD. Unlike many of the older office buildings, it has adequate parking facilities. The other Class A office buildings in the CBD have comparable access and parking facilities.

Step 2: Market Delineation

Step 2.1: Identify the Market
Most office buildings lack contiguous market or trade areas that characterize retail facilities (i.e., concentric trade areas defined by time-distance relationships and sales volume percentages) and residential subdivisions (i.e., commuting time to employment centers). The clients of financial institutions, investment firms, and professional offices are attracted more by the firm's or the practitioner's reputation than by the convenience of its location. The users of office space tend to be diffused over a broad metropolitan area.[4] Thus, the market delineation starts with the subject and competitive node where the subject is located. This identifies the type of office segment in terms of tenant types and location. The market delineation then moves to the broad area where the users originate. This area in many cases is county or metro-wide.

Case Study Application of Step 2.1: Delineate the Market Area
The subject is a multitenanted, Class A office building suitable for institutional/professional, general commercial, and quasi-industrial tenants and the clientele and employees that they tend to draw. Consequently, the appraiser considers office-based employment for the entire city metro area when making the demand forecast.

Also, the city metro area was the only geography with employment forecast. Thus, a forecast for the subject submarket of the CBD only was not made because current or forecast employment data were not available. In some cases, current and forecast employment data for a small area are available, but the reliability of the forecast generally declines significantly the smaller the geographic area of the forecast. Therefore, it should be used with caution.

---

4. Local office users include users such as dentists, veterinarians, and insurance agencies. Many of these function as neighborhood or community retail, serving nearby households. See Chapter 12 for information on typical tenants in neighborhood shopping centers.

Step 3: Forecast Demand

Step 3.1 Conduct Trend Analysis Using Inferred Methods

In performing inferred demand analysis, the appraiser takes general data and makes inferences about the future from past performance. For example, if the trend in office occupancy is good, and the economy remains strong, one could infer that the same would be characteristic of future occupancy.

Similarly, in many markets absorption figures for the last quarter are quoted as a sign of a good or bad office market. If the data reflect good absorption (net absorption, which is move-ins minus move-outs), and the future economy appears to be good, then positive historical net absorption might be a good barometer of the future.

Inferred data should not be considered in isolation, however. Inferred and fundamental data are used together, with one serving as a check on the other.

Case Study Application of Step 3.1: Inferred Demand Analysis

The analyst studies city growth and office space occupancy trends. The city has experienced a steady increase in population and employment over the past 10 years. All signs point to continued growth, so it can be inferred that demand for Class A office space will continue to increase.

Current citywide occupancy for all types of office space is about 82%; Class A space is performing better at 84% occupancy. During the past five years, Class A occupancy rose to 95%, but because of moderate overbuilding three years ago, the market experienced a downturn that resulted in the current 84% occupancy. Nevertheless, during this time, positive net absorption has been reported. From these data it can be inferred that demand for Class A office space has been increasing. If the current trend continues, it will continue to increase.

Step 3.2: Conduct Fundamental Analysis Using Segmentation Method

Step 3.2 has multiple sub-steps in which the future workforce is identified and quantified, the office space demanded is estimated and segmented by class, and the final demand figure is adjusted for vacancy.

Step 3.2(1): Forecast the Workforce

Employment data for the total United States, individual states, counties, and metropolitan areas are available from U.S. Department of Labor, Bureau of Labor Statistics. State employment agencies also have city employment data. Employment projections are provided by U.S. Department of Commerce-Bureau of Economic Analysis (BEA), state, local government agencies. The most common local agency that provides small-area employment forecasts is the regional planning agency associated with transportation planning. To receive funding, this agency is mandated by the federal department of transportation to forecast local small-area employment (and population) over a 20-year period. Also, some commercial vendors such as Woods and Pool provide county-level employment forecasts. The forecast can be for total employment or for employment subgroups. Whether to use the more detailed forecast for each employment category or the total employment forecast depends on the scope of the appraisal and whether the economic base is expected to remain proportionally stable. On the other hand, if different employment groups are growing at different rates, then the more detailed forecast of employment by subgroups is more reliable. The subgroups forecast is a Level D type analysis.

In analyzing employment data the appraiser should carefully review its parameters. The appraiser can do so by determining whether the data refer to individuals who are locally employed or to employed individuals who are local residents. Census data yield information on local resident employment, but they do not necessarily indicate that these residents work locally. An appraisal's demand forecast focuses on local employment and is not as concerned about where the employees live. The appraiser also can determine if the forecast is for all employment, for nonagriculture, or for employment covered by unemployment insurance only.

Case Study Application Step 3.2(1): Forecasted Employment
Three different sources were used to forecast employment. The forecasts were available for the subject county and then were allocated to the city according to the current ratio of city jobs to total county jobs. In addition, one forecast–the local council of government's regional transportation planning commission–was city specific and did not require any adjustment (see Exhibit 13.4). In this example, only the mid-range forecast is represented. In practice, it is recommended that high- and low-range forecasts also be prepared.

Exhibit 13.4	City Employment Forecast	
Forecast Source	**Current Local Employment**	**Employment in Five Years**
State labor department	99,000	121,950
Local council of government	99,000	110,321
Commercial vendor	99,000	112,000
Average of three forecasts		114,757

All three forecasts are considered to be reliable and will be used; their mid-range is the average. The five-year growth rate is extended out for the 10-year forecast.

Step 3.2(2): Estimate the Size of the Workforce Occupying Space in Subject-Type Office Buildings
The subject is a freestanding multitenant office building. The previous employment forecast is for workers who work in many different venues–from selling goods, to working on an assembly line in a factory, to working behind a desk in an office building such as the subject.

There are two ways of estimating the number office workers: basing the estimate on all employment groups or basing it on the dominant groups as a proxy for stand-alone office demand.

The first method requires making an estimate of all types of office workers in each separate employment group and then separating the total office workers from the number to determine the number of total officer workers who would likely go into stand-alone office buildings like the subject.

The procedure for the first category is to review all of the employment data categories and estimate the number of office workers in each one. For example, manufacturing employment data could be reviewed and the numbers from the executive, administrative, professional specialty, and technically related support jobs extracted since these categories of jobs are performed by employees most likely to work in office space. This procedure is then completed for all other types of employment groups—from mining to public administration—until office workers in all employment categories have been estimated.

The appraiser's aim in valuing a multitenant office building is to find the demand for office workers in private stand-alone office buildings. Thus, if the number of total employees to total office workers is disaggregated, the office workers performing other functions must be disaggregated, followed by office workers in private stand-alone office buildings like the subject. This task is difficult because there are no specific data that identify the employees in all the employees groups who are employed in stand-alone office buildings. Kimball and Bloomberg, as well as Carn, Rabianski, Racster, and Seldin provide examples of estimating total office jobs in each separate employment category and then allocating it to stand-alone office buildings.[5, 6]

The second method of forecasting the number of office workers in stand-alone office buildings shown in this case study is to choose only the employment groups that are most likely to house most of its employees in stand-alone office buildings such as the subject. Examples include information services, financial service activities, and professional and business services. This method uses these dominant office employment groups as a proxy for all stand-alone office workers. While it is recognized that other employment groups from industries such as manufacturing and mining will house some of its workers in stand-alone offices, those employees will be in the minority. Since the dominant office subgroups also will have employees who do not work in stand-alone office buildings, it is assumed that these numbers will offset those for employees who belong to other groups.

Making this forecast is not straightforward for two reasons. First, there is no accepted definition of office employment sectors. Second, historical data from the Bureau of Labor Statistics (BLS) have changed employment clas-

---

5. J.R. Kimball and Barbara S. Bloomberg, "Office Space Demand Analysis," *The Appraisal Journal* (October 1987).

6. Neil Carn, Joseph Rabianski, Ronald Racster, and Maury Seldin, *Real Estate Market Analysis-Techniques & Applications* (Englewood Cliffs: Prentice-Hall, 1988).

sifications over the years, which makes historical comparisons of office employment percentages difficult. The problem has been compounded by the change to the North American Industry Classification System (NAICS) in 1997, which changed office classifications significantly. For example, many analysts defined office employment under the SIC data system to include communications, publishing, finance, insurance and real estate (FIRE), legal services, business services, membership organizations, engineering, and management services not classified elsewhere.

Under NAICS, office employment is defined by some analysts as including information, financial activities, and professional and business services.[7] Three major industries with increasing employment–health care, education, and social services–are excluded by many analysts because of the analysts' judgment that most of the jobs performed by employees in these industries are not housed in stand-alone office buildings. In health care, for instance, most jobs are still performed in hospital settings and similar outpatient settings. Also, many analysts exclude most educational and social services office jobs because they also are typically performed in institutional settings. Furthermore, governmental jobs typically are not performed in private stand-alone office buildings and therefore are excluded from consideration as an office demand proxy.

Based on the background paper from the New York Study, in 2000, about 33% of the total jobs defined above (with the previously noted exclusions) were performed in office buildings; whereas, in Dallas, Texas, based on the same criteria, about 23% of the total jobs were performed in office buildings.

Exhibit 13.5 illustrates the categories that are considered to employ significant numbers of office workers in stand-alone office buildings. Note that this opinion can vary from analyst to analyst as noted by the following analysis by two highly regarded national economic data firms.

Two highly respected private national firms that provide economic data generate different conclusions when estimating office employment. One firm uses 27 subcategories including federal government and some health-related categories. The other firm uses 10 broader categories but does not include government or health-related categories. Thus, the estimates of stand-alone office employment as a percentage of total employment in a major Texas metro area in 2004 was 28% of total employment by one firm, and as expected, a lower number, 23%, of total employment, by the other firm that excluded government and health-related categories. Both perform very good analyses and both conclusions can be used if the appraiser evaluates the methodology to determine if it fits the subject property's market study situation.

The percentage of office workers, even when using the same employment groups, can vary from city to city–typically from about 20% to 34% of total employment in a market area, depending on the market's local

---

7. Background paper, "Supply and Demand: City and State May Be Planning Too Much Office Space" published by New York City Independent Budget Office, August 2004.

Exhibit 13.5   Private Sector Groups with Significant Office Employment

NAICS #	NAICS Sector	Comment
51	Information	Establishments engaged in the production and distribution of information and cultural products as well as transmitting and data processing. This includes software publishing.
52	Finance and Insurance	Comprised of establishments primarily engaged in financial transactions. This includes among others such establishments as: commercial banks, savings institutions, real estate credit, mortgage bankers, securities brokerages, insurance companies, and investment trusts.
53	Real Estate and Rental and Leasing	Comprised of entities that are primarily engaged in renting, leasing or otherwise allowing use of tangible or intangible assets. Representative establishments in this category are offices of real estate agents and brokers, real estate managers, real estate appraisers, automotive leasing agents, consumer goods rental, and equipment leasing.
54	Professional, Scientific and Technical Services	Comprised of establishments that specialize in professional services such as legal, accounting, payroll, architecture and engineering, testing laboratories, computer systems, advertising, commercial photography, veterinary services and translators.
55	Management of Companies and Enterprises	This sector is comprised of establishments that hold and manage the securities, companies, and facilities of others. This is a nongovernmental entity.
56	Administrative and Support and Waste Management and Remediation Services	This sector is comprised of establishments performing routine support activities for the day-to-day operations of others. Some examples include office administrative services, employment placement agencies, telephone call centers, credit bureaus, court reporting, travel agencies, investigative and security services, services to buildings like janitorial services, landscaping, waste collection, treatment, disposal, and management services.

Other Sub-Sectors That Have Significant Office Employment

NAICS	Sub-Sector/Comment
6114/16	Business Schools and Computer Management Training
6117	Education Support Services
621	Ambulatory Health Care Services/Physicians' Offices, and Other Health Care Providers Outside of Hospitals and Nursing Homes
6241	Individual and Family Services
6243	Vocational Rehabilitation Services
7113	Promoters of Entertainment Events
7114	Agents/Artists' Managers
813	Religious/Grant-Making/Professional Organizations

economic base. Due to a changing job mix in the city, this percentage will also vary over time even for office workers employed in the same city.

During the last decade, most estimates of total office jobs in all categories typically have been about 50% to 60% of total employment. Thus, based on the previous studies of office jobs located in stand-alone buildings, the number would be about one-third to one-half of all office jobs.

The method or detail that is appropriate for the appraiser to use depends on the type of office building being appraised and the submarket in which it competes. For example, if the subject competes in a market area for which medical facilities tend to be major users of the competitive office space, then that employment group should be used in the appraisal. However, the next appraisal might be based on a different competitive submarket that does not compete for medical space usage, in which case the medical group for that assignment would be omitted.

Case Study Application Step 3.2(2): Forecasted Percentage of Employment in Office Buildings

For the subject, the appraiser used the method of reviewing employment by NAICS supersectors (see asterisk for Exhibit 13.6 for a definition of supersectors) and selecting the sectors that were most likely to house most of its employees in stand-alone office buildings. Exhibit 13.6 shows the percentage of total employment by each sector. The sectors selected that include the employees most likely to be housed in stand-alone office buildings were added to arrive at an overall percentage of total employment of employees most likely to occupy office buildings. Applying these percentages to the employment forecast yields a forecast of the number of employees who most likely will occupy multitenant office space.

Exhibit 13.6	Percentage of Non-farm Employment by NAICS Industry Supersectors			
NAICS Supersector*	NAICS ID	State	City	Selected as Proxy for Stand-alone Office Employment
Natural Resources and Mining	1133,21	1.6%	1.1%	
Construction	23	5.8%	5.1%	
Manufacturing	31-33	9.3%	10.4%	
Trade, Transportation, and Utilities	42,44,45,48,49,22	20.6%	21.4%	
Information	51	2.4%	4.0%	4.0%
Financial Activities	52,53	6.2%	8.9%	8.2%
Professional and Business Service	54,55,56	11.3%	13.0%	13.0%
Education and Health Services	61,62	12.2%	10.2%	
Leisure and Hospitality	71,72	9.2%	9.1%	
Other Services	81	3.8%	3.8%	
Government	92	17.5%	13.7%	
Total Estimate for Office Study %		100%	100%	25.2%

Source: Bureau of Labor Statistics and appraiser's analysis for making a judgment on office sectors.

* Supersector is a grouping used by the BLS to summarize data for various geographies. See Appendix B for a more complete listing of NAICS sectors and descriptions.

As an alternative method, if local data on occupied multitenant office space are available, and the future employment mix in the area is expected to remain stable, the appraiser can estimate the percentage of the total workforce that occupies multitenant office space using the following three steps.

1. Divide the total amount of occupied or stand-alone office space (or multitenant, if the scope is to be narrowed further) by the average

square footage of space per worker to find the overall office employment in stand-alone office space.

2. Divide the overall office employment calculated in Step 1 by the
total employment to obtain the percentage of the total workforce
occupying office space.

3. Apply this percentage to the total employment forecast.

This procedure is similar to the ratio method presented in Step 3.3.

The metropolitan area has a population of 180,000, which along with
employment, is projected to increase by 3% per year. Current data indicate that 99,000 workers (55% of the population) are employed locally.
Based on NAICS supersectors, the appraiser estimated that 24,750 workers (25%) have jobs that require stand-alone office space (see Exhibit
13.6). It is anticipated that high-tech industry in particular will experience growth, ensuring a new source of employment for the community.

The five-year growth in the number of employees that will demand
office space is calculated at 3,932. Thus, total demand in five years
may be forecast at 28,682 employees (current demand of 24,750 plus
growth of 3,932). The Local Council of Governments' and a commercial data vendor's area forecasts both indicate that this growth rate
should continue for the next 10 years. Thus, demand for the next 10
years may be projected based on an expected growth rate of 3% per
year (see Exhibit 13.7).

Exhibit 13.7	Office Space Demand—Citywide			
		Current	Year 5	Year 10
Total citywide employment		99,000	114,757	133,000
Percentage occupying office space		25%	25%	25%
Total employed in office space		24,750	28,689	33,250
Percentage of office workers in Class A office space		32.5%	32.5%	32.5%
Total citywide demand for Class A office space jobs		8,044	9,324	10,806
Avg. sq. ft. per employee		180	180	180
Total citywide occupied Class A office demand in sq. ft.		1,447,875	1,678,321	1,945,125
Plus frictional vacancy @ 5%		76,204	88,333	102,375
Gross estimate of total citywide Class A office demand in sq. ft.		1,524,079	1,766,654	2,047,500

Step 3.2(3): Estimate the Size of the Workforce Occupying Space in the Subject's Class of Office Building

This step is accomplished by multiplying the figure derived in Step
3.2(1) by the specific percentage for that class of building.

Case Study Application of Step 3.2(3)

In this metropolitan area, Class A office buildings have a higher-than-
average occupancy level and make up 32.5% of the existing inventory
of occupied office space. This figure reflects the percentage of office

workers using Class A space and may be used to determine the number of citywide workers in Class A space in five years: 32.5% x 28,682, or 9,322 (see Exhibit 13.7).

Step 3.2(4): Estimate the Requisite Space per Office Worker

Another consideration in office building analysis is the amount of space required per office worker. The amount of office space per worker varies with the industry, the employee's rank, the state of the economy, and current rental rates. Typical standards for office space are 220 square feet per worker in high-tech industries, 200 square feet per employee in offices associated with manufacturing and distribution, and 136 square feet per employee in financial and governmental offices.[8]

Broken down by employee rank, the average space allotment per general office worker is 65 to 80 square feet; per supervisor, 100 to 120 square feet; per administrative assistant, 150 square feet; per executive assistant, 300 square feet; and per executive, 400 to 500 square feet. The Building Owners and Managers Association (BOMA) considers 175 to 200 square feet per office worker an average area requirement.

The ratio of office space per worker must be estimated separately for each specific market area since supply and demand, economic conditions, and industry needs vary in different market areas and are continually changing. The problem is compounded for appraisers who must use the ratio in the forecast of office space demand, which usually covers a 10-year period. This extended period means that the forecast must reflect successive office market cycles.

After the number of office workers occupying space in a specific class of office building has been estimated, the figure is multiplied by the standard area required per office worker, which was estimated at 180 square feet. If local historical data on the amount of office space and number of office workers are available, a more representative figure may be obtained by dividing occupied space by the current number of employees.

The appraiser must also forecast the size per worker for the future not necessarily based on the current ratio. If the current ratio of space per job is expected to be the same in the future, then it can be applied. However, if the current market is undersupplied, then it is likely that many businesses are doubling up on space to save money, since rents should be high in such a market. Similarly, if the market is significantly oversupplied, then the current ratio of space is probably high, since rents are usually relatively low. The forecast should also include changes expected in office employment practices. For example, the ratio has been declining in recent years because of company cutbacks to reduce costs; open space plans to reduce overall office space; the computer age, which has eliminated or reduced the need for some offices; and new working arrangements such as office hoteling, where

---

8. *Office Space Supply Study,* Technical Report 978, Texas A & M Real Estate Center, February 1993.

workers reserve office space to work onsite on certain days of the week and telecommute the other days.

Because this figure will vary at different points in the market cycle, an average allotment over the forecast period should be considered.

Case Study Application of Step 3.2(4): Forecast the Square Feet Per Employee

Although the current average area required per office worker is estimated at 180 sq. ft., larger markets with major law firms and major corporate headquarters typically require an average area of 200 to 250 per sq. ft. The 2004 New York Independent Budget office study estimated current space per employee at about 225 sq. ft.[9] The Texas A & M study estimated the average required area per worker at about 289 sq. ft back in Houston in 1993.[10] The Houston study was performed during a time when office rents were low (thus, the large amount of space per employee), and the market itself is more oriented toward large oil corporations and law firms. These factors contribute to the expectation of a higher space per employee. The subject is not located in a major market area and does not have large national law firms or major corporate headquarters. Therefore, historically, it has maintained an historical consistent range of about 175 to 200 square feet per job. Thus, the current estimate is for the market to remain steady for the foreseeable future at 180 square feet per employee (see Exhibit 13.7).

Step 3.2(5): Calculate Demand for the Specific Class of Office Space

The number of Class A workers estimated in Step 3.2(2) is multiplied by the average area per office worker derived in Step 3.2(4) to determine Class A space presently in demand.

Case Study Application of Step 3.2(5)

Multiplying the 9,322 Class A workers forecast in Year 5 by the average area of 180 square feet per office worker results in a demand projection of 1,678,000 square feet (rounded) of occupied Class A space in five years (see Exhibit 13.7).

Step 3.2(6): Adjust Demand for Frictional Vacancy Rate

The demand figure is adjusted to reflect the balanced market vacancy rate for the specific class of buildings. The result is a gross estimate of supportable Class A office space. This figure is used in marginal demand studies and proposed construction feasibility analyses. In appraisal applications, however, the subject capture forecast is based on the occupied demand estimate.

Case Study Application of Step 3.2(5): Adjust for Frictional Vacancy

The forecast demand figure of 1,678,321 square feet in Year 5 is adjusted upward by the frictional vacancy rate of 5% (see Exhibit 13.7).

---

9. New York City Independent Budget Office, August 2004.

10. Texas A & M Real Estate Center, February 1993.

The calculations in Exhibit 13.7 show the procedure for estimating existing and anticipated demand.

The reasonableness of forecast demand calculations can be checked using known data, sometimes called model calibration. Inferred methods based on a general comparison of forecast data to historical data can also be used.

The calibration method uses the demand forecast for known data. In this case, the supply survey indicated a current estimate of 1,430,040 square feet of occupied Class A space (see Exhibit 13.8). The current demand for occupied space indicated in Exhibit 13.7 is 1,447,875 square feet. These two figures are very close and thus, the demand model is considered reliable. (A more extensive calibration analysis could be made by comparing data over the past 10 years.)

The accuracy of the demand model can also be checked using inferred analysis. Projected demand is compared with historical net absorption. If there is little difference between the two, and the forecast employment is similar to past employment, the model appears reasonable. Considerable variation in the figures may indicate that the market has recently undergone a significant upturn or downturn, that additional growth is expected, or that the projections in the model are not well founded.

Step 3.3: Conduct Fundamental Analysis by the Ratio Method

All appraisal methods have technical advantages and disadvantages. Thus, alternative approaches are recommended throughout an appraisal to serve as checks on each other. The alternative method applied here is based on a ratio of total employment to total occupied space.

Exhibit 13.8	Office Market Demand Analysis by Ratio Method				
Line No.	Year	Current	+ 5 Yrs.	+ 10 Yrs.	Comments/Source
1	Total employment in primary area	99,000	115,000	133,000	Survey data: BLS, Council of Govt.
2	Total occupied Class A office space citywide (sq. ft.)	1,430,040			Survey data: Local Sources
3	Ratio of sq. ft. of occupied Class A office space per employee	14.4	14.5	14.5	Calculation (2/1) for current ratio is assumed constant for forecast
4	Total demand for occupied Class A office space citywide (sq. ft.)		1,667,500	1,928,500	Calculate Line 3 × Line 1

Case Study Application of Step 3.3: Fundamental Demand by Ratio Method
Total employment in the subject city is currently 99,000 workers. The supply survey that follows (Step 4.1) indicates that the city has 1,430,040 square feet of occupied freestanding Class A office building space. Thus, current demand in the city is approximately 14.5 square feet of office

building space per employee (1,430,040/99,000). The city's forecast indicates a total of about 115,000 jobs in five years (Step 3.2(1)). Thus, using the ratio method, total demand in five years should be 1,667,500 square feet of Class A office space. Assuming that employment continues to grow at an annual rate of 3%, total employment in 10 years would approximate 133,000 workers. Using the same ratio (14.5 square feet per worker), total demand for Class A office space in 10 years is calculated at 1,928,500 square feet (133,000 × 14.5). Comparing these results to those of the segmentation method (Exhibit 13.7) results in almost identical forecasts. The procedure may be refined further by comparing the 14.5 ratio with the average ratio over the past five years. The underlying assumptions of this method, i.e., that the future mix of employment and the current ratio of office space per employee will remain the same, are potential weaknesses. (The ratio method could not be used for the CBD directly because current and forecasted employment for the CBD area was not available.) Exhibit 13.8 shows the calculations for this forecast.

Comparable City-Ratio Method

Another related ratio method could be used that features a comparison to comparable cities. In many metro areas multiple suburban cities can be compared according to the ratio of land uses to employment (or population). This is considered a separate method from the preceding ratio method, but is noted as another related method based on the same principle as the sales comparison method in the valuation section. That is, if neighboring City A is similar to the subject city but is slightly larger than the subject city, it should have about the same ratio per population of office as the comparable city does when the subject city reaches the same population (or jobs).

Step 3.4: Reconcile the Results of Various Methods and Forecast Demand

A summary of the alternative demand forecast follows.

Method	Conclusions
Trend (Inferred) Methods	
· Growth trends	Positive
· Historical occupancy	Moderately positive citywide
Fundamental Methods	
· Segmentation method:	1,678,000 occupied sq. ft. in 5 years, and 1,945,000 sq. ft. in 10 years
· Ratio method:	1,677,500 sq. ft. in 5 years, and 1,928,500 in 10 years

In this example, historical demand and forecast demand are very similar. The appraiser should compare the rate of growth in employment during this period to the rate indicated in the forecast. It is reasonable for the forecast rate to approximate the historical rate.

The segmentation method and the ratio method produced very similar results. In theory, the segmentation method is more reliable because it accounts for more of the variables. In practice, however, the reliability of the segmentation method depends on an accurate estimation and forecast of all the variables. Since the methods applied in the case study application yielded similar results, further refinement of the forecast is not necessary.

Step 4: Measure Competitive Supply

Step 4.1: Inventory Competitive Supply

The appraiser obtains local data on existing office space, current occupancy and vacancy levels, office buildings under construction, renovations and proposed or likely office buildings. Although data on existing buildings and office space under construction generally are readily available, data on proposed office buildings may be difficult to gather. Collecting the data is only part of the problem. The timing of possible building starts must be forecast as well as the amount of new space expected. The following list describes a possible procedure for this analysis.

1. Research planned projects.
   - Interview building officials and planning department staff in the local jurisdiction about recent inquiries concerning planned projects.
   - Review preliminary and final plats submitted for office use and determine their status.
   - Review announcements of proposed buildings in local newspaper and information from the chamber of commerce to determine current status of projects.
   - Survey brokers, lenders, and developers active in the area.
2. Compile a list of possible projects and assess the probability that they will be developed. For each project, consider:
   - Who is the developer and what is his or her track record?
   - How close is the developer to obtaining permission?
   - How much space has been pre-leased?
   - Does the developer have multiple projects?
   - How attractive is the location?
3. Analyze the probability of other projects being developed.

   Compare marginal/residual demand against existing buildings and projects under construction only. This helps the analyst discern the market participants' thinking on future windows of opportunity. If it appears that the market sees the potential for high marginal/residual demand, it is probable that some new competition can be expected during this period.
4. Consider other factors that affect new construction.

   Other factors that may affect the supply situation should also be considered, e.g., the demolition of office buildings, the rehabilitation and upgrading of office buildings from an old Class C building to a Class A building, and the adaptation of older buildings to office use.

Case Study Application of Step 4.1: Estimate Supply

There are currently about 5,333,700 square feet of office space citywide, and the overall occupancy rate is 82%. Occupied Class A office space in multitenanted buildings accounts for 32.5% of total occupied office space in the city.

Approximately 2,720,000 square feet of the citywide total office space are in the central business district. Multitenanted Class A buildings account for approximately 15% of the CBD space. The CBD has an overall occupancy rate of about 80%.

The southwest node has about 1,557,250 square feet of space with an 88% occupancy rate. The northeast node contains approximately 1,056,450 square feet and has a 79% occupancy level. Approximately 60% of the office buildings in the southwest are Class A, while about 35% are classified as Class A in the northeast suburban nodes. Exhibit 13.9 summarizes the amount of office space in the market.

Class A space is the specific market for the subject. This part of the citywide office market is summarized in Exhibit 13.10 that follows.

Several projects are planned for the area. One project was announced to scrap an old building in the CBD and build a 100,000-sq.-ft. new Class A office building. The announcement appeared in the paper, but no plat was filed with the city. Some brokers believe it is a land sale

Exhibit 13.9 Current Office Space Inventory in the City

Space Type & Location	No. of Bldgs.	Net Rentable Sq. Ft.	% of Total Space in Area	Occupied Space	% of Occupied Space	Vacant Space	% Vacant
Class A	4	408,000	15%	322,320	15%	85,680	21%
Class B	12	1,088,000	40%	926,480	42%	161,520	15%
Class C	15	1,224,000	45%	952,123	43%	271,877	22%
Total CBD	31	2,720,000	100%	2,200,923	100%	519,077	19%
Class A	9	928,500	60%	789,225	58%	139,275	15%
Class B	14	628,750	40%	576,942	42%	51,808	8%
Totals SW Node	23	1,557,250	100%	1,366,167	100%	191,083	12%
Class A	5	374,700	35%	318,495	38%	56,205	15%
Class B	10	681,750	65%	514,538	62%	167,212	25%
Totals NE Node	15	1,056,450	100%	833,033	100%	223,417	21%
Citywide Totals	69	5,333,700		4,400,123		933,577	18%

Based on survey of office buildings over 4,000 sq. ft.

Exhibit 13.10 Current Occupancy Survey of Class A Stand-Alone Office Space

	Net Rentable Sq. Ft.	% of Total Sq. Ft.	Occupied Sq. Ft.	% of Total	% Occupied
CBD	408,000	24%	322,320	23%	79%
Southwest Node	928,500	54%	789,225	55%	85%
Northeast Node	374,700	22%	318,495	22%	85%
Total Citywide	1,711,200	100%	1,430,040	100%	84%

ploy to flip the property to speculators. However, the developer stated that he plans to go ahead when he secures financing. Given the current market and the developer's reputation, this project is not likely to come to fruition soon, if ever.

Another project was announced in the southwest area for a 52,000-sq.-ft. office building. There has been an option on the site and some preliminary platting and zoning with the city. This is a very good Class A office location, but given the currently oversupplied market, there is only a 50% probability that the project will come to fruition.

The northeast area has announced a 100,000-sq.-ft. building. The site has closed, zoning and final platting is complete, and the project is at the permit phase. Reportedly, financing also has been secured. This area of town is a good location, and the high vacancy in Class B space is not expected to affect the project.

Exhibit 13.11 shows the results of the planned space analysis.

Exhibit 13.11 Forecast of New Office Space Construction						
Bldg.	Location	Planned Sq. Ft.	Probability of Start	Probability Area (Sq. Ft.)	Probable Start Date	Comment
1	CBD	100,000	0%	0	10+ Years	Local promoter announced, but brokers say it is a land sale ploy
2	Southwest	52,000	50%	26,000	5 Years	Announced an option on site, but current oversupplied market makes project questionable
3	Northeast	100,000	99%	99,000	2 to 5 Years	Land purchased, final plat approved, financing secured, and building permit applied for
Total Citywide		252,000		125,000		

Final Competitive Supply Estimate

Current competitive supply is measured by adding the Class A space in the CBD to the two suburban nodes (see Exhibit 13.9). The forecasted additional 125,000 square feet of Class A office space currently planned should also be included in the supply projections.

The data above do not include sublet space, space for which the tenant still pays rent but has vacated and is trying to release. However, this is an important part of the supply analysis if the data can be secured. Even though the space is not technically vacant, the availability of a substantial amount of such space indicates a weak market. In this case study there was very little sublet space, so it was not recorded or analyzed.

Step 4.2: Analyze Competitive Supply

In addition to determining the inventory of existing and future competitive supply, supply analysis yields information that can be used along with the findings of the location analysis to perform an inferred demand analysis.

The information in Exhibit 13.10 of Class A inventories by location can be compared to the location ranking derived in Step 1.3(1) and shown in Exhibit 13.3. The latter indicated that the CBD should be capturing 24% of citywide demand, which confirms the result of the survey of actual capture, and which shows that the CBD is capturing 22.5% of Class A occupied space. The CBD is capturing almost 50% of all occupied building space (Classes A, B, and C); thus, it has captured the majority of the city's older office building space.

A wider range of office products is typically built in suburban nodes than are available in the CBD. In the subject's case, the CBD is dominated by four large multitenanted office buildings with large floor plans, whereas the suburban nodes offer large and small spaces with a mix of amenities. Thus, location alone may not indicate potential capture. In the location ranking, two factors concerning future conditions were rated. The supply analysis, on the other hand, is historical. The two perspectives must be reconciled; however, in this case they were very consistent. In the final analysis, the appraiser is more interested in future benefits than historical experience.

Step 5: Analyze Market Equilibrium/Disequilibrium

Step 5.1: Compare Supply and Demand to Determine Marginal Demand

In many parts of the appraisal, the appraiser considers the point in the real estate cycle that the market is experiencing. Marginal demand analysis helps the analyst make this judgment.[11]

The procedure for determining marginal demand begins by comparing data on existing and future competitive supply with the estimates of current and anticipated demand. This is done with two objectives in mind. First, the appraiser must identify whether there is unsatisfied, or marginal, demand. Marginal demand is the demand that remains after all available space is subtracted from the projected demand for space. Marginal demand cannot be satisfied unless additional space, over and above proposed and newly constructed space, is added to the inventory.

Second, the appraiser seeks to determine how long the absorption of existing vacant office space and space under construction will take. This determination depends on the growth of demand. The point when existing vacant space, space under construction, and proposed office space will be absorbed represents a window of opportunity when new development might be expected.

Case Study Application of Step 5: Marginal Demand Analysis

Marginal demand is estimated by subtracting the competitive existing and projected supply citywide and the subject node from supportable current and projected Class A office space.

---

11. Information on the market cycle is used in the income capitalization approach to project increases or decreases in the subject rent and occupancy and to assess the portion of the discount rate that represents risk. It is also used to support the market conditions adjustment in the sales comparison approach and economic obsolescence in the cost approach.

The time needed to absorb the existing citywide vacant space and space under construction can be calculated by dividing the total excess space by the square foot demand per year.

Total excess space: 187,121 sq. ft. (available vacant space)
+ 125,000 sq. ft. (space under construction)
312,100 sq. ft. (rounded)

Square foot demand increase per year: 242,148 sq. ft.* (the anticipated growth in demand)/5 years
= 48,500(r) sq. ft.

312,100/48,500 = 6.44 years, or about 6 to 7 years as a point estimate. (Note: for brevity, the high and low range forecasts are not presented.)

* Five-year forecast supportable demand minus total current supportable demand (see Exhibit 13.12)

Exhibit 13.12   Citywide Class A Office Marginal Demand

	Current	Year 5	Year 10
Gross estimate of total citywide Class A office demand sq. ft.*	1,524,079	1,766,654	2,047,500
Less current competitive sq. ft.	1,711,200	1,711,200	1,836,200
Less estimate new construction	0	125,000	0
Net (excess) shortage	(187,121)	(69,546)	211,300

* Demand includes 5% for frictional vacancy.

Thus, the current citywide office space surplus of 187,100 square feet and the 125,000 square feet planned should be absorbed over the next six to seven years. Note that market occupancy during next five years will range from 83% to 91% during this period and when the vacant space is absorbed, the market occupancy will be 95% a balanced market. This suggests that the next six years will be highly competitive and rents will stay relatively stable.

CBD Marginal Demand Analysis
The marginal demand for space in the CBD is also a useful analysis to further refine the market conditions in which the subject operates. These data will also be used in the next step, determining the specific capture rate for the subject.

CBD Capture Rate
The major variable in this step is the future capture rate for the CBD. As noted, the location analysis shows a potential capture rate of 24%–slightly higher than the CBD current actual capture of 22.5% of the Class A market (322,320/1,430,040). The CBD capture rate has been falling over the last few years and is expected to fall in the future with new competition in the outlying nodes. When the northwest area's new 100,000-sq.-ft Class A building comes onto the market, and the southwest node's new 52,000-sq.-ft. building, is completed, the CBD capture rate should fall even further. Exhibit 13.13 shows a pro rata share cap-

Exhibit 13.13   CBD Capture Rate by Pro Rata Share

Location	Current	% of Total	5 Years	% of Total	% Change in Pro Rata Share	Comment
CBD Class A building sq. ft.	408,000	23.8%	408,000	22.2%	-6.8%	CBD share declines
Current competitive Class A space in NW and SW nodes	1,303,200	76.2%	1,428,200	77.8%	2.1%	New construction of 125,000 sq. ft. in Year 5
Total Class A space in city	1,711,200	100%	1,836,200	100%		

ture analysis that suggests that the CBD will lose about 7% of its current capture rate.

The pro rata share analysis conclusion of a 6.8% decline in the capture rate is based on the CBD Class A buildings continuing to compete citywide as they currently do. This is considered optimistic because the new buildings should have a competitive advantage with respect to age and condition alone.

Thus, the following marginal demand shown in Exhibit 13.14 reflects this falling capture rate for the CBD. The rate is based on occupied space, whereas the preceding analysis used a capture proxy to built space.

Exhibit 13.14   CBD Marginal Demand for Class A Office Space

	Current	Year 5	Year 10
Gross estimate of total citywide occupied Class A office demand in sq. ft.	1,447,875	1,678,321	1,945,125
Est. percentage capture CBD	22.3%	21.0%	20.0%
Total occupied demand in sq. ft. from employees in CBD	322,320	352,447	389,025
Plus frictional vacancy @ 5%	16,964	18,550	20,475
Total CBD demand for Class A space	339,284	370,997	409,500
Less current competitive sq. ft.	408,000	408,000	408,000
Less estimate new construction	0	0	0
CBD marginal demand for Class A space	(68,716)	(37,003)	1,500

Based on the CBD marginal demand analysis, the occupancy at the subject property will be slow to rise, but could reach the 95% range in five to 10 years if it can compete equally with the current competition, if no new building and class B/C space is renovated to create new competition, and if the forecasted increase in citywide employment is realized.

This information is used in the next step, the subject capture estimate, to provide a context for the capture forecast.

Step 6: Forecast Subject Capture (Market Penetration)

This step is the final step in the marketability analysis for the subject and can be considered a revenue forecast for the subject office building. At this point, all of the components of the market study are refocused on the competitive outlook for the subject property. The capture estimate becomes the launch point for the last part of the appraisal—the application of the three approaches—in which the appraiser determines how the subject's capture affects the property's value.

A forecast of the subject's capture rate is made after examining all the data, including the historical capture rate of the subject, the marginal demand forecast for the total market, and the ratings assigned in the first step of the market analysis process.

Step 6.1: Derive Inferred Estimate of Subject Capture

Growth trends for the subject city appear to be positive. City employment and population are forecast to grow at a rate of 3% per year. It can be inferred that the subject's occupancy level will continue to increase at a similar rate. If so, the subject should attain a 90% occupancy level in the next few years.

Current market occupancy in the CBD is about 80%, similar to the subject's occupancy. Thus the subject may be considered typical of the Class A market, and the analyst may infer that subject occupancy will increase at a rate similar to the market rate.

Step 6.2: Derive a Capture Rate by Fundamental Analysis

It could be inferred from the market marginal demand estimate that the subject should expect little or no increase in occupancy or rent levels for the next five to seven years. This outlook is at odds with the inferred analysis. Consequently, a more detailed fundamental forecast and capture analysis will be required to reconcile and support the specific income forecast in the income capitalization approach section of the appraisal.

A good starting point for a fundamental capture analysis is the current capture rate of the subject. The subject has a current occupancy level of 80%, and there is a total citywide estimated demand for 1,447,875 square feet of occupied Class A space (see Exhibit 13.15), so the subject capture rate is 5.5% of total citywide demand (80,000/1,447,875) and 5.6% of actual survey occupancy of 1,430,040. The difference could also lie in the survey data, since the actual survey does not include buildings less than 4,000 sq. ft. If all factors and competition stay the same in the future, then the subject's existing capture rate applied to forecast Class A space would yield the following.

Exhibit 13.15 Subject Capture of Citywide Demand by Current Capture Rate			
	Current	Year 5	Year 10
Total citywide occupied Class A office demand in sq. ft.	1,447,875	1,678,321	1,945,125
Current subject capture rate	5.5%	5.5%	5.1%*
Indicated subject occupancy	79,633	92,308	99,201

* Rate reduced since subject is full.

Only the mid-range forecast is presented here. High- and low-range estimates are omitted for the sake of brevity. Nevertheless, it is recommended that the appraiser present a complete analysis, including the range of the estimates, to improve the reliability of the forecast and to reflect the probability of each outcome.

This analysis suggests that it will take the subject five to 10 years to achieve full occupancy. However, since competition will change in the future, the general estimate above needs to be refined.

If the appraiser feels that the subject would compete equally with all the buildings in all the areas of town in the future, and there is no expected new competition, then the analysis might stop here. However, there is a question about whether or not the CBD will capture citywide Class A office space in the future at the same rate as in the past. It does not appear that the CBD is maintaining its fair share (see Exhibit 13.13). The CBD represents 24% of the current Class A space, but only 22.5% of the capture. While it is close to a fair share, there may be a problem, since growth is occurring in the suburban nodes and not in the CBD. An additional 100,000 square feet of space is to be built in the northeast suburban node within the next few years and probably 52,000 square feet in the southwest node in the next five years. Exhibit 13.14 suggests that CBD's pro rata share of the market will be shrinking.

Subject Capture from CBD Class A Demand

Based on actual occupancy in the CBD (see Exhibit 13.16), the subject is capturing 24.8% of the CBD Class A occupied space (80,000/322,320). The subject pro rata share of the total Class A space is 24.5% (100,000/408,000 sq. ft.). Thus, it appears that the subject is very similar to the other Class A buildings in the CBD.

The next step in the fundamental capture rate analysis is to adjust the pro rata share for differences in the building. The following quantifiable rating provides an analysis of whether or not the building has been operating up to market potential and whether this might be expected to change in the future.

Case Study Application of Step 6.2: Analyzing the Competition by Quantifiable Rating

The subject property rents for $20 per square foot, which is competitive with the rent charged for similar buildings. The subject has an 80% occupancy rate–average for Class A buildings–and is easily accessible within the CBD. Unlike many older office buildings, it has adequate parking facilities. The other Class A office buildings in the CBD have comparable access and parking facilities. Exhibit 13.16 rates the subject with the other major Class A buildings in the CBD. The rating does not factor in the differences in rent. It assumes that it is not a factor. The final capture estimate will consider the rent component, however.

The following scoring system features a ranking of equal to, worse than, or the same. The higher the ranking, the better the factor. (See Chapter 12 for a more detailed description of the ranking scoring method.)

Exhibit 13.16 Competitive Class A Office Building in CBD—Marketability Rating

ID #	1		2		3		4		
			Across		**Four Blks.**		**Six Blks.**		**Rank of**
Rating Criteria	**Subject**	**Description**	**Street**	**Description**	**Away**	**Description**	**Away**	**Description**	**Factor**
Avg. Asking Rent (NNN)		$20.00		$23.00		$18.00		$17.50	
Occupancy in Sq. Ft.		80,000		120,000		63,000		59,320	
Location Factors									
Proximity to major roads	3	3 Blks.	3	3 Blks.	2	4 Blks.	1	Six Blks.	3
Proximity to support amenities	2	Good	2	Good	1	Moderate	1	Moderate	10
Visibility from street	1	Good	1	Good	1	Good	1	Good	2
Ease of access to site	1	Good	1	Good	1	Good	1	Good	9
Compatibility adjacent land use	1	Good	1	Good	1	Good	1	Good	11
Bldg. Factors									
Size of bldg. (sq. ft.)	3	100,000	4	150,000	1	75,000	2	83,000	1
Exterior appearance bldg. and site	1	Good	1	Good	1	Good	1	Good	4
Age and condition of bldg.	1	Good	1	Good	1	Good	1	Good	12
Adequacy and cost of parking	1	Good	1	Good	1	Good	1	Good	5
Utility and tech. infrastructure	1	Good	1	Good	1	Good	1	Good	6
Interior design/lobby/ elevator	1	Good	2	V. Good	1	Good	1	Good	7
Security features	1	Avg.	1	Avg.	1	Avg.	1	Avg.	8
Hours of operation	1	5 days no nights	2	7 days & nights	1	5 days no nights	1	5 days no nights	9
Image of bldg.	2	Good	3	V. Good	2	Good	1	Avg.	13
Tenant quality	1	Good	2	AAA	1	Good	1	Good	14
Management	2	Good	2	Good	1	Avg.	1	Avg.	8
Total Score	161		205		138		123		627
Percentage of Scores	25.7%		32.7%		22.0%		19.6%		
Pro Rata by Bldg. Size	24.5%		36.8%		18.4%		20.3%		
Pro Rata by Occupied Space	24.8%		37.2%		19.5%		18.4%		
Total Competitive Space	408,000								
Total Occupied Space	322,320								

Note: The higher the number, the better the ranking; i.e., 2 is better than 1.

   In the comparative rating of major Class A professional office buildings in the CBD, the subject received an intermediate score. However, given the competition and market demand, the subject is performing about as well as it can in terms of marketability factors.

   The preceding capture analysis did not consider differences in rents. Exhibit 13.16 shows the asking rents for the competitive properties. Exhibit 13.17 shows a rent comparison based on the score received in

Exhibit 13.17 Competitive Rent Comparison

ID #	Building	Rent Per Sq. Ft.	Competitive Ranking Score (see Exhibit 13.16)	% Difference in Score (compared to subject)	Indicated Rent Per Sq. Ft.
1	Subject		161		
2	Bldg. Across Street	$23.00	205	21%	$18.06
3	Bldg. Four Blks. Away	$18.00	138	-17%	$21.00
4	Bldg. Six Blks. Away	$17.50	123	-31%	$22.91
	Averages	$19.50			$20.66

the rating. According to the rent comparison, the subject's current rents are slightly below market. However, given the strong competition located across the street, and the future market outlook, future increases in rent are doubtful.

In the next step of the market analysis, the subject's future capture rate will be estimated based on the reconciled results of the marketability rating, rent comparison, and the other data considered.

Case Study Application of Final Capture Conclusions

The subject's current actual capture rate of CBD occupied space was 24.8%, while the rating chart indicated that it should be capturing more of the market than it currently does. The final analysis gave weight to the current capture and the rating conclusions. The conclusions derived from applying this method are shown in Exhibit 13.18.

The subject capture of citywide demand in Exhibit 13.15 is higher than the capture rate of the CBD segmented demand in Exhibit 13.18. The reason is that the citywide capture rate was based on the subject's continuing its current capture rate of competitive building in the city, whereas the CBD capture rate is based on a declining capture of the future citywide demand.

Exhibit 13.18 Subject Capture Forecast by CBD Demand

	Current	Year 5	Year 10	Comment/Source
CBD occupied demand	322,320	352,447	389,025	Based on citywide capture rate declining slightly
Subject capture rate	24.82%	25.0%	25.0%	Rating and actual reconciled
Total subject occupancy	80,000	88,112	97,256	mid-range forecast

The CBD share of citywide demand was forecast to decline in the future; thus, the subject's share would also be expected to decline. The inferred methods suggest a slightly more optimistic scenario. The results of the future-oriented fundamental analysis, which is segmented to the subject submarket, are typically given more weight.

In fundamental analysis, the more sensitive variables are considered by asking such questions as:

- Is the employment forecast consistent with current market expectations?
- Are adequate data available to separate demand for office space of the subject-type office–i.e., Class A space?
- Is the method used to estimate the capture rate based on sound conclusions and data?

The reconciliation of the subject capture indicators for this case study application are set forth in Exhibit 13.19.

Market/Marketability Study Conclusions

Low-range forecast	*Occupancy.*	Level to slightly increasing in Years 1 through 5, then slowly increasing in Years 5 through 10 to 85% occupancy.
	Rents.	Declining at real rate of 0.5% per year to maintain a slight increase in occupancy.
Mid-range forecast	*Occupancy.*	Improving to 95% occupancy between Years 5 and 10, and then leveling off.
	Rents.	Must remain level or decline slightly over the next five years if a slow increase in occupancy can be reasonably expected. After Year 7, a slight real rate of increase can be expected after citywide marginal demand appears positive.
High-range forecast	*Occupancy.*	Increasing to 95% in five years and maintaining this rate through Year 10.
	Rents.	Real rate of increase to remain level over the next five years, then increase by 2% per year for Years 5 through 10.

Note: The high- and low-range forecasts are presented for illustration. The calculations are not shown. The estimating procedure is the same, but low and high employment projections are used.

The mid-range forecast is compared to the subject's current capture ratios in Exhibit 13.18 as a final check on reasonableness.

Exhibit 13.19 Office Market/Marketability Study Recap

Line		Current	Year 5	Year 10	Comment/Source
	Citywide Marginal Demand				
1	Total citywide employment	99,000	114,757	133,000	Forecast
2	Percentage occupying office space	25%	25%	25%	Est. from NAICS office sectors
3	Total employed in office space	24,750	28,689	33,250	Line 1 × Line 2
4	Percentage of office workers in Class A office space	32.5%	32.5%	32.5%	Est. by current office sq. ft. mix
5	Total citywide demand for Class A office space jobs	8,044	9,324	10,806	Line 3 × Line 4
6	Avg. sq. ft. per employee	180	180	180	Forecast
7	Total citywide occupied Class A office demand in sq. ft.	1,447,875	1,678,321	1,945,125	Line 5 × Line 6
8	Plus frictional vacancy @ 5%	76,204	88,333	102,375	(Line 7/.95) – Line 7
9	Gross estimate of total citywide Class A office demand in sq. ft.	1,524,079	1,766,654	2,047,500	Line 7 plus Line 8
10	Less current competitive sq. ft.	1,711,200	1,711,200	1,836,200	Class A space
11	Less estimate new construction		125,000	0	Est. probability
12	Citywide Class A marginal demand— net (excess) shortage	(187,121)	(69,546)	211,300	Line 9 minus Line 10 minus Line 11
	CBD Marginal Demand for Class A Office Space				
13	Gross estimate of total citywide occupied Class A office demand in sq. ft.	1,447,875	1,678,321	1,945,125	Taken from Line 7
14	Est. percentage capture (subject area)	22.3%	21.0%	20.0%	Declines due to new suburban competition
15	Total occupied demand in sq. ft. from employees in CBD	322,320	352,447	389,025	Line 13 × Line 14
16	Plus frictional vacancy @ 5%	16,964	18,550	20,475	(Line 15/95%) – Line 15
17	Total CBD demand for Class A space	339,284	370,997	409,500	Line 15 plus Line 16
18	Less current competitive sq. ft.	408,000	408,000	408,000	Actual survey
19	Less estimate new construction	0	0	0	
20	CBD marginal demand for Class A space	(68,716)	(37,003)	1,500	Line 17 minus Line 18 minus Line 19
	Subject Capture				
21	CBD occupied demand	322,320	352,447	389,025	From Line 15
22	Subject capture rate	24.82%	25.0%	25.0%	Rating and actual reconciled
23	Total subject occupancy	80,000	88,112	97,256	Mid-range forecast

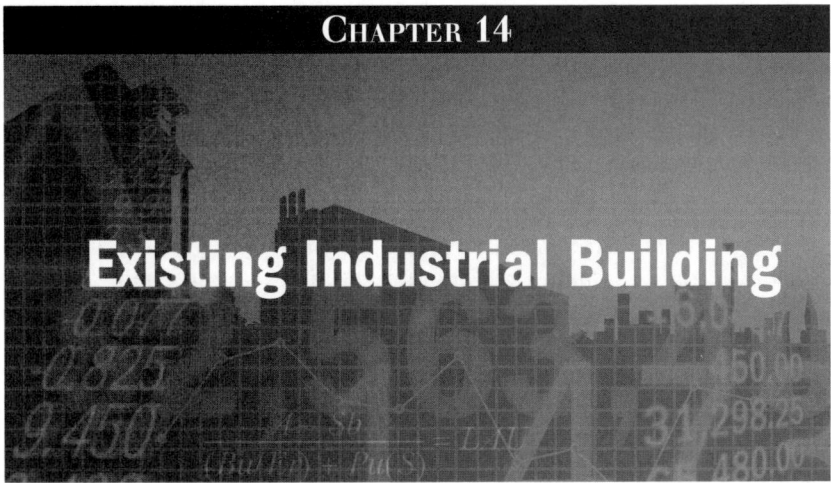

CHAPTER 14

Existing Industrial Building

Chapter Objectives

- To describe industrial building market trends
- To discuss sources of demand for industrial properties
- To introduce the market analysis process for an industrial building using a case study approach

Introduction

This chapter presents a step-by-step procedure for analyzing the market for an industrial building as part of a valuation assignment. First, an overview of the industrial building market, basic concepts and terminology, and the analytical process are presented. Then a case study application of the market analysis of an industrial building is presented in summary format as it might appear in an appraisal report.

Industrial Building Market Trends

Industrial properties have changed along with the evolution of transportation and technology. In the first half of this century manufacturing was centered in the core of major cities close to water or rail transportation. This linked raw products to manufacturing, and the manufactured products to consumers, who lived in faraway places.

The manufacturing process evolved to the point where components were manufactured in far-removed places and assembled in one final assembly plant. This was made possible in part by changes in transportation, particularly, the advent of the automobile, and, in the 1950s, the interstate highway system. The interstate highway system also changed the urban social landscape as suburbs emerged, enabling Americans to escape the crowded cities to occupy single-family housing on their outskirts. This phenomenon also changed industrial properties in two ways. First, workers did not have to live close to their jobs. The plants could be scattered throughout different locations, which were closer to raw products, cheaper labor, and to end users of the products manufactured. Second, it changed the way products were dispensed to the consumers. Shopping centers, auto dealers, and industrial plants all sprang up in far-flung corners of the metro area. The means of distribution adjusted to accommodate these changes.

In the recent past, technological improvements, such as product computer tracking and Internet sales, have changed the manufacturing and distribution process as well. For example, products can be tracked so precisely that nearby distribution centers can respond quickly, reducing the shelf life of the products.

Thus, the market analysis of industrial properties must begin with an awareness of and focus on the current trend in industrial properties and the source of their demand. In its most basic context, demand comes from: 1) new growth, i.e., expansion of the economic base, or 2) the relocation of industry from obsolete facilities. Both sources are driven in large part by the changes in industrial production trends.

Concepts and Terminology

Market analysis for an industrial building requires the segmentation of demand and supply. Generally, industrial real estate is used for production (manufacturing or processing), storage, research and development purposes, or often some combination of the three. These three areas are the typical starting point for industrial market segmentation, the precursor to demand analysis as part of a market analysis.[1] The industrial building markets that are the subject of this chapter include:[2]

Warehousing
Warehousing/distribution facilities that are used for collecting, inventorying, packaging, and dispersing products without added value process-

---

1. As an emerging alternative to the traditional three types of industrial property, the Urban Land Institute's *Guide to Classifying Industrial Property* divides industrial property into six categories:
   - Warehouse/distribution
   - Manufacturing facilities
   - Flex buildings
   - Multitenant buildings
   - Freight forwarding facilities
   - Data switch centers

   These major categories are further broken down into a total of 12 subcategories. For further discussion, see Johannson L. Yap, and Rene M. Circ, *Guide to Classifying Industrial Property* (Washington, D.C.: Urban Land Institute, 2003).

2. This chapter does not directly address a third type of industrial building—manufacturing facilities. These buildings are built for a specific use for which a market study would be required. This type of assignment is usually a Level D assignment and is not the typical appraisal assignment for most appraisers. For more detail on this type of building, see *Appraising Industrial Properties* (Chicago: Appraisal Institute, 2005).

ing. The typical storage/distribution space has less than 40% office finish, 16 ft. or higher ceilings, and contains truck-loading facilities.

Research & Development (Flex Space)

This activity includes buildings for office or showroom space, office tech, and research and development space. Typically, more than 40% of the space is finished office with attached warehouse space that may or may not have truck-loading space.

Industrial Demand Indicators

Forecasting demand for industrial properties is one of the more difficult appraisal tasks because there is not a direct link between the source of demand and the required building space. While retail can be linked directly to buying power in the market area, and housing can be linked to household growth and office to employment, industrial demand is not as straightforward.

Exhibit 14.1	Industrial Segments and Sources of Demand	
Market Segment	**Typical Activity in Buildings**	**Sources of Demand**
Warehouse/Distribution	Collecting, inventorying, packaging, and dispersing products without added value processing	Need for storing goods to serve area, state, or national economic base and population
Flex Space (Research & Development)	Product development, company office space	Technical, regional, and national population and economic base expansion
Manufacturing	Assembling components into intermediate or end-user products	The production of goods to serve a specific industry

Typical sources for industrial demand are economic base expansion or current users occupying obsolete space who need to upgrade. Users of industrial properties are almost always involved in export activities, so it is logical to measure the growth in the number of users as the main demand indicators. This is not an easy measurement, however. Estimating the quantity of goods coming into the market that requires warehousing is more difficult than forecasting the number of new employees who may need office space or estimating the level of retail buying power that exists in the market. Moreover, obtaining the data required to measure the amount of goods that need warehouse space is not practical for most appraisal assignments that have time and budget constraints.

In the last few years most models of industrial demand have correlated occupied space with either total employment, employment for a specified industry (such as warehouse and distribution employment for warehouse studies), gross domestic product, inventories, freight flow, and population. It has not been decided which of these is the best indicator.

Torto Wheaton Research cited the difficulty in finding the best demand indicators, noting that what truly fills up a warehouse is the physical volume of the goods shipped.[3] Based on their research, they have found that the best demand indicator for warehouse space is the number of employees who work in warehouses. They arrived at this conclusion after tracking for a number of years the data on occupied goods with other indicators such as the value of goods and volume of goods correlated to the space used. They concluded further that the best indication of the need for new warehouses in a market is the increase in the numbers of workers hired. Unlike occupants of office space, warehouse workers do not create the demand for warehouse space; they are a more reliable *symptom* of demand. Torto Wheaton cautions that adjustments in employment may be needed as productivity changes over time.

Other researchers have noted limitations in this method. For example, AMB Property Corporation (NYSE:AMAB) pointed out limitations to the industrial-specific employment method, stating that manufacturing employment does not take into account changes of productivity and manufacturing trends. Further, they maintain that all manufacturing-related firms are classified under one code, e.g., all 38,000 employees of the Coca Cola Company are classified as manufacturing.[4]

Rabianski and Black found that 69% of wholesale trade employees are actually located in office space.[5]

Mueller and Laposa also recognize the difficulty in finding warehouse demand indicators but offer a slightly different perspective,[6] proposing "the path of growth method." This method correlates concentrations of warehouse space to population growth. They found that when industrial warehouse buildings are viewed separately, stronger relationships between warehouse demand and population growth are found than with industrial employment growth. They concluded that the changing consumer environment and fulfillment strategies such as just-in-time inventories that many retailers have adopted have led to a shift in warehouse demand toward the path of transportation arteries. Thus, the location of warehouse space is consumer driven, and linkages to consumers become paramount.

Mueller and Laposa's studies found the national average for occupied warehouse space per capita in the United States was 44.1 sq. ft. They compared metro areas using a location quotient analysis and determined that metro areas with more square feet per capita than the national average were serving a larger area. They also found that the local population for the smaller markets was a good indicator, but the larger markets required adjustments for a larger service area. Thus, occupied space per population or, at the least, total employment as adjusted to the different market segments was judged by the authors to be the better indicator of demand, a major conclusion of their study.

---

3. Torto Wheaton Research, *About Real Estate*, Volume 5, Number 4, January 26, 2004.

4. AMB Property Corporation," Determinants of Industrial Real Estate Demand" *Real Estate Review* (Summer 2002): 57–61.

5. Rabianski, J.S. and R.T. Black, "Why Analysts Often Make Wrong Estimates About the Demand for Industrial Space," 27 *Real Estate Review* 1(1997): 68–72.

6. Glenn R.Mueller, Ph.D. and Steven P. Laposa, "The Path of Goods Movement" *Real Estate Finance* (Summer 1994).

W.T. Hughes noted that much industrial property is not population serving.[7]

AMB proposes another approach for finding demand indicators, the "Industrial Absorption Approach."[8] This method is based primarily on the Federal Reserve Board's Index of Manufacturing Output (IMO) in which they correlate occupied stock from Torto Wheaton Research data for 54 markets with various employment indicators from total employment to industry-specific employment data together with manufacturing output, business inventories, real GDP, and population. Their research indicated that the manufacturing output had the highest correlation to demand for warehouse space (.88). Total employment was second (.80); industry-specific employment third (.66 to .79); business indicator, which is inventories and real GDP, fourth (.18-.23); and population last (.06). Their article suggests that this model is very accurate for net absorption six months into the future.

Anne Frejetal uses a demand model based on gross metropolitan product and population change as interrelated demand functions. These variables are correlated with the change in the occupied space ratio in a double logarithmic functional form.[9]

The final decision that the appraiser makes as to the best indicator for warehouse demand will be based on the level of the appraisal assignment, data availability, and the type of industry studied.

Demand Models for Level C Studies

The appraiser's dilemma is centered on two major factors: the level of study that is practical for the assignment and the segmentation of demand into a small area and, ultimately, to one property. Most appraisals are constrained by limited budgets and time. Thus, the method that the appraiser uses must be based on easily available data and must be a method that can be performed in a short time. Furthermore, the typical appraisal assignment requires segmentation of demand into a small area and finally to one property. This means that the data used must be adaptable to small-area forecast. Thus, the forecast demand model must be adaptable to bottom-up analysis, defined as a Level C study.

The general approach for the appraiser is to look at detailed research on the topic of demand forecast models, decide which one is more reliable for the assignment, choose the economic principles on which the model is based, and then apply the concepts using a Level C, more simplified forecast model.

Appraisal assignments will also differ according to the technique used. When possible, it is desirable to use more than one model as a check for the results of each model. The following case study uses both an employ-

---

7. W.T. Hughes. "Determinants of Demand for Industrial Property." *The Appraisal Journal* (April 1994).

8. AMB Property Corporation.

9. Anne Frejetal, *Business Park and Industrial Development Handbook,* 2nd ed. (Washington, D.C.: ULI-Urban Land Institute, 2001): 33.

ment-based model and an occupied-space-to-total-employment method. Both have advantages and disadvantages. The advantage is that both models start with a long-range forecast of total employment. Other data such as gross national product (GNP) typically are based on short-term forecasts. Most valuation models that appraisers use are based on long-term forecasts—particularly the income and cost approaches. The appraisal assignment also requires that forecasting be segmented from the macro location to the micro location. Typically, long-term employment forecasts can be secured for a county, city, and often a smaller geographic area.

The Market Analysis Process for an Industrial Building

The market analysis process for industrial buildings is similar to that for office buildings. In fact, in many cases there is considerable overlap between the two, particularly with flex space. An overview of the process is presented in Exhibit 14.2: Market Analysis Process for an Existing Industrial Building. The six-step process includes:

1. Property productivity analysis
2. Specification of the market of most probable property users
3. Demand analysis and forecast
4. Competitive supply analysis and forecast
5. Supply and demand relationship
6. Capture estimate for the subject

Each of the six steps is divided further into sub-steps. The results are applied to the appraisal, to testing highest and best use alternatives, and to supporting the three approaches to value. The case study example follows this sequence.

The market analysis process is not static. It varies according to the availability of data, the techniques the appraiser chooses, and the changing conditions of the market. For example, different techniques might be used to analyze markets of differing sizes. Demand is typically estimated on a citywide or countywide basis and then allocated to the subject's submarket. In large metropolitan areas, it is usually segmented to reflect the building type and specific node, defined as a cluster of properties with similar or complementary uses. Generally, it includes a nucleus of commercial type buildings or activities but also mixed use of more intense activities such as entertainment. For a smaller city, the appraiser may forecast demand and analyze competitive buildings citywide. In this case, demand is segmented into a specific submarket and to a specific type of competitive buildings.

Case Study Description

The following application is a Level C market analysis for the appraisal of an existing industrial building.

Exhibit 14.2 Market Analysis Process for an Existing Industrial Building

Step 1: Analyze productivity attributes of the subject property

    1.1 Identify the type of industrial building by function and class.

    1.2 Analyze the site and building. Rate the subject in relation to the typical competition and/or the industry standard.

    1.3 Analyze the location.

        1.3(1) Analyze the macro location. Identify the submarkets, clusters or nodes of industrial buildings within the metropolitan area. Rate the cluster or node in which the subject is located relative to other competitive clusters or nodes within the metropolitan area in terms of land use linkages and the direction and rate of urban growth.

        1.3(2) Analyze the micro location of the subject, i.e., the characteristics of the subject's location within its node.

Step 2: Delineate the market of property users

    2.1 Identify the market of property users by studying the tenants, and the building function. Most industrial markets do not have a contiguous market area; the market area is generally diffused over a broad metropolitan area.

    2.2 Forecast employment growth in the market.

Step 3: Forecast demand

    3.1 Conduct trend analysis using inferred methods.

    3.2 Conduct fundamental analysis using segmentation method.

        3.2(1) Forecast the workforce occupying industrial space. Forecast employment by occupational category and multiply this figure by the percentage of employees in each category occupying industrial space.

        3.2(2) Estimate the size of the workforce occupying space in the subject's class of building. Multiply the figure derived in Step 3.2(1) by the specific percentage for that class of building.

        3.2(3) Estimate the requisite space per industrial worker.

        3.2(4) Calculate the demand for the specific class of industrial space by multiplying the number derived in Step 3.2(2) by the figure derived in Step 3.2(3).

        3.2(5) Adjust demand for the "normal" vacancy rate.

    3.3 Conduct fundamental analysis by the ratio method.

    3.4 Reconcile the results of the various methods applied and forecast demand.

Step 4: Measure competitive supply

    4.1 Inventory current competitive supply within subject's submarket.

    4.2 Forecast competitive buildings that are under construction and proposed. The competitive supply inventory may also be affected by demolitions, renovations, and the adaptation of space under other uses to industrial use.

Step 5: Analyze market equilibrium/disequilibrium

    5.1 Compare supply and demand to determine marginal demand.

Step 6: Forecast subject capture (market penetration)

    6.1 Derive a general (inferred) estimate of subject capture. Analyze the competitiveness of the subject vis-à-vis the competition in view of the marginal demand forecast. Examine historical occupancy rates for the subject and competition against historical marginal demand.

    6.2 Derive a capture rate for the subject's submarket by fundamental analysis. Rate the subject against competitive submarket.

    6.3 Derive a capture rate for the subject by comparison to competitive properties within the same submarket.

    6.4 Reconcile subject capture indications. Reconcile the competitive rating in Step 6.2/6.3 with the inferred capture rate or the subject derived in Step 6.1.

    6.5 Estimate future occupancy and rental rate based on all elements of the market/marketability study from the property productivity analysis to market study and subject market penetration (capture) analysis conclusions.

The case study is a 250,000-sq.-ft. warehouse/distribution building located in one of the northern counties of a large (four-county) metropolitan area with a population of more than 3,000,000 people. The subject county and the adjacent county together are considered part of the same market, the "Far North Market" area. The metropolitan central business district (CBD) is about 25 miles south of these far north counties, but the urban area is contiguous between. Within the Far North Market area are three submarkets:

• Allen Heights
• Palmdale
• Denia Landing Area

These two Far North counties are the fastest growing counties in the metropolitan area. The metropolitan area has also experienced extensive growth over the last decade, but in the last two years it lost jobs during an economic downturn. The subject Far North area that falls within two counties of the metro area has increased its number of jobs despite recent overall negative job growth in the metro area, but the Far North employment market, like the overall economy, has experienced a significant decline in job growth during the last year.

The subject's building is located in a deed-restricted industrial park in the Denia Landing submarket, which has four other similar industrial parks and a number of stand alone warehouse/distribution and R&D buildings.

The subject is located one block from a major freeway that connects to metro CBD. Rail service is provided in the industrial park, and a metro commuter station is one mile from the subject. The subject is also about 10 miles from the major metro airport and three miles from a major shopping mall, hotels, and office buildings.

The three tenants in the subject building occupy nearly equal space. Their leases are up for renewal in one, three, and five years, respectively. All seem to be doing well and have expressed a desire to re-lease, depending on the rate. The average subject's lease is $5.50 per sq.ft./yr. NNN.

Because the building is relatively new, fully leased, located in an established industrial park, and is in good condition, an alternative use for the subject as improved is highly unlikely. Given the relative certain condition of use for the subject and its significantly greater impact on the final value conclusion, the land as if vacant highest and best use would constitute a Level A analysis in most cases; therefore, the highest and best use of the subject as if vacant is not presented. Nor are alternative uses such as for remodeling typically critical to value, a situation that would also constitute a Level A analysis.

The most important purpose of the market/marketability study is to support the future rent and occupancy forecast needed in the income approach, the adjustments made to comparable sale properties from different markets in the sales comparison approach, and the estimate of economic obsolescence (if relevant) in the cost approach.

Step 1: Analyze Property Productivity

Step 1.1: Identify the Type of Industrial Building

The subject is a four-year-old, tilt-wall warehouse/distribution building in good condition. The building is designed for multiple tenants. Currently it is 100% leased with three tenants. The building has about 20% office space and the remainder is warehouse space.

Step 1.2: Analyze the Site and Building

A preliminary rating is developed by comparing the subject office building to the typical competition and/or the industry standard. The purpose of this rating is to assess the subject building's major strengths and weaknesses and to focus the market study on the industrial submarket that the building is designed to serve.

Besides providing a general understanding of the subject property, the preliminary rating helps the appraiser identify the characteristics to look for in determining which properties constitute the competitive supply. Subsequent ratings will enable the appraiser to estimate subject capture and to segment demand by location and building type.

The subject should be analyzed to assess how it compares to the current and future competition. The following factors should be considered in a typical industrial building analysis.[10]

Micro-Location Analysis Factors (Immediate Area)

- Proximity to major thoroughfares and access onto site for trucks. The fundamental purpose of the facilities is stated in the name–warehouse/distribution, thus, all factors related to getting material in and out of the facility is paramount.
- Proximity to complementary land use. This factor recognizes the need for an office/warehouse to have nearby land use support from related industrial services such as printing, repairing, security firms, to higher-end users such as hotels and restaurants.

Site Factors

- Land-to-building ratio. This factor pertains to the lot size compared to the building size according to the building's function. The important question is whether the site is large enough for parking and truck maneuvering. If the site does not conform to the following general rule, land-to-building ratio must be addressed further.
- Appraisers use the land-to-building ratio (sometimes called the *land-to-building footprint ratio*) to judge whether any additional land not needed to support the improvements is excess land or surplus land. The land-to-building ratio is calculated as follows:

$$\text{ratio} = \frac{\text{square footage of land}}{\text{square footage of building footprint}}$$

---

10. For a more complete discussion, see *Appraising Industrial Properties*, published by the Appraisal Institute and the Urban Land Institute handbook series-Business Park and Industrial Development Handbook, 2nd ed., published by the ULI Washington, D.C.

In most markets, the typical land-to-building ratio is between 2.5 and 3.5.[11]

- Truck maneuvering area. In recent years, the maximum truck length of 65 feet has grown to exceed 70 feet. To accommodate semi-trailers of these lengths, the recommended combined distance from the loading dock to the outside edge of the turnout area is approximately 150 feet. This distance will readily accommodate today's largest semi-trailers, which are approximately 73 feet long. The approximate relationship between truck maneuvering distance and truck length is 2.05 ft: 1 ft."

- Parking for cars and trucks. An adequate parking ratio depends on the labor requirements of the facility based on its current use and its potential uses. For industrial parks a standard parking requirement is 2.4 per 1,000 square feet of gross building area. Facilities that have substantially less parking may have a limited number of potential users, especially if access to public transportation is poor."

Building Improvements

- Construction quality and appearance. This factor pertains to more than just cost and appearance. It addresses quality over functionality. For example, the floor thickness requirement for a warehouse is an issue that should be considered. Typical warehouse applications require five to eight inches of reinforced concrete flooring. Some industrial facilities have thicker floors to support specialized machinery, such as commercial printing presses or manufacturing equipment.

- Building size, and design. These factors can vary from warehouse area, percentage of office space, flexibility for multitenants, ceiling heights, security features, and other issues that relate to productivity.

- Ceiling heights. Warehouses typically fall into three groups by truss height and price per square foot, as shown in the following exhibit.

Exhibit 14.3	Ceiling Heights
12–14 feet	Typically considered substandard for most contemporary warehouse/inventory storage uses; currently found most often in older buildings or in multitenant buildings designed as new businesses incubators
15–20 feet	Adequate for comfortable operation of many smaller warehouse/inventory storage applications
21–35 feet	Characteristic of a contemporary, efficient warehouse

- Bay spacing. Clear height dictates the vertical space available for storage or placement of special equipment within the structure, whereas bay spacing (also known as bay depth) is the horizontal distance between load-bearing walls. In the analysis of real estate,

---

11. Material in this section is based on Chapter 2 of *Appraising Industrial Properties*, Appraisal Institute, 2005.

bay spacing is a quantitative measure of space available for facility operations, including traffic flow around and within the building. The following table shows typical standards for bay spacing.

40×40 to 48×48 feet	Below current standards for most warehousing operations
52×52 feet	Adequate
60×60 feet	Emerging standard for state-of-the-art distribution facilities

- Loading facilities. Just-in-time logistics requires a high level of operational efficiency, which is hard to achieve in outdated loading facilities.

Application of Step 1.2
Exhibit 14.4 lists the factors used to rate the subject. In a Level C study, a quantitative method is generally applied to structure the analysis and help the reader follow the reasoning. (For a more complete discussion of this rating method, refer to the retail shopping center application in Chapter 12.)

Step 1.3: Analyze the Location
Because the demand for industrial space is diffused over a broad metropolitan area, the analysis must first consider the subject's macro location.

Exhibit 14.4   Industrial (Warehouse/Distribution) Building—Property Rating

| | | Inferior | | | Typical* | | Superior | |
| | | | | | | | | |
Sub-rate-> (Rate factors by inserting "X")	High	Moderate	Slight	Neutral	Slight	Moderate	High
Micro Location (immediate area)							
Proximity to major thoroughfare				X			
Access onto site for trucks				X			
Access and visibility for customers				X			
Proximity to complementary uses				X			
Site							
Parking for cars and trucks				X			
Circulation on site for trucks				X			
Topography				X			
Land-to-building ratio				X			
Building Improvements							
Construction quality				X			
Exterior appearance			X				
Size of warehouse area				X			
Size of office area				X			
Condition and effective age				X			
Security features				X			
Flexibility of design for multitenants		X					
Quality of interior finish				X			
Obsolescence (overall)							
Exterior design				X			
Interior layout and design			X				
Rating Conclusions							
Sub-rate number of items	0	1	2	15	0	0	0
Times category score	0	2	4	5	6	8	10
Category score	0	2	8	75	0	0	0
Total subject score	85						
Percentage above or (below) all average	-6%						

* Typical new construction in competitive areas.

Step 1.3(1): Analyze the Macro Location

Analysis of the macro location encompasses the overall metropolitan matrix, reflecting urban growth patterns, the clusters or nodes of industrial buildings, and the quality of the vital linkages that connect these buildings to the community and support facilities. The analyst's objective is to identify the subject node and to determine how it compares to competitive nodes currently and project how it will compare in the future.

In location analysis for industrial buildings, the metropolitan market is divided into submarkets. In a large metropolitan area such as illustrated in this case study, clusters of submarkets can be segmented as an interim step. For example, in this case study, the location analysis is divided into metropolitan segments. The subject is in the far north part (two-county area) of the metro areas (six-county area), whereas the remainder of the metro area is divided into four quadrants for a total number of five metro study sections: far north (subject), and the remaining areas northwest, northeast, southeast, and southwest.

Application of Step 1.3(1)

The Apex metropolitan area has been a fast-growing metropolitan area, and the Far North area has been the predominant direction of growth in the metropolitan area. Exhibit 14.5 and Exhibit 14.6 show growth trends in the study area. The subject far north area exhibits a faster growth rate than all of the other areas combined.

Note that the subject northwest quadrant increased employment during the previous year, while the metropolitan total employment declined. The subject area also increased its share of employment over the years from 13.8% of total employment four years ago to 16.2% of total employment currently. However, the current economic downturn affecting the metro area is also affecting the Far North counties (sub-

Exhibit 14.5	Employment Trends in Metro Area				
Year	Remainder Metro Area	% Change	Far North Counties (Subject Area)	% Change	Total Employment
4 yrs. previous	1,474,894		236,000		1,710,894
3 yrs. previous	1,541,295	4.5%	253,000	7.2%	1,794,295
2 yrs. previous	1,572,349	2.0%	275,000	8.7%	1,847,349
1 yr. previous	1,631,211	3.7%	293,000	6.5%	1,924,211
Most recent year end	1,596,251	-2.1%	308,000	5.1%	1,904,251

Exhibit 14.6	Metro Population Growth					
Metro Quadrants	20 Yrs. Ago	% of Total	10 Yrs Ago	% of Total	Current	% of Total
Far North metro	289,682	14.8%	539,551	21.1%	1,027,602	29.0%
Remainder metro	1,669,705	85.2%	2,015,801	78.9%	2,511,000	71.0%
Total metro	1,959,387	100%	2,555,352	100%	3,538,602	100%

ject submarket). During the current year employment growth in the Far North Metro area is less than half of the last year's employment growth of 15,000. Thus, this year's employment growth is expected too be positive but in the 3,000 to 7,000 job growth range.

The direction of population growth in the metropolitan area has also been moving toward the northwest quadrant (subject area). For instance, 20 years ago, the subject quadrant made up only 14.8% of the total population, while currently it makes up has 29%, as shown in Exhibit 14.6.

Metro Research surveys industrial data in 18 submarkets. (See Exhibit 14.7.) The subject Far North area includes three of these submarkets. Note that the subject Far North Metro had three of the top six submarkets with 26.8% of total metro area new warehouse/distribution construction during the last four years. The subject submarket is called the Denia Landing Area.

Macro location factors influence urban growth, and particularly location elements desired for office/warehouse/distribution facilities such as represented by the subject case study. These factors are detailed in Exhibit 14.8 that follows, but they cluster around:

- Growth trends
- The development climate in the area

Exhibit 14.7		Metro Submarkets Rank by New Warehouse Building				
Metro Area	**Rank**	**Submarket**	**Total Warehouse/ Distribution Space (Sq. ft.)**	**% of Total Bldg. Space**	**Warehouse/Distribution Bldg. Built in Last Four Years**	**New Bldg. as % of Total New Constr.**
NW	1	East Airport Area	20,010,057	6.9%	13,250,018	24.2%
NE	2	Northeast Grand Area	31,817,994	10.9%	6,322,863	11.5%
Far North	3	Denia Landing Area	10,162,844	3.5%	5,976,698	10.9%
Far North	4	Palmdale Area	9,445,764	3.2%	4,596,921	8.4%
SW	5	Lone Ridge Area	18,952,652	6.5%	4,250,660	7.8%
Far North	6	Allen Heights	5,115,963	1.8%	4,112,401	7.5%
SW	7	Southwest Park Area	7,422,755	2.5%	3,678,492	6.7%
SE	8	East Timber Area	10,162,844	3.5%	2,418,742	4.4%
NE	9	Rocky Point Area	3,851,995	1.3%	2,357,251	4.3%
NW	10	Hanes North Area	24,857,531	8.5%	1,350,765	2.5%
NE	11	Addison Village	14,193,695	4.9%	1,267,522	2.3%
SE	12	Redbird Area	11,833,636	4.1%	1,253,710	2.3%
NW	13	Brooks Creek Area	43,713,088	15.0%	1,205,893	2.2%
NW	14	North Valley Area	39,361,572	13.5%	1,205,343	2.2%
NE	15	Roaring Springs Area	3,623,651	1.2%	660,761	1.2%
NE	16	Central Park Area	19,712,903	6.8%	547,509	1.0%
SE	17	Southeast Park Area	6,935,572	2.4%	330,762	0.6%
SW	18	North River Area	9,929,897	3.4%	0	0.0%
		Total Metro Area	291,568,483	100%	49,012,821	100%

- Public infrastructure to support warehouse distribution
- Available land
- Available labor
- Quality-of-life issues

These factors are also considered in light of the current situation and the future. The long-term future is important because a market value appraisal assignment requires valuation analysis based on long-term prospects for the facility being appraised.

The five study areas of the metropolitan area are rated in terms of their competitiveness. The rating description and factors are similar to that for office uses. The score is based on a ranking system, i.e., each area is rated against all other areas for the factor being considered based on a ranking score of equal to, better than, or worse than. Thus, a score of "1" means that an area is rated the worst for that factor compared to another area. The rating chart does indicate that that area is considered a bad or substandard for a particular factor, only that the factor when compared to another area is considered inferior to that area.

Based on information about the five metro areas, the appraiser assigned the macro locational ratings shown in Exhibit 14.8. These ratings will provide support for the allocation of citywide demand among the areas and help determine subject future market penetration and economic (rent) demand (marketability).

Step 1.3(2): Analyze the Micro Location
Micro location can be analyzed in terms of competing submarkets within a metro area. For example, the subject is in the Far North metro sector, which was rated in the macro location analysis. Within the Far North metro sector are three submarkets in this case study:

- Allen Heights
- Palmdale
- Denia Landing Area

Application of Step 1.3(2): Analyze the Micro Location
These three submarkets can be rated with rating factors similar to those used for the macro rating. Exhibit 14.9 shows how this is done.

This analysis is usually performed at this step and then more detail in the market penetration (Step 6.2). Step 6.2 combines the site/building analysis with the micro location attributes of the subject and then compares these marketability features to major competitive buildings, usually from the subject's submarket.

This micro location analysis refers to the following attributes: the subject's relative location within the node, traffic conditions around the subject site (e.g., one-way streets, curb cuts, and median cuts), pedestrian access to and from the support facilities for the subject building, adjacent land uses, the availability and convenience of parking,

Exhibit 14.8 Industrial Macro-Location Analysis Chart

ID #	Rating Criteria	Far North (Subject Area)	Northwest	Northeast	Southeast	Southwest	Importance Factor
1	Travel time to employee housing	3	3	2	1	2	10
2	Travel time to executive housing	4	3	2	1	2	7
3	Travel time to passenger airport	3	4	2	1	2	3
4	Support facilities in area (hotels, restaurants, multitenant office)	3	3	2	1	1	5
5	Most public expenditures in last 5 years (infrastructure)	3	3	2	1	1	8
6	Forecast most public expenditures in next 5 years	4	3	2	1	1	8
7	Quantity of prestige companies in area	3	3	2	1	2	5
8	Area of most new industrial building in last 5 years	4	3	2	1	2	14
9	Area forecast to have most employment growth in next 10 years	4	3	2	1	1	13
10	Proximity to air freight	3	4	2	1	2	11
11	Proximity to rail	2	2	2	1	1	10
13	Proximity and access to interstate hwy.	3	3	1	2	2	12
14	Current travel time to customers	3	4	2	1	1	9
15	Current travel time to vendors	4	3	2	1	1	9
16	Expected travel time to customers in 10 years	4	3	2	1	1	8
17	Expected travel time to vendors in 10 years	4	3	2	1	1	8
18	Area with most land ready for new industrial buildings (infrastructure)	2	2	1	3	2	4
19	Land cost	1	1	2	1	2	2
20	Taxation cost	2	3	1	1	1	3
21	Educational attainment in area	3	3	2	1	1	5
22	Proximity to universities and training schools	3	3	2	1	1	6
23	Air/water quality and compliance cost	1	1	1	2	2	1
24	Utilities type and capacity in area	2	2	2	1	1	9
25	Crime in area	3	4	2	1	1	7
	Total score	566	532	334	198	246	1,876
	Percentage of total scores	30%	28%	18%	11%	13%	100%

Note: Higher number = better location.

Exhibit 14.9 Industrial Submarkets Location Analysis Chart

ID #	Rating Criteria/Submarket Areas	Denia Landing Area (Subject Submarket)	Allen Heights	Palmdale Area	Importance Factor
1	Travel time to employee housing	2	1	1	10
2	Travel time to executive housing	1	2	3	7
3	Travel time to passenger airport	2	1	1	3
4	Support facilities in area (hotels, restaurants, and multitenant office)	1	2	3	5
5	Most public expenditures in last 5 years (infrastructure)	1	1	1	8
6	Forecast most public expenditures in next 5 years	3	2	1	8
7	Number of prestigious companies in area	3	3	2	5
8	Area of most new industrial building in last 5 years	2	3	1	14
9	Area forecast to have most employment growth in next 10 years	2	2	1	13
10	Proximity to air freight	3	2	1	11
11	Proximity to rail	2	2	1	10
13	Proximity and access to interstate highways	3	2	1	12
14	Current travel time to customers	3	2	1	9
15	Current travel time to vendors	1	1	2	9
16	Expected travel time to customers in 10 years	3	2	1	8
17	Expected travel time to vendors in 10 years	2	2	1	8
18	Area with most land ready for new buildings	2	2	1	4
19	Land cost	1	1	2	2
20	Taxation cost	2	2	1	3
21	Educational attainment in area and adjacent	1	2	3	5
22	Proximity to universities and training schools	2	1	3	6
23	Air/water quality and compliance cost	1	1	1	1
24	Utilities type and capacity in area	1	1	1	9
25	Crime in area	1	2	2	7
	Total score	354	325	246	925
	Percentage of total scores	38%	35%	27%	100%

Note: Higher number = better location.

nuisances, natural amenities, the subject's future location within the projected pattern of growth for the node, and any special building amenities the subject may possess.

The importance of these factors varies for different types of industrial buildings. For a research and development industrial building the important factors are similar to those for a multitenant office building. However, for office/warehouse properties such as the subject, ease of access, proximity to vendors, rail, airport, and to the destination all are factors that become more important.

Application of Step 1.3(2): Building Location Analysis

The subject is easily accessible and has as good locational factors as any other building in the Denia Landing Area submarket.

Step 2: Delineate the Market of Property Users

Most industrial buildings do not have the contiguous market or trade areas that characterize retail facilities (i.e., concentric trade circles defined by time-distance relationships and sales volume percentages) and residential subdivisions (i.e., commuting time to employment centers). Industrial facilities such as professional office buildings are driven by the national economies translated to the local metropolitan and area and the subject submarket based on locational factors.

The property productivity analysis identified the property as competitive for office/warehouse/distribution. The submarket for the case study was identified as the Far North Metro area. The demand for future space likely will come from the overall expansion of the metro economic base. As older buildings located in the south of the metro area become obsolete and the tenants desire to relocate to the Far North Metro area, demand will also increase for the Far North Metro area.

Step 2.1: Identify the Market of Property Users

Exhibit 14.10 shows the metro employment and the employment categories market. An "X" identifies the employment categories that are most likely to occupy the warehouse/distribution centers—similar to the case study.

The NAICS (the North American Industrial Classification System) was introduced in 1997. This system of classification replaced the 1987 SIC (Standard Industrial Classification) system. The classification of employees in different categories changed; thus historical comparisons are difficult to make beyond 1997.

Employment data classifications have built-in limitations. For example, although the goal is to isolate employment related to warehouse /distribution systems, generally employment for a specific industry is classified by the primary activity of the establishment. This

Exhibit 14.10 Last Year-end Employment in North Metro Market Area

NAICS #	Description of Category		% of Total Employment	Key Categories for Warehouse Distribution Employment
11	Agriculture	4,557	1.5%	
21	Mining	777	0.3%	
23	Construction	18,537	6.2%	
31–33	Manufacturing	36,337	12.2%	
22 & 48–492	Transportation and utilities	11,037	3.7%	
493	Warehousing	398	0.1%	X
42	Wholesale trade	15,138	5.1%	X
44–45	Retail trade	70,987	23.9%	
52,53	FIRE	14,756	5.0%	
54–72	Services and other	75,058	25.3%	
92	Public administration	49,187	16.6%	
	Totals	296,769	100.0%	5.2%

Source: State Work Force Commission, employment of covered jobs in the county.

means that an accountant at a manufacturing facility would be classified as a manufacturing employee rather than a financial services employee. Also, employees of a large company can be classified in many different sectors, depending on the facilities in which they work. For instance, an oil company is classified as mining, but the employees at the headquarters building would be classified as service workers, pipeline operators would be classified as transportation workers, and refinery workers as manufacturing employees.

Step 2.2: Forecast Employment Growth in Market Area

The market study requires a forecast of future demand. Thus, the future number of employees in the above-identified group of potential users of the space will constitute the bulk of future demand. Sources are forecast then become the next concern in the market study.

Composite or aggregate data on monthly employment percentages for selected metropolitan areas are published by the U.S. Department of Labor, Bureau of Labor Statistics. Employment projections are also provided by economics departments of many universities and such local organizations as the local council of governments. This aggregate data must be analyzed, adjusted, and refined to forecast future employment. The appraiser must then adjust the employment forecast to reflect the appraiser's judgment of the most likely future for the subject demand indicators.

In analyzing employment data the appraiser should carefully review its parameters, particularly to determine whether it refers to individuals who are locally employed or to employed individuals who are local residents.

The forecasters predict that the previous rapid job growth will slow down considerably during the next decade. The metro area experienced job reductions the previous year even though the subject Far

---

Exhibit 14.11 Past Employment Trends in Far North Metro

Year	Far North Metro Total Employment (Subject Area)	Increase
4 years previous–year end	236,000	
3 years previous	253,000	17,000
2 years previous	275,000	22,000
1 year previous	293,000	18,000
Most recent year end	308,000	15,000
Total 4-year increase		72,000
Average increase/year		18,000

Forecast Employment Growth for Far North Metro

Source	Current Employment (all types)	Forecast Average Increase Per Year for Next 10 Years
Regional Planning Agency	308,000	10,322
Commercial Data Vendor	308,000	8,426

North area experienced an increase in employment. However, like the slowdown in the overall metropolitan area, the Far North Metro area has been experiencing very slow employment growth during the current years. It is expected to be less than half that of last year. The slowdown is expected to be temporary, and the job growth should approach forecast levels, but no one expects job growth to increase at the previous level—at least not for many years.

Thus, the appraiser's estimated forecast for job growth in the Far North Metro area would be:

Forecast Year 1–2

Low Range	2,000 per year on average
Mid-Range	4,000 per year on average
High Range	10,000 per year on average

Forecast Year 3–10

Low Range	7,000 per year on average
Mid-Range	10,000 per year on average
High Range	13,000 per year on average

Step 3: Forecast Demand

The appraiser considers inferred and fundamental forecast demand data and reconciles it for final demand forecast.

Step 3.1: Current Market Trend Analysis—Inferred Demand Indicators

Inferred Demand by Metropolitan Data

The data in Exhibit 14.12 shows that warehouse distribution is more than 90% occupied and that warehouse distribution makes up 72% of all industrial space. These two data points suggest a good market for warehouse/distribution.

Exhibit 14.13 shows the net absorption of space in the metropolitan area by type of industrial category. Net absorption is the good absorption number, since it is calculated as gross absorption minus move outs. This gives a number of new demand. In the metro area the data shows warehouse/distribution is by far the greatest user for industrial

Exhibit 14.12 Metro Industrial Space				
Type	Total Current Space	Vacancy Rate w/Sublet	Occupied Space	% of Total Occupied Space
Flex/R&D	102,478,000	9.9%	92,332,678	25.1%
Manufacturing	12,301,000	13.5%	10,640,365	2.9%
Warehouse/Distribution	291,568,000	9.2%	264,743,744	72.0%
Totals	406,347,000	9.51%	367,716,787	100.0%

Notes: Includes buildings 15,000 sq. ft. or larger. Includes owner-occupied buildings. Does not include buildings under construction or government buildings.

Source: Commercial Data Vendor Year-End Industrial Report.

Exhibit 14.13	Metro Industrial Space (Net) Absorption			
Type	Last Year	2 Yrs. Ago	3 Yrs. Ago	4 Yrs. Ago
Flex/R&D	1,346,000	1,023,000	1,488,000	1,624,000
Manufacturing	352,000	-40,000	210,000	214,000
Warehouse/Distribution	6,215,000	3,349,000	6,038,000	9,843,000
Totals	7,913,000	4,332,000	7,736,000	11,681,000

properties in demand and experienced the greatest demand during the last four years.

Inferred Demand By Submarket Data
Exhibit 14.14 shows occupancies and absorption by Far North Metro submarkets compared to the overall metro area. At a vacancy rate of -4.7 percent, the subject Denia Landing Area has the lowest vacancy rate of its two closest competitors and for the metro as a whole. The subject submarket also has the most properties under construction, currently at 2.6 M sq.ft. The low vacancy rate is a good sign for demand, and the significant amount of new construction can be positive, although the large volume of new construction could also be a precursor to an oversupply.

Step 3.2: Forecast Demand by Fundamental Analysis Methods
Step 3.2(1): Forecasting Demand—Method 1: Segmentation
The market delineation section (2.2) provided a forecast of future job growth in the subject Far North Metro market area. This section also provided a percentage of total employment associated with warehouse distribution. (See Exhibit 14.10.) Exhibit 14.15 shows a complete demand forecast by the segmentation method.

Forecasting Demand—Method 2, The Ratio Method
If local data on occupied industrial space, such as the subject industrial building are available, and the future employment mix in the area is expected to remain proportionally stable, the appraiser may use a ratio of total-employment-to-occupied-buildings such as the subject and then apply this ratio to the forecast.[12]

Application of Step 3.3
The first step in this method is to calculate the square feet of subject type real estate to total jobs. Exhibit 14.16 shows that in the Far North Metro area there are 73.8 sq. ft. of occupied warehouse/distribution space for every job in the same geographic area. Four years ago in the in Far North Metro area there were 58.1 sq. ft. of warehouse/distribution per job. This is an increase in square footage per job of about 3.9 sq. ft. per year on average. At this rate, in five years the Far North Metro area would

---

12. The ratio method can be tied to any demand indicator judged to be the most reliable. For example, population increase is the most common alternative to job increase.

Exhibit 14.14 Market Absorption Trends

Submarket (Subject in Denia Landing Area)	Total Bldg. Sq. Ft.	Vacancy Rate					Sq. Ft. Under Const./Renov.	Net Absorption (Sq. Ft.)				
		4 Yrs. Ago	3 Yrs. Ago	2 Yrs. Ago	1 Yr. Ago	Current		4 Yrs. Ago	3 Yrs. Ago	2 Yrs. Ago	1 Yr. Ago	Current
Allen Heights												
Flex/R&D	1,702,131	2.4%	2.9%	3.2%	1.8%	6.6%						5,000
Manufacturing												
Warehouse/Distribution	5,115,963	8.2%	5.0%	6.8%	7.8%	16.4%	700,000	2,129,000	638,000	39,000	-102,000	-77,000
Denia Landing Area												
Flex/R&D	3,653,188	24.9%	4.0%	3.9%	8.2%	11.9%	335,000	117,000	760,000	230,000	123,000	210,000
Manufacturing	416,979											
Warehouse/Distribution	10,162,844	10.0%	15.6%	7.8%	8.3%	4.7%	2,600,000	250,000	688,000	2,185,000	559,000	324,000
Palmdale Area												
Flex/R&D	4,336,022	6.4%	7.6%	9.8%	3.3%	14.8%	525,937	32,000	60,000	279,000	356,000	-79,000
Manufacturing	10,325											
Warehouse/Distribution	9,445,764	19.2%	13.6%	8.6%	4.5%	6.8%	500,000	-17,000	1,022,000	768,000	1,003,000	290,000
Metro Area												
Flex/R&D	102,478,699	8.5%	6.9%	6.9%	5.0%	8.7%	689,937	1,717,000	3,315,000	1,839,000	3,428,000	-118,000
Manufacturing	12,301,763											
Warehouse/Distribution	291,568,483	4.2%	7.7%	6.3%	5.1%	9.2%	5,923,000	11,608,000	5,714,000	11,663,000	8,670,000	731,000
Total Metro	406,348,945											

Source: Commercial data vendor

Exhibit 14.15 Warehouse/Distribution Space Mid-Range Demand Forecast by Segmentation Method

Line	Forecast New Demand	Current Year End	Year 1	Year 2	Year 3	Year 4	Year 5	Comments/Source
1	Total employment in Far North Metro area	308,000	312,000	320,000	330,000	340,000	350,000	Source: State employment commission, Bureau of Labor Statistics, and commercial data vendor
2	Forecast yearly increase of new employment (all categories) in Far North Metro area		4,000	8,000	10,000	10,000	10,000	Source: Commercial data service, local regional planning agency, state comptroller's office, and appraiser's analysis
3	Percentage employment in warehousing and wholesale trade	5.2%	5.3%	5.5%	5.8%	6.0%	6.0%	Warehouse space more concentrated in future; thus, increase over next five years toward metro 7.9% employment in these sectors. However, subject Far North Metro area not expected to reach as high concentration as the metro area.
4	Estimated warehouse and wholesale employment	16,016	16,536	17,600	19,140	20,400	21,000	Calculation–Line 1 × 4
5	Avg. sq. ft. per employee	1,419	1,420	1,420	1,420	1,420	1,420	Source: Current year calibration and average of industrial groups from Gruen 1986 Study for ULI*
6	Total occupied demand for warehouse/distribution space	22,721,881	23,481,120	24,992,000	27,178,800	28,968,000	29,820,000	Line 4 × 5

*   *Survey by Industry: Ag and Mining – 500 SF; Construction 450 SF; Manufacturing – 600 SF; High Tech – 500 SF; Tr/PU – 600 SF; Wholesale Trade – 2,900 SF. Overall Average = 925 SF. Source: Cognetics, Inc. "America's Future Industrial Space Needs for the Year 2000". National Association of Industrial and Office Parks, 1989, page 27, Table 3-17.*

Survey Results per Building Type: Light Industrial – 624 SF; R&D – 485 SF; Warehouse – 2,746 SF; Industrial Service – 724 SF; Commercial Service – 1,643 SF. Average per this data is 1,245. Source: Gruen, Gruen and Associates, Employment and Parking in Suburban Business Parks: A Pilot Study (Washington D.C.: Urban Land Institute, 1986) page 10.

Exhibit 14.16 Warehouse Distribution Space per Total Jobs in Area

	Total Warehouse/Distribution Bldg. Area (Sq. Ft.)	% Vacant	Estimated Occupied Space	Total Jobs	Sq. Ft. of Space Per Job
Current					
Far North Metro area	24,724,571	8.1%	22,721,881	308,000	73.8
Total Metro area	291,568,483	9.2%	264,744,183	1,904,521	139.0
Four Years Ago					
Far North Metro	15,802,000	13.1%	13,731,938	236,362	58.1
Metro area	227,100,000	4.2%	217,561,800	1,711,256	127.1

have 93.3 sq. ft. of warehouse space per total job. Although the increase is not expected to continue at such a rate, the trend to increase industrial density is expected to increase over the next few years. This ratio can now be applied to Exhibit 14.17 to show the total job forecast for the Far North Metro area.

Adjust Demand for "Normal" Vacancy Rate

The demand figure is adjusted to reflect the typical vacancy rate for the specific class of buildings. The result is a gross estimate of supportable space. This figure is used in marginal demand studies and proposed construction feasibility analyses. In many appraisal applications, however, the subject capture forecast figure derived in Step 3.2(4) is not adjusted for normal vacancy since the appraisal forecast in the income approach is for occupied space only.

Checking Reasonableness of Demand Forecast Model

Calculations for industrial forecasts like all market forecasts should be checked for their reasonableness. One method for doing this is to apply known historical data to occupied space and then to apply the model historically to see if it predicts what actually happens. This is sometimes called *model calibration*. Other methods include reviewing inferred data, such as historical occupancies and growth and making a general comparison of forecast data to historical data to see if it appears reasonable based on what the appraiser expects in the market.

Step 3.4: Reconcile the Results of Methods and Forecast Demand

In Exhibit 14.18, historical demand and forecast demand are very similar. The appraiser should compare the rate of growth in employment during this period to the rate indicated in the forecast. It is reasonable for the forecast rate to approximate the historical rate.

The segmentation method and the ratio method produced very similar results. In theory, the segmentation method is more reliable because it accounts for more of the variables. In practice, however, its reliability depends on an accurate estimation and forecast of all the variables. Since the methods applied in the case study application yielded similar results, further refinement of the forecast is not necessary.

Exhibit 14.17 Warehouse/Distribution Space—Mid-Range Demand Forecast by Ratio Method

Line	Forecast New Demand	Current Year End	Year 1	Year 2	Year 3	Year 4	Year 5	Comments/Source
1	Total employment in Far North Metro area	308,000	312,000	320,000	330,000	340,000	350,000	Source: State employment commission, Bureau of Labor Statistics, and commercial data vendor
2	Forecast yearly increase of new employment (all categories) in Far North Metro area		4,000	8,000	10,000	10,000	10,000	Source: Commercial data service, local regional planning agency, state comptroller's office and appraiser's analysis
3	Ratio of occupied warehouse/ distribution sq. ft. per total jobs in metro area	73.8	75.00	77.00	80.00	85.00	90.00	Warehouse space more concentrated in future; thus, increase over next five years similar to increase over last five years.
4	Total demand for occupied space in Far North Metro market area (sq. ft.)	22,721,881	23,400,000	24,640,000	26,400,000	28,900,000	31,500,000	Calculation—Line 1 × 3

Exhibit 14.18 Re-cap of Demand Studies

Analysis Method	Conclusions	Comment
Current Market Trends (Inferred Demand Method)		
Employment growth in area	Very positive	Suggest high occupancy and rental rates
New warehouse building in area	Third most active in total metro area	Suggest good long-range prospects, but current rapid growth could produce short-term oversupply
Fundamental Demand Methods		
Segmentation method	New demand increase of 1.4M sq. ft. per year on average for next five years	Mid-range forecast for Far North Metro area
Ratio-to-total-employment method	New demand increase of 1.7M sq. ft. new demand per year on average for next five years	Mid-range forecast for Far North Metro area

Step 4: Measure Competitive Supply

Step 4.1: Inventory Competitive Supply

The appraiser must obtain local data on existing space, current occupancy and vacancy levels, buildings under construction, and those that are proposed or likely to be built. Although data on existing buildings and space under construction are generally readily available, data on proposed buildings may be difficult to gather. Collecting the data is only part of the problem. The timing of possible building starts must be forecast as well as the amount of new space expected. The procedure is the same as for other property types. The following list describes a possible procedure for this analysis.

1. Research planned projects
   - Interview building officials and planning department staff in the local jurisdiction regarding recent inquiries concerning planned projects.
   - Review preliminary and final plats submitted for office use, and determine their status.
   - Review announcements of proposed buildings in local newspaper(s) and information from the Chamber of Commerce to determine current status of projects.
   - Survey brokers, lenders, and developers active in the area.
2. Compile a list of possible projects and assess probability that they will be developed. For each project, consider
   - Who is the developer and what is his or her track record?
   - How close is the developer to obtaining permission?
   - How much space has been pre-leased?
   - Does the developer have multiple projects?
   - How attractive is the location?

3. Analyze the probability of other projects being developed.

   Compare marginal/residual demand against existing buildings and projects under construction only. This helps the analyst discern market participants' thinking about future windows of opportunity. If it appears that the market sees the potential for high marginal/residual demand, it is probable that new competition can be expected during this period.

4. Calculate feasibility rent.

   Along with positive marginal demand, compare current rents to required rents for new construction. If current rents are well below rents needed for new construction, it may take more time for rents to escalate despite the strong market demand. Exhibit 14.19 is an example of this type of calculation.

5. Complete a probability forecast of new space.

   Other factors that may change the supply should also be considered. These include the demolition, rehabilitation, and upgrading of buildings, and the adaptive re-use of older buildings, all of which affect the potential supply of industrial space. (See Chapter 13 for example of application.)

Application of Step 4.1: Inventory Current Supply

Exhibit 14.20 shows a summary of the current space in the Far North Metro area submarket.

Step 4.2: Forecast New Construction

A full Level C analysis requires a building-by-building analysis of new construction (see office demand section of Chapter 13). Even if a detailed building-by-building analysis is not conducted, a general inference about market demand based on marginal demand conclusions can be made about a market's strength. For example, if rents are nearing a point where new construction is feasible, it is logical that if the forecast for job growth is the same as the last 10 years, the demand for new construction should be a repetition of that for the last 10 years. Thus, the expectation of a similar level of new construction for the next 10 years is feasible.

Application of Step 4.2: Forecast New Construction

The following is an example of forecasting new construction using this method.

- During last four years 8,922,530 sq. ft. of warehouse/distribution space was built in Far North Metro area. This was 2,230,632 sq. ft. per year, on average.
- Employment grew by 18,000 new jobs per year on average in the Far North Metro area for last four years.
- Forecasted (mid-range) is 10,000 new jobs per year on average for next five years, or 44% fewer.

Exhibit 14.19 Rent Required for New Construction

Data inputs

Construction cost	$45.00 per sq. ft.	Building size	130,000 sq. ft.
Land cost	$4.50 per sq. ft.	Land size	435,600 sq. ft.
Operating expense:		% Bldg. rented	100%
Variable	$1.50 per sq .ft.	Current rent	$8.75 per sq. ft.
Insurance	$0.115 per sq. ft.		
Taxes	$0.75 per sq. ft.		
Management/replacement			
Allowance	3% of *EGI*		
Current overall rate	10%		
Normal vacancy	5%		

Calculations of Required Rent	Size (Sq. Ft.)	$ (Sq. Ft.)	
Calculation of Total Cost			
Construction cost	130,000	× $45.00 =	$5,850,000
Land cost	435,600	× $4.50 =	$1,960,200
Total cost			$7,810,200
Calculation of Feasibility Rent			
Required *NOI*	$7,810,200	× 10% =	$781,020
Add Operating Expenses:			
Variable	130,000	× $1.50 =	$195,000
Insurance	130,000	× $0.12 =	$15,600
Taxes	130,000	× $ 0.75 =	$97,500
Subtotal Expenses			$308,100
Management			33,666
(*NOI* + Exp/(1 − Mgmt%) − *NOI* + Exp)			
Total All Expenses			$341,168
Effective gross income			$1,122,188
Vacancy and collection loss			$59,063
Potential gross Income			$1,181,250
Calculation of Required Rent for New Construction			
	PGI ÷ *NRA*		
	1,181,250 ÷ 130,000 =		$ 9.09

Exhibit 14.20 Current Warehouse/Distribution Space

Submarket	Total Bldg. Sq. Ft.	Current Vacancy Rate	Current Occupied Space	Sq. Ft. Under Construction or Renovation
Allen Heights				
Warehouse/Distribution	5,115,963	16.4%	4,276,945	700,000
Denia Landing Area				
Warehouse/Distribution	10,162,844	4.7%	9,685,190	2,600,000
Palmdale Area				
Warehouse/Distribution	9,445,764	6.8%	8,803,452	500,000
Subtotal Far North Metro Area	24,724,571	8.1%	22,721,881	3,800,000

Source: Commercial data vendor

- Thus, if new construction responds accordingly, there would be 44% less newly constructed square footage, or 4,996,616 during the next four years, or about 1,250,000 sq. ft. (rounded) per year on average (see Exhibit 14.21).

Exhibit 14.21 Estimate of New Construction by Historical Comparison Method

	Sq. Ft. Bldg.	Comment
Total—last 4 years	8,922,530	Actual Built
Average historical per year	2,230,633	
Forecasted average yearly increase	1,249,154	Based on 56% of historical since employment forecast is 44% less than historical
Number of years in forecast	5	
Total new construction forecasted	6,245,771	

Step 5: Analyze Market Equilibrium/Disequilibrium

Step 5.1: Compare Supply and Demand to Determine Marginal (Residual) Demand

In many parts of the appraisal, the appraiser considers the market's position in the real estate cycle. Analysis of marginal demand helps the appraiser make this judgment.

The procedure begins by comparing data on existing and future competitive supply with the estimates of current and anticipated demand. This is done with two objectives in mind. First, the appraiser must identify whether there is unsatisfied, or marginal, demand. *Marginal demand* is the demand that remains after all available space is subtracted from the projected demand for space. Marginal demand cannot be satisfied unless additional space, over and above proposed and newly constructed space, is added to the inventory.

Second, the appraiser seeks to determine how long the absorption of existing vacant office space and space under construction will take. This determination depends on the growth of demand. The point when existing vacant space, space under construction, and proposed office space will be absorbed represents a window of opportunity when new development might be expected.

In the previous example, total new space built in the last four years was 8,922,530 sq. ft. If the forecast for employment is a 50% per year decline on average, then new construction should also be less than historical after the space in the current pipeline is absorbed. Exhibits 14.22 and 14.23 show the ratio method and the segmentation method for forecasting demand for warehouse/distribution space.

Conclusions of Residual Demand Analysis

All methods show the market to be oversupplied for next few years. Thus, buildings will be highly competitive for tenants. Marginal build-

Exhibit 14.22 Warehouse/Distribution Space Mid-Range Demand Forecast by Ratio Method

Line	Forecast New Demand	Current Year End	Year 1	Year 2	Year 3	Year 4	Year 5	Comments/Source
1	Total employment in Far North Metro area	308,000	312,000	320,000	330,000	340,000	350,000	Source: State employment commission, Bureau of Labor Statistics, and commercial data vendor
2	Forecast yearly increase of new employment (all categories) in Far North Metro area		4,000	8,000	10,000	10,000	10,000	Source: Commercial data service, local regional planning agency, state comptroller's office, and appraiser's analysis
3	Ratio of occupied warehouse/distribution sq. ft. per total jobs in metro area	73.8	75.00	77.00	80.00	85.00	90.00	Warehouse space more concentrated in future; thus, increase over next 5 years as per increase over last five years
4	Total demand for occupied space in North Metro Market area (sq. ft.)	22,721,881	23,400,000	24,640,000	26,400,000	28,900,000	31,500,000	Calculation—Line 1 × 3
	Competition Analysis							
5	Total warehouse distribution space (sq. ft.)	24,724,571	28,524,571	29,774,571	31,024,571	32,274,571	33,524,571	Actual survey of warehouse distribution buildings on ground. Many metro areas have vendor with data services.
6	Current building under construction in North Metro submarket	3,800,000						Actual under construction
7	Planned new space		1,250,000	1,250,000	1,250,000	1,250,000	1,250,000	Due to forecasts of a 50% slowdown in employment per year on average, new construction should also be less than historical after space in current pipeline is absorbed.
	Residual Demand Analysis							
8	Estimated year-end vacant space (sq. ft.) in North Metro submarket	2,002,690	5,124,571	3,134,571	4,624,571	3,374,571	2,024,571	Total space built (Line 5) minus total demand (Line 4)
9	Estimated vacancy rate	8.1%	18.0%	17.2%	14.9%	10.5%	6.0%	Line 8/Line 5

Line	Forecast New Demand	Current Year End	Year 1	Year 2	Year 3	Year 4	Year 5	Comments/Source
1	Total employment in North Metro area	308,000	312,000	320,000	330,000	340,000	350,000	Source: State employment commission, Bureau of Labor Statistics, and commercial data vendor
2	Forecast yearly increase of new employment (all categories) in Far North Metro area		4,000	8,000	10,000	10,000	10,000	Source: Commercial data service, local regional planning agency, state comptroller's office, and appraiser's analysis
3	Percentage employment in warehousing and wholesale trade	5.2%	5.3%	5.5%	5.8%	6.0%	6.0%	Warehouse space more concentrated in future; thus, increase over next five years toward metro 7.9 % employment in these sectors
4	Estimated warehouse and wholesale employment	16,016	16,536	17,600	19,140	20,400	21,000	Calculation—Line 1 × 4
5	Avg. sq. ft. per employee	1,419	1,420	1,420	1,420	1,420	1,420	Source: Current year calibration and avg. of industrial groups from Gruen 1986 Study for ULI
6	Total occupied demand	22,721,881	23,481,120	24,992,000	27,178,800	28,968,000	29,820,000	Warehouse/distribution sq. ft.
	Competition Analysis							
7	Total warehouse distribution space (sq. ft.)	24,724,571	28,524,571	29,774,571	31,024,571	32,274,571	33,524,571	Actual survey of warehouse distribution buildings on ground. Many metro areas have commercial vendors with data services.
8	Current building under construction in North Metro submarket	3,800,000						Actual under construction
9	Planned new space		1,250,000	1,250,000	1,250,000	1,250,000	1,250,000	Due to forecasts for an average 50% per year slowdown in employment, new construction should also be less than historical
	Residual Demand Analysis							
10	Estimated year-end vacant space (sq. ft.) in North Metro submarket	2,002,690	5,043,451	4,782,571	3,845,771	3,306,571	3,704,571	Total space built (Line 7) minus total occupied demand (Line 6)
11	Estimated vacancy rate	8.1%	17.7%	16.1%	12.4%	10.2%	11.1%	Line 10/Line 7

ings will probably lower rents to maintain tenants, and better buildings will likely keep rents at their current levels. Market-wide vacancies should be higher than 15% for next two to four years.

Step 6: Forecast Subject Market Penetration (Capture Analysis)

This step can be considered a reconciliation of the market analysis section of the appraisal. It could also be seen as a marketability analysis for the subject. At this point, all the pieces of the market study are refocused on the competitive outlook for the subject property. The capture estimate becomes the launch point for the last part of the appraisal–the application of the three approaches–in which the appraiser determines how the subject's capture affects property value.

The appraiser then makes a forecast of subject's capture after examining the data, which includes the historical capture rate of the subject, the marginal demand forecast for the total market, and the ratings assigned after completing the first and fourth steps of the market analysis process.

Step 6.1: Derive a Preliminary (Inferred) Estimate of Subject Capture By Inferred Methods

Growth trends for the subject Far North Metro area are very positive, suggesting that the subject should maintain high occupancy and rents for the foreseeable future. However, market vacancies in the 15% to 20% range are forecasted for next few years. The subject property rating was slightly below average, so future rents and occupancy for subject do not appear to be high.

Step 6.2: Derive a Capture Rate

The marginal(residual) demand estimate suggests that the subject should expect little or no increase in occupancy or rent levels for the next two to four years. This outlook is at odds with the inferred analysis. Consequently, a more detailed fundamental forecast and capture analysis will be required to reconcile and support the specific income forecast in the income capitalization approach section of the appraisal.

Denia Landing Area Market Penetration

The first step in this analysis is to determine the current and future capture rate for the subject submarket, the Denia Landing Area, as illustrated in Exhibit 14.25.

Exhibit 14.25 shows the current capture rate exceeding 42.6%, while the rating for submarkets (see previous location analysis section) found the area would capture 38% based on the rating score conclusions. The final capture rate is based on the appraiser's judgment within the constraints of the alternative data indicators.

Exhibit 14.24 Far North Metro Warehouse/Distribution Building

Submarket	Total Current Bldg. Sq. Ft.	% of Total Far North	Building Built in Last 4 Years	% of Total New Bldgs.
Allen Heights				
Warehouse/Distribution	5,115,963	20.7%	4,122,401	28.1%
Denia Landing Area				
Warehouse/Distribution	10,162,844	41.1%	5,976,698	40.7%
Palmdale Area				
Warehouse/Distribution	9,445,764	38.2%	4,596,921	31.3%
Total Far North Metro area				
Warehouse/Distribution	24,724,571	100.0%	14,696,020	100.0%

Exhibit 14.25 Warehouse/Distribution Denia Landing Capture Rate Analysis

Method	Capture Rate	Comment
Percentage of new building in Denia Landing in last 4 years	40.7%	See Exhibit 14.24
Current capture rate for Denia Landing	42.6%	Based on current-occupied-space- to-current-demand calculation
Capture rate for Denia Landing by rank score	38.0%	See Exhibit 14.9 in location analysis section
Average capture rate for Denia Landing	40.4%	Average of above three capture indications

Step 6.2(1): Apply Denia Landing Area Capture Rate to Demand Forecast Denia Landing Area Submarket—Future Conditions Outlook

The next step is to apply the Denia Landing area capture rate to the North Metro area total demand estimates of the previous section. Exhibit 14.26 shows this analysis. The outlook for the Denia Landing market conditions is for the area to continue to have significant vacancies, due in large part to the new construction currently happening and expected in the future.

Determination of Subject Capture Rate

A good starting point for determining the subject capture rate is the current capture rate of the subject. The subject has a current occupancy level of 100%, which is 250,000 square feet occupied. The Denia Landing submarket currently has 9,685,190 sq. ft. of occupied warehouse/distribution space. Thus, the subject current capture rate is 2.58% (250,000/9,685,190).

If the appraiser felt that the subject would compete equally in the future with all the buildings in the areas of submarket, the analysis might stop here. However, there is a question concerning future competition in the area.

Exhibit 14.26 Warehouse/Distribution-Denia Landing Submarket—Market (Capture) Penetration

	Current	Year 1	Year 2	Year 3	Year 4	Year 5	Comments/Source
Far North Metro area total occupied demand (sq. ft.)	22,721,881	23,440,560	24,816,000	26,789,400	28,934,000	30,660,000	Average of two fundamental methods
Denia Landing capture rate	42.6%	42.0%	41.5%	40.0%	40.0%	40.0%	See Exhibit 14.25
Denia Landing total occupied demand (sq. ft.)	9,685,190	9,845,035	10,298,640	10,715,760	11,573,600	12,264,000	
Current warehouse/distribution space in area	10,162,844	10,162,844	12,762,844	13,237,844	13,712,844	14,187,844	
Expected opening of space under construction/forecast		2,600,000	475,000	475,000	475,000	475,000	Based on location rating of 38% of Far North Metro area forecast total new construction
Total warehouse/distribution space in Denia Landing submarket		10,162,844	13,237,844	13,712,844	14,187,844	14,662,844	
Residual demand for warehouse/distribution space	-477,654	-2,917,809	-2,939,204	-2,997,084	-2,614,244	-2,398,844	
Indicated percentage occupied for Denia Landing area	95.3%	77.1%	77.8%	78.1%	81.6%	83.6%	

Capture by Pro Rata Share Analysis

The subject submarket has 152 separate buildings. The average size is 66,860 sq. ft. (10,162,844/152). The subject is 250,000 sq. ft. or 3.7 times as big as the average building. The subject pro rata share on a building basis is .66% (1/152). However, the subject is 3.7 times larger; thus the pro rata share is adjusted upwards by 3.7 to give an indicated pro rata share capture rate of 2.43% (.66% × 3.7). Exhibit 14.27 illustrates this analysis.

Adjusting Pro Rata Share

The pro rata share method to this point assumes that all buildings are equal. The general location is similar, since they are all in the Denia Landing submarket, but each building will vary slightly by location, building design, functionality, and condition.

Adjustment Method 1—General Rating Adjustment

One way to adjust the pro-rata share is to use the previous general property rating (Step 1.2) and adjust the pro rata share accordingly. That is the subject rated –6% of the average, so the adjusted pro rata share would be 2.3% (2.43% less 6% of 2.43).

The next step is to adjust the pro rata share over time with the expected increase in competition. Exhibit 14.26 shows the results of this step.

Adjustment Method 2: Rating Score with Competitive Buildings

This method rates and compares the subject to all competitive buildings. Such a task for 152 buildings would be prohibitive for most one-time appraisal assignments, but if completed, it would be useful and cost-effective for multiple assignments in the same submarket. In lieu of rating all competitive buildings, the subject could be rated against the top competitors. The rating score can then be a relative number and the percentage difference in the rating score could be used to adjust the subject pro rata share.

Reconciliation and Final Determination of Subject Capture Rate

The rating and pro rata share methods yielded results that are very similar to the current capture rate. Thus, the current capture rate is given most weight because it reflects how the current market actually rates the subject. The capture rate is adjusted for changing pro rata share as the area grows(see Exhibit 14.26). Exhibit 14.28 shows the results of applying this rating amount to the forecasted demand.

Step 6.3: Reconcile Subject Capture Indicators

Low-range forecast   Occupancy. Declining significantly next five years then slowly increasing to 90% occupancy for Years 5 through 10.

Rents. Declining at real rate of 1% per year to maintain market share.

Exhibit 14.27 Subject Pro Rata Share Analysis

	Current	Year 1	Year 2	Year 3	Year 4	Year 5
Current warehouse/distribution space in Denia Landing submarket	10,162,844	10,162,844	12,762,844	13,237,844	13,712,844	14,187,844
Expected opening of space under construction/forecast		2,600,000	475,000	475,000	475,000	475,000
Total warehouse/distribution space in Denia Landing submarket	10,162,844	12,762,844	13,237,844	13,712,844	14,187,844	14,662,844
Subject size	250,000	250,000	250,000	250,000	250,000	250,000
Subject pro rata share	2.46%	1.96%	1.89%	1.82%	1.76%	1.70%
Less adjustment for property rating	6.0%	6.0%	6.0%	6.0%	6.0%	6.0%
Subject's adjusted capture rate	2.31%	1.84%	1.78%	1.71%	1.66%	1.60%

Exhibit 14.28 Subject Market (Capture) Penetration

	Current	Year 1	Year 2	Year 3	Year 4	Year 5
Far North total occupied demand (sq. ft.)	22,721,881	23,440,560	24,816,000	26,789,400	28,934,000	30,660,000
Subject capture rate	42.6%	42.0%	41.5%	40.0%	40.0%	40.0%
Denia Landing total occupied demand (sq. ft.)	9,685,190	9,845,035	10,298,640	10,715,760	11,573,600	12,264,000
Subject capture rate	2.6%	1.8%	1.8%	1.7%	1.7%	1.6%
Estimated subject market occupancy	249,878	177,211	185,376	182,168	196,751	196,224
Size of subject	250,000	250,000	250,000	250,000	250,000	250,000
Estimated subject market occupancy rate	100%	71%	74%	73%	79%	78%

Mid-range forecast Occupancy. Declining to 70% to 80% range in next five years and then slowly improving to 90% occupancy between Years 5 and 10.

Rents. Must remain level in real terms over the next five years and then increase with inflation.

High-range forecast Occupancy. Increasing, but staying in the 90% range, on average for foreseeable future.

Rents. Real rate of increase to remain level over the next five years, then increase 2% per year for Years 5 through 10.

The high- and low-range forecasts are presented for illustration. The calculations are not shown. The estimating procedure is the same, but low and high employment projections are used.

CHAPTER 15

Existing Apartment Complex

Chapter Objectives

- To describe the residential real estate market and the factors that influence supply and demand
- To discuss the principles of the market analysis process for residential property
- To introduce the market analysis process for a residential property using a case study approach
- To project occupancy and rents level conclusions for an existing apartment complex based on a market analysis

Introduction

This chapter demonstrates the step-by-step procedures applied in a market analysis for a residential apartment complex. Concepts and terminology unique to the residential property market are reviewed, and the analytical process is presented.

Apartment buildings, condominiums and subdivisions are residential properties that fall into the categories of income-producing and speculative real estate. A subdivision or a condominium appraisal is not presented here, but it would include most of the same procedural steps. A market analysis for a condominium or subdivision differs from a market analysis for an apartment building primarily in the following ways:

- Data are segmented for single-family or condominium housing rather than multifamily housing

- In some markets such as resort cities, demand sources can include nonresident demand more often than multifamily appraisals, and
- Several of the rating attributes used to estimate subject capture are different

The Residential Market

Residential properties are the building blocks of communities. Because of the far-reaching social benefits that accrue from stable communities, the government has traditionally promoted homeownership, most notably by allowing income tax write-offs for personal home mortgage interest. Residential real estate development is a mainspring of the economy, so government organizations have long worked to improve conditions in the housing market as a means of stimulating general economic growth. As an economic commodity, residential property has a dual character as both a usable good and a material asset. Traditionally, residential property has been considered a consumer good, a means of satisfying basic needs for shelter and comfort. However, in inflationary times, and when financing costs are relatively inexpensive, it is perceived as an investment instrument. During the first half of the 2000s, the cheap financing helped spur investor purchases not only in blocks of condominiums and apartment projects but in single-family housing as well. This perception has not always been favorable for the homeowner or investors, especially when the residential market cycled down as in other markets. Residential markets, as other commercial real estate markets, have always returned to the economics of the user; i.e., how much the user can and will pay for a property.

To understand the cycles of the residential real estate market, a historical perspective is needed. In the mid-twentieth century the character of residential development underwent a profound transformation. An economic depression, which nearly brought construction to a standstill in the 1930s, and the diversion of national resources to the war effort during the early 1940s, created a severe housing shortage after the war. Pent-up demand and the rapid rate of household formation after World War II triggered an unprecedented building boom. Despite short-lived cyclical contractions in housing starts, postwar levels of building activity have been maintained to the present day.

Postwar development centered on suburban areas. The typical pattern of residential development combined the creation of lots with the building of houses to produce complete unit packages, each consisting of a finished single-family house on an improved lot.

During the 1950s and 1960s, subdivisions typically contained uniformly spaced, detached single-family houses. In the 1970s, several factors brought about changes in development patterns. Concern for the environmental impact of development and energy conservation as well as escalating costs led to more intensive residential development, reflected in smaller houses, more attached units, and cluster plans. Sophisticated design techniques were used to maintain the privacy and individuality of units and preserve other amenities associated with low-density housing.

During the 1980s, cheap financing costs spurred construction of single-family homes, condominiums, and apartments, activity that was followed by a major market crash resulting from the savings and loan scandals of that era. The late 1990s to the early 2000s ushered in a resurging economy and low interest rates. This brought about a new surge in new single-family housing as low interest rates enabled many new households to afford homeownership. This exerted strong pressure on apartment building because many renters found that they could now afford to purchase single-family housing. Even during the economic downturn of the 2000s, low interest rates continued to spur home building. This spilled over, contributing to the condo craze in major markets in the middle part of the decade.

Condominiums were bought not only by new residents but also by buyers in the second-home market, and in increasing numbers the third-home market. Many households now had a home in the city, a condo on the beach, and a cabin in the mountains. The investors' market also viewed the condominium market as a commodity market for price appreciation and resale. The abundance of capital liquidity also resulted in a strong demand for investment in apartments, contributing to a capital bubble that led to some of the lowest cap rates in history for apartment projects. It also led to significant building to accommodate a demand created by abundant and significant capital chasing a limited quantity of real estate. The low interest rates also impacted apartment rental housing but usually in the opposite way. When the interest rates are low, homeownership costs begin to approach apartment rents, which means that many apartment dwellers opt for single-family ownership. The opposite occurs during times of high interest rates. Thus, housing, as all real estate types, undergoes cycles and as is true of most real estate types, these cycles are closely tied to jobs. Unlike other real estate types, however, the residential market is not exclusively tied to the vagaries of the job market.

Factors That Influence Demand

Changes in demographics, lifestyles, consumer preferences, and economic circumstances continue to affect the demand for residential development. Over the past 30 years, the median age of the U.S. population has been increasing, while average household size has decreased. Consequently, the need for larger single-family houses may decline over the long term.

Gentrification, the renovation of older homes, and the conversion of multiunit rental properties into condominiums and cooperatives have seen a resurgence in many metropolitan neighborhoods. The proportion of single Americans in the population, including people who are divorced, widowed, or never married, has increased. Their preference for smaller residential units has been felt in both suburban and urban markets. The influx of women into the workforce has also influenced housing development significantly. Working couples desire housing that requires minimal maintenance and often consider smaller units to be more efficient and practical. Affluent, double-income households with the disposable income to satisfy their demands may also require more residential amenities.

Factors That Influence Supply

Supply-side factors such as the amount of available housing stock and the costs of new development and construction also affect residential housing. Housing market inventories keep track of vacancy and absorption rates for properties on the market as well as losses in existing stock and conversions of properties from nonresidential uses. These data are especially important in estimating supply in older rust belt cities.

The cost of vacant land and the expenses associated with development have increased over the past two decades. Twenty years ago the cost of raw land represented approximately 18% of the price of an overall property; between the late 1970s and the late 1980s, however, the building site accounted for an average of 26% of the total sale price for the typical market in 2000.

Concepts and Terminology

Compared to markets for other types of property, the residential real estate market has an especially strong consumer orientation. This requires the appraiser or market analyst to stay attuned to shifts in consumer tastes and preferences and to changes in household formation patterns and lifestyles. The marketability of housing depends heavily on accessibility to jobs and the availability of public utilities and support facilities (e.g., schools, shopping centers, and recreational areas). The residential market can be broken down into the following types of properties: single-family residential, rental apartments (two- to four-unit buildings and multitenanted projects), retirement housing, and cooperatives and condominiums.

Single-Family Residential Properties

Detached single-family housing is still the preference of the typical residential consumer. A single-family residence is a consumption good with an economic life that generally extends over many decades. Residential demand may be segmented according to the size, age, and income of the household. For example, starter households with or without small children are generally characterized as having limited means; move-up households are those whose growing size requires more space; established households are affluent households with older children and can afford a variety of amenities; and empty nester or move-down households are those that seek smaller accommodations.

Rental Apartments

Rental apartments range from small, two- to four-unit properties to multitenanted developments. Like office buildings, apartment complexes may also be divided into building classes based on their location, construction, condition, management, tenancy, and amenities. These qualities determine the rent levels that an apartment building is capable of generating.

Three principal demographic groups create demand for apartments: the young and upwardly mobile; a growing class of moderate-income, permanent renters; and empty-nesters, who require less space and want to keep maintenance to a minimum.

Retirement Housing

Retirement housing options include scaled-down townhouses, senior apartments, and congregate living facilities. This last category may be divided further into adult congregate living facilities (ACLF) for those who are able to maintain a semi-independent lifestyle, and continuing-care retirement centers (CCRC), for those who require care.

Cooperatives and Condominiums

Empty nesters and affluent singles are the two main user groups that constitute the demand for cooperatives and condominiums, as many amenity-laden condominiums are well beyond the means of starter households. Many resort areas find that the nonresident second-home market is a major factor in the condominium market for user-end sales.

Residential Measurements

Four terms are used to describe the area of residential properties: gross living area, gross building area, gross leasable area, and net leasable area.

Gross living area (GLA), which is sometimes referred to as above-grade living area (*AGLA*), is the total area of finished, above-grade residential space. Unfinished areas and attics are not included. Gross living area is the most common measurement applied to houses.

Gross building area (GBA) is the total area of all floor levels, measured from the exterior of the walls. The floor area of the superstructure and the substructure basement are included in gross building area.

Gross leasable area (GLA), also referred to as gross rentable area (*GRA*), is the total floor area designed for the occupancy and use of tenants, including basements, corridors, and stairways.

Net leasable area (NLA), which is sometimes referred to as net rentable area (*NRA*), is the amount of space rented to the individual tenants, excluding common areas such as basements, corridors, and stairways.

Principles in the Market Analysis of Residential Property

In estimating demand, the analyst must consider the demographic characteristics of household formation. Thus, when analyzing the data for this task the appraiser should be aware of various factors of household formations. First various age groups within a population form households at different rates. Similarly, the rate of household formation also varies with income. For example, high rents may discourage household formation among young, unmarried adults. Thus, the traditional method of dividing total population by average household size produces a general estimate that ignores different rates of household formation among cohort groups. For a Level C market study this may be acceptable but if the appraiser is aware of significant variance in the population, then a more detailed Level D analysis may be warranted.

The use of small-area population projections, which are usually made without considering basic development conditions (e.g., utilities, infrastructure, land prices, or available acreage), can also be misleading. The analyst should study projections for the overall metropolitan area and whether or not it is likely that the subject small area can actually capture its forecasted share given its location factors. Because small-area demand is important, the case study application stresses a detailed location analysis.

In calculating changes in the inventory of competitive supply, the analyst must adjust for vacancy, lost units, and units added through conversions. Data on the loss of units and conversions are especially difficult to obtain. Losses and conversions are generally higher in older rust belt cities than in newer sunbelt cities. However, in the last decade in condo markets that experienced a bubble, many newer apartments were converted to condominiums.

Many areas such as resort, recreational areas, and lake communities find the strongest demand coming from nonresidents. This second (and third) home population can be the biggest demand drivers. The analyst will have to perform specialized research for these areas because most population forecasts do not include nonresidents. The U.S. Census does account for the seasonal homes, but the data on population and occupancy are usually not directly available.

The appraiser's market forecast should identify long-term trends rather than short-term indicators, which may be poor predictors. Short-term factors include current mortgage interest rates, vacancy or absorption rates, and the inventory of available competitive supply and space under construction. Mortgage rates are extremely volatile, and vacancy rates cannot be forecast with any accuracy beyond two to five years. The appraiser, therefore, should instead consider factors that are bellwethers of long-term trends. They include the economic base, which indicates the future growth potential of the community and the likelihood of economic cycles; planned improvements to the infrastructure; and demographics. Reasoned judgment should be applied to the available data, even if the data are fragmented.

The forecasting process must be tempered by the realization that the future may be a significant departure from the past or even the current market. For example, most markets experience large spikes in apartment construction that may be sustained for a number of years. Then as the market cycles down apartment construction may all but stop for a number of years. For the appraiser to carry forward either the up market or down market as a long-term forecast would usually be a mistake because the average of the two cycles is more representative of long-term trends. Consider the following example, which shows the historical apartment mix. The analyst must now decide which percentage mix will be used for the future. Exhibit 15.2 shows the results of using a different percentage mix for making a forecast.

Exhibit 15.1	Historical Unit Mix in Example City					
	10 Years Ago	% of Total Units	Five Years Ago	% of Total Units	Current	% of Total Units
Single-family units	3,800	63%	5,000	64%	6,500	54%
Apartment units	2,000	33%	2,200	28%	5,000	41.3%
Other units	260	4%	570	7%	600	5%
Total residential units	6,060	100%	7,770	100%	12,100	100%

If the analyst uses the current apartment mix based on the current high spike in apartments, then he or she is expecting this high mix to continue in the future. (See Exhibit 15.2.) The forecast is compounded as the difference in using the current high mix versus the historical long-term trend increases from 24% higher five years out to a 37% higher forecast 10 years out. In most markets the high spike mix does not continue.

Exhibit 15.2	Forecasted Apartment Unit Demand by Various % Mix		
	Current	5 Years into Future	10 Years into Future
Alternative 1 Avg. Apt. Mix Historically			
Forecasted households	12,100	16,000	20,000
% Apartment mix	41.3%	33%	30%
Apartment demand	5,000	5,280	6,000
Alternative 2 Current Apt. Mix for Forecast			
Forecasted households	12,100	16,000	20,000
% Apartment mix	41.3%	41%	41%
Apartment demand	5,000	6,560	8,200
% Difference in demand conclusions		24%	37%

The Market Analysis Process for a Residential Property

Exhibit 15.3 describes the process for the case study application. Only the market analysis portion of the valuation appraisal is presented.

Case Study Description

The following application describes a Level C market analysis prepared as part of an appraisal assignment. The subject property is an existing, 312-unit apartment complex located in Leadville, a suburban location in a major metropolitan area. The complex consists of 18

Exhibit 15.3   Market Analysis for a Residential Property

Step 1: Analyze the productivity attributes of the subject property.

    1.1 Analyze the legal attributes of the property.

    1.2 Analyze the physical attributes of the property.

    1.3 Analyze the locational attributes of the property.

Step 2: Delineate the market of property users.

    2.1 Determine the boundaries of the market area based on time-distance relationships. Distances to employment and support facilities (e.g., shopping centers, schools) are important, as are the locations of competitive housing that appeals to the same consumers as the subject.

    2.2 Analyze the tenant profile of the market area potential consumers.

Step 3: Forecast demand.

    3.1 Conduct inferred (trend) analysis. Compile data on general growth, market occupancy and rent trends, and the subject history to infer future demand.

    3.2 Conduct fundamental analysis by the segmentation/affordability method

        3.2(1) Estimate the current and projected resident population within the defined market area.

        3.2(2) Establish the current and projected average household size, and divide the population estimates by the household size averages.

        3.2(3) Segment the number of current and projected households by housing unit type.

        3.2(4) Segment the number of households by income levels to determine the percentage of households that are or will be able to meet the monthly mortgage payment on the housing or the monthly rent on the rental unit.

        3.2(5) Adjust the number for a normal vacancy rate.

    3.3 Conduct fundamental analysis by the ratio method.

    3.4 Reconcile forecast.

Step 4: Measure competitive supply.

    4.1 Inventory existing competitive properties, properties under construction, planned properties for which building permits have been obtained, and proposed properties. Tally the inventory of existing and anticipated competitive supply for the projection period.

    4.2 Analyze the competitive supply. Rate the subject against competitive subdivisions, districts, or apartment buildings according to criteria such as location, age, and amenities.

Step 5: Analyze market equilibrium/disequilibrium. Compare existing and potential demand with current and anticipated competitive supply to determine marginal demand.

    5.1 Input data on existing and anticipated demand for the subject property (Step 3).

    5.2 Input data on existing competitive properties and properties under construction, planned properties for which building permits have been obtained, and proposed properties (Step 4.1).

    5.3 Subtract the total inventory of existing and anticipated competitive supply for the projection period (Step 5.2) from the estimate of existing and anticipated demand for the subject property (Step 5.1) to determine the net excess or shortage in the market.

Step 6: Forecast subject capture.

    6.1 From inferred demand and fundamental demand market forecast, estimate the subject capture in terms future occupancy expectations and corresponding rent required to realize that capture.

Note the numbering system employed in this six-step process. Sub-steps are indicated with sequential numbers in parenthesis. Thus, Step 3.2 is followed by Steps 3.2(1), 3.2(2), 3.2(3), and so on.

detached, two-story buildings and is called the Pine Grove Apartments. The apartment project is 80% occupied. The appraiser will need to examine the current and anticipated demand/supply situation to determine whether the property will maintain, lose, or increase its present occupancy and income level. The purpose of the market analysis is to provide information to be used in the three approaches to value.

The subject is located in a suburban city of 46,800 people in a metropolitan area. The city has a strong local economic base and a significant number of the population commutes to the nearby central city. The subject is located in the northwestern part of the city. The city has experienced very rapid apartment growth over the last 10 years. The population and local employment have also grown significantly, and more growth is forecast at about the same pace.

The local apartment market experienced its major growth spurt during the last 10 years. Currently about 7,000 units compete with the subject. The overall market, like the subject, is oversupplied and below stabilized occupancy. The apartments are located in four major sectors of the city and all compete against each other citywide. The following case study applies the six-step process to apartments.

Step 1: Analyze Subject Property's Productivity

The appraiser begins the market analysis by investigating the legal, physical, and locational attributes of the subject apartment complex.

Step 1.1: Analyze the Legal Attributes of the Property

The subject site is zoned for multifamily residential use, and the existing buildings meet the density requirements set forth in the zoning ordinance. The leases on the apartment units are one year in duration, so they do not have any significant impact on the property's marketability.

Conversion of the complex to condominium units is a possibility, but it would require a zoning change. The city has had one condominium project that was not successful; thus, proposals for other conversions have been received negatively by city planners.

Step 1.2: Analyze the Physical Attributes of the Property

The apartment buildings stand on a rectangular site of 14.5 acres (631,620 square feet). Site drainage and utilities meet the standards of the municipal code. The apartments are set back from the intersection of two public roads (i.e., a primary, six-lane thoroughfare and a secondary, four-lane street) and are accessible by two private roadways. The subject complex is clearly visible from the primary road and a billboard on the secondary road helps drivers locate the complex from that direction.

Each of the 18 buildings in the 312-unit apartment complex has an exterior entry. In addition to the housing apartment units, there are two other buildings, one of which contains an office and recreation room and the other, a laundry. Total gross building area is 235,582 square feet; total net rentable area is 234,208 square feet. The average unit size is about 751 square feet. Each building has siding of brick and wood and a composition roof. The style is best described as modern vernacular. The overall condition and quality of the units are average. The effective age is the same as the physical age—six years. Project amenities include a tennis court, a swimming pool, and one covered parking place per unit. The apartment clubhouse is small compared to most in the market. Each unit has a porch or patio. The 312 apartment units in the complex are of three types:

- 152 units with one bedroom and one bathroom (678 square feet of net rentable area)
- 80 units with two bedrooms, one bathroom, and one lavatory (800 square feet of net rentable area)
- 80 units with two bedrooms and two bathrooms (907 square feet of net rentable area)

The purpose of the productivity analysis is to identify the submarket the real estate product serves and its competitiveness within that market. The improvement analysis is the first step in making this determination and is accomplished by rating the subject against current industry standards. The rating chart in Exhibit 15.4 provides both a checklist of items to be studied and a starting point for the analysis of the subject's productivity attributes.

Exhibit 15.4   Subject Apartment Building Rating

Impact on Productivity	Veto Factor	High	Inferior Mod.	Slight	Typical Average	Slight	Mod.	Superior High
Design and appearance of property					X			
Quality of construction (materials and finish)					X			
Condition of improvements					X			
Room sizes and layout					X			
Closets and storage					X			
Plumbing (adequacy and condition)					X			
Electrical, tech. and appliances					X			
Unit amenities					X			
Recreational amenities			X					
Parking				X				
Number of items	0	1	1		8	0	0	0
Times category score (weighting)	0	2	4		5	6	8	10
Subtotal score	0	2	4		40	0	0	0

Total subject score is 46. This suggests that the subject is about 8% below the average apartment complex in town.

Note: A more complete description of the use of the rating technique applied is presented in Chapter 12.

The subject's improvements are generally in good condition and may be considered competitive with modern projects. However, the subject's swimming pool and recreation building are moderately inferior to most newer apartments in the metropolitan area. Also, the subject's number and location of parking places are ranked below most competitive properties.

Step 1.3: Analyze the Locational Attributes of the Property

The subject's location is considered in terms of natural features, land use trends, linkages, local support services, and proximity to major cities in the region. No natural features distinguish the northwest sector, where the subject is located, from other areas of the city where competitive apartment projects are found. The zoning patterns in the subject area are consistent with city planning policies. The abutting land uses are complementary, and nearby retail centers, schools, recreational facilities, and professional offices serve the residents of the subject apartments adequately.

A breakdown of the developed acreage in the community indicates a land use mix that supports housing. Approximately 35% of the developed acres in the community are residential, (all types) and there has been a 30% increase in residential development in the last 10 years. In analyzing land use, the appraiser has also investigated growth trends in specific sectors of the community. The northwest (subject) sector is expected to remain a stable, moderate-income residential area with some additional development of single-family housing. By contrast, the northeast sector has minimal support facilities and is largely underdeveloped, so existing multifamily complexes in that area do not represent serious competition for the subject. Moreover, because there is little likelihood of further development in the northeast sector, it is not likely to compete with the subject area in the future. The southwest sector, like the subject area, is rated a good growth area, but it is primarily classified as single-family, and the city has discouraged further apartment development in the area.

The southeast sector has the largest concentration of apartment projects in the community. This sector constitutes the corridor of growth for the area. A regional mall, a mixed-use development, and two office buildings have all either been recently completed or are under construction. The southeast sector, therefore, represents the main competition for the subject area.

The northwest (subject) sector has good access linkages. Traffic counts indicate that the subject is located just south of one of the most heavily traveled thoroughfares in the community. Congestion may become a problem for the apartment complex, but it seems that this will have no effect in the short term. Plans to develop employment centers in the southeast sector of the city are likely to put the subject at a competitive disadvantage.

Location Rating

As part of the location analysis, the appraiser prepares a competitive location rating (see Exhibit 15.5). This rating procedure is composed of two steps. First, each area of the city is compared with another area according to various factors. For example, Area A and Area B are compared to determine whether Area A is better than, equal to, or worse

Exhibit 15.5   Apartment Competitive Location Analysis Chart

Factor	Rating Criteria	NW	NE	SW	SE	Rank by Importance
		Segment of Market Area				
1	Proximity to existing development	2	1	2	3	1
2	Public planning/development support for apartments	2	1	2	3	2
3	Location in path of new residential growth	2	1	3	4	3
4	Proximity to major roads - ease of access and visibility (existing or approved)	1	2	1	3	7
5	Reputation/prestige of area (social reputation, crime in area, etc.)	2	1	2	3	9
6	Proximity and ease of access to shopping centers (convenience and shopper goods)	2	1	2	3	8
7	Proximity and ease of access to employment centers	1	1	1	2	10
8	Aesthetics/natural features in area	3	1	2	3	4
9	Proximity to entertainment/cultural areas (theaters, parks, golf, restaurants)	2	1	2	2	6
10	Proximity and reputation of schools in area	2	1	2	2	5
Total	(Individual score times weighting)	97	62	96	147	Total all scores 402
Percentage of Total Scores		24%	15%	24%	37%	

than Area B with regard to each specific factor. The higher the rating assigned to an area, the higher its score. This process is then repeated for other paired areas. Second, the four districts are ranked relative to one another using a calibrating process. The resulting scores are then totaled. (The capture percentage used in Step 3 of the analysis is supported, in part, by this ranking.) A higher score identifies an area's superiority. The rating procedure focuses on general urban growth characteristics, not a specific land use. Nevertheless, urban growth is extremely relevant to residential uses.

The competitive submarkets were identified in analyzing the direction of overall growth. Leadville, the subject city, is divided into four submarkets: northeast, northwest, southwest, and southeast. (The subject is located in the northwest submarket.)

Step 2: Delineate the Market

The market area and property users must be delineated before demand and competitive supply are analyzed. The purpose of market delineation is to focus the demand forecast and competition rating on the competitive market area and the specific users, or submarket, of the subject property. In this step the appraiser identifies the market area and characteristics of the likely users—i.e., status (owner or renter), occupational profile, and income level, which indicates their ability to afford the housing. A more in-depth analysis of demand is carried out in Step 3. Competitive supply is also considered in Step 2 as an indicator of the boundaries of the market area.

Step 2.1: Determine the Boundaries of the Market Area

After analyzing the time-distance relationships to employment and support facilities as well as the market area for competitive housing, the appraiser concludes that the market area for the apartment project coincides with the boundaries of the city in which it is located. The citywide market area corresponds to the area where nearly all the competitive projects are found and is the area where prospective renters are told by realtors to look for properties. This area (total suburban city) also provides better demand data because it is large enough to yield the reliable forecast data but small enough to focus demand toward the subject's submarket.[1]

The urban community covers a fairly compact area of approximately 20 square miles. Of the local population, 70% commute to work in the nearby central city. The length of the commute from the subject to these major employment centers is about the same as the commute from any of the major clusters of multifamily housing in the community. In fact, the time-distance relationships to employment centers are similar for all of the residential areas.

The market study boundary is the foundation of the market study because it is the area for which the population forecast will be made. This forecast then sets the number of the resident households expected in this market.

Some markets may have secondary demand sources such as tourists. This could affect market studies for single-family and condominiums and, to a lesser degree, long-term rental projects such as the subject apartments. In the metropolitan suburban city that is the subject of this case study, there was no significant demand from tourists, owners of second homes, or business users.

Step 2.2: Analyze the Tenant Profile for the Subject Property and Neighborhood

By conducting a random survey and analyzing management records, the appraiser develops the following percentage breakdown of the current tenants of the subject property:

40%	Single professionals under 30
30%	Married couples under age 30 without children
20%	Married couples under age 35 with children
10%	Retired couples

Tenant Income and Rent Affordability

Tenant income is estimated based on current rents. The subject units rent for $650 to $800(excluding electricity). It is generally estimated that the average household in this market spends about 28% of their income on housing. Thus, the income range of most tenants is estimated at $28,000 to $35,000 ($650 × 12 mos./0.28; $800 × 12 mos./0.28).

---

1. For a more complete discussion of defining the market area, see Joseph S. Rabianski, "Apartment Housing Market Area Delineation," in forthcoming issue of *The Appraisal Journal*, Winter 2006.

Citywide Income and Subject Renter Segment

Because the competitive market area is assumed to be citywide, the income pattern for the city is studied. The current income pattern for the city is shown in Exhibit 15.6. A review of the data indicates that about 13.9% of the population cannot afford the subject rents (7.3 + 6.6). (Because it takes a minimum income of $28,000 to afford an apartment in the subject property, it is estimated that 20% of households with incomes of $15,000 to $24,999 cannot afford the subject rents).

Exhibit 15.6	Percentage Distribution of Household Income
Less than $20,000	7.3%
$20,000 to $29,999	6.6%
$30,000 to $49,999	17.3%
$50,000 to $74,999	22.7%
$75,000 to $99,999	18.3%
$100,000 to $149,999	19.9%
More than $150,000	7.9%

Source: XYZ Data Co. and U.S. Census.

At the top end of the income range it is estimated that households with incomes above $150,000 would not choose the subject apartments. Thus, it is estimated that a total of about 20% of the households will be unable to afford or would not choose the subject apartment types because of economic reasons. Though it is recognized that the top end estimate is optimistic, a review of the subject tenants found that a few were in the moderate to high-income category. Because the city lacks high-income apartments, some tenants who prefer apartment living chose the subject type apartments despite their high incomes. Thus, the top end recognizes this part of the market segment.

Consumer Spending Patterns

The appraiser compared data on spending patterns within local zip code areas obtained from XYZ data service with the purchasing patterns indicated in a national survey. The XYZ data showed that the subject area surpassed national averages in nearly all categories. Compared to apartment dwellers across the nation, residents of the subject were property were above-average consumers in the following areas:

- Sporting goods (28.9%)
- Dining out (17.8%)
- Auto and accessories (19.2%), and
- Apparel (21.2%)

These spending patterns suggest a lifestyle on a par with or superior to the typical apartment dweller's lifestyle.

Age Distribution and Household Size

Exhibit 15.7 provides an age breakdown of the population of the subject city. About 60% of the residents are younger than age 35. A young population is beneficial to the subject apartment project because it constitutes the likely occupants of apartments. The age distribution suggests a large market base for the subject and further confirms the occupant profile. However, nearly 25% of the city's population is younger than age of 14, which suggests a large number of families who typically seek single-family homes rather than apartments.

Exhibit 15.7	Age Distribution (%)
0–4 yrs.	7.8%
5–14 yrs.	17.0%
15–24 yrs.	17.6%
25–34 yrs.	17.1%
35–44 yrs.	17.6%
45–54 yrs.	11.6%
54–64 yrs.	6.4%
65–74 yrs.	3.2%
75+ yrs.	1.7%

Source: XYZ Data Co. and U.S. Census data

Step 3: Forecast Demand

Next, the appraiser studies the existing and anticipated relationships between the demand and supply for competitive apartment units within the community. Future demand is then forecast using the inferred and fundamental methods shown below.

Inferred Methods
- General area growth trends
- Residential construction trends
- Historical absorption
- Real rental rents

Fundamental Methods
- Forecast studies of multifamily residential demand based on the segmentation of population growth between single-family and multifamily households and the ability to afford the subject units
- Ratio Method–comparing ratio of apartment units to jobs in the city

Step 3.1: Conduct Inferred (Trend) Analysis
Exhibit 15.8 shows the historical growth pattern of the city of Leadville, where the subject is located.

Exhibit 15.8   Population Growth of Leadville

Population 10 years ago	24,573
Current population	46,800
Annual growth rate	6.7%
Avg. absolute growth	2,223/Yr.

Source: Council of Governments.

Historical growth data show that Leadville has grown at a compound annual rate of 6.7% percent. The projected population growth for the city is also positive.

Future Demand Conclusions Based on Growth Trends

The population growth for the market area is quite high relative to other comparably sized cities. Based on the historical pattern of population growth and the expectation that the rate will continue, demand for future multifamily uses is considered very positive. These data viewed in isolation suggest that the subject should lease up to full occupancy in a very short time.

Demand Based on Residential Construction Trends

Exhibit 15.9 shows multifamily residential building activity for the last 10 years. Construction activity was very high 7 years ago, dropping slightly the next three years, and then came to a standstill two years ago. According to the Leadville Planning Department, as of the date of valuation, no construction permits had been issued for three years. The city had about 6,495 units built during the last 10 years, or an average of 650 units in the 10-year period studied.

Conclusions Based on New Construction

It can be inferred from the building permit data that demand for new multifamily units is weak. No permits have been issued for the past three years, and no plats or building permits have been released this year. Previous overbuilding has resulted in a fall off of construction in the past several years. This overbuilding is obviously the reason for the high vacancy rates citywide. Given the lack of recent construction activity and the continued growth in population, however, it would seem, based on this data, that the subject should still lease up in the next year or two.

Demand Based on Historical Absorption

Another indicator of demand is the current trend in occupancy levels. XYZ data service conducts annual apartment surveys, which can be used to discern historical occupancy levels. Exhibit 15.10 indicates the occupancy trend in the Leadville market for the last four years.

Occupancy levels in Leadville for multifamily units have increased from the levels four years ago, when the full impact of the overbuilding was felt. During the past year, occupancy has increased moderately.

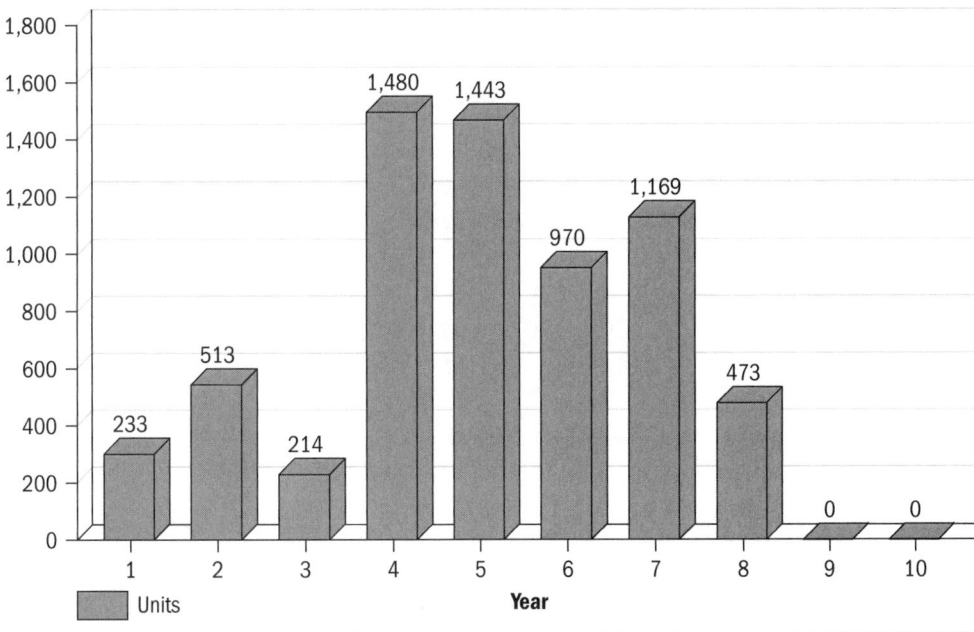

Exhibit 15.9 Multifamily Units Added in Leadville

Number of Units Added

Source: City Planning Dept.

Exhibit 15.10 Occupancy Levels in Leadville for Class A and Class B Apartment Unit Types in City

4 years ago	75%
3 years ago	78%
Last year	80%
Current	83%

Conclusion Based on Absorption Trends

Compared to the past several years, the demand for multifamily units appears to be increasing. An XYZ company survey reported that approximately 500 units were absorbed last year and an average of 250 units per year were obsorbed over the last four years. Based on increasing occupancy rates and subsequent absorption, the demand for multifamily units in Leadville appears to be very positive. A 5% annual increase in occupancy for the subject may be inferred based on these data. Thus in two to three years the subject should achieve 95% occupancy based on this inferred data.

Demand Based on Real Rental Rates

Actual rental rates can also be used to infer demand for multifamily units. Rents are typically related to occupancy levels–i.e., as occupancy levels increase, rents are also expected to increase. Data on historical and current rent levels are presented here to determine whether occupancy levels are an appropriate indicator of demand. Rent levels are used later in the equilibrium analysis (Step 5) as an indication of when new construction is expected to occur. Exhibit 15.11 summarizes the rental rates in the city of Leadville for the last four years. The rates are adjusted for inflation using the metro area CPI; thus, the figures reflect real rates, exclusive of inflation.

Exhibit 15.11	Average Rental Rates in Leadville For Class A Apartments	
Year	**Real Rate per Sq. Ft.**	**% Increase**
4 yrs. ago	$0.90	0
2 yrs. ago	$0.80	-11%
Last yr.	$0.82	2.5%
Current	$0.90	10%

Figures represent fourth quarter survey results. Source: XYZ Data Co.

Conclusion Based on Real Rental Rates

The recent increase in rent levels may be considered a consequence of the rapid increase in occupancy levels in the Leadville apartment market. These increases are believed to reflect an increase in real demand, not an increase in occupancy resulting from special marketing or rent inducements. For the subject property, the trends in occupancy and rents are very positive.

Step 3.2: Conduct Fundamental Analysis by Segmentation/Affordability Method

A fundamental forecast is based on the premise that an area's ability to support multifamily units is a direct function of the number of people and composition of households in the area, both current and anticipated over the next few years. To conduct this type of study, data on existing and projected demand in the market area must be disaggregated to establish the percentage of housing units that will be apartments and the number of households with income levels sufficient to meet the monthly rent for units in the subject property type. Exhibit 15.13 illustrates the application of Steps 3.2(1) through 3.2(5) in developing a demand estimate.

Step 3.2(1): Estimate Current and Projected Population

Measuring the current and forecast population within the market area is the appraiser's first step. In this case, four sources were used: the Local Council of Governments, the City of Leadville, the State Highway Planning Department, and the XYZ Data Service.

In the past 10 years, the population has grown at an average rate of 6.7% per year, resulting in an increase of 22,227 people. Population is expected to continue to grow even though the economy appears to be

Exhibit 15.12 Leadville Current Housing Unit Mix

Category	Type	Number	% of Total
Single family	Detached	10,413	51%
Multifamily	More than 4 units per structure; rental	8,000	39%
Condo/townhouse/duplex	Multiunit structure; most owner-occupied	1,500	7%
Other	Mobile homes	500	2%
Total of all unit types in Leadville		20,413	

Source: City Planning Dept.

slowing down slightly. The forecasts of growth in Leadville in the next 10 years range from a population increase of 14,000 to 30,000, with a mid-range forecast of approximately 22,000. This forecast is about the same as was experienced in the last decade. The wide range of growth forecast is typical in an area such as the subject city that has had a rapid growth spike.

The population forecast sets the number of people expected in this market area over the study period. Thus, the appraiser's task is to determine the number of housing units that this population will use, the percentage of these that will be apartments, and the number of households that can afford the subject type units. The following step shows how this forecast can be accomplished.

Step 3.2(2): Establish the Current and Projected Average Household Size

Household size declined from 2.8 members per household 10 years ago to 2.6 currently and is expected to continue to decline, but at a slower rate. The Site To Do Business (STDBonline.com), commercial data vendor forecast household size would drop to 2.55 in five years. This drop for the last decade reflects the changing housing mix and the large number of apartments built during the last 10 years. This continued downward trend would be reflected in the demand calculations.[2]

Step 3.2(3): Segment Housing by Unit Type

Currently the percentage of apartment units in the city is 39%.

During the large increase in apartment construction five to seven years ago, the apartment mix spiked higher than 40%. This is significantly higher than the historical mix in the city 10 years ago, before the last decade's apartment boom, but is only slightly higher than the target mix of the city's comprehensive plan of 35%. The city is concerned about the amount of apartment building during the last decade and has instituted a moratorium on new apartment zoning despite the fact that vacant land has already been zoned for apartments. The moratorium on new zoning should slow the apartment building. Current policy is based on the city's returning to the comprehensive plan's guideline of 35%. To determine whether this is reasonable and expected in the market, a study of a comparable

---

2. In a Level D analysis, household formation should be studied on a cohort basis, as age-group household formation can vary.

city in the metro area provides a market analogy to help determine the long-range forecast mix. This comparable city has a similar economic base as the subject city and similar socioeconomic characteristics. It also underwent a major building boom of apartments in its past. The comparable city's mix has fluctuated between 33% and 37%, and its current mix is 34%. The city is currently at the same population level that the subject is expected to reach in the next 10 years. Thus, the comparable market data are consistent with the subject city's plan for a 35% mix.

Census data can also be used to forecast apartment unit mix by using renter households as an apartment unit proxy. The census data found 43.7% of the total housing units were renter occupied. However, these data do not distinguish between renters of apartments or single-family homes. Thus, the number of apartment renters would be fewer. Other census data can be used to refine the percentage of apartments. The percentage of units per structure data showed that 35% of the units in the city had more than five units in a structure. Thus, it can be surmised that these are apartments. The data on which these forecasts are based were six years old as of the date of this study; nevertheless, they offer a historical perspective.

Step 3.2(4): Segment Households by Income Levels to Determine the Percentage of Households That Can Meet Monthly Housing Payments

For a household to be able to pay $650 in monthly rent, the lowest rent for a subject unit, its income must exceed $28,000.[3] Higher income households are not likely to rent in the subject market segment. Thus, it is estimated that 20% of the households would not choose the subject apartment market segment because of economic reasons.

In markets that have a substantial percentage of high-end multi-family housing a more refined stratification might be required, which would segment out the higher income households.

Step 3.2(5): Adjust for Normal (Frictional) Vacancy

At any given time, some units will be vacant because of seasonal occupancy or the need to refurbish units. A vacancy rate of about 5% is often applied to the demand forecast to reflect a market in equilibrium. In nonvaluation studies such as feasibility analyses for proposed construction, this adjustment is used to estimate the supportable project size. However, in the capture step, the valuation analyst is most interested in the demand for occupied space.

Other types of demand—move-up demand, latent demand—must be considered and nonresidents can also generate demand for apartments.

Move up demand is generated by the upward mobility of lower-income households. The subject apartment complex is an average multifamily residential project and is unlikely to attract much of this demand. Furthermore, the apartments are not located in the southeast growth corridor and may lose some of their tenants to complexes in that sector of the city. Move-up gains and lateral losses may be expected to cancel each other out.

---

3. Based on 28% of income spent on housing.

Latent demand, also called *pent-up demand*, typically results from under building in an area. If, during the last few years, apartment building had not kept pace with the population increase, latent demand might be present, but it does not apply to the case study.

Nonresident demand is demand from tourist and second-home residents. This demand can be quite significant for the single-family and condominium market, particularly in resort cities, but it is not significant for long-term rental units. The subject property that is the focus of this case study is not affected by this demand source.

Exhibit 15.13 presents the demand calculations described in Steps 3.2(1) through 3.2(5).

Step 3.3: Demand by the Ratio Method

The ratio method is based on the economic tie between apartment demand and increase in employment in the area. The current jobs in the city are compared to the current number of occupied apartment units. The city is in a strong employment growth cycle. Jobs are a leading indicator of apartment demand, since many workers require or desire this type of housing. Thus, it is reasonable to expect this current relationship in the future.

The ratio method is based on the current relationship between jobs and apartments remaining the same in the future. The current apartments in town were considered overbuilt, and the mix in the city was reduced in the previous method. This method does not allow for this adjustment; thus, we see a slightly higher demand forecast. However, this method is similar to the previous method. Exhibit 15.14 shows these calculations.

Step 4: Measure Competitive Supply

The first part of the analysis calls for an inventory of available and anticipated competitive supply. Quantitative supply data can be obtained from many sources. Apartment associations, private market research companies, and some municipal governments maintain lists of existing apartments and unit totals. City planning commissions may be able to provide information on anticipated supply. The appraiser can also conduct a survey to obtain data not available from secondary sources.

In the second part of the supply analysis, a qualitative ranking of competitive apartments is developed. Appraisers rely on their judgment to complete the qualitative survey and rate the subject against the competition.

Step 4.1: Inventory of Existing Competitive Properties, Properties Under Construction, Planned Properties, and Proposed Properties

Using quantitative data obtained from municipal lists of existing apartments and unit totals, the appraiser estimates citywide supply at about 8,000 multifamily units. Not all of these units compete with the sub-

Exhibit 15.13   Apartment Demand by Segmentation Method—Mid-Range Forecast

Line ID	Demand Forecast	Current	Year 1	Year 2	Year 3	Year 4	Year 5	Year 6	Year 7	Year 8	Year 9	Year 10	Comment
1	Population forecast	46,800	49,000	51,200	53,400	55,600	57,800	60,000	62,200	64,400	66,600	68,800	
2	Average increase per year		2,200	2,200	2,200	2,200	2,200	2,200	2,200	2,200	2,200	2,200	Analyst's forecast
3	Persons per household	2.60	2.59	2.58	2.57	2.56	2.55	2.53	2.52	2.51	2.50	2.49	Decreasing
4	Occupied housing unit demand (total households)	18,000	18,919	19,845	20,778	21,719	22,667	23,715	24,683	25,657	26,640	27,631	Line 1 divided by Line 3
5	Percentage of apartment units	39%	38%	37%	36%	35%	35%	35%	35%	35%	35%	35%	Analyst's forecast
6	Potential demand for apartments	7,020	7,189	7,343	7,480	7,602	7,933	8,300	8,639	8,980	9,324	9,671	Line 4 × Line 5
7	Percentage able to afford units in subject economic segment	80%	80%	80%	80%	80%	80%	80%	80%	80%	80%	80%	Based on minimum and maximum income
8	Total potential demand for occupied units in subject economic segment	5,616	5,751	5,874	5,984	6,081	6,347	6,640	6,911	7,184	7,459	7,737	Line 6 × Line 7
9	Plus frictional vacancy @ 5%	296	303	309	315	320	334	349	364	378	393	407	
10	Total potential demand for units in subject economic segment	5,912	6,054	6,183	6,299	6,401	6,681	6,990	7,275	7,562	7,852	8,144	Line 8 plus Line 9

ject. Some are inferior units with low rents occupied by tenants with household incomes below the range specified for the subject. Others are small projects that have no amenities, such as fourplexes, and thus do not compete with the subject. The data method was to survey all apartment projects with 25 units or more in city and then rate the properties as to market segment. The following data sheet and rating shows an example of this rating. (Exhibit 15.15) The subject is considered a Class A space. The other apartment units considered inferior were Class C and Class D. Based on the rating of competitive space it was determined that about 7,000 units that are considered competitive Class A and highly rated Class B apartment units. The survey indicates that the occupancy rate for apartment projects for Class A and B in the community averages approximately 80%, comparable to the subject's occupancy rate. Of these 7,000 competitive units, about 90% were built, like the subject, in the last 10 years.

The appraiser learns from the city planner that no new plats or building permits for apartments have been filed in the past year. The current oversupply has brought apartment development activity to a halt for the last few years. Thus, new competition in the next couple of years is unlikely. However, occupancy and rents are increasing, and there is high demand from institutional investors for apartment properties. These factors strongly suggest that building will begin in the not-too-distant future. Rents are only slightly below new construction requirements. Thus, when market occupancy approaches the 90% range, new construction is expected.

Step 4.2: Analyze Competitive Supply and Rate the Subject Against the Competition

The appraiser/analysts has rated the all apartment complexes surveyed in the city in terms of three major criteria: location, age, and amenities.

Location

Each of the areas where apartment buildings are clustered was assigned a rating on a scale of 1 to 4. The better the location within the community, the higher the rating. The areas were scored based on the results of the location rating in Step 1.3 (see Exhibit 15.15). The southeast sector received the highest rating of 4, while the northwest and southwest were both rated 3. Because the northeast sector had a significantly inferior location rating, it was rated 1.

Age

The ages of the apartment complexes were rated 1 to 5. Complexes constructed in the last three years received a rating of 5. Those constructed four to six years ago were rated 4. A rating of 3 was assigned to complexes built seven to nine years ago. Those constructed 10 to 15 years ago received a rating of 2, and older projects were assigned a rating of 1.

Line	Forecast New Demand	Current Year	Year 1	Year 2	Year 3	Year 4	Year 5	Year 6	Year 7	Year 8	Year 9	Year 10	Comment
1	Total employment in Leadville	29,028	30,228	31,428	32,628	33,828	35,028	36,228	37,428	38,628	39,828	41,028	Source: State employment commission, local council of governments
2	Forecast yearly increase of new employment (all sectors) in city		1,200	1,200	1,200	1,200	1,200	1,200	1,200	1,200	1,200	1,200	
3	Occupied apartment units in city	5,616											
4	Ratio of jobs per occupied apartment units	5.169	5.20	5.20	5.20	5.20	5.20	5.20	5.20	5.20	5.20	5.20	
5	Total demand for occupied units in city	5,616	5,813	6,044	6,275	6,505	6,736	6,967	7,198	7,428	7,659	7,890	Calculation—Line 1 divided by Line 4
6	Plus frictional vacancy @ 5%	296	306	318	330	342	355	367	379	391	403	415	
7	Total demand for apartment units	5,912	6,119	6,362	6,605	6,847	7,091	7,334	7,577	7,819	8,062	8,305	

Amenities

For rating purposes, amenities were divided into three groups. First, the appraiser considered the amenities within the apartment units. When a greater variety of amenities (e.g., appliances, fireplaces, patios, and high-tech connections) were provided, a higher rating was assigned to the unit. The second category covered the amenities found on the site (e.g., swimming pool, tennis court, sauna/hot tub, and clubhouse). The third category included the amenities within walking distance of the apartment complex (e.g., shopping areas, restaurants, recreational facilities, employment areas). Each of the three categories of amenities was rated on a scale of 1 to 5. Scores were assigned based on the number of amenities in each category, and the totals were divided into five groups with ratings from one to five. Exhibit 15.15, a sample of the 35 properties included in the appraiser's competitive supply survey, is shown along with their ratings.

Exhibit 15.15 Sample of 35 Projects Surveyed and Rated

No.	Name	Age of Project	Number per Units	Avg. Rent Occupancy Sq. Ft.	Rate	Rating Amenities*	Score
1.	Arbor Apts.	5 yrs.	300	$0.93	85%	P, LR, S, CL, O, DD, WD, CF, F, C, SC, PB	23.5
2.	Atrium Apts.	7 yrs.	244	$0.87	83%	P, LR, T, S, CL, DD, WD, CF, F, C, SC, PB, PB, SC	22.0
3.	Berkshire	8 yrs.	232	$0.87	90%	P, LR, S, DD, C	21.5
4.	Beacon Hill	6 yrs.	180	$0.90	86%	P, LR, S, CH, DD, WD, CF, F, C, O SC, PB	21.5
5.	Bryn Mawr	8 yrs.	356	$0.87	84%	P, LR, S, CL, HT, DD, F, C, PA	21.5
6.	Chestnut Hill	7 yrs.	212	$0.88	90%	P, LR, S, CL, DD, WD, CF, F, C	21.0
7.	Devonshire	7 yrs.	126	$0.85	85%	P, LR, S, CL, O, DD, WD, F, CF	20.5
8.	**Pine Grove** (subject)	5 yrs.	312	$0.83	80%	P, LR, T, CP, S, CI, DD, WD, F, C, SC, PB	20.0
Nos. 9–34 omitted for brevity							
35.	Yorkshire	15 yrs.	228	$0.70	80%	P, LR, S, DD, C	11.0

* Apartment unit amenities include: dishwasher/disposal system (DD), washer/dryer connections (WD), ceiling fan (CF), fireplace (F), cable TV—landlord pays (CL), cable TV/Internet—tenant pays (CT), burglar alarm (B), microwave oven (M), patio (PA), and other (O).

On-site amenities include: pool (P), laundry room (LR), covered parking (CP), tennis court (T), security (S), clubhouse (CH), hot tub/sauna (HT), racquetball court (RB), and other recreational facility (O).

Amenities within walking distance include: shopping center (SC), park (PK), and professional office building (PB).

The location ratings, age ratings, and the three amenities ratings were added to produce the ratings shown in Exhibit 15.15. The apartment complexes were ranked using their competitive supply ratings. (Note: Ratings for a sample of the 35 properties surveyed are included in Exhibit 15.15, but for brevity, Properties 9 through 34 are not shown.) The subject's score was considered one of the better projects in the city; it ranked eighth best in the city out of 35 projects and was considered a Class A property. However, because all of the projects in the market are similar in age and amenities, the subject ranking is not that significant.

Because the citywide demand forecast includes all likely occupants of rental units with sufficient income to afford the subject units (80% of all renters), the appraiser must consider the total citywide competition, which is represented by the other properties of similar class rating and rent structure.

Step 5: Analyze Market Equilibrium/Disequilibrium

Steps 5.1, 5.2, and 5.3: Compare Demand and Competitive Supply

Exhibit 15.16 shows a projection of demand and competitive supply over the next four years. In Steps 5.1 and 5.2, the findings of the demand analysis (Step 3) and competitive supply analysis (Step 4.1) are entered into the equilibrium analysis grid. The difference between supply and demand is calculated in Step 5.3, where either a net excess or shortage is identified. The five years shown in the projection represent the time over which demand and supply begins to approach a balanced market, assuming a mid-range forecast.

The calculations in Exhibit 15.16 suggest that in five years the market will be reaching equilibrium. In appraisals of existing properties, equilibrium analysis is used to forecast rent cycles and new competition. In the case study application, new construction can be expected when the market shows a positive net demand. Rents may also peak at this time. The relationship between rent increases and new construction should be considered in greater detail.

Based on the relationship between projected demand and the current supply of units, the demand for multifamily units justifies the construction of new units in approximately four years. However, rents must be high enough to support the project and to obtain financing. In Exhibit 15.17 the rent level required for construction of a new multifamily Class A development to be feasible is calculated. The analysis assumes a new apartment building of typical size with a typical number of units and on-site amenities.

The calculations indicate that rent levels of about $1.00 per sq. ft. per month are needed to support the construction of a new multifamily development. The appraiser should recognize that the level of required rent might change depending on the construction cost, design, density, land cost, and expenses associated with the project as well as the investors' perceptions. Nevertheless, the figure derived is considered a good gauge of the rent required to justify new construction.

Current rent levels in the Leadville market, which were established in the survey of better-rated apartment units were approaching $.90 per square foot (Step 4.2). Rent levels will need to increase by approximately 10% in real terms before new construction is anticipated. Given the increasing demand and lack of recent new construction, it is con-

Exhibit 15.16 Apartment Residual Demand by Segmentation Method—Mid-Range Forecast

Line	Market Demand Forecast	Current	Year 1	Year 2	Year 3	Year 4	Year 5	Comment
1	Population forecast	46,800	49,000	51,200	53,400	55,600	57,800	
2	Average increase per year		2,200	2,200	2,200	2,200	2,200	Analyst's forecast
3	Persons per household	2.60	2.59	2.58	2.57	2.56	2.55	Decreasing
4	Occupied housing unit demand (total household)	18,000	18,919	19,845	20,778	21,719	22,667	Line 1 divided by Line 3
5	Percentage of apartment units	39%	38%	37%	36%	35%	35%	Analyst's forecast
6	Potential demand for apartments	7,020	7,189	7,343	7,480	7,602	7,933	Line 4 × Line 5
7	Percentage of population able to afford subject economic segment	80%	80%	80%	80%	80%	80%	Based on minimum and maximum income
8	Total potential demand for occupied units in subject economic segment	5,616	5,751	5,874	5,984	6,081	6,347	Line 6 × Line 7
9	Plus frictional vacancy @ 5%	296	303	309	315	320	334	
10	Total potential demand for units in subject economic segment	5,912	6,054	6,183	6,299	6,401	6,681	Line 8 plus Line 9
Market Competition								
11	Year starting competitive supply	7,000	7,000	7,000	7,000	7,000	7,000	
12	New construction	0	0	0	0	0	0	Analyst's forecast
13	Total competitive supply	7,000	7,000	7,000	7,000	7,000	7,000	
14	Residual demand	(1,088)	(946)	(817)	(701)	(599)	(319)	Line 10 minus Line 13
15	Estimate market occupancy rate in subject market segment	80%	82%	84%	85%	87%	91%	Line 8 divided by Line 13

cluded that rents will be able to increase at the 8% to 10% rate experienced in this market in the past year. Thus, it will be about two to three years before rents are feasible for new construction.

Forecasting the future date when new construction will begin requires consideration of other supply-side factors in addition to rent. These factors include the availability of land and financing, proper zoning, and a market that is attractive to developers.

Based on the marginal demand and rent analysis, significant new construction is anticipated to occur in about ± five years.

The quantity of new construction is another question. Over the past 10 years, an average of 650 units per year have been built in this market (Step 3.1). This overbuilding is not expected to continue in the fu-

Exhibit 15.17   Rent Level Required for New Multifamily Construction

Assumptions

Average unit size	600 sq. ft.
Number of units	175
Total net leasable area (*NLA*)	105,000 sq. ft.
Construction cost	$40,800 per unit; $68.00 per sq. ft. of *NLA*
Land size	7 acres
Land and site cost	$914,760; $3.00 per sq. ft.
Overall cap rate	9%
Operating expenses	40% of gross income

Construction cost

	175 × $40,800	$7,140,000
Land and site cost		$914,760
Total cost		$8,054,760
Required *NOI*		
$8,054,760 @ 0.09		$724,928
Required effective gross income		
$724,928 ÷ 0.60		$1,208,213
Say		$1,208,200 @ 95% occupancy
Required rent per square foot		
$1,208,200 ÷ 99,750 sq. ft. of *NLA*		$12.11 per sq. ft. per year, or $1.00 per sq. ft. per month

ture because of new, more stringent zoning for apartments and because this situation represented a market bubble in an emerging suburb, which has historically leveled out in other suburbs in 10 years. Thus, construction of 300 to 450 units per year, on average, is probable over the four- to 10-year forecast period.

Step 6: Forecast Subject Capture

The subject market was analyzed with both inferred and fundamental methods. The appraiser's conclusions are summarized below.

- General growth trends. Strong lease-up potential was indicated for the subject property.
- New construction. The lack of recent construction suggests less competition for the subject and is another positive indicator of the subject's potential for quick lease-up, given the strong growth trends cited above.
- Historical absorption. Over the previous two years, absorption averaged 250 units per year; last year it was 350 units. If last year's trend continues, and the subject's capture increases by 5% annually, the subject will achieve 95% occupancy in two to three years.
- Rent increase. Last year real rents increased 10%; thus, it can be inferred that the subject's rents will increase accordingly.

Fundamental methods were used to estimate the subject's capture rate, which was then applied to the forecast of the real demand for space in the market. The rate can be analyzed in a number of ways. Three methods are presented here and the results are reconciled.

- The subject's current capture rate. Current capture is calculated as follows. Of the approximately 7,000 competitive units citywide, about 80% are occupied, indicating 5,600 occupied units. The subject currently has 250 occupied units. Thus the subject's capture rate is 250 / 5,600, or 4.4%.

- The pro rata share method. This method employs the ratio of subject units to competitive units. There are 7,000 competitive units, including the 312 subject units. Thus the subject's pro rata share is 4.5% (312 / 7,000). Comparing the current capture rate of the subject with its pro rata share suggests that the subject's performance is slightly below average.

- Competitive rating method. The scores shown in the supply survey and rating chart (Exhibit 15.15) are examined. The subject had a rating, or score, of 20, and the scores of all competitive projects surveyed totaled 474. Based on these figures, the subject's indicated percentage of capture is 4.2% (20 / 474).

Given the indications described above, it is reasonable to conclude that the subject's current actual capture rate will continue until new competition materializes. The prospect of new construction may necessitate an adjustment of the capture rate. The previous equilibrium analysis forecasts probable construction of approximately 350 units annually beginning in about five years. The pro rata share method may be used to gauge how the new units will impact the subject capture rate. The subject's current pro rata share is 4.5% (312 / 7,000), but with 350 units added, the pro rata share will be reduced to approximately 4.3% (312 / 7,350 = 4.3%). If construction continues to add an average of 350 units annually, as expected, a similar reduction in the subject's pro rata share can be expected each year.

Estimate Subject Capture
In Exhibit 15.18 the subject's possible capture is calculated based on the mid-range population forecast presented earlier in the case study.

Final Conclusions on Subject Marketability
The preceding analysis was based on a mid-range population forecast and employed both inferred and fundamental methods. The inferred methods suggested strong lease-up potential for the subject. The fundamental methods concluded a more moderate lease-up outlook. First, the fundamental techniques indicated that lease up would not be as strong as indicated by the inferred methods. Second, the fundamental methods revealed a cyclical trend that is expected to peak in four to seven years, with the subject's best occupancy slightly below 90% occupancy.

Table 15.18 Apartment Demand by Segmentation Method—Mid-Range Forecast

Line ID	Market Demand Forecast	Current	Year 1	Year 2	Year 3	Year 4	Year 5	Year 6	Year 7	Year 8	Year 9	Year 10	Comment
1	Population forecast	46,800	49,000	51,200	53,400	55,600	57,800	60,000	62,200	64,400	66,600	68,800	
2	Average increase per year		2,200	2,200	2,200	2,200	2,200	2,200	2,200	2,200	2,200	2,200	Analyst's forecast
3	Persons per household	2.60	2.59	2.58	2.57	2.56	2.55	2.53	2.52	2.51	2.50	2.49	Decreasing
4	Occupied housing unit demand (total households)	18,000	18,919	19,845	20,778	21,719	22,667	23,715	24,683	25,657	26,640	27,631	Line 1 divided by Line 3
5	Percentage of apartment units	39%	38%	37%	36%	35%	35%	35%	35%	35%	35%	35%	Analyst's forecast
6	Potential demand for apartments	7,020	7,189	7,343	7,480	7,602	7,933	8,300	8,639	8,980	9,324	9,671	Line 4 × Line 5
7	Percentage of population able to afford subject economic segment	80%	80%	80%	80%	80%	80%	80%	80%	80%	80%	80%	Based on min. & max. income
8	Total potential demand for occupied units in subject economic segment	5,616	5,751	5,874	5,984	6,081	6,347	6,640	6,911	7,184	7,459	7,737	Line 6 × Line 7
9	Plus frictional vacancy @ 5%	296	303	309	315	320	334	349	364	378	393	407	
10	Total potential demand for units in subject economic segment	5,912	6,054	6,183	6,299	6,401	6,681	6,990	7,275	7,562	7,852	8,144	Line 8 plus Line 9
Market Residual Demand													
11	Year starting competitive supply	7,000	7,000	7,000	7,000	7,000	7,000	7,000	7,350	7,700	8,050	8,400	
12	New construction	0	0	0	0	0	0	350	350	350	350	350	Analyst's forecast
13	Total competitive supply	7,000	7,000	7,000	7,000	7,000	7,000	7,350	7,700	8,050	8,400	8,750	
14	Residual demand	(1,088)	(946)	(817)	(701)	(599)	(319)	(360)	(425)	(488)	(548)	(606)	Line 10 minus Line 13
15	Estimate market occupancy rate	80%	82%	84%	85%	87%	91%	90%	90%	89%	89%	88%	Line 8 divided by Line 13
Subject Capture Estimate													
Subject Pro Rata Share		4.5%	4.5%	4.5%	4.5%	4.5%	4.5%	4.2%	4.1%	4.0%	3.7%	3.6%	
16	Estimated subject capture rate (rounded)	4.4%	4.4%	4.4%	4.4%	4.4%	4.3%	4.1%	4.0%	3.8%	3.6%	3.5%	Analyst's forecast
17	Estimated subject occupancy—units	249	255	261	266	270	273	272	276	273	269	271	Line 8 × Line 16
18	Estimated subject occupancy rate	80%	82%	84%	85%	87%	87%	87%	87%	87%	86%	87%	Subject 312 units

The purpose of this analysis is to forecast future income for a valuation appraisal. The conclusions drawn from the inferred methods are based on historical data, which described a period of unprecedented building activity. Since the forecast data are considered reliable, the conclusions based on the fundamental methods have been given more weight in estimating future occupancy and rent levels.

Projected Occupancy and Rent Level Conclusions

Low-range forecast   *Occupancy.* Level to slightly increasing in Years 1 through 5, then slowly increasing in Years 5 through 10 to 85% occupancy.

Low-end forecast   *Occupancy.* Level to very slightly rising Year 1 through Year 5, then slowly increasing to 85% occupancy Year 5 through Year 10.

     Rent. Declining at real rate of 0.5% per year to maintain the slight gain in occupancy.

Mid-range forecast   *Occupancy.* Increasing to 90% in Year 5. New construction occurs, and from Year 6 to Year 10, occupancy declines. By Year 10, occupancy about 85%.

     Rent. Increasing at a real rate of 4% per year for three years. From Year 4 to Year 10 rents decline at a rate of 0.5% per year to maintain occupancy.

High-end forecast   *Occupancy.* Increasing to 95% in five years, and maintaining this level through Year 10.

     Rent. Remaining level at the same real rate over the next five years; increasing at 2% per year for Years 5 through 10.

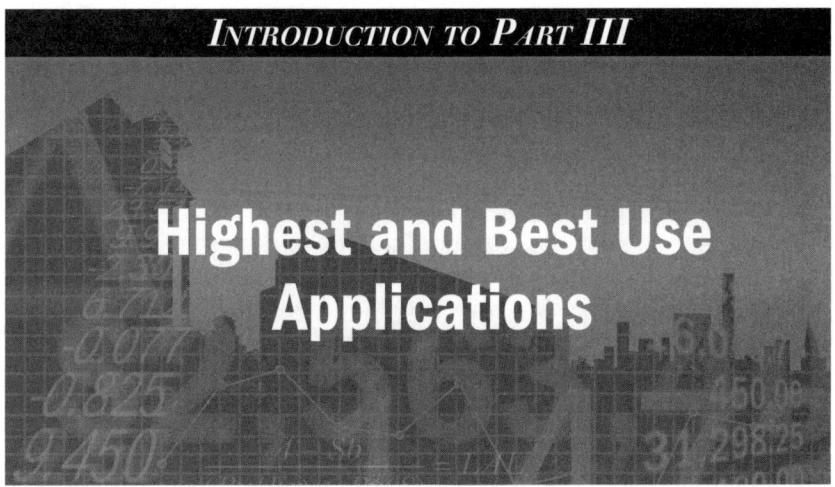

Highest and Best Use Applications

The first part of this book provided the conceptual basis of market analysis as an integral part of appraisals. The second part presented four case study applications demonstrating the application of market analysis. Part III provides a link between the mathematical models employed to test financial feasibility in highest and best use and the data inputs required in these models–specifically the forecast of occupancy and rent for the subject property. It underscores the primary themes of the book, that market analysis is the heart of appraisal, and that it is a process, not a mechanical procedure.

This process provides the data inputs such as effective demand; the subject's capture rate and timing that are critical to the conclusion of highest and best use, and the application of the three approaches to value.

The applications in Part III show that the traditional four criteria used to determine highest and best use and the six-step market analysis process presented in this book are interrelated. The conclusion of highest and best use requires an additional step, however: financial analysis of alternative probable uses to determine which use results in the highest value. Thus, the six-step market analysis process and the financial analysis of alternative probable uses (Step 7) comprise the comprehensive study process applied to determine highest and best use. The highest and best use conclusion is completed by the final step, reconciliation and specification of the use, timing, and market participants.

The case studies in the book represent Level C analyses. This is not to suggest that the same level of study is required for each alternative use examined in highest and best use analysis. Some probable uses and the timing of them are more obvious than others, and thus may warrant less study and documentation. Moreover, some alternative probable uses will result in less value and thus require a less detailed study. Alternatively, use decisions on especially complex properties may often require Level D analyses.

This book focuses on the twofold purpose of market/marketability analysis in valuation appraisals. First, the six-step process (market/marketability analysis) supports the capture forecast required for each alternative probable use in highest and best use analysis. Second, market analysis provides the economic information needed to apply the three approaches to value, i.e., the revenue (market capture) forecast used in the income approach, the analysis of property productivity considered in the sales comparison approach, and the estimate of functional and economic obsolescence incorporated into the cost approach.

The case studies presented in Part III include highest and best use applications involving vacant land and an improved property. Many of the tables presented in these applications appear as Excel files in the CD at the back of the book. The first application, in Chapter 17, illustrates how the timing of a mix of uses impacts the highest and best use decision. The case study in Chapter 18 shows how a highest and best use study functions with a proposed use. The last chapter demonstrates that the current highest and best use of vacant improved property may not be the same as the use envisioned for the property when it was built.

CHAPTER 16

Highest and Best Use Decisions

Chapter Objectives

- To define the term *highest and best use*
- To describe the three-part conclusion of highest and best use
- To demonstrate how the six-step market analysis process is linked to highest and best use decisions
- To describe the land use alternatives as they relate to highest and best use
- To introduce the measures to test for the four criteria of highest and best use: physical possibility, legal permissibility, financial feasibility, and maximum productivity
- To explain mathematical procedures for alternative use
- To describe the impact of market analysis on highest and best use decisions
- To apply marketability analysis to arrive at a highest and best use conclusion using a case study approach

Introduction

This chapter is an overview of concepts and the link between market analysis (the six-step process) and highest and best use decision criteria. The highest and best use and market analysis are the fulcrum of the appraisal. Highest and best use analysis determines the use of the property to be valued and the economic basis of that value. The valuation models (three approaches) measure the value of the highest and best use. Components of this chapter include:

- Basic concepts involved in highest and best use analysis
- Land use alternatives and levels of highest and best use analysis
- The reasonably probable and appropriately supported aspects of highest and best use
- Information and measures used to test the performance of a property's use in relation to the four criteria for highest and best use
- Problems demonstrating highest and best use financial analysis
- The relationship between highest and best use decisions and the six-step market study process

Basic Concepts and Terminology

Highest and best use is the reasonably probable and legal use of vacant land or an improved property that is physically possible, appropriately supported, financially feasible, and results in the highest value. The four criteria that highest and best use must meet are legal permissibility, physical possibility, financial feasibility, and maximum productivity.[1]

First and foremost, highest and best use is a probability study based on the most probable size, intensity, and quality in the market, given the subject's physical and locational constraints and opportunities.

Second, it is a study that must be appropriately supported, meaning that an economic demand must exist for the property and must translate into enough buying power to realize that demand. Finally, it must be a use selected that produces the highest (most probable) value from among alternatives.

A highest and best use study provides an economic basis for the chosen use by addressing the four factors of value: utility, desire, scarcity, and effective purchasing power.

Utility addresses the question: What real estate product does the subject provide; desire: Is there a demand for this real estate product; scarcity: How competitive is the subject; and effective purchasing: What is the financial reward for the subject use? Conclusions for the highest and best use guide the application of the three approaches to value.

The Three-Part Conclusion of Highest and Best Use

The conclusions of highest and best use must specify the study's determination of three main elements pertaining to a property: physical use, time, and market participants.

Physical use should be specific to the submarket served, identifying the submarket as not only retail, for example, but neighborhood retail or some other specific retail use.

Time, probable use date, or occupancy forecast is a forecast of the approximate time vacant land is expected to be used. This is not an exact date but a range of dates. For an improved property for which no alternative is feasible, timing refers to future rents and occupancy forecast.

---

1. *The Dictionary of Real Estate Appraisal,* 4th ed. (Chicago: Appraisal Institute, 2002).

Market participants constitute the typical user of space and the most probable type of buyer. This last part of the highest and best use conclusion recognizes the two markets the appraiser analyzes simultaneously: the user market and the buy/sell market. These markets sometimes operate in separate realms, but at some point they almost always return to the economics of the user market.

For years, appraisal literature has addressed each of the three elements in a highest and best use analysis of a property, but the traditional practice has been to emphasize physical use over timing and market participants. Thus, the six-step process is a vital aid in the highest and best use study because it addresses not only physical use but also the timing for the use of the property. Each of the applications in this book highlights analytical techniques for measuring timing and identifying market participants. The conclusions derived from this aspect of the analysis then form the basis for establishing the valuation models used in the appraisal.

The three parts of the highest and best use conclusions also establish the criteria for selecting comparable sales, which means that each sale must be as similar to the subject as possible relative to physical use, timing, and market participants. If there are differences, adjustments must be derived from one of the three highest and best use conclusions.

Physical use, timing, and market participants also provide the basis for estimating physical, functional, and external obsolescence used in the cost approach. Similarly, these elements support the basis for forecasts required to apply the income capitalization approach properly, such as that for future occupancy and rents.

Thus, the two major parts of a valuation appraisal are reflected in the purposes of highest and best use analysis. In the first part highest and best use is established; in the second part value itself is measured. The value of a property can be measured with accuracy *only* when the factors that establish the basis for its value are properly analyzed. Consequently, in most cases the study of market forces that affect use and value require in-depth study equal in degree to that accorded to measuring that value through the application of the appropriate techniques and procedures of the valuation approaches. Such a study would be a marketability study, or a market analysis focused on a subject property.

The Six-Step Market Analysis Process: A Framework for Highest and Best Use Decisions

The six-step market analysis process introduced in this book helps the appraiser test for highest and best use. It answers questions about physical and legal constraints and provides key inputs into the tests to determine financial feasibility and maximum productivity. Moreover, it helps appraisers specify and support highest and best use conclusions in terms of use, timing, and market participants.

This process applied to property use alternatives functions as a screen with Step 1, the land use filters of physical, legal, and locational determinants of use as a starting point. It also yields information on economic demand that often points to the elimination of certain uses (or changes in existing improvements) that might be tested for financial feasibility.

The following is a recap of the six-step process presented in Chapter 1 with comments to show the emphasis on alternative highest and best use decisions. Step 7, the financial analysis of alternatives for highest and best use, is added to complete the process.

Step 1: Property Productivity Analysis

- What uses are probable for the property based on the property's physical, legal, locational attributes?

In answering this question, Steps 2-7 are repeated for each use.

Step 2: Market Delineation

- Who are the potential typical users or likely purchasers of the property for each alternative?

Step 3: Demand Analysis

- Is each alternative use needed? (economic demand for each use)

- Population	→	Households	→	Housing Units
- Income	→	Effective Buying Power	→	Retail Sq. Ft.
- Jobs	→	% Use Office	→	Office Sq. Ft.

Step 4: Supply Analysis

- What is the competition for each alternative, and how much competition exists?

Step 5: Market Equilibrium Analysis

- When will this market require new construction for each alternative?

Step 6: Capture Analysis

- How much of this market can the subject capture for each alternative?
  - Are the property's attributes competitive?
  - Is the location competitive?
  - How much of the demand can be captured?
  - How much is the land worth for each alternative, and how much rent can be charged?

Step 7: H&B Use Financial Analysis

- Which alternative use is worth the most; i.e., which is the highest and best use?

The property productivity analysis (Step 1) yields alternatives to consider and eliminates those that are not as productive (competitive) as others. This is an important part of highest and best use analysis. The most sensitive data input in terms of impact on value, however, is the timing estimate (subject capture of market demand), which is the result of all the steps combined.

Although the six-step process does not supply the final tests for highest and best us, i.e., tests of financial feasibility and maximum productivity, it does yield the required data for performing a financial feasibility analysis, which then becomes a mathematical analysis of alternatives. The maximally productive use determination is a reconciliation of the data. The reconciliation is the appraiser's final judgment of the most reliable data. Another term for this analysis is data risk analysis—determining the data that provide the most probable future.

At any step in the application of the process, when all uses except one alternative use are eliminated, the remaining steps should focus on the market/ marketability of that single alternative.

Land Use Alternatives and Levels of Highest and Best Use Analysis

The level of market analysis required to support the three approaches to value differs according to market conditions and the type of appraisal. Similarly, alternative probable uses considered in highest and best use analysis may require different levels of study. Thus, the appraiser also considers the level of study appropriate for each alternative probable use. Because highest and best use analysis is a decision-making process, each alternative probable use should be studied in sufficient detail to allow the analyst to make a logical, supportable decision on that use in terms of specification, timing, and identification of market participants (see Exhibit 16.1).

Critics of improved property appraisals generally do not argue that the conclusion among alternative probable use conclusions is wrong but that the forecast developed in the income approach is inadequately supported. On the other hand, the most frequent criticism of vacant land appraisals is that the alternative probable uses have not been adequately analyzed and, in particular, the timing for each use has not been given sufficient attention. This criticism suggests that the factors that have the greatest impact on value require the most detailed market analysis.

For properties with improvements that are relatively new and have (or have a reasonable potential for) a positive net operating income (*NOI*), alternative uses are not a critical concern. Of course, they must still be considered, but they may, in many cases, be less detailed. The highest and best use of the land as though vacant must be considered. However, because demolition of the improvements is unlikely, and the land value is usually a relatively small portion of overall property value, it is reasonable for the analysis of the land as though vacant to be less extensive. On the other hand, future capture rates and rent levels are critical to the determination of the value of improved properties, both prospective properties and currently leased properties. Therefore, in the valuation of improved properties, the focus of market/marketability analysis is on the property as improved rather than the land as though vacant.

The appraisal of vacant land is different. The specific use among alternative probable uses selected as the highest and best use is identified as that which results in the greatest value. When valuing vacant land, each alternative probable use must be considered for its impact on the land value. A highest and best use is chosen from among alternative probable uses under which land value can vary widely. The

Exhibit 16.1   The Six-Step Process and Four Parallel Tests

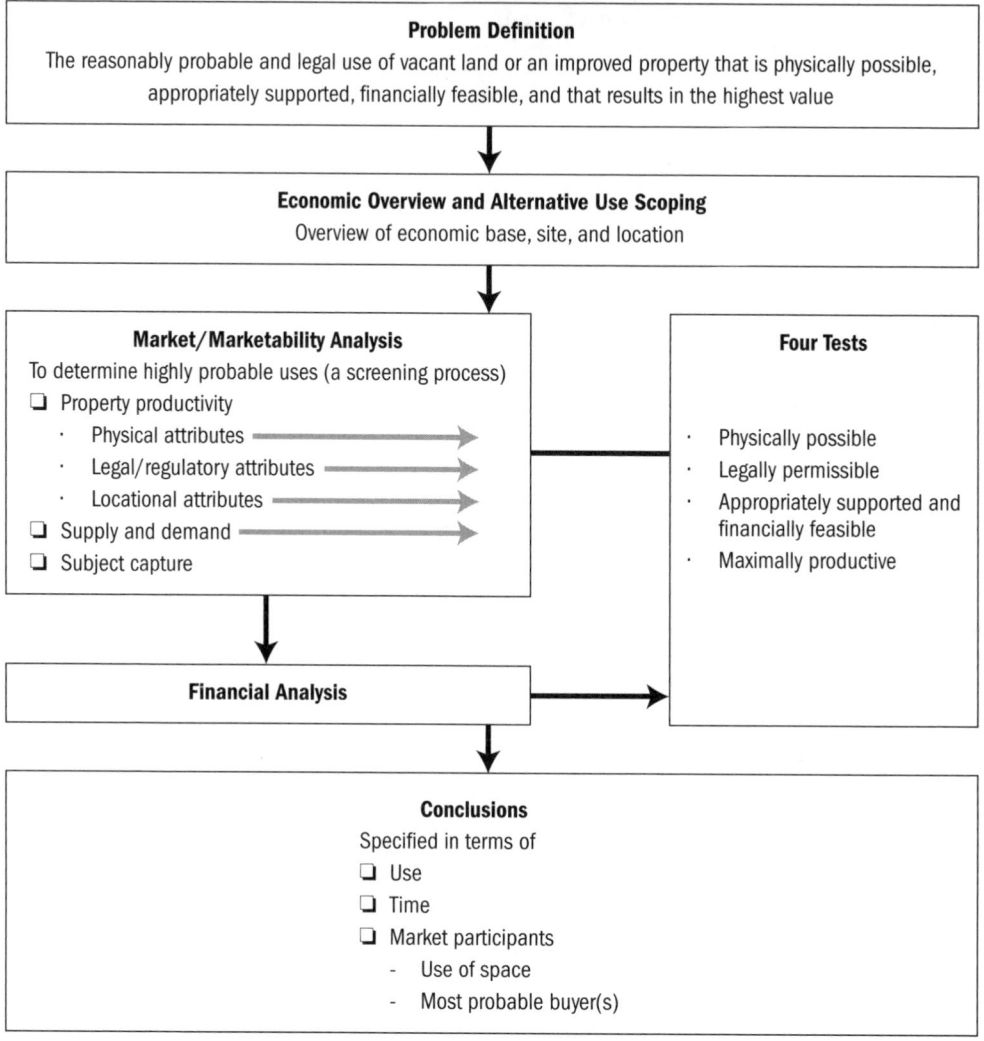

Problem Definition
The reasonably probable and legal use of vacant land or an improved property that is physically possible, appropriately supported, financially feasible, and that results in the highest value

Economic Overview and Alternative Use Scoping
Overview of economic base, site, and location

Market/Marketability Analysis
To determine highly probable uses (a screening process)
❑ Property productivity
  · Physical attributes
  · Legal/regulatory attributes
  · Locational attributes
❑ Supply and demand
❑ Subject capture

Four Tests

· Physically possible
· Legally permissible
· Appropriately supported and financially feasible
· Maximally productive

Financial Analysis

Conclusions
Specified in terms of
❑ Use
❑ Time
❑ Market participants
  - Use of space
  - Most probable buyer(s)

market analysis for each highly competitive alternative use requires an equally detailed level of study. The following are guidelines on the level of market/marketability analysis and degree of documentation required for a given assignment.

Vacant Land

Vacant land almost always has alternative use possibilities; thus, all probable alternatives should be considered. The extent of analysis required depends on the uncertainty of the future use, its timing, and how critical this determination is to value. In most instances, land that has a probability of multiple use and more uncertain timing for that use requires the most study. The criteria presented in Chapter 2 can provide guidelines on the amount of study needed.

Whatever the level of study used, a highest and best use conclusion requires a forecast of the most *probable* use, not all *possible* uses. Therefore, the property productivity analysis (site, improvements, legal, and locational attributes) usually eliminates most alternatives.

The appraisal of vacant land, as with all appraisals, requires some level of a market study to support the highest and best use conclusions. In many cases this study is more comprehensive than that for improved properties. In addition to market demand for alternative uses, vacant land requires an analysis of competition, i.e., other vacant land. The appraiser must exercise caution in performing a market analysis that results in the determination of highest and best use. A given site may be particularly well suited for a specific use, but a number of other sites may be available that are equally or more appropriate. Therefore, he or she must put the highest and best use conclusion to the test to ensure that existing and potential competition from other sites has been fully acknowledged.[2]

Improved Properties

Improved properties require two highest and best use considerations: 1) as if vacant, and 2) as improved. An "as improved" property can fit multiple scenarios such as a remodel, renovation, or conversion.

Land As If Vacant

An improved property will continue in its current use until the land as vacant, *less* demolition cost, is more valuable than the property as improved. Therefore, all highest and best use studies must consider the land as though vacant to eliminate the demolition alternative and determine if there is external obsolescence.

The extent of the analysis will vary depending on how critical the land value is to the overall property value. Threshold testing is recommended, which involves analyzing the land if it was valued as one of the highest in the area. If the land as though vacant at the threshold testing value does not approach the value of the property as improved, a detailed study of alternative uses for the land as though vacant is less critical. An example of this would be an existing 50,000-sq.-ft. shopping center on five acres.

Price of the land at extreme high-end price   5 acres × $8 per sq. ft. = $1,742,400

Price of property as improved at low-end price $45/sq. ft. × 50,000 sq. ft. = $2,250,000

These are not value estimates but are analytical tests at extreme prices to determine the threshold at which more study would be required. In this case, even under extreme conditions, the land value does not approach the value as improved. Thus, the analysis of the land as if vacant could, in most cases, be a Level A market analysis.

---

2. *The Appraisal of Real Estate,* 12th ed. (Chicago: Appraisal Institute, 2001).

Property As Improved

If a property's improvements contribute to value so that the value of the improved property is equal to or greater than the value of the land as though vacant and available for its highest and best use, *minus* demolition costs, the existing improvement must be considered as contributing to the property's current highest and best use. The highest and best use question then becomes: Are alterations (renovation, remodeling, or conversion) necessary to achieve the highest and best use? The future economic performance of these improvements, therefore, is the primary highest and best use and, in turn, value question.

The extent of the analysis depends on several crucial questions, but the major one is the future ability of the existing improvements to provide an economic return to maintain the property's value at a higher level than would be the case with alternative uses. Pertinent questions in this analysis are:

- How long and at what level (occupancy and rents) will the current improvements perform?
- How long will the current improvements contribute to the property value?
- Can the current improvements be remodeled, renovated, or converted, or should they be demolished in the future?
- If remodeling, renovation, conversion, or demolition is indicated, what is the time frame for implementing these changes?

If any alternatives to the existing use are highly competitive, the appraiser should proceed with greater detail. If the improvements are to be demolished, a full analysis of the vacant land for each new alternative use must be performed. If changes to the improvements do not change the use category, the physical and legal characteristics of the property, the location, geographic market area, and market segment may require reanalysis to fully address the advisability of any alteration to the existing use. Consider, for instance, the type of analysis that would be required if a proposal were made to convert a single-story freestanding health clinic to multistory dental-orthodontic office space.

In certain situations it is possible to consider alterations that can be accomplished without changing the basic physical structure of the improvements. Alternative operations (e.g., limited or expanded service to increase the property productivity) or alternative market segments (e.g., targeting to different users or customers) are valid alternative uses. Examples of such alternative uses might be:

- Conversion of an existing strip center from primary retail (e.g., video store, laundry, one-hour photo, or restaurants) to secondary retail (second-hand furniture store, pawnshop, small-engine repair, or sales)
- Limiting service operations of a restaurant from seven days a week to weekend operations
- Changing an apartment from rental units to condominiums

In considering these types of alternative uses, the appraiser must ensure that the highest and best use establishes the basis for the market value of the real property. Some appraisers believe such alternative uses should not be considered in highest and best use analysis because they are related to business value, not real property value. Whatever value it is called, if it affects overall value, it will probably affect the real estate contributing to that overall value.

Regardless of the alternatives to be considered, it is suggested that when the property being appraised is improved, the appraiser first complete a market analysis study of the property at its current use and then a preliminary analysis of the most optimistic value of the subject property at reasonable alternative uses. If the property at its current use is forecast to lease up or stays leased in a manner that ensures an indicated value at or above the values of the other alternatives, then the current use is selected as the highest and best use, and other alternatives are not analyzed further.

However, if the improvement productivity analysis reveals significant physical or functional obsolescence or significant changes in the rate or direction of growth, alternative uses or the timing for future demolition must be considered.

When appraising vacant buildings or properties that have an extremely low or negative *NOI*, alternative uses and/or alternative operation of the current improvements should be considered in detail. Usually this requires applying all the steps of the market analysis process as well as the financial analysis of all alternatives.

Proposed Properties

If the assignment is to value the property at a proposed use, a detailed market study of such use is typically required.

The highest and best use analysis of a proposed property is similar to the analysis conducted for an improved property. Because the proposed improvement, even when new, may not be the highest and best use of the land as though vacant, alternative uses should be considered. In some cases detailed market studies of such alternative uses are required.

If the value of the land at its highest and best use is different from the value of the land at its proposed use, external obsolescence is evident. While an analysis of alternative uses would not affect market value, it may affect investment decisions about the type of project that is most desirable.

Addressing the Reasonably Probable and Appropriately Supported Aspects of the Highest and Best Use Definition

Underlying all highest and best use analyses are the issues of reasonable probability and adequate support. Questions pertaining to these issues are frequently asked in the analysis for two reasons:

- To select use alternatives that should be tested, and
- To judge the appropriateness of conclusions from the application of each of the highest and best use criteria

This discussion presents both the theory and procedures necessary to understand and apply highest and best use analysis techniques in valuation appraisal assignments. The nature of the property and the market in which it is located often narrow the use question quickly. Although the same criteria are applicable in simple and complex highest and best use analyses, the scope of work needed to test a property's ability to meet the four criteria varies. Consideration of reasonably probable and adequate support for alternative uses, therefore, is crucial for appraisers in determining the appropriate depth of highest and best use analyses.

Because reasonable probability of and adequate support for a selected use are explicitly required when defining highest and best use, it is important to understand when and how to address these definitional aspects. Precise measures have been established for testing the physical possibility, legal permissibility, financial feasibility, and maximum productivity of alternative uses, but determining reasonable probability and adequate support has been left to the appraiser's judgment. The six-step market analysis process presented in this book provides data and tools for supporting this conclusion and ensures its sound application in selecting uses to be tested and assessing the reasonableness of conclusions reached in the analysis.

This process requires greater or lesser detail, depending on the highest and best use analysis being performed. Many potential uses are eliminated through Levels A and B market analysis techniques. When alternative uses are highly competitive, however, a detailed Level C analysis is often required.

The initial assessment of reasonable probability and adequate support is based on an analysis of market acceptability. Information on market acceptability is taken from the property productivity analysis (a step in the market analysis process) and from a preliminary analysis of demand in an identified market area. Because any alternative use depends on current and expected land use and linkage characteristics and on the availability of a market segment with effective buying power for that use, the analysis of these characteristics is crucial in the initial judgment about the physically possible and legal uses that should be studied in detail in the highest and best use analysis. It is practical to investigate alternative uses for land or improvements existing on the land only when there is reasonable probability of current or anticipated market support for potential alternative uses. The mere existence of a building on a site does not preclude the probability of an alternative use.

At times it is mandatory for an appraiser to investigate extensively the reasonable probability of a zoning change. Reasonable probability in the market is a central consideration that determines the extent of the analysis required to judge whether an alternative use meets the criteria of legal permissibility. (See the vacant land case study for example of zoning change probability analysis.)

Adequate support for a reasonably probable, physically possible, and legally permissible use is the first issue addressed in assessing the financial feasibility of a use alternative. Sound judgment on the adequacy of support is based on an analysis of the supply, demand, and equilibrium characteristics of a defined market area and the buying power of identified market participants (market segment). Information from the results of this analysis allows the appraiser to estimate absorption and capture for the subject property at a specified use. For each alternative use, a use-specific demand, supply, and equilibrium analysis is required to provide the basis of absorption and capture estimates for the property at that use. The information derived from this analysis pertains to the likely financial performance of a property—for example, the property's potential income under a specified use. This income information is required to test financial feasibility.

Information and Measures to Test for the Four Criteria

Physical Possibility

The physical possibility of a use is determined by a study of the property itself. This study is conducted in the first part of the property productivity analysis (Step 1 of the six-step process).

Legal Permissibility

The legal permissibility of a use is determined by analyzing the public and private restrictions on the use of vacant and improved properties. This analysis should be conducted in the second part of the property productivity analysis (Step 1 of the six-step process). However, if a use resulting from a reasonably probable zoning change is considered, the analysis required for its inclusion as a legally permissible use to be tested further for financial feasibility can be extensive and involves a detailed study of locational attributes as well as an analysis of supply and demand.

The probability of a change in zoning requires special considerations. Zoning can take many forms in addition to traditional district zoning. Traditional zoning districts allow most uses by right and are usually straightforward. Other types of districts are more problematic for appraisers. Some examples include planned unit developments (PUDs), smart growth requirements, specific use permits, conditional use permits, and special districts (e.g., entrance way districts, historic districts). These districts vary in requirements, but most do not allow a use by right. Many of these types of zoning ordinances require approval of some form of site plan. Others allow uses subject to a site plan. A close review of these zoning ordinances is required because, in many cases, they allow the governing body the right to approve or disapprove the use. Thus, in many of these districts the use that will be permitted cannot be fully determined without a full zoning hearing by the governing body.

The governing body is usually required to approve some economic use of the land, but the extent is not certain. The land's current value is based on the market perception that such a change will be approved. Only when the approval of the plan is a virtual certainty does the value of the property actually change to the higher and better use.

Because of the various types of zoning ordinances (and politics) analysis of the reasonable probability of a zoning change is necessary in highest and best use analysis. A sample procedure for analyzing the probability of a zoning change is described as follows.

First, legally unacceptable uses such as those that are clearly not compatible with adjacent uses and uses that have a clear history of being denied by zoning authorities at the subject's location or similar locations in the city should be eliminated.

Next, a productivity analysis of the subject property should be completed, including a preliminary land development forecast of the subject's area. The uses that seem to be reasonable from an overall area land-planning standpoint should also be determined.

The land use alternatives that appear to be reasonable for the area can then be rated for the probability of a zoning change. If the subject is not zoned according to the appraiser's preliminary land development forecast, the probability of a zoning change could be based on the following considerations.

- The site is not physically suitable for the use currently allowed by zoning, but is physically suitable for the land development forecasted for the subject.
- The use forecast for the subject is compatible or can be designed to be compatible with adjacent land uses.
- The forecasted probable use of the subject conforms to the city's comprehensive plan.
- Conditions in the subject area have changed since the date the current zoning for the subject became active.
- A public good can be shown for the use of the subject property. This implies that at least some level of economic demand should be considered along with other public interests.
- There is a history of approved zoning changes to similar properties in similar locations in other parts of town.
- No nearby neighborhood association is known to oppose similar zoning change requests that would accommodate the forecast use for the subject.

The last step, as in all analytical studies, is to reconcile and make a final judgment on the probability of a zoning change. If all of the conditions listed above are met, the probability of a zoning change may be considered high. If only a few are met, more consideration as to the probability of a change is required. It is important at this point to remember that the probability of a zoning change is almost never 100%.

Financial Feasibility

If the reasonable probability of adequate support for a physically possible and legal use is evident in the subject property's market, the detailed information needed to substantiate this support is gathered when analyzing demand and supply and their optimum point of interaction for the property at that use. The demand, supply, capture, and absorption analyses required for testing financial feasibility depend on an accurate analysis of the property's productivity attributes (i.e., site, improvements, legal, and location attributes) as well as an analysis of the geographic and economic market in which the property is located. Consequently, a detailed and documented market analysis study is needed to establish adequate support for a use. The level of this study depends on the previously discussed factors. (See Chapter 2, Levels of Market Analysis.)

Even if adequate support for a use is established, it will not be financially feasible if the costs involved in developing the property for that use and ensuring its performance at that use outweigh the financial benefits. Therefore, before the financial feasibility of a use can be tested, costs must be accurately measured. These costs are development costs, land acquisition costs, the cost of obtaining necessary approvals and permits, and land building costs, which are some of the hard costs. In addition, soft costs must be included, such as architectural, engineering, management, and entrepreneurial costs.

For change in use to improved properties, only the reproduction or replacement costs expended for the alteration to the existing use are considered. These do not include the cost of any current structures that would continue to contribute to the value of the property at the alternative use.

The test for financial feasibility compares the numerical conclusions reached in the analyses of demand and supply and their interaction to the cost to produce and maintain the appropriately supported uses. This is done using financial models designed to measure specific aspects of profitability. Because these models depend on estimates of cost, income, risk, and expected rates of return, cost approach and income capitalization approach techniques are required in the analysis of financial feasibility.

Maximum Productivity

This test could also be called reconciliation, another word for the final analytical step to assess the data to determine the risk or reliability and confidence in all the data points used in the analysis. If all the data and analysis techniques are considered equally reliable, then the highest and best use that is maximally productive is the alternative that yields the highest value.

To ensure the accuracy of the maximally productive use conclusion, the appraiser may want to employ some form of reconciliation. For example, point estimates derived through financial feasibility tests may be misleading; occasionally ranges and causes for variance in the ranges will point to the need for qualitative analysis to determine the reasonableness of the highest and best use conclusion.

Mathematical Procedures for Determining Maximum Productivity for Alternative Uses

The model chosen to help guide the final highest and best use decision must realize three characteristics.

1. It must consider the amount and timing of all cash flows until the property reaches peak income performance, and some reasonable time period past this point. It must also consider whether or not the cash flows will continue to be realized over the economic life of the property.
2. It must take into account the appropriate risk for each use considered.
3. It must be able to consistently select the alternative property use that will produce the highest financial reward, assuming that all alternatives have the same probability for realizing the forecasted cash flows.

The maximally productive analysis applies financial decision models to each alternative use; the one calculated to return the greatest number of dollars is normally the highest and best use. In theory, these financial decision models are straightforward; the cost of the alternative use is considered the cash outflow, and the *NOI* or tract sell-off is considered cash inflow. The decision model is then applied to determine the alternative use that provides the greatest financial reward.

These models will work if the estimate of initial cost and the forecast of cash inflows are accurate and all alternative uses have an equal probability of being realized. Because this does not often occur in real estate, an additional analysis of the model's results is usually required. This extra analysis is called *risk analysis.*

Adjusting for Risk in Financial Analysis of Alternatives

The three methods for adjusting for risk in the financial analysis of forecasted alternatives are adjusting the discount rate, adjusting the forecast, and inspection and reconciliation.

The more uncertain the forecast, the higher the discount rate, and the more certain the forecast, the lower the discount rate. It can also relate to property type–that certain types of properties and markets are judged more risky by their nature. The property type discount rate can sometimes be found in national surveys of investor's yields by property type. As to the adjustment of the discount rate based on certainty of the market forecast, this is, for the most part, based on the appraiser's judgment, since he or she made the forecast. In some cases the risk can be compared to the risk of alternative investments.

The second method is to adjust the forecast. If each alternative forecast is adjusted where each has the same probability of occurrence, then the discount rates can remain the same. The adjustment can be accomplished in many parts of the analysis–from the initial employment/population forecast to the final subject capture estimate.

The last method is by inspection and reconciliation. By analyzing the data for one set of forecasts, that for whatever reason, is judged less reliable or less likely to occur, the analyst can simply choose the alternative judged to be the most probable outcome. For example if Alternative A's present value is $1 million but is not expected to lease up for eight years, while Alternative B's present value is $750,000 but is expected to lease up in four years, the appraiser makes a judgment that the shorter forecast has less risk and therefore picks Alternative B as the highest and best use. This is the same procedure that is used in the sales comparison approach in which the appraiser adjusts three comparable sales to arrive at an indicated value.

Problems in Demonstrating Highest and Best Use Decisions

The following problems have two purposes:

1) to provide examples of the application of appropriate mathematical models, and

2) to show the critical nature of the demand and capture forecast numbers (timing) in the models. These problems focus on decision points and judgments required in highest and best use analysis. Because many conclusions required to make appropriate judgments and decisions are derived in the market analysis of reasonably probable uses, these conclusions are presented as givens in these problems.

Exhibit 16.2 shows the highest and best use process when timing for use is incorporated into the conclusions.[3] The following problems will demonstrate the application of the timing for use element into the highest and best use decisions.

Exhibit 16.2 shows that the first procedure following the completion of the market analysis study is to test whether or not rents are currently high enough for new construction. This is part of the overall estimate of timing (absorption) conclusions. If the market analysis study concludes that the subject has current demand for users but current rents are too low for new construction, then new construction would not occur until sometime in the future when rents are higher. Exhibit 16.3 illustrates the mathematical procedure for calculating feasibility rent, the rent (income) required to attract new construction for a specific property type.

Mathematical Procedures for Alternative Use Financial Analysis

Two methods for financial analysis can be applied to determine which of the alternative uses of a property will provide the highest value. They are the sales comparison approach by user-end sales and the land residual method.

Sales Comparison Approach by "User-End" Sales Method

This method involves considering sales to users and then adjusting for timing until the use of the property is demanded. The user-end sale is defined as a sale to a company that immediately constructs the

---

3. Source: Richard Parli, Appraisal Institute instructor and author on market analysis and highest and best use.

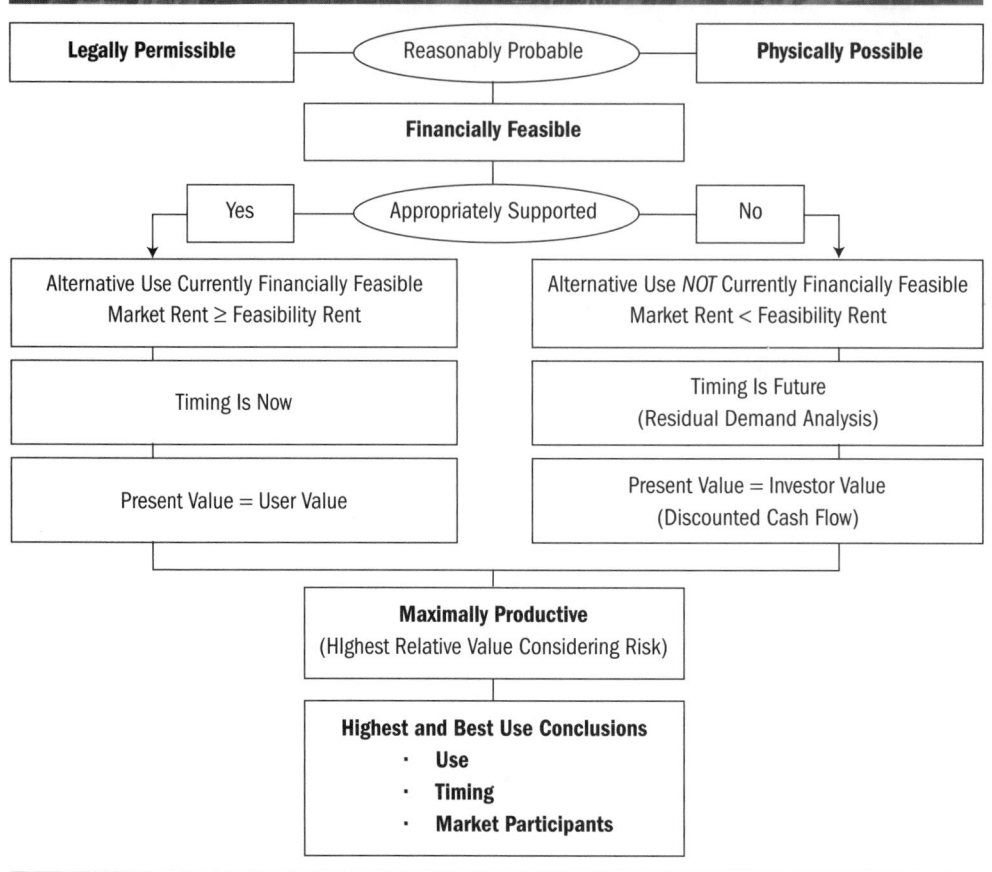

Exhibit 16.2 Highest and Best Use Decision Process—Highest and Best Use Financial Analysis Methods

Legally Permissible — Reasonably Probable — Physically Possible

Financially Feasible

Yes — Appropriately Supported — No

Alternative Use Currently Financially Feasible
Market Rent ≥ Feasibility Rent

Alternative Use *NOT* Currently Financially Feasible
Market Rent < Feasibility Rent

Timing Is Now

Timing Is Future
(Residual Demand Analysis)

Present Value = User Value

Present Value = Investor Value
(Discounted Cash Flow)

Maximally Productive
(HIghest Relative Value Considering Risk)

Highest and Best Use Conclusions
- Use
- Timing
- Market Participants

building that houses the business, e.g., selling to a major grocery store, which then builds the grocery store and shopping center. This is opposed to a speculative investor sale in which land is bought for holding with the hope of selling the land to a major grocery store or shopping center developer in the future.

The following example is a 10-acre vacant tract with three possible uses or timing for use alternatives. The site is fully developed and is ready for the building to be constructed. Thus, there is no additional site development cost for alternative use.

The following data conclusions were reached after a six-step process market study was performed and feasibility rent analysis. The appraiser forecasted that when the market was in balance, new construction would occur at the site of the subject property. The mid-point forecast for the alternative use of the property for apartment construction, construction of a retail shopping center, and multitenant office building are presented as follows.

Exhibit 16.3 Rent Required for New Construction

Data Inputs

Construction cost	$65.00 per sq. ft.	Building size:	100,000 sq. ft.
Land cost	$7.00 per sq. ft.	Land size:	435,600 sq. ft.
Operating expense	30% % of *EGI*	% Bldg. rentable:	100%
Overall rate	10%		
Normal vacancy	5%		

Calculation of Required Rent	**Sq. ft.**	**Cost per sq. ft.**	
Building and site improvement cost	100,000 ×	$65.00 =	$6,500,000
Land cost	435,600 ×	$7.00 =	$3,049,200
Total cost			$9,549,200

Calculation of Feasibility Rent

Required *NOI*	$9,549,200 ×	10% =	$954,920
Add operating expenses	(*NOI*/1 − Exp. ratio) − *NOI* =		$409,251
Effective gross income (*EGI*)			$1,364,171
Vacancy and collection loss			$71,798
Potential gross income			$1,435,970

Calculation of Minimum Required Rent for New Construction

PGI	**divided by**	**NRA**	**Req. rent**
$1,435,970		100,000 =	$14.36

Alternative Use 1: Apartments

- Yield rates: 10% to 12%
- Current market positive residual demand and rents currently feasible for new construction
- User land value $3.00 per sq. ft.
- Holding cost: $25,000 per year

Alternative Use 2: Retail Shopping Center

- Yield rates: 12% to 14%
- Market conditions
  - Three years to positive residual demand and for rents to be feasible for new construction
- User land value: $7.00 per sq. ft.
- Holding cost: $25,000 per year

Alternative Use 3: Multitenant Office Building

- Yield rate: 12% to 15%
- Market conditions
  - Six years to positive residual demand and for rents to be feasible for new construction
- User land values: $8.00 per sq. ft.
- Holding cost: $25,000 per year

Of the three alternatives, which represents the highest and best use? To answer this question, the user-end values must be discounted for timing of the sale and then the present value of all alternatives must

Exhibit 16.4   User Price Sales Method—Retail Shopping Center Alternative

Data Input

Income

User sale price	$7.00 per sq. ft.
Land size	10.0 acres
Year of sale	3

Expenses

Land holding/mgmt. cost	$25,000 per year

Financial Data

Discount rates

Low	12.00%
Mid	13.00%
High	14.00%

Analysis

Year	1	2	3	4
Sale price	$0	$0	$3,049,200	$0
Less holding expenses	$25,000	$25,000	$25,000	$0
Cash flow	($25,000)	($25,000)	$3,024,200	$0

	Discount rate	Present value	Value per sq. ft.
Present value @	12.00%	$2,110,315	$4.84
	13.00%	$2,054,220	$4.72
	14.00%	$2,000,082	$4.59

Exhibit 16.5   User Price Sales Method—Multitenant Office Alternative

Data Input

Income

User sale price	$8.00 per sq. ft.
Land size	10.0 acres
Year of sale	6

Expenses

Land holding/mgmt. cost	$25,000 per year

Financial Data

Discount rates

Low	12.00%
Mid	13.00%
High	14.00%

Analysis

Year	1	2	3	4	5	6
Sale price	$0	$0	$0	$0	$0	$3,484,800
Less holding expenses	$25,000	$25,000	$25,000	$25,000	$25,000	$25,000
Cash flow	($25,000)	($25,000)	($25,000)	($25,000)	($25,000)	$3,459,800

	Discount rate	Present value	Value per sq. ft.
Present value @	12.00%	$1,662,723	$3.82
	13.00%	$1,573,875	$3.61
	14.00%	$1,490,411	$3.42

be compared. The current highest value then becomes the highest and best use. The results of these present-value calculations on a per-square-foot basis are shown in the apartment alternative, retail, and multitenant office alternative that follows.

User Price Sales Method

The apartment alternative value is $3.00 per sq. ft.
                                                      −no discounting required

The model does not forecast real growth in land value for users (See Exhibits 16.4 and 16.5.). It forecasts that user economics will stay the same for at least five years out. In some situations, growth in user land values could be forecast to increase depending on the buying power expectations of the future market area and the cost and extent of alternative sites. However, the analyst should be careful not to appreciate "user-end" land value just on rising inflation, unless it can be shown in the market that inflation alone is driving up land prices. Also, the user-end land values for this model are based on economics of use rather than speculative land cycles bubbles that might be occurring in a market.

Based on the preceding financial analysis, the highest present value would be the retail-shopping alternative. The appraiser would also perform the same analysis to obtain a low and high forecast. Assuming that the high and low forecast yielded the same results, the highest and best use for the property would be:

Use: retail
Timing for use: 2 to 4 years
   Market participants
     ·   User   community retailers
     ·   Most probable buyer   speculative investor

This conclusion now sets the criteria for the appraiser to select comparable sales and make any adjustments in the valuation section of the appraisal. The most appropriate sales are vacant land sales to speculative investors who hope to resell the property to retail end-users in the next 2 to 4 years.

Land Residual Method

The land residual method requires an estimate of building cost and operating cost as well as lease up forecast. The start date and lease up forecast are derived from the six-step market analysis study. The model is called land residual because only the building costs are included at start date. Thus, the remainder present value is attributed to the land component, since it was not part of the cost.

The same alternatives presented in the first method are applied using a land residual discounted cash flow. The retail and office alternative DCF are shown because they are the two forecast land uses. (See Exhibits 16.6 and 16.7.) The apartment alternative is current, so land value is current as quoted in data for the sales comparison approach by the user-end sales method.

Exhibit 16.6   Retail Shopping Center Alternative—Land Residual Analysis

Data Input

Income

Rent/sq. ft. > $14.35

Expenses

Operating expenses	30% of *EGI*	
Holding expense	$25,000 per year	
(Mgmt., taxes, marketing)		

Site and Building Information

Bldg. total sq. ft.	100,000
Bldg. cost per sq. ft.	$65.00
Year built	3
Land size	10.0 acres

Year	Occupancy
1	0%
2	0%
3	0%
4	85%
5	95%
6	95%
7	95%

Financial Data

	Low	Mid	High
Discount rates	12.00%	13.00%	14.00%
Terminal cap rate	10.0%		
Selling expenses	3.00%		
Rent increase per year	3.0%—starting Year 2		
Cost increase per year	3.0%		

Analysis

Year	1	2	3	4	5
Potential gross income	$0	$0	$0	$1,568,063	$1,615,105
Less collection and vacancy loss	$0	$0	$0	$235,209	$80,755
Effective gross income	$0	$0	$0	$1,332,854	$1,534,350
Less operating expenses	$0	$0	$0	$399,856	$460,305
Less holding expenses	$25,000	$25,750	$26,523	$0	$0
Net operating income	($25,000)	($25,750)	($26,523)	$932,998	$1,074,045
Plus reversion					
Less building cost	$0	$0	($6,895,850)		
Total cash flow	($25,000)	($25,000)	($6,922,373)	$932,998	$11,492,281

	Discount rate	Land residual value	Land value/sq. ft.
Present value @	12.00%	$2,143,908	$4.92
	13.00%	$1,969,933	$4.52
	14.00%	$1,806,992	$4.15

Exhibit 16.7 Multitenant Office Alternative—Land Residual Analysis

Data Input

Income	Rent/sq. ft. > $19.00	Year	Occupancy
Expenses			
Operating expenses	35% of *EGI*	1	0%
Holding expense	$25,000 per year	2	0%
(Mgmt., taxes, marketing)		3	0%
		4	0%
Site and Building Information		5	0%
Bldg. total sq. ft.	110,000	6	0%
Bldg. cost per sq. ft.	$85.00	7	85%
Year built	6	8	95%
Land size	10.0 acres	9	95%

Financial Data	Low	Mid	High
Discount rates	12.00%	13.00%	14.00%
Terminal cap rate	10.00%	**Terminal Year**	8 Applied to Trailing Year
Selling expenses	3.00%		
Rent increase per year	3.0%	Increase Start Yr. 2	
Cost increase per year	3.0%		

Analysis

Year	1	2	3	4	5	6	7	8
Potential gross income	$0	$0	$0	$0	$0	$0	$2,495,569	$2,570,436
Less collection and vacancy loss	$0	$0	$0	$0	$0	$0	$374,335	$128,522
Effective gross income	$0	$0	$0	$0	$0	$0	$2,121,234	$2,441,915
Less operating expenses	$0	$0	$0	$0	$0	$0	$742,432	$854,670
Less holding expenses	$25,000	$25,750	$26,523	$27,318	$28,138	$28,982	$0	$0
Net operating income	($25,000)	($25,750)	($26,523)	($27,318)	($28,138)	($28,982)	$1,378,802	$1,587,244
Plus reversion								$15,396,271
Less building cost					$0	($10,839,213)		$0
Total cash flow	($25,000)	($25,750)	($25,523)	($27,318)	($28,138)	($10,868,194)	$1,378,802	$16,983,516

	Discount rate	Land residual value	Land value/sq. ft.
Present value @	12.00%	$1,881,837	$4.32
	13.00%	$1,661,698	$3.81
	14.00%	$1,462,909	$3.36

The land value hierarchy is the same as for the first method because retail is still the highest value of land. However, the values in the land residual method are slightly different than those for the user sales method because the land residual considers more detailed variables such as income and expenses, lease up time, and more specific cash flow timing. The highest and best use conclusion is also the same for all the discount rates, but the 13% discount rate is considered the most reliable, given the capitulation rate assumptions. Regardless, both models and all discount rates arrive at the same highest and best use conclusion that retail will produce the highest land value on the property.

Impact of Market Analysis and Highest and Best Use Decisions on Value

The following case study shows how the six-step market analysis process is used in highest and best use decisions and, in turn, its impact on the valuation conclusions.

The case study presents a number of land sales near the subject. The traditional approach would be to choose the sale located across the street on a corner like the subject; therefore, it would become the sale given the most weight. However, the six-step process concluded that demand for land put to use as the corner property across the street no longer exists. The question then arises whether the appraiser can ignore a sale located across the street simply because the forecast concluded that current demand was lacking.

A more detailed review of all the sales shows widely varying prices that depended on what they were used for, and not where they were located. Thus, if the sales comparables were chosen and adjusted only for location, the value conclusion would be one number; if they were selected based on use potential, then the value indication would be another number.

Case Study Description

The subject is a square, one-acre pad site located at the corner of two major thoroughfares and zoned for retail use. All utilities are in place. The site slopes gently and is not in a flood area.

Step 1: Property Productivity Analysis
Step 1.1: Site Analysis
The size of the subject restricts its use to small-scale development. Access and curb cut rights are favorable for retail development. The site's physical features are ideal for development, but its size restricts the competitiveness of alternative uses in this market since all recent developments-except fast food and convenience stores- are on much larger sites.

Step 1.2: Legal Analysis Summary

The site is zoned for retail use, but alternative zoning may be considered. The zoning is traditional pyramid district zoning; therefore, rezoning is not needed for less intensive alternative uses such as apartment. However, more intense uses, such as industrial, would not be allowed on the site. The subject site does not have any special legal advantage such as monopolistic zoning, deed restrictions in the area, or curb cut rights.

Step 1.3: Location Analysis

The subject is located on a corner pad site immediately adjacent to a retail shopping center. It has access to the street and separate interior access to the retail shopping center. It has excellent linkages to adjacent offices and to local apartment and single-family residential areas. The site is situated to intercept consumers going to the adjacent shopping center and is easily accessible during rush hour. In addition, linkage to the office area provides lunchtime consumers for the restaurants.

The subject area is rated one of the best growth areas in the city. Numerous new fast food and convenience stores have been built on sites similar to the subject's site. It is considered a highly competitive site for both of these uses. Alternative uses such as stand-alone retail or office buildings are not likely, given the large amount of local space in the market and the fact that few of these facilities are built on sites as small as the subject.

Conclusions of Property Productivity Analysis

Based on the physical, legal, and locational attributes of the subject site, all uses except fast food and convenience stores are eliminated from further study.

Step 2: Market Delineation

The site is located next to neighborhood shopping center at a major intersection. Thus, its trade area is near residential and daytime employment in the area.

Steps 3, 4, & 5: Demand, Competition, and Market Conditions

Step 3.1: Inferred Demand

The following summarizes the major inferred demand indicators.

- Retail growth in the city is increasing.
- Local convenience stores and fast food restaurants are doing more business than any similar small-scale retail enterprise in the city.
- Recent land sales in the subject's immediate market area are set to be developed with both convenience stores and fast food restaurants.
- Citywide population is increasing.
- The level of disposable income in the subject's immediate market area is one of the highest in the city.
- Nearby shopping centers and office buildings are more than 90-percent occupied.

- Very few major corners have more than one new convenience store.

Step 3.2: Fundamental Demand and Market Conditions Analyses

The conclusions of the fundamental demand and market conditions analysis are as follows.

Convenience store demand is high in the city and supply is low, so a positive marginal demand exists, given the broad study area. However, in the subject's submarket (primary market area of one mile), the current two convenience stores will be able to meet the convenience store demand for the next four to seven years.

For use as a fast food restaurant, demand is high in the city, while supply is low. The immediate market area of the subject also has high demand and low supply for fast food (marginal demand is positive).

Step 6: Subject Capture Analysis

The subject capture analysis determined that if a convenience store were built on the subject site, it would probably capture its pro rata share with the convenience store across the street. This capture is approximately half of what the typical convenience store would require to operate profitably.

If a fast food restaurant were built on the subject site, it would be expected to capture its pro rata share of the current market, which is considered more than enough to operate profitably.

Step 7: Highest and Best Use Financial Analysis

A yield rate in the 11% to 15% range is considered representative of the subject property and the market forecast risk. The final range or point estimate must be based on the capture forecast and the risk associated with each alternative. Exhibit 16.8 shows five recent user-end land sales that are identical to the subject in size, utilities, curb cuts permits, zoning, access, location, and market area served.

Highest and Best Use Financial Analysis of Alternatives

The highest and best use decision depends on the analysis of future demand. The fast food alternative would use Sales 2, 3 and 4, and there would be no discounting because demand would be current. Therefore, the value for this alternative use would be $10 per sq. ft.

For the convenience store alternative, however, it would have to be discounted for holding time, if the appraiser has confidence in the forecast. The following shows these calculations:

Value by Convenience Store Alternative

Future value of site:	$16 per sq. ft.
Timing for user sale:	4 to 7 years—say, 5 years
Most optimistic discount rate:	11%
Present value:	$8.65 per sq. ft.

Exhibit 16.9 shows this analysis.

Exhibit 16.8 Comparable User-End Land Sales

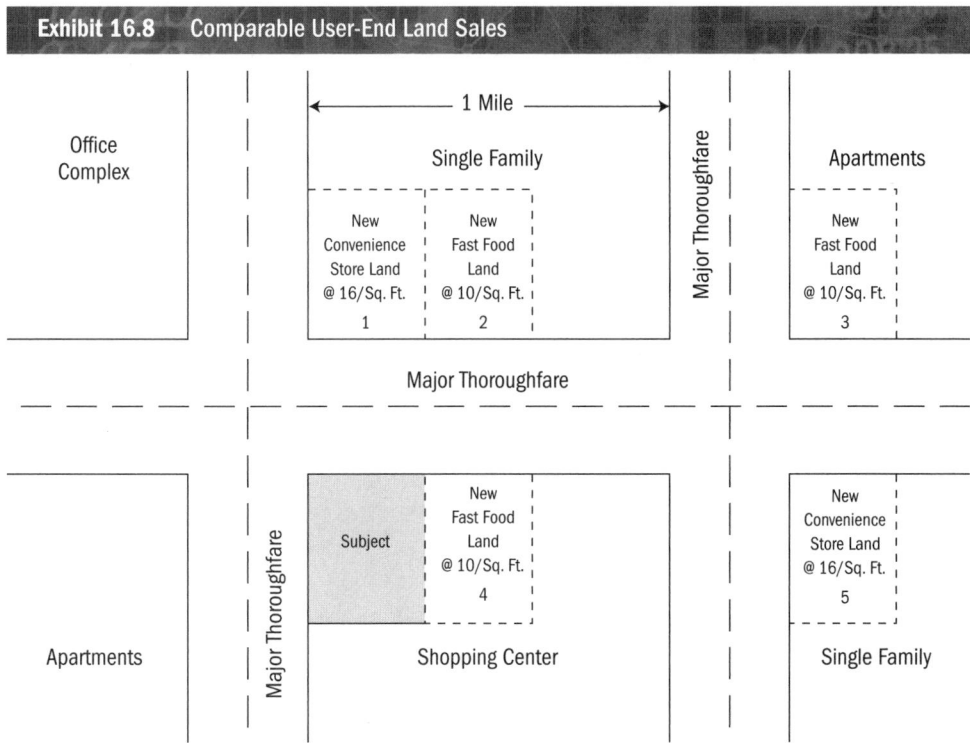

Not to scale.

Exhibit 16.9 User Price Sales Method—Convenience Store Alternative

Data Input

Income

User sale price	$16.00 per sq. ft.
Land size	1.0 acres
Year of sale	5

Expense

Land holding/mgmt. cost	$10,000 per year

Financial Data

Discount rates

Low	11.00%
Mid	12.00%
High	13.00%

Analysis

Year	1	2	3	4	5	6	7
Sale price	$0	$0	$0	$0	$696,960	$0	$0
Less holding expenses	$10,000	$10,000	$10,000	$10,000	$10,000	$0	$0
Cash flow	($10,000)	($10,000)	($10,000)	($10,000)	$686,960	$0	$0

	Discount rate	Present value	Value per sq. ft.
Present value @	11.00%	$376,653	$8.65
	12.00%	$359,426	$8.25
	13.00%	$343,110	$7.88

Highest and Best Use Conclusion

Thus, based on the preceding financial analysis of alternatives and the confidence in the alternative use forecast, the highest and best use of the subject property would be:

Use: restaurant

Timing for use: current

    Market participants:

       ·   User of space: fast food

       ·   Most probable buyer: user—business

Value Conclusions

Based on fast food highest and best use conclusion, the market value of the property as of the date of the appraisal would be about $10 per square foot, based on the fast food comparable sales.

CHAPTER 17

Mixed-Use Vacant Land

Chapter Objectives

- To define mixed-use vacant land and its related market forces
- To discuss the challenges in appraising vacant land
- To apply market analysis to mixed-use vacant land using the case study approach
- To develop a highest and best use reconciliation for a mixed-use vacant property

Introduction

In valuing vacant land, appraisers often face challenges involving zoning, availability of comparables and their appropriateness, and problems related to economic feasibility and timing of land use. Zoning issues surface when the most probable use of a property is not the same as the use as it is currently zoned. For instance, when properties located near the subject that are developed under the same permissible use experience high vacancy rates, the subject's use may be inappropriate, and a different one may be indicated.

Problems related to the availability of comparables can arise when the only comparable sales available to the appraiser involve buyers who had a specific use or uses in mind for the properties they purchased. If the subject's highest and best use, however, is as a long-term holding, then the properties with which it is compared are not truly comparable, requiring a significant time adjustment. The appraiser's dilemma lies in supporting a time adjustment without the benefit of having recent sales of very similar properties.

Challenges pertaining to the appropriateness of comparables occur when properties that represent truly comparable sales are difficult to identify, especially when the use or timing of the use for the subject has not been established.

Finally, difficulties related to economic feasibility and the timing of land use arise when appraisers are required by clients, and sometimes by professional standards, to support the economic feasibility and probable timing of the land use when recent comparable sales to users are lacking.

In addition to these problems, a property that could be classified as multiuse in combination with other uses raises the question of which mix of uses represents the combination that will produce the highest land value. These are only a few of the many problems that confront appraisers of vacant land. The focus of this chapter is on estimating the optimum mix of land uses in performing a valuation appraisal.

The highest and best use determination is a special challenge in appraising vacant urban land. Sometimes the highest and best use is apparent, but the timing for that use is difficult to establish, and timing has a great effect on value. This is illustrated by an appraisal assignment for a difficult piece of vacant land in which an appraiser was advised to talk to the market to determine its value. In doing so, he consulted the oldest real estate salesman in town. When the appraiser asked what the land was worth, he was told, "It depends on what you can use it for." The salesman knew how to value land, but because vacant land has no income stream, its current value must be derived from its future use.[1]

To reflect value accurately, comparable sales must have a similar use potential and similar timing for that use. Timing refers to the absorption of the completed property. It is also a critical element of the development approach to value, a variant of the income capitalization approach to be used to support the sales comparison, and also as an alternative to the sales comparison approach when sales data are unavailable. The most critical part of the development approach is supporting the anticipated timing of development.

An appraisal's complexity increases when the subject has mixed-use potential. Excess vacancies in nearby properties under the use or uses allowed by the current zoning may indicate that another use, or combination of uses, should be considered for the property.

The nature of demand for raw land varies with the motives of its most probable buyers. For instance, the dynamics of a market in which land parcels are sold to user-investors in anticipation of development may be very different from those of a market in which tracts of vacant land are held by speculator-investors. A user-investor will either purchase and develop the property immediately, or buy the land to develop it within a few years. This investor regards the land as a component of a property that will yield an anticipated return after it is developed. Speculator-investors consider an undeveloped parcel differently—they view it as a commodity to be resold. They will buy land only to resell it for

---

1. John S. Mitchell, "What Is Land Worth?" *Urban Land* (June 1988).

short-term gain. Short-term speculators are at the mercy of real estate cycles; they stand to reap big profits if the speculative land market goes up and incur large losses if the market goes down. Other speculator-investors use vacant land to warehouse capital assets over a long term.

The forces constituting the demand for vacant land generally interact with each other because they have a common interest. The ultimate success of the user-investor and the long-term investor depends on the ultimate user's demand for land. The success of a short-term speculator-investor is dependent on his or her ability to predict short-term market cycles, which may or may not be driven by user economics. Although economic theory suggests that short-term land markets are driven by the real demand of users, in reality other market forces are at work. Short-term market fluctuations reflect the real estate market's response to zoning and the availability of capital and the tendency of participants in these markets to make decisions based on incomplete information. Other short-term buyers are pure speculators of the resale market. As one successful land reseller said," I do not sell real estate, I sell illusions."

In the 1980s, for example, abundant investment capital increased the demand. In the 1990s, however, land users generated very little demand for land, and speculation slowed until the late 1990s created new sources of capital as occurred with the dot.com boom. In the 2000s the speculative land market again slowed, followed by new sources of capital from oil and natural resources. With each cycle, the land values rose, often based on speculation, but they eventually leveled off (or declined) based on the economics of what end-users could afford to pay for the land to use in a commercial property venture.

The activity of speculator-investors in short-term, boom markets often drives the prices of raw land up so high that they exceed what may be considered a reasonable economic cost to current user-developers. The resulting constriction of supply, however, sustains high prices. Eventually, user-investors may find the high land prices justified after the increasing pressure of user demand makes development economically feasible. On the other hand, if the pressure of user demand is insufficient to support the high prices, speculator-investors will likely lower their asking prices to bring them in line with user-investor economics. The user market maintains more uniform prices over time than the speculator market. For example, in 2004, retail grocery store anchor sites for neighborhood retail land sold to developers (end-users) in Denton County, Texas, for only slightly more than similar sites with similar demographics sold for in 1986. During this time, however, the speculative market has escalated and declined significantly three times. Thus, appraisers must understand not only the character of the short-term market for a vacant parcel of land, but also the long-term user demand for it. They can do so by asking the following questions:

- Is the market driven by user-investors or by speculator-investors?
- How do these two types of demand forces interact?

Land such as improved properties forces appraisers to analyze two markets simultaneously: the buy-sell market and the user market. In the long run, the economics of real estate have often shown that value, at some point in the future, will always be dependent on the economic constraints of the user market.

The case study presented in this chapter shows how market analysis can address these questions in an appraisal. The methodology used to determine the highest and best use of the parcel has been adapted from the technique described many years ago by Richard Peisner in his article, "Optimizing Profits from Land Use Planning."[2] To apply this technique, the appraiser obtains market data on the annual absorption rates for the specific uses and calculates the present value of the land under each use over the projection period. The appraiser examines the discounted land values from the various uses in conjunction with estimates of the acreage absorbable under each use to determine the mix of land uses that will bring the greatest return. The case study also illustrates the link between market/marketability analysis, highest and best use analysis, and the three approaches to value.

Case Study Description

An appraiser has been hired to estimate the market value of a 66-acre tract of vacant land with a potential for mixed use. The subject is located along two major thoroughfares in a rapidly growing metropolitan area. It is three-quarters of a mile west of a major north-south freeway lined with new, multistory office and retail buildings. It is about one-quarter of a mile south of a proposed north loop interchange, which will be completed in the next three to five years. The current zoning specifies office and retail use, but the highest and best use of the property may not correspond to the zoning. The vacancy rate for office and retail buildings in the overall metropolitan area is high.

The only comparables available are older sales of land bought by speculator-investors who anticipated a gain from its resale.

Over the past few years, development in the area approaching the subject tract has ceased. Until about three or four years ago, it had been booming, most notably just east of the subject on the north-south freeway. Even before the boom years, there was steady development in the general direction of the subject area. Recently, however, speculative activity has declined dramatically, while past speculative investment has restricted the available supply, driving up land prices. In terms of user-investor economics, the pressure of demand would have to increase substantially to justify the high land prices of the recent past.

Highest and Best Use Analysis

The analysis of highest and best use is a screening process for examining alternatives uses. The use considered most probable is selected

---

2. Richard B. Peisner, "Optimizing Profits from Land Use Planning," *Urban Land* (September 1982).

for further analysis. The study begins with an economic overview and scoping analysis. In this step the appraiser focuses the study and quickly eliminates the obvious alternatives that are not feasible.

The detailed part of the study begins with a productivity analysis of the subject tract. In this step the appraiser determines how the attributes of the tract define the range of possible uses and identifies the use that may be especially suitable. The subject's attributes include physical attributes (shape, size, contour, and drainage); legal and regulatory attributes (zoning and easements); and locational attributes (accessibility, linkages, adjacent land uses, relation to urban growth patterns, and locational ranking according to use-specific criteria). The analysis eliminates uses deemed inappropriate. Thus, it can be seen that the emphasis of the property productivity analysis of site and location is different for land than it is for an improved property with very little prospects for alternative use consideration. Exhibit 17.1 compares and contrasts the location analysis for improved property and vacant land.

Exhibit 17.1   Location Analysis

Improved Property Study Emphasis
- Static factors (roads, utilities, and rivers)
  The emphasis is on the competitiveness of the subject location for the current use.
- Dynamic factors (direction of growth issues)
  The emphasis is on the future competitiveness of the location for the current use.

Vacant Land Study Emphasis
- Static factors
  The emphasis is on the most likely potential use at some future time.
- Dynamic factors
  The emphasis is on the timing for use (also used as inferred demand data).

Uses that are not eliminated are examined in later steps, which are market delineation, supply and demand analysis, equilibrium analysis, and subject capture analysis. The appraiser considers the specific market for each probable use.

If it is clear that the subject site has mixed-use potential, the appraiser must specify the optimal land use plan, i.e., the mix of uses that will result in the highest return on the land, given the acceptable level of risk. Future area demand and the subject's probable capture rate are the major aspects of this study. In the final step, the appraiser estimates the value per acre of land under each type of land use (user value less development costs), the amount of acreage to be developed under each specific land use, and the timing for each use. The timing estimate is based on the marginal demand outlook for each land use, or the amount of acreage that is likely to be absorbed in the coming years. The appraiser uses projected absorption rates with financial analysis to determine the land-use mix that indicates the highest present value.

The six-step market/marketability and financial analysis of alternatives study process described provides the data input for the four tests of highest and best use. In the productivity analysis, the appraiser establishes that the use mix is physically possible and legally permissible. Location analysis rounds out the productivity study, linking it with the market analysis and subject capture step, which establishes a foundation for testing financial feasibility. The last step, in which the appraiser considers the mix of uses resulting in the highest present value, is a test of maximum profitability, which constitutes the fourth and final test of highest and best use.

The process applied in the case study is illustrated in Exhibit 17.2. The market/marketability analysis portion of the highest and best use analysis includes the six-step market/marketability study process that feeds into the financial analysis of alternatives and finally into the reconciliation and conclusion step for highest and best use.

Exhibit 17.2	Vacant Land Highest and Best Use Analysis Process

Step 1:   **Analyze property to eliminate uses and determine most probable use(s).**
- Perform a complete fundamental analysis such as an alternative use rating.
- Complete an inferred analysis by reviewing general data.

Steps 2, 3, 4, & 5:   **Perform complete market studies to determine the most probable timing in the market for new development.**
- Review general data and make an inferred estimate.
- Complete residual demand studies for uses found probable in Step 1.

Step 6:   **Estimate the subject capture.**
- Use inferred data such as case studies of similar tracts.
- Perform fundamental capture analysis by competitive tract rating.

Step 7:   **Complete a financial analysis of alternative land-use mixes to determine which use is highest value.**

Step 8:   **Perform highest and best use reconciliation and conclusions.**
- Use
- Timing (capture/absorption rates)
- Market participants
  - User(s) of space
  - Most probable buyer(s)

The graphic on the next page illustrates this process.

Case Study Application

Illustrated below is a highest and best use analysis as it would appear as part of a valuation appraisal of the 66 acres.

Figure 17.3   Highest and Best Use Analysis Process

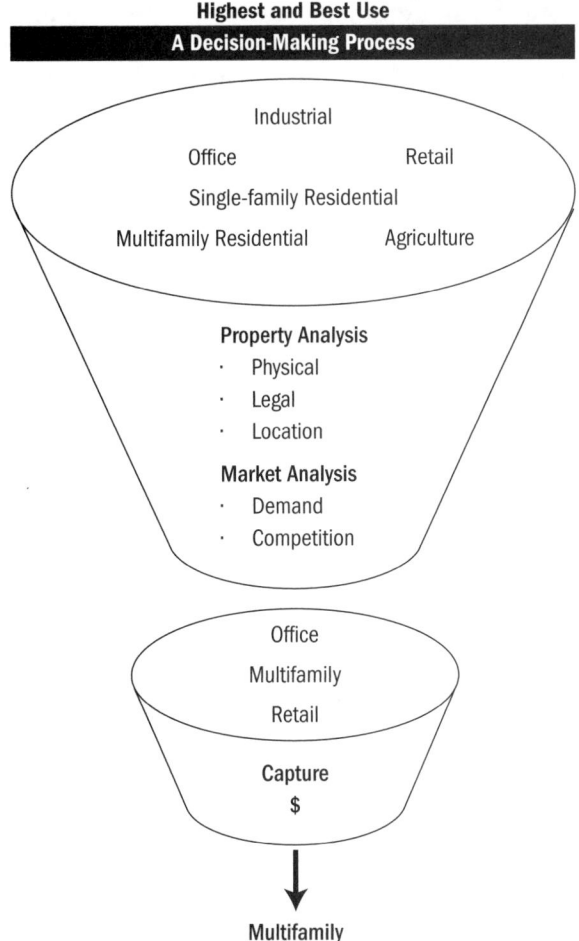

Highest and Best Use
A Decision-Making Process

Industrial

Office   Retail

Single-family Residential

Multifamily Residential   Agriculture

Property Analysis
· Physical
· Legal
· Location

Market Analysis
· Demand
· Competition

Office

Multifamily

Retail

Capture
$

Multifamily

Step 1: Property Productivity Analysis

Step 1.1: Site Analysis

In performing the site analysis, the appraiser identifies specific restrictions on the use of the site and potential opportunities to develop it under alternative land uses. The four factors to be considered in site analysis are:

- Immediate access to the site
- Physical restraints and/or advantages
- Immediately adjacent land uses
- Legal restraints and/or advantages

Site Description

Among the physical characteristics of the subject tract are its shape, size, contour, and drainage. The subject is a 66-acre rectangular site aligned with the surrounding grid of land parcels. Its dimensions are approximately one-half mile (2,640 feet) by one-fifth of a mile (1,090 feet). Its slope is moderate and does not present any impediment to development. An existing pond on the site is fed by a creek that flows across a narrow floodplain. The pond could be used for retention to capture additional runoff after the site is developed. However, constructing such a pond would reduce the developable area of the tract by at least two and one-half acres. An alternative solution would be to fill in the pond with landfill and channelize the creek with culverts. Current electricity, water, and sewer service is adequate.

Several regulatory constraints and legal entitlements are associated with the subject tract. The site is subject to two different zoning districts. The frontage along the two thoroughfares is zoned for general retail use, while the remainder is zoned for high-density office use. The city planning department is not averse to changing the zoning, either by reducing the allowable density to accommodate multifamily apartments or by increasing the density to allow for light industry (i.e., office showrooms and industrial flex space). Local floodplain regulations require that runoff be contained.

Analytic Process

One way to perform a site analysis is to develop a topographical map of the subject, outlining features that represent restraints on its use and features that present opportunities for its development. These features can be mapped individually on transparencies, which are then overlaid to produce a graphic analysis of site areas where opportunities or problems may arise. This procedure is similar to the McHarg overlay technique.[3] The checklist shown in Exhibit 17.4 features the characteristics typically studied in site analysis. Exhibit 17.5 on page 413 depicts the characteristics of the subject site.

Conclusions Derived from the Graphic Analysis of the Site

The following conclusions from the typographical analysis of the site are listed as follows:

- Views and slopes. The northern half of the tract is suitable for residential development.
- Access points. Curb cuts are required 250 feet from major corners, but this requirement should not limit land use. If an interior east-west street is desired, it will have to connect to Virginia Avenue on the west side of the subject. This street cannot be extended to an eastward connecting street, however, because there are existing apartments to the east of the subject. The interior street cannot exit to the south since the connection with New York Avenue, a major

---

3. I. McHarg, *Design with Nature* (New York: Natural History Press, 1969).

Exhibit 17.4   Site Analysis Checklist

Characteristic	Comment
Slopes	The slopes of different areas of the site are shown on the map. Analyzing them provides a basis for identifying probable uses. For example, slopes of less than 2% are best suited for retail and industrial uses. Those of more than 15% are not recommended for road grades. Steep slopes may be preferred for residential development.
View	View is a function of both the site characteristics and the off-site perspective. The subject is located at the top of a ridge. The primary concern is whether the off-site view puts the site at a disadvantage. A good view is considered positive for residential, office, and restaurant uses.
Access	Access points to a vacant tract is controlled by curb-cut regulations and the parcel's alignment with existing or platted streets. These features should be marked on the site map. A connection with the road may be required at a specific point, but in most cases, the alignment with interior roads is flexible.
Floodplain	Usually a 100-year flood line is drawn on the site map. Existing or planned ponds and other drainage features should be indicated as well.
Adjacent land uses	Adjacent land uses go a long way in determining the ultimate use of the land. In the site analysis, these uses are usually labeled and their borders with the subject are measured. The exact land use should be cited. In the subject case, apartment buildings are a nearby land use. The land immediately adjacent to the subject is an open, landscaped area, which could be used by occupants of the subject for recreation. This abutting area helps shape the land-use possibilities for the subject.
Legal/regulatory	Zoning is high intensity but would require a change for lower intensity uses such as apartments. Floodplain regulations specify containment of runoff. A right-of-way will run with the road that connects with St. James Place, the tract's western border. (The final location of this road is the developer's option.)
Noise	Sites near major generators of noise may have a noise contour above 65 decibels. A 65-decibel contour is the recognized limit for residential uses. Higher levels indicate that noise abatement measures will be required to accommodate other uses.
Utilities	The capacity of, distance to, and access points for utilities should be marked on the site map. For large tracts under less costly uses such as residential, the access point is usually located in the area developed during the first phase of the project. High-intensity land uses such as office and retail use can sometimes support the higher costs of an off-site extension. The interior area of the subject tract has substantial residential potential, but the most probable use of the front of the tract is for retail development. The absence of any current demand for a retail use could change the prospects for residential land use. If the demand for residential use is immediate but the cost of an off-site utility extension makes it unfeasible to develop the back part of the tract at this time, then the retail use at the front of the site may have to be reconsidered. If the tract has an alternative use as a long-term holding, future demand will have to be high enough to justify the holding costs.
Tree cover	The portion of a site covered by trees should be marked on the site map. The cost of clearing is included among construction costs. Tree-covered areas are a positive amenity for uses such as residential subdivisions, apartments, and office parks.
Soil/rock	Underlying soils and rock strata that differ significantly from those of competitive tracts can impact land use. Extensive rock deposits can make construction of sewer lines very expensive and discourage residential use. High shrink-swell type soils can present an obstacle to industrial land use. This feature is considered in relation to the competition and the engineering costs to correct deficiencies.

thoroughfare, would be too close to another major north-south street, St. James Place. Therefore, the only possible exit would be at Virginia Avenue. To avoid the cost of bridging the creek, the interior street should be located to the west of the creek area.

- Floodplain. The amount of area in the floodplain raises questions about the development costs. To justify the costs of floodplain modification, the land use selected must be fairly intensive and well supported. The situation is further complicated because the city requires retention features for floodplain modification, i.e., the runoff flow must meet the specific parameters set for residential use. The creek and existing ponds could be worked into the design of the tract and provide scenic amenities for residential and possibly office use. However, these features divide the tract into two halves: one to the north of the creek, and another to the south.

- Abutting land uses. To the west of the subject is single-family residential use, to the east are apartments, and to the south are retail/office units, which are 70% occupied. The land to the north is vacant but zoned for office use. For the subject, the land use question is whether the higher-density uses will connect from south to north, or the less-intense residential uses will connect from east to west. This question cannot be resolved in the site analysis, in which the appraiser identifies only the site and abutting land uses and indicates that either alternative or some combination of uses is possible.

- Noise contours. The commuter airport near the subject creates decibel readings of more than 65 in the southeast corner of the site. This suggests that a residential use for this area is doubtful.

- Utilities. The access point for utilities can be a major factor in phasing the development of large tracts. In this case, utility connections have already been installed at the site, so utility access is not a determinant of use.

- Natural features (e.g., trees and soils). The presence or absence of certain natural features can significantly influence land use decisions. Trees are not found on the subject site, which is typical of the area. The subject soils have high shrink-swell properties, but so do the soils of all the competitive tracts in this area. The shrink-swell problem can be corrected with proper engineering. Thus, these features have no impact on alternative land uses.

Public Planning and Zoning

The zoning of the subject and adjacent areas and the probability of a zoning change are analyzed next. The portion of the subject tract along the two thoroughfares is currently zoned for general retail use, and the remainder is zoned for office use. The adjacent areas to the east and northeast of the subject are zoned for multifamily, neighborhood retail, and office uses. The area to the west of the subject has a more residential character, with retail uses limited primarily to major intersections of the proposed north loop freeway.

The area just southeast of the subject is zoned for light industrial/office park use. This area has been platted, and streets were finished within the last year and a half, but no lots have been sold yet. South of the subject is a development of single-family and patio homes with some garden office facilities. Northeast of the subject, at the intersection of the north-south freeway and the proposed new north loop freeway, a tract has been zoned for a shopping mall. Zoning to the northeast, northwest, and west of the subject is predominantly residential mixed with some commercial uses to support residential development.

Exhibit 17.5 Site Analysis Map

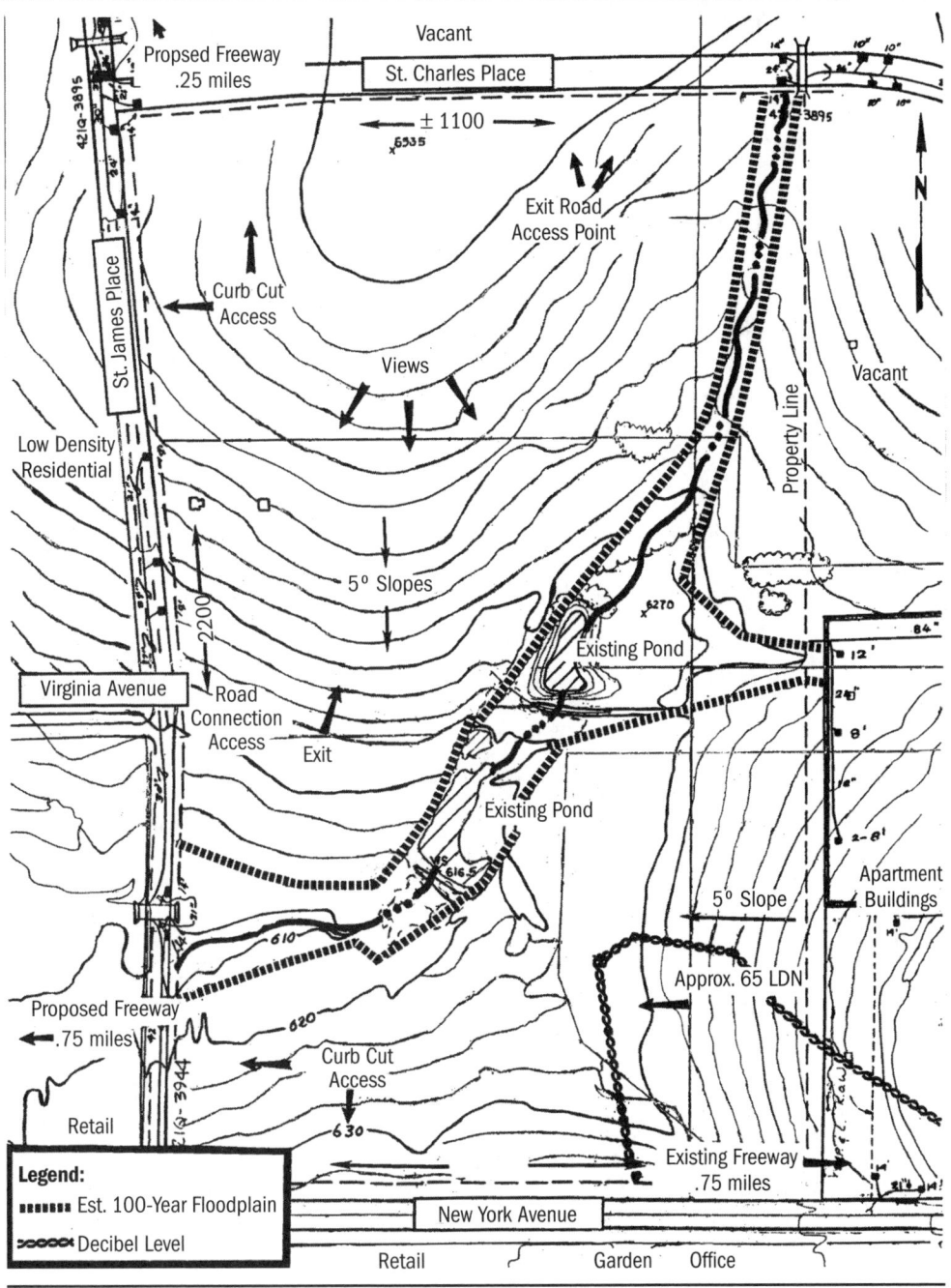

The analyst must consider the likelihood of a change in the current zoning of the subject and adjacent sites. The first step in this analysis is to eliminate uses that are clearly not compatible with existing uses in the area as well as those that have been previously denied in the subject area or comparable areas of the city. The second step is to rate the probable alternative uses for the subject tract. In doing so, the analyst considers the following conditions:

- The subject site may not be suitable for the use under the current zoning, but it is physically suitable for other use.
- The new zoning use is compatible with adjacent land uses.
- The new zoning use conforms to the city's comprehensive land use plan.
- Conditions in the subject area have changed since the current zoning became effective.
- The new zoning use of the subject contributes to the public good (e.g., a police station, firehouse, playground, and school) and is supported by civic or public interests.
- Zoning changes for comparable properties in similar locations in other parts of the city have been approved.
- No nearby neighborhood association opposes the new zoning use.

If the new zoning alternative use or uses satisfy all these conditions, the probability of a zoning change may be considered very high. If some of these conditions are met, the probability is moderate. The analyst should note, however, that the probability of a zoning change is almost never 100% certain.

The typical approval time should also be considered. If it is extremely long, the estimated timing for the use should account for the time required for rezoning. Exhibit 17.6 shows this rating analysis.

Alternative Zoning Analysis Conclusion

The previous exhibit shows the conclusions of the rating score, which is interpreted in light of the probability of zoning for the various uses. Exhibit 17.7 shows the scoring guidelines used in this analysis.

The rating conclusion was that office and retail zoning (as currently zoned) is considered good zoning policy for the area. The residential uses are also probable for the area, but the apartments will take more site planning to accommodate anticipated neighborhood opposition to them. The industrial use is considered moderately low probability to secure zoning. Thus, in conclusion, the zoning and public plans for the subject area are conducive to mixed-use development of the tract.

Site and Zoning Analysis Conclusions

Exhibit 17.8 summarizes the site analysis. So far, the analysis has focused only on the specific site. Further analysis of the subject's location may alter the conclusions presented in this exhibit.

Exhibit 17.6 Probability Analysis of Changing Zoning

Decision Factors	Retail*	Office*	Industrial	Apts.	Single Family	Importance Rank
	Zoning Alternatives					**Importance**
Site features suitable for land use allowed by zoning	3	2	1	3	2	3
Compatible with adjacent land use	3	1	-3	3	1	6
Conforms to comprehensive plan	3	3	-3	1	-3	4
Change in conditions since zoned	0	0	0	0	0	1
Public good shown	1	1	2	0	0	2
History of similar zoning approval in area	3	3	-2	3	3	5
Neighborhood support	1	1	-3	-2	2	7
Gross Score	14	11	-8	7	5	
Total Weighted Score	63	48	-54	32	29	

Rating Criteria

Description of Score	Score
Highly positive	+3
Moderately positive	+2
Slightly positive	+1
Neutral, no impact	0
Slightly negative	-1
Moderately negative	-2
Highly negative	-3

* Current zoning on property.

Exhibit 17.7 Rating Guidelines for Rezoning Probability

	Score
Highly probable for rezoning	over 60
Moderately probable for rezoning	30 to 60
Slightly positive for rezoning	0 to 29
Low probability for rezoning	-1 to -29
Moderately low probability for rezoning	-30 to -60
Very low probability for rezoning	over -60

Exhibit 17.8 reveals that many site features are conducive to residential development of the northern half of the subject. The southern half of the tract appears to have greater potential for retail and office use, primarily because it fronts one of the most heavily traveled east-west thoroughfares in the city, and properties across the street have been developed under similar uses. Nevertheless, the site analysis has not eliminated any uses, although industrial ranks very low, and single-family ranks low at least on the southern half. Therefore, the appraiser must continue to consider the full range of usage possibilities for the subject. The next step, location analysis, will help focus the study on the most probable uses.

Exhibit 17.8 Site Analysis for Alternative Uses

Factor	Single-Family	Apartment	Retail	Office	Industrial
			Impact on Alternative Uses		
Northern Half of Tract					
Slopes	1	2	0	0	-2
View	2	2	0	1	0
Access	1	2	-3	-2	2
Floodplain	1	2	-2	-1	-2
Abutting land uses	3	3	-3	-2	-3
Noise	1	1	1	1	1
Utilities	1	1	1	1	1
Trees/soils	0	0	0	0	0
Legal features	3	2	1	1	-1
Total Score	13	15	-5	-1	-4
Southern Half of Tract					
Slopes	1	2	0	0	-2
View	1	2	0	1	0
Access	-1	2	3	2	2
Floodplain	1	2	-1	-1	-2
Abutting land uses	-3	2	3	2	1
Noise	-3	-1	0	0	0
Utilities	1	1	1	1	1
Trees/soils	0	0	0	0	0
Legal	1	2	3	3	3
Total Score	-2	12	9	8	3

Rating Scale	
Highly important for use	3
Moderately important for use	2
Slightly important for use	1
On balance, neither negative or positive	0
Slightly negative for use	-1
Moderately negative for use	-2
Highly negative for use	-3

Step 1.2: Location Analysis

The locational attributes of real estate indicate where growth is most likely to occur. The demand analysis performed in Steps 3, 4, and 5 will help the appraiser estimate the amount of growth that might be expected. Areas with locational features most favorable to growth tend to capture growth at a faster rate than other areas.

Both static and dynamic features comprise location. Static features include linkages and land use associations. Linkages refer to the movement of people, goods, services, and information to and from the subject site and are measured in terms of time and cost. Land-use associations may be complementary or incompatible. In terms of growth, complementary uses have a positive impact, while incompatible uses have a negative effect.

Because locational relationships change over time, the dynamic aspects of location also need to be addressed. Dynamic features include the character of urban growth as well as its direction and rate.

Step 1.2(1): Describe the Subject's Location

Major thoroughfares provide access to the 66-acre site along its southern and western borders. A secondary street provides access along the northern side of the tract. Commuters traveling from suburban communities on the north to the office park districts farther south account for much of the traffic on the thoroughfares. To provide direct access to the site, curb cuts will have to be made along the two thoroughfares, and an east-west access road to the interior of the tract will have to be built to line up with an adjacent east-west secondary street.

Linkages with other sectors in the metropolitan area are readily available. A major north-south freeway lies three-quarters of a mile to the east, and the site of a proposed north loop freeway is approximately one-fourth of a mile to the north. The freeway should be completed in three to five years. The subject does not have direct access to these freeways, but linkages to the subject will be improved with the completion of the freeway. The traffic count in the immediate vicinity of the subject is approximately 20,000 vehicle trips per day and is expected to double in the next 10 to 15 years. Traffic congestion in the area could, therefore, become a problem and might negatively impact the tract's potential for residential use.

The subject is located along the northern periphery of a major metropolitan area. Land uses in the immediate area include residential and strip commercial development. To the north and the northeast, there are moderate-income, family-type apartment complexes. Middle-income residential communities extend five miles to the northwest of the tract. Beyond these communities lie higher-income neighborhoods. A middle-income, single-family, patio-home development is located to the southwest of the subject. If residential development is considered for the tract, it would likely appeal to middle-income, rather than upper-income, residents.

Retail facilities to the south of the subject include a local shopping center, several strip developments, and convenience stores. These represent support facilities for the residents in the area.

Light industrial flex space has been planned for an area one-half mile southeast of the subject. This area was platted with streets a year ago, but no lots have been sold yet; nor has any construction started.

With respect to metropolitan growth patterns, the tract lies three-quarters of a mile west of the north-south freeway, a major corridor lined with multistory office buildings. This office corridor has an excellent reputation both locally and nationally. The completion of the proposed north loop freeway northwest of the subject tract will likely stimulate further office development in the vicinity.

An understanding of the metropolitan matrix and major regional employment centers also helps the appraiser assess the probable character of development for the tract. The central business district, which is approximately 20 miles south of the site, contains 30 million square feet of office space. A second concentration of office buildings three to four miles southeast of the subject is centered around an interchange on the north-south freeway. The office corridor that lines the freeway is an extension of this node. The second office district contains 10 million square feet of office space as well as retail and light industrial space. A third office node is located eight miles west of the subject tract. It has 10 million square feet of office space plus retail, hotel, and light industrial space.

Step 1.2(2): Apply the Location Analysis

The location analysis focuses on probable future land use(s) for the subject, given the broad growth trends in the area. Growth trends are analyzed in a number of ways. In one analytic approach, locational factors are examined under five major categories:

- Existing land use and linkages
- Direction of growth and land-use intensity
- Growth rate (dynamic attributes)
- Zoning and planning
- Neighborhood land-use forecast

Different analytical techniques can be applied. The example shown here is based on a graphic analysis in which the appraiser maps the specific elements being considered, e.g., land-use linkages, land-use patterns, and historical growth rates. As a final step, a narrative summary and future land-use map are compiled.

Land Uses and Linkages—Projected Roads and Thoroughfares

Exhibit 17.9 is a map of existing roads in the area of the subject and those that will be completed within the next five years. A five-year time frame was selected because the subject is located in an area where substantial development has occurred within the last five years. If the land use of a tract located some distance from current development were being considered, then roads projected for completion in five to 10 years might be mapped. For still more distant tracts, roads planned 20 years into the future could be mapped using the city's long-range thoroughfare plan as a guide. Most roads indicated on the long-range thoroughfare plan will not be in place until after the subject property is developed, so this plan is given little weight in the location analysis. Land use is influenced more by immediate linkages than by linkages that may exist in 20 years. (The 20-year plans of some cities represent long-range wish lists rather than expectations of thoroughfares that will be actually completed 20 years in the future.)

A land-use map is important for identifying potential critical mass locations, which are sometimes called major intensity nodes. Urban growth models suggest that growth occurs along transportation linkages and that concentrations of different socioeconomic groups also influence growth patterns. Exhibit 17.9 shows land-use linkages and the moderate- and high-income residential developments located in the subject area. The only new road of significance is the proposed north loop freeway to be completed just north and west of the subject in the next few years. This new freeway will help link the subject to other complementary land uses and open up new markets for the subject. On the downside, more intense land uses may develop at the major

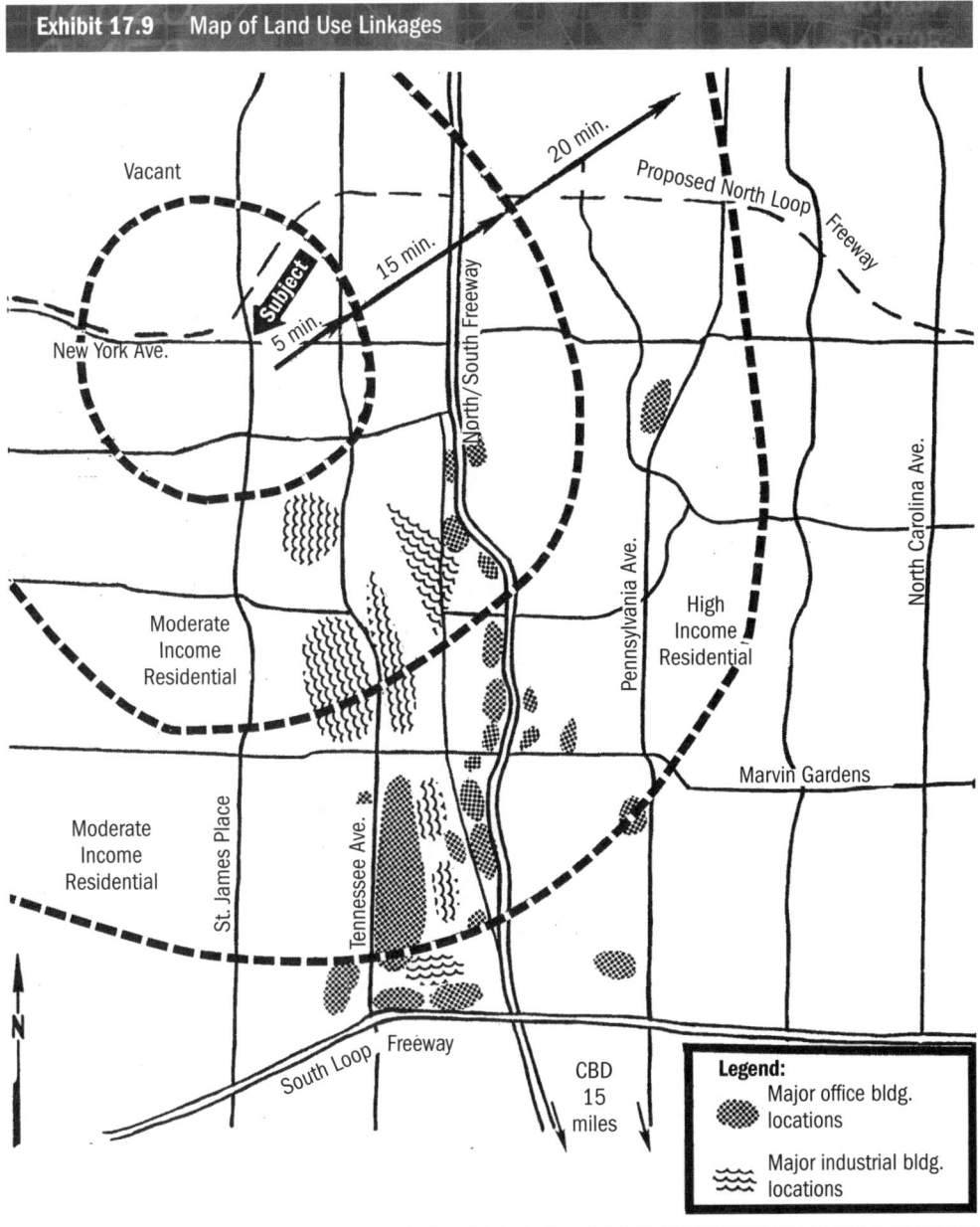

Exhibit 17.9   Map of Land Use Linkages

intersections of the new freeway and draw clientele away from the retail node on the southwest corner across from the subject that is currently developing. Such development would also tend to relegate the retail uses around the subject to small-scale, drive-by retail establishments rather than larger destination retail.

Direction of Growth and Intensity of Land Use

The analyst identifies current growth trends, focusing on patterns in the intensity of use, to determine if the subject will be located in a high-, medium-, or low-intensity area. In doing so, he considers whether the subject will be located in an area where intense land uses such as multistory office or retail use dominate. Again, the analytical technique demonstrated is graphic, mapping land uses by intensity. The following categories are identified on the existing land use map (Exhibit 17.10):

- High-intensity commercial–multistory office buildings and regional retail centers.
- Moderate-intensity commercial–concentrations of garden office (e.g., doctors' offices, and insurance offices), community retail, and restaurant facilities. Small, scattered, neighborhood retail uses are not usually included in this category because they do not typically set the growth pattern of an area. Of course, there may be exceptions. If neighborhood retail use is able to expand in one location, it may evolve into a community retail node. When such situations are found, they are identified on the map as moderate-intensity commercial.
- Moderate-intensity industrial–industrial park and flex space buildings. All industrial land uses in the subject area are considered to be in this category. The graphic analysis technique identifies concentrations rather than isolated industrial land uses.
- Moderate-intensity apartment (20 to 35 apartment units per acre). All the apartments in the subject area are considered moderate intensity.
- Low-intensity residential–one- to four-family units

Based on these criteria, the pattern for development in the subject area is plotted in Exhibit 17.10. The contour lines on the map set the boundaries of the high-intensity growth area. In the case study application, high-intensity land use is of major concern. The subject is zoned for moderate-intensity land use (general retail and office), and the analysis of growth patterns confirms that a high-intensity use is improbable. High-intensity land uses have been developed on a north-south axis along the freeway, in keeping with the radial corridor growth model. Land uses in the immediate area of the subject, however, are likely to be moderate to low intensity.

Conclusions of Analysis of Land Use Patterns

High land-use intensity can be seen on both sides of the north-south freeway corridor between St. James Place to the west and Pennsylvania Avenue to the east. The greater the distance from the high-intensity, north-south freeway, the lower the land use intensity, as evidenced by the presence of apartment and residential uses.

The development pattern in the area to the east and the west of the north-south freeway resembles a funnel. The highly intense development at the intersection of the south loop freeway and north-south freeway tends to be constricted north of the intersection. Based on proposed developments, the high-intensity corridor is likely to expand in the vicinity of the proposed new freeway intersection.

Exhibit 17.10   Map of Existing General Land Uses

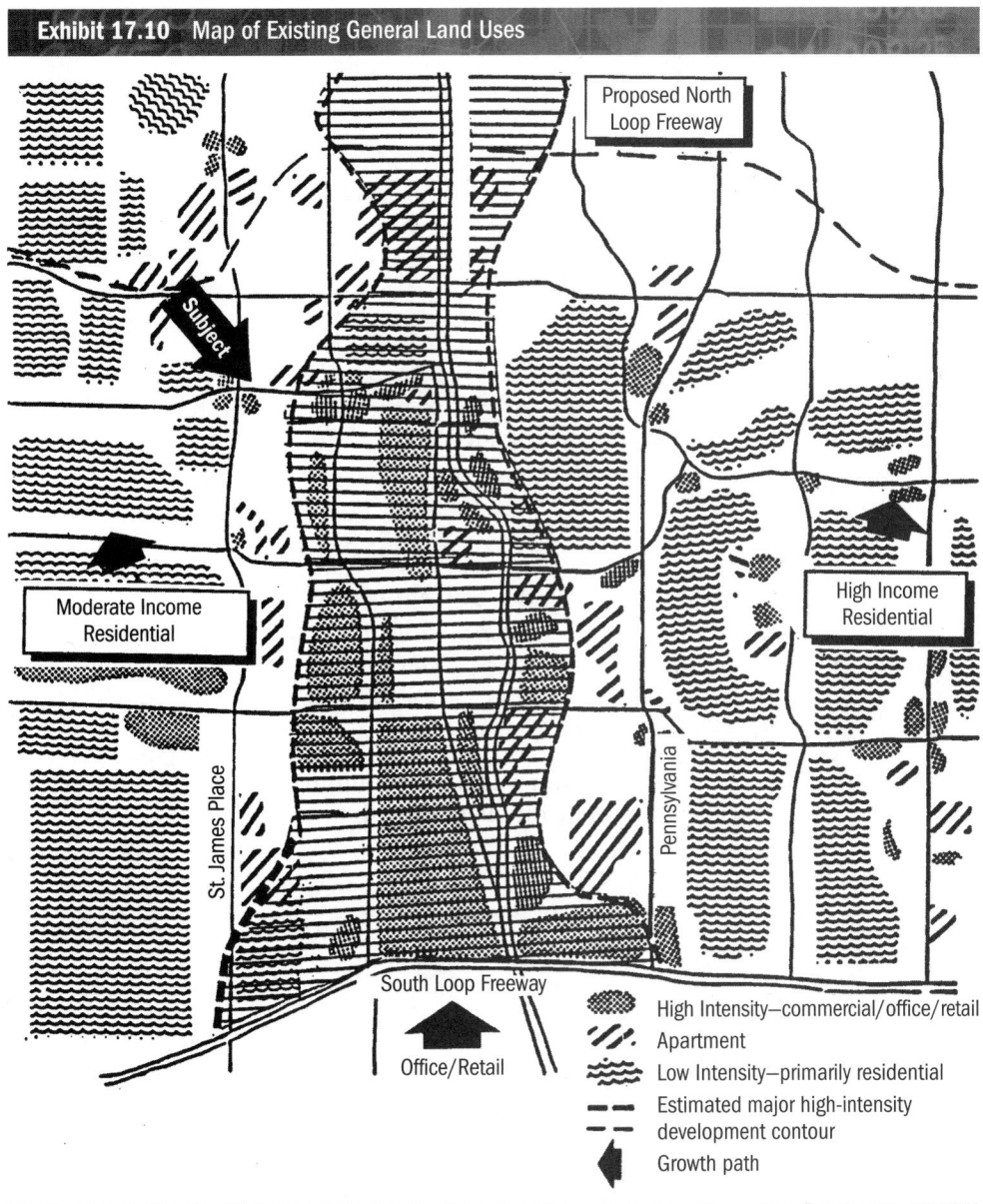

Based on this analysis, it appears that the subject lies in a transitional area between the more intense uses to the east near the north-south freeway and the area of less intense land use to the west. A contour line of the probable area to be developed under high-intensity land use is shown in Exhibit 17.10.

Rate of growth is another significant factor. The rate of growth is a function of infrastructure, regulatory trends, demographics, and demand. At this stage in the process, the analyst takes a preliminary look at the rate of growth from a locational perspective. The technique presented here maps the areas of urban growth over time. The historic boundaries shown in Exhibit 17.11 indicate the point when the area became urbanized. This information was compiled by studying aerial photographs taken over a period of time. An urban area is defined as an area in which at least 60% of the land was developed. The periphery of urban growth at the beginning of each decade is shown on the map. The growth rate for the area within the contour lines of the growth corridor is then estimated from the timing and direction of previous development.

The subject area is not located within the path of the growth corridor but at its edge. Assuming that demand continues, the subject will become part of a growing urban area within two to five years.

Step 1.2(3): Rate the Subject Use Potential by Location

The purpose of the location rating is to relate the subject's locational features to its most probable use. At this point in the analysis, demand has not been considered. In the next section, the analyst will screen probable uses on the basis of demand.

In the rating procedure, specific criteria are applied to evaluate various potential uses of the subject site. According to the analysis, the subject location is most suitable for multifamily, garden office, and community retail uses; moderately suitable for an industrial park; and least suitable for regional retail, single-family, and multistory office. The rating procedure is illustrated in Exhibit 17.12 on pages 424 and 425.

The site and location analyses indicate that all uses are probable alternatives for the subject site. The lowest-rated, improbable uses were multistory office, regional retail, and single-family residential. Single-family use might be acceptable on the northern half of the tract, but given the limit size (33 acres) and the current relatively low price per acre for single-family use compared to other uses, this use does not seem financially feasible at this time. Thus, single-family use will not be considered further unless it is found in later parts of this study that alternative uses are in such low demand that their per-acre price approaches single-family values.

The top-rated uses are:

1. Multifamily residential
2. Garden office
3. Community retail

Exhibit 17.11 Map of Historical Rate of Growth

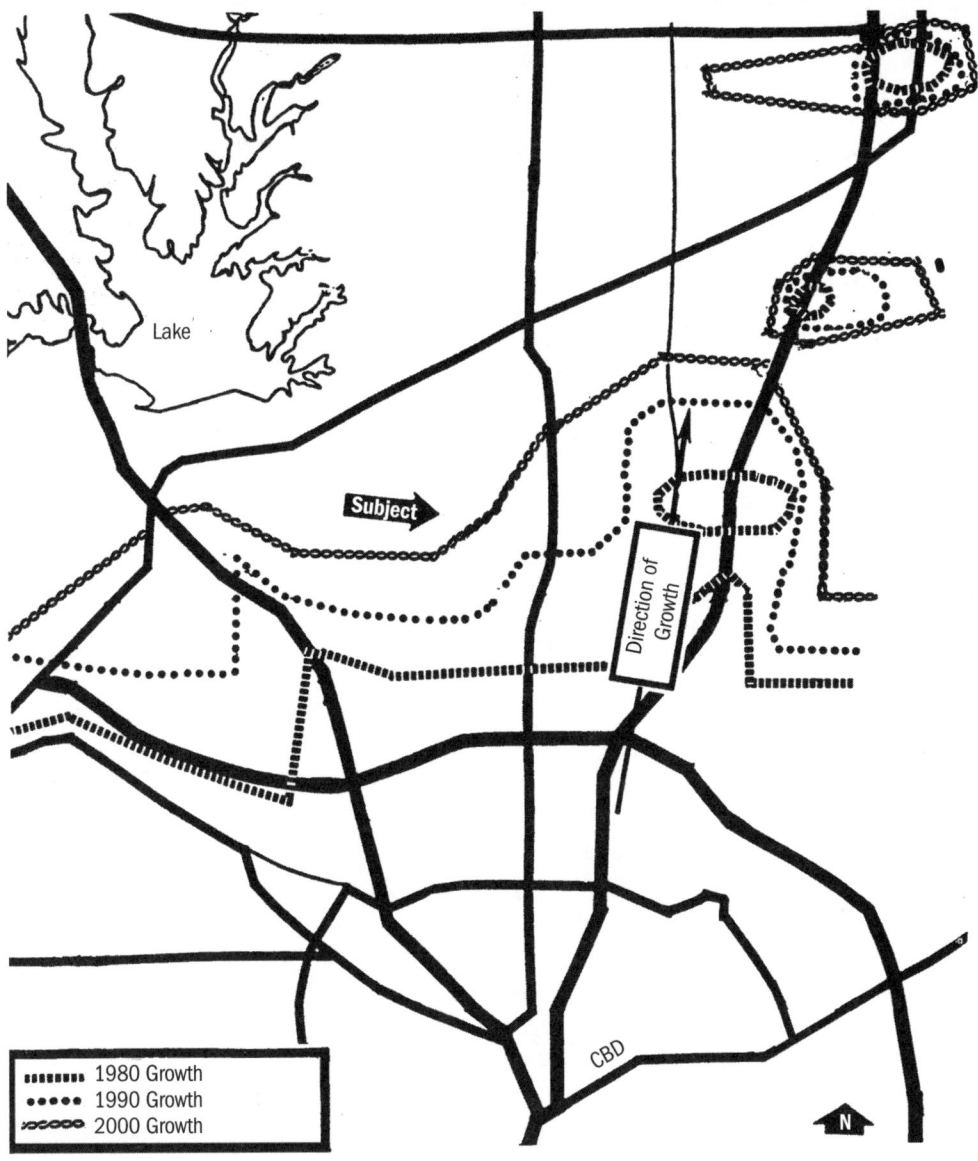

Lake

Subject →

Direction of Growth

CBD

N

▪▪▪▪▪▪▪ 1980 Growth
●●●●● 1990 Growth
∞∞∞∞ 2000 Growth

An industrial use is also rated higher than average but is not considered probable for this site for the following reasons:

- Demand for an industrial use is questionable.
- Land values under retail and office uses are six times higher than those under an industrial use.

- In locational analysis the tract was assigned a marginal rating for an industrial use.
- Zoning the tract for an industrial use is questionable.
- An industrial park was developed just southeast of the subject last year, but no lots have yet been sold.

Exhibit 17.12 shows the most probable development of the subject under a mix of apartment, garden office, and community retail uses.

Exhibit 17.12 Summary of Subject Location Analysis

| | Ratings | | | | |
	1 Poor	2 Average	3 Good	4 Excellent	Relative Score
Multistory Office					
Proximity to major activity nodes (linkages to other offices & support facilities)	X				
Proximity to major transportation linkages (freeway)		X			
Proximity to executive housing	X				
Proximity to Fortune 500 firms	X				
Direction of multistory office growth	X				
Public planning and zoning	X				
Total score					7
Garden Office (Doctors, Insurance)					
Proximity to housing market				X	
Proximity to major thoroughfares				X	
Proximity to complementary retail uses				X	
Proximity to office occupants' housing		X			
Direction of garden office growth			X		
Public planning and zoning			X		
Total score					20
Regional Retail					
Proximity to regional housing market		X			
Traffic volume by site		X			
Proximity to major activity center (office)	X				
Proximity for direct access to freeways	X				
Direction of regional retail growth	X				
Public planning and zoning	X				
Total score					8
Community Retail					
Proximity to housing				X	
Traffic volume by site			X		
Proximity to other community shopping facilities			X		
Density of area housing			X		
Direction of community retail growth			X		
Public planning and zoning			X		
Total score					19

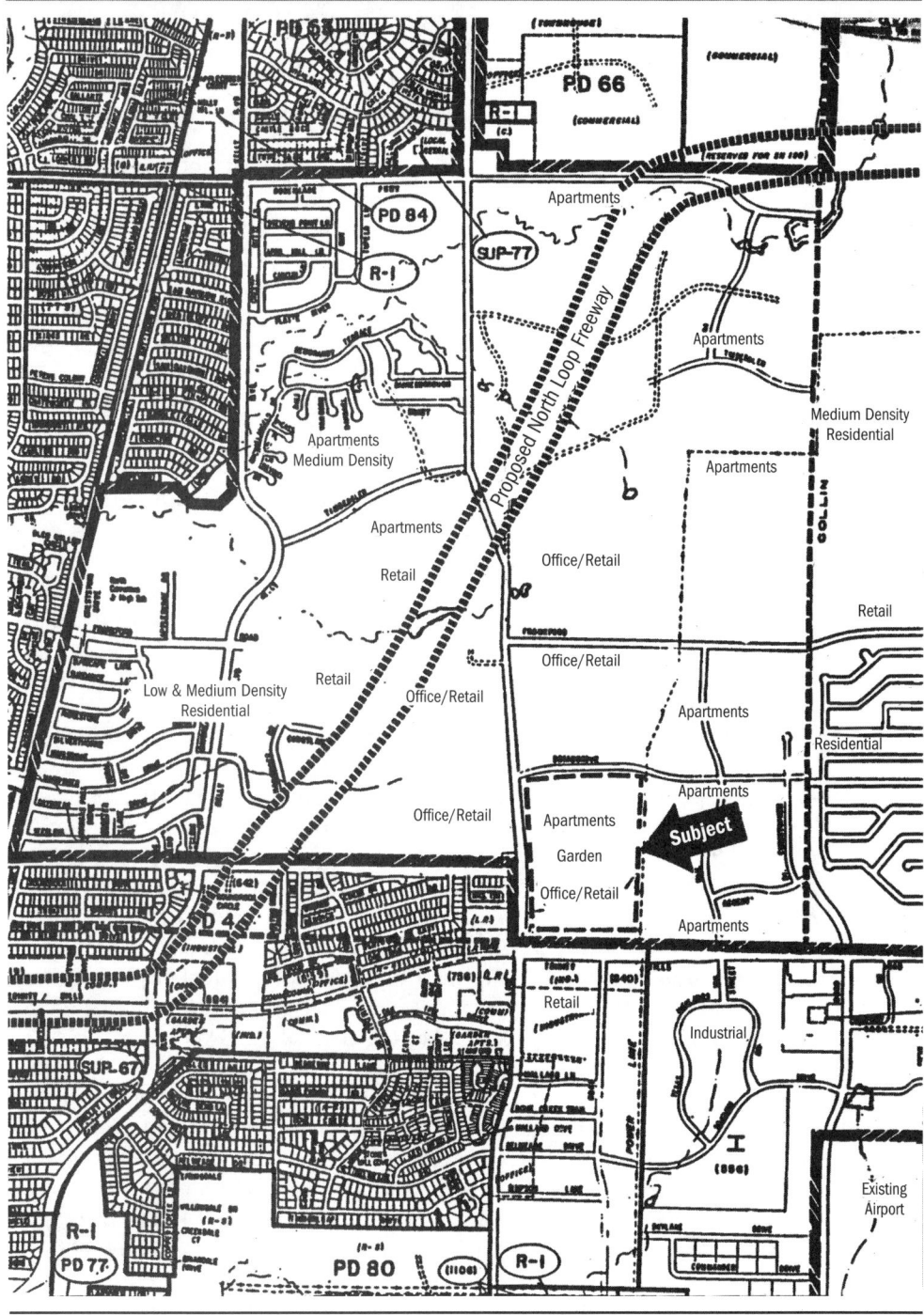

Step 2: Delineate the Market

A market area is defined by the specific use or uses of the property and the users it is likely to attract. The tenants and clientele who constitute the demand for the mix of uses in the subject tract will not all be drawn from areas with identical boundaries. Available data often have to be adjusted to correspond to the market areas defined by the location of property users. In this application, the overall city (suburban city as part of a metro area) may be considered the market area for two of the prospective uses: the multifamily residential development, and the office. Citywide demographics are used to measure the potential demand for these uses—i.e., the potential tenants of multifamily housing and the office work force. The demand for retail space, the third potential use, is largely a function of the effective purchasing power of the population in the trade area of the retail facility. Thus, the boundaries of the market area for a moderate-intensity, commercial use are defined based on the likely tenant, in this case community retail type center.

Steps 3, 4, and 5: Analyze Demand and Supply for Each Possible Use

The appraiser gathers data on the demand for and supply of properties under the three uses deemed most suitable: multifamily apartment, moderate-intensity retail, and office.

Multifamily Apartment Demand Analysis

The entire city constitutes the market area for multifamily apartment units. Based on a study of various demographic forecasts, the current citywide population of 67,500 may be expected to increase to 85,200 in four years, and 107,585 in eight years. Household size now averages 2.58 persons but is expected to decline at a rate of 1% annually. Thus, in four years, there should be 33,543 demand units (85,200/2.54) and in eight years, 43,034 demand units (107,585/2.5). Multifamily units are forecast to account for 35% of the residents in the community, while single-family and other miscellaneous type units account for 65%. Thus, total potential demand for multifamily units in four years will approximate 11,740 units (0.35 × 33,543) and in eight years, 15,062 units (0.35 × 43,034).

If the multifamily units considered for the tract are to appeal to middle-income tenants, approximately 25% of the potential demand should be disaggregated from the total projection to represent high-income tenants who seek more expensive apartments and low-income tenants who cannot afford the rents. The actual potential demand for middle-income apartment units would amount to approximately 8,805 tenant households (0.75 × 11,740) in four years and 11,296 tenant households (0.75 × 15,062) in eight years.

Exhibit 17.14 shows how the projections of actual unit demand were derived.

Exhibit 17.14 Multifamily Demand

	Current	Year 4	Year 8
Citywide population	67,500	85,200	107,585
Divided by household size (declining 1% per yr.)	2.58	2.54	2.50
Total housing unit demand	26,163	33,543	43,034
Times % forecasted multifamily unit mix	35%	35%	35%
Estimated total occupied multifamily unit demand	9,157	11,740	15,062
Less 25% of high-or low-income households	2,289	2,935	3,765
Multifamily households in middle income range	6,868	8,805	11,296
Plus frictional vacancy @ 5%	361	463	595
Total potential multifamily unit demand	7,229	9,269	11,891

Multifamily Supply Analysis

There are currently 10,750 existing multifamily units. Of these, approximately three-quarters fall within a rental range affordable to middle-income tenants. Thus, the available competitive supply of 8,062 units (0.75 × 10,750) exceeds existing demand (6,868) by 1,194 units. The vacancy rate in the market area is at 15%, and no new units are under construction or planned.

Residual Demand Analysis

In little more than one and one-half years there should be positive residual demand in the market. Current oversupply is 833 units. Average new demand per year is 510 units (9269 – 7229/4 yrs.). Residual demand for the multifamily residential use is calculated below in Exhibit 17.15:

Exhibit 17.15 Multifamily Residual Demand

	Current	Year 4	Year 8
Total potential multifamily unit demand	7,229	9,269	11,891
Less current competitive supply of multifamily units	8,062	8,062	8,062
Less estimate new construction	0	0	0
Net (excess) shortage	(833)	1,207	3,829

Forecast Apartment Demand Compared with Historical Absorption

The average annual demand equals 510 units per year (9,269-7,299/4 yrs). At 20 units per acre, the average annual demand for land would be about 25 acres. In the last 10 years, approximately 250 acres have been developed for apartment units in the city, which is about the same as forecast.

Forecast Multifamily Apartment Growth Conclusion

The development of 25 acres per year into apartment units seems reasonable, given the rapid population growth forecast. The last 10 years' development pace did not result in overbuilding because population growth continued. The growth forecast is considered reasonable and is supported by the historical absorption rates. Thus, citywide growth in apartment unit development can be forecast as follows:

- Conservative - an average of 15 acres annually
- Most probable- an average of 25 acres annually
- Optimistic - an average of 35 acres annually

There will be sufficient residual demand to begin new apartment unit development in one to three years. It should be noted that any forecast of the timing of new construction typically includes a feasibility analysis to determine whether future rents justify the construction. These analyses are presented for the highest and best use applications, but are not shown here. The preceding forecast was consistent with the feasibility analysis of future rents.

Moderate-Intensity Retail Demand and Supply Analyses

A community retail facility on the subject site would probably have a market area of about three miles. Due to freeway location, the actual market area is an irregular rectangle shape. The number of supportable square feet of retail space is primarily a function of the purchasing power of the households within this market area.

Population forecast and average area household income was estimated, and it was found that approximately 60% of this income is spent on taxes and nonretail items, so the retail purchasing power per household is about 40% of gross income. Demand projections for moderate-intensity retail use are shown in Exhibit 17.16.

Exhibit 17.16 Community Retail Demand Forecast			
Year	Current	In 4 Yrs.	In 8 Yrs.
Total number of households in 3-mile primary trade area	12,790	16,400	21,000
Average household income	$70,524	$70,524	$70,524
Total household income in primary trade area	$902,001,960	$1,156,593,600	$1,481,004,000
Percentage of income spent on retail	40%	40%	40%
Total retail sales potential	$360,800,784	$462,637,440	$592,401,600
Percentage of retail sales by community shopping center*	73%	73%	73%
Total community shopping center sales	$263,384,572	$337,725,331	$432,453,168
Sales required per sq. ft.	$275	$275	$275
Supportable occupied sq. ft. of retail space from households in primary trade area	957,762	1,228,092	1,572,557
Plus frictional vacancy @ 5%	50,409	64,636	82,766
Total forecast demand (sq. ft.) in primary market area	1,008,171	1,292,729	1,655,323

* Excludes major department stores except discount stores, and excludes auto sales and other exclusive specialty retail space.

Residual Demand Estimate

The appraiser estimates the total available retail space within the market area (which is about a three-mile area of the subject) to be 1,368,240 square feet. Given the current oversupply, no new construction is expected until the market comes into balance. Currently, demand exceeds supply, as Exhibit 17.17 demonstrates:

Exhibit 17.17 Community Retail Residual Demand Analysis—Mid-range Forecast			
Year	**Current**	**Year 4**	**Year 8**
Total forecast demand (sq. ft.) in primary market area (approx. 3-mile radius)	1,008,171	1,292,729	1,655,323
Less existing sq. ft. of competitive space	1,368,240	1,368,240	1,368,240
Less forecasted new competition	0	0	0*
Net (excess) shortage of supportable sq. ft. of retail space	-360,069	-75,511	287,083

*Probably new construction in Year 5 but left 0 for current market condition analysis.

Based on the residual demand forecast and analysis of rents required for new construction, it is estimated that it will take at least four years before new construction can be expected in this market area.

Forecast Retail Demand Compared with Historical Absorption

The forecast of four to eight years in the future indicates that approximately seven acres of new retail space will be needed within the market area each year:

(1,292,729 − 1,008,171)/4 yrs. = 71,139/10,000 sq. ft. of bldg. per acre = 7 acres)

According to the city planning department, 250 acres of retail space has been developed citywide in the past 10 years. This indicates an average of more than 25 acres per year citywide. The subject market area is about 1/3 of the city's area; thus, the forecast is slightly less than historical actual.

Forecast Retail Growth Conclusion in Market Study Area

In reconciling historical absorption with forecast demand, the appraiser gave far greater weight to the forecast, which is based on fundamental analysis. The appraiser reasoned that because the last decade was characterized by highly speculative practices, construction was not totally driven by fundamental demand. Part of this speculation was the big box retailers competing directly with each other to establish market presence. These conditions are not expected to be repeated in the next eight years. The citywide data also described a larger area than the subject's market area. Thus, the average annual growth in retail demand for the subject market area indicates that development should occur in about four years. (The yearly new demand acreage is based on 70,844 avg. sq. ft. of new demand per year divided by 10,000 avg. building size per acres.) The estimates are as follows:

Conservative—   an average of 3 acres annually
Most probable— an average of 7 acres annually
Optimistic—   an average of 11 acres annually

Office Market Demand Analysis

The city boundaries encompass most of the market area identified for the subject. Thus, current and future employment citywide is studied to establish the demand for office space. Sources of the demand forecast were derived from the council of governments, employment commission, and the appraiser's analysis of city economic development data.

The employment categories were analyzed by NAICS sectors to determine the categories that best represented office workers. It was found that the metro area had about 25% in these categories. However, given the extensive amount of office space in the city and in the nearby north/south freeway corridor, it was estimated that in this submarket there were about 35% to 40% of total employment in office buildings. Data from the city's economic development director showed this had been rising from about 25% a decade ago, and the city expected the percentage to increase in the future. Given the new high tech office, however, it is forecast that space per employee will be declining. Exhibit 17.18 shows the results of the demand forecast.

Exhibit 17.18 Office Space Demand			
Year	Current	Year 4	Year 8
Total employment—forecast	30,527	38,070	56,901
Percentage occupying office space	37%	38%	40%
Total employed in office space	11,356	14,543	22,988
Avg. sq. ft. per employee	200	180	180
Estimated total occupied demand (in sq. ft.)	2,271,209	2,617,693	4,137,841
Plus frictional vacancy @ 5%	119,537	137,773	217,781
Total demand (sq. ft.)	2,390,746	2,755,467	4,355,622

Supply Analysis

The city planning department estimates that the city currently has 4,100,000 square feet of existing office space. This figure does not include industrial buildings (flex space) or office space in retail shopping centers. According to a real estate data company report, Northwest County Area 10 has about 4,039,300 square feet of office space. Area 10 does not include all areas within the city, which accounts for the difference between the report's figure and the estimate provided by the city planning department. Neither study included the adjacent north-south freeway area (adjacent but outside of this market area), which has more than 9,797,000 square feet of office space of which only about 75% is currently occupied.

A share of the citywide employment projection must be segmented to the subject market area. Because of the amount of vacant space nearby, reliable market segmentation is critical, or a significant margin of error could result. The city planning department has processed preliminary plats for an additional 712,000 square feet of office space in the subject market area, but there is no information on when development will begin. Given the current oversupply and corresponding low rents, construction is not anticipated in the near future.

A comparison of supply and demand suggests that it will take up to eight years before supply and demand would achieve a reasonable balance. The calculations are shown in Exhibit 17.19.

Exhibit 17.19 Office Residual Demand

Year	Current	Year 4	Year 8
Gross estimate of total citywide office demand in sq. ft.	2,390,746	2,755,467	4,355,622
Less current competitive sq. ft.	4,100,000	4,100,000	4,100,000
Less estimate new construction		0	0
Net (excess) shortage	(1,709,254)	(1,344,533)	255,622

Yearly Average Demand

Typically, 10,000 to 20,000 square feet per acre are developed under suburban office use, so the annual office demand increase per year in demand is about 245,600 sq. ft., or 15 acres per year, on average, for the next eight years as shown in Exhibit 17.20.

Exhibit 17.20 Average New Office Demand—Current to Year 8

Avg. increase per year (sq. ft.)	245,609
Avg. bldg. size (sq. ft.) per acre	16,000
Avg. yearly increase in market demand (in acres)	15

Forecast Office Demand Compared with Historical Absorption

Over the last 10 years, the city has experienced an average of 10 acres platted for multitenant office use each year. However, a closer look at the data shows that 80% of this office space (1,600,000 sq. ft.) was created in the last five years, indicating an average of 16 acres per year for the last five years.

Forecast Office Growth Conclusion for the City

Based on fundamental analysis, a high-range forecast of the annual demand for new office space indicates that 256,600 square feet will be added over the next eight years. At this rate, new demand will fill up the current 1,829,800 square feet of vacant space in seven years. Neverthe-less, a closer look at the forecast shows that the major surge in em-ployment will not occur until the latter part of the eight-year forecast period. Thus, new demand will not be realized for nearly eight years. The annual average of new demand over the next eight years comes to 15 acres per year. This figure is very close to the actual growth experi-enced over the last decade. Office building construction outpaced ac-tual growth in employment, creating an overbuilt market, and it now appears that it will take up to eight years to absorb the current supply of vacant space. After this time, building can be expected to resume, as the city has excellent long-term growth potential.

Fifteen acres per year is chosen as the top end of the range because the forecast data are averaged, and the employment surge is not ex-pected for at least four years. A comparison to historical overbuilding rate of growth was also considered in the final conclusion. Thus, the final conclusion for citywide office average growth per year in new demand beginning eight years out is:

Conservative—an average of 10 acres per year
Most probable—an average of 12 acres per year
Optimistic—an average of 15 acres per year

Apartment and retail uses demonstrate the most predictable short-term use potential. Demand for office use is eight years out, and is more problematic.

Use	Most Probable New Development Start	Average	Yearly Demand
Apartment	1 to 2 years	25.0 acres/year	15 to 35 acres/year
Retail	4.0 years	7.0 acres/year	3 to 11 acres/year
Office	8.0 years	12.0 acres/year	10 to 15 acres/year

Step 6: Subject Capture Estimate

The competition for vacant land is other vacant land that has similar use potential. Thus, this step requires the appraiser to identify com-petitive vacant tracts located in the same geographic area of the de-mand forecast. The tracts would require utilities and similar zoning prospects as the subject and would need to be located on a major road like the subject. Appraisers can use the following sample survey sheet for the competitive tract inventory:

ID#

Location:	Corner location, 1/2 mile west of subject on New York Avenue
Owner:	ABC Development Company
Comment/analysis:	Company has good track record of developing land as retail centers.
Status:	Owner plans to develop as mixed-use development when market improves.
Land area:	55 acres
Zoning:	All commercial; zoning allows for multifamily and garden office uses.
Utilities:	All at site
Land condition:	Level, no floodplains

After the competitive tracts are identified, they are rated preliminarily according to different use-specific criteria. This initial rating groups the competitive tracts according to those that are most likely to be developed first. Usually this means selecting the top-rated tracts, typically the top third that have highest scores. If the subject itself is one of the top-rated tracts, it should compete along with the others as soon as new demand is realized in the market. If it is not, then it will likely have to wait until the market demand is absorbed by the top tracts in the market. In the subject case study the subject is one of the top tracts in the market. After the top tracts are identified, they become the prime candidates for development in the city for the next few years. These tracts are then studied in more detail and again rated.

Segmentation of Competitive Tracts

The subject has mixed-use potential; thus, various parts of it are competitive with different vacant tracts in the market. For example, the subject's retail front part is competitive with other tracts that have prime retail potential. On the other hand, the entire subject could be used for office space or apartments. Apartment and office use tend to be built on tracts with similar locational characteristics so they can compete with other competitive tracts.

Rating Matrix Method

Rating competitive tracts in relation to the subject is a way of to gauge the market share that the subject will likely capture. The procedure is a two-step process. The first step compares each tract with the other tracts and rates it as better than, equal to, or worse than the comparable according to the specific rating factor. The higher the rating, the higher the score is. This process is repeated in pairs. The second step positions each pair with each other so that all pairs are ranked according to each other. This procedure is considered a calibrating process. The resulting scores are totaled, and the capture percentage is estimated. The higher score is considered superior. Exhibit 17.21 is an example of how two sets of competitive tracts are rated.

Of the competitive tracts, the subject was rated one of the best tracts in the area in both sets. Thus, it is considered above average compared to competitive tracts suitable for mixed-use development.

Pro Rata Share Capture Method

The first step in the capture estimate is to compare on the basis of pro rata share. If all tracts are equal, they should compete equally. Exhibit 17.22 shows the pro rata share based on amount of acreage. Another method is to calculate the pro rata share based on the number of competitive properties. The subject calculated pro rata share for office/apartment tracts based on acreage was 14%; for the competing retail tracts it was 16%. The next step in the capture analysis is to adjust the pro rata share capture percentage by a specific property rating method.

Exhibit 17.21   Vacant Land Competitive Ranking Analysis—Community Retail

		Competitive Tracts							
ID	**Rating Criteria**	**1 (Subject)**	**2**	**3**	**4**	**5**	**6**	**7**	**Importance Factor**
1	Proximity to current households (quantity)	6	4	3	1	2	3	1	9
2	Proximity to current or planned retail (cumulative attraction)	4	3	3	1	2	1	2	5
3	Location in path of new residential growth	5	4	5	1	3	2	2	8
4	Major road location	5	4	6	1	3	2	2	7
5	Access and visibility from road	6	4	5	1	2	3	3	6
6	Traffic count by area	5	3	6	1	5	4	2	4
7	Size and drawing power of current tenants in immediate area	4	3	4	2	3	2	2	10
8	Reputation (prestige) of area	5	2	5	1	4	3	2	3
9	Area of most planned public expenditures in next 5 yrs.	4	3	5	1	2	2	2	2
10	Amount of vacant land available	6	4	3	7	3	2	5	1
	Total Score	274	193	246	71	154	131	110	1179
	Percentage of Total Scores	23%	16%	21%	6%	13%	11%	9%	100%
	Pro Rata Share by Size	16%	14%	12%	22%	12%	7%	17%	**Total Acres**
	Size of Tracts (acres)	33	30	25	45	25	15	35	208

Analysis of subject and competitive tracts suggests that most expected retail acreage is based on location and site features.

Capture Rate Conclusions

According to the pro rata share estimate, the subject's share is 14% to 16%. The ranking analysis indicates that the subject, with a capture rate of 23% for retail and 19% for office and multifamily apartment, is significantly superior to most competition. This conclusion is illustrated in Exhibits 17.23 through Exhibits 17.26.

The office forecast was lower for the first four years, and increased significantly in the last four years.

The approach presented here is based on economic modeling rather than forecasting the actual sequence of development, the procedure applied in feasibility studies. Economic modeling is used because the long-term predictions made in forecasting the actual phasing of development are often unrealistic. Furthermore, the appraisal is of a vacant tract with an optimal land-use mix based on a probability model. In the case study application, office use is included in the mix of potential uses, but it is seldom developed on a per-acre basis. In the subject market, development in six-acre phases is most typical. However, marginal demand for office use is forecast to be eight years out. Market-wide demand averages 10 to 15 acres per year, with a mid-range point estimate of 13 acres; the subject capture at 23% suggests approximately three acres per year. Thus, if demand is forecast eight years out, it will be 10 years before a six-acre phase of garden office development can begin on the subject

Exhibit 17:22 Vacant Land Competitive Ranking Analysis—Office and Apartment Potential

		Competitive Tracts								
ID	Rating Criteria	1 (Subject)	2	3	4	5	6	7	8	Importance Factor
1	Proximity to current apartment complexes	5	4	3	1	2	1	1	1	9
2	Proximity to current or planned office	4	3	3	1	2	2	3	3	9
3	Proximity to current employment centers (non-office)	4	3	5	1	3	2	2	4	5
4	Proximity to higher-income housing	3	4	5	1	3	2	2	2	7
5	Proximity to most new construction of residential in last five years	4	3	5	1	2	3	2	3	6
6	Major road frontage	5	3	6	1	4	2	3	2	4
7	Proximity to complementary facilities in area (hotels, restaurants, shopping centers, entertainment areas, and country clubs)	2	3	4	2	3	2	2	1	2
8	Quality of node's tenants	4	2	5	1	3	2	3	2	5
9	Reputation (prestige) of area for office and apartments	4	2	5	2	1	2	4	3	8
10	Area of most planned public expenditures in next 5 years	4	3	5	1	2	2	2	2	3
11	Amount of vacant land available	5	3	6	1	2	3	2	4	1
	Total Score	239	180	262	69	137	116	143	142	1288
	Percentage of Total Scores	19%	14%	20%	5%	11%	9%	11%	11%	100%
	Pro Rata Share by Size	14%	6%	27%	10%	5%	7%	15%	16%	Total Acres
	Size of Tracts (acres)	66	30	125	45	25	35	70	75	471

Note: Ranking method 1 = worst

Exhibit 17.23 Subject Multifamily Unit Capture Estimate

Avg. increase per year (units)	510
Avg. density (units) per acre	20
Avg. yearly increase in market demand (units)	25
Subject capture rate	19%
Avg. yearly subject capture (acres/yr.)	5

Exhibit 17.24 Subject Office Capture Estimate to Year 4

Avg. increase per year (sq. ft.)	91,180
Avg. bldg. size (sq. ft.) per acre	15,000
Avg. yearly increase in market demand (acre)	6
Subject capture rate	19%
Avg. yearly subject capture (acre/yr.)	1.2

Exhibit 17.25 Subject Office Capture Estimate—Current to Year 8	
Avg. increase per year (sq. ft.)	245,609
Avg. bldg. size (sq. ft.) per acre	16,000
Avg. yearly increase in market demand (acre)	15
Subject capture rate	19%
Avg. yearly subject capture (acre/yr.)	3

Exhibit 17.26 Subject Retail Capture Estimate	
Avg. increase per year (sq. ft.)	71,139
Avg. bldg. size (sq. ft.) per acre	10,000
Avg. yearly increase in market demand (acre)	7
Subject capture rate	23%
Avg. yearly subject capture (acre/yr.)	2

tract, allowing time for demand to increase to sufficient levels. Of course, the exact date for the subject could be earlier or later than forecast.

The economic modeling technique demonstrated here does not attempt to forecast a specific date for the absorption of six acres. Instead, it establishes the average annual demand for each specific use. In other words, the subject might be either the first tract to be developed or the last tract. This tends to smooth out forecast cash flows and their probable timing. In a market value appraisal, highest and best use is essentially a probability study, not a feasibility study for actual development. This is the rationale for using an economic modeling approach. An alternative would be to forecast the exact timing of development, which many appraisers do. Other appraisers undertake even more detailed analyses, estimating cash flows and actual construction and lease-up costs (see land residual method in Chapter 16).

Step 7: Financial Analysis and Optimal Land Use Plan

To perform a financial analysis, the appraiser assigns user values (i.e., the value of the developed land under a specific use, sometimes called retail value) and absorption estimates to each possible land use. The mix of uses that yields the highest present value is the highest and best use. Development costs, holding costs, and sales expenses are also estimated.[4] The primary purpose of estimating the dollar amounts is to provide a means of comparing the use mixes and determining the most probable land-use mix for the subject property.

---

4. If all the development costs are the same for each alternative, they do not necessarily have to be estimated in highest and best use, since the question of what is the highest value is relative. However, for a more complete analysis and to support the valuation section, a complete development approach, which includes development costs, can be completed in the highest and best use section.

In each of the models, nine of the 66 acres (14%) are allocated to interior roads and the floodplain identified in the site analysis. To determine the optimal land-use mix on the remaining 57 acres, the appraiser selects a discount rate and estimates typical user values. The user values are as follows:

Multifamily use   @ $4.00/sq. ft. per acre
Retail use   @ $8.00/sq. ft. per acre
Office use   @ $10.00/sq. ft. per acre

The market forecast did not determine any real growth in disposable income; nor was there evidence in the user sales market that user-end sales prices were appreciating more than inflation. Most user-end sales in this market had not appreciated as much as inflation. Thus, for this constant dollar model the user-end sales prices are not adjusted upward for future value in real terms.

Next, the appraiser estimates development costs. These costs are minimal and about the same for each use. The only major cost is the construction of the interior road, Virginia Ave. If development costs, such as on-site costs, occur with the user sales, they can be averaged per acre as shown in this case study. However, if upfront costs are required, such as off-site costs, then the cost is usually a lump sum and is taken off the total present value calculation for each alternative. There were no off-site costs in this case study. Since this is a constant dollar model the costs are not adjusted for inflation.

The appraiser then forecasts the average absorption of alternative uses over time. Absorption was concluded to begin when demand exceeds supply and rents are sufficient to justify new construction. Exhibit 17.27 illustrates the process of analyzing land-use alternatives to arrive at a mid-range forecast.

Selection of Discount Rate for Discounted Cash Flow Model

The discount rate applied is based on "real terms" adjusted downward for inflationary expectations and represents an investment return to a

---

Exhibit 17.27   Financial Analysis of Land-Use Alternatives—Mid-Range Forecast

Data Input

Site Data

Gross acres	66
Less interior road and floodplain	14.0%
Development acres	56.7

Land Use Type	User Price per Sq. Ft.	Less Mgmt./Sells/Tax Cost	Less Development Cost/ Acre (on-site)	Net Sale Price Per Sq. Ft.	Absorption Avg. Acre Per Year	Absorp. Year Start	Discount Rate
Apartment	$4.00	10.00%	$30,000	$2.91	5	1	12.00%
Retail	$8.00	10.00%	$30,000	$6.52	2	4	12.00%
Office	$12.00	10.00%	$30,000	$10.11	2	8	12.00%

typical third party based on the risk inherent in the absorption forecast. The rate is also adjusted downward for the long-term basis of the DCF and is not considered a short-term discount rate.

The market/marketability analysis focused on real growth in the subject's market area and not on growth due to inflationary pressures beyond it. The subject market area was not forecast to experience real growth in disposable incomes over the forecast period; thus, it is not expected that user land sales will appreciate much, if any, in real terms. To maintain consistency throughout this analysis, and not confuse real growth with nominal growth, the discount rate is adjusted for inherent inflationary expectations.

The next major estimate in the discount rate is the risk factor. The risk factor is primarily a function of the confidence level of the forecast elements. Therefore, the detail of the analysis in the market study must be considered when estimating the discount rate. A very general market study, with little or no support for absorption, would tend to have a low confidence level; therefore, more risk is associated with the cash flows and should be recognized in the discount rate. On the other hand, a detailed market study with specific capture support and forecast within a range, recognizing downside possibilities as well as upside possibilities, makes the forecast absorption confidence higher. Thus, the discount rate (risk) would tend to be lower since the absorption forecast confidence level is higher, which is the case in this forecast.

Finally, the length of the financial analysis is considered. Short-term expectations of returns are typically higher than long-term expectations. This is a function of risk and the nature of compound interest. Short-term forecasts require a high degree of precision and are subject to many fluctuations in the market. On the other hand, long-term forecasts tend to even out the up and down spikes found in most markets over time. Also, the long-term nature of compound interest is significant and increases the value the longer the term. Thus, the long-term nature of the case study economic model requires some downward adjustment in the rate when compared to a current short-term rate expectation.

One method of determining the discount rate is analyzing alternative investments adjusted for the subject economic model and risk discussed earlier. This analysis should also address market expectations evidenced by real estate investor surveys and land sales. However, investor survey data should also be adjusted to compare forecasted expectations to the forecast conclusions in the appraiser's market/marketability study to determine if the absorption times are similar. If not, the investor survey must be adjusted to the expectations of the appraisal forecast.

The task is to run combinations of the land-use mix possibilities until the highest value mix is attained. The exact highest and best use economic mix can be calculated by using a computer. However, a selected analysis of various mixes can quickly zero in on the mix that is close to the mathematical highest value mix. The procedure is to run all one-use alternatives and then proceed with various combinations until the values tend to cluster. In Exhibit 17.28, Model 1 is the computer-calculated highest value land-use mix. This exhibit is a simplified version of the Excel spreadsheet containing the seven alternatives. The complete models are contained on the CD that accompanies this book.

These are only an analytical sample of the many other possible combinations.

Baseline Alternative

These development alternatives are also compared to the baseline alternative long-term speculative land as evidence by comparable land sales in the area. These would be sales of acreage tracts (40 to 100

Exhibit 17.28 Financial Analysis of Alternative Land-Use Mixes

Use Mix	Acres of Land Use	Net $/Sq. Ft. (Net of Development Cost)	Avg. Acres Absorbed Per Year	Year Start Date	Present Value of Land* @ 12% (Rounded)
Model 1					
Apartment	26	$2.91	5	1	$2,352,910
Retail	17	$6.52	2	4	$2,082,747
Office	14	$10.11	2	8	$1,818,532
Total	57				$6,254,189
Model 2—As Currently Zoned					
Apartment	0	$2.91	5	1	NA
Retail	27	$6.52	2	4	$2,638,775
Office	30	$10.11	2	8	$2,713,943
Total	57				$5,352,718
Model 3					
Apartment	0	$2.91	5	1	NA
Retail	40	$6.52	2	4	$3,018,980
Office	17	$10.11	2	8	$2,053,350
Total	57				$5,072,330
Model 4					
Apartment	0	$2.91	5	1	NA
Retail	17	$6.52	2	4	$2,082,747
Office	40	$10.11	2	8	$2,976,369
Total	57				$5,059,115
Model 5					
Apartment	40	$2.91	5	1	$3,149,881
Retail	10	$6.52	2	4	$1,456,969
Office	7	$10.11	2	8	$1,087,269
Total	57				$5,694,118
Model 6					
Apartment	57	$2.91	5	1	$3,832,298
Model 7					
Retail	57	$6.52	2	4	$3,234,891
Model 8					
Office	57	$10.11	2	8	$3,189,233

Note: Calculation by Excel spreadsheet, which is taken out to eight decimal places. Numbers here are rounded.

acres) on New York Ave., or a similar major street that have sold recently and have the same highest and best use as the subject. The speculative investor sales would be to buyers of a property similar to the subject who chose not develop the property but planned to hold it for resale. These sales, if available, are considered the baseline alternative sales because they would be a known value from the buy/sell market for comparison to the values suggested by the user/development market. If the speculative investor sales were higher than the user/development values indicated above, then the speculative investor buyers of large acreage tracts such as the subject would be the highest and best use. For the subject case study these types of speculative investor sales were not available.

Conclusion

The mix of multifamily, retail, and office uses proposed as Model 1 result in the highest present value. This model would be the best economic fit to develop the highest and best use concept plan if all the forecasts had equal probability. Highest and best use is not arrived at by a mechanical process. The financial analysis will provide input data to be further scrutinized. The risk associated with each value in the analysis must be assessed. For example, the land-use mix specified in Model 5 is similar to that of Model 1. Model 5, which is 9% less valuable than Model 1, has more acreage allocated to multifamily use and could be considered less risky than Model 1 because there is current demand for multifamily space. Whereas office space represents 29% of the value of Model 1, it is only 19% of the value of Model 5. Office use is the most uncertain because of its long projection period. The element of uncertainty or risk can be addressed in three ways:

- The discount rate can be adjusted.
- The forecast for the more uncertain land uses can be revised along more conservative lines.
- The different risks and values can be reconciled.

Each method has its advantages and disadvantages. Adjustment of the discount rate for different land-use mixes is the approach most often used, but it is sometimes difficult to support the rate adjustment. Appraisers, like investors in the market, do not always agree on the trade-off between risk and the expected returns.[5] Market-derived discount rates should also be adjusted for the specific property and to the risk of the specific forecast in the discounted cash flow.[6] The use of a common discount rate to evaluate alternatives perceived to be within the same risk category does allow

---

5. Gaylon E. Greer and Michael D. Farrell, *Investment Analysis for Real Estate Decisions*, 2d ed. (Chicago: Dearborn Financial Publishers, 1988).

6. The use of a market-derived rate does not imply that estimated future cash flows could be forecast with more or less accuracy; it means that market participants view certain types of properties as being more or less risky. It does not contain project-specific risk information on whether the particular property being analyzed is more or less risky than the market norm. See William Weaver and Stuart Michelson, " A Practical Tool To Assist in Analyzing Risk Associated with Income Capitalization Approach Valuation or Investment Analysis," *The Appraisal Journal* (October 2003): 335–341.

for a more consistent comparison of the data input and the assumptions underlying the decision-making process.[7] This application uses such a method and makes the final adjustment for risk in the reconciliation.

Reconciliation of the Financial Analysis

The value of Model 1 is about 6% greater than that of Model 5, but 30% of the value of Model 1 depends on office space compared to 19% in Model 5. Thus, the central risk question is the reliability of the forecast for office. If the confidence in the office forecast were questionable, then Model 5 would be the highest and best use selection. However, as in this case the office forecast was considered slightly conservative, then Model 1 would be the highest and best use selection.

Thus, the land use allocation of Model 1, or some combination of Model 1 and Model 5, may be concluded as the best indicated financial fit for the subject.

To conclude the highest and best use analysis, the appraiser returns to the tract and fits the chosen mix to the physical constraints of the site. While the financial analysis of land use mixes provides guidance on the allocation of acreage among specific land uses, the land use model must be adapted to the physical features of the land. Exhibit 17.29 represents the concept plan for the highest and best use of the tract.

Highest and Best Use Reconciliation

This section brings together the site, location, supply and demand, capture, and financial analyses to identify the most probable use for the subject property. The land-use conclusion forecast for the subject is based on its site characteristics, and locational attributes, and on the supply and demand relationships in its market. The land-use conclusion is not an engineering study or a specific development plan. The land-use concept plan is for valuation analysis purposes only and must not be construed as the proposed development plan. The actual developer may have special financing advantages or anticipate revenues from an anchor tenant with drawing power that is atypical of the market. The developer could use this study as a starting point, however, but would need to commission a detailed engineering plan and feasibility analysis before development could proceed. Lengthy discussion with the city would also be required before the land-use plan of the tract could be finalized. This highest and best use study does, however, indicate the long-term development potential of the site, given the market conditions at the time of the appraisal. The supply and demand study indicated that any nonresidential use for this site would not be realized for at least four to six years.

---

7. This technique controls risk rather than adjusts for risk. See Etter, "Putting a Leash on Risk: Towards Evaluating Commercial Properties," *Tierra Grande: Journal of the Real Estate Center at Texas A&M University* (Spring 1994). See also the discussion of the incorporation of risk analysis into policy guidelines in Greer and Farrell text.

Exhibit 17.29 Concept Plan for Highest and Best Use of Subject Tract

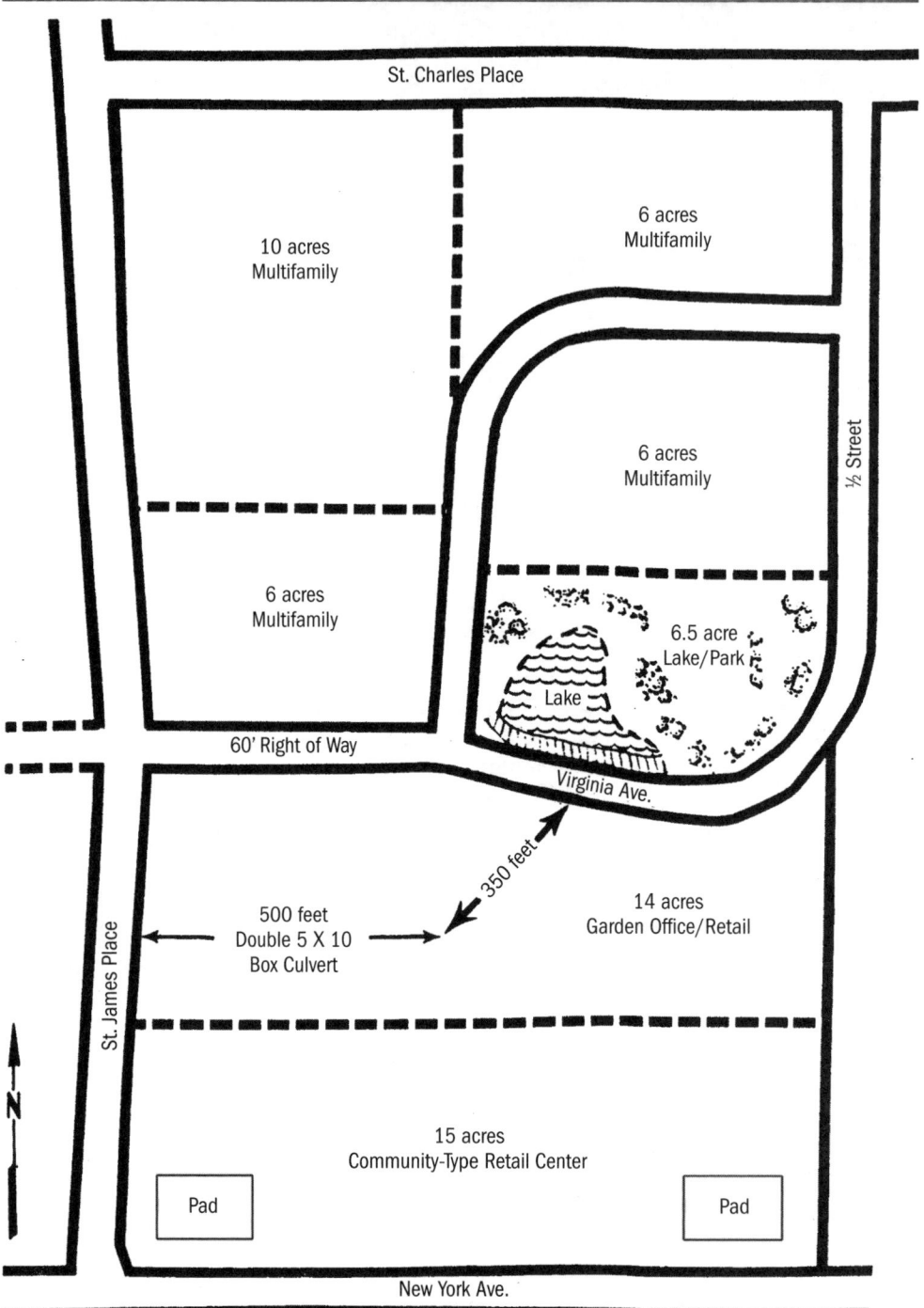

Land-Use Conclusions and Major Considerations

The land-use conclusion recognizes five major specifications for the design of the tract that were considered earlier in the site analysis.

1. Access to the interior from St. James Place, which runs along the western boundary of the tract, should be at the Virginia Avenue intersection.

2. The frontage and adjacent land use along New York Avenue is recommended for higher-intensity uses. The logical divide between less intensive residential land use to the north and more intensive retail/office land use to the south would be the access road connecting St. James Place to the interior. Physical constraints can often necessitate modification of the allocation of acreage in the financial analysis. This means less multifamily acreage than the financial Model 5 suggested. The 40-acre allocation in Model 5 is reduced to a 28-acre allocation in the concept plan. The reduction in multifamily acreage results in an increase in the acreage to be developed under retail and garden office use.

3. An outlet is needed at St. Charles Place, which runs along the northern boundary of the tract.

4. In all probability, the city will discourage an outlet road from the interior directly onto New York Avenue, which runs along the southern boundary of the tract.

5. The topography and drainage of the tract will likely necessitate that some type of retention facility be constructed in the general location of one of the existing ponds, preferably the upper pond. A lake park (5.6 acres) is recommended both as drainage for the residential development in the northeast quadrant and as an amenity feature aesthetically designed to give the project a competitive advantage and increase its absorption in this highly competitive market. The box culvert in the southwest quadrant allows for drainage of the acreage under proposed garden office and retail use.

Location

Location analysis showed that the subject was located in a transition area between more intensive land uses along the north-south freeway to the east and less intensive residential use to the west. More intensive uses such as multitenant office use were not probable for the site.

Market Demand

Market analysis indicated long-term demand for all the land uses, but short-term demand only for apartment units.

Marketability

The subject site is one of the more competitive sites in the market area and can be expected to have an above-average capture rate.

Financial Analysis

Financial analysis suggests an optimal land use mix of apartment, retail, and office space, with apartment units the dominant use. The mix is similar to Model 1. The highest and best use concept plan represents the appraiser's conclusion of the subject's highest and best use.

Land Concept Plan

The current zoning of the frontage along New York Avenue, and the results of the location analysis, both suggest that a community retail center should be built on this part of the tract. From a location standpoint, the back portion of the tract shows potential for residential or office use. The financial analysis indicates that a multifamily residential use would yield the highest present value because residual demand for that use will be realized much sooner than demand for the other potential uses.

Highest and Best Use Specification

Based on the results of the site, location, and market analyses, a forecast of the most probable future land use for the subject is made. This forecast is illustrated in Exhibit 17.29. The subject has two especially competitive future corners pads, which would most probably accommodate land uses that complement community retail—i.e., a fast-food restaurant, bank, or gasoline station.

Timing for Use

The market analysis projected the following timing for demand for various uses of the subject tract:

Apartment:	1 to 3 years
Retail:	3 to 5 years
Office:	6 to 15 years

The subject location was rated one of the better tracts for all uses, so it should have a capture rate superior to most of its competitors.

Market Participants

The users of the property will reflect the categories of market demand for each of the proposed uses, i.e., moderate-income apartment residents, the local clientele of a community retail center, and community residents who use the services provided by occupants of a garden (neighborhood) office development. In view of the long-term development potential for the land, the most probable buyer for the subject would be a speculative investor who plans to hold it and resell it.

Case Study Application to Valuation Models

The highest and best use conclusions now set the criteria for selecting comparable sales, and the three-part conclusion establishes the bases for adjusting sales for any differences. The highest and best use study can also be used in the development approach to value, as the financial analysis is considered one method of such an approach. A more detailed method would be the land residual method or a detailed cost, lot sell-off, land development value model. Regardless of the development model used, the highest and best use analysis explicitly provides the timing element, which is the most critical aspect of the development models.

CHAPTER 18

Proposed Retail Shopping Center

Chapter Objectives

- To apply highest and best use to a proposed retail shopping center using a case study approach
- To demonstrate how to perform a demand analysis for a supermarket
- To demonstrate how to conduct a financial feasibility analysis by threshold testing
- To develop a highest and best use conclusion based on a market analysis of a proposed retail shopping center

Introduction

This highest and best use study is based on a Level C market analysis of a vacant land tract for which a neighborhood shopping center/supermarket is proposed. Note that the data are analyzed in slightly different format than the previous chapter, but the study process includes the same analytical steps. This case study shows that there are different ways to look at data, but the overall analysis study steps are the same. The study process includes these seven steps:

1. Property productivity analysis and alternative use scoping. The physical, design/amenity (shape of the tract), legal/regulatory, and locational attributes of the vacant land are examined to establish the potential use(s) of the parcel. The most likely use of the subject

parcel was determined to be retail, specifically a neighborhood shopping center/supermarket. Multifamily housing represented a less probable, alternative use.

2. Market area definition. The primary and secondary trade areas are identified.

3. Demand forecast. The appraiser makes an estimate and forecast of the population for the market area, probable per capita food expenditure, and net leakage out of the market area. The demand for the goods sold at a neighborhood shopping center is also estimated using an alternative ratio.

4. Competitive supply inventory. The square footage of current and anticipated competitive space in the subject's market area are inventoried.

5. Marginal demand estimate. Existing and forecast demand is compared to current and anticipated supply to determine the net market support for the supermarket.

6. Subject capture estimate. The likely share of the market that the subject retail center will capture is estimated.

7. Financial feasibility analysis. After property productivity and supply and demand analyses have been completed, a financial feasibility test is conducted to identify the potential values of the land resulting from development for retail use and multifamily housing use. Retail use was found financially feasible, but the multifamily residential use was not, retail use being substantially more profitable.

Step 1: Analyze Property Productivity

To conduct a property productivity analysis, the appraiser examines the physical, design/amenity (shape of the tract), legal/regulatory, and locational attributes of the site. After a thorough examination, a preliminary highest and best use conclusion can be developed.

Step 1.1: Analyze the Physical Attributes
The subject tract is a 10-acre site with physical attributes that are well suited to a variety of different land uses, including multifamily housing, office, warehousing, and a neighborhood shopping center/supermarket.

Step 1.2: Analyze the Design/Amenity Attributes
The property is relatively level with a slightly irregular shape. It was purchased as a portion of a larger tract, and its irregular shape was part of the purchase agreement submitted by the buyer, who bought the tract for use as a neighborhood shopping center. The tract's boundaries were designed with the contours of a neighborhood shopping center in mind. This shape ensures that excess land

will be kept at a minimum when the land is developed as a shopping center.

The tract offers no special features for alternative land uses, but it could also accommodate an apartment complex, a warehouse, or an office building.

Step 1.3: Analyze the Legal/Regulatory Attributes

The tract offers a special benefit that most of the competitive properties do not have. The local zoning ordinance permits the sale of beer and wine. When the city voted on the zoning, the tract was already located within the city limits. Competing tracts had not yet been incorporated into the city at the time of the vote, and therefore did not receive this legal benefit. Such an important legal attribute will have a significant effect on any supermarket that anchors the neighborhood shopping center. For alternative land uses, the legal/regulatory attributes of the tract offer no special advantages.

Under the cumulative zoning ordinances in the city, both office and multifamily residential uses would be acceptable. Warehouse development is not allowed under the existing zoning, and a change would have to be requested. Members of the city planning staff have indicated that they would oppose such a change.

Step 1.4: Analyze the Locational Attributes

The attributes of both the micro location and the macro location appear favorable for the development of either a multifamily apartment complex or a neighborhood shopping center. Microlocational features include ease of ingress and egress and its location on the beltway around the city. Complementary land uses for both multifamily housing and a shopping center are relatively close.

Office and warehousing uses require different microlocational attributes. Although access to the tract is excellent for both uses, complementary land uses are seriously deficient. Most office and industrial space is found in other areas of the city, and it appears that the tract's location would not be favorable for either of these uses.

The tract's macro location is in the city's northeast quadrant, within the secondary growth path of the development. Although growth has been in abeyance for the past several years, this particular growth axis is well established, and as soon as the current economic slump ends, new development in the northeast quadrant of the city is very likely to resume.

The prospect of economic recovery bodes well for both multifamily housing and retail uses. For warehouse and office uses, the tract's macrolocational attributes are less than desirable. Most warehouse, distribution, and manufacturing uses are found to the south and west of the site, while new office space has tended to cluster around the new mall to the southeast.

Step 1.5: Perform Preliminary Highest and Best Use

While the physical attributes of the tract support a number of land uses, other attributes indicate that a multifamily apartment project or a neighborhood shopping center is the most likely use. Furthermore, it appears that the shopping center has the advantage. Three features are favorable to developing the tract as a shopping center:

1. The boundaries of the tract were designed to accommodate a neighborhood shopping center.
2. The zoning advantage permits beer and wine to be sold on the tract, giving it an edge over other competitive sites.
3. The micro and macro locations are well suited to a neighborhood shopping center.

Exhibit 18.1 shows that the attributes of the subject tract are rated on their suitability for multifamily housing and a neighborhood shopping center. The grid suggests that the retail use would be more likely, although a multifamily apartment project remains a potential alternative use. The rating of the attributes does not completely eliminate the multifamily residential use from consideration. Use of the tract as a multifamily housing project will be reexamined in the financial feasibility analysis (Step 7) by threshold testing. *Threshold testing* is an analytical procedure employed in highest and best use studies in which an alternative use is tested using especially optimistic forecast data (i.e., marginal demand projection and capture rate) to give the use every possible chance to succeed. If threshold testing reveals that the alternative use does not compare favorably with the other financially

---

Exhibit 18.1 Property Productivity Analysis Rating Grid—Alternative Land Use Ratings

Attributes	Subject's Features	Effect on Multifamily Housing	Rating	Effect on Neighborhood Shopping Center	Rating
Physical:					
Size	10 acres	Positive	+3	Positive	+3
Topography	Level	Positive	+3	Positive	+3
Design:					
Shape	Designed for neighborhood center	Negative	-1	Positive	+3
Legal/Political:					
Beer/wine/sales	Permitted	Neutral	0	Positive	+3
Zoning	Retail	Negative	-1	Positive	+3
Location:					
Access/visibility	Excellent	Positive	+2	Positive	+3
Linkages	Excellent	Positive	+2	Positive	+2
Neighborhood	Good	Positive	+1	Positive	+1
Direction of growth	Good	Positive	+1	Positive	+1
Ratings total			+10		+22

feasible uses, the alternative use can be eliminated from further consideration.

Ordinal numbers from +3 to -3 rate the suitability of the subject tract for two uses. A rating of +3 indicates that the attribute has a strong positive rating, whereas a -3 suggests that the tract is undesirable in this regard. A zero indicates that the effect is neutral. The land use with the highest total rating is the one best suited for that tract of land. The numerical ratings do not indicate that the retail use is 2.2 times better than the multifamily residential use. The ratings only suggest that the shopping center use is likely to be the more profitable use of the land at the time of the appraisal.

Highest and Best Use: Supply and Demand Analysis

Based on the property productivity analysis, the appraiser decides to test the market for the retail use. If the market did not indicate support for a retail use, the market for multifamily residential use would be tested. In the financial feasibility analysis (Step 7), threshold testing of both uses is undertaken to determine whether the multifamily housing project is indeed a viable alternative use.

In Step 2, the primary and secondary market areas for the subject are defined. The market areas of major competitors are also identified. The supply and demand analysis performed in Steps 3 through 5 investigates whether market support exists for a neighborhood shopping center. In these steps, two market areas are defined (Market Area 1 and Market Area 2), one for each of the two sets of population data used. Then independent demand and supply estimates are developed for each of the two population data sets to establish the extent of demand for a retail center in the designated market area and the competitive supply (Steps 3 and 4). Finally, an estimate of the marginal demand for retail space in the market area is made and the supportable retail space is allocated among a supermarket, general retail stores, and pad site(s) (Step 5).

Step 2: Define the Market Area

The primary and secondary market areas for the subject are identified. The primary market area is defined as the area within a three-mile radius of the subject. The primary market area is identified with Census Tracts 1 and 2. The secondary market area covers the northeast quadrant of the city, extending from the center of the downtown area to the suburban periphery, about 25 miles out. Census Tracts 1, 2, 3, and 4 define the primary and secondary market areas.

Exhibit 18.2 shows the subject's retail market area and the retail market areas for the major competing supermarkets. The breakpoints between the market areas for the various stores have been estimated using a retail gravitation model. The identification of these breakpoints allows the analyst to plot the individual market areas.

Exhibit 18.2   The Subject and Competing Market Areas

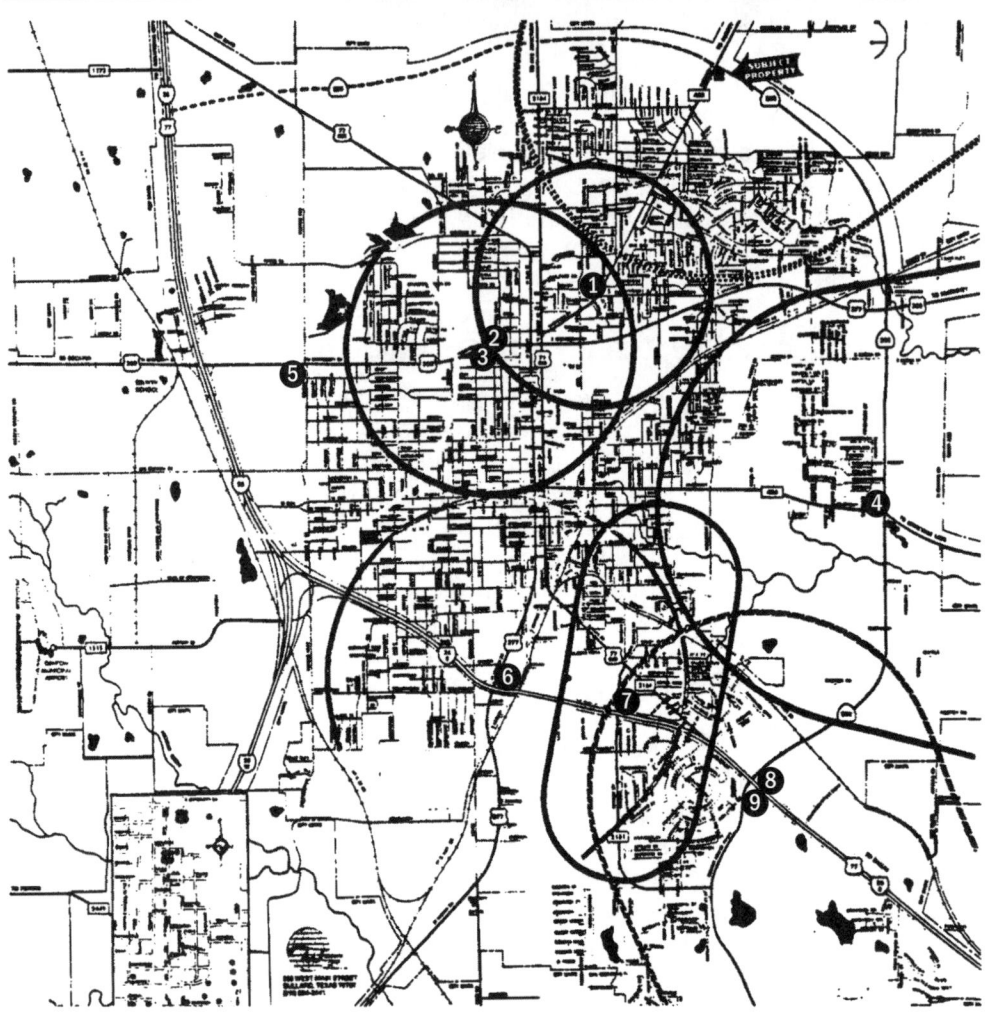

Supermarket	Name	Location	Distance/Time from Subject	Size in Sq. Ft.
1	Piggly Wiggly	Sherman Drive	1.8 mi./4 min.	30,750
2	Kroger	University Dr. @ Caroll Blvd.	2.8 mi. 7 min.	45,750
3	Winn Dixie	Sunset Blvd. @ University Dr.	3.0 mi./8min.	26,280
4	Piggly Wiggly	McKinney St. @ Loop 288	3.7 mi./5 min.	20,740
5	Skaggs	University Dr. @ Bonnie Brae	4.3 mi./10min.	45,000
6	(Proposed) Albertsons	Ft. Worth Dr. @ IH-35	4.3 mi./10 min.	N/A
7	Winn Dixie	Teasley Ln. @ IH-35	4.7 mi./15 min.	45,100
8	Kroger	Loop 288 @ IH-35	6 mi./11 min.	44,400
9	Skaggs	Loop 288 @ IH-35	6.8 mi./12 min.	66,400

Step 3: Forecast Demand

Population growth in the city has been variable but continuous for the past 30 years as shown in Exhibit 18.3.

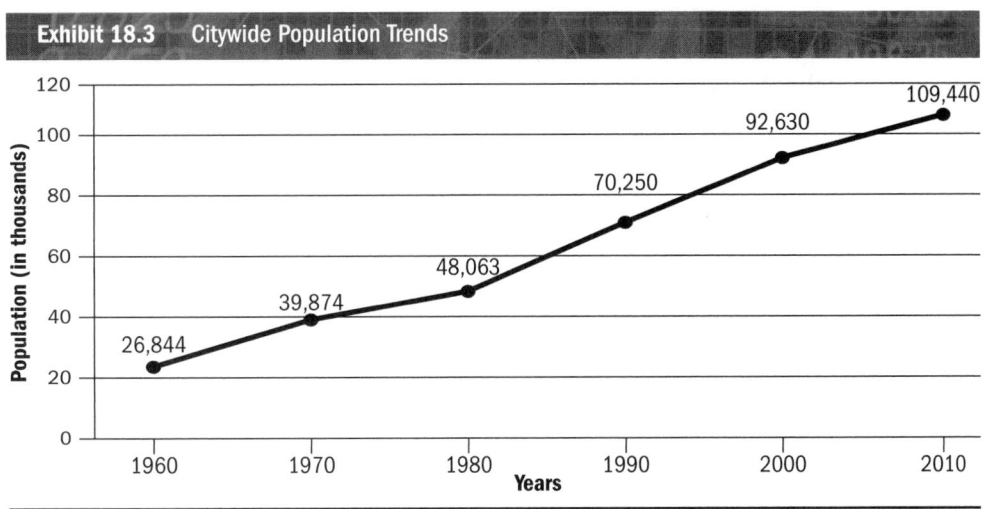

Exhibit 18.3   Citywide Population Trends

Market Area Demand

Historical population trends for Market Areas 1 and 2 are graphed in Exhibit 18.4.

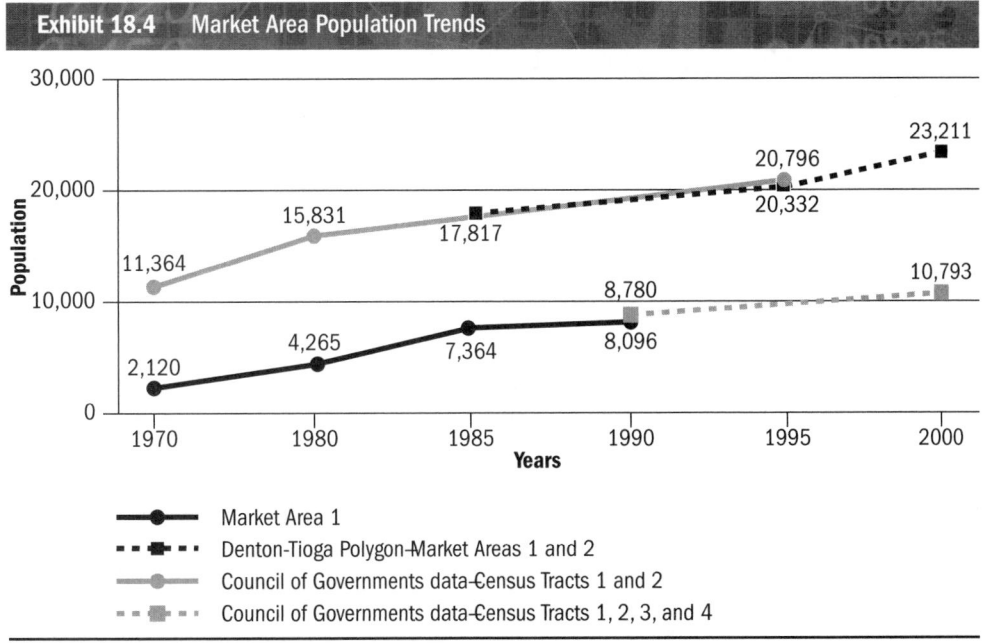

Exhibit 18.4   Market Area Population Trends

Seven data sets were used to estimate demand for the proposed supermarket, but only two are analyzed here. Steps 3.1 through 3.4 explain the methods the analyst applied to Data Set 1 to estimate supportable supermarket space in the market area. The focus on the supermarket was chosen since the total center was dependent upon the grocery feasibility of the supermarket. Data Set 1 focuses on the food expenditures of the area population. Continuing with the demand estimate derived from this data set, an inventory of competitive supply is developed in Step 4 and marginal demand is estimated in Step 5. Exhibit 18.5 shows the process employed to refine the demand data and arrive at the marginal demand estimate. Estimates of supportable supermarket space derived from the seven different data sets are shown in Exhibit 18.6.

Exhibit 18.5 Demand for Supermarket Space in the Market Area—Data Set 1	1994	1999
Demand Estimate		
Step 3.1 Primary trade area population*	9,774	10,812
Step 3.2 Annual per capita food expenditure[†]	× $1,516	× $1,516
	$14,817,384	$16,390,992
Step 3.3 Net leakage estimated @ 25%[‡]	($3,704.346)	($4,097,748)
Step 3.4 Estimated demand	$11,113,038	$12,293,244
Supply Inventory		
Step 4.1 Total competitive supermarket space in trade area	00	00
Step 5.1 Net market support—excess demand (demand minus supply)	$11,113,038	$12,293,244
Average sales/sq. ft.[§]	$312	$312
Supportable supermarket space in trade area	35,619 sq. ft.	39,401 sq. ft.

* Primary trade area consists of Census Tracts 1 and 2. Data are taken from the Council of Governments. The data for the primary trade area were adjusted to reflect only the portions of the traffic survey zones that are in the trade area.

† Annual per capita expenditures are based on Bureau of Labor Statistics, Department of Labor, *Consumer Expenditure Survey Results* (Washington, D.C.: U.S. Government Printing Office). Because the market area has a high median income level, the fourth and fifth decile food expenditures were averaged.

‡ Net leakage is the estimated amount of food expenditures that will be lost to stores outside the trade area. Although 25% is a high leakage factor, it is considered reasonable because of the nature, extent, and size of the trade area.

§ A rough guide employed by supermarket site location specialists is $6/sq. ft./week, or $312/year. This will vary depending on a variety of factors.

In an attempt to double-check the estimates derived, the appraiser used several different population data sets and generated various ranges for the forecast. The results of this sensitivity analysis are shown in Exhibit 18.6.

Data Set 2 quantifies the area demand for retail goods (excluding food) sold at a neighborhood shopping center. To estimate this demand, an alternative method employing a ratio technique is applied. This method is demonstrated in Alternative Steps 3.1, 3.2, and 3.3. Alternative Steps 4.1 and 5.1 show how this alternative demand estimate is adjusted for competitive space and a marginal demand estimate is derived. Exhibit 18.7 shows the steps in the process of refining the data derived from this alternative ratio technique.

Exhibit 18.6   Seven Forecasts of Supportable Supermarket Space

Supportable Supermarket Space in Square Feet

Data Set No.	Current	5 Yrs.
1	35,619	39,401
2	37,593	36,453
3	28,507	34,469
4	48,331	76,929
5	42,949	62,895
6	33,412	36,953
7	44,862	49,181
Average size	37,735	49,469
Standard deviation	+7,040	+15,419
Range	28,507 to 48,331	34,469 to 76,929
Mean plus 1 standard deviation	30,695 to 44,775	34,050 to 64,888
Highest and Best Use supermarket size		35,000 to 45,000 sq. ft.

Exhibit 18.7   Demand for Shopping Center Space in the Market Area (Alternative Ratio Technique)

Year	Data Set	Space Requirement Per Capita* in Sq. Ft.	Population	Total Retail Space Required in Sq. Ft.	Less Existing Space	Sq. Ft. of Excess Demand
Market Area 1						
1994	1	3.06	9,774	29,908	0.00	29,906
1999	1	3.06	10,812	33,084	0.00	33,084
Market Area 2						
1994	2	3.06	20,798	63,642	(30,750)[†]	32,892
1999	2	3.06	23,211	71,026	(30,750)	40,276

*   Retail sales were taken from Reported Gross and Taxable Sales, provided by the Comptroller of Public Accounts. Categories included were miscellaneous general merchandise; auto & home supply stores; men's and boys' clothing; women's clothing; sporting goods; miscellaneous retail. These sales figures totaled $122,340,419. County population was estimated to be 281,100. Thus, county per capita demand for neighborhood shopping center retail space = $122,340,419 / 281,100 = $435.22.

Retail sales per sq. ft. were derived from information in the Urban Land Institute's Dollars and Cents of Shopping Centers, 1994. No price index adjustment was used because it is believed that sales have been rather stable or slightly lower due to economic uncertainty in the area.

Demand per capita $435.22
Retail sales per sq. ft. = $142.33; 3.06 sq. ft. retail space required in neighborhood shopping per capita center retail space

†   Existing space in the defined area: 30,750 sq. ft.

Demand Analysis (Supermarket Space)

To estimate market demand for a supermarket, the appraiser spoke with employees in the real estate departments of several supermarket chains. Most of the supermarket personnel offered little help, preferring not to divulge information about their company's location strategy. Only two supermarket chains were willing to talk about their customer bases. From these discussions the appraiser concluded that as the minimum level of support, the chains would be willing to develop a store in an area with 5,000 customers. One chain targeted weekly sales at $6.00 per square foot or $312.00 per square foot annually as sufficient demand. Using this information, the appraiser developed the calculations shown in Exhibit 18.8.

Exhibit 18.8 breaks down the supportable retail space in the market area into three categories: supermarket, general retail, and pad site. It shows estimates of the maximum square footage to be developed in the defined market area.

Exhibit 18.8	Total New Retail Space Demand in the Defined Market Area		

	Retail Space in Square Feet	
Type of Space	**Recommended**	**Maximum**
Supermarket	40,000	50,000
General retail	35,000	40,000
Pad site	19,600[*]	19,600[*]
Totals	94,600	109,600

[*] Based on three sites of 26,136 sq. ft., with a 4:1 land-to-building ratio.

Step 3.1: Population in Trade Area

Population in the primary and secondary trade areas is estimated for current year and five years in the future.

Step 3.2: Per Capita Food Expenditures

Annual per capita expenditures on food are estimated using data from the Bureau of Labor Statistics' *Consumer Expenditure Survey Results.* Although the economy had taken a downturn since the data were published, no adjustment of the data appears to be warranted. The neighborhood is an upper-income area of the city, so an average of the two highest deciles for the data are used.

Multiplying the annual per capita expenditure for food by the estimated population in the market area indicates that the total expenditures on food in the market area will be $14,817,384 in 1994 and $16,390,992 in 1999.

Step 3.3: Net Leakage

In the preceding step, the total potential expenditure on food in the market area was estimated. However, some of these expenditures will not be made at supermarkets in the defined market area. Expenditures will leak out to other market areas and stores. In Step 3.3 the appraiser estimates this loss of sales to outside the market area to be 25%. The 25% figure is high relative to rule-of-thumb estimates, which range between 10% and 25%, depending on the structure of the market area and the design of the store.

Step 3.4: Estimated Demand

Leakage is subtracted from the per capita expenditures to arrive at an estimate of supermarket expenditures for the market area. The calculations are

$$\$14{,}817{,}384 - (\$14{,}817{,}384 \times 0.25) = \$11{,}113{,}038$$

Step 4: Inventory the Competitive Supply

Step 4.1: Total Competitive Supply

Exhibit 18.2 showed the sizes and estimated market areas of the competitive supermarkets. Each competitor has its own market area. It revealed no competitive supermarkets in the subject's market area and only one planned supermarket (Albertson's). The map in Exhibit 18.9 shows competitive vacant sites in the subject's market area.

Step 5: Estimate Marginal Demand

To arrive at an estimate of marginal demand for supermarket space, the competitive supply is subtracted from supportable supermarket space. Since the defined market area has no competing supermarkets, zero appears on the line for competitive space in Exhibit 18.5.

If there had been competitive space, the estimated demand would have had to be adjusted to obtain the estimate of marginal demand (i.e., net demand required to support new supermarket space). For example, if there had been an existing 30,000-sq.-ft. supermarket in the defined market area, its annual sales could have been estimated at $9,360,000 ($312 in sales per square foot per year × 30,000 square feet = $9,360,000).

Demand was estimated in Step 3.4 at $11,113,038, of which the 30,000-sq.-ft. supermarket would absorb $9,360,000. The $1,753,038 difference would represent marginal demand and would not be enough net expenditure to warrant a new supermarket. Marginal demand, which is the focus of Step 5, is the measure of excess demand in the market area, calculated as supportable demand minus competitive supply.

Step 5.1: Net Market Support

Using the average estimated supermarket sales required per square foot, the appraiser can calculate the amount of new supermarket space that market area demand can support. In Exhibit 18.6, supportable supermarket space is calculated at 35,619 square feet for 1994 and 39,401 square feet for 1999. Thus, between 35,000 and 40,000 square feet of supermarket space can be supported by the market area.

The appraiser applies an alternative technique to Data Set 2 to estimate the demand for the neighborhood shopping center. The steps followed in applying the technique are outlined below. Exhibit 18.7 illustrates how the market demand data derived from this alternative ratio technique are refined into an estimate of marginal demand for the neighborhood shopping center.

Alternative Step 3.1: Per Capita Expenditure on Retail Goods

The per capita expenditure on retail goods at a neighborhood shopping center, excluding supermarket sales, is estimated based on sales tax data and population estimates. (Sales tax data for counties and cities are available from the state accounts comptroller.) Selected categories of retail sales considered pertinent to the subject were identified in the tax

Exhibit 18.9 Competitive Vacant Sites

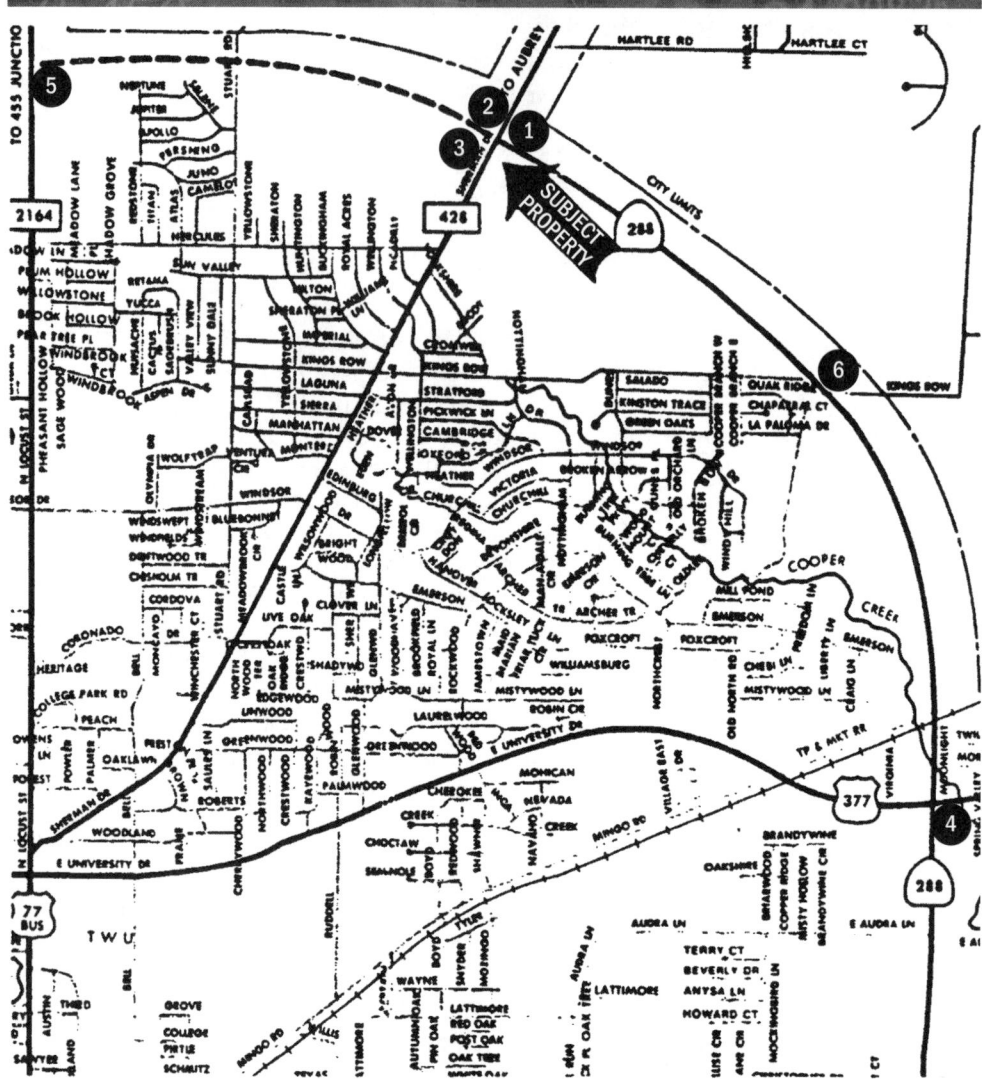

Site #	Location	Comments
1	NEC Loop 288 @ Sherman	Strong competitor. Good location.
2	NWC Loop 288 @ Sherman	Divided among multiple owners.
3	SWC Loop 288 @ Sherman	Divided among multiple owners.
4	Loop 288 @ University Dr.	Serious floodplain and fill problems on all corners.
5	Proposed Loop 288 @ SH2164	Good location. Depth of demand from neighborhood not as well developed as subject.
6	NC Loop 288 @ Kings Row	Beer/wine sales prohibited.

data. From the selected categories on the tax receipts, the appraiser estimates the total per capita sales for the county to be $435.22

Alternative Step 3.2: Retail Sales per Square Foot

From the Urban Land Institute's data, *Dollars and Cents of Shopping Centers*, the appraiser obtained an estimate of $142.33 in retail sales per square foot for neighborhood shopping centers.

With this information the per capita retail space requirements for shopping center stores in the county can be calculated. $435.22 per capita sales / $142.33 retail sales per sq. ft. = 3.06 sq. ft. per person demand for neighborhood retail space.

Alternative Step 3.3: Supportable Retail Space

Multiplying the square-footage space requirement of 3.06 by the population in the market area yields an estimate of the amount of shopping center space supported by market area demand. For 1994 (current) the estimate is 29,908 square feet ($3.06 \times 9,774$); for 1999 the estimate is 33,084 square feet ($3.06 \times 10,812$).

Alternative Step 4.1: Competitive Space

Existing competitive space in the market area must be subtracted from the amount of supportable retail space in the market area. Since there was no existing or anticipated competition in Market Area 1 (as defined by Data Set 1), no adjustment was required. In Market Area 2, represented by Data Set 2, there are 30,750 square feet of existing competitive space, which must be subtracted from the estimate of supportable retail space (see Exhibit 18.7).

Alternative Step 5.1: Marginal Demand

Marginal demand in the market area is the amount that remains after competitive space is subtracted from supportable retail space. Note that after the adjustment for competitive retail space is made, the estimated marginal demand figures derived from the two data sets are reasonably similar. The difference in the two sets of population estimates reflects the different sizes of the two defined market areas.

Step 6: Estimate Subject Capture

Because the subject tract has no competition in the immediate market area and an excellent location, it will capture 100% of the marginal demand forecast. If competition existed in the market area or the subject's location was less desirable, the subject's capture rate would have to be estimated. Generally, the test of financial feasibility requires an estimated capture rate for the subject property.

Highest and Best Use Conclusion

The property's locational attributes indicate a probable retail use, but other attributes suggest alternative uses. For example, the property's physical attributes could support multifamily housing, warehouse/industrial, or office uses. The zoning advantage points to a retail use, as do the complementary properties and land uses found nearby. Finally, the design of the site supports a retail use. Thus, the aggregate of property attributes indicates a retail use, specifically a neighborhood shopping center/supermarket.

The market analysis shows that there is demand for a neighborhood retail facility in the defined market area. It appears that a 40,000-sq.-ft. supermarket can be supported by marginal demand and that another 35,000 to 40,000 square feet of general retail space is also viable.

Threshold testing of the multifamily residential use (Step 7) is presented in the following pages to verify that the use assessment is correct. As mentioned earlier, threshold testing is an analytical procedure commonly employed in highest and best use analyses. An alternative use is tested based on especially optimistic forecast data (i.e., marginal demand and capture rate) to give the alternative use every possible chance to succeed. If the threshold testing establishes that the alternative use does not compare favorably with the other financially feasible uses, the use is eliminated from further consideration.

Step 7: Analyze Financial Feasibility Using Threshold Testing

To conclude the highest and best use study, the appraiser conducts a financial feasibility analysis by threshold testing. There are several ways to test the viability of a proposed development project. In this case, the client is a developer, so financial feasibility is examined from the perspective of a developer. The developer wants assurances that his investment in the project will be justified. This is established once the value of the developed property reaches or exceeds a breakeven point at which project costs are covered. Hence, the developer uses the breakeven point as a risk control measure to ensure that the development will have sufficient cash flow to warrant the investment.

Exhibit 18.10 compares the basic financial feasibility of a retail center and a multifamily apartment project. At the top of the exhibit, 13 market-based assumptions for each use are listed. A breakeven model is employed.[1] The retail development appears capable of supporting a land value of $4.41 per square foot on a construction budget of $39.54 per square foot. Both figures are within the parameters set for the project. A multifamily housing use was tested with appropriate variables and the results differed significantly. The land value would be

---

1. James A. Graaskamp, Fundamentals of Real Estate Development, Development Component Series (Washington, D.C.: Urban Land Institute, 1981), 21.

Exhibit 18.10 Feasibility Tests: Land under Retail Use Versus Land under Multifamily Housing Use

Feasibility Test #1: Retail Land Breakeven (Default Ratio) Model

Market-Based Assumptions
Market-Based Variables

1. Site cost/sq. ft.	$4.13
2. Site size in sq. ft.	435,600
3. Construction budget (direct & indirect) costs/sq. ft.	$38.00
4. Building size in sq. ft.	80,000
5. Equity dividend ratio	3.5%
6. Breakeven ratio (default ratio)	80.0%
Loan	100.00%
Rate	10.50%
Term	25.0 yrs.
7. Debt service constant	11.33%
8. Market rent/sq. ft.	$8.00
9. EGI operating expense ratio	31.0%
10. Vacancy rate	8.0%
11. Operating expenses/sq. ft.	$2.48
12. Risk reserve	$0.00
13. Cash replacement reserves	$0.00

Breakeven (Default Ratio) Model
Developer's BEP Model
The Computations
Justified Cash Equity Investment

Potential gross income	$640,000
× (1 − default ratio)	20.0%
= Cash available after operating expenses & debt service	$128,000
− Vacancy & collection loss	($51,200)
− Risk reserve	$0
= Cash available for investors	$76,800
/ Equity dividend rate	3.5%
= Justified equity cash investment	$2,194,266

Justified Mortgage Loan

Potential gross income	$640,000
× Default ratio	80.0%
= Cash outlays for operating expenses & debt service	$512,000
− Operating expenses	($198,400)
− Cash replacements	$0
= Cash available for debt service	$313,600
/ Debt service constant	11.33%
= Justified mortgage loan	$2,767,829

Total Justified Investment

Justified equity investment	$2,194,286
+ Justified mortgage loan	$2,767,829
= Total justified investment	$4,962,115

Justified Construction Budget

Total justified investment	$4,962,115
− Land value	($1,799,028)*
= Construction budget (direct & indirect)	$3,163,087
/ Square feet in building	80,000
= Justified budget/sq. ft.	$39.54

Justified Land Value

Total justified investment	$4,962,115
− Construction budget	($3,040,000)
= Justified land value	$1,922,115
/ Square feet in land	435,600
= Justified land value/sq. ft.	$4.41

Feasibility Test #2: Retail Land Breakeven (Default Ratio) Model

Market-Based Assumptions
Market-Based Variables

1. Site cost/sq. ft.	$4.13
2. Site size in sq. ft.	435,600
3. Construction budget (direct & indirect) costs/sq. ft.	$32.00
4. Building size in sq. ft.	105,000
5. Equity dividend ratio	3.5%
6. Breakeven ratio (default ratio)	75.0%
Loan	100.00%
Rate	10.26%
Term	25.0 yrs.
7. Debt service constant	11.33%
8. Market rent/sq. ft.	$5.76
9. EGI operating expense ratio	22.0%
10. Vacancy rate	14.0%
11. Operating expenses/sq. ft.	$1.27
12. Risk reserve	$0.00
13. Cash replacement reserves	$0.00

Breakeven (Default Ratio) Model
Developer's BEP Model
The Computations
Justified Cash Equity Investment

Potential gross income	$604,800
× (1 − default ratio)	25.0%
= Cash available after operating expenses & debt service	$151,200
− Vacancy & collection loss	($84,672)
− Risk reserve	$0
= Cash available for investors	$66,528
/ Equity dividend rate	3.5%
= Justified equity cash investment	$1,900,800

Justified Mortgage Loan

Potential gross income	$604,800
× Default ratio	75.0%
= Cash outlays for operating expenses & debt service	$453,600
− Operating expenses	($133,056)
− Cash replacements	$0
= Cash available for debt service	$320,544
/ Debt service constant	11.13%
= Justified mortgage loan	$2,881,264

Total Justified Investment

Justified equity investment	$1,900,800
+ Justified mortgage loan	$2,881,264
= Total justified investment	$4,782,064

Justified Construction Budget

Total justified investment	$4,782,064
− Land value	($1,799,028)*
= Construction budget (direct & indirect)	$2,983,036
/ Square feet in building	105,000
= Justified budget/sq. ft.	$28.41

Justified Land Value

Total justified investment	$4,782,064
− Construction budget	($3,360,000)
= Justified land value	$1,422,064
/ Square feet in land	435,600
= Justified land value/sq. ft.	$3.26

* 10 acres x 43,560 sq. ft./acre × $4.13 site cost/sq. ft. = $1,799,028.

$3.26 per square foot with a supportable construction budget of $28.41 per square foot, 11% below the $32 actual cost to construct apartment units in the current market. Thus, the test confirms the appraiser's belief that the site is best suited to retail use.

Specification of Highest and Best Use

The highest and best use conclusion for the property is use as a neighborhood shopping center. The timing of this use is current. The market participants specified are the neighborhood residents, who represent the users of the shopping center, and a developer, who would be the likely buyer of the vacant tract.

CHAPTER 19

Vacant Retail
Shopping Center

Highest and Best Use Analysis Process

The highest and best use analysis process entails three steps: performing the six-step process, analyzing the most competitive alternatives, and reconciling the data to arrive at a conclusion.

Six-Step Process

The six-step process is completed to provide the data for screening alternatives to determine the most competitive ones. It yields the forecast data required to assess the financial expectations of each alternative.

Financial Analysis of Alternatives

The most competitive alternatives are analyzed based on financial performance expectations.

Final Highest and Best Use Conclusions (Reconciliation—Maximally Productive)

All of the data are synthesized to estimate the most probable-productive use of the property.

Case Study Description

The case study is the highest and best use part of a market value appraisal of a 10-year-old vacant 36,000-sq.-ft. property in two buildings previously used for specialty retailing and restaurant, but is now vacant. The buildings have a common brick and wood (cedar) façade, are in good condition, and are connected by a covered porch.

The site's large front yard is landscaped, which is considerably more attractive than typical retail strips in town, which have little or no landscaping. It has 300 parking spaces (one space per 120 sq. ft. of gross building area), and the concrete parking lot is in good condition. The number of spaces is more than is required by the zoning.

The current site utilization is shown below:

Property Element	Square Feet	Percentage of Total Site
Parking 300 spaces × 400[1] sq. ft.	120,000	61%
Building area (1-story buildings)	36,000	19%
Loading and maintenance areas	10,000	5%
Landscaping, courtyard, and walkways	30,000	15%
Total area of site	196,000 sq. ft. (4.5 acres)	

The property was previously occupied by a restaurant and upscale specialty stores, including a clothing store, jeweler, and electronics store. The last of the tenants recently vacated the store in favor of the new mall area about two miles from the subject, where all of the tenants have relocated.

The site is zoned retail, which allows for a wide range of uses, including such former uses as retail and restaurant, office (restricted to two stories), and apartments at 18 units per acre.

---

1. Required square feet per parking space includes maneuvering space.

The property is located on a major road in a growing segment of a major metropolitan area. The primary concern about location is that most new retailers have moved toward a new highway bypass and mall located approximately 1 1/2 miles south of the subject. Exhibit 19.1 shows the subject and its location.

Exhibit 19.1 Site Plan for a 10-Year-Old Small Shopping Center

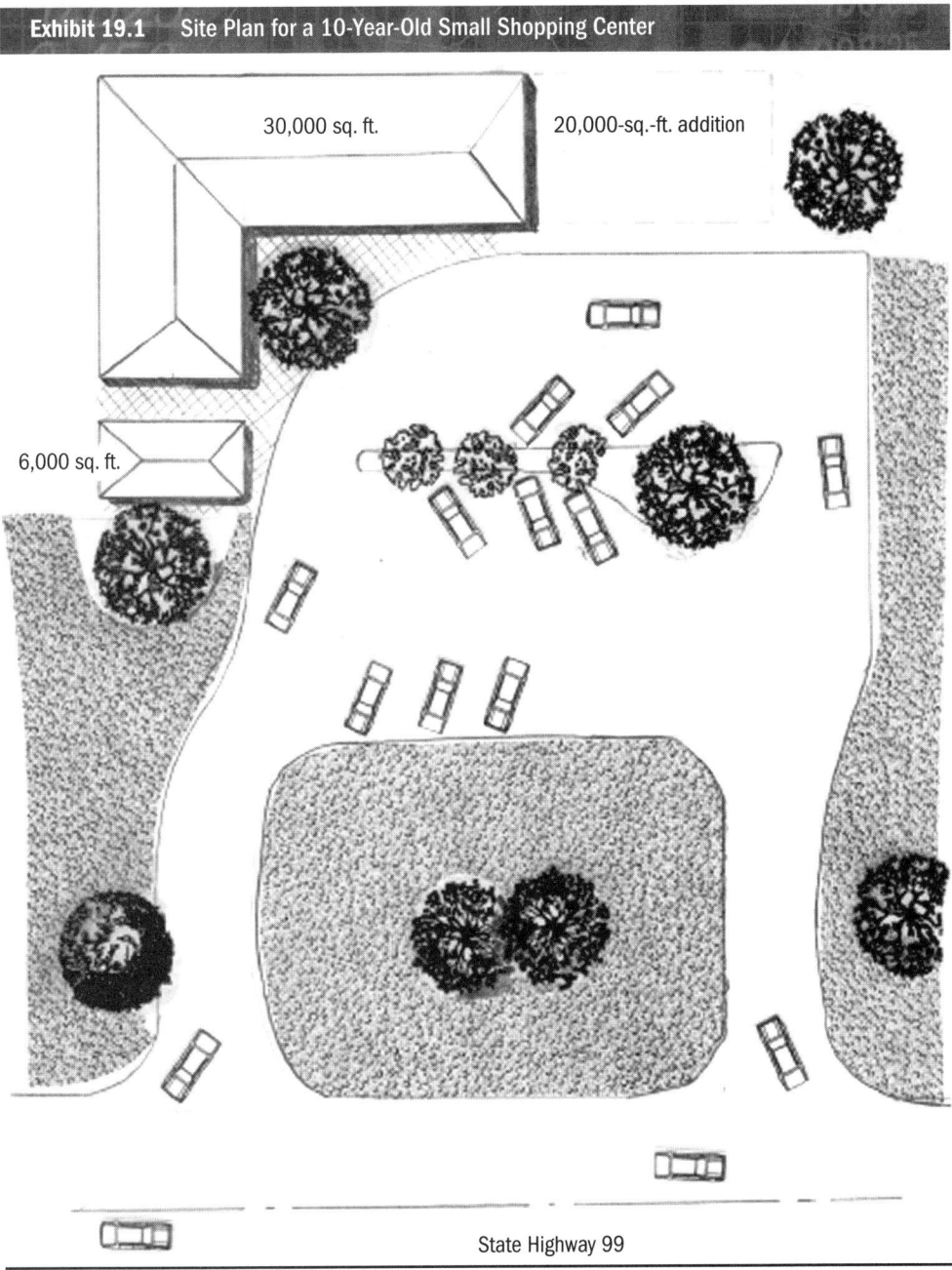

30,000 sq. ft.

20,000-sq.-ft. addition

6,000 sq. ft.

State Highway 99

Scoping Analysis

The scoping analysis is a brief overview of all possible alternative uses of the property to eliminate those that are obviously not feasible. It is based on general logic and inferred data that are commonly available. In many instances, the site, building improvements, and location factors will screen out many alternatives. In addition, the real estate economic trends commonly known in the area will further screen out others.

The intent of this step is to focus the main part of the highest and best use study on the most competitive alternatives.

Most Competitive Alternatives for the Subject

Assumed vacant (the demolition alternative; the land assumed vacant)

1. Restaurant/specialty retail (the current use alternative)
2. Restaurant/neighborhood retail (new marketing strategy alternative)
3. Restaurant/office remodel alternative
5. Restaurant/office addition alternative with addition in Year 1
6. Phasing alternative of restaurant/office addition with addition in latter years
7. Total office remodel and addition

Based on this general analysis, the focus of the case study will be on these alternatives.

Step 1: Analyze the Property's Productivity Property Rating

Exhibit 19.2 summarizes the property rating for retail use. The rating compares the property's features with those of the major competitors in the market area. The data show that the center rates below average in property features. Because the center is vacant, the tenant factors are all rated highly negative. If the center were occupied, it would rate above average, given the higher quality site features. The building is rated excellent for exterior appearance. Features of the site that rated positive were landscaping and parking. The landscaping is very good, since the city requires only 10%, and the quality of the plant material and maintenance is good. The number of parking spaces exceeds the required number for restaurant and retail use; thus, it is rated positive.

The subject building is compared to other competitive retail centers in close proximity. Although the design and appearance of the subject is superior to typical retail in the area, the lack of tenants, particularly anchor tenants, makes the subject highly inferior to the competition for retail use.

Location Analysis

The subject is located on the main street in a suburb of a large metropolitan area. The street is also a state highway that crosses the city. The land

Exhibit 19.2 Property Rating Summary for Retail Use

Comparison to Standard Impact on Productivity	Veto Factor	Inferior			Typical	Superior		
		High	Moderate	Slight	Average	Slight	Moderate	High
Site								
1. Grades (topography)					X			
2. Land-to-building ratio					X			
3. Ease of access (curb-cuts)					X			
4. Landscaping								X
Parking								
5. Number							X	
6. Interior circulation					X			
Building Improvements								
7. Exterior appearance								X
8. Design flexibility							X	
9. Street visibility					X			
Tenant Mix and Marketing Features								
10. Size and drawing power of anchor		X						
11. Image of center		X						
12. Tenant Compatibility Mix		X						
Immediately Adjacent Land Use								
13. Land use compatibility					X			
14. Reputation of immediate area					X			
15. Cumulative attraction					X			
Other								
16. Legal constraints/opportunities						X		
Subject number of items		3	0	0	8	1	2	2
Times category score		0	2	4	5	6	8	10
Subject score		0	0	0	40	6	16	20

use fronting this highway in the vicinity of the subject is predominantly commercial and apartments. Apartments and vacant land lie to the east of the subject. Some of the apartments have been built in the last few years. Primarily 10-to-20-year-old single-family residences are to the west and southwest of the subject. About one mile east of the interstate is a major office/industrial park with campus-type developments. This 400-acre office/industrial park is approximately five years old and is about 20% developed, which is considered good absorption for this market.

Within the last two years a major retail mall was opened about 1 ½ miles southeast of the subject. This mall fronts the interstate and is adjacent to a new bypass of the state highway that is scheduled to open within two years. This bypass is a new routing of the highway that fronts the subject.

Land Use Along Main Street

Exhibit 19.3 shows the land use fronting Highway 99 (subject street) at a length of 2 ½ miles from the interstate on the north to the new state highway bypass on the south.

Profile of Tenant Types Along Highway 99 within 1 Mile of Subject

A review of the types of tenants along State Highway 99 can be used to draw an inference about the possible user expected for the subject. Exhibit 19.3 summarizes the tenant types and the approximate amount of space occupied. These tenants are located within the shopping centers along Highway 99 and are also located in stand-alone buildings.

The tenant along Highway 99 indicates a large concentration of restaurant uses. Restaurants account for approximately 25% of the total tenants and the total space occupied. Convenience stores and service stations account for the next highest number of tenant uses. Insurance offices and other service offices rank third.

Current Land Use Growth Trends

Most of the new single-family residential growth in the city has occurred west of subject, and apartment development has been active just east of subject.

State Highway 99 (subject) frontage and the intersections of major thoroughfares have historically been the dominant area for retail development. Retail growth in the last two years has occurred in the southeast around the new mall. The retail businesses built in the last five years within two miles of the subject along Highway 99 have all been neighborhood convenience-type stores, which included a new grocery store, a dry cleaner, a car wash, and a service station.

Exhibit 19.3	Land Use Fronting Highway 99			
Tenant Type	**# Along Hwy. 99**	**% of Total**	**Estimated Total**	**% of Total GLA**
Grocery store	1	1.1%	30,000 sq. ft.	11.1%
Drug store	2	2.4%	20,000 sq. ft.	7.4%
Clothing store	5	5.8%	18,000 sq. ft.	6.7%
Specialty retailer	7	8.1%	31,000 sq. ft.	11.5%
Rental stores	3	3.5%	10,000 sq. ft.	3.7%
Medical services	6	7.0%	10,000 sq. ft.	3.7%
Restaurants	22	25.6%	70,000 sq. ft.	25.8%
Clothing cleaners	5	5.8%	9,200 sq. ft.	3.4%
Coin laundry	3	3.5%	8,500 sq. ft.	3.1%
Convenience/Service				
Stations	11	12.8%	20,300 sq. ft.	7.5%
Beauty salon	7	8.1%	10,800 sq. ft.	4.0%
Auto service	2	2.3%	18,000 sq. ft.	6.7%
Insurance and other				
Service office	8	9.4%	9,100 sq. ft.	3.4%
Child care center	1	1.1%	5,600 sq. ft.	2.0%
Used car dealership	3	3.5%	N/A	0%
Total	86	100%	270,500 sq. ft.	

Note: Includes sit-down and drive-up restaurants

Most restaurant development has been concentrated around the new mall but restaurant development is still occurring on Highway 99 in the vicinity of the subject and in the northeastern part of the city along major thoroughfares and the interstate highway.

Office development has been limited to the office/industrial park just east of the interstate and scattered small office projects throughout the city.

Exhibit 19.4 summarizes new commercial development in the city that has occurred in the last five years.

Exhibit 19.4	New Development in City in Last Five Years		
Land Use Type	Northwest Part of City	Central Part of City*	Southeast Part of City†
Restaurants	10	12	14
Retail	11	4	23
Apartments	4	14	2
Office	0	0	3

* Within 1 mile of subject in the vicinity of the Highway 99 corridor.

† Primarily within 1/2 mile of new mall and new office business park.

Traffic Counts

The subject is currently located on a major through state highway whose current traffic count is 23,000 cars per day. Even after the new state highway bypass is completed and through traffic is rerouted, local traffic is expected to maintain the current traffic volume, with increases forecast in the future.

Location Rating

The subject location (2-mile frontage along Highway 99 from the interstate to new Highway 99 bypass) is rated for various land uses, which are summarized in Exhibit 19.5.

Highest and Best Use Alternatives Conclusions Based on Property and Location Features

The property and location analysis suggests the following major land use alternatives that would require further study to determine which use is estimated to provide the maximally productive use for the property:

Alternative 1: Assumed Vacant—The Demolition

The most active real estate development in the immediate area in the last five years has been apartments. Because of the proximity and extent of the new apartment development, this alternative needs to be considered. It would involve demolition of the existing building improvements to construct apartments.

Alternative 2: Restaurant/Specialty Retail—The Current Use

The property has building improvements in good condition and until recently, had been occupied with restaurant and specialty retail. Thus, the current (or in this case) most recent use is nearly always an alternative that requires further study.

Alternative 3: Restaurant/Neighborhood Retail—New Marketing Strategy

The subject was improved for restaurant and retail use. The former retail classification was regional/community in the form of specialty retail. Because the center lost all of its tenants to the new regional mall, a new retail use of the property might be in order. The advantages of this alternative are that the building would not require remodeling costs, and the public perceives the property as a retail store.

Alternative 4: Restaurant/Office Remodel

This is an alternative use that would require the least amount in remodeling costs. In this case, office use is most probable, given the subject location and the improvements design, which is easily adapted to office use.

Alternative 5: Restaurant/Office Remodel and Addition Year 1

This alternative is a further expansion of the previous office remodel alternative. Because the office use is a change in land use from the site's original plan, the optimum site utilization should be explored. In this case, the building can be expanded for office use primarily due to the reduced requirement for parking for office use compared to retail use. The reduced parking requirement frees up land that can be developed for office use.

Alternative 6: Restaurant/Office Remodel and Addition Year 5

This alternative is a refinement of the previous alternative by varying the time of entry of the office addition into the market.

Alternative 7: Total Office Remodel and Addition

This alternative considers the subject as a total office project.

The subject's highest and best use will depend heavily upon the supply and demand factors in the market, which is the focus of the next part of this case study.

The next section, the Financial Analysis of Alternatives, will apply the economic demand estimate to financial models.

The results of the financial models will provide the data to estimate the use that will provide the highest economic return to the property.

Step 2: Delineate the Market

The market areas will vary according to the alternative property type. The neighborhood retail alternative will be within about 1 1/2 miles,

Exhibit 19.5   Ranking of Land Use Alternatives

Rating Factors	Very Poor -3	Below Avg. -1	Avg. 0	Above Avg. 1	Very Good 3	Total Score
Office—(garden office)						
Proximity to major activity nodes				1		
Proximity to freeways/thoroughfares				1		
Proximity to housing					3	
Proximity to newest office development		-1				
Visibility from major thoroughfares					3	
Public planning and zoning				1		
Office total score						8
Retail (regional/community)						
Linkage to households in 5-mile radius			0	1		
Proximity to direction of new residential growth in trade area				1		
Proximity to major activity centers		-1				
Proximity to freeway(s)-veto factor	-3					
Proximity to direction of regional retail growth	-3					
Public planning and zoning support for retail			0			
Regional retail total score						-5
Retail (neighborhood)						
Linkage to housing in 1- to 2-mile radius				1		
Proximity to new residential growth				1		
Traffic volume by site				1		
Density of immediate area housing					3	
Proximity to new neighborhood retail growth	-3					
Public planning and zoning			0			
Neighborhood retail total score						3
Restaurant						
Linkage to housing in 1- to 2-mile radius				1		
Proximity to office and hotels				1		
Traffic volume by site				1		
Density of immediate area housing					3	
Proximity to other restaurants				1		
Public planning and zoning			0			
Restaurant total score						7
Multifamily						
Proximity to employment for typical tenants					3	
Proximity to cultural activities (restaurants and entertainment)				1		
Proximity to major thoroughfares/freeways					3	
Proximity to comparison shopping				1		
Direction of multifamily growth					3	
Public planning and zoning				1		
Multifamily total score						12

while the community retail will be 3 miles, and office and apartment alternatives will be citywide. The following gives an overview of the market area characteristics.

Population and Household Growth in the City

Exhibit 19.6 provides data for the city as a whole and the area within one mile of the subject. The data show current and forecasted population and households. The forecasted population is the mid-range, with the high and low range estimated at about a 15% spread.

Exhibit 19.6   Population and Household Growth in the City

	Population			Households		
Area	Current	+10 years	% Increase per Yr.	Current	+ 10 Years	% Increase per Yr.
City	48,250	73,280	4.26%	17,570	28,930	5.11%
One mile of subject	11,692	16,809	3.67%	4,990	8,430	5.38%

Employment Growth in City

The employment data represent local employment; that is, actual jobs located in the city. These data are both current data and forecasted. The employment forecast represents the mid-range estimate with a 20% spread, for the high and low range as summarized in Exhibit 19.7.

Exhibit 19.7   Employment Growth in the City

	Total Employment		
	Current	+10 Years	% Increase per Yr.
City	18,260	29,850	4.3%

Steps 2, 3, 4, 5 & 6: Perform Market and Marketability Analyses for Each Alternative

Apartment Market Analysis

According to the previous data, a current demand for apartments in the subject's immediate area is evidenced by new building construction and population growth. The location analysis rated the subject location very positive for apartment development.

Thus, because much inferred data suggest immediate demand, a detailed fundamental forecast is not judged to be necessary. Based on inferred data, it is estimated that the subject site, assumed vacant, would be competitive in the current market for apartment development at 18 units per acre.

Restaurant Market and Marketability Analysis

The building design, previous use, and location all suggest that a restaurant use might be a viable alternative or part of other alternatives for the property. This section assesses market demand for this use at this location.

Inferred Demand for Restaurant

- Location Rating
  The subject area was rated high for restaurant use.
- Gross Sales Trends

  Exhibit 19.8 shows the gross sales for restaurants in the city.

Exhibit 19.8	Historical Gross Sales for Eating Places							
Year (Current & Previous Years)	Adjusted Gross Sales*	% Change	Number of Stores Reporting	% Change	Avg. Sales per Store	Sales per Capita-City	Sales per Capita- Metro-Area	Sales per Capita State
5 yrs. prev.	$28,110,162		73		$385,071	$769		
4 yrs. prev.	$31,034,842	10.4%	79	8.2%	$392,846	$834		
3 yrs. prev.	$30,395,855	-2.1%	85	7.6%	$357,598	$741		
2 yrs. prev.	$34,215,963	12.6%	84	-1.2%	$407,333	$777		
Last year	$35,162,396	2.8%	84	0.0%	$418,600	$770		
Current year	$40,410,141	14.9%	88	4.8%	$459,206	$863	697	527

* Note: Adjusted for inflation—i.e., sales in current dollars

- The gross sales data for restaurant sales in the city showed a 14.9% increase in real dollars during the last year. This can be attributed in large part to the new restaurants and customers coming to the mall that opened in the last two years. However, sales in the city have increased in each of the five years except one. The average sales per capita are higher than state and metropolitan averages. Thus, the city is a good area for restaurant use.

- Restaurant Building Activity
  The location section provided data that showed 36 new restaurants built in the city in the last five years; 12 of these restaurants were located in the subject immediate area of the two-mile strip along Highway 99. This is considered positive for the city and the subject immediate area for restaurant use.

- Current Tenant Mix
  The location section provided data on a survey of current tenants within one mile of the subject along Highway 99. These data found that 25% of the tenants were restaurant use, which is positive for the subject in terms of future release of the subject for restaurant use.

- Population and Employment Growth
  The city in general and the subject's immediate area both are forecast to have good growth rates with employment growth especially good. The employment growth is one very positive factor for restaurant use.

Fundamental Residual Demand Analysis of the Restaurant Market

Exhibit 19.9 presents a fundamental demand analysis of the restaurant market. The analysis is considered conservative because:

- The household data are only for a one-mile radius of subject. Sit-in restaurants typically draw from a larger area.
- The demand from daytime employment is not estimated, but it should be recognized that it does exist in this market.

The conservative data assumptions are used to assess the primary demand for the subject market–the nearby households. If the market showed positive demand from the households that would generate the largest income for subject type restaurant, it would be considered a good market.

Exhibit 19.9   Sit-in Restaurant Residual Demand within 1 Mile of Subject by Buying Power Method

Year	Current	Five Years	10 Years	Comment
Households in 1-mile radius	4,990	6,710	8,430	
Median household income	$ 47,000	$47,000	$47,000	Constant-dollar calculations
Total household income	$234,530,000	$315,370,000	$396,210,000	
Percentage of income spent on retail	38%	38%	38%	Source: Bureau of Labor Statistics
Retail buying power	$89,121,400	$119,840,600	$150,559,800	
Percentage of retail expenditures spent on restaurant	13%	13%	13%	Source: State sales tax data
Restaurant buying power in 1 mile of subject	$11,585,782	$15,579,278	$19,572,774	
Percentage of restaurant buying power spent at sit-in (subject type bldg.)	52%	52%	52%	Source: Commercial data vendor
Total buying power for sit-in restaurants by households in one mile of subject	$6,024,607	$8,101,225	$10,177,842	
Demand from secondary sources	0	0	0	Leakage out is estimated to equal leakage in
Total sit-in restaurant demand	$6,024,607	$8,101,225	$10,177,842	
Required sale per sq. ft.	$210	$210	$210	Source: *Dollars & Cents of Shopping Centers* by Urban Land Institute, adjusted to local rents
Estimated amount of supportable sit-in restaurant space demand in one mile of subject in sq. ft.	28,689	38,577	48,466	
Less current occupied sit-in restaurant space in one mile of subject	23,500	23,500	23,500	Source: On-the-ground surveys; see description section
Residual demand for new sit-in restaurant space (sq. ft.) based on current occupied space	5,183	15,295	24,966	

Subject Marketability (Capture) for Restaurant Use

The preceding residual demand study showed that the market has excess demand from households within one mile of the subject based on occupied space. In addition, it is expected that additional demand will be realized from secondary sources such as the daytime employment in the area. Assuming that the current restaurant occupants remain where they are, the subject and competitive vacant space would be dividing up the new residual demand.

The subject's ability to compete in this market is analyzed by a system for rating the competition. The subject for sit-in restaurant use is a 6,000-square-foot building that sits at the front of the subject property and was previously used for restaurant use.

Exhibit 19.10 depicts a rating system based on a ranking technique where competitive facilities are ranked with all other competition. It highlights the major competition and the rating comparison of the subject to the competition. The higher the ranking (score), the higher the competitive position.

- Currently Built Vacant Space Designed for Sit-in Restaurant Use
  The following rates the subject with currently vacant space designed for a sit-in restaurant. The following is space that was previously used (and is improved) for restaurant use. Building 4 is a stand-alone building like the subject, while the other three competitive spaces are parts of shopping centers. The competitive restaurant space is located within one mile of the subject in the same area used for the demand calculations.

Exhibit 19.10 Capture Potential of Vacant Space Designed for Restaurant Use

		Ranking Factors						
Factor Importance		6	5	4	3	2	1	
Bldg #	Square Feet	Proximity to Supportive Facilities (Office/Hotels) and Other Restaurants	Bldg./ Space Condition	Bldg. Space Design Appeal	Visibility of Space	Frontage and Access	Traffic Volume by Site	Total Ranking Score (Wt.)
1	3,000	1	2	2	3	1	2	37
2	2,800	3	1	1	1	1	4	36
3	5,072	2	2	3	2	2	3	47
4	3,500	4	2	2	1	1	1	48
Subj.	6,000	4	3	4	4	2	2	73
Total	20,372							

- New Construction

   The market is showing current positive demand for new space and is forecast to grow. However, according to the city planning staff, there are not any new restaurant platting, zoning, or preliminary inquiries. Regardless, competition from new construction is expected because of the positive buying power in the market.

   The competitive position of the subject with possible new construction is estimated by comparing it with competitive vacant sites within one mile of the subject. Exhibit 19.11 rates the competitive vacant tracts with the subject site.

Exhibit 19.11 Small Tract Restaurant Capture Potential

		Ranking Factors						
Factor Importance		6	5	4	3	2	1	
Tract #	**Acreage**	**Proximity to Supportive Facilities (Office/ Hotels)**	**Proximity and Links to Residential**	**Proximity to Other Resteraunts**	**Visibility of Site**	**Frontage and Access**	**Traffic Volume by Site**	**Total Ranking Score (Wt.)**
1	1	3	2	3	3	1	2	53
2	2	3	2	2	1	1	4	45
3	2	3	2	3	3	1	3	54
4	0.68	4	2	2	1	1	2	49
5	1.2	3	1	3	4	1	1	50
6	0.8	1	2	3	3	2	1	42
7	2.1	1	3	4	3	3	3	55
8	0.68	4	1	1	3	1	3	47
9	1.1	3	3	4	3	2	3	65
10	2.3	2	3	3	4	1	3	56
11	0.85	3	2	2	3	1	1	48
12	1	3	1	2	4	2	2	49
13	1.2	2	2	1	2	3	1	39
14	1.3	4	3	3	2	2	2	63
Subj.	1	3	3	3	4	2	3	64
Total	19.21							

Subject Marketability for Restaurant Use Conclusions

The subject was rated highest in terms of competitive vacant space and the place where new competition might locate.

Thus, the subject is considered very competitive and could expect to realize a new restaurant tenant in the next one to three years. The improving market and positive residual demand after Year 5 suggest some real rate growth in rents.

Regional/Community Retail Market/Marketability Analysis

The city is considered to be a good market for regional retail since the new mall is reported to be fully occupied and numerous satellite regional retail centers have developed next to the new mall. The relocation of the subject's previous tenants shows a shift in regional retail preference from the subject area to the new mall area. (Note: The subject's previous tenants' use was regional/community-type retail use.)

The subject area (see location analysis) was not rated high for regional retail, primarily due to the development of the new mall. The current market in the subject central city area shows a considerable number of vacancies in community centers. These community centers, which are located next to the freeway, are considered to be in superior location than the subject.

Thus, based on these data, the subject area and, particularly, the subject, are not considered to be competitive for regional/community type retail.

Neighborhood Retail Market/Marketability Analysis

The building design and previous use of the subject property was for specialty (regional/community) retail. However, the building could also be used "as is" for neighborhood retail tenants. The location rated the subject area as positive for neighborhood retail. This section assesses market demand for this use at this location.

Inferred Demand for Neighborhood Retail

- Location Rating
  The subject area was rated positive for neighborhood retail but not as high as other uses, such as office and apartment. Thus, the location is not considered ideal for neighborhood retail use.

- Recent Building Activity
  The location description section provided data that showed that 38 new retail developments were built in the city in the last five years. Of this total, only 11% were built in the subject area. This is considered positive for the city but negative for the subject area.

- Current Tenant Mix
  The location section provided data on a survey of current tenants within one mile of the subject along Highway 99. These data found that nearly 50% of the users were convenience-type retail. The data are positive for the subject in terms of future release of the subject for neighborhood (convenience) retail.

- Population and Employment Growth
  The city in general and the subject immediate area both are forecast to have good growth rates, with employment growth especially good. The employment growth is a positive factor for neighborhood retail use.

- Current Retail Shopping Center Occupancy in the Market

  Exhibit 19.12 summarizes the retail survey (complete survey in description section) of shopping centers within one mile of the subject along Highway 99. The survey found 11 centers (including the subject) with two community centers located next to the interstate and nine centers along Highway 99 both north and south of the subject.

  The typical lease rate in these centers for non-anchor space is about $9 to $11 (including pass through) per square foot, which is well below rents required for new construction. The high vacancy rate in the area explains why rents are low. All of these factors are negative for the subject as a neighborhood retail center.

Exhibit 19.12 Retail Shopping Centers within 1 Mile of Subject				
	Total Sq. Ft.	Occupied Sq. Ft.	Vacant Space	Occupancy Rate
Totals of all centers	578,563	246,583	331,980	43%
Averages of all centers	52,597	22,417		43%
Total neighborhood centers only (not incl. subj.)	276,455	106,805	169,650	39%

Fundamental Demand Analysis for Neighborhood Retail

Exhibit 19.13 shows the results of a residual demand study for neighborhood retail within one mile of the subject.

The fundamental demand study found the market to be severely oversupplied for the next 10 years.

Subject Marketability for Neighborhood Convenience Retail

Based on the data above, noting in particular the existing vacancy in the area and the negative residual demand for the next 10 years, it appears that the subject's prospects for retail use is highly unlikely, even if it were rated the best center in the area. The property productivity analysis rated the subject only average for retail use compared to the general competition in the area.

Thus, the subject is forecast to have very slow absorption with low rents for this use alternative. Exhibit 19.14 shows a pro rata capture of total market demand.

Office Market/Marketability Analysis

Although it was designed and used previously for specialty (regional/community) retail, the building can be easily adapted for office use. This analysis assumes that the subject is remodeled to compete with Class A/B office buildings in this market. (The next step in the highest and best use process, the financial analysis, will determine if this assumption is maximally productive for the property.) This section assesses the market demand for this use at this location and the subject's ability to compete for this demand with the remodel assumption.

Year	Current	Five Years	10 Years	Comment
Households In 1-mile radius	4,990	6,710	8,430	
Average household income	47,000	47,000	47,000	Constant-dollar calculations
Total household income	234,530,000	315,370,000	396,210,000	
Percentage of income spent on retail	38%	38%	38%	Source: Bureau of Labor Statistics
Retail buying power	89,121,400	119,840,600	150,559,800	
Percentage of retail buying power spent for neighborhood convenience goods	30%	30%	30%	Source: State sales tax data; includes: hardware stores, variety stores, food stores, auto and home supplies, fast food restaurants, drug stores, and misc. stores
Total buying power for neighborhood convenience goods within 1 mile of subject	26,736,420	35,952,180	45,167,940	
Demand from secondary sources	0	0	0	Leakage out is estimated to equal leakage in
Total neighborhood convenience retail demand	26,736,420	35,952,180	45,167,940	
Required sale per sq. ft.	245	245	245	Source: *Dollars & Cents of Shopping Centers* by Urban Land Institute
Estimated amount of supportable neighborhood retail (sq. ft.) in 1 mile of subject	109,128	146,744	184,359	
Plus frictional vacancy @ 5%	5,744	7,723	9,703	
Total supportable space	114,872	154,467	194,062	
Less current occupied neighborhood retail space in 1 mile of subject	106,805	106,805	106,805	
Less current vacant space in neighborhood centers	169,650	169,650	169,650	
Less new construction anticipated	0	0	0	
Residual demand for neighborhood shopping center space in market	(161,583)	(121,988)	(82,393)	

Note: The data above do not include vacant space in community shopping centers in one-mile study area.

Exhibit 19.14 Neighborhood Retail Pro Rata Share Capture/Total Demand

Year	Current	Five Years	Ten Years
Existing total sq. ft. of neighborhood centers in 1 mile of subject	276,455	276,455	276,455
Estimated new construction	0	0	0
Subtotal sq. ft.	276,455	276,455	276,455
Plus subject sq. ft	30,000	30,000	30,000
Total competitive space	306,455	306,455	306,455
Subject as percentage of total supply	9.79%	9.79%	9.79%
Total demand (sq. ft.) convenience retail in 1 mile	109,128	146,744	184,359
Est. subject occupancy by pro rata share (sq. ft.)	10,683	14,365	18,048
Percentage occupancy of subject	36%	48%	60%

Inferred Demand for Office Use

- Location Rating

  The subject area was rated high for office use (see previous location section for rating location).

- Recent Building Activity

  Only three office buildings were built in this city in the last five years and none were in the subject's location. All were owner-occupied buildings built in the office/industrial park located east of the subject toward the new mall. This, in general, is unfavorable for office use, unless a pent-up or forecasted new demand occurs in the near future.

- Population and Employment Growth

  The city is forecast to have good growth rates, with employment growth especially good. The employment growth is one very positive factor for office use.

- Current Building Occupancy in the City

  Exhibit 19.15 shows office building occupancy in the city. The survey is for Class A and B multitenant and owner-occupied buildings. Office space in shopping centers (which is considered Class C office space in this market) and office as part of manufacturing or other similar mixed use is not included. All of the following space would be considered competitive with the subject when the assumed remodel or addition is taken into account.

Exhibit 19.15 Office Space (Class A & B Space in Buildings Over 5,000 Sq. Ft.)

	Occupied (Sq. Ft.)	% of Total	Vacant (Sq. Ft.)	% Vacant	Total Sq. Ft.	% of Total
North part of city	298,624	34%	84,566	22%	383,190	36%
Central part of city (approx. within 1 mile of the subject)	178,000	20%	19,428	10%	197,428	18%
Southeast part of city (mall area and office/park area)	405,650	46%	81,421	17%	487,071	46%
Total in city	882,274	100%	185,415	17%	1,067,689	100%

Note: Includes multitenant and owner-occupied buildings; does not include office use in shopping centers or the subject.

Current office rents for office space in this market is about $16 per square foot, and the tenant pays for janitorial services and utilities.

The data suggest a positive prospect for office in the subject area.

Estimation of New Office Construction in This Market

Because occupancy is approaching a balanced market, an assessment of new competitive construction is a major part of the market study.

This study has two parts. First, the city is required to inventory any projects in the construction or planning stages. Second, a forecast of

unannounced projects is required to make a judgment of the prospects for the market beyond the announced ones.

- Announced or Planned Projects
  A review with the city did not find any projects under construction
  or planned. If some had been found, the appraiser would have to
  perform research with the developers concerning status, financing,
  and pre-leasing before a judgment about the probability of completion and the projected date could be made.
- Unannounced Projects
  Forecasting new construction beyond the announced projects is a
  market judgment based on future market outlook, the availability of
  vacant land or properties that could be redeveloped, availability of
  construction money, and rent feasibility for new construction. The
  following are some of the conclusions drawn from this case study.

Future Market Outlook

One way to assess the future market outlook is to complete a residual
demand study without considering new construction. If the future residual demand is positive, then new construction is more probable.
The residual demand study found a very positive residual demand for
the next 10 years.

Vacant Land for Office Use

The subject area along Highway 99 has numerous sites that could be
developed as office space, and a number of retail shopping centers such
as the subject that could be redeveloped. Thus, availability of land does
not appear to be a deterrent to new development in this market.

Availability of Construction Money

The current market has experienced a big influx of money sources
looking for products to invest in. This is expected to continue for the
next few years. This not only provides large quantities of money, but
also on the mortgage loan side, has kept interest rates low. All of this is
positive for new construction.

Feasibility Rents

Exhibit 19.16 shows calculation estimates of rents required for new
construction and a general estimate of the time when this could be
expected, given the improving market conditions and an estimate of
the real rate increase in rents.

Feasibility Rent and New Office Construction Conclusions

The current rents in the subject competitive market area is about $15
per square foot. The rents would have to increase (in real dollars) about
2% per year to realize feasibility rents for new construction. The market shows a very positive residual demand in the next three to five

Exhibit 19.16 Rent Required for New Office Construction

Data Inputs

Construction cost	$95.00 per sq. ft.	Building size:	30,000 sq. ft.
Land cost	$3.25 per sq. ft.	Land size: *70,916*	108,900 sq. ft.
Operating expense	$3.50 per sq. ft.	% Bldg. rented:	90%
Overall rate	10%		
Normal vacancy	5%		

Calculations of Feasibility Rent

	Sq. Ft.	Cost per Sq. Ft.	
Building and site improvement cost	30,000 ×	$95.00	= $2,850,000
Land cost	108,900 ×	$3.25	= $353,925
Total cost			$3,203,925
Required *NOI*	$3,203,925 ×	10%	= $320,392
Add operating expense	30,000 ×	$3.50	= $105,000
Effective gross income	$425,393		
Vacancy and collection loss @ 5%	$22,389		
Potential gross income	$447,782		

Calculation of Required Rent for New Construction

PGI	/	*NRA*	=	Req. Rent
$447,782	/	27,000	=	$16.59

years (assuming no new construction). Thus, it appears reasonable that some new construction would occur during this time.

The subject property could be feasible for new construction in a shorter time frame if the current improvements (e.g., parking lot) can be used to reduce the construction cost. This may also be true of some competitive shopping centers that, like the subject, are having lease up problems. The financial analysis section that follows addresses the financial feasibility of this alternative for the subject. One way to address this possibility at other centers is to look at current occupancy. If the center has current tenants, it will be some time, in most cases, before they would or could legally be required to vacate. Thus, in the subject market, a review of the competitive centers finds all but the subject with some occupancy. Thus, the probability of new construction via remodeling existing centers seems some years off for all except the subject.

Exhibit 19.17 presents a fundamental demand study for office use in the subject area of town. The method presented is based on the ratio of office occupancy in Class A/B buildings compared to the current total employment level. Then, the forecasted employment is correlated to a forecast ratio of office occupancy to total employment.

No new construction is assumed. This shows the overall market demand before judgment about new construction. The preceding estimated new construction would occur. The impact of the new construction will be addressed in the marketability (market capture) section.

Exhibit 19.17 Office Market Analysis—Citywide Segmentation Method

Year	Current	+Five Years	+10 Years	Comment
Citywide employment	18,260	24,055	29,850	Mid-range forecast
Ratio sq. ft. occupied office/employment	48.32	50	52	Includes multitenant and owner-occupied; ratio increased toward metro average as city urbanizes
Total citywide occupied office demand (sq. ft.)	882,270	1,202,750	1,552,200	
Percentage capture central part of city (subject area)	20.18%	20%	20%	Judgment based on current capture rate
Office space demand in central part of city (occupied)	178,000	240,550	310,440	
Plus frictional vacancy @ 5%	9,368	12,660	16,339	
Total supportable space	187,368	253,211	326,779	
Current square feet of competitive office buildings in central part of city	197,428	197,428	197,428	Does not include the subject
Estimated new construction in central part of city	0	0	0	New construction probable in Years 5 through 10, but will be considered in following marketability section
Residual demand for office space in central part of city	-10,060	55,783	129,351	

Subject Marketability Analysis for Office Use

The marketability forecast incorporates the property's attributes with the market demand and competition estimates the future rent and occupancy prospects for the subject property.

- Remodel/Addition Assumption
  This marketability forecast assumes that the property has been remodeled and the addition is constructed to be competitive with the better office space in the city.
- Office Capture Analysis by Pro Rata Share Method
  This marketability (capture) analysis technique compares the subject on a pro rata share, based on size. This method has the built-in judgment that the subject can compete equally with all buildings in the market area. With the remodel assumption and the subject location, this is a reasonable estimate.

Exhibits 19.18 and 19.19 show the pro rata share estimations based on the total market demand capture assumption for the remodel alternative and the addition Year 1 alternative, respectively.

Subject Marketability for Office Use Conclusion

Based on the analysis above and the preceding market and property analysis, it appears that the subject's future rents and occupancy would be as follows for both the remodel or addition alternative

Low Range: *Occupancy:* Lease up in two to four years after improvements are complete

Exhibit 19.18 Pro Rata Share Capture/Total Demand—Remodel Alternative

Year	Current	Five Years	Ten Years
Existing total sq. ft. in central part of city	197,428	197,428	197,428
Estimated new construction	0	30,000	100,000
Subtotal sq. ft.	197,428	227,428	297,428
Plus subject sq. ft	30,000	30,000	30,000
Total competitive space	227,428	257,428	327,428
Subject as percentage of total supply	13.19%	11.65%	9.16%
Total demand (sq. ft.) for central part of city (occupied)	178,000	240,550	310,440
Est. subject occupancy sq. ft.	23,478	28,024	28,436
Subject percentage occupancy	78%	93%	95%

Exhibit 19.19 Pro Rata Share Capture/Total Demand Addition Year 1 Alternative

Year	Current	Five Years	Ten Years
Existing total sq. ft. in central part of city	197,428	197,428	197,428
Estimated new construction	0	30,000	100,000
Subtotal sq. ft.	197,428	227,428	297,428
Plus subject sq. ft	50,000	50,000	50,000
Total competitive space	247,428	277,428	347,428
Subject as percentage of total supply	20.21%	18.02%	14.39%
Total demand (sq. ft.) for central part of city (occupied)	178,000	240,550	310,440
Est. subject occupancy by pro rata share	35,973	43,347	44,672
Subject percentage occupancy	72%	87%	89%

	Rents:	$15 per sq. ft. to start, with 3% to 5% real rate increases about Year 5 and again about Year 10
Mid-Range:	*Occupancy:*	Lease up in two to three years after improvements are complete
	Rents:	$15 per sq. ft. to start, with 8% to 10% real rate increases about Year 5 and again about Year 10
High Range:	*Occupancy:*	Lease up in one to two years after are improvements complete
	Rents:	$15 per sq. ft. to start, with 10% to 15% real rate increases about Year 5 and again about Year 10

Step 7: Financial Analysis of Alternatives

This step in the highest and best use process takes the conclusions of the market/marketability study (six-step process) and applies financial analysis to each of the alternatives under study. These alternatives are:

1. Assumed vacant (the demolition alternative)
2. Restaurant/specialty retail (the current use alternative)
3. Restaurant/neighborhood retail (new marketing strategy alternative)
4. Restaurant/office remodel alternative
5. Restaurant/office addition alternative with addition in Year 1
6. Restaurant/office addition alternative with addition in Year 5
7. Total office remodel and addition in Year 1

Financial Data
Market Rates
- Retail and Restaurant Space: Current market rents of $11.50 per sq. ft., with expenses of $1 for variable and $2.50 for fixed

- Class A/B Office Space: Current market rents of $15.00 per sq. ft., with expenses of $1 for variable and $2.50 for fixed

- Yield Rates: Non-inflation yield rates of 10% to 14%, with office rates toward the lower end and retail toward the higher end. However, all of the forecasts have been adjusted to equal expectations for occurrence.

- Cap Rates: Retail: 11% to 14%
  Office: 10% to 12%

Land Cost
Current sites on Highway 99 recently sold to apartment developers for $3.00 to $3.50 per sq. ft. All of the land sales could be used for retail, office, or apartment.

Land Sale of 2- to 6-acre tracts in other parts of town:

- Owner-occupied office in new business park southeast of subject, $3.50 to $4.00/sq. ft.
- Retail sites to users around the new mall, $6.00 to $7.00/sq. ft.

Remodel and Addition Cost Data
The subject 30,000-sq.-ft.-buildings were designed for use as retail. They are one-story block construction with a decorative brick front. To be competitive with Class A/B office space, however, the façade and some interior space would have to be improved extensively.

The restaurant building is a 6,000-sq.-ft. building located on the front part of the property. It has extensive improvements and was previously used for a restaurant. It could also be remodeled for Class A/B office space. The remodel cost would be higher than the retail building because of the extensive kitchen equipment, which would have to be removed and additional interior walls built.

The property also has space to accommodate about a 20,000 square feet of additional office space. This additional space can be found by the changing parking ratio from retail to office.

The current improvements are such that the land used for the addition could not be sold separately because it is not a separate economic unit. However, the excess land could be used to add an additional building if it is designed to be part of the original building complex. This is accomplished primarily by building in the parking lot in front of the current buildings.

The new addition could also use the existing parking lot for its required parking. The ability to use the existing parking lot and other site improvements such as the landscaping results in reduced cost compared to a building on a vacant lot.

Thus, the total cost for the remodel/addition alternatives for the subject are:

- Remodel existing retail building for Class A/B office–$20/sq. ft.
- Remodel existing restaurant building for Class A/B office–$25/sq. ft.
- A 20,000-sq.-ft. addition (new building.) of Class A/B office–$70/sq. ft.

Financial Analysis of Alternatives

The following shows the financial analysis of the alternatives described.

Alternative 1: Apartment

• Land value @ $3.50 per sq.-ft.	$686,700
• Less demolition cost	$ 20,000
• Value as apartment	$666,070

Alternative 2: Release as Specialty Retail

A financial analysis was not completed on this alternative because it was eliminated from further study (see previous discussion).

Alternatives 3 Through 7

The financial models shown in Exhibits 19.20 through 19.24 take the revenue forecast for each alternative use market/marketability study along with the cost to remodel, and applies each to a DCF analysis. The purpose is to determine whether an improvement alternative (such as remodeling) will make the property more valuable than it would be if nothing were done under the two other alternatives (vacant land or continue current use). Each use takes into account the time value of money based on the anticipated lease up and cost to implement each alternative.

Exhibit 19.20 Oak Point Shopping Center—Neighborhood Retail Alternative 3

Data Input

Income

Restaurant Current Market Rent/sq. ft.	$11.50	
Multitenant Current Market Rent/sq. ft.	$11.50	

Occupancy

Restaurant
Yr. Occup. 2

Expenses

Variable (MT)	$1.50 per sq. ft.
Fixed	$2.00 per sq. ft.

Building Data

Restaurant sq. ft.	6,000
Multitenant sq. ft.	30,000
Total sq. ft.	36,000

Rent Increases (Real Rate Inc.)

Restaurant Space		Multitenant Space		Multitenant Space		Expense Increases		Capital Cost	
Year	% Increase	Year	% Increase	Year	Occup.	Year	% Increase	Year	Cost
1	0%	1	0%	1	10%	1	0%	0	$0
2	0%	2	0%	2	20%	2	0%	1	$0
3	0%	3	0%	3	30%	3	0%	2	$0
4	0%	4	0%	4	40%	4	0%	3	$0
5	5%	5	0%	5	50%	5	0%	4	$0
6	0%	6	0%	6	60%	6	0%	5	$0
7	0%	7	0%	7	70%	7	0%	6	$0
8	0%	8	0%	8	80%	8	0%	7	$0
9	0%	9	0%	9	85%	9	0%	8	$0
10	5%	10	0%	10	85%	10	0%	9	$0
								10	$0

Financial

	Low	Mid	High
Discount Rates	10.00%	12.00%	14.00%
Terminal Cap Rate	11.00%		
Selling Expenses	6.00%		

Analysis

Year	1	2	3	4	5	6	7	8	9	10
Effective Gross Income										
Restaurant	$0	$69,000	$69,000	$69,000	$72,450	$72,450	$72,450	$72,450	$72,450	$76,073
Multitenant	$34,500	$69,000	$103,500	$138,000	$172,500	$207,000	$241,500	$276,000	$293,250	$293,250
Total Effective Inc.	$34,500	$138,000	$172,500	$207,000	$244,950	$279,450	$313,950	$348,450	$365,700	$369,323
Less Expenses										
Variable	$4,500	$9,000	$13,500	$18,000	$22,500	$27,000	$31,500	$36,000	$38,250	$38,250
Fixed	$72,000	$72,000	$72,000	$72,000	$72,000	$72,000	$72,000	$72,000	$72,000	$72,000
Total Expenses	$76,500	$81,000	$85,500	$90,000	$94,500	$99,000	$103,500	$108,000	$110,250	$110,250
Net Operating Income	($42,000)	$57,000	$87,000	$117,000	$150,450	$180,450	$210,450	$240,450	$255,450	$259,073
Plus Reversion										$2,213,892
Less Capital Cost	$0	$0	$0	$0	$0	$0	$0	$0	$0	$0
Total Cash Flow	($42,000)	$57,000	$87,000	$117,000	$150,450	$180,450	$210,450	$240,450	$255,450	$2,472,965

Discount Rate	Present Value	Less Yr. 0 Cost		Net Present Value
10.00%	$1,631,416	$0	=	$1,631,416
12.00%	$1,401,668	$0		$1,401,668
14.00%	$1,209,379	$0		$1,209,379

Present Value @ 10.00%	$1,631,416
Present Value @ 12.00%	$1,401,668
Present Value @ 14.00%	$1,209,379

Exhibit 19.21 Restaurant Office Mixed Use—The Remodel Alternative 4

Data Input

Income

Restaurant Current Market Rent/sq. ft.	$11.50
Multitenant Current Market Rent/sq. ft.	$15.00

Occupancy

Restaurant Yr. Occup.	2

Expenses

Variable (MT)	$1.50 per sq. ft.
Fixed	$2.00 per sq. ft.

Building Data

Restaurant sq. ft.	6,000
Multitenant sq. ft.	30,000
Total sq. ft.	36,000

Rent Increases (Real Rate Inc.)

Restaurant Space		Multitenant Space		Multitenant Space		Expense Increases		Capital cost	
Year	% Increase	Year	% Increase	Year	Occup.	Year	% Increase	Year	Cost
1	0%	1	0%	1	35%	1	0%	0	$600,000
2	0%	2	0%	2	65%	2	0%	1	$0
3	0%	3	0%	3	85%	3	0%	2	$0
4	0%	4	0%	4	95%	4	0%	3	$0
5	5%	5	10%	5	95%	5	0%	4	$0
6	0%	6	0%	6	95%	6	0%	5	$0
7	0%	7	0%	7	95%	7	0%	6	$0
8	0%	8	0%	8	95%	8	0%	7	$0
9	0%	9	0%	9	95%	9	0%	8	$0
10	5%	10	10%	10	95%	10	0%	9	$0
								10	$0

Financial

Discount Rates	Low	10.00%
	Mid	12.00%
	High	14.00%
Terminal Cap Rate		11.00%
Selling Expenses		6.00%

Analysis

Year	1	2	3	4	5	6	7	8	9	10
Effective Gross Income										
Restaurant	$0	$69,000	$69,000	$69,000	$72,450	$72,450	$72,450	$72,450	$72,450	$76,073
Multitenant	$157,500	$292,500	$382,500	$427,500	$470,250	$470,250	$470,250	$470,250	$470,250	$517,275
Total Effective Inc.	$157,500	$361,500	$451,500	$496,500	$542,700	$542,700	$542,700	$542,700	$542,700	$593,348
Less Expenses										
Variable	$15,750	$29,250	$38,250	$42,750	$42,750	$42,750	$42,750	$42,750	$42,750	$42,750
Fixed	$72,000	$72,000	$72,000	$72,000	$72,000	$72,000	$72,000	$72,000	$72,000	$72,000
Total Expenses	$87,750	$101,250	$110,250	$114,750	$114,750	$114,750	$114,750	$114,750	$114,750	$114,750
Net Operating Income	$69,750	$260,250	$341,250	$381,750	$427,950	$427,950	$427,950	$427,950	$427,950	$478,598
Plus Reversion										$4,089,833
Less Capital Cost	$0	$0	$0	$0	$0	$0	$0	$0	$0	$0
Total Cash Flow	$69,750	$260,250	$341,250	$381,750	$427,950	$427,950	$427,950	$427,950	$427,950	$4,568,431

Discount Rate	Present Value	Less Yr. 0 Cost		Net Present Value
Present Value @ 10.00%	$3,664,976	$600,000	=	$3,064,976
Present Value @ 12.00%	$3,206,554	$600,000		$2,606,554
Present Value @ 14.00%	$2,819,981	$600,000		$2,219,981

Data Input

Income

Restaurant Current Market Rent/sq. ft.	$11.50
Multitenant Current Market Rent/sq. ft.	$15.00

Occupancy

Restaurant Yr. Occup.	2

Expenses

Variable (MT)	$1.50 per sq. ft.
Fixed	$2.00 per sq. ft.

Building Data

Restaurant sq. ft.	6,000
Original sq. ft.	30,000
Addition sq. ft.	20,000
Total sq. ft.	56,000

Rent Increases (Real Rate Inc.)

	Restaurant Space	Multitenant
Year	% Rent Increase	% Rent Increase
1	0%	0%
2	0%	0%
3	0%	0%
4	0%	0%
5	5%	10%
6	0%	0%
7	0%	0%
8	0%	0%
9	0%	0%
10	5%	10%

Multitenant Occupancy

Year	Original	Addition
1	35%	0%
2	65%	40%
3	85%	80%
4	95%	95%
5	95%	95%
6	95%	95%
7	95%	95%
8	95%	95%
9	95%	95%
10	95%	95%

Expense Increases (Real Rate Inc.)

Year	% Increase
1	0%
2	0%
3	0%
4	0%
5	0%
6	0%
7	0%
8	0%
9	0%
10	0%

Capital Cost

Year	Cost
0	$600,000
1	$1,400,000
2	$0
3	$0
4	$0
5	$0
6	$0
7	$0
8	$0
9	$0
10	$0

Financial

	Low	Mid	High
Discount Rates	10.00%	12.00%	14.00%
Terminal Cap Rate	11.00%		
Selling Expenses	6.00%		

Analysis

Year	1	2	3	4	5	6	7	8	9	10
Effective Gross Income										
Restaurant	$0	$69,000	$69,000	$69,000	$72,450	$72,450	$72,450	$72,450	$72,450	$76,073
Original Multitenant	$157,500	$292,500	$382,500	$427,500	$470,250	$470,250	$470,250	$470,250	$470,250	$517,275
Addition	$0	$120,000	$240,000	$285,000	$313,500	$313,500	$313,500	$313,500	$313,500	$344,850
Total Effective Inc.	$157,500	$481,500	$691,500	$781,500	$856,200	$856,200	$856,200	$856,200	$856,200	$938,198
Less Expenses										
Variable	$15,750	$41,250	$62,250	$71,250	$71,250	$71,250	$71,250	$71,250	$71,250	$71,250
Fixed	$72,000	$112,000	$112,000	$112,000	$112,000	$112,000	$112,000	$112,000	$112,000	$112,000
Total Expenses	$87,750	$153,250	$174,250	$183,250	$183,250	$183,250	$183,250	$183,250	$183,250	$183,250
Net Operating Income	$69,750	$328,250	$517,250	$598,250	$672,950	$672,950	$672,950	$672,950	$672,950	$754,948
Plus Reversion										$6,451,370
Less Capital Cost	$1,400,000									$0
Total Cash Flow	($1,330,250)	$328,250	$517,250	$598,250	$672,950	$672,950	$672,950	$672,950	$672,950	$7,206,317

	Present Value		Less Yr. 0 Cost		Net Present Value
	$4,379,914		$600,000	=	$3,779,914
	$3,684,225		$600,000	=	$3,084,225
	$3,100,770		$600,000	=	$2,500,770

	Discount Rate
Present Value @	10.00%
Present Value @	12.00%
Present Value @	14.00%

Exhibit 19.23 Restaurant/Office Mixed Use—The Remodel and Yr. 5 Addition Alternative 6

Data Input

Income

			Occupancy		**Expenses**	
Restaurant Current Market Rent/sq. ft.	$ 11.50		Restaurant		Variable(MT)	$1.50 per sq. ft.
Multitenant Current Market Rent/sq. ft.	$ 15.00		Yr. Occup.	2	Fixed	$2.00 per sq. ft.

Building Data

Restaurant sq. ft.	6,000
Original sq. ft.	30,000
Addition sq. ft.	20,000
Total sq. ft.	56,000

Rent Increases (Real Rate Inc.)

	Restaurant Space	Multitenant		Multitenant Occupancy			Expense Increases (Real Rate Inc.)		Capital Cost	
Year	% Rent Increase	% Rent Increase	Year	Original	Addition	Year	% Increase	Year	Cost
1	0%	0%	1	35%	0%	1	0%	0	$600,000
2	0%	0%	2	65%	0%	2	0%	1	$0
3	0%	0%	3	85%	0%	3	0%	2	$0
4	0%	0%	4	95%	0%	4	0%	3	$0
5	5%	10%	5	95%	0%	5	0%	4	$0
6	0%	0%	6	95%	40%	6	0%	5	$1,400,000
7	0%	0%	7	95%	80%	7	0%	6	$0
8	0%	0%	8	95%	95%	8	0%	7	$0
9	0%	0%	9	95%	95%	9	0%	8	$0
10	5%	10%	10	95%	95%	10	0%	9	$0
								10	$0

Financial

	Low	Mid	High
Discount Rates	10.00%	12.00%	14.00%
Terminal Cap Rate	11.00%		
Selling Expenses	6.00%		

Analysis

Year	1	2	3	4	5	6	7	8	9	10
Effective Gross Income										
Restaurant	$0	$69,000	$69,000	$69,000	$72,450	$72,450	$72,450	$72,450	$72,450	$76,073
Original Multitenant	$157,500	$292,500	$382,500	$427,500	$470,250	$470,250	$470,250	$470,250	$470,250	$517,275
Addition	$0	$0	$0	$0	$0	$132,000	$264,000	$313,500	$313,500	$344,850
Total Effective Inc.	$157,500	$361,500	$451,500	$496,500	$542,700	$674,700	$806,700	$856,200	$856,200	$938,198
Less Expenses										
Variable	$15,750	$29,250	$38,250	$42,750	$42,750	$54,750	$66,750	$71,250	$71,250	$71,250
Fixed	$72,000	$72,000	$72,000	$72,000	$72,000	$112,000	$112,000	$112,000	$112,000	$112,000
Total Expenses	$87,750	$101,250	$110,250	$114,750	$114,750	$166,750	$178,750	$183,250	$183,250	$183,250
Net Operating Income	$69,750	$260,250	$341,250	$381,750	$427,950	$507,950	$627,950	$672,950	$672,950	$754,948
Plus Reversion										$6,451,370
Less Capital Cost	$0	$0	$0	$0	$1,400,000	$0	$0	$0	$0	$0
Total Cash Flow	$69,750	$260,250	$341,250	$381,750	($972,050)	$507,950	$627,950	$672,950	$672,950	$7,206,317

Discount Rate	Present Value	Less Yr. 0 Cost		Net Present Value
Present Value @	10.00%	$4,178,694	$600,000	=	$3,578,694
Present Value @	12.00%	$3,579,786	$600,000		$2,979,786
Present Value @	14.00%	$3,082,020	$600,000		$2,482,020

Exhibit 19.24 Total Office—The Remodel All and Addition Alternative 7

Data Input

Income

Restaurant Current Market Rent/sq. ft.	$11.50		
Multitenant Current Market Rent/sq. ft.	$15.00		

Occupancy

Restaurant	Yr. Occup.

NA

Expenses

Variable (MT)	$1.50 per sq. ft.
Fixed	$2.00 per sq. ft.

Building Data

Restaurant sq. ft.	36,000
Original sq. ft.	20,000
Addition sq. ft.	
Total sq. ft.	56,000

Rent Increases (Real Rate Inc.)

	Restaurant Space	Multitenant
Year	% Rent Increase	% Rent Increase
1	0%	0%
2	0%	0%
3	0%	0%
4	0%	0%
5	0%	10%
6	0%	0%
7	0%	0%
8	0%	0%
9	0%	0%
10	0%	10%

Multitenant Occupancy

Year	Original	Addition
1	35%	0%
2	65%	40%
3	85%	80%
4	95%	95%
5	95%	95%
6	95%	95%
7	95%	95%
8	95%	95%
9	95%	95%
10	95%	95%

Expense Increases (Real Rate Inc.)

Year	% Increase
1	0%
2	0%
3	0%
4	0%
5	0%
6	0%
7	0%
8	0%
9	0%
10	0%

Capital Cost

Year	Cost
0	$750,000
1	$1,400,000
2	$0
3	$0
4	$0
5	$0
6	$0
7	$0
8	$0
9	$0
10	$0

Financial

	Low	Mid	High
Discount Rates	10.00%	12.00%	14.00%
Terminal Cap Rate	11.00%		
Selling Expenses	6.00%		

Analysis

Year	1	2	3	4	5	6	7	8	9	10
Effective Gross Income										
Restaurant	$0	$0	$0	$0	$0	$0	$0	$0	$0	$0
Original Multitenant	$189,000	$351,000	$459,000	$513,000	$564,300	$564,300	$564,300	$564,300	$564,300	$620,730
Addition	$0	$120,000	$240,000	$285,000	$313,500	$313,500	$313,500	$313,500	$313,500	$344,850
Total Effective Inc.	$189,000	$471,000	$699,000	$798,000	$877,800	$877,800	$877,800	$877,800	$877,800	$965,580
Less Expenses										
Variable	$18,900	$47,100	$69,900	$79,800	$79,800	$79,800	$79,800	$79,800	$79,800	$79,800
Fixed	$72,000	$112,000	$112,000	$112,000	$112,000	$112,000	$112,000	$112,000	$112,000	$112,000
Total Expenses	$90,900	$159,100	$181,900	$191,800	$191,800	$191,800	$191,800	$191,800	$191,800	$191,800
Net Operating Income	$98,100	$311,900	$517,100	$606,200	$686,000	$686,000	$686,000	$686,000	$686,000	$773,780
Plus Reversion										$6,612,302
Less Capital Cost	$1,400,000									$0
Total Cash Flow	($1,301,900)	$311,900	$517,100	$606,200	$686,000	$686,000	$686,000	$686,000	$686,000	$7,386,082

Discount Rate		Present Value	Less Yr. 0 Cost		=	Net Present Value
Present Value @	10.00%	$4,500,588	$750,000			$3,750,588
Present Value @	12.00%	$3,789,225	$750,000			$3,039,225
Present Value @	14.00%	$3,192,680	$750,000			$2,442,680

Reconciliation of Alternatives (Maximally Productive Analysis)

This is the final step in the highest and best use analysis. This step involves making a final assessment of the data analyzed and determining the final highest and best use(s).

This step can be called the risk analysis of the data and the various analysis techniques used. The data considered to be the most reliable and most representative of the market reaction are given the greatest weight in the final conclusions of highest and best use.

Analysis of Alternatives

The alternative that will yield the highest value with the least acceptable risk in the market is the alternative(s) that is the highest and best use.

Qualitative Analysis

Alternative 5, the mixed-use office remodel and addition in Year 1, is the highest value. However, the phasing alternative (6) with addition in Year 5 is only about $100,000 less valuable than the alternative (5) with addition in Year 1 or the total office alternative 7. This presents a risk consideration since the phasing alternative (6) allows for an additional measure of risk reduction by testing the lease up forecast. The phasing alternative (6) offers the advantage of actually revealing the market reaction to re-use as office before additional funds are committed to the additional office. The phasing alternative not only allows for testing the absorption but also allows for entry into the market when rents are expected to increase in real terms by 20% over a five-year period (10% in Year 5, and 10% in Year 10).

Quantitative Analysis

The preceding DCF analysis is the base analysis used for quantitative analysis. However, since three alternatives (5, 6, and 7) are relatively close in value, and they required added risk of constructing additional office space, further risk analysis is helpful.

One method of analysis is to compare the additional cash flow realized from the addition compared to the cost to realize the additional cash flow. Exhibit 19.25 shows the comparison of internal rate of return on the addition investments by comparison to the no-addition alternative.

Exhibit 19.25 Rate of Return on Addition		
Alternative	*IRR*	**Risk Assessment**
5	15.14%	Moderate high
6	13.32%	Moderate
7	14.4%	High

Alternative 5, the mixed use with office addition in Year 1, not only has the highest value but also the higher IRR for the addition cost compared to rate of return (see Exhibit 19.26). The final highest and best use conclusion will be a risk judgment of whether the added value and return is compensable with the added risk. For example, Alternative 6 is judged to have the least risk but also has the least value and IRR (see Exhibit 19.27). The analyst must judge whether the added value and/or IRR increase of 1% to 2% would be recognized in the market, given the added risk.

Alternative 7, the remodel for office and addition, has nearly the same overall value as Alternative 5, the restaurant /office remodel mixed use; however, Alternative 7 is the most risky since it is not phased and is totally dependent on forecasting the office market but loses the risk reduction advantage of mixed use projects such as Alternative 5.

Exhibit 19.29 highlights the highest and best use study to this point.

Highest and Best Use Conclusions

Highest and best use is defined as "the reasonably probable and legal use of vacant land or an improved property, which is physically possible, appropriately supported, financially feasible, and results in the highest value."

Two separate highest and best use analyses are required. The first assumes the land to be vacant and available for development; the second pertains to the land, as it exists, with existing improvements in place.

Subject Property Determinants, "As If Vacant"
Legal Constraints/Opportunities
A legally permissible use must be allowable within the context of legal restrictions encumbering the use of the site, if any, particularly zoning regulations and any privately imposed restrictions that limit site development.

The subject is zoned commercial. Retail or office use would be the most compatible use, given the zoning classification.

However, the zoning district also allows apartment at 18 units per acre.

Physical Possibility
For a projected use to be physically possible, site size, shape, topography, frontage, and depth must be conducive to development for the use contemplated.

Size/Shape
The site's size (4.5 acres) is conducive to office, retail, or apartment development. Typical multitenant office developments and apartments within the submarket area are built on 4 to 7 acres. The size of the site suggests multitenant office development, retail, or apartment use.

Exhibit 19.26 Alternative 5—Addition Rate of Return with Construction in Year 1 Compared to No Addition

Year	1	2	3	4	5	6	7	8	9	10
Alternative 5 office-addition Yr 1 income	$69,750	$328,250	$517,250	$598,250	$672,950	$672,950	$672,950	$672,950	$672,950	$7,206,317
Alternative 4 remodel income-no addition	$69,750	$260,250	$341,250	$381,750	$427,950	$427,950	$427,950	$427,950	$427,950	$4,568,431
Income difference	0	$68,000	$176,000	$216,500	$245,000	$245,000	$245,000	$245,000	$245,000	$2,637,886

	Income Difference Present Value	Less Cost of Addition	Net Present Value
Present Value @ 12%	$1,727,672	$1,400,000	$327,672
Present Value @ 15%	$1,412,539	$1,400,000	$12,539
IRR = 15.14%			

Exhibit 19.27 Alternative 6—Addition Rate of Return with Construction in Year 5 Compared to No Addition

Year	1	2	3	4	5	6	7	8	9	10
Alternative 6—office addition Yr 5 income	$69,750	$260,250	$341,250	$381,750	$427,950	$507,950	$627,950	$672,950	$672,950	$7,206,317
Alternative 7—remodel income -no addition	$69,750	$260,250	$341,250	$381,750	$427,950	$427,950	$427,950	$427,950	$427,950	$4,568,431
Income difference	$0	$0	$0	$0	$0	$80,000	$200,000	$245,000	$245,000	$2,637,886

	Income Difference Present Value	Less PV @ 6% for Additional Cost	Net Present Value
Net Present Value			
Present Value @ 12%	$1,167,630	$1,046,161	=	$121,469
Present Value @ 13%	$1,074,244	$1,046,161	=	$28,083
IRR =	13.32%		

File ID:Retail Re-Use DCF.xls / Addition IRR

Exhibit 19.28 Alternative 7 Total Office—Remodel All and Addition Year Compared to No Addition

Year	1	2	3	4	5	6	7	8	9	10
Alternative 7 - all office and addition	$98,100	$311,900	$517,100	$606,200	$686,000	$686,000	$686,000	$686,000	$686,000	$7,386,082
Alternative 4 - remodel income	$69,750	$260,250	$341,250	$381,750	$427,950	$427,950	$427,950	$427,950	$427,950	$4,568,431
Income difference	$28,350	$51,650	$175,850	$224,450	$258,050	$258,050	$258,050	$258,050	$258,050	$2,817,651

	Income Difference Present Value	Less Cost for Restaurant Remodel and Addition	Net Present Value
Net Present Value			
Present Value @ 12%	$1,832,671	$1,550,000	$282,671
Present Value @ 14%	$1,600,769	$1,550,000	$50,769
IRR =	14.49%		

Exhibit 19.29   Highest and Best Use Analysis Recap

Alternatives	1 Demolition for redevelopment as apartments	2 Release the property as restaurant and specialty retail (former use)	3 Release the property as restaurant and neighborhood retail	4 Remodel retail as office for mixed-use bldgs. restaurant/office	5 Remodel and addition as mixed-use restaurant/office—with addition in Yr. 1	6 Remodel and addition as mixed-use restaurant/office—with addition in Yr. 5	7 Total office remodel and addition Yr. 1
Evaluation Factors							
Site	Good	Good	Average-not on corner	Good	Good	Good	Good
Improvements	NA	Average	Average	Class A/B	Class A/B	Class A/B	Class A/B
Legal	No zoning or lease problem or advantage	No zoning or lease problem or advantage	No zoning or lease problem or advantage	No zoning or lease problem or advantage	No zoning or lease problem or advantage	No zoning or lease problem or advantage	No zoning or lease problem or advantage
Location	Very good	Very poor-veto	Average	Good	Good	Good	Good
Market demand	Very good	Very low at this location	Moderate	Good	Good	Good	Good
Marketability (subject capture)	Very good	Very poor	Poor	Good	Good	Good	Good
Financial value (rounded)	$600,000 to $700,000	NA-very low	$1.2M to $1.6M Pt. $1.40M	$2.2M to 3.0M Pt. $2.6M	$2.5M to $3.78M Pt. $3.084M	$2.5M to $3.6M Pt. $2.980M	$2.4M to $3.75M Pt. $3.039M
Risk assessment	Low	Extremely high since regional retail such as the specialty retail is relocating to new mall area	Very high due to oversupply of neighborhood retail in this market	Moderate	Moderately high risk of large up-front cost requiring longer absorption	Moderate—addition delayed, which can better gauge the expected rent spikes in Yr. 5	High totally dependent on office market and loses marketing advantage of mixed use
Internal Rate of Return					15.14%	13.32%	14.49%

Access

The site is an interior site on a major highway. It has good access to and from the highway. The interior location and secondary access characteristics would be conducive to development of office use or apartment and reasonable for retail use.

Current Site and Abutting Land Uses

The current and abutting land uses include office, retail, and apartment uses. Based on the abutting land uses, the most likely use is office, retail, or apartment use.

Conclusion

Site determinants of use suggest multitenant office, retail, or apartment use.

Financial Feasibility

To be financially feasible, a contemplated use should generate positive net income. After reviewing the preceding development constraints, economic feasibility is the final remaining consideration. Feasible developments have certain characteristics in common, which appear to enhance the probability of success of the property.

- There must be a likely population growth or support (economic demand) in the market area.
- The present and future growth of the area must be relatively homogeneous and not violate the principle of conformity.
- The political and economic climate must be stable.
- There must be a balance of supply and demand in order for the property to generate sufficient income to cover rent or debt service. Excessive supply of a proposed use in the subject's market is a direct indication of unfeasibility.

In response to each of these items, the following observations have been made:

- Retail is severely overbuilt in this area.
- Office demand is increasing, but new construction is not forecast for 4 to 6 years. Land values are similar to those for apartment use.
- Apartment demand is current, and new construction has occurred nearby.

Highest and Best Use "As If Vacant"

The highest and best use "as if vacant" is for apartment use.

- Use: Apartment at 18 units per acre
- Timing: Current, on average, one year
- Market Participants:
    - Users: Moderate income young professionals
    - Most Probable Buyer: Apartment developers

Subject Highest and Best Use-As Improved

The same highest and best use test as if vacant is applied to the subject as improved.

Physically Possible

The subject improvements are designed for retail and restaurant use; however, they could be easily remodeled for alternative use such alternative use as office.

Legally Permissible

The zoning could accommodate office or retail. There are no leases on the property that would encumber its use.

Financially Feasible

This factor considers all of the preceding market analysis, which showed a strong office demand at this location.

Highest and Best Use Conclusions (Maximally Productive)-As Improved

The alternative with the highest value was Alternative 5, restaurant with remodel with addition for office in Year 1. However, Alternative 6 had about the same value but less risk since it was the same as 5, except to delay the office until Year 5. This allows a longer look at the office market and allows phasing in of the office component.

Thus, the highest and best use of the property as improved is for current mixed use with restaurant with the plan to remodel the current retail part for office and add another building in about five years for additional office use.

- Use: Mixed Use Restaurant and Office
- Timing: Current, on average, one year
- Market Participants:
    - Users: Moderate Profile Professional
          Service Office Tenants
    - Most Probable Buyer: Developers

Application of Market Analysis Concepts in the Approaches to Value

This epilog describes how market analysis relates to property value—the bottom line of most appraisals. The market/marketability analysis is the underpinning of a property's value, while the valuation approaches measure that value. In other words, incorporating the findings of the market/marketability analysis into the three approaches and the reconciliation of value brings the analysis to its logical conclusion. The specific uses of market analysis in the three approaches to value are outlined below.

The Appraisal of Vacant Land

Identification of Appropriate Comparables

The valuation section of an appraisal represents a detailed financial analysis of the property under the highest and best use specified in the market/marketability analysis. First, the three major conclusions of highest and best use, timing, and market participants, supply the criteria for selecting comparable sales. These three criteria become the screen for sifting through sales data to determine those that are the most comparable to use for further analysis. For example, assume that a property's highest and best use was determined as follows:

- Use: Neighborhood Retail Shopping Center
- Timing: 3 to 6 years
- Market participants, or most probable buyer: Speculator investor

Now consider two sales. Sale 1 is to a grocery store located across the street from the subject that bought and developed a neighborhood shopping center. Sale 2, located down the street, was bought by a speculator investor with plans to sell to a grocery store shopping center developer in three to six years. Of the two sales, Sale 2 is the superior comparable.

Comparable Sales Adjustment and Highest and Best Use Conclusions

The three-point conclusions of highest and best use also become the basis of adjustments to differences in the sales.

Adjustment for Physical Differences

The use determination entails all of the factors of Step 1, property productivity analysis, in the six-step process, as it encompasses all the physical site factors such as shape, floodplain, and utilities; all of the legal factors of zoning and deed restrictions; and all the physical location factors. Thus, any or all of these factors can be adjusted for in the sales comparison grids.

Market Conditions Adjustment

The timing element also becomes the basis for a market conditions adjustment. The highest and best use analysis of vacant land provides information used to estimate an adjustment for changes in market conditions. Comparable tracts of vacant land may have been sold to users or investors, and market expectations at the time of sale, which may have occurred one to two years earlier, may have been different from those on the date of the appraisal. The best sales data available are often historical sales to purchasers who bought the land with a specific use in mind. These sales provide an indication of the anticipated land value under the specific use. A study of marginal demand can establish the time horizon for development of the subject, and the prospective values of the subject under the specific use plan can be estimated. Discounting the prospective value yields an estimate of the present value of the subject land, which can be compared to the values indicated by past sales.

Economic Feasibility/Development Approach

The conclusions of the six-step process provide the absorption forecast for developing the feasibility analysis. Appraisers must investigate the economic feasibility of the use of the real estate. Industry guidelines require the appraiser to identify the motives behind sales transactions because the economic feasibility of a parcel of real estate under a specific use does not always explain market transactions. Factors such as hyper-speculation practices, special tax situations, insolvency that results in the liquidation of holdings, and even misinformation help account for the sale and purchase of real estate. To test value estimates derived from these types of comparable sales, and to determine whether the intended use of a property is indeed economically feasible, the development approach is often applied. A forecast of marginal demand enables an appraiser to draw up a land use concept plan on which the application of the development approach depends.

Furthermore, a Level C market analysis generates the specific information on use and timing required in the development approach. This analysis provides an alternative value indication to weigh in comparison to the conclusions by the sales comparison.

The Appraisal of Improved Properties

Sales Comparison Approach

The market/marketability analysis yields information about the attributes of comparable improved properties. This information is the basis for the adjustments made to the sale prices of comparable properties for changes in market conditions and differences in physical and locational attributes. The locational attributes become more than identifying the street where the subject is located compared to other sales. The location analysis adjustment encompasses the neighborhood market dynamics of the sales when compared to the subject. For example, where a retail property is concerned, is the sale located in a neighborhood with the same buying power as the subject? If not, an adjustment to the sale would be warranted. The market/marketability analysis can also provide insights into other property characteristics such as the quality of management, the profile of the tenancy, and the nature of special lease provisions, which have special relevance to income-producing properties. These characteristics are considered when analyzing the income produced by the subject and comparables and the potential income they are capable of generating. Information on these characteristics provides the basis for adjustments made on the market data grid.

Market analysis may also shed light on the reasonableness or appropriateness of an overall rate of return (R_O). Overall rates of return are a unit of sales comparison used to convert a single year's income expectancy (NOI) into an indication of property value. An overall rate of return is derived by analyzing actual market data on the sale prices and net operating incomes of comparable properties. If the rates are extremely low, the market would expect future prices, i.e., resales, to be higher to realize their desired overall return. (Yield is equal to the overall rate minus the expected change in value converted to a yearly factor.)

Overall capitalization rates derived from historical data reflect past conditions, but the overall rates applied in a current value estimate must be responsive to changes taking place in the current market. If the demand forecast developed in market analysis does not seem likely to sustain the income expectations reflected in the overall rates derived from historical sales data, current values may no longer be supportable, and a decline in the market will be indicated. In such a case, a higher overall capitalization rate might be selected because an inverse relationship exists between R_O and value. If the demand forecast seems to support development, property values are likely to increase. In a developing market, a lower overall capitalization rate might be selected.

Cost Approach

The knowledge of market conditions derived from market analysis is essential to the application of the cost approach. The appraiser uses this information to determine whether the property has incurred functional obsolescence (i.e., is the physical structure competitive in the user market?), external obsolescence, or has an economic advantage (i.e., is the market over built or under built and does the subject have some competitive advantage or disadvantage?). The cost approach is based on the premise that the depreciated cost of the improvement(s) plus the value of the land will equal market value when supply and demand are in balance. The approach also recognizes that properties can gain or lose value because of external market conditions such as an economic upswing or an economic recession. In a down market, the appraiser considers the loss in rent for the anticipated period as a charge for external obsolescence, which is deducted from the depreciated cost of the subject improvement. Similarly, if a property is below industry standards to attract tenants as determined by Step 1, the property productivity analysis, and then there may be curable functional obsolescence that must be deducted in the cost approach.

Income Capitalization Approach

The market/marketability six-step process produces the data, analysis and conclusions for the revenue forecast in discounted cash flow income capitalization techniques.

To perform a discounted cash flow (DCF) analysis for a property, an appraiser prepares a reconstructed operating statement forecast (pro forma) based on data pertaining to the property's current and forecast occupancy levels, rents, and operating expenses. The estimates of *NOI* developed for each year of the projection period are supported by the conclusions of the market/ marketability analysis. In the DCF model, the projected cash flows are refined further to reflect all factors that affect *NOI*. These factors reflect property performance and include gross potential income, vacancy and collection losses, fixed and variable operating expenses, and debt service. The information gathered in the market/marketability analysis enables the appraiser to test the reasonableness of each element forecast in the DCF model by asking: Will the rents and occupancy levels in the market continue to rise or fall? Will rents and occupancy levels increase initially but head downward over the forecast period?

The income streams estimated in the reconstructed operating statement are discounted using a rate derived from analyzing the relationship between demand and competitive supply. If the market/marketability forecast indicates a strong market for the subject, the investment risk and discount rate will probably be lower. If the market/marketability forecast indicates a weak market, the investment risk and discount rate will probably be higher. The findings of the market/marketability analysis help set the range for the discount rate.

The choice of a discount rate also depends on the appraiser's confidence level in the absorption/capture forecast. The level of detail found in the market analysis must be considered. A low level of confidence will be associated with a general market/marketability study, which offers little support for the absorption forecast. The cash flows projected on the basis of such a forecast are riskier, and thus the selection of a higher discount rate is warranted. On the other hand, a high confidence level is associated with a detailed market/marketability study, which offers persuasive support for the capture forecast and thereby narrows the range of upside and downside possibilities. The cash flows projected on the basis of such a forecast are more secure, and the choice of a lower discount rate would be justified.

APPENDIX A

Market Analysis Guidelines

Purpose and Scope of NCREIF Suggested Guidelines

Recognizing the importance of market analysis in an appraisal, the Valuation and Research Committees of NCREIF [National Council of Real Estate Investment Fiduciaries] conducted a careful study of the issues with the objective of providing practical guidelines to the appraisal industry. The result is the following outline, which contains suggested elements of a complete market analysis for appraisals of investment-grade real estate. However, the level of detail and analysis in each appraisal is dictated by the nature of the assignment, time and expense constraints, and other specific considerations of the particular assignment.

This document is the first attempt at consolidating the thoughts of the members of NCREIF and this issue. Because of the dynamic nature of the subject matter, the *Market Analysis Guidelines* will likely be updated from time to time. We encourage industry input on this subject. Please contact any of the NCREIF committee members or the committee co-chairs.

NCREIF Suggested Market Analysis Guidelines

Market Area Delineation

1. Define and describe the metropolitan area.
    a. Identify the economic base industries of the metropolitan area, with emphasis on activities that influence the quantity, quality (risk), and duration of the specific space market.
    b. Identify possible and expected changes in the economic base.
2. Delineate the market study area(s). The market study area encompasses the competitive demand for and supply of space that is simi-

lar to the subject property. It is the subject's competitive market in terms of geographical area, product type, and price.

3. Demarcate the boundaries of the market on a market area map.
4. Explain reasons for selecting the boundaries of the market area.

Demand Analysis

The purpose of demand analysis is to show the development of historical relationships as a basis for forecasting future demand. However, merely extending the historic trend beyond the present to project future demand is not acceptable. It is necessary to identify changes in relationships and patterns that may affect trends and influence expectations, and to explain the assumptions that underlie these projected changes and their implications.

The submarket area strength conclusion in the population, demographic, and economic analysis serves as a background to and a frame of reference for the submarket demand analysis. Link these conclusions to the metropolitan economic base analysis and expected changes.

The suggested procedure for demand analysis is as follows:

1. Determine the major market demand factors (e.g., employment, population, shipping, trade, income) that affect the specific property type.
2. Define the unit of demand for the property type (e.g., households, retail sales, office employment, per capita occupancies for the property type).
3. Present historic and projected demand data for the metropolitan area and the specified market study area. It is important to use a reliable service for population, employment, and other demographic projections.
4. Relate the effect of total market demand on submarket demand (i.e., historic and prospective market share analysis for each submarket).
5. Relate the effects of U.S. macroeconomic demand factors to local market demand to the extent that the local market is influenced by macroeconomic factors. These factors are:
   a. GDP growth projections
   b. U.S. consumption trends
   c. Employment trends
   d. Federal trade policies
   e. Currency fluctuations
   f. Interstate commerce policies
   g. Changing technologies
   h. Cost of capital
   i. Capacity utilization levels
   j. Political influences
   k. Other

Demand Analysis by Property Type

Office Demand Analysis

1. Determine appropriate demand factors.

   a. Office-using employment such as FIRE, service, professional, technical, and sales. If aggregating employment data according to Standard Industrial Classification (SIC) codes, four-digit codes provide the appropriate level of specificity for office-using industries.

2. Develop use ratio (i.e., percentage of total employment that is office using).

3. Calculate total office employment demand.

4. Present historical use ratios and forecast changes in future use ratios.

5. Present historical demand and forecast changes in future demand.

   a. Marginal demand (i.e., increase over base)

   b. Migrational demand (i.e., intra-urban or office class migration)

6. Develop demand factor ratio (i.e., space per employee).

7. Calculate average annual demand for all office space, both owner-occupied and multitenant.

8. Calculate total forecast demand.

Industrial Demand Analysis

The procedure used for industrial demand analysis is the same as for office demand analysis. However, in addition to employment in manufacturing, wholesale, retail, transportation, communications, and public utilities (two- to four-digit SIC codes), demand factors may also include U.S. and regional economic growth that affects local demand; population growth; overall employment growth; household growth; retail sales (applicable in market analysis for retail storage and wholesale distribution properties); and cargo flows by transport type (e.g., truck, rail, water, air) and product type (e.g., high or low bulk). Some of these factors may also be used in office demand analysis.

Multifamily Residential Demand Analysis

1. Determine appropriate demand factors.

   a. Demographics by income, age, and family size

   b. Employment (e.g., labor force trends, future growth by industry segments)

   c. Population growth/decline

   d. Household formation and household size forecasts

   e. Migration trends

2. Perform internal mobility analysis (i.e., demand for units due to change in households, upgrades, demolition). Segment rental markets and owner markets according to percentage of demand.

3. Conduct rent vs. buy analysis (i.e., calculate percentage of population that can afford to buy units at the price they can afford to buy) to segregate effective demand from total demand.

4. Develop ability-to-pay model (from housing cost to finance payment [debt service] to debt service, to loan amount [loan-to-value ratio], to housing price, to required income, to submarket by income groups).

5. Present total demand.

6. Apply appropriate demand factor (e.g., units per population).

7. Profile appropriate tenants (e.g., single professionals, families, retirees).

8. Calculate average annual demand.

9. Forecast future demand.

Retail Demand Analysis

1. Determine appropriate demand factors.
   a. Population/employment growth
   b. Households and household size breakdown
   c. Average household income and disposable income
   d. Trade area disposable income

2. Project level of retail sales based on trends in population, household patterns, personal income, consumer purchasing habits, historical retail sales, and shopping center sales.

3. Calculate disposable income factor (i.e., money remaining after taxes).

4. Present total disposable income, both historical and forecasted.

5. Apply retail sales factor (i.e., retail sales as a percentage of disposable income).

6. Calculate total retail sales.

7. Apply shopping center sales factor (i.e., general merchandise, apparel, home furnishings, and other merchandise normally sold in malls [GAFO] or department store type merchandise [DSTM]).

8. Calculate total shopping center sales.

9. Calculate total shopping center sales per household.

10. Calculate total shopping center sales for trade area.

11. Calculate sales per square foot, broken down by retail store type.

Supply Analysis

Supply analysis begins with a review of the historical relationships between demand growth and supply growth. It includes defining the generally accepted attributes for specific building types (e.g., Class A, B, and C office; regional vs. neighborhood retail), relating these to the specific tenant profile and the current market capacity to satisfy that specific demand. The total space inventory is described by both quantity and quality. It is described by location, quality (e.g., premier regional mall, Class A office building, luxury multifamily), type (e.g., owner-occupied, rental), size, age, and other classifications related to property type (e.g., shopping center classification, unit types for multifamily).

The items covered in supply analysis include existing inventory (e.g., total square feet, number of properties, building area); existing available space; historical construction trends (e.g., total square feet, number of properties, average building area); inventory under construction, expansion, or revision; cost-feasible rent level necessary for new construction; and inventory proposed and the probability of completion.

The suggested procedure for supply analysis is as follows:

1. Present an inventory of competitive supply in the market and submarket.
2. Analyze the salient characteristics of this supply.
3. Show historic supply trends in the market and submarket.
4. Explain the reasons for past supply growth (as a reaction to increased demand, overbuilding without regard for demand, and special circumstances).
5. Define where the market is in the current supply cycle.
6. Identify the factors that will affect new supply in the future as a basis for forecasting future supply (i.e., relationships and patterns as they relate to the trends identified in the demand analysis). Link conclusions to the metropolitan economic base analysis.
7. Forecast near-term supply in square feet or units per year, using construction starts, permitted starts, planned starts, and dates of completion.
8. Forecast long-term supply, using potential future inventory based on a balanced market demand-supply model. Correlate with land availability in the subject area. Link analysis to the metropolitan analysis with respect to direction and potential growth.
9. Review specific constraints to future supply, such as financing availability, regulatory climate, and infrastructure capacity.
10. Relate the effect of metromarket on submarket supply. Relate statistics to historical and present market conditions.

Absorption Analysis

The suggested procedure for absorption analysis is as follows:

1. Describe historical absorption patterns (e.g., amount of space absorbed, rate of absorption) in the macromarket and the submarket. Relate the effect of macromarket demand on submarket demand. Relate to components of demand and prevailing market conditions. This may be accomplished by a fair-share analysis and penetration analysis by submarket. Historic demand and supply statistics should correlate to historic absorption patterns. If not, reconcile and explain differences.
2. Use forecast demand trends to relate to market conditions (e.g., evidence of potential national, regional, or local changes that would alter demand). Make adjustments for unique considerations in the submarket.

a. Present historic total demand factor.

b. Calculate historic growth rate.

c. Forecast future growth rate.

d. Calculate property type use ratio.

e. Apply property type demand factor.

f. Calculate annual space demand.

g. Calculate total forecast space demand.

h. Calculate future annual forecast demand.

3. Analyze available space and, to the extent possible, "hidden" space (e.g., sublet space), and calculate amount of time needed to absorb all available space and space under construction (known as "years to absorb"). Distinguish between owner-occupied and multitenant space.

a. Present total inventory.

b. Calculate availability rate.

c. Present amount of occupied space.

d. Calculate net absorption per year. Net absorption is defined as the change in total occupied square feet from period to period.

4. Analyze cost-feasible rent levels for the type and class of property being analyzed and how they relate to current and historical rental rates. This provides a benchmark similar to the supply aspect of the space analysis. Correlation of cost-feasible rental rates to market rental rates can provide inference to future absorption rates and probable real rental rate increases in the future.

Vacancy Analysis

The suggested procedure for vacancy analysis is as follows:

1. Present historical, current, and forecasted vacancy and occupancy trends. Relate to market conditions. Link absorption estimates to occupancy levels.

2. Develop an equation from historic supply, demand, and absorption statistics to explain historic vacancy rates and discuss changes that would modify the equation.

3. Use the equation and the forecast inputs from the supply, demand, and absorption work to forecast future vacancy rates.

It is important to correlate assumptions of structural or stabilized vacancy rates with the assumptions in the discounted cash flow analysis (e.g., tenant attrition rate, down time between leases, credit loss).

Market Rental Rate Analysis

The suggested procedure for rental rate analysis is as follows:

1. Describe typical lease terms, including free rent and other concessions. Effective rent is a key consideration. For example, flat face rental rates accompanied by a reduction in rental concessions equate to an increase in effective rental rates.

2. Present historic rental rate trends. Relate to absorption and vacancy trends and market conditions.

3. Differentiate rental rates by building quality class (e.g., Class A vs. Class B office; warehouse vs. R&D [research and development] space; regional mall vs. community retail space; high-rise vs. garden apartments). Address rental rate differentials resulting from building age.

It is important to link rental rate growth assumptions to demand indicators in the attempt to ascertain the users' ability to pay (e.g., occupancy cost as a percentage of retail sales in shopping centers, household income growth and the percentage applicable to housing for multifamily properties, increases in service revenues for office tenants). Supply constraints may not be the sole determinant of upward movement in rental rates. Rental rate changes can be correlated to inflation and expense growth assumptions to make clear the real rental rate growth assumptions.

North American Industry Classification System (NAICS)

After 60 years of use, the outdated Standard Industrial Classification (SIC) system was retired and replaced in 1997 by the new North American Industry Classification System (NAICS). NAICS is the product of a collaborative effort between the United States, Canada, and Mexico. The notice that made NAICS effective in the United States was issued in April 1997, and the first NAICS U.S. manual was published in mid-1998. For the first time ever, direct comparison of economic data across North American borders has been made possible.

Unlike previous SIC revisions, the NAICS changes are fundamental. It now recognizes hundreds of new businesses in the U.S. economy, largely in the fast-growing service sector. NAICS has doubled the number of top-level groupings of industrial classification. The highest level of NAICS classification is called the sector, and corresponds roughly to the division in SIC. There are 20 broad sectors in NAICS, compared to only 10 divisions in SIC. It also has increased the descriptive detail for businesses in the service sector, adding new sectors such as information, professional, scientific and technical, administrative and support, waste management, remediation, and accommodation and food service.

A Different Numbering System

The numbering system for NAICS coding is unrelated to SIC system. It provides five levels of classification (compared to four in SIC) using detailed codes with a maximum of six digits (also up from four in SIC), and detailed classifications called "U.S. Industry" rather than "Industry" assigned by the SIC.

This material was extracted in part from the U.S. Department of Labor, Bureau of Labor Statistics Web site (www.bls.gov).

NAICS was organized so that industries would be comparable across the United States, Canada, and Mexico at the 5-digit level, known as the "NAICS Industry Level." The sixth digit of a NAICS classification may be used differently in the United States, Canada, and Mexico. A comparison of the organizational structures of SIC and NAICS is illustrated in Exhibit B-1 below.

Exhibit B-1	Comparison of SIC/NAICS Organizational Structures		
SIC		**NAICS**	
Level	**Code**	**Level**	**Code**
			XX
Major Group	XX	Subsector	XXX
Industry Group	XXX	Industry Group	XXXX
Industry	XXXX	NAICS Industry	XXXXX
		U.S. Industry	XXXXXX

At the heart of NAICS is a production-based concept of classification; i.e., it classifies each establishment into a detailed industry based on the production processes that it uses. Under the SIC system, some establishments were classified according to production processes, while others were classified using different criteria, such as class of customer. Thus, reclassification under NAICS substantially changes how many and which businesses are included in certain sectors. Examples of this reclassification are readily found in the wholesale/retail trade and in auxiliary establishments.

Under the SIC, wholesalers and retailers were classified according to the class of customer they served. NAICS groups them according to the way each establishment operates. For instance, retailers typically sell merchandise in small quantities, using public-oriented methods such as mass-media advertising and high-traffic locations. Wholesalers, on the other hand, are often closed to the public, sell goods in large quantities and rely on business-oriented sales methods such as specialized catalogs and warehouse locations. Thus, establishments that previously were considered to be engaged in wholesale trade, such as the sale of used auto parts or office furniture, could be considered retail trade if they were open to the public.

Auxiliary establishments, which provide services such as warehousing, personnel, or data processing to other organizations within the same company, are classified in the same industry as their parent companies under the SIC. NAICS, however, classifies them establishments according to the services they provide.

NAICS 2002

NAICS 2002 is a revision of NAICS 1997. Both are the same as for 16 of the 20 sectors. However, construction and wholesale trade are substantially changed, a number of retail classifications are modified, and the information sector has been reorganized.

Exhibit B-2 shows the 2002 sector and subsector codes and titles.

Exhibit B-2	2002 NAICS Sector and Subsector Codes and Titles

North American Industrial Classification System (NAICS) 2002 (3-Digit Level)

Sector 11   **Agriculture, Forestry, Fishing, and Hunting**
- Subsector 111   Crop Production
- Subsector 112   Animal Production
- Subsector 113   Forestry and Logging
- Subsector 114   Fishing, Hunting, and Trapping
- Subsector 115   Support Activities for Agriculture and Forestry

Sector 21   **Mining**
- Subsector 211   Oil and Gas Extraction
- Subsector 212   Mining (Except Oil and Gas)
- Subsector 213   Support Activities for Mining

Sector 22   **Utilities**
- Subsector 221   Utilities

Sector 23   **Construction**
- Subsector 236   Construction of Buildings
- Subsector 237   Heavy and Civil Engineering Construction
- Subsector 238   Specialty Trade Contractors

Sectors 31–33   **Manufacturing**
- Subsector 311   Food Manufacturing
- Subsector 312   Beverage and Tobacco Product Manufacturing
- Subsector 313   Textile Mills
- Subsector 314   Textile Product Mills
- Subsector 315   Apparel Manufacturing
- Subsector 316   Leather and Allied Product Manufacturing
- Subsector 321   Wood Product Manufacturing
- Subsector 322   Paper Manufacturing
- Subsector 323   Printing and Related Support Activities
- Subsector 324   Petroleum and Coal Products Manufacturing
- Subsector 325   Chemical Manufacturing
- Subsector 326   Plastics and Rubber Products Manufacturing
- Subsector 327   Nonmetallic Mineral Product Manufacturing
- Subsector 331   Primary Metal Manufacturing
- Subsector 332   Fabricated Metal Product Manufacturing
- Subsector 333   Machinery Manufacturing
- Subsector 334   Computer and Electronic Product Manufacturing
- Subsector 335   Electrical Equipment, Appliance, and Component Manufacturing
- Subsector 336   Transportation Equipment Manufacturing
- Subsector 337   Furniture and Related Product Manufacturing
- Subsector 339   Miscellaneous Manufacturing

Sector 42   **Wholesale Trade**

Subsector 423   Merchant Wholesalers, Durable Goods

Subsector 424   Merchant Wholesalers, Nondurable Goods

Subsector 425   Wholesale Electronic Markets, Agents, and Brokers

Sectors 44–45   **Retail Trade**

Subsector 441   Motor Vehicle and Parts Dealers

Subsector 442   Furniture and Home Furnishings Stores

Subsector 443   Electronics and Appliance Stores

Subsector 444   Building Material, Garden Equipment and Supplies Dealers

Subsector 445   Food and Beverage Stores

Subsector 446   Health and Personal Care Stores

Subsector 447   Gasoline Stations

Subsector 448   Clothing and Clothing Accessories Stores

Subsector 451   Sporting Good, Hobby, Book, and Music Stores

Subsector 452   General Merchandise Stores

Subsector 453   Miscellaneous Store Retailers

Subsector 454   Nonstore Retailers

Sectors 48-49   **Transportation and Warehousing**

Subsector 481   Air Transportation

Subsector 482   Rail Transportation

Subsector 483   Water Transportation

Subsector 484   Truck Transportation

Subsector 485   Transit and Ground Passenger Transportation

Subsector 486   Pipeline Transportation

Subsector 487   Scenic and Sightseeing Transportation

Subsector 488   Support Activities for Transportation

Subsector 491   Postal Service

Subsector 492   Couriers and Messengers

Subsector 493   Warehousing and Storage

Sector 51   **Information**

Subsector 511   Publishing Industries (Except Internet)

Subsector 512   Motion Picture and Sound Recording Industries

Subsector 515   Broadcasting (Except Internet)

Subsector 516   Internet Publishing and Broadcasting

Subsector 517   Telecommunications

Subsector 518   Internet Service Providers, Web Search Portals and Data Processing Services

Subsector 519   Other Information Services

Sector 52   **Finance and Insurance**

Subsector 521   Monetary Authorities—Central Bank

Subsector 522   Credit Intermediation and Related Activities

Subsector 523   Securities, Commodity Contracts, and Other Financial Investments and Related Activities

Subsector 524   Insurance Carriers and Related Activities

Subsector 525   Funds, Trusts, and Other Financial Vehicles

Sector 53   **Real Estate and Rental Leasing**
             Subsector 531   Real Estate
             Subsector 532   Rental and Leasing Services
             Subsector 533   Lessors of Nonfinancial Intangible Assets (Except Copyrighted Works)

Sector 54   **Professional, Scientific, and Technical Services**
             Subsector 541   Professional, Scientific, and Technical Services

Sector 55   **Management of Companies and Enterprises**
             Subsector 551   Management of Companies and Enterprises

Sector 56   **Administrative and Support and Waste Management and Remediation Services**
             Subsector 561   Administrative and Support Services
             Subsector 562   Waste Management and Remediation Services

Sector 61   **Educational Services**
             Subsector 611   Educational Services

Sector 62   **Health Care and Social Assistance**
             Subsector 621   Ambulatory Health Care Services
             Subsector 622   Hospitals
             Subsector 623   Nursing and Residential Care Facilities
             Subsector 624   Social Assistance

Sector 71   **Arts, Entertainment, and Recreation**
             Subsector 711   Performing Arts, Spectator Sports, and Related Industries
             Subsector 712   Museums, Historical Sites, and Similar Institutions
             Subsector 713   Amusement, Gambling, and Recreation Industries

Sector 72   **Accommodation and Food Services**
             Subsector 721   Accommodation
             Subsector 722   Food Services and Drinking Places

Sector 81   **Other Services (Except Public Administration)**
             Subsector 811   Repair and Maintenance
             Subsector 812   Personal and Laundry Services
             Subsector 813   Religious, Grantmaking, Civic, Professional, and Similar Organizations
             Subsector 814   Private Households

Sector 92   **Public Administration**
             Subsector 921   Executive, Legislative, and Other General Government Support
             Subsector 922   Justice, Public Order, and Safety Activities
             Subsector 923   Administration of Human Resource Programs
             Subsector 924   Administration of Environmental Quality Programs
             Subsector 925   Administration of Housing Programs, Urban Planning, and Community Development
             Subsector 926   Administration of Economic Programs
             Subsector 927   Space Research and Technology
             Subsector 928   National Security and International Affairs

BLS Standard for Sector Aggregation Titles for NAICS

Data are sometimes consolidated by what are called "supersectors," which are defined in Exhibit B-3 below.

Exhibit B-3	BLS Definition of Supersectors

Goods-Producing

Natural Resources and Mining

| Sector 11 | Agriculture, Forestry, Fishing, and Hunting |
| Sector 21 | Mining |

Construction

| Sector 23 | Construction |

Manufacturing

| Sectors 31–33 | Manufacturing |

Service-Providing

Trade, Transportation, and Utilities

Sector 42	Wholesale Trade
Sectors 44–45	Retail Trade
Sectors 48–49	Transportation and Warehousing
Sector 22	Utilities

Information

| Sector 51 | Information |

Financial Activities

| Sector 52 | Finance and Insurance |
| Sector 53 | Real Estate, Rental, and Leasing |

Professional and Business Services

Sector 54	Professional, Scientific, and Technical Services
Sector 55	Management of Companies and Enterprises
Sector 56	Administrative, Support, Waste Management, and Remediation Services

Education and Health Services

| Sector 61 | Education Services |
| Sector 62 | Health Care and Social Assistance |

Leisure and Hospitality

| Sector 71 | Arts, Entertainment, and Recreation |
| Sector 72 | Accommodation and Food Services |

Other Services

| Sector 81 | Other Services (Except Public Administration) |

Government

| Sector 92 | Public Administration |

Unclassified

| Sector 99 | Unclassified |

Bibliography

General Surveys and Anthologies

Appraisal Institute. "Real Estate Cycles: Trends and Analysis." Technical report from the 1993 Annual Research Symposium, Chicago.

___. *Real Estate Market Analysis and Appraisal.* Research Report 3. Chicago: American Institute of Real Estate Appraisers, 1988.

___. *Real Estate Market Analysis: Supply and Demand Factors.* Technical report from the 1992 Annual Research Symposium. Chicago: Appraisal Institute, 1993.

Carn, Neil, Joseph Rabianski, Ronald Racster, and Maury Seldin. *Real Estate Market Analysis.** Englewood Cliffs, N.J.: Prentice-Hall, 1988.

Clapp, John M. *Handbook for Real Estate Market Analysis.** Englewood Cliffs, N.J.: Prentice-Hall, 1987.

DeLisle, James R. and J. Sa-Aadu, eds. *Appraisal, Market Analysis and Public Policy in Real Estate: Essays in Honor of James A. Graaskamp.* The American Real Estate Society. Norwell, Mass.: Kluwer Academic Publishers, 1994.

Fanning, Stephen F. and Jody Winslow. "Guidelines for Defining the Scope of Market Analysis in Appraisals." *The Appraisal Journal* (October 1988).

McKinley, Michael D., ed. *Appraising Industrial Properties.* Chicago: Appraisal Institute, 2005.

Ratcliff, Richard U. *Real Estate Analysis.* New York: McGraw-Hill Book Company, Inc., 1961.

Vernor, James D., ed. *Readings in Market Analysis for Real Estate.* Chicago: American Institute of Real Estate Appraisers, 1985.

---

* Contains excellent bibliography on data sources and data services available for market analysis.

Economic Base Analysis, Census Data, Location Theory, City Planning, Real Estate Trends, and Finance/Investment

Alonso, W. and J. Friedmann. *Regional Development and Planning.* Cambridge, Mass.: MIT Press, 1964.

Andrews, Richard B. *Urban Land Economics and Public Policy.* New York: The Free Press, 1971.

___. "Situs: Variables of Urban Land Use Location," *Urban Land Economics and Public Policy.* New York: The Free Press, 1971.

Christaller, Walter. *Central Places in Southern Germany.* Englewood Cliffs, N.J.: Prentice-Hall, 1966.

Crispell, Diane. *Demographic Know-How: Everything You Need to Find, Analyze, and Use Information About Your Customers,* 3d ed. Ithaca, N.Y.: American Demographic Books, 1993.

Etter, Wayne E. "Putting a Leash on Risk: Toward Evaluating Commercial Properties." *Journal of the Real Estate Center at Texas A&M University* (Spring 1994).

Feagin, J.R. *The Urban Real Estate Game.* Englewood Cliffs, N.J.: Prentice Hall, 1983.

Greer, Gaylon E. and Michael D. Farrell. *Investment Analysis for Real Estate Decisions.* 2d ed. Chicago: Dearborn Financial Publishers, 1988.

Heilbrun, James. *Urban Economics and Public Policy,* 2d ed. New York: St. Martin's Press, 1981.

Isard, Walter. *Methods of Regional Analysis.* Cambridge, Mass.: MIT Press, 1960.

Jackson, John Brinckerhoff. *A Sense of Place, a Sense of Time.* New Haven, Conn.: Yale University Press, 1994.

Kostof, Spiro with the collaboration of Greg Castillo, *The City Assembled: The Elements of Urban Form Through History.* New York: Little, Brown, 1992.

Kostof, Spiro. *The City Shaped: Urban Patterns and Meanings Through History.* New York: Little, Brown, 1991.

Kunstler, James Howard. *The Geography of Nowhere: The Rise and Fall of America's Man-Made Landscape.* New York: Simon and Schuster, 1993.

Lessinger, Jack. *The Crash of Suburbia: The Coming Boom of Small Towns.* Seattle: Socioeconomics, 1990.

___. *Penturbia: Where Real Estate Will Boom After the Crash of Suburbia.* Seattle: Socioeconomics, 1991.

___. *Regions of Opportunity: A Bold Strategy for Real Estate Investment with Forecasts to the Year 2010.* Seattle: Socioeconomics, 1986.

Lösch, August. *Economics of Location.* New Haven, Conn.: Yale University Press, 1954.

Malkiel, Burton G. *A Random Walk Down Wall Street*, 5th ed. New York: Norton, 1990.

Martin, W.B. "How to Predict Urban Growth Patterns." *The Appraisal Journal* (April 1984).

McShane, Clay. *Down the Asphalt Path: The Automobile and the American City*. New York: Columbia University Press, 1994.

Myers, Dowell. *Analysis with Local Census Data: Portraits of Change*. San Diego: Academic Press, Inc., a subsidiary of Harcourt Brace Jovanovich, 1992.

___. "Ransacking the Federal Census." A paper delivered at the annual meeting of the American Real Estate Society, 1992.

Pfouts, R.W., ed. *The Techniques of Urban Economic Analysis*. West Trenton, N.J.: Chandler Davis Publishing Co., 1960.

Rabianski, Joseph. "The Accuracy of Economic/Demographic Projections Made by Private Vendors of Secondary Data." *The Appraisal Journal* (April 1992).

Tiebout, Charles M. *The Community Economic Base Study*. Supplementary Paper No. 1. New York: Committee for Economic Development, December 1962.

Whyte, William Hollingsworth. *City: Rediscovering Its Center*. New York: Doubleday, 1989.

Zeckendorf, William. *Zeckendorf: The Autobiography of William Zeckendorf*. New York: Holt, 1970.

Appraisal Literature

Clapp, John. *Real Estate Absorption for Appraisal, Investment, and Lending*. Conn.: Land Publications.

Graaskamp, James A. *The Appraisal of 25 N. Pinckney: A Demonstration Case for Contemporary Appraisal Methods*. Madison, Wis.: Landmark Research, Inc., 1977.

___. *Fundamentals of Real Estate Development*. Development Component Series. Washington, D.C.: Urban Land Institute, 1981.

Monographs and Articles About Specific Property Types
Office Buildings

Alexander, Ian. *Office Location and Public Policy*. New York: Chancer Press, 1979.

Building Owners and Managers Association. *Downtown and Suburban Office Building Experience Exchange Report*. Washington, D.C.: BOMA.

Garreau, Joel. *Edge City: Life on the New Frontier*. New York: Doubleday, 1991.

Gordon, Edmond S. *How to Market Space in an Office Building*. Boston: Warren, Gorham, and Lamont, Inc., 1976.

Kimball, J.R., and Barbara S. Bloomberg. "Office Space Demand Analysis." *The Appraisal Journal* (October 1987).

White, John R., ed. *The Office Building: From Concept to Investment Reality.* A joint publication of the Appraisal Institute, American Society of Real Estate Counselors, and Society of Industrial and Office Realtors.® Chicago, 1993.

Urban Land Institute. *Office Development Handbook.* Washington, D.C.: ULI, 1982.

Residential

Kimball, J.R., and Barbara S. Bloomberg. "The Demographics of Subdivision Analysis." *The Appraisal Journal* (October 1986).

Myers, Dowell. *Housing Demography: Linking Demographic Structure and Housing Markets.* Madison: University of Wisconsin Press, 1991.

___. "Housing Market Research: A Time for Change." *Urban Land* (October 1988).

Urban Land Institute. *Residential Development Handbook.* Washington, D.C.: ULI, 1978.

U.S. Department of Commerce, Bureau of the Census. *Construction Reports.* Washington, D.C.: U.S. Government Printing Office.

Shopping Centers

American Planning Association. "Changing Retail Trends," *Planning* (January 1991).

Berry, Brian L.J. "Spatial Theories of Marketing Systems, Abstract and Operational" in Robert L. King, ed. *Marketing and the New Science of Planning.* Chicago: American Marketing Association, 1968.

Berry, Brian and J.B. Parr. *Market Centers and Retail Location: Theory and Applications.* Englewood Cliffs, N.J.: Prentice-Hall, Inc., 1988.

Clapp, John. *Acorn Hill Mall: A Case Study for Retail Market Analysis.* Conn.: Land Publications.

___. *Retail Gravitation Analysis.* Conn.: Land Publications.

Nelson, Richard L. *The Selection of Retail Locations.* New York: F.W. Dodge, 1958.

Rabianski, Joseph, and James D. Vernor. *Shopping Center Appraisal and Analysis.*, Chicago: Appraisal Institute, 1993.

Reilly, William J. *Methods for the Study of Retail Relationships.* Austin: Bureau of Business Research, University of Texas, 1929. Reprinted in Austin in 1959.

Rocca, Ruben A., ed. *Market Research for Shopping Centers.* New York: International Council of Shopping Centers, 1985.

Urban Land Institute. *Dollars and Cents of Shopping Centers.* Published triennially. Washington, D.C.: ULI.

Urban Land Institute. *Parking Requirements for Shopping Centers.* Summary Recommendations and Research Summary Report. Washington, D.C.: ULI, 1986.

Urban Land Institute. *Shopping Center Development Handbook,* 2d ed. Community Builders Handbook series. Washington, D.C.: ULI, 1985.

Vacant Land and Proposed Development (Mixed-Use Developments)

McMahan, John. *Property Development: Effective Decision Making in Uncertain Times.* New York: McGraw-Hill, 1976.

Peisner, Richard B. "Optimizing Profits from Land Use Planning." *Urban Land* (September 1982).

Reports and Forecasts on Real Estate Market Trends

(Compiled by David A. Mulvihill and published in *Urban Land* (August 1994.)

Baring Consensus Forecast
  Baring Advisors
  2 Grand Central Tower, Suite 4000
  140 East 45th Street
  New York, NY 10017-3144
  212-697-3340
  March issue of firm's *U.S. Property Report.* Ranking of top investment markets based on analysis of more than 30 separate forecasts.

Commercial Property Trends
  Oncor International
  3040 Post Oak Boulevard, Suite 500
  Houston, TX 77056
  713-961-0600
  Annual. Information on commercial property and economic trends in 55 markets in the United States, Canada, and Europe.

Dodge/Sweet's Construction Outlook
  McGraw-Hill, Inc.
  1221 Avenue of the Americas
  New York, NY 10020
  212-512-3853
  Annual. Forecast of construction activity in the residential, commercial, public works, and manufacturing sectors.

Emerging Trends in Real Estate
  RERC Real Estate Research Corporation and Equitable Real Estate Investment Management, Inc.
  RERC Real Estate Research Corporation
  2 North LaSalle Street, Suite 400
  Chicago, Illinois 60602
  312-346-5885
  Annual. Information on general economic trends, investment trends, capital sources, specific markets, and property types.

Hospitality Directions
Coopers & Lybrand
1301 Avenue of the Americas
New York, NY 10019-6013
212-259-2620
December issue of quarterly journal. Twelve-quarter forecast of average hotel occupancy rates, room rates, total receipts, room supply, and construction.

The Host Report
Arthur Anderson & Co., SC
The Arthur Anderson Real Estate Services Group
633 West Fifth Street
Los Angeles, CA 90071
800-959-1059
Annual. Operating statistics and supply and demand information for U.S. full-service, limited-service, and all-suite hotels based on information from Smith Travel Research, with specific information on 21 major markets.

Market Trends
Julien J. Studley, Inc.
300 Park Avenue
New York, NY 10022
212-326-1000
Annual. Overall U.S. and international real estate market trends and specific commercial property market information for a limited number of major markets.

Property Report
The Yarmouth Group
Swiss Bank Tower
10 East 50th Street
New York, NY 10022
212-355-4810
Annual. General economic and real estate trend information for office, retail, industrial, and lodging markets in 18 U.S. and European markets.

Real Estate Market Forecast
Landauer Real Estate Counselors
335 Madison Avenue
New York, NY 10017
212-687-2323
Annual. U.S. economic information as well as specific performance information for the office, retail, industrial, residential, and hotel sectors and for two dozen U.S. metro areas.

Real Estate Value Trends

Valuation Network, Inc.
608 2nd Avenue South
Northstar East, Suite 700
Minneapolis, MN 55402
800-345-1277

Annual. List of economic and demographic growth markets and top investment markets for the office, industrial, retail, and apartment sectors.

Top Construction Markets

Cahners Economics
Cahners Publishing Company
275 Washington Street
Newton, MA 02158
617-964-3030

Annual. U.S. economic, demographic, and employment information and predictions for the top 50 construction markets for each upcoming year in both residential and nonresidential sectors.

Trends in the Hotel Industry

PKF Consulting
PKF Consulting Headquarters
425 California Street, Suite 1650
San Francisco, CA 94104
415-421-5378

Annual. National and regional operating and financial data for U.S. hotels and motels as well as overall demographic and economic information pertinent to the lodging industry.

Index

This index uses two types of cross-references. *See* references refer the reader from one term to another term–often the more common usage–under which page numbers are listed. *See also* references refer the reader from one term, under which page numbers are listed, to a second, related term, under which more information can be found.

above-grade living area (*AGLA*), 347

absorption rates, 5, 20–23, 358–359, 370

    for prospective uses of vacant land, 429–431, 433

accessibility, 51, 55–58

    and curb cuts, 410

    and land prices, 71–72

    macro-level, 55–57

    micro-level, 57–58

    and multiple nuclei model, 80–82

    of office buildings or office parks, 271, 277

    and rent theorists' model, 84–90

    See also physical location

adult congregate living facilities (ACLF), 347

age

    of apartment complexes, 365–367

    of shopping centers, 214

age distribution. *See* demographics

agglomeration, economics of, 56

agricultural land use. *See* land use

air-conditioning. *See* heating, ventilation, and air-conditioning

air rights, 38

Alonso, William

    rent theory of, 58, 85–86

alternative use scoping, 5–6, 85–86

AMB Property Corporation, 310

amenities

    of apartment complexes, 365–367

    market segmentation by, 116, 125

    in office buildings, 271, 279

    of area, 59–61

    and residential properties, 345

    in shopping centers, 200, 214, 450–451

    See also design/amenities ratings; environment

analogs, 163-164

    and market definition, 120

    and urban growth rate, 208

anchor tenants, 201, 206, 214

Andrews, Richard
and land use changes, 99, 209
apartment complex
and building property rating, 352
and competitive location rating, 353–354
and competitive property rating, 365–368
and forecasting demand by ratio method, 383
and fundamental demand forecasting by segmentation method, 360–363
and inferred demand indicators, 357–360
market analysis for, 343–373
and market area delineation, 354–356
and market penetration analysis, 370–372
and market residual demand, 369
and segmentation by affordability, 362
and segmentation by unit type, 361–362
and unit mix determination for forecasting, 349
See also residential properties
Applebaum customer spotting technique, 121
appraisal
and client needs, 26
appraisal process
and market analysis, 5–6
and scientific method, 6–9
appraisal reports
and levels of analysis, 27–30
approaches to value. *See* appraisal process; cost approach; development approach; income capitalization approach; sales comparison approach
assembling movement, 57–58
axial (radial corridor) model, 82–84

basic employment, 103–108, 111
basic industries, 103–105
bid-rent curves, 84–87
"bubble" market, 175–176
building area
of shopping centers, 199
building codes and permits, 66, 145, 158
building envelope, 41–43
building lines, 272
building management. *See* office buildings

Building Owners and Managers Association (BOMA), 271
building rentable area
in office buildings, 271
building terms
for offices, 271
for residential property, 346–347
for shopping centers, 194
buildings
design and layout of, 200, 277–278
structure of, 36–37
See also apartment complex; office buildings; retail shopping center
building usable area
in office buildings, 271
built environment, 59–60
Bureau of Labor Statistics (BLS), 153, 233
Burgess, Ernest W., 74–76
and concentric zone model, 74–76
business cycles, 170–171, 174, 348
See also real estate cycles
buying power, 153, 228, 234–235
See also consumer spending

capture analysis
for an apartment complex, 370–373
concepts, 171–183
implications of alternative methods, 180–181, 261
for an industrial building, 337–341
for an office building, 300–305
for optimal use of vacant land, 434–438
for a proposed retail center, 461
for a retail shopping center, 258–268
for a vacant retail center, 477–478, 485–486
capture methods,
two alternatives, 180–181
capture rate
calculated from new demand, 180–181
calculated from total demand, 180
concept, 179–180
long and short term, 179–180
CBD. *See* central business district

census tracts

and trade areas, 118, 219

central business district (CBD), 71, 74–76, 123–124

and concentric zone model, 74–76

and office space development, 270, 272

and rent theorists' models, 84–88

central city

rebirth of, 93

cities

size and age, 72

See also urban growth; urban structure

city planning, 65–66

and physical environment, 59–60

and retail shopping centers, 255, 259

See also public planning; urban growth; urban structure

civil rights

vs. property rights, 38–39

client needs, 26

clustering, 56, 80–81, 223, 280

coalescence

in concentric zone model, 77

commercial office space, 270

commercial property, 27

common areas, 194

community preferences

and market structure, 40–41

comparable city-ratio method, 294

compatibility, principle of, 201

competitive rating procedures

for apartment complexes, 363–368

for office space, 276–280, 298–300

for shopping centers, 215–216, 254–256

for vacant tracts, 434–438

See also capture rate; competitive supply; competitive supply analysis

competitive supply

definition of, 142

estimating, 144–146

and level of analysis, 143–144

and market segmentation, 142–143

competitive supply analysis, 5, 11, 142–146, 255–256

for an apartment complex, 363–368

for an industrial building, 331–334

and location, 210–216

for an office building, 295–298

for a proposed retail center, 459, 461

for prospective uses of vacant land, 428, 430, 432–434

and residential property, 348

for a retail shopping center, 253–258

for a vacant retail center, 474–477

concentric zone model, 74–76, 99, 138

condominiums, 38, 347, 351

constant dollars, 233

construction

data sources, 156–157

residential trends in, 358, 368–370

See also buildings; building terms

consumer spending, 153–154, 234, 240, 356

at neighborhood shopping centers, 459–461

continuing-care retirement centers (CCRC), 347

convenience goods, 238, 242

convenience stores, 196–197, 231, 470

cooperatives, 347

corridors

in office buildings, 278

cost approach, 504

and office buildings, 275

and shopping centers, 268

Co-Star, 157

county business patterns, 154

critical variables, 150

cumulative attraction, principle of, 190, 201

customer spotting, 121–122, 239

cycles. *See* business cycles; real estate cycles

data sources and collection, 149–167

    on apartment complexes, 363–365

    on competitive supply, 143–146

    on construction/space inventory, 156–157

    on convenience and shopping goods, 238

    on demographics, 152–153

    on employment, 154, 284–285

    on household income, 152–153, 234

    on employment by industry, 154

    and market segmentation, 116–117

    and real estate market trends, 159

    and real estate space inventory, 156–157

    on retail shopping centers, 204, 216, 220

    on retail store tenants, 242–243

    sources listed, 152–157

    on supply and demand, 151

    See also primary data; secondary data

DCF. *See* discounted cash flow analysis

demand

    for apartment complexes, 347

    and business and real estate cycles, 170–177

    definition of, 127–129

    and market segmentation, 129–131

    for office space, 270

    reasons to examine, 128

    and residential markets, 345–346

    and secondary data, 150–157

    for single-family homes, 346

    sources of, 132

    techniques for examining, 131–137

    and urban growth, 137–138

    See also competitive supply; effective demand; latent demand; marginal demand; move-down demand; move-up demand; supply and demand

demand analysis, 186

    for an apartment complex, 357–363

    for an industrial building, 309–312, 325–331

    for an office building, 284–295

    for a proposed retail center, 455–459

    for prospective uses of vacant land, 428–434, 445

    for a retail shopping center, 227–253

    for a vacant retail center, 472–486

    See also fundamental analysis; inferred analysis; market analysis

demand forecast. *See* demand analysis; forecasting

demographics

    and demand for prospective uses of vacant land, 428

    and market segments, 116–117

    and residential markets, 345–349, 355–357

    sources of data, 152–153

    See also data sources and collection

design/amenities ratings, 146

    See also property rating procedures

development

    phasing of, 436–438

development approach, 502

discounted cash flow (DCF) analysis, 268, 439–440, 504–505

dispersive movement, 57–58

disposable income. *See* buying power; consumer spending

distance. *See* accessibility; subjective distance; transportation

Downs, Anthony, 95

ecology models. *See* social ecology models

economic base, 348

    defined, 101

    and urban structure, 72–73

economic base analysis, 20, 101–111

economic cycles. *See* business cycles; real estate cycles

economic environment, 63–65

    See also land use

economic location, 51–53, 88–90

economic modeling, 436–438

    See also financial feasibility analysis; forecasting

economic theory

    and market analysis, 4–5

economy

    circular flow of, 103

edge cities, 90–92

effective demand, 4–5, 10

efficiency ratio

    in office buildings, 271

electrical systems

    in office buildings, 277

elevators

    in office buildings, 278

eminent domain, 41, 44–45

employment, 72, 101–110

    and economic base analysis, 103–104

    and office space demand, 284–292

    and real estate cycles, 171–173

    and real estate markets, 103–104

    sources of, 103–104

    See also basic employment; nonbasic employment

employment multiplier

    application of, 108–110

    estimating, 104–108

empty nesters, 347

environment

    impact on site use, 59–66

equilibrium analysis

    for an apartment complex, 368–370

    concepts, 176–177

    for an industrial building, 334–337

    for an office building, 298–300

    for a proposed retail center, 453

    for prospective uses of vacant land, 428

    for a shopping center, 256

    See also supply and demand analysis

escheat, 41

estimate

    vs. forecast, 131

existing supply

    vs. new supply, 144–146

export industries, 103–104

exurbia, 92–93

feasibility analysis. *See* financial feasibility analysis

fee simple estate, 38

filtering

    and high-income residential markets, 77–80

financial analysis

    of optimal vacant land use mix, 438–445, 502–503

    See also financial feasibility analysis

financial feasibility analysis, 487–501

    and development approach, 502–503

    for proposed retail center, 462–464

    for vacant retail center, 487–501

Financial Institutions Reform, Recovery and Enforcement Act (FIRREA), 12, 26

financing terms, 72–73

FIRREA. *See* Financial Institutions Reform, Recovery and Enforcement Act

flex space, 308–309

floodplains, 411–412

floor rentable area

    in office buildings, 271

floor size

    in office buildings, 278

forecast demand. *See* demand analysis

forecasting, 131–132, 375

    for appraisers and lenders (long-term), 230

    for developers (phase-specific), 436–438

    and residential properties, 348–349

    for retailers (short-term), 230

    techniques, 21–24

    See also capture analysis; marginal demand

Frejetal, Anne, 311

friction

    and location analysis, 37–38, 55

frictional vacancy, 246

   See also normal vacancy

frontage and visibility

   of shopping centers, 199

fundamental analysis

   of an apartment complex, 357, 360–363, 370–373

   concepts, 23–24

   defined, 18–20

   of an office building, 284, 293–295, 301–306

   of prospective uses of vacant land, 428–434

   of a shopping center, 228, 246–253, 259

Garreau, Joel, 90

general merchandise, apparel, furnishings, and other (GAFO), 191

general warranty deed, 42

gentrification, 97, 345

government, four powers of, 41

government offices, 271, 281

government regulations, 24–26, 39–41

   and urban structure, 72–73

   See also legal constraints; zoning

Graaskamp, James, 203

Gratz, Roberta B., 93

gravity models, 120–121, 220–221, 223–224

   See also Reilly's law of retail gravitation

gross building area (*GBA*), 194, 271, 347

gross floor area (*GFA*), 194

gross leasable area (*GLA*), 191, 194, 347

gross living area (*GLA*), 347

gross rentable area (*GRA*), 347

gross sales area (*GSA*), 194

ground cover. *See* vegetation

growth patterns. *See* urban growth

growth rate

   analysis of, 212

Harris, Chauncy D., 80–82

   and multiple nuclei model, 80–82, 88–90

heating, ventilation, and air-conditioning (HVAC), 278–279

heritage

   and psychological environment, 61–62

highest and best use, 5, 8, 32, 50–52, 59, 63–65, 70, 97–99

   basic concepts and terminology, 378

   and levels of analysis, 375–376

   and proposed retail center, 452–453, 462

   and six-step process, 380, 382

   and threshold testing, 383

   of vacant land, 466–468

   of vacant retail center, 495–499

   See also financial feasibility analysis; forecasting

household income, 230–236, 345, 347, 356, 362

   See also consumer spending

households, 103, 357

   formation of, 345, 347

   in primary trade area, 213, 228–230

   size of, 228–230, 362

housing

   data, 152–153

   estimating demand for, 136–137

   See also residential properties

housing starts, 173, 300

Hoyt, Homer

   and sector model, 74, 77–80

Hughes, W.T., 311

Hurd, Richard

   and axial (radial corridor) model, 74, 82–84

HVAC. *See* heating, ventilation, and air-conditioning

hypermarts, 191

improved land, 376, 503–505

   See also vacant land

improvements, 27

   on-site and off-site, 36–37

   See also buildings

income
    mean vs. median, 232–233
    in primary trade areas, 230–232
    and real estate markets, 101–103, 172–174
    and urban structure, 72
    sources of data, 152–154
    See also household income
income capitalization approach, 504–505
    data inputs for, 267, 273
industrial buildings
    and estimating market penetration, 337–341
    and fundamental demand by ratio method, 326
    and fundamental demand by segmentation method, 328
    and location rating, 317–322
    market analysis for, 307
    and market delineation, 323–324
    and market/marketability analysis process, 313
    and market residual demand, 334–337
    and measuring competitive supply, 331–334
    and property productivity analysis, 315–322
    and segments and sources of demand, 309
industrial demand indicators, 309–311
industrial space
    defined, 308–309
    types of, 271
industry. *See* basic industries; nonbasic industries
industry standards
    for retail use, 198–202
inferred analysis, 18–22
    for an apartment complex, 357–360, 373
    for an office building, 284, 301
    for a proposed retail center, 455–461
    for prospective uses of vacant land, 428–434
    for a shopping center, 227, 252, 259
    for a vacant retail center, 475–486

inflation
    and income forecasts, 233–234
    inflated vs. constant dollars, 233–234
    and residential property prices, 346
    and rental rates, 360
information
    produced from data, 150
infrastructure, 60
institutional and political environment, 65–66
institutional/professional office space, 271
insurance, 64–65
interest rates
    and economic environment, 64
    and real estate cycles, 173–174, 345
investment
    and economic environment, 64
    in land, 405–406
    See also speculation; speculator-investors; user-investors
investment analysis, 11, 19
    See also financial analysis; financial feasibility analysis; fundamental analysis

"jumping"
    in concentric zone model, 77

Koebel, Theodore C., 95
Kotkin, Joel, 93

labor force. *See* employment
Lancaster, John C.
    consumer theory of, 32
land
    supply of, 72
landscaping
    and office buildings, 278
    and shopping centers, 200
land-to-building ratios, 199

land use, 34–40, 44, 50–52, 63–65
  agricultural, 95
  associations of, 53–55, 81
  categories of, 355
  and community preferences, 40–41
  and concentric zone model, 74–76
  cyclical patterns of regulation, 40–41
  economics of, 63–65
  and prestige, 61–62
  and property attributes, 34–37
  and real estate markets, 63–65
  residential, 79–80
  and shopping centers, 209
  and situs process, 51–52
  and status, 61–62
  and vacant land, 469–471, 499
  See also highest and best use; linkages;
    neighborhoods; urban growth
land use maps
  concept plan, 384
  and linkages, 353
land use succession, 97–98
Laposa, Steven P., 310
latent demand, 363
leasehold estate, 39
legal attributes
  and potential land use, 451
  and productivity analysis, 38–40, 351
legal constraints
  and shopping centers, 202
  See also government regulations; zoning
Leinberger, Christopher, 92
Lessinger, Jack, 92
levels of market analysis
  criteria for determining, 24–27
  described, 20–24
levels of marketability analysis, 181–183
lifestyles. See psychological environment;
  social and cultural environment
lighting
  and office buildings, 277
linkages, 57–58, 209, 353, 417–420

location, 47–67
  three levels of, 47–50
  See also economic location; location
    analysis; physical location; situs
location analysis, 50–52
  of an apartment complex, 353–354, 365
  of an industrial building, 317–322
  of an office building, 272, 280–283,
    297–298
  of a proposed retail center, 451
  of prospective uses, 207–209, 212–216
  of vacant land, 416–427
  See also macro-location analysis;
    micro-location analysis
location quotient, 106–108
location rating grid
  for apartment complexes, 354
  for industrial buildings, 321–322
  for office space, 282
  for retail shopping centers, 210, 214
  for prospective uses of vacant land, 422,
    424–425
lots
  and office buildings, 277

macro-location analysis, 280–282, 468–469
maintenance
  and economic and psychological
    environment, 65
major intensity nodes, 418
malls. See retail shopping center
marginal demand, 23, 259
  for apartment and retail uses, 459, 461
  for shopping centers, 461
  See also equilibrium analysis
marketability, 300–301, 382
marketability analysis, 177–183
  calculating capture rate in, 180–181
  levels of, 181–183
  and the six-step process, 178–179
  and valuation, 178
  See also capture rate analysis

market analysis

and absorption rates, 5

and appraisal process, 5–6

and client needs, 26

and highest and best use, 5

and land use, 97–99

levels of, 20–27, 143, 375–376

and market conditions, 26–27

and market participants, 5

process for an apartment complex, 349–350

process for an industrial building, 312

process for an office building, 273–275

process for a proposed retail center, 449–450

process for a shopping center, 194–196

process for vacant land, 406–407

process for a vacant retail center, 465

and property complexity, 27

purpose of, 375

and research process, 9–13

and situs process, 50–52

steps in case study applications, 186

trends for residential property, 348–349

market area analysis. *See* market delineation

market areas, 115

and retail shopping centers, 216–227

techniques for defining, 118-123

See also retail market areas; trade areas

market boundaries, 52–59, 71–73, 118–123, 355

See also market delineation; trade area

market conditions, 26, 176–177

adjustment for vacant land, 502

See also equilibrium analysis

market cycles

and business cycles, 170–171

interaction of long- and short-term, 172–174

and market conditions (residual and demand analysis), 176–177

and real estate cycles, 172

recognizing the "bubble" market, 175–176

market delineation, 52, 113

for an apartment complex, 354–357

for an office building, 283

and peripheral competition, 222

procedures for segmenting markets, 116–121

for a proposed retail center, 453

for prospective uses of vacant land, 428

reasons for, 114

and regulatory enforcement, 39–40

for a retail shopping center, 216–227

and urban structure theory, 71–73

for a vacant retail center, 472, 474

See also market areas; trade areas

market disequilibrium or equilibrium, 256

See also equilibrium analysis

market participants. *See* speculator-investors; user-investors

market penetration. *See* capture analysis

market research process, 9–13

market segmentation, 116–123

and competitive supply, 142–143

defined, 130

and demand, 129–131

See also market delineation

Marshall, Alfred, 49

McHarg overlay technique, 410

mean income, 232–233

median income, 232–233

medical and dental offices, 270–271

metropolitan statistical area (MSA), 153–154, 156

and location analysis, 49

micro-location analysis, 282–283, 451

mineral rights. *See* subsurface rights

mixed-use development, 27

of vacant land, 426

model calibration, 293

modeling

to refine data, 166–167

models, analytical

definition of, 149

experimentation with, 163–164

of urban land use, 74–84

mortgages and foreclosures, 348
  and economic environment, 64
move-down demand, 346
move-up demand, 273, 346, 362
multiple nuclei model, 74, 80–82, 88–90
  and rent theory, 88–90
Mueller, Glenn R., 310
Muth, Richard F., 87

NAICS. *See* North American Industry Classification System
National Council of Real Estate Investment Fiduciaries, 507–513
natural features
  of sites, 52, 59–60
  of vacant land, 412
  See also soil composition; topography; vegetation
NCREIF. *See* National Council of Real Estate Investment Fiduciaries
neighborhood, 51–67
  accessibility, 55–58
  activities of, 53–55
  land use associations in, 53
  boundaries of, 52
neighborhood shopping centers, 191–194, 217, 449–464, 472
Nelson, Richard L., 190
  technique for estimating trade area size, 122–123
net leasable area (*NLA*), 347
net rentable area (*NRA*), 347
new urbanism, 93–95
noise contours, 412
nonbasic employment, 103–105, 110
normal vacancy, 246, 362, 364, 372
North American Industry Classification System (NAICS), 111, Appendix B

occupancy rates
  in apartment complexes, 359, 373
  in office buildings, 272
  See also vacancy rates
office buildings
  class and quality of, 123–124, 271–272

office districts, 282
office market areas, 123–124, 270
office nodes, 123
office space, 271–272
  demand for, 292–293, 482
  estimating demand for, 135–136
  layout of, 278
  per employee, 285, 289, 291
operating costs
  data on, 162
overall capitalization rates (R_O), 503
overflow effect
  and urban growth, 77

pad sites, 400
parking
  area, 194
  index, 194
  and office buildings, 277
  ratio, 194
  and shopping centers, 199
Peisner, Richard, 406
Pellucid Corporation, 157
pent-up demand. *See* latent demand
per capita sales demand method, 246–249
physical attributes, 34–35
  of apartment complexes, 351–352
  and highest and best use, 34–35
  of industrial buildings, 315–317
  and market segmentation, 116
  of office buildings, 277–279
  and productivity analysis, 32–37
  of retail shopping centers, 199–201
  of vacant land, 409–416
physical environment, 59–60
physical location, 47
  and location analysis, 50–52
  and retail shopping centers, 213–214
planning. *See* city planning; public planning
police power, 41
political organization
  and neighborhoods, 65–70

population
    alternative techniques for analyzing data, 459–461
    projections, 109, 360–361
    and real estate cycles, 172
    and real estate markets, 97, 118
    See also demographics
prestige
    and psychological environment, 61–62
price
    and economic environment, 63–64
    and residential properties, 346
primary data, 173–176
    defined, 161
    estimating supply with, 144–146
    issues with using, 164
    sources of, 164–165
primary trade area, 191–193
private property
    and powers of government, 41
probability study, 230
productivity
    and real estate market structure, 88–90
productivity analysis, 8, 35–49, 186
    of an apartment complex, 351–354
    definition and purpose, 32–33
    impact of overall environment on site, 59–65
    of an industrial building, 315–323
    and legal attributes, 38–39
    and location, 50–51
    of an office building, 276–283
    and physical attributes, 34–37
    and property accessibility, 55–58
    and property use, 32–34
    of a proposed retail center, 450–453
    and rating of alternative uses, 453
    of a retail shopping center, 197–216
    of a vacant retail center, 450–453
    of a vacant site, 409–428
property attributes
    and market segmentation, 146

property productivity analysis. *See* productivity analysis
property rating procedures
    for an apartment complex, 353–354
    for an office building, 280
    for a shopping center, 202–207
property types
    and levels of market analysis, 27
    and market segmentation, 116
property use. *See* land use
pro rata share capture method
    applied to vacant land, 435–438
    applied to shopping centers, 260–261
proximity. *See* accessibility; physical location
psychological environment, 61–62
public planning
    and vacant land, 412, 414
    See also city planning
public policy
    and market delineation, 39–40
public services
    and neighborhoods, 66
purchasing power. *See* buying power

quantitative data. *See* data sources and collection

R & D space. *See* research and development space
Rabianski, Joseph, 157, 310, 355
random movement, 58
Ratcliff, Richard, 76
rating procedure. *See* competitive rating procedures; property rating procedures
rating matrix capture method
    applied to vacant land, 435
ratio method, 246, 247, 326, 363
ratios
    used to estimate demand, 132–137
raw land, 27, 346, 405–406
    See also vacant land

real estate
    as alternative investment, 11–13
    and highest and best use, 32–33
    legal concept of, 38
    as a space-time product, 44
    supply and demand, 5
real estate cycles, 172–176, 300, 342
    See also business cycles; speculation
real estate demand. *See* demand
real estate markets, 113–114
    characteristics of, 97–99
    defining, 114
    and urban structure, 70–73
    See also market delineation; market segmentation
real rental rates
    used to infer demand, 359–360
regional shopping centers, 191–194, 218
regulatory requirements. *See* government regulations; legal constraints
Reilly, William, 120
Reilly's law of retail gravitation, 120, 220
rent
    and apartment complexes, 368–370
    and economic environment, 63–65
    and household formation, 347–348
    and location, 81, 84–89
    and tenant income, 355, 359–360, 362
    See also real rental rates
rentable area, 271
rental apartments. *See* apartment complex
rent theorists' models, 84–89
REIS, 157
research and development space, 271, 276
residential land use. *See* land use
residential properties, 343–351
    See also housing
residual analysis, 176, 267
    See also equilibrium analysis
residual demand. *See* marginal demand
retail capture. *See* capture analysis
retail center. *See* retail shopping center

retail market areas, 116–123, 455–461
    data on, 153–156
    retention of sales in, 242–245
    See also trade areas
retail sales tax data, 240–241, 457
retail shopping center
    definition of, 188
    market analysis for existing, 187–268
    market analysis for proposed, 449–464
    market analysis for vacant, 465–499
    and office building development, 281
    sources of data on, 238
    types of, 191–193
    See also neighborhood shopping centers; regional shopping centers; retail market areas; superregional shopping centers; vacant retail center
retail space
    estimating demand for, 132–135
    estimating demand for proposed, 455–458
    estimating supply of competitive, 253–256
    forecasting demand for existing, 227–253
    supportable, 246
retail spending. *See* consumer spending
retail trade survey, 153
retirement housing, 347
roads
    projected, 418–419
    proximity to shopping centers, 213

sales comparison approach, 14, 503
    data inputs for, 196, 267, 273, 276
    and market conditions, 186-187
    and models, 149-150
sales tax data. *See* retail sales tax data
sales per square foot, 194
satellite stores, 255
scarcity
    in value theory, 4
scatteration, 80
Schmitz, Adrienne and Deborah L. Brett, 113, 193
scientific method and appraisal process, 6–9

scoping. *See* alternative use scoping

secondary data, 150–160

    estimating demand with, 159–161

    estimating supply with, 143–144

    evaluating, 157–159

    refining with modeling, 166–167

    on shopping centers, 212, 219, 254

    sources of, 152–157

secondary trade area, 196, 205, 239

    sources of demand, 244

sector (wedge) model, 74, 77–80, 84, 138

secular cycles, 172

security

    in office buildings, 279

service sector. *See* nonbasic employment

shopping center. *See* retail shopping center

signage, 201

single-family homes, 346

    demand for, 344–345

site, 9–12

    and location analysis, 47–50, 422–427

    use and overall environment, 59

site analysis, 37–38

site efficiency analysis

    and shopping centers, 198–202

    and vacant land, 410–425

    See also entries for individual site characteristics, e.g., parking, topography, utilities

site improvements. *See* improvements

site orientation

    and property use, 35

Site To Do Business (STBD), 155–156

situs, 50–52, 59, 80, 209

    definition of, 48

    and land use succession, 97–98

    process, 51

    and residential land use, 77–80

six-step process overview, 13–15

size-of-the-center capture technique, 260–261

"sliding"

    in concentric zone model, 77

smart growth, 95–96

Smith Travel Research, 157

social and cultural environment, 60–61

social ecology models, 74–84

Society of Industrial and Office Realtors, 157

soil composition, 60

    and property use, 34–35

space inventory and operating costs

    sources of data on, 156–157

    See also office space; retail space

space-time product, 44

speculation

    in raw land, 404–406

speculator-investors, 404–405

    See also user-investors

stairways

    in office buildings, 278

Standard Industrial Classification (SIC) codes, 238, 287

status

    and psychological environment, 61–62

store dimensions, 200

street layout, 277

    See also roads

structural vacancy. *See* frictional vacancy

subjective distance, 123

substitution, principle of

    and land use, 81

    and market definition, 119

subsurface rights, 38

subsurface utilities, 60

suburban office markets, 123–124

suburban residential development, 344

suburban urban core cities. *See* edge cities

supermarkets, 457–459

superregional shopping centers, 191–194, 218

supply

    estimating with primary data, 144–145

    estimating with secondary data, 143–144

    existing, 145

    planned, 146–147

    of sites, 147

    under construction or planned, 145–146

supply analysis. *See* competitive supply analysis

supply and demand, 14, 97–98, 127–129, 141–143, 186

and data collection, 20–24

of land, 404–405

and location, 44

for prospective uses of vacant land, 428–434

of residential properties, 346

See also competitive supply; competitive supply analysis; demand; demand analysis; equilibrium analysis

sustainable growth, 95

taxation, 41, 72

See also retail sales tax data

technology, 72

and economic environment, 63–65

tenant finish, 278

tenants

in apartment complexes, 355–357

in office buildings, 270–272

quality of, 279

in shopping centers, 201–202, 214, 218–220, 240, 245

See also anchor tenants

territoriality

and psychological environment, 61–62

threshold testing, 452–453, 462–464

timeshare, 38

timing

of use, 404, 426

See also forecasting

topography, 59–60

and market boundaries, 52

and property use, 34–35

and shopping centers, 199, 205–206

and urban structure, 71, 80–81

and vacant land, 410–411

Torto Wheaton Research, 157, 309–310

trade areas, 53, 191–194, 217–227

breakdown by sales and driving time, 113, 118–122, 193

and site, 49

size by shopping center type, 192

and time/distance variable, 52

See also retail market areas

traffic

and accessibility, 55–57

and location, 52

projections of, 417

and shopping centers, 213

transportation, 72

and axial model, 82–84

and multiple nuclei model, 80–82, 88-89

and rent theorists' models, 84–88

and sector model, 77–80

See also traffic

transportation corridors, 70–71

transshipment point, 78

trapping point, 58

trend analysis. *See* inferred analysis

truck service facilities, 201

Ullman, Edward L., 74

and multiple nuclei model, 80–82, 84

Uniform Standards of Professional Appraisal Practice (USPAP), 24–26

and secondary data, 157–159

unimproved land. *See* vacant land

urban growth

and apartment complexes, 357–358

concepts and models, 74–90

and demand, 137–139

future, 96–97

and office buildings, 280

predicting direction of, 138

and prospective uses of vacant land, 417–418, 420-422

recent trends, 90–96

and retail shopping centers, 209–210

See also rent theorists' models; social ecology models; urban structure

urban land economics, 49–51

Urban Land Institute, 243, 276

urban situation value, 49

urban structure, 69–99

    definition of, 70

    forces influencing, 71–74

    future, 96–97

    land use succession and urban growth forms, 97–98

    recent trends in, 90–95

    rent theorist's models, 84–89

    social ecology models, 74–84

usable area/space

    in office buildings, 271

user-investors, 405–406

    See also speculator-investors

USPAP. *See* Uniform Standards of Professional Appraisal Practice

utilities

    and office buildings, 277

    and shopping centers, 199

    and vacant land, 412

utility

    in value theory, 4

vacancy rates

    in apartment complexes, 362

    in office buildings, 292

    in residential properties, 348

    See also occupancy rates

vacant land, 346, 376

    market analysis for, 446

    valuation of, 404–406, 501–502

    See also improved land

vacant retail center

    market analysis for, 465-499

valuation process. *See* appraisal process

vegetation, 60

wages. *See* income

warehousing, 308–309

wind direction, 60

Woods and Poole, 156

working women

    and housing preferences, 345–346

Xceligent Corporation, 157

Zeckendorf, William

    and "Hawaiian technique," 38

Zell, Sam, 173

zones of conflux, 57

zoning, 41–43

    and highest and best use, 404

    policies in Texas, 39–40

    and shopping centers, 202, 255

    and vacant land, 412–415

    See also government regulations; legal constraints